PROCEEDINGS OF THE FIFTH CALIFORNIA ISLANDS SYMPOSIUM

Volume 1

29 March to 1 April 1999

Sponsored by the Minerals Management Service

Editors

David R. Browne
Kathryn L. Mitchell
Henry W. Chaney

Santa Barbara Museum of Natural History   2002

DISCLAIMER

This report has been reviewed by the Minerals Management Service (MMS) and approved for publication. The opinions, findings, conclusions, or recommendations expressed are those of the authors and do not necessarily reflect the views or policies of the MMS. Mention of trade names or commercial products does not constitute endorsement for use. This report has been technically reviewed according to contractual specifications; however, it is exempt from further review by MMS editors.

Printing History

Original CD-ROM Edition

> February, 2000
> Minerals Management Service
> OCS Study
> MMS 99-0038

> Prepared by
> MBC Applied Environmental Sciences
> 3000 Redhill Avenue
> Costa Mesa, California 92626
> Under MMS Contract No. 14-35-01-96-RC-30801

> Contact information for CD-ROM Edition:
> U.S. Department of the Interior
> Minerals Management Service, Pacific OCS Region
> 770 Paseo Camarillo
> Camarillo, California 93010-6064

Revised Printed Edition

> © 2002
> Santa Barbara Museum of Natural History
> Santa Barbara, CA 93015-2936

> ISBN 0-936494-31-X (Volumes 1 and 2)
> ISBN 0-936494-32-8 (Volume 1)
> ISBN 0-936494-33-6 (Volume 2)

> Contact information for Printed Edition:
> Santa Barbara Museum of Natural History
> Attn: The Museum Store
> 2559 Puesta del Sol Road
> Santa Barbara, California 93105-2936

FIFTH CALIFORNIA ISLANDS SYMPOSIUM
STEERING COMMITTEE

Minerals Management Service Representatives:

David Browne, Chairman
Mark Pierson
James Lima
Catherine Dunkel
John Romero
Craig Ogawa

Santa Barbara Museum of Natural History Representatives:

Henry Chaney, Co-Chairman
Eric Hochberg
John Johnson

Minerals Management Service Contractor:

Kathryn Mitchell, MBC Applied Environmental Sciences

ACKNOWLEDGEMENTS

The Fifth California Islands Symposium was planned and conducted by a team of people representing various Federal agencies and nonprofit organizations. Without their dedicated effort and willingness to share their expertise, this Symposium could not have effectively met its objective of presenting the latest scientific research related to the California islands. The Fifth California Islands Symposium Steering Committee and its associated team consists of :

Minerals Management Service

Ellen Aronson
Marilyn Bishop
Patricia Bowen
David Browne, Symposium Chairman
Richard Brumer
Jane Carlson
Rodney Cluck
Mary Elaine Dunaway
Catherine Dunkel
Michael Hargrove
James Lima
Bill Mallonee
Craig Ogawa

Julie Pember
Mark Pierson
Fred Piltz
J. Lisle Reed, MMS Regional Director
Larry Roberts
John Romero
Loretta Slusher
Linda Smith
Michelle Tetley
Carmen Unchangco
Barbara Voyles
Richard Wilhelmsen
Rochelle Williams-Hooks

Minerals Management Service Contractor

Kathryn and Charles Mitchell, MBC Applied Environmental Sciences

Santa Barbara Museum of Natural History

David Anderson, Co-Executive Director
Robert Breunig, Former Executive Director
Henry Chaney, Symposium Co-Chairman
Kathy Conti

Joanne Hankey
Eric Hochberg
John Johnson
Brian Rapp, Executive Director

National Park Service

Gary Davis

Catherin Schwemm

Channel Islands National Marine Sanctuary, NOAA

Ben Waltenberger

Santa Cruz Island Foundation

Marla Daily

Danielle Greene

ACKNOWLEDGEMENTS

The following individuals gave an extraordinary and professional effort in the development of the Fifth California Islands Symposium and its proceedings:

*David Browne: Overall project management, Symposium procurement process, Symposium planning, document editing, Symposium information dissemination, and proceedings organization and media development

*Mark Pierson: Symposium procurement process, Symposium planning, document editing, Symposium information dissemination, and proceedings media development

*James Lima: Symposium planning, document editing, Symposium information dissemination, and proceedings media development

*Kathryn Mitchell: Symposium announcements, poster, program document, Symposium planning, Symposium logistics, subcontractor procurement, and proceedings media development, paper compilation, editing, and printing

*John Romero: Public relations, planning Poster Session and agency displays

*Henry Chaney: Symposium planning, subcontractor procurement, Symposium logistics

*Eric Hochberg: Symposium planning

*Catherin Schwemm: Symposium procurement support

*Ben Waltenberger: Symposium procurement support

*Catherine Dunkel: Document editing, Symposium information dissemination, and proceedings media development

*Craig Ogawa: Symposium planning

Fred Piltz: Symposium procurement process, management support

Loretta Slusher: Announcement mailings, administrative support

Richard Brumer: Announcement mailings

Bill Mallonee: Symposium procurement process

*Kathy Conti: Subcontractor procurement

Herb Leedy: Symposium videotaping coordination

Harold Syms: Proceedings media development

Those marked with an asterisk (*) also contributed to the Symposium as a presenter, session chair, and/or paper reviewer. All of the above were instrumental in making the Fifth California Islands Symposium a success.

In all large endeavors, there is an inner circle of individuals whose efforts make that project possible. I want to express my deep appreciation to Mark Pierson, James Lima, Catherine Dunkel, and John Romero of the MMS, Kathryn Mitchell of MBC Applied Environmental Sciences, and Henry Chaney of the Santa Barbara Museum of Natural History for their enthusiastic and creative assistance in the conduct of the Fifth California Islands Symposium and the development of its proceedings.

David R. Browne
Fifth California Islands Symposium Chairman
April 1999

MISSION STATEMENTS

The Department of the Interior Mission
As the Nation's principal conservation agency, the Department of the Interior has responsibility for most of our nationally owned lands and natural resources. This includes fostering sound use of our land and water resources; protecting our fish, wildlife, and biological diversity; preserving the environmental and cultural values of our national parks and historical places; and providing for the enjoyment of life through outdoor recreation. The Department assesses our energy and mineral resources and works to ensure that their development is in the best interests of all our people by encouraging stewardship and citizen participation in their care. The department also has a major responsibility for American Indian reservation communities and for people who live in island territories under U.S. administration.

The Minerals Management Service Mission
As a bureau of the Department of the Interior, the Minerals Management Service's (MMS) primary responsibilities are to manage the mineral resources located on the Nation's Outer Continental Shelf (OCS), collect revenue from the Federal OCS and onshore Federal and Indian lands, and distribute those revenues.

Moreover, in working to meet its responsibilities, the **Offshore Minerals Management Program** administers the OCS competitive leasing program and oversees the safe and environmentally sound exploration and production of our Nation's offshore natural gas, oil and other mineral resources. The MMS **Royalty Management Program** meets its responsibilities by ensuring the efficient, timely and accurate collection and disbursement of revenue from mineral leasing and production due to Indian tribes and allottees, States and U.S. Treasury.

The MMS strives to fulfill its responsibilities through the general guiding principles of: (1) being responsive to the public's concerns and interests by maintaining a dialogue with all potentially affected parties and (2) carrying out its programs with an emphasis on working to enhance the quality of life for all Americans by lending MMS assistance and expertise to economic development and environmental protection.

TABLE OF CONTENTS

Volume 1

KEYNOTE ADDRESS

PHYSICAL OCEANOGRAPHY AND CLIMATOLOGY

TERRESTRIAL ECOLOGY

Volume 2

MARINE ECOLOGY

GEOGRAPHIC INFORMATION SYSTEMS

PLATFORM ECOLOGY, OCEAN CIRCULATION, AND RESOURCE MANAGEMENT

PALEONTOLOGY, ARCHAEOLOGY, AND ANTHROPOLOGY

SOCIAL SCIENCE AND EDUCATION

POSTERS

CALIFORNIA'S CHANNEL ISLANDS:
A ONE-WAY TRIP IN THE TUNNEL OF DOOM

Larry D. Agenbroad

Dept. of Geology/Quaternary Studies, Northern Arizona University, Flagstaff, AZ 86001
(520) 523-2379, FAX (520) 523-9220, E-mail: larry.agenbroad@nau.edu
and
Santa Barbara Museum of Natural History, Santa Barbara, CA 93105
(805) 682-4711, FAX (805) 569-3170

ABSTRACT

Islands have impoverished biological communities when contrasted with continents. Islands are classified as "continental" (being, or having been attached to the mainland), or "oceanic" (separated by deep ocean straits from the mainland). Islands are isolated, their faunas are often described as impoverished, or depauperate, and they often have unique biological forms. Islands are extinction loci. Some islands contain the remains of Pleistocene proboscideans. The Northern Channel Islands of California are compared to island characteristics on the global scale. Extinction of some Channel Islands fauna is documented, and it still may be at work.

Keywords: California Channel Islands, pygmy mammoths, extinction, oceanic islands, Pleistocene.

INTRODUCTION

"Islands, in general, are biologically anomalous."

"Islands are a haven and breeding grounds for the unique and anomalous."

"They (islands) are natural laboratories of extravagant evolutionary experiments."

"Islands are where species go to die."

".......insular evolution.....tends to be a one-way tunnel towards doom."

The preceding quotes and many similar ones came from a book published in 1996 by David Quammen, entitled, "The Song of the Dodo." The subtitle is, "Island biogeography in an age of extinctions." In the book, Quammen describes and discusses the reasons for the unique biology of islands and why extinction might be considered the "norm" for island biota. The California Channel Islands (Figure 1) are no exception.

There is an extensive history of island research and researchers, many of whom Quammen (1996) discusses or describes. Additional researchers will be discussed in this

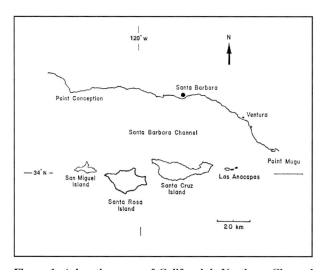

Figure 1. A location map of California's Northern Channel Islands.

presentation, beginning with Paul Sondaar, a Dutch scientist interested in fossil faunas of islands, and how they got to the islands, were changed by the islands, and ultimately became extinct.

Let me say, at the onset, that I am not a biogeographer, in the traditional sense of the word. Nor am I a biologist who has studied modern island flora and fauna. I will lay claim to the fact that I am a paleontologist who specializes in mammoths and other extinct Pleistocene megafauna (> 45 kg live weight). It has been my good fortune to become involved in the study of the Northern Channel Islands of California, because three of these islands contain the only pygmy mammoth population in the world!

MATERIALS AND METHODS

I would like to cover some basic facts about islands, island proboscidean biogeography, and island faunas (Table 1). Then I would like to apply these general characteristics to four specific islands: San Miguel, Santa Rosa, Santa Cruz, and Anacapa. What you must keep in mind is that these modern islands do not tell the entire geohydrologic story.

There are six islands, or island groups that produced the remains of fossil proboscideans (Table 2; Figure 2). These

Table 1. Island characteristics.

a. islands are classed as 'oceanic', or 'continental'
b. islands are biologically impoverished and unbalanced
c. islands are isolate
d. islands are restricted (area, environments)
e. islands are large, or small
f. barren islands acquire biologic populations
g. island fauna undergo size change
h. islands have unique selective pressures
i. oceanic islands lack large carnivores
j. islands are localities of extinction (doom!)

are: 13 islands in the Mediterranean Sea; several islands in the Indonesian archipelago; a few islands in the Philippine archipelago; the Japanese archipelago; Wrangel Island in the Siberian Arctic Ocean; and the Northern Channel Islands of California. Only Wrangel Island and the northern Channel Islands of California have fossil mammoths. A recent article (Thikonov 1997) states that the Wrangel mammoths are no longer considered to be dwarfs. That means the California Channel Islands of San Miguel, Santa Rosa, and Santa Cruz are unique! They have the only pygmy mammoth fossils in the world!

Table 2. Proboscidean fossils on islands or island groups (Shoshani and Tassy 1996; Agenbroad 1998).

Locality	Islands	Proboscidean
Mediterranean Sea	Sardinia, Crete, Sicily, Malta	pygmy elephants
	Cyclades islands, Dodecanese	*Elephas falconeri*
	islands, Cyprus,	*Elephas leonardi*
	Crete	*Elephas mnaidriensis*
Indonesian archipelago	Timor, flores, Sumba, Java,	pygmy stegodons
	Sulawesi	elephants
		Stegodon florensis
		Stegodon sompoensis
		Stegodon tinioriensis
		Stegodon hypsilophus
		Elephas celebensis
		Elephas hysandrindicus
		Elephas maximus
Philippine archipelago	Mindanao	stegodons and elephants
	Luzon	*Stegodon luzonensis*
		Stegodon mindanensis
		Stegodon trigoncephalus
		Elephas beyeri
Japanese archipelago	Ryukyu islands	elephants
	Taiwan*	
Wrangel Island		mammoths
		Mammuthus primigenius
California Channel	San Miguel	mammoths
Islands	Santa Rosa	*Mammuthus columbi*
	Santa Cruz	*Mammuthus exilis*

*Taiwan is not usually considered part of the Japanese archipelago.

RESULTS

Elaboration of Island Characteristics and their Application to the Northern Islands

Classification

Islands are classified as 'oceanic' or 'continental.' (Darlington 1957; Sondaar 1977; Quammen 1996). Continental islands are those that are, or have been attached to the adjacent continent by a land bridge. These islands have a larger, more diverse fauna than oceanic islands. Oceanic islands are those separated from an adjacent continent by a

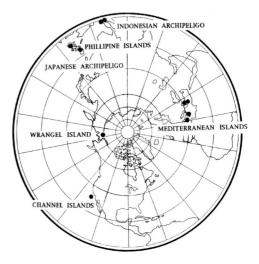

Figure 2. Islands or island groups known to have remains of fossil proboscideans.

deep water strait. They have been uplifted from the ocean floor by tectonic, or volcanic forces. Oceanic islands are depauperate (biologically) as compared to continental islands.

It has been stated, repeatedly, in the literature that the Northern Channel Islands were connected to the coast of California by a land bridge. That notion was based on the premise that elephants could not swim, and since elephant (mammoth) remains were found on the Northern Channel Islands they must have been connected to the mainland (Fairbanks 1897; Stock and Furlong 1928; Chaney and Mason 1930; Stock 1935, 1943; Valentine and Lipps 1967; Von Bloecker 1967; Weaver and Doerner 1967; Hooijer 1976; Madden 1977; Azzaroli 1981). Wenner and Johnson (1980) provided sufficient evidence to conclude that the Northern Channel Islands are to be classed as "oceanic" islands. They were never connected by a land bridge—at least in the mammoth period (the late Pleistocene).

Biologic Impoverishment

Oceanic islands have only a small representation of the species diversity of the nearest mainland (Johnson 1983). Wenner and Johnson (1980) provided tables of southern California fauna as contrasted to the Northern Channel Islands. They indicate at least 127 species of mainland land vertebrates (excluding avifauna). In contrast, they list the Northern Channel Islands as having only 12 or 13 species native to the island, including extinct ones. Table 3 provides a list of fossil fauna from the islands. Extant, endemic land mammals on Santa Rosa Island include the island fox (*Urocyon littoralis santarosae*), the spotted skunk (*Spilogale gracilis amphias*), and the deer mouse (*Peromyscus maniculates streatori*) (Orr 1968). Three other species of living deer mice are proposed from Santa Cruz Island and one extinct form (*Peromyscus anyapahensis*), from Anacapa Island. This provides a total of thirteen fossil species and up to seven species of extant vertebrates (omitting extant snakes).

Either assessment is sufficient to illustrate the extreme biological impoverishment of the Channel Islands as compared to coastal southern California. Isolation is easily demonstrated by a deep water strait present between the Northern Channel Islands and the California coast (Wenner and Johnson 1980). This was so, even in the eustatic sea level fluctuations of the Pleistocene. During an ice age, sea level was lowered by as much as 100 m by the fact that precipitation was stored on the continents as snow and ice, creating the ice sheets, glaciers, permafrost, and snow fields characteristic of an "Ice Age." The lowering of sea level by as much as 100 m made a drastic change to the Pleistocene coastline of California, and an even more impressive change to the shoreline of the Ice Age island named Santarosae (Figure 3) by Phil Orr (1968). The modern Channel Islands are simply the subaerial mountain tops of Pleistocene Santarosae. Using a simplistic map of the Santarosae land area compared to the land area of the modern islands, approximately

Table 3. Fossil vertebrate, terrestrial fauna from the Northern Channel Islands (Guthrie 1998).

Land Vertebrates

Columbian mammoth	*Mammuthus columbi*
pygmy mammoth	*Mammuthus exilis*
ornate shrew	*Sorex ornatus*
"giant" deer mouse	*Peromyscus nesodytes*
"giant" meadow vole	*Microtus miguelensis*
Anacapa deer mouse	*Peromyscus anyapahensis*

Avifauna

Condor (?)	*Gymnogyps californicus*
vampire bat	*Desmodus stocki*
caracara	*Caracara prelutosa*
flightless goose	*Chendytes lawi*
owl	*Asio prelutosa*
gannet	*Morus reyanus*
auklet	*(currently undescribed)*

Reptiles

(Pacific) San Miguel rattlesnake	*Crotalus viridis*

Note: (?) remains on San Miguel w/extinct vole (condor is "extinct" on the islands).

76% of ancient Santarosae was submerged, as sea level rose with the post-Pleistocene warming and resultant meltoff, returning water to the ocean. During sea level lowering the strait separating Santarosae was reduced to approximately 6 to 9 km. It has been demonstrated (Wenner and Johnson 1980) that elephants (and probably mammoths) could easily have swum the strait formed by Pleistocene sea level lowering.

Paul Sondaar (1977) presents data that suggests oceanic islands are represented by only a few large mammals. Large mammals found most often on oceanic islands are good swimmers. They include elephants, deer, and hippopotami. Similarly, such islands lack large carnivores (poor

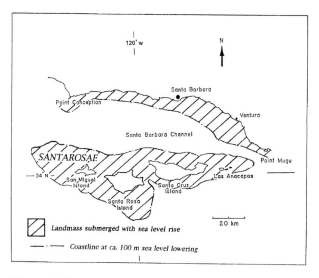

Figure 3. The modern Channel Islands compared to the Pleistocene island Santarosae. The Pleistocene coastlines of Santarosae and the mainland are due to approximately 100 m sea level drop. The modern islands represent the mountains of Santarosae after post-Pleistocene eustatic sea level rise.

swimmers). He goes further, to state that if an oceanic island has one or more members of his "elephant-deer" fauna, they got there by a "sweepstakes" route (Sondaar 1977; Wenner and Johnson 1980). Quammen (1996) makes a more definitive statement, "Every terrestrial animal on an oceanic island, and every plant, is descended from an animal or plant that arrived there by cross-water dispersal after the island was formed." The smaller animals were most likely castaways (or waif migrants) which clung to debris from mainland floods until they arrived at the island. This would have been even more feasible during lowered sea level. There is, however, no known Pleistocene record for foxes nor skunks on the islands.

Orr (1968) reported the collection of one fox skull he collected from the upper part of the Tecolote Formation (± 16,000 yr BP). He goes on to state the specimen was "lost at sea." Paul Collins (SBMNH) found the specimen in other collection material, compared it with fox specimens from San Miguel and Santa Rosa islands, and found it to be within the range of modern specimens (Collins 1993). Until the skull is dated, it is uncertain as to whether it is a Pleistocene fox, or a Holocene fox whose den was in Pleistocene sediments.

Island foxes have low genetic variability (Roemer et al. 1994), are threatened by canine diseases, and are classed as a threatened species by the California Department of Fish and Game (Crooks and Van Vuren 1994).

Island Fauna and Size Change

Darwin noted that on islands, large mainland animals often became smaller, whereas small mainland animals often became larger. He attributed dwarfism to a process of pathologic degeneration (Sondaar 1977). The change of size noted above is commonly known as "Foster's Rule" (Foster 1964). Sondaar (1977) suggests that rather than degenerate forms, that smaller large mammals and larger small animals may be an adaptive response producing an animal better suited for island life. In the absence of carnivores, large size loses its adaptive value and selective pressures for becoming smaller are: 1) increased mobility, 2) less food consumption, and 3) a reduction in range requirement. He (Sondaar 1977) also notes that a common development of island elephants, deer, and hippos is a shortening of the distal part of the legs. This fact allows for low speed locomotion in a varied, mountainous environment (Sondaar 1977). The overall size reduction also lowers the center of gravity of the animal (over its mainland ancestral form) which is advantageous (and a selective advantage) in a rugged mountainous island, allowing negotiation of steeper slopes, giving access to rugged grazing areas.

DISCUSSION

All of the features, discussed above, are demonstrable for *Mammuthus exilis* on the Channel Islands. It is my theory that as sea level rose, reducing the resource area(s), crowding the remaining island, that mainland size mammoths (*M. columbi*) that originally colonized Santarosae were selected against, giving rise to their smaller (pygmy) descendents who could reach resources that were unavailable to the larger forms. The ratio of *M. columbi* remains to *M. exilis* is approximately 1 to 10 in the on-going controlled survey for mammoth remains, initiated in 1996.

Island environmental pressures were selective for smaller, more mobile mammoths that could reach rugged resources unavailable to the larger form and which needed a smaller amount of those resources for survival, than did the ancestral, mainland form.

Extinction

Three causes of extinction on oceanic islands are discussed by Sondaar (1977). They include: 1) introduction of new, mainland species by way of a land bridge; 2) arrival of humans; and 3) periodic overpopulation leading to overgrazing of vegetation resulting in malnutrition and starvation. An additional category, with similar results would be drought, or lightning strike fires.

The first two causes have little to do with the pygmy mammoths of the Northern Channel Islands. However, the arrival of humans was Orr's (1968) favorite theory for the extinction of island mammoths. Results of the third cause would be dramatic population reduction, limiting the surviving genetic diversity of the survivor's gene pool, and selection for traits advantageous to the island environment. Sondaar (1977) feels this would cause rapid evolution of the island forms but make them more susceptible to extinction.

Quammen (1996) gleaning from others, cites four sources of "population uncertainty:" 1) demographic: variation in birth rates, death rates, and ratio of sexes; 2) environmental: fluctuation of weather, food, disease, competition; 3) natural: floods, droughts, wild fires; and 4) genetic: reduction of alleles in the gene pool increasing the frequency of harmful traits, and inbreeding of surviving populations.

There is another negative factor which has been alluded to in the previous discussions, that is dividing or splitting habitats. It is generally accepted that small populations in fragments of former habitat are especially vulnerable to the four sources of population uncertainty.

Recall now that Santarosae is being inundated by the post glacial melt of continental ice. Approximately 11,000 years ago, the modern four islands became separate (isolate) and are the mountainous remainder of ancient Santarosae. The extinction causes, or "population uncertainties" are focused on small, isolated, inbreeding populations, and, as we know, *Mammuthus exilis* is extinct!

Is the "Tunnel of Doom" Still Active?

My answer is "yes." The most recent victim, in my opinion, is the Island fox (*Urocyon littoralis*). There is one tentative report of the fox in the Pleistocene (Orr 1968), however it may have represented a den in Pleistocene sediments, rather than a Pleistocene fox. There is no question this charming little animal was (and is) present in the Holocene. It has been suggested that it may have been brought to the islands as pets, by Chumash people (Orr 1968; Johnson 1983), and they are as early as 11,700 Yr BP according to the record in Daisy Cave, San Miguel Island (Erlandson et al. 1996; Guthrie 1998).

The possible Pleistocene specimen was the same size as extant animals, which led to some question of its Pleistocene antiquity (Collins 1993). Those remains were thought to have been "lost at sea" (Orr 1968; Guthrie 1998), however, it was relocated by Paul Collins (Johnson 1983). Whether Pleistocene or Holocene, the indications of last August are that the Island Fox has become very scarce on the islands. National Park Service fox trapping efforts during my August 1998 stay on the island of Santa Rosa yielded scant results—a sharp contrast to August 1994, or August 1996. The suspected cause of declining fox numbers is heartworm. But isn't that (disease, not heartworm) one of the extinction factors that Quammen (1996) postulated for island animals. The disease appears to be transferred from the mainland to the island by mosquitos (Paul Collins, pers. comm. 1998).

There are possibly other examples I could cite, but as I said at the beginning of this presentation, I am not a biological or zoological researcher working on extant populations. My research subjects, the pygmy mammoths (*Mammuthus exilis*), have already made their trip through the tunnel! They met DOOM! They are extinct!

I, for one, regret their loss. Imagine a 1 to 2 m tall mammoth—one I refer to as a "house mammoth," or an "attack mammoth." I would love to have seen the reaction of a German Shepherd, or Rottweiler that jumped the fence into my yard!

The world's only island-inhabiting mammoth! I only missed it by ± 11,000 to 12,000 years. We still do not know the events that shaped this exceptional creature. It will take more field research, and many more absolute dates to understand the timing and sequence of events that took place in transit, through the tunnel. In particular, the timing (rate) of dwarfing; the possible causes of population pressures, if there are more than we have already discussed (and I think I've seen hints, in the field, that can be dated). The possibility of contemporaneity with the earliest Chumash; the final date of mammoth extinction.

I am often asked, "Won't you be excited when you find a mammoth bone with a spear point in it?" My response is, "I've got a different perspective. I'm looking for a human ribcage with a tusk in it." A second common question is, "How is your research relevant (to modern times)?" Well, I feel it shows us what has happened in an oceanic island environment in very recent time (geologically speaking) and may be still at work, as in the case of the Island fox. The Tunnel of Doom is still functioning (Figure 4).

Figure 4. A schematic of the one-way trip through the "tunnel of doom." Selected mainland forms enter the island (tunnel) to become modified by island adaptations and finally become extinct. (Artwork by Carl Buell).

LITERATURE CITED

Agenbroad, L. D. 1998. Pygmy (dwarf) mammoth of the Channel Islands of California. The Mammoth Site of Hot Springs, South Dakota, Inc. Hot Springs.

Azzaroli, A. 1981. About pigmy mammoths of the Northern Channel Islands and other island fauna. Quaternary Research 16:423-425.

Chaney, R. W. and H. L. Mason. 1934. A Pleistocene flora from Santa Cruz Island, California. Carnegie Institution of Washington. Publication 415.

Collins, P. W. 1993. Taxonomic and biogeographic relationships of the Island Fox (*Urocyon littoralis*) and Gray Fox (*U. cinereoargenteus*) from western North America. Pages 351-390 *in* Hochberg, F. G. (ed.), Third Channel Islands Symposium: recent advances in research on the California islands. Santa Barbara Museum of Natural History, Santa Barbara.

Crooks, K. R. and D. Van Vuren. 1994. Conservation of the Island Spotted Skunk and Island Fox in a recovering island ecosystem. Pages 379-385 *in* Halvorson, W. L. and G. J. Maender (eds.), The Fourth California Islands Symposium: Update on the status of resources. Santa Barbara Museum of Natural History. Santa Barbara.

Darlington, P. J. 1957. Zoogeography: the geographical distribution of animals. John Wiley and Sons, Inc. New York.

Erlandson, J., D. Kennett, B. Ingram, D. Guthrie, D. Morris, D. Tveskov, G. West, and P. Walker. 1996. An archaeological and paleontological chronology for Daisy Cave (CA-SMI-261), San Miguel Island, California. Radiocarbon 38:1-19.

Fairbanks, H. W. 1897. Oscillations of the coast of California during the Pliocene and Pleistocene. American Geologist 20:213-245.

Foster, J. B. 1964. Evolution of mammals on islands. Nature 202:234-235.

Guthrie, D. A. 1998. Fossil Vertebrates from Pleistocene Terrestrial Deposits of the Northern Channel Islands, Southern California. Pages 187-192 *in* Weigand, P. W. (ed.), Contribution to the Geology of the Northern Channel Islands, Southern California. Pacific Section American Association of Petroleum Geologists.

Hooijer, D. A. 1976. Observations on the pygmy mammoths of the Channel Islands, California. Pages 220-225 *in* Churcher, C. S. (ed.), Athlon: Essays on palaeontology in honor of Loris Shano Russel. Miscellaneous publications of the Royal Ontario Museum. Ontario.

Johnson, D. L. 1972. Landscape evolution on San Miguel Island, California. Ph.D. dissertation, Univeristy of Kansas, Lawrence, Kansas.

Johnson, D. L. 1978. The origin of island mammoths and the Quaternary land bridge history of the Northern Channel islands, California. Quaternary Research 10:204-225.

Johnson, D. L. 1980. Problems in the land vertebrate zoogeography of certain islands and the swimming powers of elephants. Journal of Biogeology 7:383-398.

Johnson, D. L. 1983. The California Continental Borderland: landbridges, watergaps, and biotic dispersals. Pages 381-527 *in* Masters, P. M. and N. C. Fleming (eds.), Quaternary Coastlines and Marine Archaeology: towards the prehistory of land bridges and continental shelves. Academic Press, New York.

Madden, C. T. 1977. Elephants of the Santa Barbara Channel Islands, Southern California. Geological Society of America Abstracts with Programs, 1977 Annual Meeting. Pages 458-459.

Orr, P. C. 1968. Prehistory of Santa Rosa Island. Santa Barbara Museum of Natural History. Santa Barbara.

Quammen, D. 1996. The Song of the Dodo. Touchstone Publishers. New York.

Roemer, G. W., D. K. Garcelon, T. J. Coonan and C. Schwemm. 1994. The use of capture-recapture methods for estimating, monitoring, and conserving Island Fox populations. Pages 387-400 *in* Halvorson, W. L. and G.

J. Maender (eds.), The Fourth California Islands Symposium: Update on the status of resources. Santa Barbara Museum of Natural History. Santa Barbara.

Shoshani, J. and P. Tassy (eds.). 1996. The Proboscidea: Evolution and palaeoecology of elephants and their relatives. Oxford University Press. Oxford.

Sondaar, P. 1977. Insularity and its effects on mammal evolution. Pages 671–707 in Hecht, M. K., P. C. Goody, B. M. Hecht (eds.), NATO Advanced Study Institute Series Number 14. Plenum Press. New York.

Stock, C. 1935. Exiled elephants of the Channel Islands, California Scientific Monthly XLI:205-214.

Stock, C. 1943. Foxes and elephants of the Channel Islands. Los Angeles County Museum of Natural History Quarterly 3:6-9.

Stock, C. and E. L. Furlong. 1928. The Pleistocene elephants of Santa Rosa Island, California. Science LXVIII:140-141.

Thikonov, A. 1997. (Brief report). Zoological Institute Russian Academy of Sciences, St. Petersburg, Russia. Department of History of Fauna. UroMam Newsletter 4:14-15.

Valentine, J. W. and J. H. Lipps. 1967. Late Cenozoic history of the southern California Islands. Pages 21-35 in Philbrick, R. N. (ed.), Proceedings of the Symposium on the Biology of the California Islands. Santa Barbara Botanic Garden. Santa Barbara.

von Bloeker, J. R., Jr. 1967. The land mammals of the southern California Islands. Pages 245-266 in Philbrick, R. N. (ed.), Proceedings of the Symposium on the Biology of the California Islands. Santa Barbara Botanic Garden. Santa Barbara.

Weaver, D. W. and D. P. Doerner. 1967. Western Anacapia—a summary of the Cenozoic history of the Northern Channel Islands. Pages 13-20 in Philbrick, R. N. (ed.), Proceedings of the Symposium on the Biology of the California Islands. Santa Barbara Botanic Garden. Santa Barbara.

Wenner, A. M. and D. L. Johnson. 1980. Land vertebrates on the California Channel Islands: Sweepstakes or bridges? Pages 497-530 in Power, D. M. (ed.), The California Islands: Proceedings of a multidisciplinary symposium. Santa Barbara Museum of Natural History. Santa Barbara.

SOURCES OF UNPUBLISHED MATERIALS

Collins, Paul, Vertebrate Zoology, Santa Barbara Museum of Natural History, 2559 Puesta del Sol, Santa Barbara, CA 93105. Personal Communication September 1998.

SURFACE CIRCULATION PATTERNS IN THE
SANTA BARBARA CHANNEL

C. D. Winant[1] and S. Harms[2]

[1] Scripps Institution of Oceanography, Center for Coastal Studies, UCSD
9500 Gilman Drive, La Jolla, CA 92093-0209
(858) 534-2067, FAX (858) 534-0300, E-mail: cdw@coast.ucsd.edu
[2] Alfred Wegener Institute for Polar and Marine Research
Postfach 12 01 61, D-27515 Bremerhaven, Germany
E-mail: sharms@awi-bremerhaven.de

ABSTRACT

Under the auspices of the Minerals Management Service (MMS), a four-year long program of measurements was conducted in the Santa Barbara Channel (SBC) to describe the circulation of waters and to relate that circulation to different forcing factors. The observational program consisted of five components. Meteorological measurements were acquired from a wide variety of sources. Currents and related physical parameters were measured at moored locations. Water-tracking drifters were deployed from 12 sites at regular intervals. Spatially intensive surveys of currents and water mass properties were conducted biannually. Maps of sea surface temperatures (SST) were obtained from satellite images several times each day. These diverse observations were synthesized into a description of the ocean circulation consisting of a finite number of characteristic patterns, or synoptic views. In the summer the four dominant patterns are labeled Upwelling, Relaxation, Cyclonic, and Propagating Cyclones. In the winter the circulation usually falls into either of two patterns labeled Flood East and Flood West. Different patterns prevail depending on the strength of two forcing functions: the stress imposed by the wind on the ocean surface at the western entrance to the channel, and the sea level difference between the Southern California Bight and the central California shelf.

Keywords: Santa Barbara Channel, Minerals Management Service, ocean circulation, currents, Southern California Bight, OSRA, oil spill risk.

INTRODUCTION

Observations of the surface circulation in the Santa Barbara Channel (SBC) (Figure 1) have been acquired over a four-year period (1993 to 1996), sponsored by the Minerals Management Service (MMS) of the U.S. Department of the Interior. The project was designed to achieve two parallel objectives. The first is to provide a description of the various components of the circulation, and a dynamical explanation suitable to guide the development of a predictive model. The second is to translate results into a form of immediate use to analysts charged with making decisions relating to development of resources.

The SBC is bounded to the north by the mainland coast of California, which is oriented from east to west in this area. The four Channel Islands: San Miguel, Santa Rosa, Santa Cruz, and Anacapa constitute the southern boundary. The passages between the islands are typically 40 m deep. The channel is about 100 km long and 40 km wide. The central basin extends to 500 m, and there are narrow, 3 to 10 km wide shelves on either side. The eastern sill has a depth of 220 m and the depth at the western sill is 400 m.

METHODS

The field effort consisted of five separate components. The first was designed to provide a comprehensive description of the atmosphere over the area of interest. Previous descriptions (Caldwell et al. 1986) suggest that the SBC is an area characterized by large variability, requiring high spatial resolution. This description is based primarily on fixed station observations from a variety of sources. The National Data Buoy Center (NDBC), also sponsored by MMS, maintains several meteorological buoys in and around the periphery of the channel (all these sites are located on Figure 1). In addition we have deployed an array of stations on four oil platforms and on two of the Channel Islands (Santa Rosa and Santa Cruz). Finally routine observations from Vandenberg AFB, the NDBC coastal stations, and the Santa Barbara Air Pollution Control District are integrated into the set of observations. Dorman and Winant (1998) summarize the results of this component.

The second component of the field effort relied on moored observations of physical parameters, horizontal currents, temperature salinity, and pressure to provide long time series (about four years long) of these parameters. The moorings, located on Figure 1, were deployed over the shelf along the 100 m isobath and at 200 m depth in the eastern entrance. In addition the meteorological buoys (53 and 54)

Santa Barbara Channel - Santa Maria Basin CCS

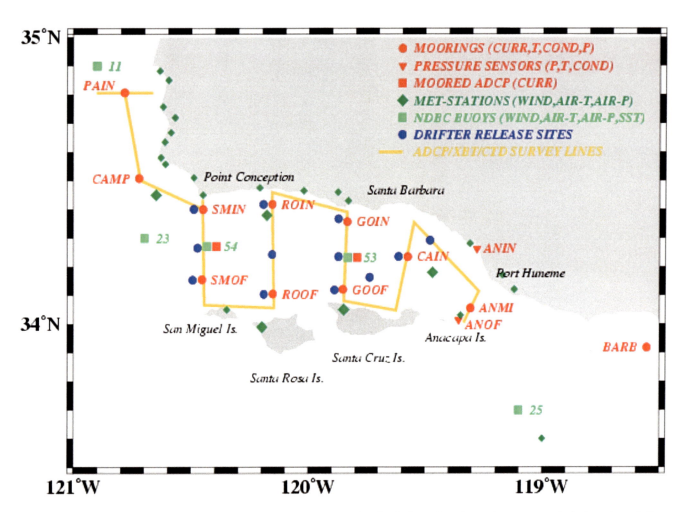

Figure 1. Santa Barbara Channel-Santa Maria Basin Coastal Circulation Study. Location of moorings, meteorological stations, drifter release sites, and survey tracks.

were equipped with current profilers. Current measurements were made at 5 and 45 m, except for the meteorological buoys where measurements are available at 16 m intervals, beginning 24 m beneath the surface. Results of this part of the field work are described by Harms and Winant (1998).

The third component of the work provides a description of near surface trajectories using drifters. These instruments are designed to follow surface water parcels, and telemeter their location back to shore several times each day. Drifters were released at the twelve locations illustrated in Figure 1, approximately every two months. Descriptive aspects of this component are summarized by Winant et al. (1999) and a statistical and dynamical interpretation is presented in Dever et al. (1998).

Spatially intensive snapshots of the flow constitute the fourth component. Shipboard surveys are conducted using Acoustic Doppler Current Profilers (ADCPs), expendable bathythermographs, (XBTs) and Conductivity-Temperature-Depth (CTD) surveys conducted at regular intervals. Daily archiving of satellite imagery provides another source of spatially intensive data (Hendershott and Winant 1996).

The fifth component consists of a number of modeling efforts aimed at synthesizing the observations as well as to provide a means of interpolating between observations which are either spatially sparse (moored measurements) or temporally sparse (surveys). The models are intended to eventually provide a capability to forecast flow situations.

RESULTS AND DISCUSSION

Synoptic Patterns of Circulation

Maps of daily averaged currents, including temperature and pressure fields were prepared for each day of the observational period. These maps were subjectively sorted to identify characteristic flow patterns, in the same way that meteorologists identify synoptic views for different weather patterns The observations can be sorted into six different synoptic states illustrated in Figure 2. These states are called the Upwelling, Relaxation, Cyclonic, and Propagating cyclone patterns, which are most commonly observed during spring, summer, and early fall; the Flood East and Flood West patterns tend to occur more frequently during the winter. About 60% of the daily average maps corresponds to one of these patterns. The remaining observations either correspond to transitions between patterns or involve much smaller scale features than can be resolved by the moored array.

As illustrated in Figure 2, there is always a cyclonic component to the circulation. The cyclonicity is strongest in summer and weakest in winter. In the Upwelling pattern, the circulation appears to result from the superposition of an equatorward (towards the southeast) current and the cyclonic eddy. In the relaxation pattern, a strong jet carries flow along the northern boundary towards the west, past Point Conception, while the flow along the Channel Islands is weak and towards the east. The Cyclonic pattern corresponds to a condition when the central eddy is at maximum strength with little net flow into the channel. The Propagating Cyclone pattern corresponds to a number of smaller cyclonic eddies which drift through the channel towards the west. Two modifications of the patterns just described occur in the winter, Flood East and Flood West. The first describe conditions in which the flow is everywhere directed towards the Southern California Bight, and the other pattern is the reverse. The patterns are similar to the Upwelling and Relaxation patterns, with reduced cyclonic circulation.

A more objective analysis of the current observations has been completed using Empirical Orthogonal Functions (EOFs). Eigenvectors and eigenvalues of the matrix of covariance coefficients between low-frequency components (periods longer than 38 hours) are determined. The EOF analysis is based on patterns from which the time average has been removed. The mean flow near the surface, as described by Harms and Winant (1998), consists of a westward flowing current on the northern shelf and a weaker eastward flow over the southern shelf. These opposing flows lead to a cyclonic circulation similar to pattern (C) in Figure 2. In the EOF analysis, each pair of eigenvalues and eigenvectors describes a mode of co-variation of currents. Details of the analysis are described by Harms and Winant (1998). Three modes account for 50% of the variance, the remainder is probably caused by smaller scale flow features. The dominant mode of circulation corresponds to a net flow through the channel, either poleward or equatorward. The second mode describes a cyclonic eddy. In combination with the mean flow, these modes are consistent with the subjectively derived patterns illustrated in Figure 2. The EOF analysis also describes how each pattern occurs as a function of season, or as a function of the external forcing.

Forcing of the Circulation

Harms and Winant (1998) suggest that circulation in the SBC is driven by a combination of two different forcing mechanisms. One is provided by the wind stress. During spring, summer, and early fall, the wind stress is very strong over the western portion of the SBC, and weaker along the northern boundary, as the strong winds which blow along

UPWELLING/ RELAXATION   CYCLONIC   FLOODS

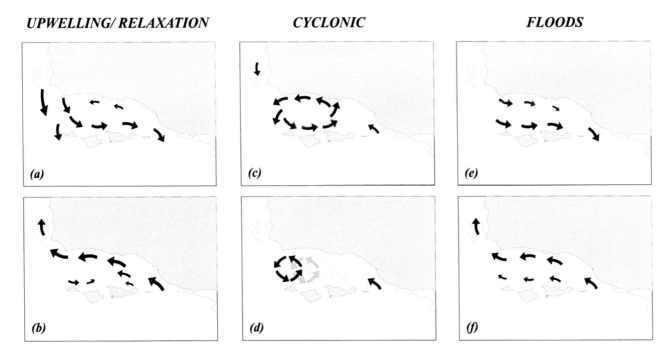

Figure 2. Schematic diagram of the six synoptic views of circulation in the Santa Barbara Channel. (a) Upwelling; (b) Relaxation; (c) Cyclonic; (d) Propagating Cyclones; (e) Flood East; and (f) Flood West.

NDBC 54 Wind Stress along 124° N

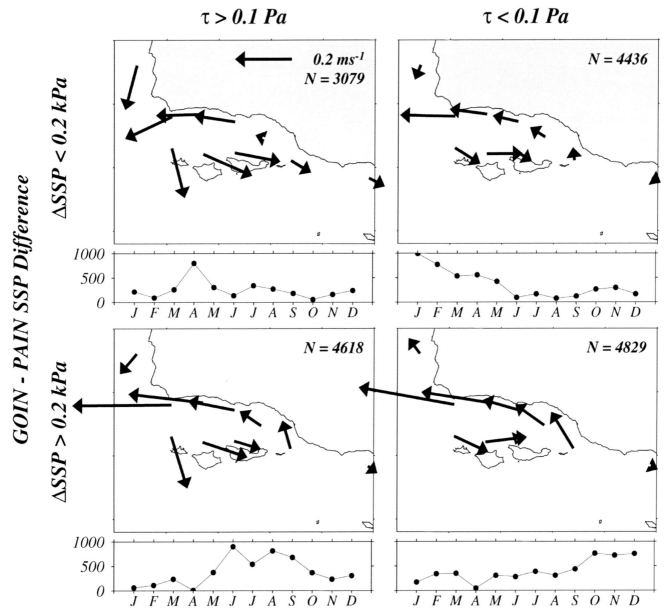

Figure 3. Conditionally averaged 5-m current velocity (ms-1) as a function of equatorward wind stress (in Pa) at NDBC 46054 along 124° N, and the along-channel SSP difference (in k Pa) between GOIN and PAIN. The number in the upper right corner of each panel is the number of realizations (hourly averages) upon which the conditional average is based.

the central California coast separate from the coast in the vicinity of Point Conception. The winds during these seasons are characterized not only by large wind stress, but by large spatial gradients in the wind stress alone. It is however not possible to explain the flow in the SBC on the basis of local wind stress alone. The most obvious reason being that the average wind stress is directed towards the southeast whereas the average current is directed in the opposite direction.

It is known that the areas on either side of the SBC, the central California coast and the Southern California Bight, have significantly different temperatures, particularly during the summer and early fall. Analyses demonstrate that areas of warmer temperature correspond to higher pressure at the surface than areas of lower temperature, and on this basis it is expected that a pressure gradient exists in the direction parallel to the coast. The mean pressure difference is the direction to oppose the mean wind stress. Quantitative estimates of the pressure difference suggest that it can have a comparable effect to that of the wind stress.

In order to define the relative effect of wind stress and alongshore pressure difference on the circulation, current observations have been sorted according to the direction and strength of each forcing function, as illustrated in Figure 3. The component of the wind stress along 124° N at NDBC buoy 54 is chosen as an index of the strength of the local wind, and the difference in synthetic surface pressure (equivalent to sea level) between stations GOIN (in the channel) and PAIN (north of Point Conception) represents the pressure gradient. Each map represents the average of all available current measurements under the illustrated conditions of wind stress and pressure difference.

The pattern of circulations changes systematically as the winds stress and pressure difference change, although the cyclonic tendency is always present. When the wind stress is strong and the pressure gradient is weak, the circulation resembles the Upwelling pattern, with a net flow through the channel towards the southwest, along the direction of the wind stress. When the wind stress is weak and the pressure difference is large, the circulation resembles the Relaxation pattern, characterized by a strong jet towards the west, consistent with the direction of the pressure difference. In intermediate situations, the flow resembles the Cyclonic pattern.

Synthesis

This research has established that the circulation of surface waters in the SBC can be described in terms of a finite number of circulation patterns, similar to the synoptic patterns used by forecast meteorologists to describe weather patterns. All patterns include a cyclonic tendency. A comparison of the synoptic patterns and two distinct forcing functions, the wind stress acting over the surface of the ocean and the pressure difference between the central California shelf and the Southern California Bight account for the different circulation patterns.

LITERATURE CITED

Caldwell, P. C., D. W. Stuart, and K. H. Brink. 1986. Mesoscale wind variability near Point Conception, California, during spring 1983. Journal of Climate and Applied Meteorology 25:1241-1254.

Dever, E. P., M. C. Hendershott, and C. D. Winant. 1998. Statistical aspects of surface drifter observations of circulation in the Santa Barbara Channel. Journal of Geophysical Research 103(C11):24,781-24,797.

Dorman, C. E. and C. D. Winant. The structure and variability of the marine atmosphere around the Santa Barbara Channel. Submitted to Monthly Weather Review, August 1998.

Harms, S. and C. D. Winant. 1998. Characteristic patterns of the circulation in the Santa Barbara Channel. Journal of Geophysical Research 103(C2):3041-3065.

Hendershott, M. C. and C. D. Winant. 1996. Surface Circulation in the Santa Barbara Channel. Oceanography 9(2):14-121.

Winant, C. D., D. J. Alden, E. P. Dever, K. A. Edwards and M. C. Hendershott. 1998. Near-surface trajectories off central and southern California. Submitted to Journal of Geophysical Research, July 1998.

CHANNEL ISLANDS AND SANTA BARBARA CHANNEL METEOROLOGY

Clive E. Dorman

Center for Coastal Studies, Scripps Institution of Oceanography, UCSD
9500 Gilman Drive, La Jolla, CA 92093-0209
(858) 534-7863, FAX (858) 534-0300, E-mail: cdorman@ucsd.edu

ABSTRACT

The lower atmosphere in this area has great structure in the vertical and horizontal. In the summer, a dense, cool marine air 300 m deep is capped by hot, dry air above. Strong and persistent westerly winds extend across the western mouth of the Santa Barbara Channel, decreasing to the east. High speed winds push between the islands. Air temperature tracks the sea surface temperature with the coldest in the western portions. The marine layer and wind structure is consistent with a transcritical flow regime responding to the local topography. In the winter, the vertical structure weakens. Extended weak wind periods are followed by strong southeast winds that reverse to strong northwest winds. Temperature changes are modest with the warmest temperatures in the central, southern portion of the bight.

Keywords: Meteorology, Santa Barbara Channel, Santa Maria Basin.

INTRODUCTION

The Center for Coastal Studies at Scripps Institution of Oceanography has been running a long-term field project to understand the ocean and atmosphere around the Channel Islands and the Santa Barbara Channel. An extensive and unusually dense surface meteorological station network was developed (Figure 1). These included shore stations supervised by the Santa Barbara and Ventura air pollution control districts, the U.S. Navy at Point Mugu, and meteorological buoys operated by the National Data Buoy Center. The Center for Coastal Studies maintained stations on three oil platforms and the western tips of Santa Cruz and Santa Rosa Islands. Although only one summer and one winter are presented here, the results are typical.

RESULTS

Annual Trend

A distinct annual trend is seen in the monthly mean wind vectors along California (Dorman and Winant 1995) and at the western end of the Santa Barbara Channel and the islands (Figure 2). The strongest speeds are in the summer (maximum is April and May 1996) and weakest in the winter (minimum is February 1996) but always from a northwesterly direction. The annual trend has similar annual phase

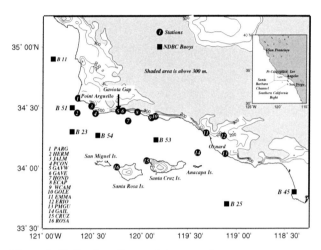

Figure 1. Station locations and topography.

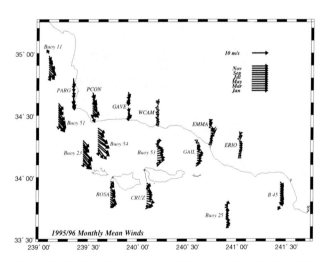

Figure 2. Wind vector mean monthly annual trend. Monthly mean winds for January (lowermost arrow) through December 1996 (uppermost arrow). Speeds are greatest in the western channel mouth in the summer.

but much weaker magnitude in the eastern end of the channel. Stations on the north channel coast and east of Point Conception, with the exception of Ventura (designated as station EMMA), have weak means with no significant annual speed trend that is typified by Gaviota east station (GAVE) and the Santa Barbara west campus station (WCAM).

The weather in the area is typified by two seasons: the summer and the winter. The remainder of this paper is organized around examining the two representative seasons. The summer structure and variations are presented first. This is followed by a shorter winter structure and variations as the winter has less complicated structure and provides a contrast with the summer season.

Summer

In the mean (Figure 3, upper), the sea-level winds approach the channel from the northwest, accelerate and turn cyclonically around Point Arguello, reaching a maximum in the middle of the western channel. Once past this point, the near-surface air slows as it continues down the center of the channel, exiting to the east into the Ventura Valley or continuing over water to the southeast toward the greater Los Angeles Valley. Compared to the center channel, winds are weaker at the islands on the south edge. Standard deviations are less than the means for the over-water stations in the western mouth.

Correlations for the summer season were computed among the stations for the wind along the principal axis (PA)

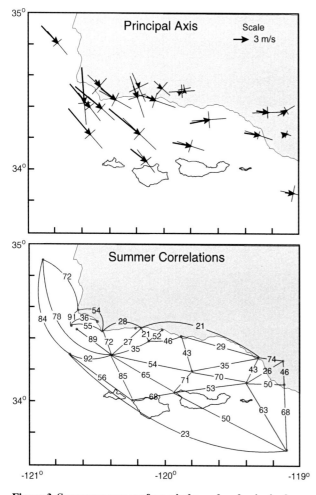

Figure 3. Summer mean surface wind speed and principal axes (PA) (upper frame). Mean is the arrow that flies with the wind. The cross at the end of the wind vector is the wind standard deviation with the long side the maximum magnitude and orientation and the short side the minimum. Wind correlations along station PA's (lower frame).

or the direction of the maximum variance which is close to mean wind direction (Figure 3, lower). The best correlations (0.7 to 0.9) are between the stations in the western mouth of the channel (B54 with others). Weak correlations (0.5 to 0.6) are between the western mouth (as represented by B54) and the eastern central stations as B53 and CRUZ. Poor correlations exists between the center line channel stations (B54, B53) and the land coastal stations Gaviota West (GODW) to EMMA and Platform Hondo (HOND). Even though it is over water, HOND is poorly related to B54 and also the coastal stations. In contrast, the two stations on exposed Point Arguello (PARG and Point Conception (PCON) are at least moderately correlated with the near, over-water stations Buoy 54 (B54), and Platform Hermosa (HERM).

The most frequently occurring summer event is high speed, sustained winds from the north followed by a short period of weak winds. Fastest winds are at the western mouth of the Santa Barbara Channel and are associated with strengthened along-coast sea-level pressure gradient and weak cyclonic circulation in the mid-level of the atmosphere. A typical case is examined for the period 2 to 11 July 1996. The main sea level synoptic features are the North Pacific anticyclone to the northwest with a heat low in the southwest U.S. north of Point Conception, the along-coast pressure gradient strengthens from the 3 to 5 July then decreases again on 9 July as the heat low expands (not shown). Sea-level pressure gradients over water are consistently weak southeast of Point Conception for the entire period despite of the variation in sea-level speeds at the western mouth. At 700 hPa an approaching trough on 3 July weakens as it moves over the California coast on 7 July and to eastern California on 9 July.

The sea-level winds along the main channel are sensitive to the above-noted synoptic variations. Examples of selected stations are shown in Figure 4 for which the wind direction has been rotated to the station's PA so as to make viewing easier. After a brief period of weak winds, strong inbound northerly winds persisted at Buoy 51 (B51) for seven days with stronger winds at B54. Once past B54, wind speeds decrease to Buoy 53 (B53), then to Platform GAIL (GAIL) (not shown), to reach a minimum speed at El Rio (ERIO) in the eastern end. Indeed, it would be hard to determine the state of the winds at the western mouth of the Santa Barbara Channel if only the El Rio observations were available. Not shown are winds at the Channel Islands of Santa Rosa (SROS) and Santa Cruz (SCRZ) which are somewhat weaker but coincident with the buoy winds at B54 and B51. The winds over the land stations were generally west-east with only an occasional clear, cross-coast, northerly velocity such as occurred at GAVE (and GAVW and HOND) for four hours early on 5 July. Finishing up this synoptic sequence, weak winds and reversals occurred on 9 July and 10 July which are the second most frequently occurring event over the open channel.

The explicit diurnal trends for cross channel stations are not shown. However, all stations wind speeds are a minimum around sunrise and increase in the afternoon. The

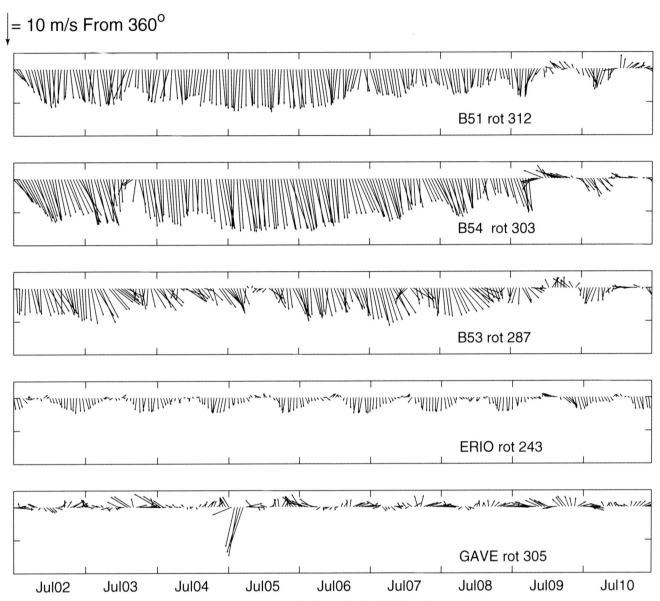

= 10 m/s From 360°

B51 rot 312

B54 rot 303

B53 rot 287

ERIO rot 243

GAVE rot 305

Jul02   Jul03   Jul04   Jul05   Jul06   Jul07   Jul08   Jul09   Jul10

Figure 4. Surface wind vector time series rotated to the PA for 2 to 11 July 1996 for selected stations.

stations on Santa Rosa and Santa Cruz islands have a small diurnal change while Buoy 54 in the center of the channel has the largest in the area.

Temperatures for the summer are shown in Figure 5. In the summer morning, the land is warmer than the sea in the Santa Barbara Channel, with a weak gradient to the east. In the afternoon, all stations are warmer, with the weakest increases over the western mouth and the greatest over the land at the eastern end. Added to the 0600 PST chart are the seasonal averaged sea-surface temperature contours from satellite infrared images as thin dashed lines. Wind-driven upwelling, associated with the fastest winds, causes the sea-surface temperature minimum in the western mouth. The air-temperature field follows the sea-surface temperature field on account of the low heat capacity of the air and the restricted exchange of the marine air with other sources.

A synopsis of the results of the Navy Variability of Coastal Atmospheric Refractivity (VOCAR) sounding

program is presented that maintained eight upper-air stations in the Southern California Bight in August and September 1993. In the morning at 0400 PST, the inversion base was lowest in the Santa Barbara Channel and highest in the southern half of the bight (Figure 6). The strength of the inversion is greater offshore. In the afternoon, at 1600 PST, all base heights are typically about 100 m lower but still is the lowest is in the Santa Barbara Channel. The strongest horizontal gradient in the inversion base height is at the western mouth of the Santa Barbara Channel. The greatest inversion strength is to the southwestern portion of the bight while it is weakest in the Santa Barbara Channel.

VOCAR winds over the Southern California Bight are relatively strong only on the western side (not shown). The winds are greatly accelerated in the afternoon, sweeping directly across the Bight with little curvature.

14

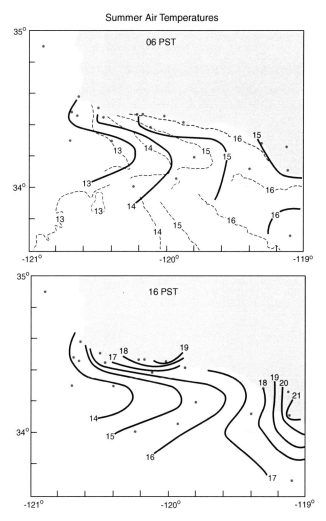

Summer Air Temperatures

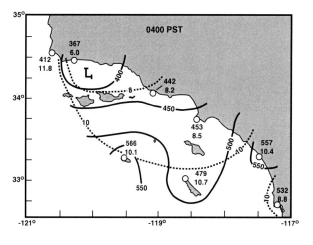

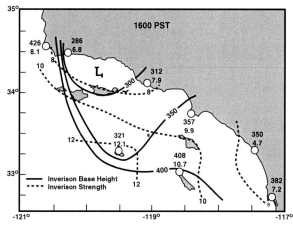

Figure 6. 0400 PST (upper frame) inversion base height (solid) and strength (dashed). Stations locations are at circles, where the upper plotted number is the air temperature inversion base height in meters and the lower number is the inversion strength in °C. 1600 PST (lower frame) inversion base height and strength. The lowest inversion base height is over the Santa Barbara Channel at both times.

Figure 5. Summer mean air temperatures at 0600 PST (upper frame) and 1400 PST (lower frame). It is coolest in the western mouth. The summer sea surface temperature estimated from satellite infrared images are superimposed on the upper chart as thin dashed lines.

Winter

Mean winter winds are for the December 1995 to February 1996 period for all stations except B11 and JALM. The December 1994 to February 1995 observations are used to compute the mean for B11 and JALM as these stations were not available for the 1995/1996 season. The winter wind mean and PA for the surface stations are from the northwest at the western mouth and turn to the east in the Santa Barbara Channel (Figure 7, upper) as during the summer. However, drainage flows down the Ventura river valley caused by colder night temperature over the elevated topography causes offshore wind at ERIO, EMMA, and GAIL. There is a mean offshore flow over the north coast stations in contrast to summer. Winter standard deviations are larger than the mean winds and also greater than the summer standard deviations.

Correlations of the over-water wind component along the PA (Figure 7, lower) are greater than in the summer, which is evidence of a larger synoptic scale. Most of the

over water stations have correlations of 0.7 to 0.8 or better with neighboring stations. The lowest correlation between a central channel stations (B54) and a near coast station (GAVE) dips to only 0.69. Even the stations away from the Santa Barbara Channel (B11, B25) are correlated with those in it. The poorest correlations are between the land stations at the eastern end of the Santa Barbara Channel.

A late-December 1995 case is typical of strong southerly sea-level winds followed by a reversal to strong northerly winds. The synoptic situation for strong southerly winds is an approaching front off California and a deep low extending from sea level to above 500 hPa (not shown). Sea level and mid-level winds are from the south along central California and the western portion of the Southern California Bight. Later, by 28 December a ridge oriented northwest-southwest developed across central California from sea level to above 500 hPa and a trough to the east of California. The result were strong winds from the northwest from sea level to the upper atmosphere over the Santa Barbara Channel.

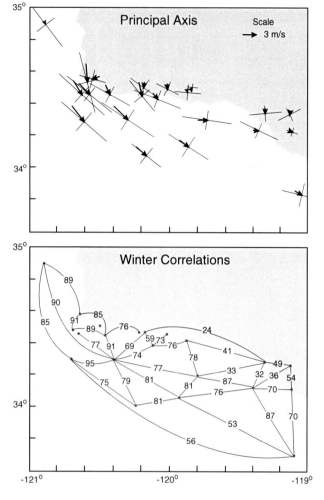

Figure 7. Winter mean surface wind speed and principle axis (PA) (upper frame). See Figure 3 for explanation. Wind correlations along station PA's (lower frame).

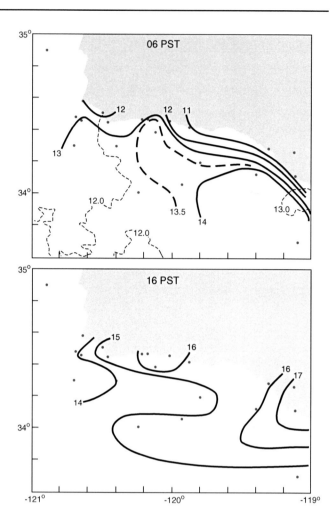

Figure 9. Winter mean air temperatures at 0600 PST (upper) and 1400 PST (lower). The winter sea surface temperature estimated from satellite infrared images are superimposed on the upper chart as thin dashed lines.

Strong southerly winds at the western Santa Barbara Channel surface stations extended from 22 to 26 December with the winds increasing in strength from the Islands to B51 (Figure 8). Winds were slower and from the east in the eastern portion of the channel. North coastal stations varied between periods of southerly and along-shore winds.

The winds reversed abruptly around midnight on 26 to 27 December to be strong from the north-northwest of the western channel until 1 January. Winds increased from B51 to maximum at B54 then mildly decreased at the islands. The north coast stations as GAVE experienced persistent offshore winds but at speeds less than at the islands. Finally, winds were weak and variable in direction at the eastern coastal station ERIO.

Winter air temperatures shown in Figure 9. In the winter morning, there is a weak air temperature maximum over the center of the channel while the strongest minimum is over the Oxnard Plain on the eastern end. By the afternoon, stronger diurnal warming has reversed the situation so that the warmest temperatures are over land. Somewhat similar to the summer, there are along- and cross-channel gradients with the coldest air at the western mouth of the channel. However, satellite-derived sea-surface temperatures (thin dashed lines in Figure 9) are nearly uniform over the Santa Barbara Channel.

↓ = 10 m/s From 360°

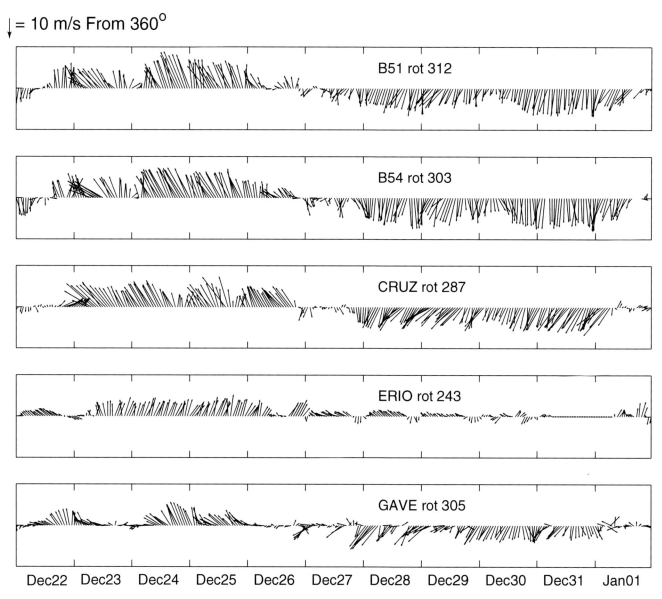

B51 rot 312

B54 rot 303

CRUZ rot 287

ERIO rot 243

GAVE rot 305

Dec22   Dec23   Dec24   Dec25   Dec26   Dec27   Dec28   Dec29   Dec30   Dec31   Jan01

Figure 8. Surface station wind vector series rotated to the PA for 22 December 1995 to 2 January 1996.

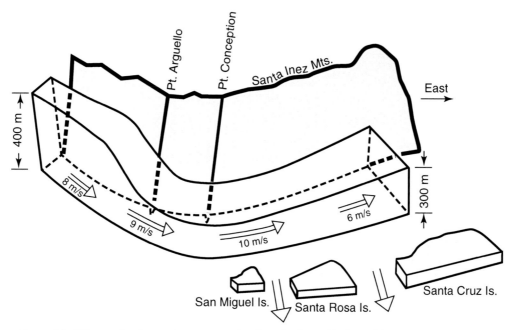

Figure 10. Schematic model of the marine layer structure turning into the Santa Barbara Channel. The marine air thins, expands, and accelerates as it turns the corner into the Santa Barbara Channel, causing the fastest winds to be at the western mouth.

Model

We propose that the dynamical explanation for the high speed winds in the western mouth of the Santa Barbara Channel is a transcritical expansion fan. Supercritical marine layer conditions were found around Point Arena (Winant et al. 1988). Subcritical upstream flow with Froude numbers between 0.5 and 1.0 will result in limited areas of supercritical or transcritical flow in the lee of a point (Rogerson 1998) which is what is found here.

The conditions in the western mouth are very much like a supercritical or transcritical expansion fan in the lee of a corner. A schematic model in Figure 10 summarizes the details. Under strong, supercritical flow to the south or southeast, the near sea level air accelerates from around Point Arguello/Point Conception to the speed maximum around B54. At the same time the atmospheric marine layer expands and thins to a minimum height and the sea-level pressure decreases. The inversion also tilts downward to the north across the channel, making the lowest inversion base along the north coast. As marine air continues eastward toward B53, it slows and the vertical dimension increases. Some of the air mass entering the western mouth exits at supercritical speeds via the gaps between the Channel Islands.

LITERATURE CITED

Dorman, C. E. and C. D. Winant. 1995. Buoy observations of the atmosphere along the west coast of the United States, 1981-1990. Journal of Geophysical Research 100:16029-16044.

Rogerson, A. M. 1998. Transcritical Flows in the Coastal Marine Atmospheric Boundary Layer. Journal of the Atmospheric Sciences. In press.

Winant, C. D., C. E. Dorman, C. A. Friehe, and R. C. Beardsley. 1988. The marine layer off northern California: An example of supercritical channel flow. Journal of the Atmospheric Sciences 45:3588-3605.

SUNDOWNERS, DOWNSLOPE WIND EVENTS AROUND THE SANTA BARBARA CHANNEL

Erik Klimczak[1] and Clive E. Dorman[2]

[1]Department of Geological Sciences, San Diego State University
5500 Campanile Drive, San Diego, CA 92182
(858) 594-5586, E-mail: eklimczak@geology.sdsu.edu
[2]Center for Coastal Studies, Scripps Institution of Oceanography, La Jolla, CA 92093-0209
(858) 534-7863, E-mail: clive@coast.ucsd.edu

ABSTRACT

Sundowners are downslope winds, occurring mainly in the late afternoon to early evening, that cause an irregular temperature increase in the Santa Barbara area. A study was made from September 1995 through August 1997, based upon a dense network of surface meteorological stations around the Santa Barbara Channel, as well as a radar profiler, and National Weather Service charts. Statistics were developed about the occurrence, wind strengths, and horizontal extent of events over the Santa Barbara Channel. A sundowner event on June 30, 1996, 0000 Greenwich Mean Time (GMT) was used to show that sundowners are mesoscale events influenced by the topography and strength of the marine layer. Although consistent with synoptic scale pressure gradients and maps indicating offshore flow, the events during this study showed offshore winds over a very limited aerial extent, with some coastal stations having onshore winds at all levels, and most offshore stations being unaffected. In general, the events during this study did not show good correlations to pressure differences between Santa Maria and buoy 54, or Bakersfield and buoy 54.

Keywords: Santa Barbara, sundowners, downslope winds.

INTRODUCTION

Downslope winds that commonly occur in the late afternoon to early evening are known as "sundowners" in the Santa Barbara area. These winds are heated adiabatically as they descend downslope from the north on the lee side of the east–west trending Santa Ynez Mountains, forming a lee side trough and a temperature increase outside of the diurnal norm. The Santa Barbara area is located just south of the Santa Ynez Mountains, along a one to five mile wide coastal plain (Ryan 1996). Fifteen surface stations and a radar profiler were used to determine the horizontal and vertical extent of sundowner winds (Figure 1). The events during this study, from September 1995 through August 1997, most frequently occurred at Gaviota West (godw), a surface station on the coast at the mouth of a canyon leading up

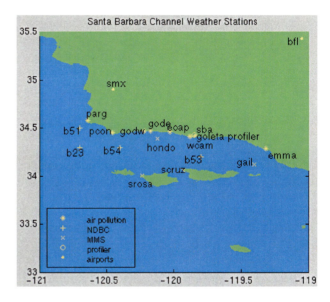

Figure 1. Location map of weather stations around the Santa Barbara Channel.

Nojoqui Pass. One possible reason for this is that Nojoqui Pass is the lowest gap in the Santa Ynez Mountains. Another is that godw is the furthest northwest of the stations studied, with the exception of buoy 51 and Point Conception (pcon), which are on the windward side of the mountains and are not affected by sundowner winds. National Weather Service charts were also used to determine the synoptic scale conditions during sundowner events.

MATERIALS AND METHODS

There were two main criteria used to find sundowner events during this study. First, days with temperatures greater than 25°C correlated with north (offshore) winds were found from monthly time series plots at Gaviota West. Then these days were used to find when there was a temperature difference of 10°C or more between Gaviota West and buoy 54. These criteria were used because 25°C is much higher than the average summer temperature of about 18°C to 19°C in this area, and because buoy 54 is usually unaffected by events and represents the regional norm if there was no sundowner event (Dorman et al., in press). When days of possible events were determined from these criteria, time series plots of about one week around the event day were made for the temperature at Gaviota West, the pressure gradients between Bakersfield (BFL) and buoy 54, and Santa Maria (SMX) and buoy 54, and the north wind component at Gaviota West (Figure 2). These plots and scatter plots of the godw/buoy 54 temperature difference vs. BFL/buoy 54 pressure difference, godw/buoy 54 temperature difference vs. SMX/buoy 54 pressure difference, godw/buoy 54 temperature difference vs. godw north wind speed, BFL/buoy 54 pressure difference vs. godw north wind speed, SMX/buoy 54 pressure difference vs. godw north wind speed, and godw temperature vs. godw north wind speed were made to determine any correlations between these pressure gradients and sundowner events (Figure 3). Correlation coefficients for temperatures between stations and north wind speed components between stations were calculated for the time of maximum temperature at Gaviota West (Tables 1 and 2). The event that occurred on June 30, 1996, 0000 GMT was then chosen to further study the synoptic and mesoscale conditions for a sundowner event. For this date, a map of the winds at all stations and a table of their temperatures was made (Figure 4), the wind speeds and temperatures at various heights from the surface to 2295 m were determined from a radar profiler at Goleta (Figure 5), and National Weather Service surface and 850 mb charts were studied to determine the synoptic scale conditions during this event (Figures 6 and 7).

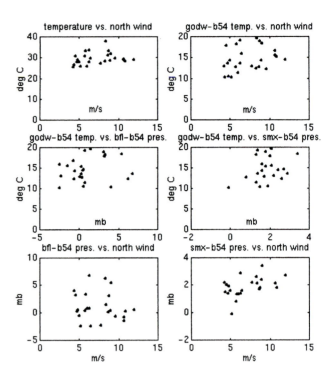

Figure 3. Scatter plots of godw temperature vs. north wind speed, godw-buoy54 temperature vs. north wind, godw-buoy 54 temperature vs. bfl-buoy 54 pressure, godw-buoy 54 temperature vs. smx-buoy 54 pressure, bfl-buoy 54 pressure vs. godw north wind, and smx-buoy 54 pressure vs. godw north wind for all sundowner events from September 1995 through August 1997.

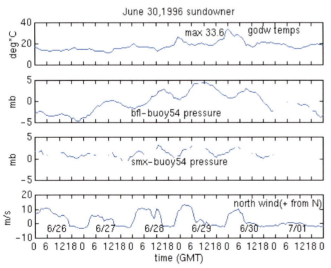

Figure 2. Time series plots of temperatures, pressure gradients, and north wind speed components.

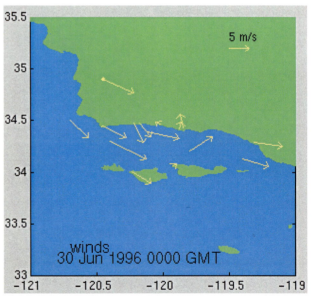

Figure 4. Map of winds on June 30, 1996, 0000 GMT and table of station temperatures.

station	temperature	station	temperature	station	temperature
pcon	21.5 C	ecap	28.3 C	srosa	18.8 C
godw	33.6 C	wcam	21.2 C	scruz	19.3 C
gode	34.1 C	buoy 54	14.4 C	gail	17.5 C
hondo	31.6 C	buoy 53	16.6 C		

Table 1. Correlation coefficients of temperatures between stations during sundowner events from September 1995 through August 1997.

station	godw	gode	ecap	wcam	buoy 54	hondo	gail	srosa	scruz
godw	1	0.7188	0.5644	0.5514	0.3275	0.7619	0.3089	0.3052	0.4417
gode	0.7188	1	0.7051	0.5263	0.0884	0.7545	0.2132	0.2094	0.3012
ecap	0.5644	0.7051	1	0.7207	0.2003	0.6867	0.3427	0.2032	0.3106
wcam	0.5514	0.5263	0.7207	1	0.3605	0.5857	0.5715	0.2724	0.4657
buoy 54	0.3275	0.0884	0.2003	0.3605	1	0.3722	0.6903	0.869	0.8807
hondo	0.7619	0.7545	0.6867	0.5857	0.3722	1	0.3793	0.4815	0.6015
gail	0.3089	0.2132	0.3427	0.5715	0.6903	0.3793	1	0.5568	0.7219
srosa	0.3052	0.2094	0.2032	0.2724	0.869	0.4815	0.5568	1	0.9096
scruz	0.4417	0.3012	0.3106	0.4657	0.8807	0.6015	0.7219	0.9096	1

Table 2. Correlation coefficients of north wind speed components between stations during sundowner events from September 1995 through August 1997.

station	godw	gode	ecap	wcam	buoy 54	hondo	gail	srosa	scruz
godw	1	0.4661	0.0727	NaN	0.3614	0.1988	NaN	-0.3124	-0.2039
gode	0.4661	1	0.4358	NaN	-0.0973	0.4021	NaN	-0.2134	0.059
ecap	0.0727	0.4358	1	NaN	-0.087	0.3747	NaN	-0.1821	0.0859
wcam	NaN	NaN	NaN	1	NaN	NaN	NaN	NaN	NaN
buoy 54	0.3614	-0.0973	-0.087	NaN	1	-0.0157	NaN	-0.0109	-0.0228
hondo	0.1988	0.4021	0.3747	NaN	-0.0157	1	NaN	-0.0516	0.3159
gail	NaN	NaN	NaN	NaN	NaN	NaN	1	NaN	NaN
srosa	-0.3124	-0.2134	-0.1821	NaN	-0.0109	-0.0516	NaN	1	0.2154
scruz	-0.2039	0.059	0.0859	NaN	0.0228	0.3159	NaN	0.2154	1

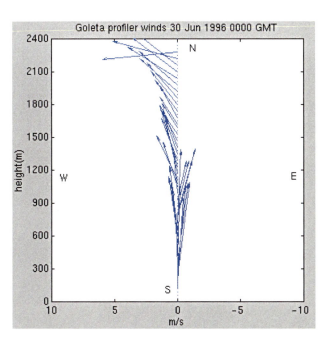

Figure 5. Wind speeds to 2295 m from the Goleta radar profiler for June 30, 1996, 0000 GMT.

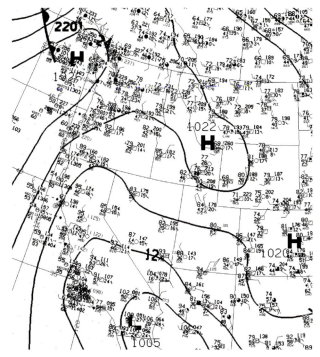

Figure 6. National Weather Service surface chart for June 30, 1996, 00Z.

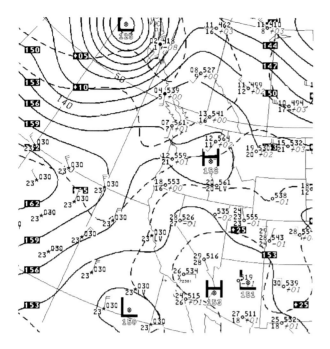

Figure 7. National Weather Service 850mb chart June 30, 1996, 00Z.

RESULTS

The sundowner events during this study occurred mainly between 2100 GMT and 0000 GMT. Figure 4 is a map of the winds and a table of the temperatures at all stations on June 30, 1996, 0000 GMT (June 29, 1996, 1700 PDT). Gaviota West and Gaviota East (gode) were most affected by sundowner winds from the north-northwest with temperatures of 33.6°C and 34.1°C, respectively. Hondo platform, the closest offshore station, was also affected by sundowner winds with a temperature of 31.6°C and winds from the west. Sundowner winds did not extend to the offshore stations buoy 51, buoy 54, Santa Rosa Island, or GAIL platform, where west-northwest winds prevailed with cool temperatures. These winds also did not affect Santa Cruz Island or buoy 53, where there were cool temperatures and winds from the southwest. El Capitan had onshore winds from the southeast and a temperature of 28.3°C. Finally, the surface station at West Campus (wcam) also had onshore winds, but from the southwest with a temperature of 21.2°C. The pressure gradient from BFL to buoy 54 was 0.7 mb, and from SMX to buoy 54 was 1.4 mb. There were very poor correlations of both north wind speed and temperatures between all coastal and nearshore stations during sundowner events, while the two island stations had a good temperature correlation (Tables 1 and 2). Winds were plotted from the surface to 2295 m using data from a radar profiler at Goleta. Profiler winds were variable and did not appear to increase from the north at height as expected (Figure 5). In fact, the winds were onshore (from southerly directions) at all levels from the surface to 2295 m.

DISCUSSION

Surface and upper air charts show that the sundowner event on June 30, 1996, 0000 GMT was associated with synoptic scale trough passage through central and southern California (Figures 6 and 7). Surface charts show a thermal low in the southeastern California desert and highs in southeast Idaho, and the Pacific Northwest. The 850 mb charts also show low pressure in the desert Southwest with higher pressure to the north. These charts are consistent with offshore flow in the Santa Barbara area, but as Figure 4 shows, this is not the case at all surface stations or the profiler in Goleta. Sundowners then must be mesoscale events, with some dependence on synoptic scale conditions. It appears that sundowners go offshore, mainly over godw, and meet the marine layer, where they then deflect off of it and veer to the east, in this case, a little further offshore than Hondo platform. Also, some coastal stations such as wcam and goleta did not experience these winds, possibly because they were bathed in marine air sheltering them. However, these stations may also be affected by sundowner events on a mesoscale in that onshore winds there are going in to fill the low created by heated downslope winds at godw.

Some events showed considerable north to south pressure gradients between SMX and buoy 54, and BFL and buoy 54. However, there does not appear to be a direct correlation between the events studied and pressure gradients, as evident by the scatter plots and statistics. Some events even had a negative gradient between BFL and buoy 54. This is in conflict with the hypothesis that sundowners are associated with synoptic scale, north to south, offshore pressure gradients between SMX and Santa Barbara, and BFL and Santa Barbara. As expected there is a closer relationship between the closer SMX station and buoy 54 pressure gradient though, and there is consistency in synoptic scale conditions when studying the surface and upper air charts for sundowner events.

Finally, an interesting observation for most events was that the winds at godw continued to increase from the north, often to speeds greater than 10 m/s, even after the time of maximum temperature. One possibility for this is that cooler marine air is brought over the Nojoqui Pass from the Santa Maria Basin after the sundowner event occurs.

LITERATURE CITED

Dorman, C. E., C. D. Winant, and J. Bane. 1997. The marine layer in and around the Santa Barbara Channel. Submitted to Monthly Weather Review.

Ryan, G. 1996. Downslope winds of Santa Barbara, California. National Oceanic and Atmospheric Administration Technical Memorandum, National Weather Service WR-240. NEXRAD Weather Service Forecast Office, Oxnard, California.

VERTICAL STRUCTURE OF THE MARINE ATMOSPHERIC BOUNDARY LAYER

Kathleen A. Edwards[1] and Clinton D. Winant[2]

[1]Center for Coastal Studies, Scripps Institution of Oceanography, UCSD
9500 Gilman Drive, La Jolla, CA 92093-0209
(858) 534-7202, FAX (858) 534-0300, E-mail: kate@coast.ucsd.edu
[2]Center for Coastal Studies, Scripps Institution of Oceanography, UCSD
9500 Gilman Drive, La Jolla, CA 92093-0209
(858) 534-2067, FAX (858) 534-0300, E-mail: cdw@coast.ucsd.edu

ABSTRACT

The marine atmospheric boundary layer (MABL) is the lowest layer of the atmosphere over the ocean. Along the California coast it is about 400 m thick in the summer. It is cooled and moistened by the ocean below and separated from warm, dry free troposphere above by a region of rapidly increasing temperature, known as the inversion layer. In June 1996, 377 vertical profiles of the MABL were recorded by an instrumented aircraft during the Coastal Waves 96 project. The speed and virtual potential temperature measured by the plane were shown to have a consistent form during the project, which covered 200 km across-shore and 800 km alongshore and took place over 11 days. The averaged dimensionless profiles show a wind jet located within the strongly statically stable inversion layer at the top of the slightly stable MABL. Different height scales for virtual potential temperature and wind speed gave the most effective scaling.

Keywords: Marine atmospheric boundary layer, coastal meteorology, California, vertical profiles.

INTRODUCTION

In summertime along the west coast, the marine atmospheric boundary layer (MABL) consists of a cool, moist layer of air about 400 m deep which is denser than the warm, dry air above (Figure 1). This vertical structure is well established and has been studied during several field experiments. Shipboard releases of instrumented balloons were the basis of a climatology showing an inversion-topped MABL with a jet in wind speed that extended far offshore (Neiburger et al. 1961). A. Miller described the strong inversion and jet in the MABL off of San Francisco (Lester 1985). During the Coastal Ocean Dynamics Experiment, the dynamics of the wind jet at the top of the MABL were investigated by Zemba and Friehe (1987) and Beardsley et al. (1987). The jet has been modeled by Holt (1996) and Burke and Thompson (1996).

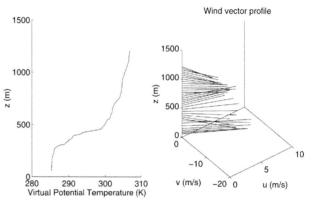
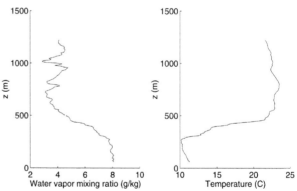

Figure 1. A typical profile of the MABL during summer taken by an instrument aircraft during Coastal Waves 96. Top left: Virtual potential temperature profile; Top right: Wind vector profile. Lower left: Water vapor mixing ratio profile; Lower right: Air temperature profile.

During June 1996, the Coastal Waves 96 field project studied the MABL within 200 km of the west coast. For 11 days of June 1996 an instrumented aircraft surveyed the MABL, recording standard meteorological variables such as temperature, humidity, and wind speed. Each survey included vertical profiles of the MABL from about 1500 m to the 30 m above the sea surface, as well as runs at level altitudes. Data was recorded at 25 Hz, rapid enough for the direct calculation of fluxes from covariances. The location of the profiles flown during all flights (Figure 2) shows that the survey region extended to about 200 km offshore and 800 km alongshore, from Cape Blanco in Oregon to Point Conception, California.

METHODS

The vertical boundaries defining the MABL are the sea surface below and the inversion layer above. Exchanges across these boundaries affect the vertical structure of the MABL. Fluxes calculated from runs at 30 m can be taken as representing fluxes across the ocean surface, since this altitude is within the surface layer. The fluxes were directly estimated from averaged covariances of the high-rate data. A histogram of fluxes from all 30 m runs (Figure 3) shows that most surface heat flux estimates were downward (negative) and most moisture fluxes were upwards (positive), indicating that the MABL was cooled and moistened by the ocean. Few runs were flown within the inversion layer, so the exchanges at the top of the MABL are not estimated here. Zemba and Friehe (1987) calculated a vertical profile of the exchange of momentum and found that it was highest near the sea surface where the drag of the sea surface slows the wind.

These exchanges of heat, moisture, and momentum give the MABL its vertical profile. The 377 vertical profiles flown during the Coastal Waves project were used to evaluate how persistent this vertical structure was during the project. Without scaling, the profiles of virtual potential temperature (Figure 4) and speed (Figure 5) appear variable. Altitude, speed, and virtual potential temperature scales were chosen by their success in collapsing the profiles onto a single shape. Speed (U) was scaled by the mean speed (U_{mean}) beneath the jet height (H_{jet}), giving $U(z)' = U(z)/U_{mean}$, where

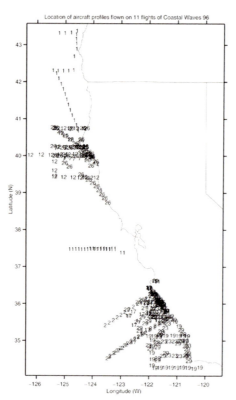

Figure 2. Profile locations indicated by the flight number. The survey region covered approximately 800 km alongshore and 200 km across shore.

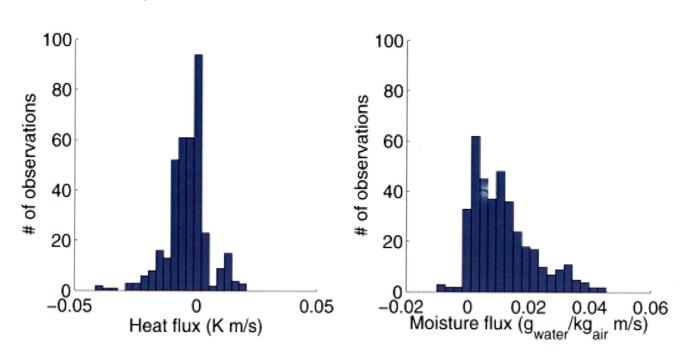

Figure 3. Histograms of fluxes calculated directly from high rate data at 30 m. Each 2 minute average counts as 1 observation. Left: Heat flux; Right: Moisture flux. Positive values are fluxes from the ocean to the atmosphere.

primes indicate dimensionless quantities. Altitude for the wind profiles was scaled with the height of the jet ($z' = z/H_{jet}$), following Forrer (1997). Virtual potential temperature (T) was scaled by the difference in temperature between the surface and the inversion base (dT), after subtracting out the mean temperature (T_{mean}) beneath the inversion base, giving $T(z)' = (T(z) - T_{mean})/dT$. The bottom of the inversion layer (H_{inv}) was chosen as the height scale for the virtual potential temperature profiles ($z' = z/H_{inv}$). Using the same height scale for the wind and virtual potential temperature profiles reduced the success of the scaling.

RESULTS

The majority the speed profiles scaled successfully (Figure 4). The mean dimensionless speed profile shows the wind jet maximum was about 25% greater than the mean speed, and the surface minimum was 25% less than the mean speed, an approximation used in Winant et al. (1988). The mean dimensionless virtual potential temperature profile shows the strongly statically stable inversion layer lying above the less stable MABL (Figure 5), with most profiles fitting into the scaling. Fedorovich (1997) scaled buoyancy profiles by the jump in buoyancy across the inversion layer and the thickness of the inversion. However, the fact that many of the profiles did not extend through the top of the inversion layer prevented use of this possibly more successful set of scales.

The height scales used for the virtual potential temperature and speed profiles were different. The success of the scaling decreased when the same height scale was used for both. A comparison of the two height scales (Figure 6) shows that when the MABL was fairly shallow, the jet height was just above the inversion base, and that the height scales

were comparable. A deep boundary layer (above 500 m) seems likely to have a jet beneath the top of the inversion base, but scatter is high. Some of the scatter may be attributed to the convective regime of the layer: when the layer was undergoing forced convection, the speed and virtual

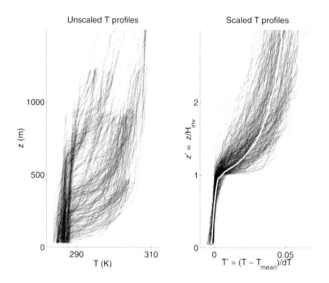

Figure 5. Left: Vertical profiles of virtual potential temperature. Right: The dimensionless virtual potential temperature profiles. Altitude was scaled with the height of the inversion base (Hinv). After the mean virtual potential temperature beneath the inversion base (Tmean) was removed, the profiles were scaled by the difference in temperature between the top and bottom of the marine atmospheric boundary layer (dT). The mean profile (white) is averaged over dimensionless altitude bins.

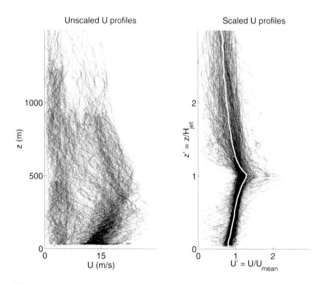

Figure 4. Left: Vertical profiles of wind speed. Right: The dimensionless speed profiles, with altitude (z) scaled by the height of the wind jet (Hjet) and speed scaled by the mean speed below the jet (Umean). The mean profile (white) is averaged over dimensionless altitude bins.

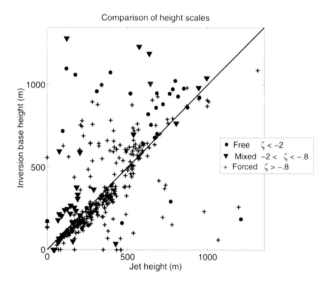

Figure 6. The height scale used in the speed profiles (Hjet) vs the height scale used in the virtual potential temperature profiles (Hinv). If the scales were the same they would lie along the strait line. The convective regime is given by z/L, where L is the Monin-Obukhov length scale calculated from the fluxes at 30 m: free convection (solid circles), mixed (triangles), or forced convection (crosses).

potential temperature scales were more likely to be close than in a free convective regime.

ACKNOWLEDGMENTS

K. Edwards is supported by an ONR AASERT fellowship.

LITERATURE CITED

Beardsley, R. C., C. E. Dorman, C. A. Friehe, L. K. Rosenfeld, and C. D. Winant. 1987. Local atmospheric forcing during the CODE experiment. 1. A description of the marine boundary layer and atmospheric conditions over a northern California upelling region. Journal of Geophysical Research 92(C2):1467-1488.

Burke, S. D. and W. T. Thompson. 1996. The summertime low-level jet and MBL structure along the California coast. Monthly Weather Review 124:668-686.

Fedorovich, E. E. and D. V. Mironov. 1997. A model for a shear-free convective boundary layer with parameterized capping inversion. Journal of the Atmospheric Sciences 52(1):83-95.

Forrer, J. and M. W. Rotach. 1997. On the turbulence structure in the stable boundary layer over the Greenland ice sheet. Boundary Layer Meteorology 35:111-136.

Holt, T. R. 1996. Mesoscale forcing of a boundary layer jet along the California coast. Journal of Geophysical Research 101(D2):4235-4254.

Lester, P. F. 1985. Studies of the marine inversion over the San Francisco Bay area: A summary of the work of Albert Miller, 1961-1978. Bulletin of the American Meteorological Society 66(11):1396-1402.

Nieburger, M., D. S. Johnson, and C.-W. Chien. 1961. Studies of the structure of the atmosphere over the eastern Pacific Ocean in summer, volume 1(1) of University of California Publications in Meteorology. University of California Press.

Winant, C. D., C. E. Dorman, C. A. Friehe, and R. Beardsley. 1988. The marine layer off norther California: An example of supercritical channel flow. Journal of the Atmospheric Sciences 45(23):3583-3605.

Zemba, J. and C. A. Friehe. 1987. The marine atmospheric boundary layer jet during the Coastal Ocean Dynamics Experiment. Journal of Geophysical Research 92(C2):1489-1496.

DRIFTER DATA SET FROM THE SANTA BARBARA CHANNEL–SANTA MARIA BASIN COASTAL CIRCULATION STUDY

Douglas John Alden

Center for Coastal Studies, Scripps Institution of Oceanography, UCSD
Mail Code 0209, 9500 Gilman Drive, La Jolla, CA 92093-0209
(858) 534-8997, FAX (858) 534-8299, E-mail: dalden@ucsd.edu

ABSTRACT

The drifter data from the Santa Barbara Channel - Santa Maria Basin Coastal Circulation Study (SBC-SMB CCS) is accessible via the Internet on the Center for Coastal Studies web and gopher sites. The drifter section of the web site also contains information on the instrumentation used, deployment dates, processing methods, and analysis. Users can map drifter track trajectories interactively using a web browser. Information on data set availability and format, and instructions for access are presented. Future plans for the web site interface are also discussed.

Keywords: Drifters, Santa Barbara Channel, Santa Maria Basin, circulation, currents, temperature, instrumentation.

INTRODUCTION

In this paper, drifter data collected since 1992 as part of the SBC-SMB CCS sponsored by the Minerals Management Service (MMS) are presented. The collection, processing, and archiving methods are explained, and access to the data sets is discussed.

Regional Coverage

Drifter deployments are primarily made within the Santa Barbara Channel (SBC) and Santa Maria Basin (SMB). There are 24 permanent sites used for drifter releases (Figure 1). In the early stages of this project (through 1995) only the 12 sites (red dots) in the SBC were used. Twelve additional sites (blue dots) in the SMB were added in 1996. The SBC-SMB CCS also includes a large component of moored instrumentation. Most of the drifter deployment sites coincide with current or historical mooring sites. Additionally, a few drifter pairs have been deployed during oil spill events to aid spill containment efforts.

DRIFTER INSTRUMENTATION

Overview

Drifter data have been collected in the SBC as part of this study since April of 1992, and in the SMB since 1996. A group of drifters is deployed every few months. The time it takes to release all the drifters in a group over the study

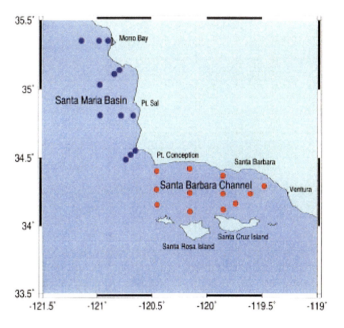

Figure 1. Map of the drifter deployment sites. Locations noted in red have been used since 1992, those in blue since 1996.

area ranges from a few hours to just over a day depending on the means of deployment. The electronics package used in the drifters is programmed to transmit data for 40 days. A complete list of the deployments to date is listed in Table 1.

Instrumentation

The drifters used in this study are similar to those used by Davis (1985). The electronics and battery are housed in a submerged vertical tube approximately 1 m in length (Figure 2). An antenna protrudes from the top of the tube and extends upward through the surface of the water. A temperature sensor is installed in the top of the tube adjacent to the antenna. Four cloth vanes of total area 1.8 m^2 are supported on rods that extend radially from the top and bottom of the tube. Four floatation elements are attached at the end of each rod by short lengths of nylon line. During deployment the top of the vertical tube is suspended 30 cm below the surface of the water. The drifter rod and vane assemblies can be collapsed for air deployment, although, the most common method of deployment has been from boats.

Table 1. Drifter deployment dates.

Deployment Number	Date	Release Numbers
2	May-93	34-48
3	Jul-93	49-64
4	Oct-93	65-76
5	Dec-93	77-92
6	Feb-94	93-104
7	Apr-94	105-116
8	Jun-94	119-131
9	Sep-94	132-148
10	Nov-94	149-161
11	Jan-95	162-180
12	Mar-95	181-193
13	May-95	194-205
14	Jul-95	206-217
15	Aug-95	218-240
16	Oct-95	241-252
17	Jan-96	253-273
18	May-96	274-295
19	Aug-96	296-319
20	Sep-96	320-340
21	Dec-96	341-364
22	Mar-97	365-392
23	Jul-97	395-420
24	Nov-97	421-444
25	Apr-98	445-459
26	Jul-98	460-484
27	Oct-98	485-506

Figure 2. Photograph of a drifter in the water.

The electronics consist of a controller with temperature circuit and transmitter. The drifter measures hourly averages of the sea surface temperature (SST) using a one-minute sample rate. Temperature samples have an accuracy of 0.01°C. Twelve hourly averages of SST are included in the data stream transmitted by the drifter. The transmitter in the drifter interfaces with ARGOS, a satellite-based location and data collection system. ARGOS satellites locate the drifters several times each day to within 150 to 1000 m, and collect drifter data. The drifters are programmed to operate for 40 days after deployment.

Most of the deployments have been from small boats. In particular, the vessels and personnel of the University of California, Santa Barbara Marine Sciences Department have been instrumental to the success of the drifter program. A few of the deployments have been made from the R/V *Sproul* during mooring recovery and deployment cruises. Some of the more recent deployments have been from the air by helicopter.

Data Processing

Raw position and temperature data are collected using ARGOS. The raw data are processed in a series of steps that results in two time series: position and temperature.

Position data files are created from locations as determined by ARGOS. The position data is not sampled at regular intervals in time due the orbit paths of the satellites. Satellites measure the Doppler shift in frequency of drifter transmissions as the satellites pass overhead. The Doppler shift

and a few other parameters are then used to determine the drifter location and assign an accuracy class to the position. Position data accuracy is classified by ARGOS in one of three categories: class 1 (350 to 1000 m), class 2 (150 to 350 m), and class 3 (±150 m). During processing, the drifter position data files are checked for the beaching of the drifter or removal of the drifter from the water; the data time series is truncated should one of these events occur.

Temperature data processing results in a time series of hourly averages of SST in °C. All drifter temperature circuits are calibrated prior to deployment. The calibration coefficients are applied to the data after transmission through ARGOS.

ANALYSIS

The SBC-SMB CCS is a multi-year program sponsored by the MMS to describe the flow, provide inputs to aid in the development of numerical models, and create general summaries of the flow for oil spill analysis. The drifters supplement the eulerian observations acquired from the moored array with a langragian component and provide insights into the near-surface circulation in the SBC and SMB. Several papers have been written with the drifter data.

Dever et al. (1998) provides a statistical analysis of the drifter data including comparisons to near-surface current meter data. Winant et al. (1998) develops synoptic descriptions of the SBC circulation. Dever et al. (1999) focuses on circulation around the Point Conception area.

Since the drifter data has been made available over the Internet, other scientists outside the SBC-SMB CCS program are using it in their research. Hobday (1998a, b) used the data to describe faunal patterns and dispersal on kelp rafts in southern California. Schroeder of the Marine Science Institute at the University of California Santa Barbara is using the data to correlate rockfish recruitment to kelp beds with various mesoscale oceanographic features.

INTERNET DATA ACCESS

The drifter data set is available via the Internet and can be accessed using a web browser or a Gopher client. A web browser is a software application such as Lynx, Microsoft Internet Explorer, Mosaic, or Netscape Navigator that is used to locate and display web pages. The URL for web browser access is:

www-ccs.ucsd.edu/research/sbcsmb/drifters

In addition to the data, the drifter web site provides information about the instrumentation used, deployment dates, processing methods, and analysis. It also has an interactive section that enables the user to create a map of drifter trajectories from any deployment.

Another method for accessing the data is via a Gopher client. Gopher is a document retrieval system developed by the University of Minnesota that pre-dates the World Wide Web. Gopher clients can access the data using the following address:

gopher-ccs.ucsd.edu/11/zoo/lbight/drifters

The gopher site only provides access to the processed data.

The drifter data from this project are archived in an ASCII format called CSA. This is a columnar format, with five lines of header information (Figure 3). In the near future all the data will be converted to netCDF, a binary format. Only drifter position data files are available at this time. Temperature time-series data files should be on-line sometime in the coming months.

```
start_time     npts    depth    release#
yymmddhhmmss   #_pts   meters
950824193800   3       1        227
time           latitude  longitude    location
yymmddhhmmss   deg        deg         quality
950824193800   34.100  -120.148   3
950825011854   34.098  -120.112   1
950825165851   34.071  -119.923   1
```

Figure 3. Sample of CSA-format file. This is the standard archive format for all drifter position data files.

LITERATURE CITED

Davis, R. E. 1985. Drifter observations of coastal surface currents during CODE: The method and descriptive view. Journal of Geophysical Research 90: 4741-4755.

Dever, E. P., M. C. Hendershott, and C. D. Winant. 1998. Statistical aspects of surface drifter observations of circulation in the Santa Barbara Channel. Journal of Geophysical Research 103:24,781-24,797.

SOURCES OF UNPUBLISHED MATERIALS

Dever, E. P., C. D. Winant, M. C. Hendershott. 1999. Near-surface drifter trajectories in the Pt. Conception area. Scripps Institution of Oceanography, UCSD, Mail Code 0209, La Jolla, CA 92093.

Hobday, A. J. 1998a. Faunal patterns and dispersal on kelp rafts in southern California. Ph.D. Dissertation. Scripps Institution of Oceanography. UCSD, La Jolla, CA 92093.

Hobday, A. J. 1998b. Abundance and dispersal of kelp rafts in southern California. Scripps Institution of Oceanography. UCSD, La Jolla, CA 92093.

Winant, C. D., D. J. Alden, E. P. Dever, K. A. Edwards, and M. C. Hendershott. 1998. Near-surface trajectories off central and southern California. Scripps Institution of Oceanography, UCSD, Mail Code 0209, La Jolla, CA 92093.

NEAR-SURFACE DRIFTER TRAJECTORIES IN THE POINT CONCEPTION AREA

Edward P. Dever, Clinton D. Winant, and Myrl C. Hendershott

Center for Coastal Studies, Scripps Institution of Oceanography, UCSD
9500 Gilman Dr. La Jolla, CA 92093-0209
(858) 534-8091, FAX (858) 534-0300, E-mail: edever@ucsd.edu

ABSTRACT

Over 450 satellite-tracked drifters deployed near Point Conception provide insights into the near-surface circulation in the region. Drifters were seeded uniformly throughout the region and in all seasons. This was done in order to sample evenly in space and time minimizing bias towards any one circulation pattern. After deployment, drifters either exited the region or beached on an island or mainland coast. Typical residence times for drifters which exited were 10 days. The near-surface drifters exhibit a response to wind forcing and pressure gradients. South and east of Point Conception, in the Santa Barbara Channel, hydrographic cruises provide evidence that baroclinic pressure gradients are important in determining drifter trajectories. Local wind forcing is also important in the southwestern Santa Barbara Channel. North and west of Point Conception, in the Santa Maria Basin, the picture is more complicated. Though the baroclinic pressure gradient is sometimes important, the barotropic pressure gradient may also play a role. Local wind forcing can also be important here. The drifters were equipped with accurate temperature sensors. These indicate the amplitude of diurnal heating and cooling as well as giving insight into temperature mixing.

Keywords: Santa Barbara Channel, Santa Maria Basin, near-surface circulation, field observations

INTRODUCTION

To learn more about circulation within the Santa Barbara Channel and Santa Maria Basin and to better assess oil spill risks, the Minerals Management Service has funded an extensive oceanographic field program, the Santa Barbara Channel - Santa Maria Basin Coastal Circulation Study (Hendershott and Winant 1996; Harms and Winant 1998). The program included over 450 surface drifters deployed at 24 locations in a rough grid pattern within the Santa Barbara Channel and Santa Maria Basin (Figure 1). It also included an extensive moored current meter array with near-surface vector-measuring current meters (VMCMs) at 5 m depth. During mooring turnaround cruises, combined conductivity-temperature-depth, expendable bathythermograph, and acoustic Doppler current profiler (CTD/XBT/ADCP) surveys were also made.

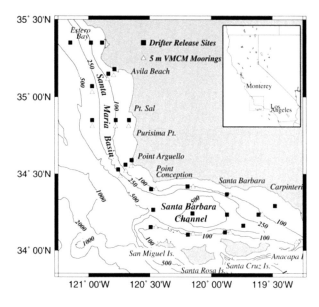

Figure 1. The Santa Barbara Channel and Santa Maria Basin, showing drifter deployment sites (solid squares) and vector-measuring current meter (VMCM) moorings (open triangles). Bottom bathymetry is also shown.

MATERIALS AND METHODS

The surface drifters used here are similar to the Davis (1985) Coastal Ocean Dynamics Experient (CODE) design. A central cylindrical case houses batteries and electronics. Four nylon sails are attached with fiberglass rods. Spherical styrofoam floats tied to the ends of the rods provide buoyancy. The nominal sampling depth of the drifters is 0.5 m. The primary difference between these drifters and the CODE type is the use of ARGOS satellite tracking rather than radio tracking. Positions were acquired for at least 40 days. Generally, four to five fixes per day are available with an accuracy of under 1 km (most often, under 300 m). Drifters and moored velocity measurements (Dever et al. 1998) compare well. Drifters also measured temperature (calibrated to 0.01°C) once per min and averaged them every hour.

Our data come almost entirely from drifters deployed on 25 occasions between May 1993 and July 1998. Additional data from a few drifters deployed in testing and for oil spill response drills also exist. To sample the seasonal variability, deployments were spaced about every 3 months. From 1993 to 1995, drifters were deployed mainly in the Santa Barbara Channel with only one or two drifters deployed in the Santa Maria Basin. Beginning in January 1996 the focus of the field effort shifted to the Santa Maria Basin with 12 drifters released there in each deployment.

During mooring turnaround cruises, drifters were deployed from the survey ship. In between these cruises, drifters were deployed from a small boat or helicopter. When survey data is available it greatly aids in interpreting the initial drifter trajectories. Ship surveys were generally completed in two days or less. To decrease survey time and increase synopticity, the primary survey method was XBTs. A temperature-salinity (T/S) relation based on historical CTD data was then used to estimate salinity from temperature. Underway velocity measurements were also acquired using a ship-mounted or towed ADCP.

Moored velocity and wind measurements also aid in the interpretation of drifter tracks. Between 1993 and 1995, eight moorings were in the Santa Barbara Channel with one or two moorings in the Santa Maria Basin. Since the beginning of 1996, 12 mooring sites within the Santa Maria Basin have been occupied along with sites at the eastern and western Santa Barbara Channel. Each mooring includes a near-surface vector-measuring current meter (VMCM) at 5 m. Winds from National Data Buoy Center (NDBC) buoys and meteorological stations on oil platforms and the coast were also acquired.

RESULTS

Residence Times and Beaching

The residence time is defined here as the length of time a drifter spends in a specified region. Two regions are considered. The first is the Santa Barbara Channel, and the second is the Santa Maria Basin. The Santa Barbara Channel has well defined boundaries consisting of the eastern and western entrances and the Channel Islands. The Santa Maria Basin has more nebulous boundaries. Here we consider it to extend from Estero Bay south to a latitude near the Channel Islands and from the coast to 121.25°W. The Santa Barbara Channel and Santa Maria Basin regions considered here are indicated on Figure 2 and are roughly equal in area.

Within the Santa Barbara Channel, relatively large temperature gradients and spatially variable wind forcing exist (Harms and Winant 1998). The combination of wind and temperature forcing leads to a commonly-observed vigorous anti-clockwise (cyclonic) feature in the western channel with weaker circulation in the east. These characteristics affect the residence time and likelihood of beaching. In the Santa Barbara Channel, drifters launched in the western channel exited most rapidly (Figure 2) and had the lowest likelihood of beaching. Several of the beached drifters launched in the northwest channel actually were caught up in the cyclonic circulation, transported south and beached on the

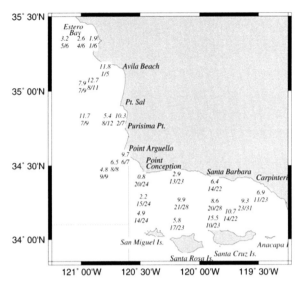

Figure 2. Residence times of drifters in the Santa Barbara Channel and Santa Maria Basin areas. The Santa Barbara Channel region considered here extends south along the solid line from the mainland between Point Arguello and Point Conception to the bottom of the map and east to the eastern boundary of the map. The Santa Maria Basin extends from the top of the map south to the dashed line west of San Miguel and east to the solid line marking the western boundary of the Santa Barbara Channel region. At each drifter launch point, the three numbers shown correspond to: median residence time of those exiting in days over the (number exiting)/(number deployed) e.g. at the northwest channel location 0.8 over 20/24 indicates a median residence time of 0.8 d with 20 exiting the Channel region out of 24 deployed.

Channel Island coasts. Drifters launched in the eastern channel had longer residence times with an increased likelihood of beaching. These drifters generally beached near their launch points.

The Santa Maria Basin shelf is generally broader than that in the channel (approximately 20 km), while the coast is distinguished by Point Arguello, Purisima Point, and Point Sal. Within the Santa Maria Basin, wind forcing is more uniform and temperature gradients arise largely due to coastal upwelling. Most drifters deployed in the Santa Maria Basin exited within 10 days. Drifters deployed in the north across Estero Bay exited the region most rapidly. Drifters launched at the inshore locations near Avila Beach and Point Sal were the most likely to beach and beached near their launch point. Interestingly, few of the drifters launched at the Point Arguello line beached. Initial offshore movement was usually followed by southward flow west of San Miguel Island in summer or northward flow through the Santa Maria Basin in fall and winter. In only one deployment (April 1998) were drifters observed to transit into the Santa Barbara Channel from the Point Arguello line.

The Roles of Baroclinic Pressure Gradients and Wind Forcing

Despite the fact that drifters sample at a depth of less than 1 m, their trajectories can show effects of both subsurface baroclinic pressure gradients and surface wind forcing (local Ekman transport). Baroclinic pressure gradients are derived from horizontal gradients of density (temperature and salinity) as measured during CTD/XBT ship surveys. When pressure gradients act to balance the acceleration due to the Earth's rotation (Coriolis force), flow tends to occur along lines of constant pressure (geostrophic flow). Likewise, direct wind forcing of near-surface flow is affected by the Coriolis force such that wind-forced flow tends to be directed to the right of the wind in the northern hemisphere (Ekman flow). The effects of both geostropic and Ekman flow are seen when the drifter trajectories are examined in light of measured wind stress and the ship survey baroclinic pressure field (dynamic topography).

The effect of the baroclinic pressure gradient is seen most clearly in the western Santa Barbara Channel where a large low exists (Figure 3). Flow tends to be cyclonic (counterclockwise in the northern hemisphere) around this low. It is evidenced both by the drifters as well as by moored current meter and ship-survey ADCP measurements, and the magnitude of the flow as estimated by the baroclinic pressure gradient is approximately that observed.

Elsewhere, the consistency of the observed flow with the dynamic topography varies. In the southwest Santa Barbara Channel, where winds tend to be strong, wind forcing tends to force drifters in a southwest direction across lines of constant pressure. In the eastern Santa Barbara Channel

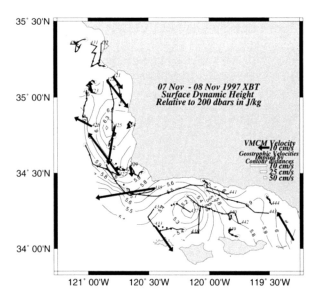

07 Nov - 08 Nov 1997 XBT
Surface Dynamic Height
Relative to 200 dbars in J/kg

VMCM Velocity
10 cm/s
Geostrophic Velocities
Implied by
Contour distances
10 cm/s
25 cm/s
50 cm/s

Figure 3. Surface dynamic topography with drifter trajectories and near-surface current meter vectors superimposed. The drifter trajectories are shown for approximately one day after deployment. Numbers indicate the start position of drifters are connected by solid lines to the open circles which indicate the last fix received on 8 November. Solid dots indicate drifter positions interpolated every six hours. In some cases they extend beyond the open circle to give a qualitative indication of drifter movement. VMCM velocity arrows are scaled such that their length corresponds to the distance a particle with that velocity would travel in one day.

the flow often bears little resemblance to that implied by topography while in the Santa Maria Basin, the baroclinic pressure gradient tends to have a smaller effect on the flow. Occasionally, as in Figure 3, it can be quite large in the Santa Maria Basin, but generally the flow implied by the dynamic topography is weaker than the observed flow. The strength of the observed flow relative to the dynamic topography may in part be due to a large contribution by the barotropic pressure gradient which is not included in the dynamic topography.

Drifter Temperature Variability

Drifter temperature variability occurs on both diurnal and lower frequency time scales. Diurnal temperature variability occurs due to daytime near-surface warming and nighttime cooling. The magnitude of the diurnal cycle is affected by the wind stress as well as the solar radiation received during the day. High wind stress causes vertical mixing of heat input by the sun down to 10 m or more and a smaller near-surface temperature change than if solar heating were confined to the top couple of meters. Thus the amplitude of the diurnal heating cycle is primarily a function of the local wind conditions rather than the seasonal variation of solar radiation. Its amplitude generally ranges from about 0.5 to 2°C.

Averaged over time scales of several days, the net surface heat flux has a relatively small effect on drifter temperatures and on these time scales temperature variability occurs primarily due to horizontal and vertical mixing. The paths of the drifters in combination with the observed surface temperatures give some insight into temperature mixing. For example, in summer temperature isolines trend roughly southeast to northwest in the Santa Barbara Channel. The warmest temperatures are found along the mainland coast while the coldest temperatures are found in the southwest and in the center of the cyclonic circulation cell. Drifters often transit around the circulation cell with periods of several days. As a drifter moves from the north coast south towards the Channel Islands its temperature almost always decreases by several degrees. Either vertical mixing with colder subsurface water or horizontal mixing with colder surface water can cause this. Later it may head east and north to complete the cyclonic circulation. During this time its temperature generally increases. This increase is probably due to horizontal mixing only as mixing with colder subsurface water can only decrease its temperature further.

The drifter trajectories complement moored measurements and provide the most direct insights into water parcel movement available. They can be used qualitatively to gauge the likelihood of pollutants released at different locations impacting the coast. In the Santa Maria Basin, drifters released near the shore had the highest likelihood of beaching. They generally beached near their release points. In the Santa Barbara Channel, drifters released in the eastern channel were the most likely to beach. They too usually beached near their release point. Drifters released in the northwest channel were less likely to beach, but those which did often traveled south and beached on the Channel Islands.

Trajectories indicate that drifter movement in the Santa Barbara Channel results largely from subsurface baroclinic pressure gradients. These pressure gradients are consistent with the observed vigorous cyclonic circulation in the western Santa Barbara Channel. In the channel, wind forcing is important mainly in the southwest and results in a tendency for southwest flow. In the Santa Maria Basin, wind stress forcing is also important while subsurface pressure gradients are weak. Though wind stress and dynamic topography influence the drifter paths, trajectories often exhibit a smaller-scale structure than either the measured wind stress or dynamic topography. In some cases this may be due to limits on our ability to resolve dynamic topography and wind stress. In other cases it clearly indicates the importance of dynamics other than geostrophy and surface Ekman flow. These processes may also influence the temperature variations observed by the drifters.

LITERATURE CITED

Davis, R. E. 1985. Drifter observations of coastal surface currents during CODE: The method and descriptive view. Journal of Geophysical Research 90:4741–4755.

Dever, E. P., M. C. Hendershott, and C. D. Winant. 1998. Statistical aspects of surface drifter observations of circulation in the Santa Barbara Channel. Journal of Geophysical Research 103:24,781–24,797.

Harms, S., and C. D. Winant. 1998. Characteristic patterns of the circulation in the Santa Barbara Channel. Journal of Geophysical Research 103:3041–3065.

Hendershott, M. C., and C. D. Winant. 1996. Surface circulation in the Santa Barbara Channel. Oceanography 9:114–121.

THE SURFACE CIRCULATION OF THE SANTA BARBARA CHANNEL AS OBSERVED WITH HIGH FREQUENCY RADAR

Libe Washburn[1], Brian M. Emery[1] and Jeffrey D. Paduan[2]

[1]Institute for Computational Earth System Science, Dept. of Geography
University of California, Santa Barbara, CA 93106-3060
(805)-893-7367, FAX (805) 893-2578, E-mail: washburn@icess.ucsb.edu
[2]Naval Postgraduate School, Code OC/Pd, Monterey, CA 93943-5000
(831) 656-3350, FAX (831) 656-3350, E-mail: paduan@oc.nps.navy.mil

ABSTRACT

We are using an array of high frequency (HF) radar systems to observe the surface circulation in the western Santa Barbara Channel. Observations of surface currents are important for understanding the basic physical processes controlling coastal circulation. In addition, the movements of river runoff plumes, buoyant pollutants such as oil, and larvae of many marine species are governed by surface currents. We have established a network of three HF radar sites along the northern boundary of the Santa Barbara Channel: at Coal Oil Point, near Refugio State Beach, and at Point Conception. Each radar system has a range of about 40 to 50 km, depending on conditions, and surface current maps are produced hourly. Preliminary analysis reveals that the surface circulation in the Channel is often dominated by eddies. Some of these eddies propagate westward at a few kilometers per day and have lifetimes of several days. Others are nearly stationary for several days. Eddies with both clockwise and counter-clockwise rotations are observed. At times, broad areas of the Channel rapidly respond to the local wind field. At other times, surface currents appear to result from remote forcing process. In addition to circulation studies, we are evaluating the performance of the HF radar systems by comparison with conventional, in situ current meters.

Keywords: Eddies, biogeographic boundaries, current measurement.

INTRODUCTION

The Santa Barbara Channel is a cross-roads for large-scale water masses moving along the California coast. Waters from the north are cooled by coastal upwelling as they move southward through sub-polar regions. Most of these waters pass outside the Channel Islands, but some are swept into the Channel through the western entrance. Warm water from the south, heated in the sub-tropics, flows northward along the coast and enters the Channel from the east. These contrasting waters swirl and mix in the Channel to form the complex patterns often visible in satellite images of sea surface temperature. These coastal currents bring together an abundance of diverse marine life from widely separated ocean regions. A series of oceanographic studies since the 1969 oil spill have greatly enhanced our knowledge of the circulation processes in the Channel. However, much remains to be learned. For example, the relationship between distributions of marine organisms and current patterns is not well understood, but is crucial for such practical issues as resource management and conservation.

The surface circulation of the Channel is of particular interest, because larvae of many marine organisms are transported by surface flows during the planktonic stages of their life cycles. Surface currents govern the dispersal of terrestrial runoff and pollutants into the coastal ocean. Accurate knowledge of surface circulation is important for navigation and the effective conduct of search and rescue operations. Surface flows in the Channel are exceedingly complex because they are produced by forces acting over a very wide range of time and space scales. The more persistent, large scale movements of water masses through the Channel result from dynamic process on scales much larger than the Channel itself. In contrast, local processes such as strong winds produce rapidly-evolving, energetic flows that vary over scales of several kilometers.

We are using a combination of remote sensing and in situ observations to study the surface circulation of the Channel. To observe directly the evolving structure of the flow field, we have deployed an array of high frequency (HF) radar systems along the mainland coast between the University of California Santa Barbara (UCSB) campus and Point Conception. This is the first time HF radar has been used to study oceanographic process in the Channel. The radar array provides higher spatial resolution than has previously been available. In this paper we provide an overview of our research employing the HF radar systems. We also discuss some of the interdisciplinary research being conducted to understand the consequences of the circulation for marine organisms.

MATERIALS AND METHODS

Measurement of ocean surface currents by HF radar is not new but has enjoyed renewed interest lately from the oceanographic community (for a recent review see Paduan and Graber 1997 and references therein). To make the measurement, a Doppler radar transmits electromagnetic energy (EMR) out over the ocean's surface and then detects the signal that is back-scattered from surface waves. The frequency of the back-scattered radar signal is Doppler-shifted because the velocities of the surface waves generally have components in the radial direction to the radar site. The received signal results from Bragg, scattering due to surface waves with wavelengths equal to one half the transmitted wavelength. For our radars, the transmitted frequency is 13 Mhz and, the wavelength is about 24 m. Thus the surface waves which back-scatter the EMR have a wavelength of 12 m. The frequency change of the received signal depends on the phase velocity of the surface waves and on the advection of the waves by surface currents. Because the waves producing the received signal have known wavelengths, their phase speed is known. The remaining part of the frequency change results from the surface current component. By measuring this change, the magnitude of surface current component along the radial path to the radar site can be determined. Use of multiple radars allows the total surface current vector to be determined over a broad area of the ocean's surface.

We have established an array of HF radar sites along the northern coast of the Channel (Figure 1) at the following locations: 1) Coal Oil Point on UCSB campus; 2) the Refugio operations center of the Channel Coast Ranger District; and 3) Point Conception. These installations were deployed in collaboration with the U.S. Coast Guard and the Channel Coast Ranger District of the California Department of Parks and Recreation. Apart from occasional power outages, the array has been collecting data hourly, around the clock since December 1997.

Each radar site has a Sea Sonde HF radar system (manufactured by CODAR Ocean Sensors, Ltd. of Los Altos, CA) consisting of a transmit antenna, a receive antenna, signal processing electronics, and a Macintosh Power PC computer. The transmitted power is about 50 watts at an adjustable frequency around 12.5 to 13 Mhz. The processing electronics and computer are mounted inside weatherproof housings at the sites. To maximize range, radar antennas are mounted as close to the water as is practical because the radar signals are attenuated rapidly over land.

The Sea Sonde systems operate autonomously to record data, which can be downloaded via modem from the three sites. The performance of the radar depends on factors such as sea state, atmospheric conditions, and wave direction. We find that the range is typically about 40 km, although longer ranges are often achieved. The coverage area from an individual site is occasionally much less than 40 km, however. This has been particularly true for the site at Point Conception. We do not know the reason for the diminished coverage, but are investigating a number of pos-

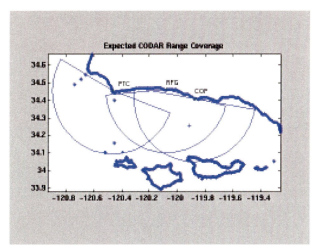

Figure 1. Approximate spatial coverage for each of the three Santa Barbara Channel HF radar sites. North and East ocean current velocity components are resolvable for regions covered by two or more HF radar sites.

sibilities including interference from other signal sources and variable oceanic conditions.

Raw data is processed into hourly maps of surface currents over an area of about 700 km^2 of the western Santa Barbara Channel (Figure 1). Data from each site is first processed to give maps of the radial component of surface current over circular sectors centered on each radar site. Radial current data from all sites are then combined to produce a vector map of surface currents over a grid of points. We organize the surface current data into monthly time series with a current measurement for each hour at each grid point. A typically monthly file is about 50 megabytes of data.

RESULTS

The radar observations show that the surface current field in the western Santa Barbara Channel evolves rapidly, although persistent features such as eddies are commonly observed. Recent results presented by Harms and Winant (1998), and Hendershott and Winant (1996), show that the circulation in the Channel varies seasonally. In summer the dominant pattern is a counter-clockwise circulation producing westward flow along the mainland and eastward flow along the north coasts of the western Channel Islands. In winter the pattern is more complex. At times, either clockwise or counter-clockwise patterns prevail, while at other times general eastward and westward movements of water result from winter storms. Using the radar array, we observed the winter-to-summer transition in circulation from December 1997 through June 1998. We computed the mean rotation rate of waters in the western Channel over this period from all available radar data. The results show that from December through February, the rotation varied between clockwise and counter clockwise patterns on time scales of about two weeks. By mid-March, the mean rotation was counter-clockwise and remained so at least through June 1998 (the extent of our analysis at the time of this writing).

This reproduced the findings of Harms and Winant (1998). It also gives us some assurance that the radar system is useful for examining circulation processes on seasonal time scales.

To illustrate the complex surface circulation in the Channel, we present an example from winter. Figure 2a shows a clockwise eddy in the western Channel on 13 December 1997. Maximum current speeds are 0.4 m s^{-1} and the eddy diameter is about 30 km. Over the next two days the eddy propagates westward at a rate of a few kilometers per day (Figures 2b, 2c). On 16 December 1997 (Figure 2d), the eddy appears to be decaying and its flow field is less organized. The study of Harms and Winant (1998) indicates that the velocity field of eddies like that of Figure 2 extends to depths of at least 45 m. Recent observations indicate a much deeper extent. In June 1998, we collaborated with Mary

Nishimoto of the Marine Science Institute (MSI) at UCSB in her survey of a counter-clockwise eddy of similar size and strength. Analysis of these data show that the eddy extended down to 200 m based on the deep temperature structure of the eddy. This indicates that these eddies are not merely surface features, but are important throughout the water column.

An important interdisciplinary goal of our research is to understand how the evolving circulation patterns affect the recruitment of marine larvae (such as those of rockfishes, urchins, and abalone) to coastal populations. It is well known that the recruitment is highly variable both spatially and temporally. However, the causes for the variability are not well understood. We are using our observations of surface currents to understand how advection and other coastal transport processes might affect recruitment. Studies from

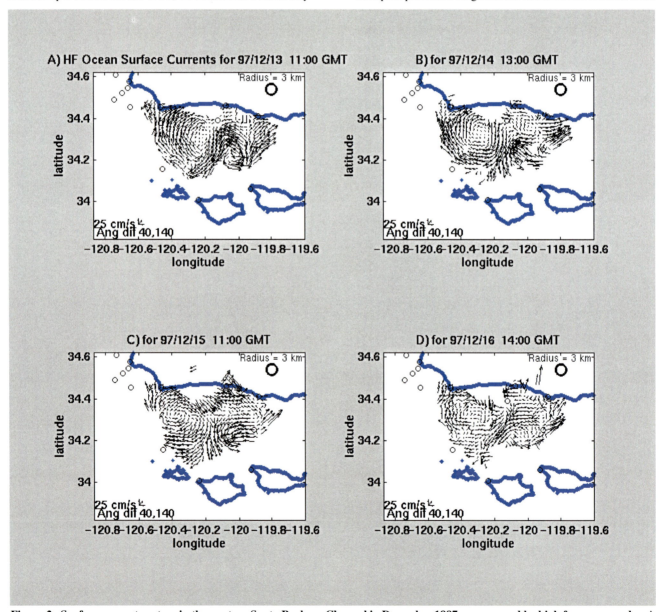

Figure 2. Surface current vectors in the western Santa Barbara Channel in December 1997 as measured by high frequency radar. A clockwise eddy is visible centered on 34.3°N, 120.2°W on 13 December (panel A). The eddy propagates westward at a few kilometers/day as seen on 14 December (panel B) and 15 December (panel C). By 16 December the eddy appeared to be dissipating (panel D). Radar stations are located at Coal Oil Point (COP), Refugio (RFG), and Point Conception (PTC). Scale at lower left indicates speed.

other areas indicate that coastal circulation processes are important in regulating recruitment (e.g., Farrell et al. 1991; Wing et al. 1995). An interesting characteristic of the Channel is that Point Conception is a significant biogeographic boundary: it is a northern range limit for many marine species. The reason why Point Conception is a biogeographic boundary is not understood at present. We are investigating the hypothesis that current patterns around the point inhibit northward transport of larvae. Other factors such as the large temperature gradients around the point may also be responsible.

To explain the spatial distributions of various invertebrate species along the California coast, a large array of intertidal sampling stations has been established from Ventura to San Simeon by Steven Gaines and colleagues from the MSI. At various piers and coastal sites, test substrates are placed below the low tide line such that larvae, if present, can settle out of the water column. The sampling indicates that occasional strong pulses of larvae arrive at the settlement sites. During these recruitment events, high numbers of larvae settle onto the substrates. Preliminary analysis suggests that some of these events may be associated with current reversals near shore. The reversals result from changes in the structure of eddies off shore as observed by our radar system. In an effort to understand the link between recruitment and flow patterns, we are extending our HF radar array to include two stations north of Point Conception: one at Point Arguello and another near Point Sal. This is being done in collaboration with Jack Harlan and colleagues of the Environmental Testing Laboratory of the National Oceanic and Atmospheric Administration (NOAA) in Boulder, Colorado.

In other studies, we use our real-time observations of surface currents to direct field sampling in specific flow features such as eddies. In June 1998 for example, surface current data obtained by our radar array were used to direct sampling of juvenile fish populations in the Channel. The field work was part of a larger effort to understand the causes of spatial and temporal variations in fish populations in the area. Mary Nishimoto, Milton Love, and colleagues at MSI are conducting the study. Over a two week period several net trawls were made in a strong counter-clockwise eddy that occupied the western Channel. Based on patterns obtained by the radar observations, many of the trawls were made in the core of the eddy. A surprising finding was that within the eddy, the abundance of several groups of juvenile fishes was greatly enhanced (by factors of 10 to 100) compared with surrounding waters. Examination of flow patterns in weeks preceding the field sampling indicates that a general counter-clockwise flow pattern had been present for several weeks before the experiment. We speculate that the weakly swimming juvenile fishes may be retained in the eddy longer than they would in its absence. Such retention may increase their survival. We are presently investigating this and other hypotheses to understand these extraordinary concentrations of juvenile fishes.

Another important goal of our study is the validation of the HF radar-derived ocean currents. Several moorings located in the coverage area of the HF radar array contain conventional current meters such as vector measuring current meters (VMCM), electromagnetic current meters, and acoustic doppler current profilers (ADCPs). Most of the moorings are maintained by the Center for Coastal Studies at the Scripps Institution of Oceanography. These current meters have well known characteristics, and provide valuable ground truth information for testing the accuracy of the HF radar. Ground truth tests are made between the radar data from a single HF site, and the component of the current meter data in the direction to that radar site. This method tests the radar data in a basic form to determine the accuracy of the radar measurement. Preliminary results suggest a high correlation ($r^2 > 0.7$) between the HF radar and moored current meter data (Figure 3), despite the inherent differences in the measurements. For example, the HF radar data measures the upper 1 m of the water column, over a large spatial area of typically 3 km^2, while the moored current meters are considered a point measurement, at 5 m water depth. While the high correlation is encouraging, improvements in the moored current meter measurements, such as removing mooring motions and advanced processing of the ADCP data to measure nearer the surface, may improve the correlation. These results should provide valuable information for interpreting HF radar data.

DISCUSSION

Our observations using HF radar systems confirm the complex nature of the surface flow of the Santa Barbara, in agreement with previous studies. We build on this previous research by obtaining observations of the flow field with much higher spatial resolution.

Comparison of surface currents derived from conventional current meters and HF radar shows that the radar systems perform satisfactorily. They are capable of mapping surface currents to about 40 km from shore with a spatial resolution of 3 to 5 km.

The radar systems have proven useful in directing field experiments so that specific flow features can be sampled with precision. This has allowed us to examine how populations of juvenile fishes are distributed in a persistent eddy in the Channel. It illustrates the importance of sampling marine communities where flow structures are concurrently observed. We feel that the radar technique will prove increasingly valuable in interdisciplinary studies of the coastal ocean.

ACKNOWLEDGMENTS

Funds for the radar system and its operations were provided by the W.M Keck Foundation and the Minerals Management Service. We thank Chief Ranger Richard Rojas of the Channel Coast Ranger District 910 of the California Department of Parks and Recreation for assistance in

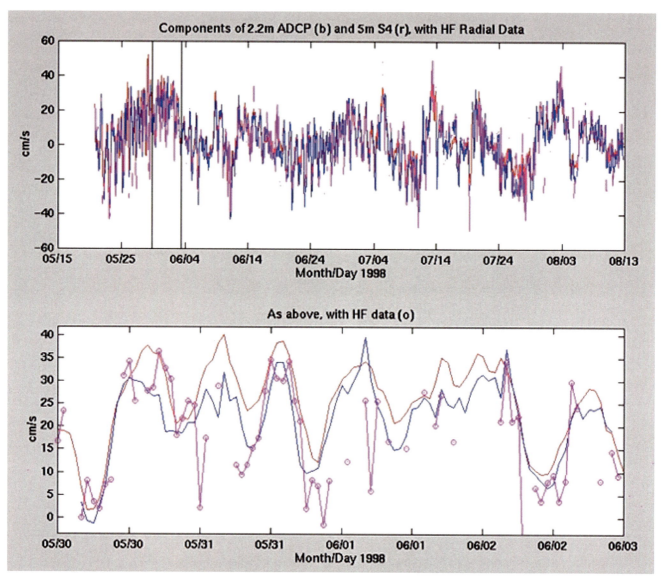

Figure 3. Time series of three independent ocean current measurements. Radial current speed measured from the COP HF radar site is plotted (magenta), along with the same component from an Acoustic Doppler Current Profiler (ADCP) at 2.2 m depth in blue, and an electromagnetic S4 current meter at 5 m depth in red. Velocity is positive in the direction toward the radar. The lower panel shows a three day section of the same time series. Comparing HF and ADCP measurements produces $r^2 = 0.67$, while comparing HF and S4 measurements produces $r^2 = 0.70$.

establishing the radar site at Refugio. We also thank the U.S. Coast Guard for allowing us to locate a radar site at the Point Conception lighthouse. Valuable assistance in setting up the radar systems and data processing has been provided by David Salazar, Ben Best, Chris Gotschalk, Krisada Lertchareonyong, and Michael Cook. We have benefited from valuable discussions with Brian Gaylord, Mary Nishimoto, Steve Gaines, Donna Schroeder, and Milton Love.

LITERATURE CITED

Farrell, T. M., D. Bracher, and J. Roughgarden. 1991. Cross-shelf transport causes recruitment to intertidal populations in central California. Limnology and Oceanography 36(2):279-288.

Harms, S., and C. D. Winant. 1998. Characteristic patterns of circulation in the Santa Barbara Channel. Journal of Geophysical Research 103(C2):3041-3065.

Hendershott, M. C., and C .D. Winant. 1996. The circulation in the Santa Barbara Channel. Oceanography. 9(2):114-121.

Paduan, J. D. and H. C. Graber. 1997. Introduction to high frequency radar: Reality and myth. Oceanography 10(2):36-39.

Wing, S. R., J. L. Largier, L. W. Botsford, and J. F. Quinn. 1995. Settlement and transport of benthic invertebrates in intermittent upwelling region. Limnology and Oceanography 40(2):316-329.

CIRCULATION PATTERNS IN THE SANTA BARBARA CHANNEL

Myrl C. Hendershott

Center for Coastal Studies, Scripps Institution of Oceanography, UCSD
Mail Code 0209, 9500 Gilman Drive, La Jolla, CA 92093-0209
(858) 534-7202, FAX (858) 534-0300, E-mail: mch@coast.ucsd.edu

ABSTRACT

Currents at depths of 5 m and 45 m as well as winds and sea surface pressures have been monitored since 1992 at moorings located in the Santa Barbara Channel and the Santa Maria Basin. Conditional averaging of the observed currents on local winds and on the measured along channel sea surface pressure difference reveals one circulation pattern individually forced by observed local winds, another individually forced by observed local gradients of sea surface pressure, and a third not attributable to either. These patterns closely resemble, but are not identical with, the upwelling, relaxation, and cyclonic synoptic patterns of Harms and Winant (1998).

Keywords: Santa Barbara Channel, Santa Maria Basin, ocean circulation, ocean currents, wind forcing, pressure gradient forcing, Minerals Management Service, sea surface pressure gradient.

INTRODUCTION

Materials And Methods

With the support of the Minerals Management Service, currents at depths of 5 m and 45 m as well as winds and sea surface pressures have been monitored since 1992 at moorings located in the Santa Barbara Channel and the Santa Maria Basin. At each mooring, sea surface pressure was constructed from simultaneous sea floor pressure gauge time series and water column temperature times series as in Harms and Winant (1994). For the present analysis, the wind stress in the Santa Barbara Channel-Santa Maria Basin will be represented by the wind at meteorological buoy NDBC54 in the western mouth of the Santa Barbara Channel; the analysis of Harms and Winant (1998; hereafter HW) justifies this choice and quantifies the amount of variance thus captured. The sea surface pressure gradient over this region will be represented by the difference between sea surface pressure at a mooring (ANMI) in the eastern mouth of the Santa Barbara Channel and that at a mooring (SMIN) just off Point Conception in the western Santa Barbara Channel. These series will be called simply "wind" and "pressure difference" in the following discussion.

All time series have been low pass filtered to remove variance associated with periods shorter than about 36 h. All correlations quoted have been computed after removal of the seasonal cycle, so that the results do *not* apply to the seasonal variation of currents. Positions of all stations to which the text makes reference are shown on Figure 1.

The unusual length of time over which data have been collected makes it possible to use conditional averaging to separate the circulation into a part driven by the wind and a part associated with the gradient of sea surface pressure. As an example, if the currents at the moorings are averaged over only those time intervals when the measured wind was below a small threshold and the measured pressure difference exceeded a large threshold, then the result is called a conditional average of the currents. It is reasonable to expect that this particular conditional average would be a pattern of currents that is strongly correlated with the pressure difference, but not with the wind. The question to be answered below is "does conditional averaging on observations of wind and pressure difference produce patterns individually directly attributable to winds and to pressure differences?"

RESULTS

Many surprising features emerge from the analysis. The first superficially surprising result (Figure 1) is that, when the 5 m currents are averaged over periods of gentle winds and large pressure differences, the 5 m currents then flow equatorward (poleward) when the sea surface pressure is higher (lower) at the east mouth of the Santa Barbara Channel (mooring ANMI) than it is beyond Point Conception (mooring PAIN). This is just the opposite of what would be expected in simple laboratory flows or in ocean flows where friction is important; in these, the flow would be away from regions of high pressure and towards regions of low pressure. What does it mean?

HW (their Figure 16) carried out a similar analysis, one, however, based upon the pressure difference between GOIN and PAIN and obtained the expected result; flow was equatorward (poleward) when the sea surface pressure was lower (higher) near the east mouth of the Santa Barbara Channel than it was beyond Point Conception. The contrary

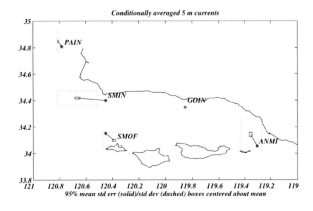

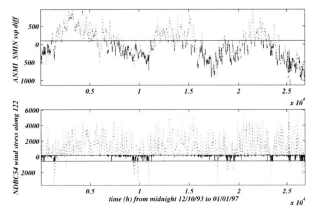

Figure 1. Top panel shows 5 m current vector in conditional average over the ANMI-SMIN sea surface pressure difference bins defined in the middle panel and wind stress bins defined in the lower panel. Mean wind stress is -0.001 dy/cm², and mean ANMI-SMIN sea surface pressure difference is -0.302 kPa (ANMI pressure is *lower* than SMIN; see text). Middle and lower panels, respectively, show 1177 days of ANMI-SMIN sea surface pressure difference and of wind stress at meteorological buoy NDBC54 along 122° starting at midnight, 12/10/1993. Full series are dotted lines, values included in conditional average bins are solid lines, bin limits are solid horizontal lines.

result of the present analysis may be understood as follows. On account of the earth's rotation, equatorward (poleward) currents give rise to pressure that is high (low) some distance directly offshore relative to pressure nearer the coast. If both the earth's rotation and friction were important, if the coast of the Santa Barbara Channel-Santa Maria Basin were straight, and if GOIN and PAIN were exactly the same distance from the coast but ANMI was a little further from the coast than SMIN, then equatorward (poleward) flow would be associated with high (low) pressure at PAIN relative to GOIN, but also with high pressure at ANMI relative to SMIN. The coast is not straight enough that this line of reasoning may be directly applied to the observations by measuring the distances from the moorings to the coast, but the difference between the present analysis based on ANMI-SMIN and that of HW based on GOIN-PAIN means that it has to be an important factor in setting up the observed

pressure field. The present interpretation is thus that the pressure field observed at the moorings is a combination of an along channel pressure difference directly set up by the wind in opposition to the wind stress and the pressure field that results on account of the earth's rotation when the wind directly forces along channel currents.

Does the local wind account for all of the observed pressure difference? The answer is no. The maximum lagged correlation between the wind stress series and the ANMI-SMIN pressure difference series is only 0.341 at a lag of 12 hours. The positive sign of the correlation and of the lag means that equatorward winds are followed by a rise in sea surface pressure at ANMI relative to SMIN, the smallness of the correlation relative to unity means that most of the measured pressure difference signal does not originate in the measured wind signal. This is consonant with the fact that, in a numerical model of the circulation in the entire Southern California Bight, Oey (1998) has found that a large monthly mean model pressure difference signal is generated in the Santa Barbara Channel by monthly mean observed nearshore winds hundreds of km equatorward of the Santa Barbara Channel. It is not yet known whether his mechanism accounts for all of the observed pressure difference within the Santa Barbara Channel at this and/or shorter periods.

The 5 m current pattern of Figure 1 is an average over those times when the wind is small and sea surface pressure at ANMI is lower than sea surface pressure at SMIN. We might next average over times when the wind is large and the pressure difference is small. If we called these two patterns the pressure dominated pattern and the wind dominated pattern, respectively, then the implicit assumption would be that if we next averaged over times when both the wind and the pressure difference are small, there would be little 5 m flow anywhere. This turns out not to be the case. A trivial reason could be is that even an error as small as a few cm in getting the bottom pressure sensors at the same depth at two different moorings would result in a nonzero offset in the pressure difference series between the two moorings even if the true pressure difference between the two moorings were zero. In that case we would just average over times of small winds and different pressure differences, and take as the offset that pressure difference that gave small flow everywhere. But no choice of pressure difference over which to average ever gave small 5 m flow at all the moorings. The best that could be done was to choose a pressure difference over which to average that minimized the flow at ANMI and PAIN.

Figure 2 correspondingly shows that in average over times of small winds, 5 m flow persists at SMIN and at SMOF even when the pressure difference over which the average is carried out has been chosen to minimize the 5 m flow at ANMI and at PAIN. If we interpret that particular pressure difference as an offset associated with (very plausible) error in bottom pressure sensor depth, then Figure 2 shows the 5 m circulation pattern that prevails when both local winds and the pressure difference are small. This null pattern must

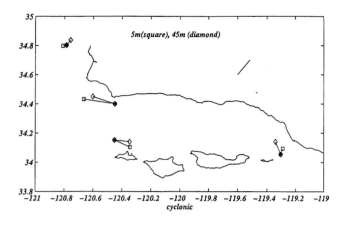

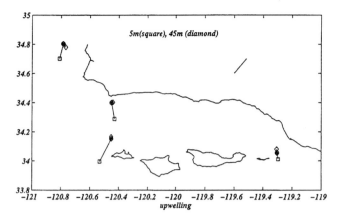

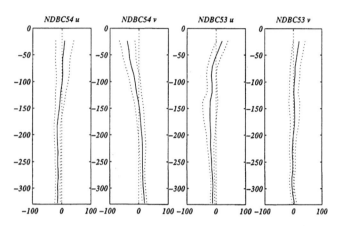

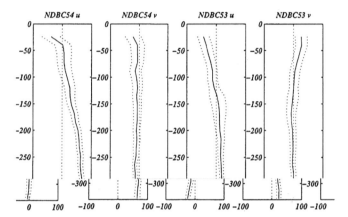

Figure 2. Upwelling pattern of currents whose amplitude is proportional to wind stress. Upper panel shows currents at 5 m (square) and 45 m (diamond). Reference arrow is 10 cm/s. Lower panels show eastward (u) and northward (v) currents at meteorological buoys NDBC54 and NDBC53 (units of mm/s) plotted against depth (m). Mean wind stress is 2.9 dy/cm², and mean ANMI-SMIN sea surface pressure difference 0.122 kPa is virtually the null bin 0.119 kPa.

Figure 3. Relaxation pattern of currents whose amplitude is proportional to along channel sea surface pressure difference. Upper panel shows currents at 5 m (square) and 45 m (diamond). Reference arrow is 10 cm/s. Lower panels show eastward (u) and northward (v) currents at meteorological buoys NDBC54 and NDBC53 (units of mm/s) plotted against depth (m). Mean wind stress 0.01 dy/cm² is virtually null, and ANMI-SMIN sea surface pressure difference is -0.330 kPa (ANMI pressure is lower than SMIN).

be subtracted from what were above called the pressure dominated and wind dominated patterns in order to obtain patterns whose amplitude may be expected to become small when the corresponding forcing agent, wind or along channel sea surface pressure difference, is small. The resulting patterns are shown in Figures 3 and 4.

Three 5 m patterns thus finally emerge from the conditional averaging; one (the wind dominated pattern minus the null pattern) whose amplitude is proportional to local wind stress (Figure 3), one (the pressure dominated pattern minus the null pattern) whose amplitude is proportional to the along channel sea surface pressure difference (Figure 4), and one (the null pattern) whose amplitude is not well correlated with either wind stress or along channel sea surface pressure difference (Figure 2). These correspond closely to the three synoptic patterns called upwelling, relaxation and cyclonic previously identified by HW. Their zero lag correlation coefficients with the wind stress are 0.61, -0.10, and 0.02 respectively; their zero lag correlation coefficients with the ANMI-SMIN sea surface pressure difference series are 0.27, -0.33, and 0.13 respectively. The upwelling

pattern is thus best correlated with the wind or the pressure difference. Even though the relaxation pattern was constructed using observations over which the wind stress averaged to virtually zero so that this pattern should reflect circulation response only to the pressure difference, the pressure difference itself is correlated with the wind and this results in partial correlation between the relaxation pattern and the wind.

The upwelling pattern is everywhere much less pronounced at 45 m than at 5 m, in accord with simple Ekman theory. The relaxation pattern at 5 m is concentrated along the California coast of the Santa Barbara Channel-Santa Maria Basin, and is only slightly attenuated at 45 m. The cyclonic pattern at 5 m within the Santa Barbara Channel is not very different from that at 45 m. Both the relaxation and cyclonic patterns do not appear to persist below about 100 m in the western Santa Barbara Channel (at NDBC54), the situation is more complicated in the interior (at NDBC53) with some suggestion of deep counter currents. A final surprise however is that at depths greater than about 100 m in

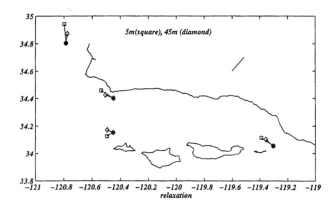

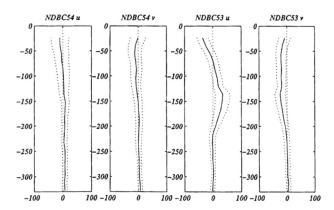

Figure 4. Cyclonic pattern of currents whose amplitude is proportional neither to wind stress nor to along channel sea surface pressure difference. Upper panel shows currents at 5 m (square) and 45 m (diamond). Reference arrow is 10 cm/s. Lower panels show eastward (u) and northward (v) currents at meteorological buoys NDBC54 and NDBC53 (units of mm/s) plotted against depth (m). Wind stress -0.043 dy/cm² is virtually null, and ANMI-SMIN sea surface pressure difference is the null bin 0.119 kPa.

the western Santa Barbara Channel, the most energetic pattern is the upwelling pattern; very strong equatorward flow below 100 m is associated with equatorward winds. The manner in which this deep flow is driven is not yet understood.

ACKNOWLEDGEMENTS

This work has been supported by the Minerals Management Service (MMS).

LITERATURE CITED

Harms, S. and C. D. Winant. 1998. Characteristic patterns of the circulation in the Santa Barbara Channel. Journal of Geophysical Research 101(C2):3041-3065.

Harms, S. and C. D. Winant. 1994. Synthetic subsurface pressure derived from bottom pressure and tide gauge observations. Journal of Oceanic and Atmospheric Technology 11(6):1625-1637.

Oey, L.-Y. 1998. A Forcing Mechanism for the Poleward Flow off the Southern California Coast. Manuscript.

MOMENTUM BALANCE FROM A HINDCAST AND NOWCAST MODEL OF CURRENTS IN THE SANTA BARBARA CHANNEL

Lie-Yauw Oey[1], Dong-Ping Wang[2], Clinton Winant[3], Myrl Hendershott[3], and Thomas Hayward[4]

[1]Atmospheric & Oceanic Science Program, Princeton University, Princeton, NJ 08544
(609) 258-5971, E-mail: lyo@splash.princeton.edu
[2]State University of New York, Stoney Brook, NY 11794
[3]Center for Coastal Studies, Scripps Institution of Oceanography, La Jolla, CA 92093-0209
[4]Marine Life Research Group, Scripps Institution of Oceanography, La Jolla, CA 92093

ABSTRACT

Previous works suggest that both wind and pressure gradient play important roles in determining the near-surface circulation in the Santa Barbara Channel (SBC). The results from a hindcast and nowcast model of currents in SBC for the recent El Niño winter and spring, from December 1997 through April 1998, were analyzed to infer the momentum balance in the channel. Two main forcing into the model were wind stresses and California Cooperative Oceanic Fisheries Investigations (CalCOFI) temperature and salinity (T/S) fields. Wind stresses were calculated by combining hourly National Data Buoy Center (NDBC) wind in the vicinity of the channel with historical, monthly COADS wind over the outer region away from the channel. Historical T/S fields were used to initialize the model, and together with CalCOFI data from December 1997 through April 1998, were assimilated into the modeled T/S by a simple nudging scheme. The assimilation of CalCOFI data introduced warmer water in the Southern California Bight (SCB).

The cross-channel balance was approximately geostrophic. The along-channel balance was primarily between wind, which was equatorward, sea-level tilt, which was poleward, and Coriolis, which was poleward if the wind was uniformly intense west and east of the channel, and was equatorward if the wind was much weaker in the east. The former wind condition induced southward cross-channel flow and would correspond to the observed 'Flood East' or 'Upwelling' scenario, while the latter northward cross-channel flow and to the 'Cyclonic' or 'Relaxation' scenario.

Keywords: Southern California Bight, eastern boundary currents, model nowcast, pressure gradients, wind curl.

INTRODUCTION

Located at the confluent region between the warm water of Southern California Bight (SCB) origin and the cooler upwelled water off the central California coast, and being partially sheltered from wind by the mountain range to its north, circulation in the Santa Barbara Channel (SBC; Figure 1) is driven by a combination of wind, windcurl, and thermal contrast. The equatorward wind in the SBC/SCB drives coastal currents near the surface which generally flow

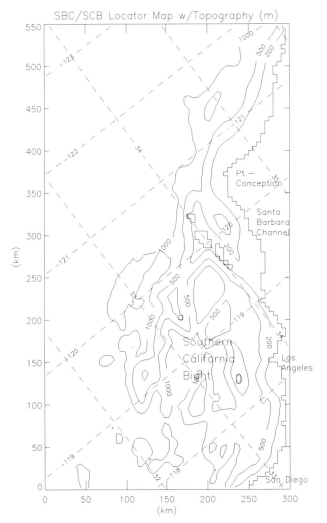

Figure 1. Santa Barbara Channel (SBC) and Southern California Bight (SCB) locator map and the model domain and topography. For computational efficiency, the deepest model's depth has been set to 2000m.

equatorward (e.g., Allen 1980). This holds true also in the SCB/SBC except that the situation is complicated by the intense windcurl at Point Conception that diminishes equatorward along the channel and the SCB coast. The equatorward weakening of the windcurl, which on the seasonal time scale peaks in summer, generates alongshore pressure gradient, and drives poleward coastal flow (Oey 1996). Thus nearshore flows in the SCB/SBC can be envsioned as being driven by these two competing (and inseparable) mechanisms. The theory was originally intended to apply to seasonal time scales, but a more careful scaling analysis suggests that it should also be applicable to shorter time (O(10 days)) and smaller spatial (channel) scales (Oey 1999).

While the above idea can explain the origin of the alongshore pressure gradients, it does not directly address how the imbalances of these and the wind drive the channel's circulation. A tour de force analysis by Harms and Winant (1998) of 1994/1995 observations shows that near-surface currents in the channel are indeed a function of both wind and pressure gradient. One objective of the present paper is to understand the interplay between these two forcing components, and to reconcile theoretical ideas with those inferred from observations.

Our analyses are based on an application of the Oey's (1996) SBC/SCB model forced by realistic wind and thermal forcing. The model produces hindcast and nowcast of currents and temperature and salinity (T/S) fields during recent El Niño conditions from December 1997 through April 1998, when waters which were warmer than during normal conditions were found off the southern and central California coasts. The choice of a model with realistic bathymetry and forced by realistic wind and T/S fields, as opposed to a model with idealized settings, offers the advantage that inferences that are specific to the SBC/SCB system can be made. The down side is that the analysis will be more complex and simplifications will be necessary. The El Niño conditions also offer the opportunity of examining effects of heating (warm waters) from the south. The present results can also be used by: (1) the Office of Naval Research (ONR) in support of their field exercises in the channel, and (2) the Minerals Management Service (MMS) as basis for their surface flow trajectory analysis and Oil Spill Risk Analysis (OSRA).

THE MODEL

The model solves the finite-difference analog of the three-dimensional primitive equations assuming that the ocean is incompressible and hydrostatic, and using the Boussinesq approximation (details in Oey and Chen 1992). The model boundary conditions, domain and topography are the same as those used in Oey (1996; Figure 1), with two exceptions. The present application employs the coarse-grid only (i.e., the nested-grid option is turned off), with grid sizes $\Delta x = \Delta y = 5$ km and 30 equally-spaced sigma layers in the vertical. Secondly, a 200 km-wide sponge layer, within which the horizontal viscosity is linearly increased to ten times its interior value, is placed along the western open boundary. In combination with a radiation condition, the sponge damped westward-propagating Rossby waves and helped to prevent the development of a western boundary current.

Initial Condition and T/S Assimilation

Integration begins on December 16, 1997 and ends on May 5, 1998. The initial T/S fields were obtained from monthly climatological data set for December. These historical T/S were also used as boundary conditions during the integration. To account for the actual T/S conditions in 1997-1998, CalCOFI data from December 1997 and February-March 1998 cruises were assimilated into the model. While there were a number of cruise tracks, Line 90 (which spans offshore from the coast between Los Angeles and San Diego; Figure 2) only was used. The rationale is that T/S forcing from this southern location would propagate north to influence circulation in the channel. If CalCOFI T/S in and/or near the channel are also assimilated, questions related to incompatibility of data in the channel must also be addressed as the model attempts to adjust both to local and remote forcing.

The assimilation was accomplished as follows. The CalCOFI data at each standard level were first interpolated (extrapolated) onto the model grid using:

$$T_{ci} = \Sigma T_{cn} E_{ni} / \Sigma E_{ni} \qquad (1a)$$

$$E_{ni} = \exp \left\{ -\left[\left(x_{cn} - x_i \right)/ x_s \right]^2 \right. \\ \left. -\left[\left(y_{cn} - y_i \right)/ y_s \right]^2 \right\} \qquad (1b)$$

where the summation Σ is over the total number 'N' of CalCOFI data points (i.e., n=1,N), T_{ci} denotes the interpolated value at the model's ith-grid point (x_i,y_i) (in degrees longitude and latitude, say), T_{cn} the nth-station CalCOFI value at (x_{cn},y_{cn}), and x_s and y_s are parameters that dictate the radius of influence of the CalCOFI data on the neighboring model grid points. Here, we take $x_s=y_s=0.25°$.

Assimilated fields, T_{ai}, are next constructed using a weighted combination of the interpolated CalCOFI values, T_{ci}, and historical values, T_{hi}:

$$T_{ai} = W_i T_{ci} + \left(1 - W_i \right) T_{hi} \qquad (2a)$$

$$W_i = \exp \left[-\min_n \left(R_{ni} \right) \right] \bullet \exp \left\{ \left(Z_i / 200 \right) \right. \\ \left. -H_v \left(t - t_0 \right).\left(t - t_0 / 30 \right) \right\} \qquad (2b)$$

$$R_{ni} = \left[\left(x_{cn} - x_i \right)/ x_s \right]^2 \\ + \left[\left(y_{cn} - y_i \right)/ y_s \right]^2 \qquad (2c)$$

where the minimum function 'min' checks over the total number 'N' of CalCOFI data points, z_i the vertical coordinate (=0 at surface and -H(x,y), where H=water depth, at the ocean bottom) in meters, t is time in days, t_0 is time that

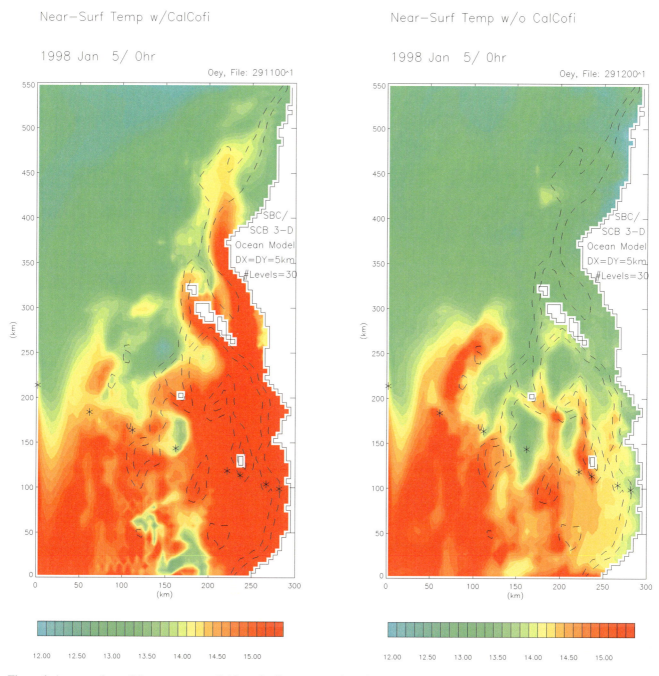

Figure 2. A comparison of the temperature fields at the first near-surface sigma level on January 5, 1998, with (left panel) and without (right panel) assimilation of the CalCOFI T/S along Line 90 (the starred points).

corresponds to April 15, 1998, and H_v is the Heaviside function. The spatial distribution of the weighting function, W_i, is such that, near the surface, it is ≈ 1 for model grid points near any of the CalCOFI stations, but decays exponentially away, and also with depth. Thus the assimilated field, T_{ai}, assumes CalCOFI for grid points near the cruise stations, and merges smoothly to historical field for points far away.

Finally, the assimilated field is inserted into the T/S transport equations as sources (i.e., the model was used in a so called 'robust diagnostic mode'):

$$\partial T / \partial t = \hat{e} + C \cdot \left(T_a - T \right) \qquad (3a)$$

$$C = W_i \big|_{z=0} \cdot \left\{ G_d + \left(G_s - G_d \right) \cdot \exp(z / 500) \right\} \qquad (3b)$$

where $G_s = 1/5$ day^{-1} and $G_d = 1/300$ day^{-1}, and similarly for the salinity, S. Thus for grid points near CalCOFI, the modeled T/S are nudged back to CalCOFI with time scales of five days near the surface and 300 days in deeper layers. Away from CalCOFI stations, the T/S are nudged towards the historical T/S (because of Equation 2) but at increasing time scales (because of $W_i|_{z=0}$ in Equation 3) the calculation becomes essentially prognostic for distances > 50 km to 100 km away. In Figure 2, we compare the near-surface temperature fields on January 5, 1998 for runs with and without the CalCOFI nudging. It shows that, because of El Niño influence, the temperature with CalCOFI nudging is 1 to 2°C higher than 'climatology' especially near the coast where it is dynamically important. By this time (20 days into the integration), the warmer water has intruded into the channel and past Point Conception.

The Wind

The wind was specified by merging the hourly wind vectors (U_w) at NDBC stations in the vicinity of the channel (see Figure 3 for station sites) with climatological winds from COADS that cover the entire model domain (and beyond), as follows. The NDBC winds were first converted to wind stresses:

$$\tau_o = C_d |U_w| U_w \qquad (m^2.s^{-2})$$

(4)

where $C_d = 1.44 \times 10^{-6}$ for $|U_w| < 11$ m.s^{-1}, and $= (0.49 + 0.065 |U_w|) \times 10^{-6}$ otherwise. These were interpolated onto the model grid points using (1) with $x_s=y_s=1.5°$, and merged with COADS wind using equation (2a) (i.e., with NDBC replacing T_{ci} and COADS replacing T_{hi}). However, the weighting function is simpler $= E_{ni}$, where the (x_{cn},y_{cn}) in (1b) is taken as fixed equal to (-120°12', 34°24'), the center of gravity of the NDBC sites used. For the simulation period, data were available at seven sites in the vicinity of the channel (those marked '⊕' in Figure 3), but was missing at station 46053 (marked '+'). Data from previous years (e.g., Harms and Winant 1998) indicates that wind at this site is weak and more similar to stations to the east and south than to stations in the western mouth of the channel. The wind at station 46053 is therefore equated to that at station 46045. Figure 3 shows an example of the result of the NDBC/COADS wind merging at two times, winter and spring. An important aspect is wind weakening from west to east of the channel, and also to the south over the Southern California Bight.

RESULTS

We first present results for the experiment (Experiment A; Table 1) in which the wind and T/S are prescribed as in previous section. However, to gain further insights, other experiments with different wind and T/S forcing have also been conducted. Figure 4 shows daily averaged surface temperature, elevation (η) and currents (u,v) at surface and at 100 m depth on March 16 and April 15, 1998. The two dates are chosen to illustrate two different dynamical regimes as wind (March 16) and windcurl (April 15) forcing

compete in driving near-coast flows in region southeast of SBC (Oey 1996,1999). In Figure 4a, flow in this region is equatorward caused by upwelling favorable wind that began to strengthen near the beginning of March. A cyclone also begins to form at the western portion of the channel. This we will see depends critically on the relative strength of the wind at NDBC stations 46054 and 46053. Cooler water, as well as a dip in free-surface elevation, can be seen at the cyclone center. By April, poleward flow is seen southeast of SBC. Its appearence can be explained in terms of equatorward weakening of windcurl along the coast in the SCB, and the subsequence set-up of an along-coast pressure gradient (compare the elevation contours in Figures 4a,b; Oey 1996,1999).

Momentum Balance

To elucidate the dynamics, we resolved the model velocities in the near-coast region into cross-isobath (x and u; positive shoreward) and along-isobath (y and v; positive poleward) components. We find that the cross-isobath momentum balance is to a good approximation geostrophic. The along-isobath momentum equation is:

$$\begin{array}{ccc} dv/dt + & fu + & g \cdot \partial\eta/\partial y \\ \text{I} & \text{II} & \text{III} \end{array}$$

$$-\partial\left(K \cdot \partial v/\partial z\right)/\partial z$$
$$\text{IV}$$

$$+ (g/\rho_o) \cdot \int_z^0 \partial\rho/\partial y \cdot \partial z' = 0$$
$$\text{V}$$

(5)

where $d/dt = \partial/\partial t + \mathbf{u} \cdot \nabla$, K the eddy viscosity coefficient (m²/s), ρ the density (kg/m³), g = 9.8 m/s², f the Coriolis parameter (s⁻¹), and a small term arising from the curvature of the isobath (coastline) is omitted. Each term in Equation 5 was calculated beginning with the 50 m isobath near the coast, and to 40 km offshore, and averaged cross-isobath and also in time (note that in the SBC, this averaging encompasses the entire channel width). We find that term I, and also term V for the near-surface grid layer, are small. Figure 5 shows the three remaining terms for the near-surface grid as a function of the alongshore distance. Plotted is also the term that represents friction acting at the base of the near-surface layer; i.e., the term IVb on the right hand side of

$$\partial\left(K \cdot \partial v/\partial z\right)/\partial z \approx \tau_o^y/\Delta z$$
$$\text{IVa}$$

(6)

$$-\left(K \cdot \partial v/\partial z\right)\big|_{base}/\Delta z$$
$$\text{IVb}$$

where τ_o^y is the along-isobath wind stress and Δz (15m) is the thickness of the layer. Figure 5 shows that this friction term is small, and wind stress therefore dominates the shear term IV, which is negative along the entire coast (i.e., equatorward; note that the negative of term IV is plotted). Thus, to a good

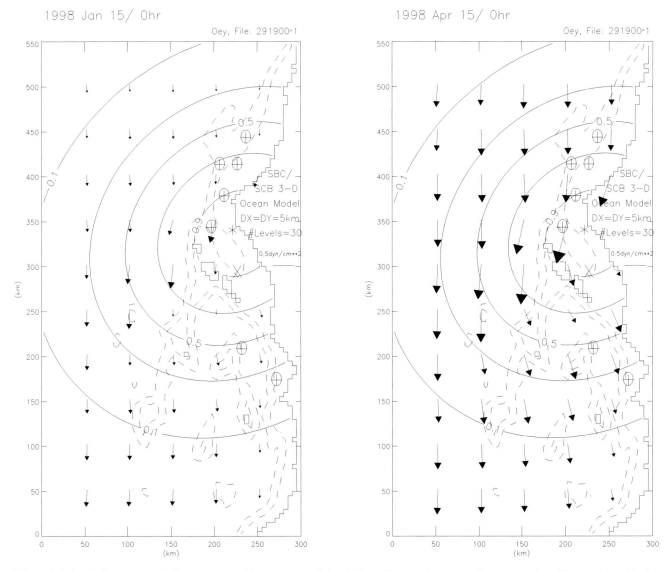

Figure 3. The 10-day averaged wind vectors on January 15 and April 15, 1998. Locations of national Data Buoy Center (NDCB) wind stations used in the simulation are marked as '⊕'. They are, from northwest to southeast: 46062, 46011, 46023 (offshore) and 46045. An additional station, marked as 'x' (NDBC station 46053) was also used (see text). The location of center of gravity of these stations is marked as '*'. The contours give the weighting function used to merge the NDBC with COADS winds (see text).

Table 1. Model experiments.

| | Winds | | T/S Assimilation | | Wind Merging Scales | NDBC Buoy # 46053 |
Experiment	COADS	NDBC	Historical	CalCOFI	X_s & Y_s	Set to:
A	*	*	*	*	1.5	46045
B	*	*	*	*	1.5	-
C	*	*	*	-	1.5	46045
D	*	*	*	-	1.5	-
E	*	*	*	*	3	46045
F	*	*	*	*	1.5	46025

A star '*' or number means that the item was applied in the model.
A dash '-' means that the item was omitted.

approximation, the alongshore balance is between the equatorward wind and the pressure gradient (III) and Coriolis (II) terms. We note also that the friction term IVb is positive, which means that the alongshore currents near the surface, being wind-driven, are more equatorward than currents in the lower layer. This is generally true also for all other experiments to be discussed below, and the frictional force is poleward opposing the wind.

Balance in the Southern California Bight

From San Diego (SD) to about 100 km north, sea level slopes upward (i.e., III is positive). This is because off 33.5°N ($y \approx 100$ km) the equatorward wind, hence its curl, is weakest, and also warmer water is being assimilated from

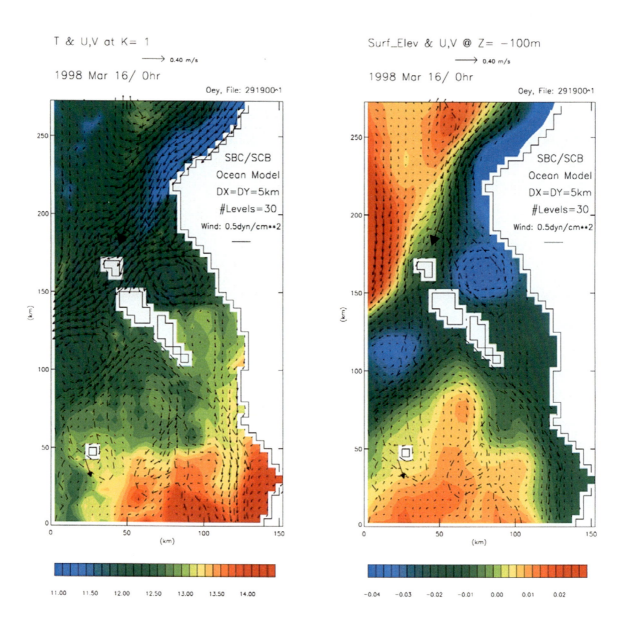

Figure 4A. The one-day averaged temperature (°C) and currents at the first model grid point near the surface (left panel), and elevation (m) with currents at z=-100m (right panel), for (a) March 16 and (b) April 15, 1998, in a blow-up region that focuses on the Santa Barbara Channel and vicinity. Five-day averaged wind stresses are also plotted as vectors with thick arrows at four locations.

CalCOFI stations. Both mechanisms interact because of density advection, but in general induce a local high. That wind weakens off 33.5°N is supported by the extensive analysis of data from buoys and ship observations by Winant and Dorman (1997), but the second mechanism is a model artifact caused by assimilation (in reality, warmer El Niño water extends from the south). The positive sea-level gradient and equatorward wind stress are balanced, geostrophically and through Ekman dynamics, by the negative Coriolis term II caused by offshore flow south of the anticyclonic high.

Further north, the pressure gradient switches to negative as sea level tilts downward by about 3 cm over the 200 km alongshore distance from Los Angeles (LA) to Point Conception (PC). Just north of LA, pressure gradient is balanced by equatorward wind stress and the acceleration caused by onshore flow (term II is positive) on the north side of the coastal anticyclone. Further north and into the eastern SBC (y ≈ 260 km), offshore flow develops consistent with wind-driven Ekman dynamics, the resulting poleward acceleration combines with pressure gradient to balance the equatorward wind stress.

Balance in the Santa Barbara Channel

From eastern SBC to the central channel (y ≈ 300 km), wind stress and hence its offshore (i.e., from north to south across the channel) Ekman flux remain approximately

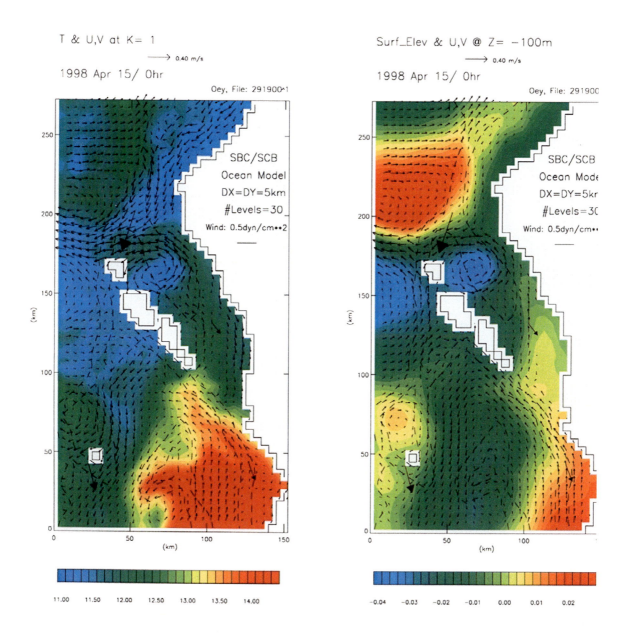

Figure 4B. The one-day averaged temperature (°C) and currents at the first model grid point near the surface (left panel), and elevation (m) with currents at z=-100 m (right panel), for April 15, 1998, in a blow-up region that focuses on the Santa Barbara Channel and vicinity. Five-day averaged wind stresses are also plotted as vectors with thick arrows at four locations.

equal to their values to the south (recall that for Experiment A, wind at 46053 = 46045), but downward tilt of sea level increases towards the cyclone low in the western channel. The excess pressure gradient forces an onshore flux that reverses the wind-driven Ekman component at the mid-channel (280 km < y < 310 km). This mechanism depends crucially on differential wind strength west and east of the channel. Figure 6 shows the balance plot for Experiment B, for which wind at 46053 was not explicitly specified, and was therefore, essentially extrapolated from the western channel station 46054 using (1) as described previously. The wind in the eastern portion of the channel is therefore similar to that in the west, and is intense during the spring transition

period beginning in March. Comparing Figure 6 with Figure 5, differences in the balance can be seen from y = 220 km (southeast of the SBC) to PC. For Experiment B, (the negative of) shear term IV (due to wind) begins to increase near y = 220 km, instead of near y = 300 km (mid-channel) for Experiment A (Figure 5). The result is that offshore (southward) Ekman flux persists in the eastern channel for Experiment B. Also, the friction term (IVb) is larger, caused by more intense mixing by strong wind in the channel, although the shear term IV is still dominated by the wind stress term IVa. Thus the summed poleward acceleration caused by the Coriolis of this Ekman flux, sea-level tilt, and friction, is balanced by the equatorward acceleration due to wind.

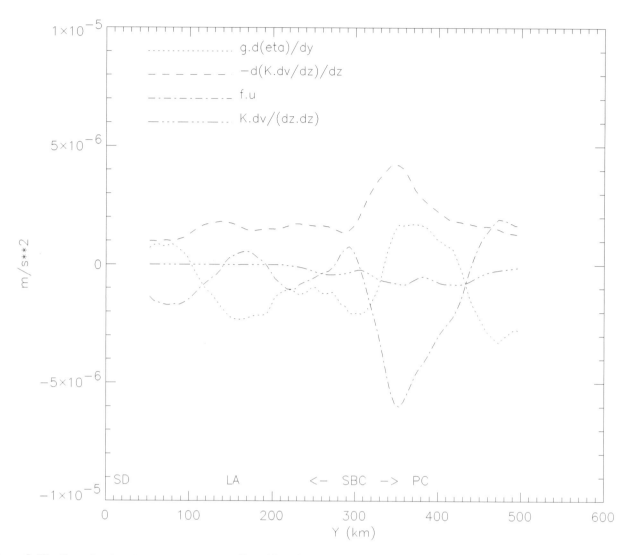

Figure 5. The three dominant terms: pressure gradient (dotted), vertical shear (dashed) and Coriolis (dash-dot), and the term that represents friction at the base of the layer (dash with 3 dots), in the along-isobath momentum balance in the model's near-surface layer for Experiment A. Geographical locations along Y are, SD: San Diego, LA: Los Angeles, SBC: Santa Barbara Channel, and PC: Point Conception.

In summary (Figure 7), the near-surface flow in SBC can be viewed as being due to an imbalance between poleward (westward) sea-level tilt and equatorward (eastward) wind stress. An excess of the former, caused by weakened wind in the eastern portion of the channel, generally leads to a south-to-north cross-channel flow that helps to reinforce the cyclonic re-circulation in the west, as well as the likelihood that poleward flow develops in the channel (State I). The reverse (State II) leads to a north-to-south cross-channel Ekman flux near the surface, and the situation is more akin to classical upwelling problems, which in general would result in equatorward flow in the channel. We have shown that the establishment of one state versus the other depends crucially on the relative magnitude of the wind stresses west and east of the channel.

The momentum balance gives no clue as to how the western cyclone is formed; i.e., if the cyclone is a result of successions of State I caused originally by equatorward weakening of the windcurl, or is locally spun up (by windcurl

or flow separation). It is clear that, however it is produced, the cyclone dynamically contributes to the sea-level tilt.

Balance at Point Conception and North

Near and to the north of Point Conception, the sea-level gradient term III changes sign to become positive, induced by the cyclone low at the western SBC. The resulting equatorward acceleration reinforces that from the intense wind stress along the central California coast. Given that friction and other terms in the alongshore balance are small, these must be balanced by a poleward acceleration due to the Coriolis term. Thus the coastal jet acquires an offshore component that is most intense just south of Point Conception where both the wind and upward sloping of the sea-level are maximum (Figure 5), and the jet has a tendency to veer offshore (Figure 4).

North of y ≈ 420 km, sea-level tilts downward. This is a model artifact due to northward advection of warmer water from the south. A warm eddy was present off y ≈450 km

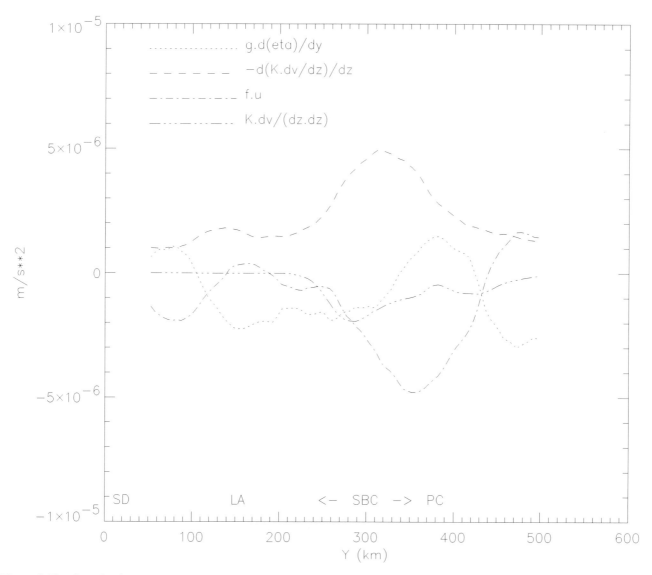

Figure 6. The three dominant terms: pressure fgradient (dotted), vertical shear (dashed) and Coriolis (dash-dot), and the term that represents friction at the base of the layer (dash with 3 dots), in the along-isobath momentum balance in the model's near-surface layer for Experiment B. Geographical locations along Y are, SD: San Diego, LA: Los Angeles, SBC: Santa Barbara Channel, and PC: Point Conception.

after about 20 to 30 days of simulation (c.f. Figure 2, left panel), and slowly dispersed westward. To its north, the eddy produced onshore flow and downward tilt of sea-level.

Balance in Other Experiments

When CalCOFI T/S was not assimilated (Experiment C or D), the strong poleward flow in December 1997 and January 1998 for Experiments A and B was now absent. However, because of upwelling in March and April, warmer water in Experiments A and B was confined to the southern region (the SCB), and the dynamic balance in the channel was similar with or without CalCOFI T/S. It is likely that, had the integration been extended to cover summer and fall, the effects of warmer water would be more apparent.

Finally, the model results also changed little when the values of x_s and y_s in the weighting function used to merge the NDBC with COADS winds were changed from 1.5° to

3° (Experiment E). The results are also not sensitive to which of the two NDBC wind data in the southeastern-most stations (46045 – Experiment A or 46025 –Experiment F) was used for the missing wind station NDBC 46053.

DISCUSSION AND CONCLUSIONS

Three dominant terms in the alongshore momentum balance of the coastal circulation in the SBC/SCB from December 1997 through April 1998 are wind, which is equatorward, pressure gradient, which is poleward, and Coriolis due to cross-shore flows, which can be poleward or equatorward. In the SBC, we have identified two distinct states of circulation that depend critically on the distribution of wind stress in the channel. For winds with approximately equal strengths west and east of the channel, the along-channel component produces southward Ekman flow

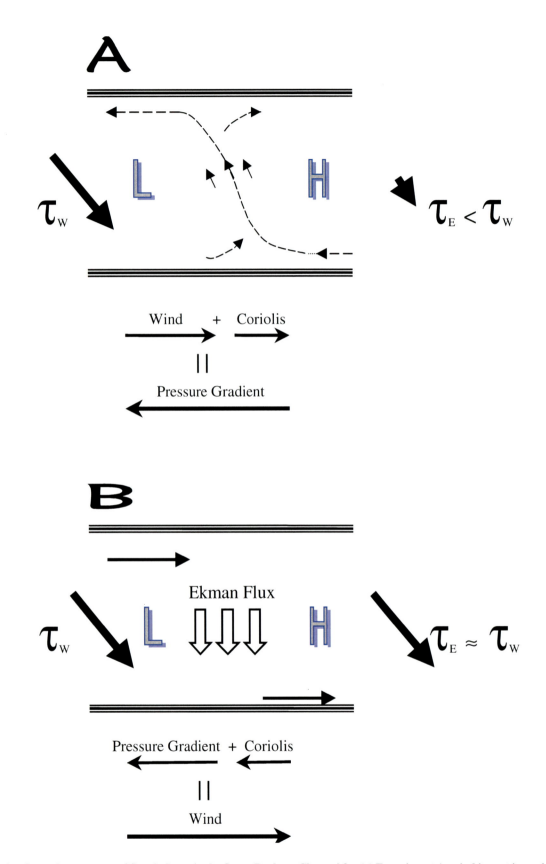

Figure 7. A schematic summary of flow balance in the Santa Barbara Channel for (a) Experiment A: wind in east is weaker than that in west, and (b) Experiment B: wind in east is of the same magnitude as that in west.

across the channel that together with the pressure gradient balances the wind. The along-channel flow then tends to be uniformly equatorward with no cyclonic recirculation in the west. This (State II) would correspond to either the Upwelling or Flood East characteristic patterns described in Harms and Winant (1998). We may expect that the same requirement of uniformity in wind, but reversed in direction, would lead to the Flood West pattern. On the other hand, for wind that is intense in the west but weak in the east, the wind-induced Ekman flow is overcome by the south-to-north cross-channel flow generated by the pressure gradient. This cross-channel flow occurs near and to the east of the mid-channel where wind stress is weak. This (State I) would tend to produce a cyclonic recirculation in the west and would correspond to either the Cyclonic or Relaxation characteristic patterns described in Harms and Winant (1998). In both states, the cross-channel flow serves as an important index that characterizes the imbalance between wind and pressure gradient.

A comparison of the pressure gradient terms in Figures 5 and 6 show that they are of comparable magnitudes, although in the non-uniform wind case (Figure 5), the presence of a cyclone in the west induced a larger sea-level tilt. This suggests that a large portion of the sea-level gradient is caused by larger scale windcurl and heating over the SCB. One also ponders upon the chicken-and-egg question of whether the cyclone is formed by an aggregate of State-I events, or is purely local induced by localized windcurl and flow separation, say, and hence helps to promote the State-I event. This clearly requires further research.

Finally, the types of dynamic balance described here are of significant practical value. They help to identify forcing patterns that may then be used as key predictive parameters in future hindcast/nowcast studies.

ACKNOWLEDGMENTS

This work was funded by the Office of Naval Research (LYO) and the Minerals Management Service (MMS). Computing was performed at the Geophysical Fluid Dynamic Laboratory, Princeton, and the San Diego Supercomputer Center.

LITERATURE CITED

Allen, J. S. 1980. Models of wind-driven currents on the continental shelf. Annual Review of Fluid Mechnics 12:389-433.

Harms, S. and Winant, C. D. 1998. Characteristic patterns of the circulation in the Santa Barbara Channel. Journal of Geophysical Research 103:3041-3065.

Oey, L.-Y. and P. Chen. 1992. A nested-grid model simulation of the Norwegian coastal current. Journal of Geophysical Research 97:20,063-20,086.

Oey, L.-Y. 1996. Flow around a coastal bend: a model of the Santa Barbara Channel eddy. Journal of Geophysical Research 101:16,667-16,682.

Oey, L.-Y. 1999. A Forcing Mechanism for the Poleward Flow off the Southern California Coast. Journal of Geophysical Research, 104:13,529-13,539.

Winant, C. D. and C. E. Dorman. 1997. Seasonal patterns of surface wind stress and heat flux over the Southern California Bight. Journal of Geophysical Research 102:5,641.

ACCESS TO CALIFORNIA COASTAL HISTORICAL AND REAL-TIME DATA VIA THE WORLD WIDE WEB AND ITS APPLICATIONS

Jerome R. Wanetick[1] and David R. Browne[2]

[1]Center for Coastal Studies, Scripps Institution of Oceanography, UCSD
9500 Gilman Drive, La Jolla, CA 92093-0209
(858) 534-7999, FAX (858) 534-0300, E-mail: jwanetick@ucsd.edu
[2]Minerals Management Service, Office of Environmental Evaluation
770 Paseo Camarillo, Camarillo, CA 93010
(805) 389-7838, FAX (805) 389-7637, E-mail: david.browne@mms.gov

ABSTRACT

In 1991, a study was undertaken by the Center for Coastal Studies (CCS) at Scripps Institution of Oceanography (SIO), funded by the Minerals Management Service (MMS), to determine the characteristic oceanic circulation patterns in the Santa Barbara Channel and Santa Maria Basin, an area of significant Outer Continental Shelf (OCS) oil and gas activity. An array of twelve current meter moorings measure continuous time series of currents, temperatures and salinities of the water column as well as bottom pressure at each mooring location. Data from the current meter at 5 m depth are telemetered daily to CCS via satellite. This is done to secure some of the measurements and to monitor the integrity of the moorings. As a side benefit to this research program, these near real-time data are collected and published on a World Wide Web site to aid MMS and other agencies in their oil spill response efforts in the study region. It is important to these oil spill response efforts that a monitoring program remain in place in the Santa Barbara Channel and Santa Marine Basin. An array of four current meter moorings and four National Data Buoy Center (NDBC) buoys is necessary to make this effort viable.

Keywords: Santa Barbara Channel, Santa Maria Basin, California, circulation study, bottom pressure, Data Zoo, oil spill response, current meters, near real-time data, historical data.

INTRODUCTION

In 1991, the Minerals Management Service (MMS) of the U.S. Department of the Interior entered into a Cooperative Agreement with the State of California, and ultimately with the Center for Coastal Studies (CCS) at Scripps Institution of Oceanography (SIO), University of California San Diego (UCSD), to study the ocean circulation in the Santa Barbara Channel and the Santa Maria Basin. This is the primary area of Outer Continental Shelf (OCS) oil and gas activity in the Pacific OCS region regulated by the MMS. The ongoing Santa Barbara Channel-Santa Maria Basin

(SBC-SMB) study has maintained twelve moorings in and around the Santa Barbara Channel since 1991.

From March 1991 until December 1995, ten current meter moorings were located in the Santa Barbara Channel, one mooring was located on the 100 m isobath off of Point Sal and one in the Santa Monica Basin (Figure 1). In January of 1996, nine of these moorings were moved north to the Santa Maria Basin (Figure 2) leaving three moorings in the Santa Barbara Channel, two at the western entrance, SMIN, SMOF and one at the eastern entrance, ANMI.

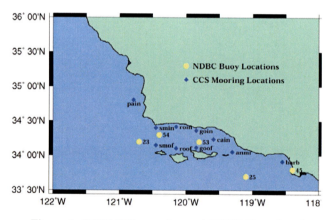

Figure 1. CCS/MMS mooring and NDBC Buoy locations, 1991 - 1995.

The original charter of the SBC-SMB study Data Management task was to archive data from historical physical oceanographic studies of the California coast. Some of these studies include the: Coastal Transition Zone (CTZ), Coastal Ocean Dynamics Experiment (CODE), Super Coastal Ocean Dynamics Experiment (SuperCODE), Observations of Persistent Upwelling Structures (OPUS), Central California Coastal Circulation Study (CCCCS), and the Northern California Coastal Circulation Study (NCCCS). The data from these studies were acquired from

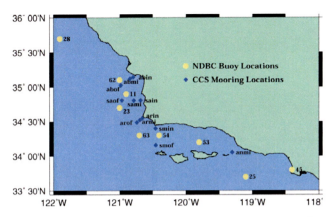

Figure 2. CCS/MMS mooring and NDBC Buoy locations, 1996 - present.

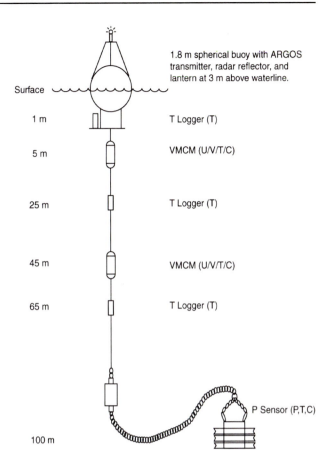

Figure 3. Typical CCS mooring configuration.

the original investigators, converted to a common ASCII format when possible, and published in an Internet-accessible archive called the Data Zoo. Along with these historical data, data collected from the SBC-SMB moorings are archived in the Data Zoo as well.

The development of the Data Zoo coincided with the development of the World Wide Web (WWW), which gives graphical access to data on the Internet via universally available browsers. With the advent of this new paradigm, the Data Zoo has evolved into not only a static archive of data, but a means of delivering oceanographic and meteorological data in near real-time. MMS currently funds the Data Zoo and its real-time component, the Oil Spill Response Website, to provide access to historical, and study data to the research community, and real-time data to assist oil spill response efforts in the Santa Barbara Channel and the Santa Maria Basin.

MATERIALS AND METHODS

In May 1996, MMS identified a need for near real-time environmental data in the Santa Barbara Channel and Santa Maria Basin to assist MMS, the Marine Spill Response Corporation, U.S. Coast Guard, the National Oceanic and Atmospheric Administration (NOAA) HAZMAT, and the oil industry in their efforts to predict oil spill trajectories and to help direct cleanup efforts during an oil spill event. A website was created to augment the Data Zoo archive which provided the near real-time data collected as part of the SBC-SMB study in an easily accessible format. The URL for the site is: www.ccs.ucsd.edu/oilspill.

The moorings deployed in the SBC-SMB study area (Figure 3) consist of three (or two depending upon the depth of the mooring) current meters at 5 m, 45 m, and 100 m depth, temperature logging thermistors located at various points along the mooring string, and a pressure sensor mounted in the mooring anchor. The current meters measure north and east current vectors, temperature, and conductivity (salinity). The thermistors provide additional temperature observations of the water column and the pressure sensor provides bottom pressure measurements at each

mooring location. The moorings are recovered, instrument data downloaded, and then redeployed every six months. To monitor the integrity of the moorings, and to assure that the mooring maintains position, an ARGOS transmitter placed on the mooring buoy transmits position and in situ data from the 5 m current meter to CCS via ARGOS, a satellite-based location and data transmission service, once or twice each day. The in situ data consists of two-hour averages of north and east ocean current vectors processed onboard each 5 m current meter. The most recent 12 of these data are averaged to give a 24-hour daily average speed and direction vectors for each mooring location.

Along with data from the present array of CCS moorings, meteorological data from the NDBC buoys in the study area are collected as well. Data from buoys 46028, 46062, 46011, 46023, 46063, 46054, 46053 and 46025 (Figure 2) are transmitted to CCS via NOAA/Unidata. Unidata is an organization of over 120 colleges, universities, and other educational institutions funded by the National Science Foundation (NSF) through the University Corporation for Atmospheric Research (UCAR/NCAR) in Boulder, Colorado. SIO is a Unidata member institution and thus has access to the direct National Ocean Data Center (NODC) data feed via the Unidata Internet Data Distribution (IDD) system. These data are hourly averaged and presented in the current/wind vector map on the Oil Spill Website (Figure 4).

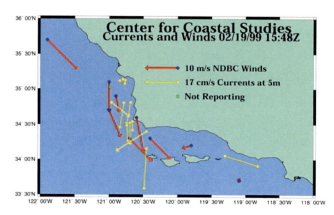

Figure 4. Interactive daily wind and current vector map, Website: www-ccs.ucsd.edu/research/sbcsmb/buoys/immap/.

Advanced Very High Resolution Radiometer (AVHRR) satellite images are downloaded daily from Seaspace Corporation, processed and placed on the Oil Spill Website (Figure 5). These images are subject to occasional cloud cover over the study area which may affect the quality of the images, thus their usefulness in determining flow regimes. The AVHRR web page allows for interactive image manipulation using a menu to select which daily image to view and to adjust the thermal color palate values for that image. This gives the user the ability to enhance different features in the image.

In the event of an oil spill, Lagrangian surface drifter buoys are deployed by CCS within the study area, their positions transmitted via ARGOS to CCS, and posted on the Oil Spill Website (Figure 6). These positions are updated as often as possible, which under normal circumstances, is approximately twice or three times daily, depending upon the transmission quality of the ARGOS satellites.

To enhance the utility of the website, links to other data sources are supplied. One of the more useful links points to the CCS Coastal Data Information Program (CDIP) Website (Figure 7). CDIP is funded by the California Department of Boating and Waterways and the U.S. Army Corps of Engineers. It supplies swell and wave now-casts using swell data measured at the Harvest oil platform off of Point Conception, and forecasts using data obtained from the U.S. Navy Fleet Numerical Meteorology and Oceanography Center in Monterey, California. These data are used as input to a Refraction/Diffraction model which outputs wave direction and energy predictions for the beaches in central and southern California, including the Santa Barbara Channel and Santa Maria Basin (O'Reilly and Guza 1991).

RESULTS

Through numerous oil spills and oil spill drills, the Oil Spill Website has proven a valuable asset in predicting oil spill trajectories. Scientists are studying the driving mechanisms of the circulation in the SBC-SMB study area by analyzing the seven-year time series collected for the

AVHRR DATA VIEWER

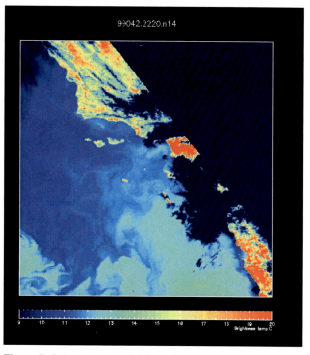

Figure 5. Interactive AVHRR satellite image viewer, Website: /www-ccs.ucsd.edu/research/sbcsmb/sat_images/ dataviewer.cgi.

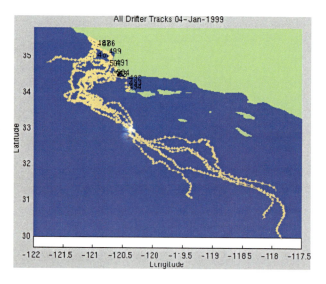

Figure 6. Lagrangian surface drifter buoy tracks, Website: www-ccs.ucsd.edu/research/sbcsmb/ drifters/realtime/ d5latest.gif.

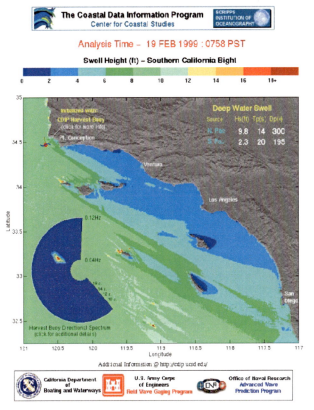

Figure 7. Coastal Data Information Program (CDIP) Southern California Bight Swell Model, Website: cdip.ucsd.edu/ models/ socal_now.shtml.

study. From these data, an understanding of the characteristic flow regimes in the region is evolving. The interaction of the California Current and the seasonal winds around Point Conception play a significant role in the forcing of these different flow regimes.

The Internet has proven an excellent means of delivering near real-time data, given its ability to make available graphical as well as textual and tabular data, in a platform independent and intuitive way. The Oil Spill Website allows users to view daily average wind and current data, as well as to view the time series and tabular data used to make these averages. This facility enables users to view trends in these data and to better forecast conditions in the study area.

As this site evolves, more functionality will be added to enhance its usefulness and reliability. Feedback from users, such as the MMS and NOAA HAZMAT, has helped CCS tailor this product to better suit the requirements of the community.

DISCUSSION

Oceanic surface currents move spilled oil over the ocean's surface. Wind has its effect on spilled oil movement indirectly by the ocean currents it forces. To accurately predict oil spill movement, we must have an understanding of the characteristic flow regimes and their causal forcing in the Santa Barbara Channel. SBC-SMB Circulation Study

results indicate that near surface circulation in the Santa Barbara Channel area is primarily driven by the wind stress and pressure gradient through the channel area. The wind stress along south central California coast is generally equatorward (upwelling favorable) and the along-channel pressure gradient is directed poleward most of the year. The time series measurements of the wind stress and the alongshore pressure gradient are significantly anticorrelated, and their relative strengths determine the particular surface flow regime in the channel area. Figure 8 (Harms and Winant 1998) exhibits the effect on the surface circulation in the Santa Barbara Channel by varying the relative strengths of the wind stress and the alongshore pressure gradient. This information is a valuable tool to the oil spill trajectory forecaster.

Figure 9 (Harms and Winant 1998) visually describes the six characteristic flow regimes of the Santa Barbara Channel area. They are the Upwelling, Relaxation, Cyclonic, Propagating Cyclones, Flood East, and Flood West flow regimes. When the wind stress is significantly larger than the alongshore pressure gradient, the Upwelling flow regime exists. When the pressure gradient dominates significantly over the wind stress, the Relaxation flow regime is formed. When the opposing wind stress and along-shore pressure gradient both become strong, the flow transitions to the Cyclonic flow regime. When the wind field is unidirectional over the entire channel area (typically during winter storm conditions), and the along-shore pressure gradient is weak or in the same direction as the wind stress, the Flow East and Flow West conditions occur. The Propagating Cyclone regime may dominate the channel flow during a transition to another flow regime, or may be superimposed on one of the other flow regimes just described.

The oil spill trajectory forecaster who understands the flow dynamics summarized above, can make a reasonable estimate of the existing flow regime in the channel area, and its relative intensity, by studying real-time data from the field array described in Figure 2. From this, intelligent estimates of a simulated flow field can be made. This capability is essential in forecasting oil spill trajectories successfully during an oil spill crisis in the Santa Barbara Channel area, with or without an oil spill trajectory model. If the forecaster has a trajectory model, the accuracy of his modeled trajectories is greatly improved by this information.

Through their research and collaboration, CCS, MMS, and industry scientists have developed this forecasting expertise. Their oil spill trajectory predictions were accurate with, and without, the use of oil spill trajectory models during the Heritage platform oil spill that occurred in May of 1995. Oil spill trajectory was accurately predicted during the September 1997 Irene platform oil spill without the use of an oil spill trajectory model.

The data used for oil spill response primarily comes from four current meter moorings and four NDBC meteorological buoys strategically located in the SBC-SMB study area, satellite imagery (two images per day during good weather), and Lagrangian surface drifter buoy tracks from buoys launched at the onset of oil spill response activities.

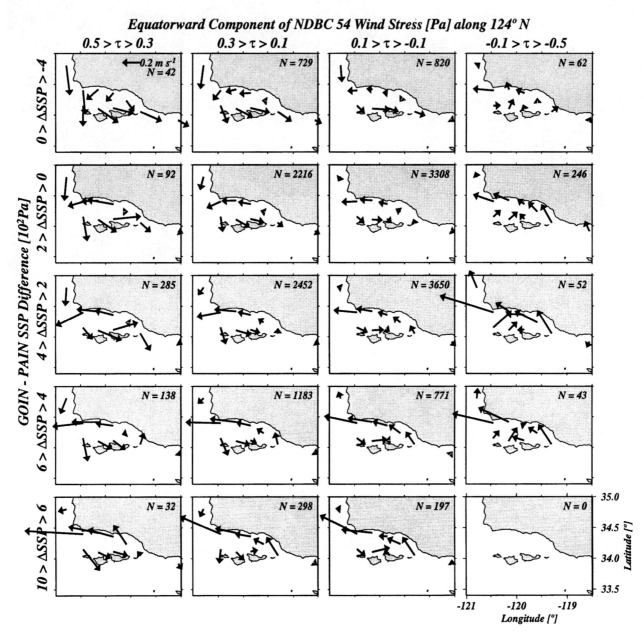

Figure 8. Varying wind stress and alongshore pressure gradient (Harms and Winant 1998).

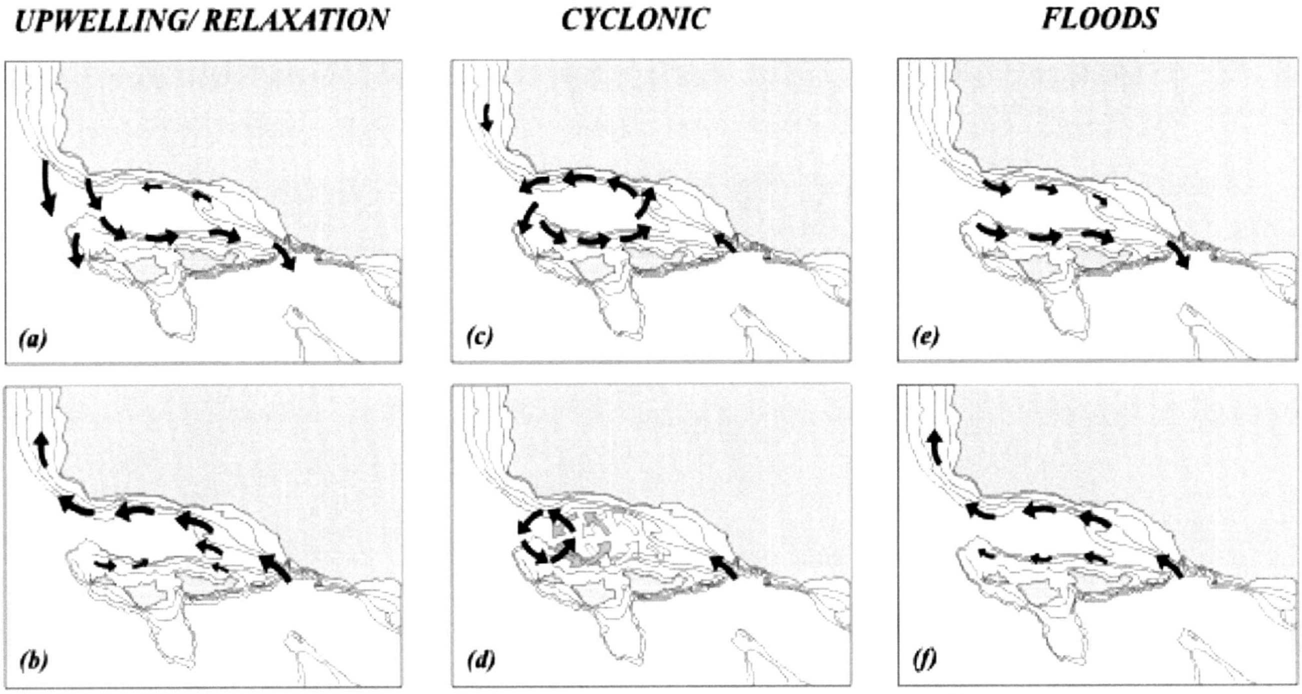

UPWELLING/RELAXATION   **CYCLONIC**   **FLOODS**

Figure 9. Characteristic flow regimes in the Santa Barbara Channel area (Harms and Winant 1998).

This suite of observations would comprise a long term monitoring program that would remain after the larger field array is finally recovered. The four current meter moorings and four NDBC meteorological buoys are indicated in Figure 2 and designated: ANMI, SMIN, SMOF, SAMI, 23, 54, 53, and 25, respectively.

The mooring array depicted in Figure 2 will be recovered from the field in November 1999. Without the valuable real-time data that these moorings provide, accurate predictions of oil spill movements that do much to protect valuable environmental and socio-economic resources in the Santa Barbara Channel, will no longer be possible. The hope is that state agencies and industry can combine resources to ensure the continuation of this valuable oil spill response resource.

LITERATURE CITED

Harms, S. and C. D. Winant. 1998. Characteristic patterns of the circulation in the Santa Barbara Channel. Journal of Geophysical Research, 103:3041-3065.

O'Reilly, W. C. and R. T. Guza. 1991 Modeling surface gravity waves in the Southern California Bight. SIO reference series, no. 91-25.

AVAILABILITY OF MOORED DATASETS FROM THE SANTA BARBARA CHANNEL-SANTA MARIA BASIN CIRCULATION STUDY

Daniel N. Larsen

Center for Coastal Studies, Scripps Institution of Oceanography, UCSD
Mail Code 0209, 9500 Gilman Drive, La Jolla, CA 92093-0209
(858) 534-2210, FAX (858) 534-0300, E-mail: dlarsen@ucsd.edu

ABSTRACT

Moored datasets including ocean current, temperature, salinity, and bottom pressure measurements have been collected and archived in the Santa Barbara Channel and Santa Maria Basin areas since 1992. This extensive dataset has undergone quality control and is now available on the Internet. Near-real-time data is also available over the Internet, and sample applications of that accessibility are presented in the context of coastal monitoring and oil spill response. Maps of the data are presented here. Information on dataset availability, format, and instructions for accessing the data are presented. Future plans for data formats and web delivery are also discussed.

Keywords: Moorings, currents, temperature, salinity, bottom pressure, Santa Barbara, monitoring, oil spill.

INTRODUCTION

In this paper, moored data collected during the Santa Barbara Channel-Santa Maria Basin Circulation Study since 1992 will be presented. The phrase *moored data* is used here to describe several datasets which are collected from a set of instruments moored at various depths. These datasets include vector measured currents, temperature, salinity, and pressure data. The collection, processing, and archiving methods are explained, and public access to the datasets is discussed.

Study Location

The mooring sites are located within the Santa Barbara Channel (SBC) and the Santa Maria Basin (SMB), between the 30 m (meter) and 200 m isobaths (Figure 1). The moorings have four-letter names, in which the first two letters represent a nearby geographical landmark (e.g. "AN" for the island of Anacapa), and the last two letters indicate whether the mooring is inshore ("IN"), offshore ("OF"), or in the middle ("MI").

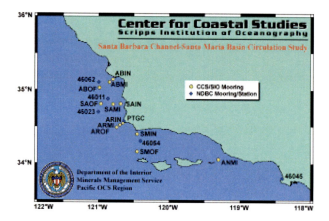

Figure 1. Study region, showing location of moorings and their names. Also shown, as a reference, are the locations of five NDBC meterological platforms.

MOORED DATASET

Introduction

The moored array consists of a total of twelve moorings deployed over the shelf along the 30 m, 100 m, and 200 m isobaths. Our standard mooring (Figure 2) consists of a surface buoy with ARGOS transmitter and temperature logger at 1 m depth, current meters at 5 m and 45 m which also record temperature and conductivity, additional temperature loggers at 25 m and 65 m depth, and a bottom anchor which houses a pressure sensor that additionally records temperature and conductivity. Individual deployments of moorings are on the order of 8 to 10 months.

Instrumentation

Ocean current is measured by vector measuring current meters (VMCM) which internally record north and east components of currents, temperature, and conductivity. The conductivity data is fed into the VMCM from an externally mounted SeaBird Conductivity Sensor SBE 4. The temperature logging instruments found at 1 m, 25 m, and 65 m depths were developed in-house. The bottom pressure sensor instrument measures both pressure and temperature directly and is fed conductivity from an external SeaBird Conductivity Sensor. The VMCMs are outfitted with an

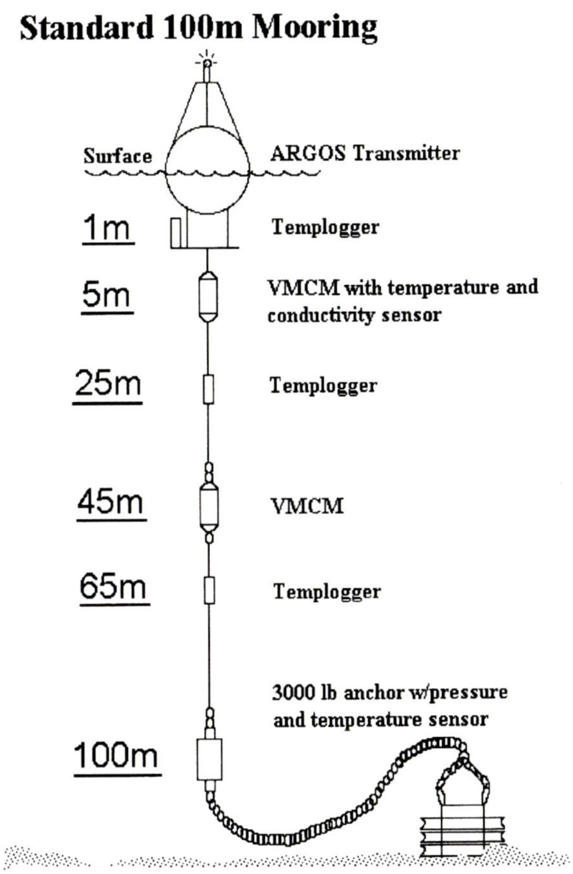

Standard 100m Mooring

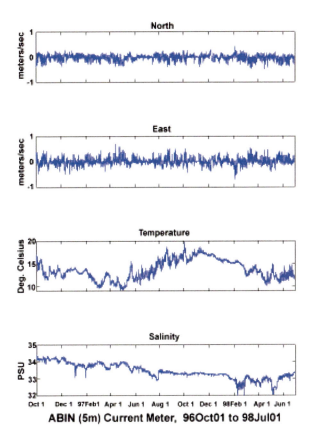

Figure 2. This diagram shows the standard layout of our 100 m mooring. In addition to the notes listed on the diagram, conductivity measurements are taken at 45 m and at 100 m.

ABIN (5m) Current Meter, 96Oct01 to 98Jul01

Figure 3. This plot shows sample data from the 5 m VMCM at the Avila Beach Inshore (ABIN) mooring. The data behind this particular plot has not completed quality control. This can be seen in the salinity plot around August 1, 1997, where the merge point of two deployments is still visible and a correction must be applied.

external serial dataport, and the top-most 5 m instrument is connected via cable to the buoy mounted ARGOS transmitter to allow for near real-time transmission of data. Data received through ARGOS includes two-hour averaged data from the 5 m instrument, as well as latitude and longitude coordinates of the mooring which is used to monitor its location.

Calibration of the instruments is performed before and after deployments. The suite of calibrations includes compass, temperature, flow, and pressure calibrations. The manufacturer performs conductivity calibrations.

Data Processing

The data from the various instruments are processed in similar manners. Each instrument records the data internally on standard PC flash memory cards. The data retrieved from these cards is processed with a suite of programs that apply the calibration information in order to convert the data from instrument values to standard engineering units. A sample plot of data collected from the inshore Avila Beach mooring (ABIN) 5 m current meter is shown in Figure 3.

Quality Control, Averaging, and Data Format

Data is recorded in four minute averages and remains at this sample interval as it undergoes further quality control measures to remove erroneous data. Once processed, the data is converted to hourly averages before being published on-line.

The moored data from this project are currently archived in an ASCII format called CSA. This is a columnar format, with five lines of header information (Figure 4). We are currently in the process of converting the data to netCDF, a binary format that is quickly becoming the oceanographic standard.

```
start_time      npts        samp_interv  depth       lat        lon
yymmddhhmmss    #_pts       seconds      meters      deg        deg
960320020000    19966       3600         5.00        35.1388    -120.7960
north           east        temp         salinity
m/s             m/s         deg_C        psu
-0.0127         -0.0051     12.6077      33.4051
0.0057          -0.0382     12.6171      33.4125
-0.0625         -0.0592     12.1619      33.4695
-0.0572         -0.1125     12.0829      33.4852
-0.0144         -0.1457     12.2183      33.4602
0.0002          -0.1341     12.1127      33.4635
0.0367          -0.1779     12.4955      33.4187
0.0777          -0.1945     12.8005      33.3811
0.1095          -0.1809     13.0036      33.3465
0.1611          -0.1290     13.1215      33.3616
...             ...         ...          ...
```

Figure 4. Sample CSA format file. This is our ASCII data archival format, consisting of five header lines. The first three header lines contain static data about the file, including start time, number of points, sample interval, latitude, and longitude. The next two lines contain header names and units of dynamic variable, such as north and east components of currents, temperature, and salinity. Next, the data itself is listed in columnar format.

WORLD WIDE WEB ACCESS

All of these datasets, as well as many other datasets, are available via the World Wide Web. The URL for the SBC-SMB Circulation Study is:

www.ccs.ucsd.edu/research/sbcsmb

From here, users can access information about all of the moored data, as well as other datasets, which comprise this study. The data itself can be downloaded from the Center for Coastal Studies' (CCS) Data Zoo, which can be accessed from the above starting point.

The near real-time delivery of the top-most current meter data is also available as part of oil spill response web site. The URL for this page is:

www.ccs.ucsd.edu/oilspill

From the Oil Spill Response Web Page users will find data and links to near real-time datasets of Advanced Very High Resolution Radiometer (AVHRR) satellite images, drifter trajectories, surface currents, surface winds, wave conditions, and swell height. The availability of this data over the web is part of a growing effort to provide high-quality environmental data that can be used in coastal monitoring and emergency response programs.

SOURCES OF UNPUBLISHED MATERIALS

Winant, Clinton D. Scripps Institution of Oceanography, UCSD, Mail Code 0209, La Jolla, CA 92093.

AVAILABILITY OF AVHRR SATELLITE DATA AND NDBC BUOY DATA FROM THE SANTA BARBARA CHANNEL-SANTA MARIA BASIN CIRCULATION STUDY

Brett N. Lesh

Center for Coastal Studies, Scripps Institution of Oceanography, La Jolla, CA 92093-0209
(858) 534-7561, FAX (858) 534-0300, E-mail: blesh@coast.ucsd.edu

ABSTRACT

Advanced Very High Resolution Radiometer (AVHRR) satellite data and National Data Buoy Center (NDBC) buoy data of the Santa Barbara Channel (SBC) and Santa Maria Basin (SMB) are acquired and archived in the Data Zoo at the Center For Coastal Studies. The AVHRR data set is acquired by polar-orbiting National Oceanic and Atmospheric Administration (NOAA) satellites and processed daily. Some images are presented here. NDBC moored buoy data and Coastal Marine Automated Network (CMAN) data are acquired and archived. Plots and maps are presented here. AVHRR, NDBC moored buoy data, and CMAN data are accessible through the Internet. Instructions on how to access the data, the format the data is in, data processing, and the availability of the data are discussed.

Keywords: Web, Internet, access data, Advanced Very High Resolution Radiometer, National Data Buoy Center , winds, satellite images, Coastal Studies ASCII, sea surface temperature, buoys.

INTRODUCTION

Advanced Very High Resolution Radiometer (AVHRR) High Resolution Picture Transmission (HRPT) satellite image data, National Data Buoy Center (NDBC) buoy data, and Coastal Marine Automated Network (CMAN) data acquired during the Santa Barbara Channel-Santa Maria (SBC-SMB) Basin Circulation Study since 1992 will be discussed. AVHRR HRPT data for channel 4 (infrared) is archived and accessible through the World Wide Web. NDBC buoy data is archived from all buoys around the Santa Barbara Channel and Santa Maria Basin. Data archived for NDBC buoys are wind speed and direction, atmospheric temperature, atmospheric pressure, and sea surface temperature (SST). Data for NDBC buoys is archived in Coastal Studies ASCII (CSA) format. CMAN stations are the same as NDBC buoys except there is no sea surface temperature. The collection, processing, and availability on the World Wide Web is discussed.

AVHRR IMAGE DATA

AVHRR HRPT data have been received since March of 1992 as part of the SBC-SMB Circulation study. This data is captured using a satellite dish and Seaspace's Terascan acquisition software and hardware system. The data is then calibrated to engineering units which is percent albedo for channels 1 and 2 and brightness temperature for AVHRR channels 3, 4, and 5. Channel 4 is used as a estimation of sea surface temperature when it is cloud free. Satellite data is important since its spatial resolution is high and images are taken in one synoptic state. There are on average four images a day that have HRPT data in the SBC-SMB area.

Instruments

The AVHRR is carried on the National Oceanic and Atmospheric Administration (NOAA) Polar Orbiting Environmental Satellite (POES) (Figure 1). POES satellites are in near-polar sunsynchronous orbit at 833 km height which allows them to cover the globe twice daily. The resolution is 1.1 km at nadir. AVHRR has 5 channels, two visible and three infrared (VIS, 0.62 Fm and 0.91 Fm; IR, 3.7 Fm, 10.8 Fm, and 12.0 Fm). The infrared channels have a noise equivalent differential temperature of approximately 0.12°C when viewing the ocean surface.

Figure 1. AVHRR Satellite.

Data Processing

HRPT data is received on a satellite dish whenever one of the AVHRR sensors is recording data and within sight of a receiver dish. These data are then calibrated and registered to the SBC-SMB area using Seaspace's Terascan software system. Now the data is ready to be looked at with the Terascan system, where the coast is navigated by hand to the coastline in the SBC-SMB area. After all this is done the images are archived in Terascan Data Format (TDF). Monthly SST means have been made for 1993 through 1998 (see Figure 2 for 1998). SST means were made by first making good daily images to reduce cloud cover. Good daily images are made by taking all images for a given day and removing all ludicrous values and picking the maximum value in each position. The mean of these reduced cloud daily images taken over each month is the monthly mean.

Web Access

AVHRR data can viewed in a few different ways on the web. Images since 1993 are saved as ".gif" files for a specific temperature range (10°C to 20°C) and can be found at the following website:

**www-ccs.ucsd.edu/research/sbcsmb/sat_images/
data_archive.cgi** (Figure 3).

You can also enhance the latest 30 images to get a better look. This page will let you enter a color pallette and a temperature range for the latest 30 images. The best way to do this is to enter a big range and then narrow it down by looking at the temperature scale and choosing the values that seem appropriate. This can be done at this website:

**www-ccs.ucsd.edu/research/sbcsmb/sat_images/
dataviewer.cgi** (Figure 4).

Some cloud free images are processed to bring out all the details. These can be found at this website:

**www- ccs.ucsd.edu/research/sbcsmb/sat_images/
clearimages.cgi.**

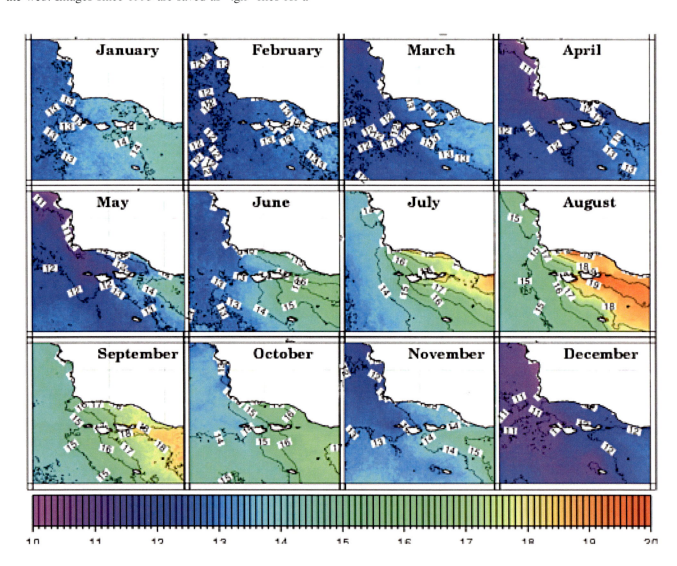

Figure 2. 1998 Monthly SST means derived from AVHRR images.

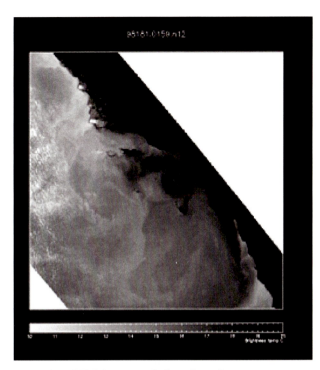

Figure 3. AVHRR image made from Dataviewer.

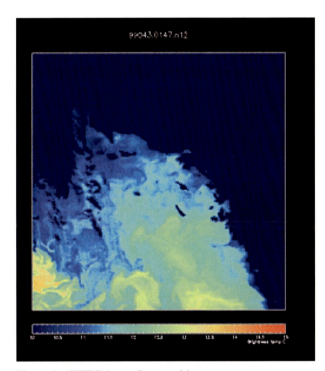

Figure 4. AVHRR image from archives.

Monthly averages can be found at website:

**www-ccs.ucsd.edu/research/sbcsmb/sat_images/
analysis.html** (Figure 2).

There have also been some movies of AVHRR data
with drifter tracks overlaid which can be found at website:
**www-ccs.ucsd.edu/ research/sbcsmb/sat_images/
movies.html.**

NDBC BUOY AND CMAN DATA

NDBC buoy data have wind direction, wind speed,
atmospheric temperature, atmospheric pressure, and SST
data, while CMAN stations have the same without SST.
These data have been taken during the SBC/SMB Circulation study. The data has been taken from 3 m buoys, 10 m
buoys, 6 m nomad buoys, and the CMAN station at Point
Arguello.

Instrumentation

NDBC buoys used in this study have been one of three
types; 3 m discus buoys (Figure 5), 10 m discus buoys (Figure 6), and 6 m nomad buoys (Figure 7). They each contain
wind direction, wind speed, atmospheric pressure, atmospheric temperature, and SST data. They were deployed by
NOAA and data is received by NDBC in real-time. Real-
time messages coded in FM-13 (buoys) and FM-12 (CMAN)
are posted on a internet server maintained by University
Corporation for Atmospheric Research (UCAR). CMAN
Station PTGC1 has all the same data except that it does not
have any sea surface temperature information. It also posts
data to the server maintained by UCAR. For positions of
NDBC buoys see Figure 8.

Data Processing

Data for NDBC buoys and CMAN stations are processed in two different ways, one is for real-time purposes
and the other is for archiving. Data for NDBC buoys and
CMAN stations is available from NDBC over the web. It is
quality controlled and put in f291 format. It is then downloaded and formatted into CSA format and archived. The
CSA files are hourly averages of ten minute data. Real-time
data received from UNIDATA in FM-12 and FM-13 format
is downloaded daily and decoded. This data is used as daily
real-time winds and is also hourly averages.

Figure 5. Three meter buoy.

Figure 6. Ten meter buoy.

Figure 7. Six meter buoy.

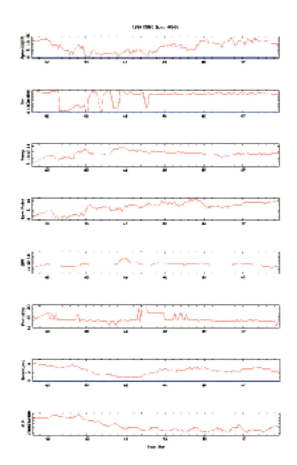

Figure 9. Times series of NDBC buoy data from web page.

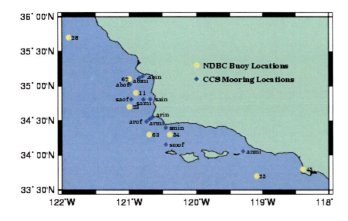

Figure 8. Positions of NDBC buoys.

CSA Format

CSA is a data format that is composed of a five line header which the data follows.The first and second lines of the header show the relevant information such as the start time, number of points, sample interval, elevation, latitude, longitude and relevant units, while the third line has the actual values. The fourth line contains the variable names and the fifth has the variable units. For example:

start_time npts samp_interv elev lat lon
yymmddhhmmss #_pts seconds meters deg deg
970101005000 8759 3600.00 10.0034.3000120.4000
north east atm_pressure atm_temp_drysea_surf_temp
 m_s m_s hPa deg_C deg_C
0.7100 -8.0700 1018.300 14.600 14.200
-0.1200 -6.8000 1018.900 14.900 14.200
-0.3500 -6.6900 1019.300 14.600 14.200
0.9600 -6.8300 1019.400 14.900 14.200
2.6600 -8.1800 1019.500 14.900 14.200

Web Access

There are a few ways to view the NDBC data. Real-time data is plotted and available daily along with ASCII columns of the latest three days of data if you click on a buoy on the following web page:

www-ccs.ucsd.edu/research/sbcsmb/buoys/ immap/ (Figure 9).

Archived quality controlled data is available in CSA format at web page:

gopher://gopher-ccs.ucsd.edu:70/11/zoo/ndbc/ buoydata.

A good explanation and source of data is located at website:

seaboard.ndbc.noaa.gov/

LITERATURE CITED

Lauritson, L. and G. Nelson. July 1979. Techniques for Data Extraction and Calibration of TIROS-M/NOAA Series Satellite Radiometers for Direct Readout Users; NOAA-NESS Publication #107.

Seaspace Corporation. October 10, 1993. Terascan Reference Manual.

NDBC. 1998. How Do You Decode Real Time Data? NDBC Web Page http://seaboard.ndbc.noaa.gov/ decode.shtml.

THE SANTA BARBARA CHANNEL-SANTA MARIA BASIN CIRCULATION STUDY: A BRIEF HISTORY

Brynn Craffey

Center for Coastal Studies, Scripps Institution of Oceanography, UCSD
Mail Code 0209, 9500 Gilman Drive, La Jolla, CA 92093-0209
(858) 534-9861, FAX (858) 534-0300, E-mail: brynn@coast.ucsd.edu

ABSTRACT

A brief history of the Santa Barbara Channel-Santa Maria Basin (SBC-SMB) Circulation Study, including field experiences of investigators while collecting and analyzing data from a variety of sources, including the National Oceanic and Atmospheric Administration (NOAA), Advanced Very High Resolution Radiometry (AVHRR) Satellites, the National Data Buoy Center (NDBC), Vector Measuring Current Meters (VMCM), Conductivity, Temperature and Depth (CTDs) measuring devices, Expendible Bathythermographs (XBTs), and Acoustic Doppler Current Profilers (ADCPs).

Keywords: Southern California Bight, Santa Barbara Channel, Santa Maria Basin, offshore, oil drilling, continental shelf, circulation.

INTRODUCTION

On February 9, 1989, responding to mounting concerns over the environmental risks associated with offshore oil drilling, President George Bush suspended oil leases for several continental shelf areas off the coasts of Florida and California. At the same time, he set in motion the governmental machinery to investigate the long-term environmental risks of outer continental shelf (OCS) exploration. He established a National Research Council (NRC) independent scientific committee to access the adequacy of the existent scientific data covering the lease areas. He also created a cabinet level task force to review environmental issues associated with exploration and drilling. Drs. Clinton Winant and Myrl Hendershott, of Scripps Institution of Oceanography's (SIO) Center for Coastal Studies (CCS), served on the former committee. (U.S. Dept. of the Interior MMS 1991)

BACKGROUND

After careful study, the NRC committee concluded there was inadequate physical oceanographic data to assess the environmental impacts of re-opening the southern California OCS to oil exploration (Committee to Review the Outer Continental Shelf Environmental Studies Program 1989). The Minerals Management Service (MMS) convened a workshop at SIO on 27 November to 29 November 1990 to chart a course of action. To remedy the lack of data, MMS proposed a study of the Southern California Bight that would span several years and cost upwards of $20 million. This sum proved too costly, prompting MMS to turn again to SIO. Scripps scientists eventually designed a study that would cost less and actually span a longer period of time. This became the Santa Barbara Channel-Santa Maria Basin (SBC-SMB) Circulation Study which, under the leadership of David Browne, has evolved into an 11-year, $15 million field study of the overall circulation in the SBC-SMB area.

WORK, PHASES, AND TASKS

To expand the time period covered by the study and at the same time reduce the overall cost required scaling back the geographic scope. Rather than study the entire Southern California Bight, scientists decided to focus on that portion of the bight already under active oil exploration and production: Santa Barbara Channel and Santa Maria Basin areas.

Initial funding carried the study through Phase I, which encompassed initial planning, preparation, and start-up, and ran from spring 1991 through March 1996. As information was collected and evaluated, it became increasingly apparent that more data were needed. So despite bureaucratic uncertainties in Washington, MMS extended the project. Phase II ran from 1994 through 1997 and was comprised of field work and analysis focused on the Santa Barbara Channel. During Phase II, the need for a reliable modeling component became evident, leading MMS to expand the study once more. Phase III, currently underway, includes a modeling component and extended the geographic area of field work and analysis to include the Santa Maria Basin.

In all the phases, the study has focused on two broad goals: first, to identify specific patterns of circulation, and second, to translate scientific results into an immediately useful form for analysts in charge of resources development. To accomplish these goals, work has been divided roughly into five main categories: meteorology, moored observations, Lagrangian observations, surveys (expanded surveys and satellite imagery), and eventually modeling. From the outset, the intellectual challenge has been to integrate seemingly disparate results from these individual components into a coherent picture of the circulation and its driving forces.

Researchers at CCS have realized significant scientific achievements all along the way. In Phase I, preliminary field observations were accomplished in SBC, resulting in the theory of "synoptic views," or ocean equivalents of the atmospheric patterns employed by meteorologists to forecast weather. The CCS Data Zoo and Website were established, eventually offering (on the MMS/SIO Oil Spill Response page) near real-time Internet access to a wide-range of data gathered by project scientists and instrumentation.

In Phase II, the circulation in the Santa Barbara Channel was described in terms of six characteristic patterns (Figure 1). Together, these synoptic views account for a major part of the variability in the field study's results over the years. The patterns' forcing mechanisms have been identified (Figure 2), including the important role played by the upwelling favorable wind stress (from the northwest winds) and the opposing alongshore pressure gradients. As a result of the research, scientists working in related areas of study have begun to re-evaluate the entire dynamics of ocean circulation in various areas, such as CODE. Moreover, the data is leading to the development of effective current forecasting methods.

Phase III is expected to achieve similarly significant scientific results in the Santa Maria Basin, north of Point Conception (Figure 3).

Throughout the study's history, there has been a clear and direct relationship between MMS's consistent support and the high quality of the work. The value and significance of CCS's research and scientific results have been in direct proportion to the persistence of MMS' funding. And, while

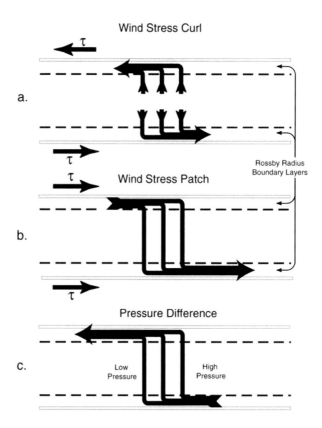

Figure 2. Illustration of the effects of wind stress curl (a) or a patch of uniform wind stress, (b) or a pressure difference, and (c) on various circulation patterns within the channel.

UPWELLING/ RELAXATION   CYCLONIC   FLOODS

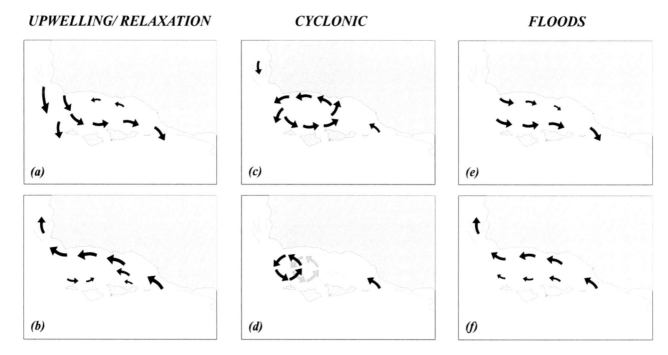

Figure 1. Different characteristic patterns of the surface circulation in the Santa Barbara Channel, derived by subjective review of 900 daily maps of average currents. These patterns account for the circulation over 60% of the time.

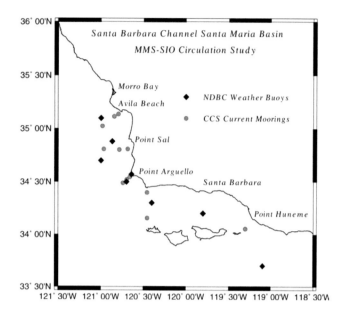

Figure 3. Site of the experiment. Circles indicate location of current meter, temperature and pressure moorings. In the Santa Maria Basin, moorings are located on three major transects extending out from Avila Beach (the AB line), from Point Sal (the SA line), and from Point Arguello (the AR line). Three moorings are maintained in the Santa Barbara Channel to determine the synoptic state of surface circulation in that area.

complying with MMS's strict procurement rules has not always been a trivial enterprise, nor always compatible with scientific research, the work has continued apace – mostly thanks to the unswerving advocacy of David Browne. Time and again, David has managed to translate the vital importance of the study and its results into language easily understandable to the Washington officials in charge of funding, thus guaranteeing continued federal support for what has become an important, ground-breaking study.

LITERATURE CITED

Committee to Review the Outer Continental Shelf Environmental Studies Program, Board on Environmental Studies and Toxicology, et. al. 1989. The Adequacy of Environmental Information for Outer Continental Shelf Oil and Gas Decisions: Florida and California. 1-12.

Santa Barbara Channel-Santa Maria Basin Circulation Study Phase 1 Proposal. 1991.

U. S. Department of the Interior, Minerals Management Service. 1991. Southern California Bight Physical Oceanography, Proceedings of a Workshop. Prepared by MBC Applied Environmental Sciences, Costa Mesa, CA. 157 p. plus appendices.

Winant, C. D., M. C. Hendershott, C. E. Dorman. 1998. Quality Review Board Minutes of Meeting No. 6.

RIVER DISCHARGE PLUMES IN THE SANTA BARBARA CHANNEL

Barbara M. Hickey

School of Oceanography, University of Washington, Box 357940, Seattle, WA 98195
(206) 543-4737, FAX (206) 616-9289, E-mail: bhickey@u.washington.edu

ABSTRACT

Satellite-derived images of ocean sea surface turbidity and in situ measurements of ocean salinity demonstrate that large areas of the coastal zone in southern California (as much as 8,000 km) can be impacted by discharge from coastal rivers. Such river plumes carry both dissolved and suspended material from California watersheds into the coastal ocean. River plumes can also substantially affect coastal current patterns, particularly in the upper ~5 m of the water column. Typical plumes from the Santa Clara River region, for example, cover a surface area of about 500 km^2 extending up to 50 km into the Santa Barbara Channel under northward regional wind conditions or 70 km southeast into the Santa Monica Basin under southward regional wind conditions. Individual plumes persist for about two to five days. Southward and offshore surface flows during upwelling-favorable wind conditions tend to spread plumes offshore of the river mouth. For example, the plume from the Santa Clara and Ventura rivers in the eastern Santa Barbara Channel frequently reaches the eastern Channel Islands during the strong upwelling events that generally follow major storms. Similarly, in high discharge years, the western Channel Islands are impacted by river discharge plumes that originate north of Point Conception.

INTRODUCTION

River plumes provide a primary mechanism by which material from coastal watersheds and storm runoff is distributed through the coastal zone. The presence of a river plume in a coastal region can also significantly change regional flow patterns, particularly in the upper ~5 m of the water column. Previous studies in the Southern California Bight have not addressed the structure and temporal variability of such features: river plumes occur only during major storms when measurements are difficult to obtain; and they occupy the shallowest portion of the coastal ocean, which is difficult to sample. This paper describes the spatial structure and temporal variability of river plumes that impact the Santa Barbara Channel. A complete discussion of this topic for the entire Southern California Bight is given in Hickey and Kachel (1999).

Significant progress has been made recently in understanding circulation in the Santa Barbara Channel (Hendershott and Winant 1996; Harms and Winant 1998).

The large scale circulation patterns described by these studies are a result of wind, wind curl and pressure gradients along the coast. In the upper 5 m of the water column, direct wind forcing (frictional currents) is also important.

River plumes, when they occur, contribute additional complexity to the resulting circulation patterns. When coastal rivers discharge into the coastal ocean, they form a buoyant plume governed by nonlinear dynamics. In the northern hemisphere, and in the absence of ambient currents, such plumes bend toward the right on entering the ocean (e.g., model results in Chao 1988; Kourafalou et al. 1996). The region in which the plume turns is highly nonlinear. Farther downstream, the plume reattaches to the coast to form a (linear) coastal current that hugs the coastline. In the presence of ambient currents, the plume may bend to the left after it leaves the river mouth (e.g., the Columbia River plume in summer); or it may remain adjacent to the coast if the prevailing coastal flow is northward. River plumes are particularly sensitive to changes in local wind conditions, which directly affect flow in the surface Ekman layer (e.g., model results in Chao 1988; Kourafalou et al. 1996). This sensitivity has been demonstrated in the Columbia plume, which moves onshore or offshore as the wind changes direction from northward to southward on scales of two to three days (Hickey et al. 1998). The response time of the Columbia plume to such changes is less than six hours (Hickey et al. 1998). The spatial structure of surface currents during large storms, when plumes occur, is of particular consequence during oil spills and other marine emergencies.

During winter and spring seasons when the principal river discharge events occur, winds with a northward component are generally associated with storms, increased rainfall and northwestward to westward surface flow in the Santa Barbara Channel ("upcoast" flow) adjacent to the coast. Winds with a southward component during those seasons are generally associated with good weather, upwelling of cold water adjacent to the coast, and eastward to southeastward ("downcoast") flow) surface currents near the coast (Hickey 1992; Harms and Winant 1998).

MATERIALS AND METHODS

Time series of daily mean river discharge as well as suspended sediment yield for selected rivers were obtained from the United States Geological Survey (USGS).

Discharge data from 1998 were provided by the United Water Conservation District.

Wind data at a centrally located buoy (National Data Buoy Center Buoy 46025) were obtained from the "Data Zoo" maintained by Scripps Institution of Oceanography (SIO). Buoy location is shown in Figure 1. Comparison with wind data at other sites (Hickey 1992) as well as analysis of wind patterns within the Bight (Winant and Dorman 1997) show that winds from this site are sufficient to provide a general indication of environmental conditions in the nearshore Southern California Bight.

Satellite images of sea surface temperature, visible imagery, and surface albedo were obtained for selected dates from Ocean Imaging, Inc. Data have a nominal spatial resolution of 1 km. A combination of the first two satellite channels (detecting red and near infrared light, respectively) was used by Ocean Imaging, Inc. to construct a measure of sea surface turbidity using the algorithm of Stumpf and Pennock (1989).

RESULTS

Three major rivers (the Santa Clara and Ventura, the Santa Maria, and the Santa Ynez) have discharge plumes that can affect the Santa Barbara Channel (Figure 1). These discharge plumes are easily identified in satellite-derived images of sea surface turbidity (Hickey and Kachel 1999).

The plume from the Santa Clara and Ventura rivers discharges into the channel near its eastern end. Roughly one-third of the plume volume originates from the Ventura River; the remaining two-thirds originates from the Santa Clara River (Hickey and Kachel 1999). The plume from the Santa Maria and Santa Ynez rivers enters the channel from its western end during periods of strong coastal upwelling.

River discharge data demonstrate that major floods from rivers in Southern California occur every few years (30% of the years since 1943) primarily during El Niño conditions (Hickey and Kachel 1999). During flood years, periods of high discharge generally occur for two to ten days on several occasions between January and April. During each storm, river discharge begins abruptly and tapers off over several days (Figure 2). Most rivers flood at roughly the same time. During the strongest El Niños, discharge can remain high for several weeks (Hickey and Kachel 1999). Between flood years, and during summer and fall in all years, southern California rivers are essentially dry.

During flood years, millions of tons of material can be delivered to the Southern California Bight in a very short period of time (one to two days), exceeding the mean annual output of the largest river on the U.S. west coast (the Columbia) (Figure 2 for 1993; see Hickey and Kachel (1999) for additional years). This material is derived from the river drainage basin, including agricultural lands, storm sewers, etc. Pollutants such as pesticides (e.g., DDT), PCB, and oil

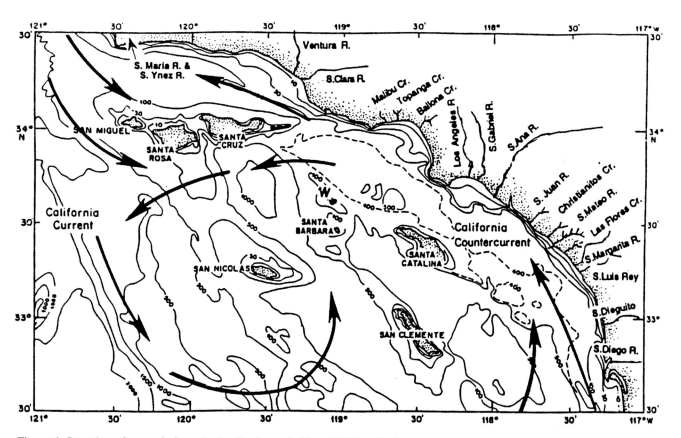

Figure 1. Location of gauged rivers in the Southern California Bight relative to coastline orientation and bottom topography. A schematic circulation pattern for large scale flow in the Bight near the sea surface is superimposed on the topography (from Hickey 1992).

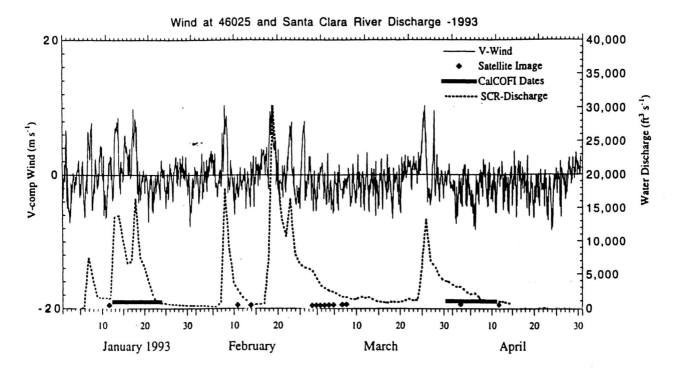

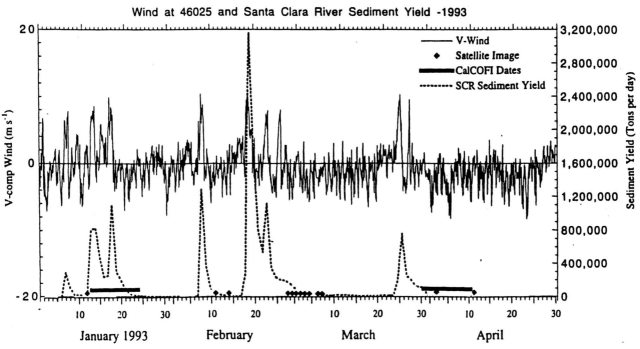

Figure 2. North–south component of wind and river discharge (upper panel) and wind and sediment yield (lower panel) during periods when satellite data were collected. Time is given in Pacific Standard Time. Dates of satellite images are shown as symbols along the x-axis. In general, southward wind is indicative of upwelling conditions and northward wind is indicative of downwelling conditions.

are transferred from their point of origin or temporary storage to coastal marshes or to the ocean.

The plume from the Santa Clara and Ventura rivers has two dominant orientations: upcoast tending or downcoast tending. Upcoast plumes are generally associated with the

occurrence of upcoast winds, hence downwelling and onshore flow that tends to keep plumes confined to the coast (Figure 3, upper panel). Downcoast plumes are generally associated with downcoast winds, hence upwelling and offshore flow that tends to spread plumes off the coast and to the south or southeast (Figure 3, lower panel). For both types of plumes, spatial structure is much less variable than the environmental conditions or recent and ongoing river discharge rate (Hickey and Kachel 1999). This suggests some limitation to growth of turbid plumes. In the images collected (winter to spring 1991, 1993, 1995, 1998), turbid plumes from the Santa Clara and Ventura rivers extended a maximum distance of about 60 km westward into the Santa Barbara Channel or 110 km southeast into the Santa Monica Basin (Hickey and Kachel 1999). Downcoast tending plumes are typically almost twice as long and more than twice as wide as the upcoast plumes, likely a result of enhancement of wind-driven flow as the Ekman layer is compressed by plume stratification. Thus, upwelling conditions are very effective at spreading fine-grained material away from river mouths. For example, the plume from the Santa Clara and Ventura rivers can envelop Anacapa Island during upwelling conditions following major floods.

Each major storm in southern California is generally followed by a strong upwelling event. During these upwelling events, turbid material from flooding rivers north of Point Conception (principally the Santa Maria and the Santa Ynez) enter the Bight from the west where they frequently envelop the western Channel Islands (Figure 3, lower panel). The intrusion of turbid water from north of Point Conception into the Santa Barbara Channel is consistent with silt content in surface sediments (Thornton 1984) as well as light transmission surveys (Drake 1972). Thus, upwelling events following major floods may be more efficient than actual storm conditions at moving finer grained particles away from river mouths along the coast and out to the Channel Islands.

The volume of freshwater discharged into the ocean during a typical five-day flood in the Santa Barbara Channel would occupy a 2 m high column of water over an area of about 10 to 100 km². The volume impacted by the discharge can be many times greater than the initial discharge volume. Lower salinity areas at the sea surface as great as 8,000 km² have been observed off the southern California coast during periods of highest discharge (Hickey and Kachel 1999). On one occasion, fresher water in the Santa Clara River region occupied an area of about 2,000 km². More typical low salinity areas in the Santa Clara region covered a surface area of about 500 km². Areas covered by turbid plumes from the Santa Clara River ranged from 100 to 1,500 km², although an area of about 3,000 km² was covered by the plume during strong upwelling following closest in time to a very high discharge event. Depth strata in which salinity is clearly influenced by river discharge range from the sea surface to 10 or 20 m from the surface (Hickey and Kachel 1999).

DISCUSSION

This paper uses satellite-derived images of sea surface turbidity to provide information on the spatial structure and temporal variability of river plumes in and near the Santa Barbara Channel. Such information is important for

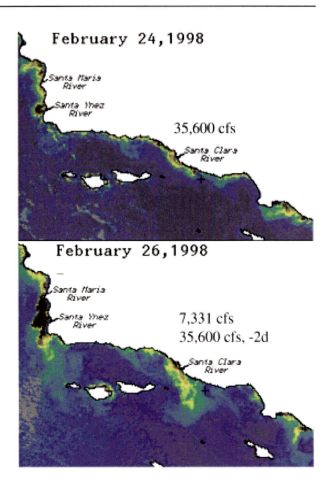

Figure 3. Satellite images of sea surface turbidity for the Southern California Bight for downwelling conditions (February 24, 1998; upper panel) and upwelling conditions (February 26, 1998; lower panel). Discharge from the Santa Clara River on the image dates and the value and date of any recent discharge maximum (subtract the number of days given from the image date) are listed. Turbidity scales are relative only.

providing an accurate picture of surface currents during storms on the California coast as well as for understanding how material in coastal watersheds is distributed to offshore coastal regions.

Results demonstrate that river plumes can readily distribute this material throughout a large portion of the coastal zone. During a particular flood, large particles may be deposited in the vicinity of the river mouth. Finer particles can be carried tens and hundreds of kilometers from the river mouth. Some of the fine material may form aggregates and settle more rapidly. While the particles are in the upper water column interactions with the biota can occur: particles may be consumed by marine animals and utilized by plants. These in turn are ingested so that any pollutants move up the food chain to birds and mammals. Marine birds, in particular, are often found at density fronts near the edges of river plumes because water convergence at the front increases food density.

Because sediment falls from the water column, the depth and area influenced by river turbidity may differ from that of water properties. Area influenced at the sea surface is likely smaller for turbidity than for salinity. However, turbidity could affect a larger area in the water column than salinity at deeper depths and the area influenced might be expected to increase with depth. Areas covered by turbid plumes shown in the majority of available satellite images may underestimate areas that would be covered at peak flood. On the other hand, fallout of particulates from the plume, as well as processes such as flocculation, which accelerate fallout rates (Baker and Hickey 1986), appears to limit the size of turbid plumes.

The greatest impact on the Channel Islands likely occurs during coastal upwelling, which spreads river discharge plumes from the eastern channel offshore toward Anacapa Island, and spreads discharge plumes from north of Point Conception into the western channel entrance where they encounter the western Channel Islands. Upwelling conditions cause plumes to thin and spread out so that the total surface area is many times that observed during the actual storms responsible for the rainfall that caused the river plumes.

Impacts on flow fields cannot be ascertained from satellite imagery. However, results from other studies (e.g., Hickey et al. 1998) and model results (e.g., Kourafolou et al. 1996) suggest that effects in the upper 10 m of the water column are significant. Current speeds of 10 to 20 cm s^{-1} above ambient flow would not be unreasonable. Moreover, current direction in the vicinity of the plume would likely be altered: for example, currents in the upper 5 to 10 m of the water column a few kilometers from a river mouth would tend to parallel density contours and be concentrated along density fronts. Hence, particularly during strong upwelling, current patterns in the upper water column might differ significantly from those observed in the absence of river plumes.

ACKNOWLEDGMENTS

Data analysis was supported by Montrose Chemical Corporation of California, Chris Craft Industries, and the Zeneca Corporation. Discharge data from the Santa Clara River were graciously provided by Mr. Ken Turner of the United Water Conservation District.

LITERATURE CITED

Baker, E. T. and B. M. Hickey. 1986. Contemporary sedimentation processes in and around an active West Coast submarine canyon. Marine Geology 71:15-34.

Chao, S.-Y. 1988. Wind-driven motions of estuarine plumes. Journal of Physical Oceanography 18:1,144-1,166.

Drake, D.E. 1972. Distribution and transport of suspended matter, Santa Barbara Channel, California. Ph.D. Dissertation, University of Southern California, 357 pp.

Harms, S. and C.D. Winant. 1998. Characteristic patterns of the circulation in the Santa Barbara Channel. Journal of Geophysical Research, in press.

Hendershott, M.C. and C.D. Winant. 1996. Surface circulation in the Santa Barbara Channel. Oceanography 9(2):114-121.

Hickey, B.M. 1992. Circulation over the Santa Monica-San Pedro basin and shelf. Progress in Oceanography 30:37-115.

Hickey, B.M. and N.B. Kachel. 1999. The influence of river plumes in the Southern California Bight. Submitted to Continental Shelf Research.

Hickey, B.M., L. Pietrafesa, D. Jay and W.C. Boicourt. 1998. The Columbia River Plume Study: subtidal variability of the velocity and salinity fields. Journal of Geophysical Research 103(C5):10,339-10,368.

Kourafalou, V. H., T. N. Lee, L. Oey and J. Wang. 1996. The fate of river discharge on the continental shelf, Part II: Transport of coastal low-salinity waters under realistic wind and tidal forcing. Journal of Geophysical Research 101(C2):3,415-3,434.

Stumpf, R.P. and J.R. Pennock. 1989. Calibration of a general optical equation for remote sensing of suspended sediments in a moderately turbid estuary. Journal of Geophysical Research 94(C10):14,363-14,371.

Thornton, S.E. 1984. Basin model for hemipelagic sedimentation in a tectonically active continental margin: Santa Barbara Basin, California Continental Borderland. Pages 377-394 *in* Stow, D.A. and D.J. Piper (eds.), Fine-Grained Sediments: Deep-Water Processes and Facies. Blackwell Scientific Publishers, Oxford, England.

Winant, C.D. and C.E. Dorman. 1997. Seasonal patterns of surface wind stress over the Southern California Bight. Journal of Geophysical Research 102(C3):5,641-5,654.

WAVE PREDICTION IN THE SANTA BARBARA CHANNEL

W. C. O'Reilly, R. T. Guza and R. J. Seymour

Center for Coastal Studies, Scripps Institution of Oceanography, La Jolla, CA 92093-0209
(858) 534-4333, FAX (858) 534-0300
E-mail: woreilly@ucsd.edu, rguza@ucsd.edu, rseymour@ucsd.edu

ABSTRACT

Wave conditions in the Santa Barbara Channel impact fishing, commercial shipping, and recreation. In addition, nearshore waves drive sediment processes such as beach erosion and harbor entrance shoaling. Accurate historical wave information is needed for engineering design, environmental impact assessment and hazard mitigation. Wave fields in the channel are complex owing to the sheltering effects of Point Conception and the Channel Islands, the reflection of wave energy from the steep coastal cliffs of Santa Cruz Island, and the irregularity of the local continental shelf bathymetry. Wave model predictions and field observations from the Coastal Data Information Program are used to illustrate these phenomena. Ongoing and planned wave modeling in the channel is described.

Keywords: Santa Barbara Channel, physical oceanography, waves.

INTRODUCTION

The complicated wind and wave conditions in the Santa Barbara Channel region are well known to mariners. The energy and direction of short period seas generated by local winds, and of long period swell radiated from distant storms, can vary greatly throughout the channel on any given day. Local seas often mirror the highly variable wind fields resulting from the mountainous coastal and island topography, and swells are dramatically affected by the sheltering of Point Conception and the Channel Islands. In addition, the complex shallow water bathymetry within the channel results in large wave height variations along the shoreline.

Wave conditions along the California coast have been monitored for the last two decades by the Coastal Data Information Program (CDIP) at Scripps Institution of Oceanography with the sponsorship of the California Department of Boating and Waterways and the U.S. Army Corps of Engineers (Seymour et al. 1993). In recent years, the program has used numerical wave models in conjunction with field measurements to predict regional wave conditions. As part of this effort, CDIP provides experimental real-time predictions of swell heights (no local seas) in the Santa Barbara Channel via the World Wide Web.

The present CDIP wave model is described and examples of the estimated swell height variability in the channel are presented. A recent field study designed to validate the wave model is discussed. The model underpredicted swell energy in the lee of Point Conception during northwest swell events, and the measurements confirm that the model underprediction is primarily the result of (unmodeled) wave energy reflection back into the channel from the coastal cliffs of Santa Cruz Island. Future plans to incorporate both island wave reflection and local wind wave generation into the model are described.

SWELL HEIGHT PREDICTION IN THE SANTA BARBARA CHANNEL

Computer models, supplemented with measurements from buoys and pressure sensors, are widely used to hindcast and forecast waves. Real-time model predictions (nowcasts) of swell wave heights (wave periods of 8 to 25 seconds) in the channel are disseminated hourly over the World Wide Web at cdip.ucsd.edu by CDIP (Figure 1).

The predictions are based on a numerical refraction-diffraction model that simulates the propagation of waves from the deep ocean into shallow water depths of approximately 10 m (Kirby 1986; O'Reilly and Guza 1993; O'Reilly 1993). As an individual wave crest propagates into shallow water its speed decreases and its height increases (shoaling). However, at the same time, variations in the water depth along a crest lead to variations in speed and bending of the crest (refraction). Refraction results in the convergence or divergence of the wave energy associated with the crest, producing changes in wave height as well as wave direction. When the convergence or divergence of wave energy becomes very strong, producing large changes in wave energy over short distances, additional wave crests of significant size evolve to move wave energy away from or into these areas and reduce the spatial variation of energy (diffraction). Wave shoaling, refraction, and diffraction can all be important in the Santa Barbara Channel and are included in the numerical model. The model does not include the generation of seas by local winds, so the predictions are presently restricted to swell arriving from more distant sources.

The model is initialized with wave measurements from either an array of sensors attached to Chevron's Harvest Platform, or a wave buoy near the platform, located approximately 10 km west of Point Conception in 200 m water depth.

The measurements are transmitted by telephone lines to the CDIP central facility at Scripps where they are processed to estimate the deep water wave spectrum (the distribution of wave energy as a function of the wave period and direction). This wave spectrum is in turn used to initialize the refraction-diffraction model that predicts the wave field within the entire Southern California Bight. (Other offshore buoys are used to initialize model predictions for regions in central and northern California.) Examples of nowcasts in the Santa Barbara Channel for incident west and south swells with 17 second periods are shown in Figures 1 and 2, respectively. The location of areas that are sheltered by the Channel Islands depends critically on the swell direction.

West (Winter) Swell

For the west swell event, relatively large swell heights are predicted to occur just east of Point Conception along

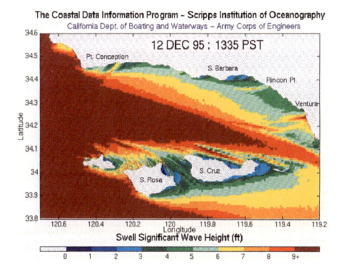

Figure 1. CDIP swell model prediction for the Santa Barbara Channel during a large west swell event in December 1995.

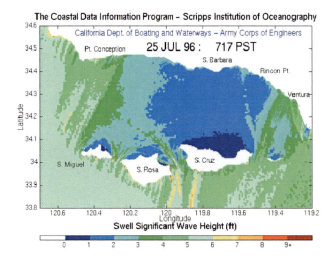

Figure 2. CDIP swell model prediction for the Santa Barbara Channel during a large south swell event in July 1996.

the south-facing coastline (e.g., Figure 1 where bands of yellow indicate larger waves than in the adjacent green regions). A submarine escarpment (steep slope) running along a SW-NE fault line across the continental shelf focuses westerly swell energy between Hollister Ranch and Drake's Point, as is well known to the local surfing community. Rincon Point also has significantly higher wave heights than the surrounding coastline during west swell events.

Wave heights are also significantly amplified along portions of the Channel Islands bordering the south side of the channel. Most of the "focusing zones" begin to develop in relatively deep water. That is, relatively large scale bathymetric features, like an escarpment or the curvature of the continental shelf bathymetry, produce these zones of higher waves along the coast. Small scale coastal features that are often associated with bigger waves, such as a popular surfing reef or headland, often fall within one of the larger focusing zones and are a final, very localized enhancement of this larger scale wave amplification.

Another area of high swell height is located at the east end of the Santa Barbara Channel just south of Ventura (Figure 1). In this case, wave focusing is caused by the massive subaerial fan of sediment deposited on the shelf by the Ventura and Santa Clara rivers. This large scale bathymetric feature extends nearly 40 km offshore and concentrates much of the wave energy propagating eastward down the channel onto a narrow stretch of coastline near the Santa Clara River mouth. When the deep water swell comes from a slightly WSW direction (e.g., the swell of an arriving winter storm) this focusing zone shifts northward directly into the Ventura area and is likely the underlying cause of the occasional storm damage to the Ventura Pier.

Finally, a significant amount of west swell energy propagates through the deep water passage between Anacapa Island and the mainland at the east end of the channel. This wave energy reaches a small section of coastline at the south end of Santa Monica Bay around Redondo Beach. This phenomenon has been linked to time periods when surprisingly large waves were observed in the Redondo Beach area relative to the rest of the Santa Monica Bay coastline.

South (Summer) Swell

Swell conditions in the Santa Barbara Channel are quite different during the summer when south swell dominates the southern California wave climate. Most of the channel and the south-facing coastline are sheltered by the Channel Islands (Figure 2). The extent to which the west end of the channel is sheltered by San Miguel Island depends on the direction of the arriving swell. South swell arriving from storms near New Zealand (a common source region) reach the west end of the channel (Figure 2) whereas swell arriving from a slightly more easterly source (storms closer to South America) are almost completely blocked from the west end of the channel (not shown).

Wave conditions at the east end of the channel are similarly sensitive to the swell direction.

South swell propagates past Anacapa Island and typically reaches the coast near Ventura and Rincon Point (Figure 2). Swell from a direction slightly east of south (e.g., a true compass heading of 160°) reaches Santa Barbara, but these events are rare.

WAVE REFLECTION FROM THE CHANNEL ISLANDS

The swell model was tested using observations in the channel during the winter of 1994-1995. Three Datawell Directional Waverider buoys were deployed in 50 m water depth near Santa Rosa and Santa Cruz Islands, and a fourth buoy was installed near the mainland east of Santa Barbara (Figure 3, sites labeled as "Scripps Buoys (1995)"). The entire east end of the channel is heavily sheltered by Point Conception from the WNW swell that dominated during the experiment period. The Santa Barbara Buoy was deep in the theoretical Point Conception wave "shadow" (Figure 4, upper panel). The model underpredicted the swell energy (overpredicted the sheltering effects) at this location (Figure 4, lower panel). The directions of the measured waves, estimated from the directional buoy data, consistently showed that the primary cause of the model underprediction is the presence of reflected wave energy coming from Santa Cruz Island (Figure 5, right panel, and shown schematically in Figure 4, top panel) that is not included in the model. This hypothesis is further supported by the buoy measurements

close to Santa Cruz Island (Figure 5, left panel) showing waves coming from two directions; one direction corresponds to waves incident from the deep ocean and the other to waves reflected from the island. Similar results (not shown) were obtained by the buoy at the northeast corner of the island. The north side of Santa Cruz Island appears to be a particularly good wave reflector owing to the large extent of sheer coastal cliffs that drop straight into water depths of 10 m or more. Interestingly, the measurements from Santa Rosa Island (not shown) show little reflected wave energy. The Santa Rosa coastline has low cliffs, but these typically have rocky shallows at their base, and the continental shelf along the island is much broader and shallower than the Santa Cruz Island shelf.

FUTURE MODEL IMPROVEMENTS

Through grants from the Minerals Management Service and the Office of Naval Research, efforts are underway to improve the CDIP Santa Barbara Channel wave predictions by incorporating wave reflection from Santa Cruz Island and wave generation by local winds.

The consistent CDIP model underprediction of wave energy in the lee of Point Conception during northwest swell events (Figure 4, lower panel) suggests that a simplified treatment of the reflected wave field may be possible for practical applications. Historical wave measurements from the channel (Figure 3) are presently being analyzed to

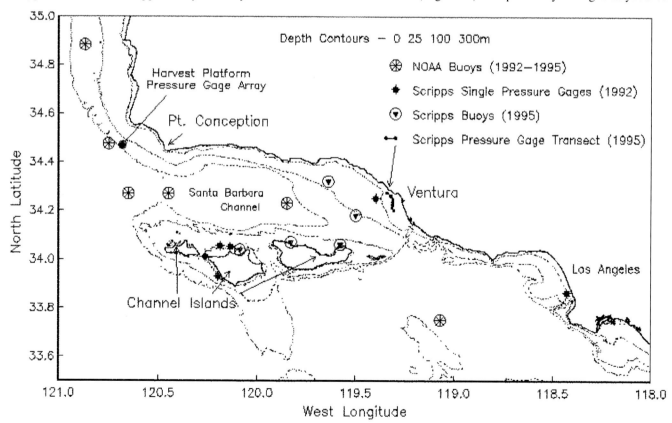

Figure 3. Historical wave data locations from 1992 to 1995 that will be used to improve swell model predictions and study local seas. NOAA buoys collected both wind and wave (mostly directional) data. Scripps directional buoy and pressure gage deployments typically spanned several winter months.

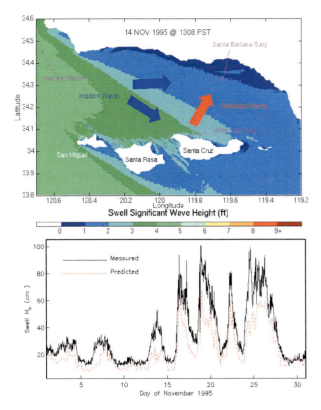

Figure 4. UPPER PANEL: Swell model prediction overlayed with schematic illustration of incident swell propagating into the channel (blue arrows) and reflecting from Santa Cruz Island (red arrow). LOWER PANEL: Underprediction of swell wave heights at the Santa Barbara Buoy (upper right of upper panel) owing to the unmodeled reflected wave energy.

determine if the reflection from Santa Cruz Island is directionally specular (e.g., waves reflect off the cliffs much like a billiard ball reflects off the side of a pool table) or directionally broad (e.g., a narrow directional beam of incident wave energy is scattered into many directions by the irregular facets of the cliff face).

The present swell model does not include local wind effects. Although long period swell waves arriving from the deep ocean are largely unaffected by local winds, sea waves continue to grow downwind of the Point Conception measurement site used to initialize the operational model. Predictions of seas, based solely on wave propagation theory (no generation), are therefore valid only over a small area near the initialization location. There are many models that predict wave generation given the wind field near the sea surface. Deep water wind-wave generation models have been used for the last decade on global scales (e.g., the third-generation WAM model, The WAMDI Group 1988). These models have more recently been modified to include shallow-water effects, but the simplified wave propagation algorithms (e.g., no diffraction) limit their accuracy in regions with complex bathymetry like the Santa Barbara Channel.

The Office of Naval Research has recently started an advanced wave prediction program to improve the SWAN model (Shallow Water Numerical model) developed at Delft Hydraulics in the Netherlands (Holthuijsen et. al. 1993). This model includes wave generation and was designed specifically for shallow water applications. The Point Conception area has been chosen as a field testing site for the SWAN model improvements (Figure 6, upper left model region),

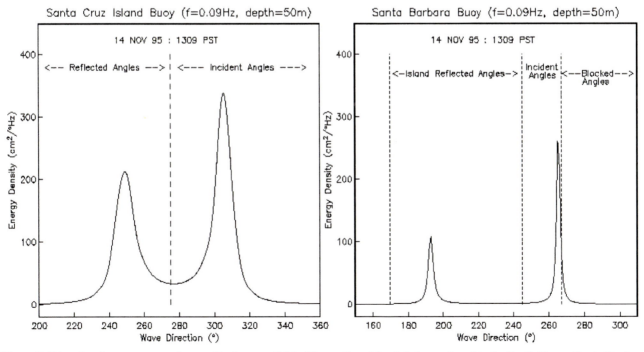

Figure 5. Directional wave spectra observed in the near field of Santa Cruz Island (left panel) and in the far field near Santa Barbara (right panel, see upper panel Figure 3 for locations). Left Panel: incident 11 second northwest swell refracts to 305° at the Santa Cruz buoy, reflects from the island and propagates at 245° towards the mainland. Right Panel: near the mainland, the incident northwest swell refracts to 265° and the swell reflected from Santa Cruz Island has refracted to 195°.

and it is anticipated that the test area will be expanded over time to include the entire Santa Barbara Channel. Of particular interest is the local generation of seas in the presence of pre-existing swell, which is a common occurrence in the channel.

Finally, CDIP plans to establish two long-term directional wave buoy stations in the channel in the next three to five years as part of a multi-year wave network expansion funded by the California Department of Boating and Waterways (Figure 6). Real-time data from these buoys will be used to validate future model improvements and enhance CDIP nowcasts through data assimilation methods. The designation of the Point Conception - Santa Barbara Channel as a "test bed" for U.S. wave model research will insure that government and commercial marine activity in this area will be the direct beneficiary of state-of-the-art wave nowcast and forecasts in the near future.

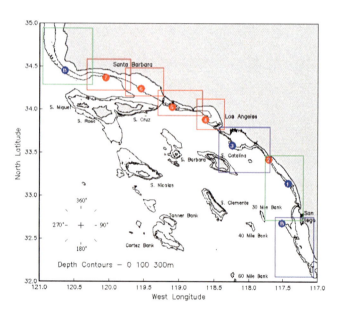

Figure 6. Locations of present (blue), planned for 1999 (green), and future (red) local CDIP buoy stations (circles) and model regions (boxes). This network is designed to provide combined sea and swell predictions for the Southern California coastline.

ACKNOWLEDGMENTS

The Coastal Data Information Program (CDIP) is supported jointly by the California Department of Boating and Waterways wave data utilization program for furthering boating access and safety, and the U.S. Army Corps of Engineers Field Wave Gaging Program. Wave model validation data was collected by CDIP and the U.S. Naval Postgraduate School (NPS), and was supervised by David Castel and Julie Thomas (CDIP), and Paul Jessen (NPS). Ongoing wave model research in the Santa Barbara Channel is sponsored by the Minerals Management Service and the Office of Naval Research Waves BE program.

LITERATURE CITED

Holthuijsen, L. H., N. Booij, and R. C. Ris. 1993. A spectral wave model for the coastal zone. Pages 630-641 *in* Proceedings of the 2nd International Symposium on Ocean Wave Measurement and Analysis, New Orleans, LA.

Kirby, J. T. 1986. Higher-order approximations in the parabolic equation method for water waves. Journal of Geophysical Research 91:933-952.

O'Reilly W. C. 1993. The southern California wave climate: effects of islands and bathymetry. Shore and Beach 61(3):14-19.

O'Reilly, W. C., and Guza, R. T. 1993. A comparison of two spectral wave models in the Southern California Bight. Coastal Engineering 19:263-282.

Seymour, R., D. McGehee, D. Castel, J. Thomas, and W. O'Reilly. 1993. New Technology in Coastal Wave Monitoring. Pages 105-123 *in* Proceedings of the 2nd International Symposium on Ocean Wave Measurement and Analysis, New Orleans, LA.

The WAMDI Group. 1988. The WAM model-A third generation ocean wave prediction model. Journal of Physical Oceanography 18:1775-1810.

THE CLIMATE OF THE CHANNEL ISLANDS, CALIFORNIA

David Yoho, Tim Boyle, and Elliot McIntire

Department of Geography, California State University, Northridge, CA 91330-8249
(818) 677-3532, FAX (818) 677-2723
E-mail: davidyoho@hotmail.com; tboyle@csun.edu; elliot.mcintire@csun.edu

ABSTRACT

Climatological data for most of the Channel Islands has been, until very recently, extremely limited. Complete understanding of the environmental interactions of the islands' physical and biological processes requires detailed information about a variety of climatic factors, including temperature, rainfall, windspeed and direction, humidity, soil temperature and moisture, and the amount of fog drip which may be present. Fortunately, this situation is now being rectified as new data become available from a variety of sources. For more than a decade the Department of Geography at California State University, Northridge (CSUN) has been developing a network of weather stations on Santa Cruz and later on San Clemente Islands. These stations, together with those of the National Park Service and other agencies, now make it possible to develop a fairly full picture of variation within and among the Channel Islands. While the record is as yet far too short to draw definitive conclusions, we are at least in a position to develop a number of hypotheses relating to these variations.

Keywords: Channel Islands, climate, weather, instrumentation.

INTRODUCTION

Beginning with a single station on Santa Cruz Island in the mid-1980s, students and faculty of the Department of Geography at California State University, Northridge (CSUN) have gradually expanded a network of weather stations which, together with those of other agencies such as the National Park Service, Ventura and Santa Barbara County Flood Control, and the U.S. Navy, now provide data from throughout the Channel Islands. The department currently maintains an array of eight stations, three on Santa Cruz Island and five on San Clemente Island. The purpose of these stations is to monitor climatological variations found in a maritime environment on and in the vicinity of the Channel Islands, providing a better understanding of the islands' unique physical and biological processes.

This paper represents a preliminary analysis of data that have been collected since 1994 to explore climatological variations and the environment. Meteorological parameters discussed include temperature, relative humidity, wind speed/direction, and precipitation. Analysis of these parameters should provide a better understanding of the

islands' influence on certain controls on micro- and mesoscale climatic regimes. Although the records from the automated stations are limited, some annual trends and variations are already identifiable. However, further studies with many additional years of data collection are necessary to develop an in-depth understanding of the climate of the Channel Islands.

PROJECT HISTORY

Work with a portable weather station on Santa Cruz Island led to a contract between CSUN and the Natural Resources Office (NRO) at North Island Naval Air Station in Coronado, California, in 1992. The purpose of the project was to assemble a network of automated weather stations and deploy them in three microhabitats on San Clemente Island. The data was to be used to monitor local meteorological variations in and around the microhabitats and would be used by numerous agencies and universities for environmental studies. Some of the projects include restoration of native flora and studies of endangered species, including the loggerhead strike (*Lanius ludovicianus*) (Hargleroad et al. 1996).

Three Automated Local Evaluation in Real Time (ALERT) weather stations were deployed in three microhabitats: coastal terraces (Eel Point), central plateau (Hoeppel) and eastern escarpment (Nanny). Hoeppel and Eel Point stations were deployed in January 1994, and Nanny was installed December 1994. Eel Point weather station is located on the western coastal terraces at an elevation of approximately 20 m. Hoeppel weather station is located on the central plateau at an elevation of approximately 350 m. Nanny is located near the bottom of the eastern escarpment at an elevation of approximately 68 m.

In addition to the ALERT stations, two portable Campbell Scientific micro-weather stations have been installed. The first was deployed in May 1996 at the Nursery site, in a small valley in the northern part of the island. The second station was deployed at Hoeppel in October 1996 while the ALERT station was under repair, and was then moved to a site near the southern end of the island at Observation Point 1 (OP1). An additional station is planned for installation in November 1998 at Observation Point 3 (OP3) also near the southern end of the island (Figure 1).

In 1995 two additional Campbell Scientific micro-weather stations were deployed on Santa Cruz Island. The first station was deployed at Prisoners Harbor on the northern side of the island at an elevation of approximately 130 m. The additional stations were installed at Christy Airfield located on the western side of the island at an elevation of approximately 75 m, and at Christy Pines in the mountains in the west-central area of the island at an elevation of approximately 450 m (Figure 2). This network of stations provides data for a detailed examination of inter- and intra-island climatic variations.

GENERAL CHARACTERISTICS OF THE CHANNEL ISLANDS CLIMATE

The only study to address the climate of the Channel Islands as a group is that of Kimura (1974), who examined the climate of the Southern California Coastal and Offshore Zone, and the following discussion is drawn from his paper. Kimura characterized this area as belonging to the Mediterranean Dry Summer Subtropical climatic type, with a cool summer regime. The zone includes the immediate coastal areas of southern California and extends westward to the 121st meridian. Temperatures are controlled by the sea and because of the moist ocean air, the relative humidity at night is generally high (90%), decreasing slightly during the day due to solar radiation. Precipitation is mostly concentrated in winter, with average values between 150 and 360 mm depending on the island.

The dominant climatic control during both summer and winter is the Pacific Subtropical Anticyclone. In summer this cell strengthens and migrates north with its eastern edge over the West Coast. Due to subsidence, air is heated by compression creating a temperature inversion at approximately 600 m. A second inversion is created near the surface from the relatively cold water flowing southward along the coast. These two inversions result in an extremely

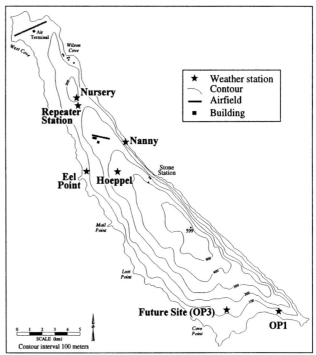

Figure 1. Location map of weather stations on San Clemente Island.

stable environment, effectively preventing the occurrence of precipitation during the summer, although early summer is the cloudiest time of year, with low-lying stratus often accompanied by light drizzle. In mid-summer, an increase in solar radiation causes a decrease in the stratus, and only night and morning coastal cloudiness remains. Thermally-induced lows over the deserts of the Southwest result in an increase in the sea-breeze along the coastal areas. Summer precipitation occurs on rare occasions as a result of moist, maritime subtropical air invading from the Gulf of California, or tropical storms which have moved well north of their usual path.

Although the Pacific Subtropical Anticyclone weakens and migrates to the south in winter, it still dominates the

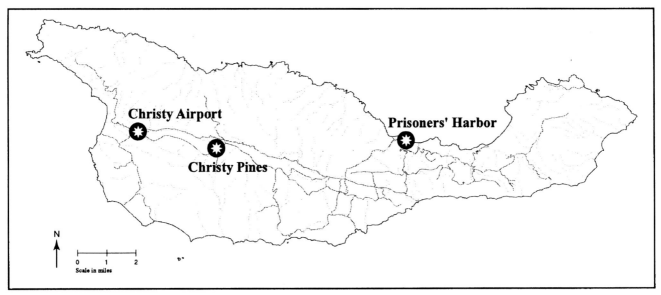

Figure 2. Location map of weather stations on Santa Cruz Island.

weather pattern. Ninety-five percent of the precipitation in this zone falls between the months of November and April. As the anticyclone migrates south, large storms that form in the Gulf of Alaska invade southern California. These storms are short in duration, usually lasting about one to two days, but on occasion some storms last up to a week, bringing great amounts of precipitation. Winds are usually southeasterly in advance of frontal storms but veer to a northwesterly direction as the fronts pass. The northwesterly winds are usually quite strong creating large swells of three meters or more. As high pressure reestablishes over the Great Basin, the flow changes to an offshore component resulting in "cold" Santa Ana conditions with gale and sometimes hurricane force winds with the relative humidity as low as 5%.

The distribution of average annual precipitation varies considerably from north to south. Catalina Island reports an average annual value of 350 mm. A little farther south and farther offshore, San Nicolas Island reports an average annual value of 180 mm while the southernmost island, San Clemente Island, reports an average annual value of 130 mm. Topography is important to the variability of precipitation. The summit of San Clemente Island (nearly 640 m) reports an average annual value of 170 mm of precipitation, virtually all as rain. Drizzle occurs frequently but rarely accumulates to more than a trace. Most of the rain in southern California is the result of frontal storms, which usually advance from the northwest and occur mostly in the winter months.

Air temperature over the Southern California Coastal and Offshore Region is controlled mainly by marine influences. Temperatures are moderated throughout the seasons throughout the year. Diurnal differences also tend to be small, with cool days and relatively warm nights. In the outer coastal waters (including San Clemente Island) lowest monthly mean temperatures are experienced in February while the warmest month is September. For the inner coastal waters the coolest month is January and the warmest is August. The difference is due to the lag time caused by the slower cooling and warming of ocean water compared to land areas. The temperature difference between warmest and coldest months is only about 4°C over the ocean.

Relative humidity readings in and around the Channel Islands vary diurnally. At night and in the early morning hours relative humidity often reaches 100% when the temperatures are the lowest. In the afternoon readings, on the average, drop to about 60% (Kimura 1974). Far lower readings occur during Santa Ana wind episodes in Fall and Winter.

The basic air flow along the Southern California Coastal and Offshore Area is northwesterly, resulting from the semi-permanent Pacific Anticyclone. This anticyclone is most dominant in the warm months, when northwest winds are strongest and most constant (Kimura 1974).

A local factor that affects the climate of the Southern California Offshore Zone is the Catalina Eddy. This vorticity is formed by north and northwesterly winds flowing around the coastal projections and mountains near Point

Conception, most common in late spring and early summer. Because the north-south mountains abruptly change to an east-west orientation, the winds recurve, causing a deepening in the cyclonic flow. As the eddy moves down the coast, the winds veer to the south and southeast. The Catalina Eddy is generally centered around Catalina Island, hence the name. As the eddy becomes intense, marine air deepens, forcing the inversion upward allowing for greater vertical mixing. This layer is often 600 to 1000 m deep, sometimes as deep as 2000 m, and influences the development of stratus clouds and fog, delays daytime temperature increases along the immediate coast and coastal valleys, and raises daily minimum temperatures.

METHODOLOGY

The data analyzed in this study was collected from the three ALERT stations on San Clemente Island and the Campbell Scientific micro-weather stations on San Clemente Island and Santa Cruz Island. Each ALERT station is 4 m tall with a diameter of 30 cm. Sensors are powered by a solar panel that feeds into a 12 volt 9.5 amp hour gel cell battery. Each station records data on wind, relative humidity, temperature, and rainfall. Additionally, Eel Point weather station is equipped with a solar radiation sensor that measures total sun and sky (global) radiation. Data at each station is recorded on a 32K-memory board and is automatically transmitted by VHF radio to a base station at field headquarters on the island at Stone Station.

Software at the base station provides fully integrated data analysis, modem support, graphics capabilities, data compression, statistical analysis, custom reports, automated reports and real-time equations. ALERT data is stored in the base station automatically at frequent intervals and is easily accessible for downloading. The Campbell Scientific micro-weather stations are also powered by solar panels. Each station is equipped with numerous sensors including wind, temperature/relative humidity, tipping-bucket rain gauge, soil temperature/moisture and leaf-wetness sensors. Data is stored in modules that are connected to data-loggers which can be easily accessed. The station at Prisoners Harbor transmits data directly to CSUN via satellite. Data discussed in this paper are based on the records from the Department of Geography stations for 1996 through the first half of 1998. Even with this limited data set, some general patterns are evident.

AIR TEMPERATURE

Diurnal differences tend to be small, contributing to cool days and relatively warm nights. The temperature patterns revealed by the analysis of data collected from ALERT and micro-logger weather stations over a period of three years confirms Kimura's analysis of the climate of the Channel Islands region. Although prevailing conditions are mild, extreme temperatures can occur throughout the year.

San Clemente Island

During 1996-1998, the annual mean temperature recorded at Eel Point was 17°C, the mean maximum was 25°C, and the mean minimum was 13°C. The warmest time of the year is August with a mean temperature of 21°C. Mean maximum temperatures for November were also high (particularly at Hoeppel and Nanny) which are attributed to Santa Ana wind conditions. Minimum temperatures are relatively warm throughout most of the year with the exception of the winter months when mean minimum temperatures of 10°C occur (Figure 3).

Hoeppel recorded an annual mean temperature of 17°C, a mean maximum of 29°C and a mean minimum of 10°C. At Hoeppel's elevation of about 350 m, temperatures appear to be less moderated by marine influences and show more temperature variability throughout the year. August has the highest mean temperature of 22°C. Mean maximum temperatures of 36°C occur in August with a secondary peak of 34°C in November, also attributed to the Santa Ana wind condition. Hoeppel also records the lowest mean minimum temperatures from the network. The mean temperature for the month of February is 12°C with a mean minimum temperature of 6°C (Figure 4).

Nanny recorded an annual mean temperature of 18°C, a mean maximum of 27°C and a mean minimum of 13°C. Although Nanny is located on the eastern side of the island near the ocean, marine influences are clearly less important than at Eel Point. August is the warmest month at Nanny with a mean temperature of 22°C. November's mean maximum temperature mirrors Eel Point and Hoeppel with 32°C, once again influenced by Santa Ana wind conditions. The lowest mean minimum temperatures are recorded in the winter months with readings of 10°C (Figure 5).

OP1 and the Nursery micro-logger stations record very similar averages. Again, the highest temperatures are recorded in August with secondary peaks in November and the lowest temperatures occur in January and February.

Santa Cruz Island

The 1996-1998 temperature data records from Santa Cruz Island weather stations are very similar to the temperature records from San Clemente Island. However, some minor differences are noted. Santa Cruz Island annual mean temperatures are 1 to 2°C lower than San Clemente Island, probably due to lower sea surface temperatures around the latter.

Prisoners Harbor recorded an annual mean temperature of 16°C, a mean maximum temperature of 22°C and a mean minimum temperature of 13°C. The warmest mean monthly temperature was recorded in September with a temperature of 19°C. The highest mean maximum temperatures are recorded in August and November with 24°C. The coldest temperatures are recorded in the months of January and February with a mean temperature of 14°C and a mean minimum temperature of 10°C (Figure 6).

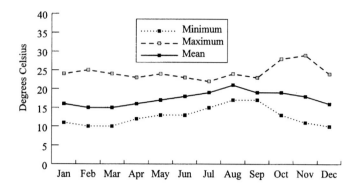

Figure 3. Eel Point monthly temperatures 1996-1998.

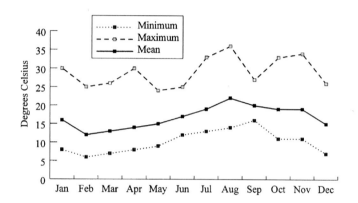

Figure 4. Hoeppel monthly temperatures 1996-1998.

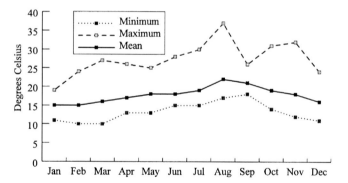

Figure 5. Nanny monthly temperatures 1996-1998.

Christy Airfield recorded an annual mean temperature of 15°C, a mean maximum of 19°C, and a mean minimum of 12°C. The warmest mean monthly temperatures are experienced in September with 19°C. Mean maximum temperatures increase to 26°C in October and November. The coldest temperatures are recorded in January and February with a mean of 12°C and a mean minimum of 9°C in December, January, and March (Figure 7).

At Christy Pines the annual mean temperature is 15°C, with a mean maximum of 23°C, and a mean minimum of 11°C. Similar to Hoeppel, Christy Pines weather station is the highest on the island at an elevation of 450 m and recorded more temperature variability. The highest mean temperature is recorded in September with 21°C. The highest mean monthly maximum is recorded in August with 32°C. The coldest mean monthly temperature occurs in February with 11°C and a mean minimum of 7°C in March (Figure 8). It should be noted that a fairly dramatic decrease in mean maximum temperatures occurred in June at Hoeppel on San Clemente Island and at Christy Pines on Santa Cruz Islands.

RELATIVE HUMIDITY

San Clemente Island

Eel Point recorded an annual mean relative humidity of 86%, a mean maximum of 100% and a mean minimum of 39%. September has the highest mean monthly relative humidity with 94%. October, November, and December experience the lowest mean readings ranging between 11 to 18%, indicative of Santa Ana wind episodes.

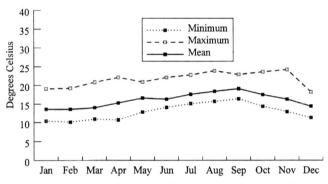

Figure 6. Prisoners Harbor monthly temperatures 1995-1998.

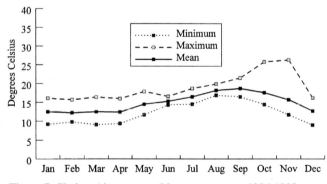

Figure 7. Christy Airport monthly temperatures 1996-1998.

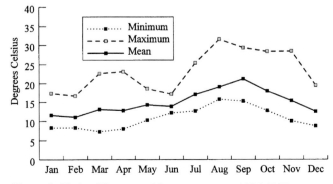

Figure 8. Christy Pines monthly temperatures 1996-1998.

Hoeppel recorded an annual mean relative humidity of 82%, a mean maximum of 98% and a mean minimum of 32%. June has the highest mean relative humidity with 94% and October through December averages the lowest readings ranging between 10 to 12% with Santa Ana winds. At Nanny the annual mean relative humidity is 82%, with a mean maximum of 100% and a mean minimum of 24%. July has the highest mean monthly relative humidity of 90% and the lowest mean monthly minimum ranging between 10 to 13% from October through December with Santa Ana winds. September experiences a significant relative humidity increase at all stations which is not evident in August or October.

OP1 and the Nursery micro-loggers record relative humidity patterns similar to the ALERT stations, with high readings recorded in June, July, and September and low readings recorded from October through December.

Santa Cruz Island

Prisoners Harbor recorded an annual mean relative humidity of 74%, a mean maximum of 100%, and a mean minimum of 12%. The highest mean monthly reading occurs in July and August with 83% while the lowest mean monthly reading occurs in April with 65%. Mean monthly minimums of less than 10% occur in April, May, October, and November.

Christy Airfield recorded an annual mean relative humidity of 79%, a mean monthly maximum of 98%, and a mean monthly minimum of 22%. The highest mean values occur in June, July, and August with 85%. The lowest means occur in October with 67% and mean minima ranging from 7 to 10% occur from October through December. Unlike Prisoners Harbor, Christy Airfield recorded a significant increase in mean monthly minimum readings from mid-April through July.

Christy Pines recorded an annual mean relative humidity of 75%, a mean monthly maximum of 100%, and a mean monthly minimum of 13%. The highest mean occurs in June with 92% with a secondary increase noted in November with 74%. The lowest mean monthly value occurs in October with 60%, with mean minimum readings of 7% in September and December. Similar to Christy Airfield, Christy Pines experiences a dramatic increase in mean minimum readings from mid-April through June.

Unlike San Clemente Island which experiences an increase in mean relative humidity in September, a decrease is evident on Santa Cruz Island. Also, mean readings are lower on Santa Cruz Island compared to those found on San Clemente Island.

PRECIPITATION

The Southern California Coastal and Offshore Zone receives 95% of its annual precipitation from November through April, and over 50% is recorded in the three winter months of December, January, and February (Kimura, 1974). Summer precipitation is very rare, although drizzle associated with the marine layer and occasionally fog-drip is recorded from June through August. Remnants of tropical storms occasionally affect the Channel Islands in the form of late summer and early fall precipitation.

Topography is clearly an important control on precipitation variability on San Clemente Island and Santa Cruz Island where precipitation patterns are quite variable from one site to the next. San Clemente Island usually receives more precipitation on the northern half and less on the southern half.

San Clemente Island

Eel Point recorded 113.79 mm of precipitation for the 1996-1997 water year (July 1 to June 30). A high percentage of the precipitation fell in November with a total for the month of 53.09 mm. February and March 1997 were unusually dry in southern California including the Channel Islands. No precipitation was recorded at Eel Point. The 1997-1998 water year totaled 285.75 mm of precipitation with the highest amounts recorded in February (112.78 mm). No precipitation was recorded from June through October in 1996 and 1997 (Table 1).

Hoeppel recorded 200.41 mm of precipitation for the 1996-1997 water year. Again, the highest amount fell in November (62.99 mm). The 1997-1998 water year recorded 491.74 mm with the highest amounts recorded in February (182.12 mm). In September 1997, 4.06 mm of precipitation was recorded, as a result of remnants from Tropical Storm Nora (Table 1).

Nanny recorded 125.22 mm during the 1996-1997 water year with 74.93 mm recorded in November. In 1997-1998 416.81 mm of precipitation was recorded with 175.77 mm falling in February. September's 3.05 mm of precipitation resulted from remnants of Tropical Storm Nora (Table 1).

Higher totals for the 1997-1998 water year are attributed to the higher storm frequency during the 1997-1998 El Niño year. The fact that Hoeppel consistently received more precipitation than the other stations is clearly linked to orographic lifting (Table 1).

Santa Cruz Island

Prisoners Harbor recorded 454.90 mm of precipitation for the 1996-1997 water year. The highest monthly total was recorded in January with 223.50 mm. All summer months in 1996 received precipitation either in the form of drizzle or fog-drip. A dramatic precipitation increase was recorded in the 1997-1998 water year with 948.65 mm recorded, with 413.74 mm falling in February (Table 1).

Christy Airfield recorded 148.86 mm of precipitation for the 1996-1997 water year with the highest monthly total recorded in January with 126.51 mm. In the 1997-1998 water year a total of 764.28 mm was recorded with the highest monthly total recorded in February with 333.23 mm (Table 1).

Christy Pines recorded 280.16 mm for water year 1996-1997 with the highest monthly total recorded in

January (126.51 mm). Of the three stations on Santa Cruz Island, Christy Pines had the highest 1997-1998 water year total of 1081.51 mm of precipitation with the highest monthly total recorded in February with 469.08 mm (Table 1).

The 1997-1998 water year totals recorded on Santa Cruz Island are quite impressive and are linked with the 1997-1998 El Niño event. Totals recorded on that island in February 1998 exceeded many annual totals recorded on San Clemente Island (see Boyle and Laughrin, 1999). Christy Pines, like Hoeppel on San Clemente Island, experienced the highest precipitation totals, also the result of orographic lifting (Table 1).

WIND

Unfortunately, due to sensor malfunction and configuration problems, ALERT wind data is unavailable for San Clemente Island between 1996 and 1998. The two microloggers, OP1 and the Nursery, are the source of wind data in this section and provide a general view of air flow over the island.

San Clemente Island

The Nursery station recorded northwest winds over 50% of the time between 1996 and 1998. On average, the speed ranged between 4 to 6 meters per second (m/s). Higher gusts from the north-northeast of between 8 to 10 m/s occasionally occur in association with Santa Ana wind episodes.

OP1 experienced different average wind directions throughout the study period. In 1996, the dominant wind flow was between the north and the northeast 56% of the time. The average speed ranged between 4 to 6 m/s. Occasionally, gusts from the north exceeding 14 m/s occurred. Southwest winds were also very common and included gusts over 14 m/s. In 1997, the pattern remained very similar to that of 1996. However, some minor fluctuations are noted. Winds exceeding 16 m/s occurred from the northeast and the south. The southerly winds are in response to the prevailing flow ahead of frontal systems that invade the area in the winter months. In 1998, the flow changed from a prevailing north-northeasterly wind to north-northwesterly and southerly winds with gusts exceeding 16 m/s. This change may be indicative of increased storm activity during the 1997-1998 El Niño Event.

Santa Cruz Island

The prevailing wind flow at Prisoners Harbor is from the northwest. Average speeds range between 4 to 6 m/s. South-southwesterly winds are also a common occurrence. Stronger gusts exceeding 10 m/s occur from the west-northwest and northerly directions. Christy Airfield recorded a majority of wind from the west-northwest direction with speeds averaging between 4 to 6 m/s. Stronger gusts to 10 m/s commonly occur from the east-northeast during Santa Ana wind episodes. Christy Pines recorded a westerly wind approximately 75% of the time with average speeds ranging between 4 to 6 m/s. Stronger gusts measure between

Table 1. Rainfall totals for San Clemente Island and Santa Cruz Island.

San Clemente Island

OP1	Jan	Feb	Mar	Apr	May	June	July	Aug	Sep	Oct	Nov	Dec	Calendar Year	Water Year
1996							0.0	0.0	0.0	8.9	41.2	24.4	74.4	141.5
1997	66.8	0.0	0.0	0.3	0.0	0.0	0.0	0.0	5.3	0.5	15.2	109.7	197.9	
1998														

Nursery	Jan	Feb	Mar	Apr	May	Jun	Jul	Aug	Sep	Oct	Nov	Dec	Calendar Year	Water Year
1996					3.3		0.3	0.3	0.3	12.7	76.5	31.5	124.7	202.4
1997	77.5	1.0	0.8	1.5	0.3	0.0	0.3	0.8	3.3	2.8	15.2	80.8	184.1	
1998														

Eel Point	Jan	Feb	Mar	Apr	May	Jun	Jul	Aug	Sep	Oct	Nov	Dec	Calendar Year	Water Year
1996	0.0	17.3	8.1	3.0	0.0	0.0	0.0	0.0	0.0	6.1	53.1	18.3	105.9	113.8
1997	35.3	0.0	0.0	1.0	0.0	0.0	0.0	0.0	0.0	0.0	14.2	69.1	119.6	285.8
1998	1.5	112.8	53.1	26.9	8.1	0.0	0.0	0.0					202.4	

Hoeppel	Jan	Feb	Mar	Apr	May	Jun	Jul	Aug	Sep	Oct	Nov	Dec	Calendar Year	Water Year
1996	0.0	0.0	0.0	0.0	0.0	0.0	0.0	0.0	0.0	20.1	63.0	32.0	115.1	200.4
1997	84.3	0.0	0.0	1.0	0.0	0.0	0.0	0.0	4.1	21.1	22.4	94.2	227.1	491.7
1998	38.6	182.1	85.1	27.9	16.3	0.0	0.0	0.0					350.0	

Nanny	Jan	Feb	Mar	Apr	May	Jun	Jul	Aug	Sep	Oct	Nov	Dec	Calendar Year	Water Year
1996	0.0	25.1	19.3	7.1	0.0	0.0	0.0	0.0	0.0	16.0	74.9	34.3	176.8	125.2
1997	0.0	0.0	0.0	0.0	0.0	0.0	0.0	0.0	3.0	4.1	29.2	72.1	108.5	416.8
1998	22.4	175.8	72.1	26.9	11.2	0.0	0.0	0.0					308.4	

Santa Cruz Island

Prisoners Harbor	Jan	Feb	Mar	Apr	May	Jun	Jul	Aug	Sep	Oct	Nov	Dec	Calendar Year	Water Year
1995						4.8	0.0	0.3	0.0	0.0	2.5	27.9	35.6	53.6
1996	0.8	0.3	1.5	18.5	1.0	0.8	0.3	0.3	0.8	35.8	38.6	154.9	253.5	454.9
1997	223.5	0.0	0.0	0.3	0.0	0.5	0.0	1.0	0.5	0.0	56.9	297.7	580.4	948.7
1998	72.9	413.7	67.8	38.1	53.1	0.8							646.4	

Christy Pines	Jan	Feb	Mar	Apr	May	Jun	Jul	Aug	Sep	Oct	Nov	Dec	Calendar Year	Water Year
1996												57.4	57.4	280.2
1997	221.2	0.0	0.0	0.3	0.3	1.0	0.5	3.3	1.5	0.0	68.8	302.0	599.0	1081.5
1998	113.3	469.1	77.5	45.5	75.7	1.0	2.5	0.0					784.6	

Christy Airfield	Jan	Feb	Mar	Apr	May	Jun	Jul	Aug	Sep	Oct	Nov	Dec	Calendar Year	Water Year
1996												21.8	21.8	148.9
1997	126.5	0.0	0.0	0.0	0.0	0.5	0.0	0.5	2.0	0.0	63.8	208.6	401.9	764.3
1998	69.9	333.2	53.1	33.3	43.9	0.8	0.0	0.0					534.1	

10 to 12 m/s from the northeast during Santa Ana wind episodes. Wind patterns on Santa Cruz Island are discussed in greater detail by Boyle and Laughrin (1999, this volume).

CONCLUSION

This paper provides a brief summary of the preliminary analysis of meteorological data collected from automated weather stations located on San Clemente Island and Santa Cruz Island operated by the Department of Geography at CSUN. Integration of these data with data from stations currently maintained by other agencies can provide a much more detailed analysis of conditions on several islands individually, and of the Channel Islands as a group. In addition, many more years of data collection and analysis involving all the Channel Islands is necessary for a thorough understanding of the meso- and micro-climate behavior offshore. Additional weather stations throughout the Channel Islands, and the integration of all existing data, give promise of soon providing students of the region with a great deal of useful, specific climatic information.

ACKNOWLEDGMENTS

The following persons and agencies contributed time, data and equipment to the preparation of this report. Their assistance is greatly appreciated. Department of Geography at California State University, Northridge; Lyndal Laughrin, Reserve Director, Santa Cruz Island Reserve; Gary Ryan, Oxnard National Weather Service; Linda Ayres, Andy Yatsko, and Jan Larson, Natural Resources Office, Naval Air Station North Island; and U.S. Navy personnel on San Clemente Island.

LITERATURE CITED

Boyle, T., and L. Laughrin. 1999. California's Santa Cruz Island Weather. Pages 93 to 99 *in* Browne, D. R., K. L. Mitchell, and H. W. Chaney (eds.), Proceedings of the Fifth California Islands Symposium. 29 March to 1 April 1999. Santa Barbara Museum of Natural History, Santa Barbara, CA. Sponsored by the U.S. Minerals Management Service, Pacific OCS Region, 770 Paseo Camarillo, Camarillo, CA 93010. OCS Study No. 99-0038.

Kimura, J. C. 1974. Climate. Pages 2-1 to 2-70 *in* Daily, M. D. B. Hill, and N. Lansing (eds.), Summary of Knowledge of the Southern California Coastal Zone and Offshore Areas, Volume 1, Physical Environment. Bureau of Land Management, Department of Interior, Contract 08550 CT4-1.

Hargleroad, G., H. Rogers, T. Boyle, and E. McIntire, 1996. San Clemente Island Climatic Monitoring Project. Report to Natural Resources Office, North Island Naval Air Station. Contract Number N68711-92-LT-2002.

BASIN-TO-BASIN WATER EXCHANGE IN THE SOUTHERN CALIFORNIA BIGHT

Barbara M. Hickey

School of Oceanography, University of Washington, Box 357940, Seattle, WA 98195
(206) 543-4737, FAX (206) 616-9289, E-mail: bhickey@u.washington.edu

ABSTRACT

An array of moored current meters was deployed for a nine-month period on the sills surrounding the Santa Monica and San Pedro basins (the SILL study). The goal was to determine the frequency and mechanisms of interaction between the Santa Monica and San Pedro basins, and the Santa Barbara Channel, Santa Cruz Basin, and the San Diego Trough. Hydrographic surveys were made on three occasions during the deployment. The sediments in the Santa Monica Basin are near-anoxic to anoxic, and the anoxic area has been growing with time. Our results from measurements on the sill (depth ~740 m) demonstrate that renewal of bottom water (addition of oxygen, as identified by the appearance of water with colder temperatures) occurs in isolated events of several days duration, with intervals of several years between renewal periods. These events are associated with processes occurring in the upper water column over the basin; in particular, with strong upwelling and southeastward flow from the Santa Barbara Channel into the Santa Monica Basin. Thus, as with much of the current and water property fluctuations in the basins of the Southern California Bight, it appears that basin anoxia is controlled in large part by large-scale environmental conditions.

INTRODUCTION

The topography of the Southern California Bight consists of a series of relatively deep offshore basins separated by ridges and islands (Figure 1). The lower portions of these basins are frequently separated from adjacent basins by sills so that renewal of water in the lower basins is only accomplished if water flows over the sill from one basin to the next. Renewal is important for maintaining oxygen levels within the basins. In general, oxygen near the bottom decreases northward from basin to basin (Hickey 1993). Some basins are nearly anoxic. In particular, anoxic sediments covered about 10% of the floor of the Santa Monica and San Pedro basin sediments 200 years ago. Today, almost the entire basin floor is near-anoxic (Gorsline 1988). Growth of the anoxic area depresses the ability of basin sediments to support marine life.

The large-scale oceanography of the Southern California Bight is dominated by the California Current system (e.g., Hickey 1979, 1992, 1993, 1998; Lynn and Simpson 1987, 1990; Bray et al. 1998). The California Current flows southeastward year-round offshore of the California Bight, bringing colder, fresher Subarctic water southward. South of Point Conception, the California Current turns southeastward and then shoreward and northwestward in a large eddy known as the Southern California Countercurrent or the Southern California Eddy. This northwestward flowing surface countercurrent and the subsurface California Undercurrent are the dominant features in the upper water column of the nearshore basins. The northwestward flow divides at the northwestern end of the Santa Monica Basin into two components, one flowing northwestward through the Santa Barbara Channel, the other flowing westward south of Santa Cruz and the other Channel Islands.

Fluctuations with dominant time scales from 3 to 30 d are superimposed on seasonal means. In winter and spring, a significant fraction of the variance is related to local wind driving at most locations (Hickey 1993; Harms and Winant 1998). In the Santa Barbara Channel, Harms and Winant (1998) have identified westward or upcoast advection in the Santa Barbara Channel during periods of winter storms ("flood west") and eastward or downcoast advection during upwelling periods ("flood east"). Seasonal maps of available current meter data in the Southern California Bight up to 1993 demonstrate that during winter and spring upwelling events, flow is southward nearshore in much of the Southern California Bight (Hickey 1993). During upwelling events,

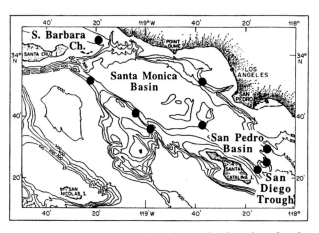

Figure 1. Bottom topography and mooring locations for the SILL study.

89

upwelled water from regions north of the Bight appears to enter the western end of the Santa Barbara Channel and move eastward along its southern boundary (Hickey 1992; Hendershott and Winant 1996). The alongshore pressure gradient is also responsible for a significant percent of the variance, particularly at longer (20 to 30 d and seasonal) time scales (Lentz and Winant 1986; Hickey 1992; Harms 1996; Harms and Winant 1998). In particular, in the Santa Barbara Channel, the alongshore pressure gradient causes currents to push warm water westward through the Channel when equatorward wind stress weakens (Harms and Winant 1998). In the Santa Barbara Channel, currents at some locations also appear to be driven equatorward by wind stress curl (Wang 1997).

A study of the Santa Monica and San Pedro sediments and the ocean circulation in the region was carried out by the Department of Energy from 1985 to 1990. Data collected in this program have been used to describe the water circulation in the region (Hickey 1991, 1992, 1993). In particular, in 1987 a study of flow across the basin sills was carried out. The goal of the study was to determine the mechanisms and frequency of exchange between the Santa Monica and San Pedro Basin and the adjacent basins. This paper summarizes results of that study.

MATERIALS AND METHODS

Subsurface arrays of moored sensors were deployed on all four sills or entrances of the Santa Monica and San Pedro basins from April to October of 1987 (Figure 1). Instruments included mechanical current meters (Aanderaas) as well as electromagnetic current meters (S4s), vector measuring current meters (VMCMs) and Doppler profilers (ADCPs). Data were processed to remove outliers and filtered to remove tidal and higher frequency fluctuations.

Conductivity, temperature, and depth (CTD) surveys were taken upon deployment and retrieval of the moored arrays. These data were calibrated to accuracies of about 0.003 psu and 0.001°C. Additional data are included from mid-basin bottle samples used to calibrate the CTD data. These data were obtained over a period of five years.

RESULTS

Time series of water properties (salinity, temperature and sigma t) just above the floor of the Santa Monica and San Pedro basins illustrate that abrupt changes, bringing colder, saltier, denser water into the basin, occur infrequently (Figure 2). In particular, during the five-year interval shown, renewal events occurred between April and May 1987, and in May 1988. Recovery to near-normal conditions occurs over a period of one to two years, a result of vertical and lateral mixing (Ledwell and Hickey 1995). A similar event was reported in the San Pedro Basin in 1984 (Berelson 1991).

Fortuitously, the moored array discussed in this paper was deployed during a year when renewal events occurred.

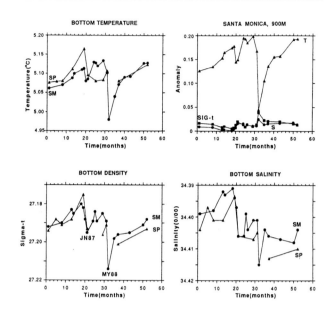

Figure 2. Five-year time series of water properties (temperature, salinity and sigma-t) as well as anomalies near bottom (~900 m) in the Santa Monica and San Pedro basins (Hickey 1992).

Temperature time series from the sill separating the San Pedro Basin from the San Diego Trough (the Avalon sill) indicate two major events, one in late May and one in mid-September (Figure 3). Temperature five meters above the bottom drops by almost 0.5°C in each of the events. Lowered temperatures are observed as high as 200 m above the sill. Note that the September event does not appear in water properties near 900 m in the Santa Monica Basin although it appears in the San Pedro Basin (as a failure to recover towards "normal" conditions) (Figure 2). The San Pedro Basin is the first basin encountered after water leaves the Avalon sill.

Subtidal temperature data reveal that three smaller renewal events took place between the two larger events that dominated the tidal time series (Figure 4). Subtidal velocity time series demonstrate that flow five meters above the floor of the sill was indeed directed into the Santa Monica Basin at the time of all five low temperature events (Figure 4). Flow was also northwestward on the sill that separates the San Pedro and Santa Monica basins (not shown).

Comparison between velocity five meters above the floor of the sill and velocity 30 m below the sea surface at a location in the mouth of the Santa Barbara Channel, illustrates that northwestward flow over the sill into the San Pedro and Santa Monica basin is strongly correlated with upper water column southeastward inflow into the Santa Monica Basin from the Santa Barbara Channel (Figure 4). Southeastward flow into the Santa Monica Basin is typically associated with major upwelling events that occur near the mouth of the Santa Barbara Channel.

Along-sill sections of oxygen, density and light attenuation taken during an event in which water over the sill is flowing southeastward out of the Santa Monica and San Pedro basins show the along-basin near sill depth gradients

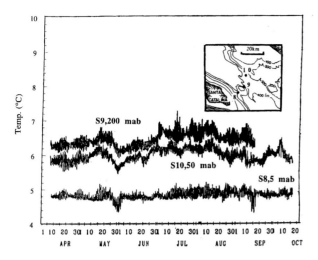

Figure 3. Time series of temperature at selected depths and locations on the Avalon sill, the sill separating the San Diego Trough from the San Pedro Basin.

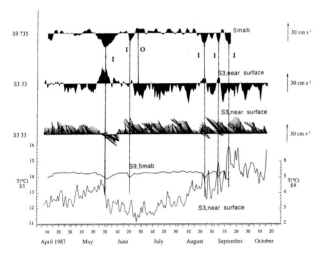

Figure 4. Time series of subtidal velocity (east-west component only) and temperature at sites on the Avalon sill (S9) as well as at a location in the mouth of the Santa Barbara Channel (S3). Negative velocity indicates flow over the sill into the San Pedro Basin or into the Santa Barbara Channel. Note that inflow over the sill is strongly related to outflow from the channel. Events discussed in the text are marked by vertical lines ("I" or "O" signifying inflow or outflow, respectively).

in oxygen (lower to the north), density (denser to the north), and light transmission (more turbid to the north). The density data suggest that the along-basin baroclinic (density-related) pressure gradient would be directed southeastward at this time. This relationship suggests that the direction of flow over the sill may be related to the along-basin pressure gradient, which is largely determined by upper water column processes.

DISCUSSION

A map of varved sediments in the basins shows that varved sediments cover almost the entire floor of the Santa

Monica Basin (Figure 5). The existence of varved sediments, indicating a lack of bioturbation, is usually associated with low oxygen levels, or near-anoxic conditions. The near-anoxic region has increased rapidly over the last two centuries, from about 10% to almost 100% at present. Results presented herein shed some light on processes controlling the rate of renewal of bottom water in the basin. In particular, results indicate that renewal occurs infrequently (several year intervals) and that renewal events are of relatively short duration (a few days).

Renewal events appear to occur during strong upwelling events in the Santa Barbara Channel. During these events, sea level is set down toward the east in the channel. Moreover, Harms (1996) suggests that sea level in the adjacent basin (Santa Monica) rises in opposition to the southeastward wind stress. The resulting northwestward pressure gradient over the basin could be responsible for the northwestward flow over the basin sill.

The density of the water crossing the sill is such that in the absence of entrainment and mixing, the water would fall to the bottom in the San Pedro Basin in a localized region near the sill. The fact that the resulting temperature anomaly at a depth near 900 m (Figure 3) is about five times less than the temperature anomaly over the sill suggests that this is not the case (Figure 2). The dense plume likely entrains ambient water as it cascades off the sill, subsequently spreading out laterally on the density surface corresponding to the density resulting after entrainment.

Renewal of bottom water in the Santa Monica and San Pedro basins does not occur every year, in spite of several strong upwelling events that occur each year. Moreover, renewal events do not appear to be strongly correlated to upper water column flow directly overhead of the sill (not shown). These mysteries and other aspects of the renewal process are the subject of ongoing research which will eventually lead to a better understanding of the mechanisms controlling renewal in these and other basins of the California borderland.

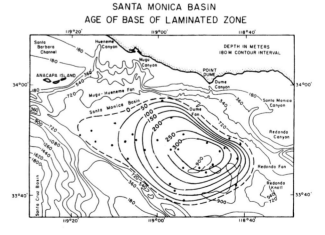

Figure 5. Thickness of varved sediments in the Santa Monica and San Pedro basins. Varved sediments are an indicator of near-anoxic conditions (Gorsline 1988).

ACKNOWLEDGMENTS

Data analysis and paper preparation were supported by the Minerals Management Service Contract #14-35-01-96-CT-30819 to B. Hickey. Data were collected with support from the Department of Energy, Contract #DE-FG05-85-ER-60333 to B. Hickey. Mr. D. Ripley was responsible for deployment and retrieval of moored arrays. Ms. S. Geier and Dr. N. Kachel were responsible for data preparation and display.

LITERATURE CITED

Berelson, W.M. 1991. The flushing of two deep basins, southern California borderland. Limnology and Oceanography 36(6):1,150-1,166.

Bray, N.A., A. Keyes, and W.M.L. Morawitz. 1998. The California current system in the Southern California Bight and the Santa Barbara Channel. Journal of Geophysical Research, submitted.

Gorsline D.S. 1988. History of contemporary anaerobic conditions in Santa Monica Basin, California Continental Borderland. Bulletin of the American Association of Petroleum Geologists 72:382.

Harms, S. 1996. Circulation induced by winds and pressure gradients in the Santa Barbara Channel. Ph.D. Dissertation, University of California, San Diego, 138 pp.

Harms, S. and C.D. Winant. 1998. Characteristic patterns of the circulation in the Santa Barbara Channel. Journal of Geophysical Research 103:3041-3065.

Hendershott, M.C. and C.D. Winant. 1996. Surface circulation in the Santa Barbara Channel. Oceanography 9(2):114-121.

Hickey, B.M. 1979. The California Current system—hypotheses and fact. Progress in Oceanography 8:191-279.

Hickey, B.M. 1991. Variability in two deep coastal basins (Santa Monica and San Pedro) off Southern California. Journal of Geophysical Research 96 (C9):16,689-16,708.

Hickey, B.M. 1992. Circulation over the Santa Monica-San Pedro Basin and shelf. Progress in Oceanography 30:37-115.

Hickey, B.M. 1993. Physical Oceanography. Pages 19-70 in M.D. Dailey, D.J. Reish and J.W. Anderson (eds), Ecology of the Southern California Bight. University of California Press, Berkeley, California.

Hickey, B.M. 1998. Coastal Oceanography of western North America from the tip of Baja California to Vancouver Island. Pages 345-393 in R. Robinson and K.H. Brink (eds), The Sea, Volume 10, Wiley and Sons, New York.

Ledwell, J.R. and B.M. Hickey. 1995. Evidence for enhanced boundary mixing in Santa Monica Basin. Journal of Geophysical Research 100(C10):20,665-20,679.

Lentz, S.J. and C.D. Winant. 1986. Subinertial currents on the southern California shelf. Journal of Physical Oceanography 16:1,737-1,750.

Lynn, R.S. and J.J. Simpson. 1987. The California current system—the seasonal variability of its physical characteristics. Journal of Geophysical Research 92(C12):12,947-12,966.

Lynn, R.S. and J.J. Simpson. 1990. The flow of the undercurrent over the continental borderland off southern California. Journal of Geophysical Research 95(C8):12,995-13,009.

Wang, D.-P. 1997. Effects of small -scale wind on coastal upwelling with application to Point Conception. Journal of Geophysical Research 102(C7):15,555-15,566.

CALIFORNIA'S SANTA CRUZ ISLAND WEATHER

Timothy Boyle[1] and Lyndal Laughrin[2]

[1]Geography Department, California State University, Northridge, CA 91330-8249
(818) 677-5632, E-mail: tim.boyle@csun.edu
[2]Santa Cruz Island Reserve, Marine Science Institute, UCSB, Santa Barbara, CA 93106
(805) 893-4127, E-mail: laughrin@lifesci.ucsb.edu

ABSTRACT

Statistics are developed from five weather stations on Santa Cruz Island. Record length is 94 years for one station and between two and eight years for the other four. Temperature and humidity variations are limited by the marine layer influence, except for the interior island valley which is isolated by topography. The 1997-1998 water year was the fourth largest rainfall total recorded since 1904. During a large storm on December 5 and 6, 1997, these weather stations recorded precipitation values ranging from 152 mm (6 in) to 254 mm (10 in) over a 36-hour period. This event was responsible for a large debris flow, which inundated a National Park Service campground and moved historic buildings off their foundations in Scorpion Harbor. Observations by park rangers reported rain totals of over 305 mm (12 in) in that time period.

Keywords: Santa Cruz Island, weather, El Niño.

INTRODUCTION

Although significant climatological research has been completed on coastal southern California, studies of the climatology of the Channel Islands have been limited and have not addressed specific islands (Figure 1). The climate of Santa Cruz Island is especially difficult to generalize because of its many microclimates. This study, still in its preliminary stages, examines air temperature, relative humidity, wind and precipitation data collected at four recently installed weather stations and a longer (94-year) record of precipitation from the Main Ranch, located in the central valley of the island. Particular attention is paid to a recent flood event, which affected Santa Cruz Island in December of 1997.

METHODOLOGY

Data for this study were collected from five sites located on Santa Cruz Island: National Park Service (NPS) Central Valley, Christy Airfield, Christy Pines, Prisoners Harbor, and the Main Ranch (Figure 2). Automated as well as standard meteorological instruments administered by NPS, California State University Northridge, and the U.C. Reserve System were used. At the Main Ranch, temperature

and precipitation data have been manually collected. In this paper, only the precipitation record is analyzed. At the four automated sites hourly readings of temperature and relative humidity were recorded at standard heights of 1.5 meter (m), whereas wind speed/direction were recorded at heights varying between 2.5 and 6 m. In the vicinity of the Main Ranch manual station, the National Park Service automated weather station was established in April of 1990. However, it has been moved three times from its original location near Centinela (elev. 155 m), to the vicinity of the U.C. Research Station approximately 1 km west of the Main Ranch (elev. 62 m), and finally to just south of the Main Ranch on a north-facing slope (elev. 152 m). This change was noted in the record but the move was not judged to be significant enough to warrant separation of the data. The Prisoners Harbor weather station was originally located in the Central Valley

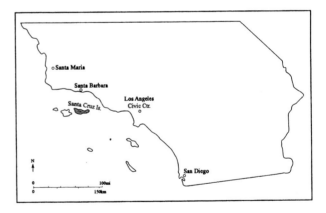

Figure 1. Southern California coastal region.

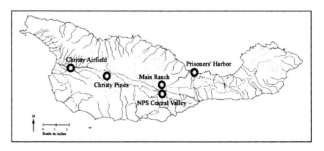

Figure 2. Location map of Santa Cruz Island weather stations.

near Cañada de la Portezuela (elev. 137 m) in the late 1980s, but in June of 1995 the station was moved to the coast (elev. 122 m) to fill a gap that existed in the coverage of the island. Only the later data by the coast was analyzed for this report. Two more stations, maintained by California State University Northridge, were added in December of 1996: Christy Pines (elev. 419 m) and Christy Airfield (elev. 64 m) (Figure 2). The siting of these new stations was designed to fill in gaps that existed in the climatic coverage of the island. Thus, data are presently being collected from four distinct geographic regions: the central valley, coastal plain, mountain peak, and northern coast.

CLIMATE

Santa Cruz Island is the largest of the California Channel Islands, with an areal extent of 248 km². It is located approximately 25 km from the coast of Santa Barbara (Figure 1) and reaches a maximum elevation of 753 m. The island is aligned approximately east-west, roughly parallel with the prevailing winds. A large fault controlled valley runs down the central axis of the island, bounded by mountains that rise to elevations of 700 m or more. The climate of Santa Cruz Island is Mediterranean Dry Summer Subtropical, with a cool summer regime (Kimura 1974; Ryan 1994). The surrounding Pacific Ocean effectively moderates seasonal and diurnal temperature and humidity ranges. A steady inflow of marine air minimizes temperature changes over much of the island. Diurnal temperature ranges tend to be small, with relatively cool days and warm nights (Kimura 1974). Seasonal variations in wind in the region are related to shifts in the location of a semi-permanent anticyclone over the eastern Pacific Ocean and the intensification of a semi-permanent thermal low over California and the Great Basin (Nelson 1977). The semi-permanent Pacific subtropical anticyclone or Pacific High is extremely important to southern California weather. The Pacific High deflects storms and produces a prevailing onshore flow of moist Pacific air at the surface into the region. At elevation, the Pacific High produces subsidence of warm, dry air restricting the location of moist marine air to the lowest few hundred meters above the surface (Rosenthal 1972).

Topography plays an important role in defining the island's microclimate. The central valley has greater temperature and humidity extremes due to its isolated location. The central valley is hotter and drier in the summer and receives more precipitation in the winter months than any other coastal station. Along the immediate Santa Cruz Island coast, low clouds predominate during the summer months, while inland valleys remain generally clear.

Summer Pattern

The most dominant climatic control for coastal southern California during both summer and winter is the semi-permanent Pacific subtropical anticyclone or Pacific High (Kimura 1974; Ryan 1994). In summer, this high pressure

cell strengthens and moves northward from over the eastern Pacific Ocean toward the northern California/Oregon coast. A clockwise flow of air around the high results in persistent northwest winds over most of the offshore area (Rosenthal 1972). Active subsidence with the high pressure results in air warmed by compression and the creation of a temperature inversion (Neiburger et al.1961; Baynton et al. 1965; Rosenthal 1972; Kimura 1974; Nelson 1977). The inversion base near the coast of southern California is approximately 400 to 600 m but rises gradually westward and is slightly higher at Santa Cruz Island. Cool water flowing southward from the California Current helps maintain this inversion at low elevations along the southern California coast (Neiburger et al. 1961; Nelson 1977). Fog and low stratus clouds are created as the overlying air is chilled by cool water. These inversions create very stable atmospheric conditions which limit convective activity and turbulent diffusion above the inversion base. Thus, during the summer months the only precipitation is light drizzle from stratus clouds.

Infrequently, during non-winter months a deepening of the marine layer known as a Catalina Eddy occurs off the coast of the southern California. An eddy is the rotational movement occurring in a flowing fluid that appears as irregular whirls. The Catalina Eddy is responsible for creating a thick persistent marine layer with stratus clouds and a weak cyclonic flow throughout the offshore region (Bosart 1983; Dorman 1985; Wakimoto 1987; Mass and Albright 1989; Clark and Dembek 1991; Thompson et al. 1996). During such events, Santa Cruz Island is inundated with a thick marine layer that persists at mountain summit locations as well as in the interior reaches of the Central Valley.

Winter Pattern

Toward the end of October and early November the stable atmosphere of summer is broken down. The Pacific anticyclone weakens and migrates southward, permitting frontal systems to enter southern California (Kimura 1974). As a result, precipitation is concentrated in the winter months, with 94% of all rainfall occurring between the months of November to April. The 94-year precipitation table at the Main Ranch (Table 1) shows an average annual rainfall of 515 mm (20.26 in). Precipitation totals increase with elevation giving the island a diverse rainfall total. Average rainfall along the coast is approximately 380 mm (14.96 in). Prevailing winds are generally from the west or northwest with surface wind patterns modified by local topography. In late fall and early winter as the Pacific anticyclone cell begins to move northwest and surface high pressure develops over the Great Basin, light offshore winds develop bringing relatively clear days to southern California (Nelson 1977; Dorman and Winant 1995). If the surface pressure over the Great Basin greatly exceeds that found along the southern California coast, very strong winds develop known as Santa Ana winds (Small 1995). These high winds create an offshore flow strong enough to reach the Channel Islands and be potentially dangerous to boaters (Small 1995).

DATA ANALYSIS

Air Temperature

Central valley temperatures were analyzed from the 1990-1998 record of the NPS automated weather station. For the time period analyzed, the mean annual temperature was 13.4°C. The highest mean monthly temperature (17.5°C) occurred in August, while the lowest mean monthly temperatures (9.4°C) occurred in December and January. During winter in the central valley, it is not uncommon to find minimum temperatures on the coldest days to be well below freezing. Extreme minimum temperatures have reached as low as –8.3°C. During summer and fall, central valley air temperatures are warm, as cool marine air is held back by the surrounding mountains. Maximum recorded temperatures reached 39.4°C.

The Christy Airfield weather station is located on a narrow coastal plain at the western end of Santa Cruz Island. The climate at this site is influenced by its proximity to the coast and location on the prevailing wind side of the island. Temperatures are moderated by the cool sea breeze throughout most of the year. Daily temperatures gradually increase as the marine layer dissipates. The mean annual temperature for Christy Airfield was 16.2°C. This relatively high annual average is principally a result of the moderating effect of the ocean and the low elevation (64 m) of the station. Mean monthly temperatures were highest in August (18.4°C) and September (19.1°C), while the extreme maximum temperature occurred on November 2, 1997 (37.2°C). Mean annual minimum temperatures in winter were as low as 9°C in December, with the extreme minimum temperature of 2.2°C recorded on February 26, 1997.

The Christy Pines weather station is also located in western Santa Cruz Island, but at approximately 419 m elevation, it is the highest weather station used in this study and the only station located on a mountain crest. The station is sited in an open area among pine trees just below a north-facing crest. A thick marine layer and the station's proximity to the coast are the strongest factors in moderating temperatures at this location. The Christy Pines mean annual temperature was 15.0°C, which is less than the Christy Airfield and Prisoners Harbor mean, but above the longer-term record of the central valley (13.4°C). This difference in mean annual temperatures is primarily due to colder winter temperatures and less influence of the marine layer in the Central Valley. The highest mean monthly temperature (21.2°C) occurred in September, and the extreme high temperature (36.0°C) occurred in August. Annual mean monthly temperatures vary according to the depth and penetration of the marine layer. For example, a significant drop in the mean monthly temperature occurred in June 1997, when the temperature averaged 13.9°C. This drop was due to an increase in the marine layer, which effectively lowered temperatures. The following July mean monthly temperature rose to 17.1°C. The lowest mean monthly temperatures (11.1°C) were recorded in February. The extreme minimum temperature reached a low of 3.7°C in March. In autumn, mean

Table 1. Precipitation record from Santa Cruz Island Main Ranch (courtesy L. Laughrin). Data taken with a standard four inch rain gauge.

	Season	Total	Jul	Aug	Sep	Oct	Nov	Dec	Jan	Feb	Mar	Apr	May	Jun
	1904	269.2							18.3	119.9	91.7	39.4	0.0	0.0
1904	1905	629.7	0.0	0.0	56.4	11.2	0.0	34.8	119.1	200.4	158.5	4.8	44.5	0.0
1905	1906	732.8	0.0	0.0	0.0	0.0	45.2	0.0	166.9	138.2	291.8	12.4	76.7	1.5
1906	1907	611.4	0.0	0.0	0.0	0.0	12.7	113.8	195.1	57.9	231.9	0.0	0.0	0.0
1907	1908	742.4	0.0	0.0	0.0	108.7	0.0	78.7	175.3	346.7	2.5	30.5	0.0	0.0
1908	1909	860.6	0.0	0.0	35.6	0.0	33.3	80.5	365.3	253.0	93.0	0.0	0.0	0.0
1909	1910	462.5	0.0	0.0	0.0	7.1	49.3	243.6	80.8	0.0	75.4	6.4	0.0	0.0
1910	1911	798.3	1.3	0.0	64.8	9.1	13.2	40.9	328.7	115.8	153.7	69.6	0.0	1.3
1911	1912	363.2	0.0	0.0	4.3	0.0	2.5	25.1	12.7	0.0	215.1	73.2	30.2	0.0
1912	1913	388.1	0.0	0.0	0.0	9.4	1.3	0.0	98.6	221.2	7.6	39.1	0.0	10.9
1913	1914	686.6	0.8	1.5	0.0	0.0	50.8	145.8	275.6	151.1	25.9	30.7	0.0	4.3
1914	1915	834.9	5.8	0.0	0.0	0.0	5.3	163.1	154.4	277.4	89.2	99.3	40.4	0.0
1915	1916	780.8	0.0	0.0	5.1	0.0	14.2	74.4	559.6	68.6	58.9	0.0	0.0	0.0
1916	1917	515.9	0.0	0.0	63.5	68.3	5.6	126.2	86.9	151.9	4.8	8.6	0.0	0.0
1917	1918	527.8	0.0	0.0	2.0	0.0	4.6	1.3	15.0	173.2	325.6	0.0	6.1	0.0
1918	1919	306.8	0.0	2.5	40.6	0.0	90.2	18.3	23.9	69.3	35.8	0.0	26.2	0.0
1919	1920	224.0	0.0	0.0	0.0	0.0	1.8	19.3	0.0	91.7	94.0	17.3	0.0	0.0
1920	1921	529.1	0.0	0.0	0.0	8.4	50.0	46.5	247.9	36.1	67.3	6.6	66.3	0.0
1921	1922	601.5	0.0	0.0	10.7	18.5	1.3	259.3	91.4	168.4	45.0	0.0	6.9	0.0
1922	1923	444.0	0.0	0.0	0.0	8.9	48.5	247.1	15.0	51.1	4.6	68.1	0.0	0.8
1923	1924	165.9	0.0	0.0	4.8	0.0	13.5	19.6	31.0	0.0	61.5	35.6	0.0	0.0
1924	1925	316.2	0.0	0.0	0.0	19.8	19.3	49.5	17.5	57.7	53.3	21.6	73.7	3.8
1925	1926	511.8	0.0	0.0	0.0	0.0	17.8	68.6	68.1	157.0	9.9	190.5	0.0	0.0
1926	1927	587.0	0.0	0.0	0.0	0.0	121.9	66.0	67.1	282.2	49.8	0.0	0.0	0.0
1927	1928	361.4	0.0	0.0	0.0	64.5	94.5	82.0	0.0	44.5	65.3	10.7	0.0	0.0
1928	1929	318.0	0.0	0.0	0.0	8.1	50.0	71.6	39.9	62.0	71.1	0.0	0.0	15.2
1929	1930	431.8	0.0	0.0	8.4	0.0	0.0	0.0	181.1	91.7	82.8	8.9	58.9	0.0
1930	1931	401.8	0.0	0.0	0.0	0.0	67.1	0.0	125.7	121.9	0.0	56.6	30.5	0.0
1931	1932	682.2	0.0	2.5	0.0	0.0	49.3	294.4	118.6	205.0	6.1	5.8	0.5	0.0
1932	1933	313.7	0.0	0.0	25.7	1.5	0.0	29.7	176.8	0.0	16.8	11.7	1.0	50.5
1933	1934	509.3	0.0	9.7	0.0	28.2	0.0	193.8	38.1	176.3	0.0	0.0	0.0	63.2
1934	1935	610.9	0.0	0.0	0.0	23.4	112.5	66.3	130.3	29.7	137.9	110.7	0.0	0.0
1935	1936	412.2	0.0	0.0	3.6	13.5	40.6	0.0	54.9	223.0	46.2	30.5	0.0	0.0
1936	1937	808.2	0.0	9.1	0.0	101.3	0.0	116.6	83.3	339.6	158.2	0.0	0.0	0.0
1937	1938	724.4	0.0	0.0	0.0	0.0	0.0	134.6	39.9	290.8	259.1	0.0	0.0	0.0
1938	1939	367.8	0.0	0.0	0.0	16.5	3.8	118.1	100.3	57.2	68.1	3.8	0.0	0.0
1939	1940	599.7	0.0	0.0	0.0	86.9	13.2	0.0	38.6	162.6	264.9	22.4	11.2	0.0
1940	1941	1426.2	0.0	0.0	0.0	41.4	18.5	366.3	401.6	226.3	231.1	139.4	1.5	0.0
1941	1942	486.2	0.0	0.0	0.0	57.9	9.4	202.2	26.9	36.3	59.9	93.5	0.0	0.0
1942	1943	583.9	0.0	0.0	0.0	14.0	5.1	52.1	313.9	81.0	76.7	41.1	0.0	0.0
1943	1944	685.5	0.0	0.0	0.0	23.4	5.6	248.4	91.7	203.5	85.1	27.9	0.0	0.0
1944	1945	445.8	0.0	0.0	0.0	0.0	98.6	17.0	23.9	123.7	182.6	0.0	0.0	0.0
1945	1946	341.4	0.0	0.0	0.0	8.1	0.0	227.6	5.6	17.8	82.3	0.0	0.0	0.0
1946	1947	254.3	0.0	0.0	0.0	6.1	115.6	68.6	10.7	15.7	37.6	0.0	0.0	0.0
1947	1948	203.2	0.0	0.0	0.0	12.4	0.0	27.9	0.0	12.7	90.4	56.6	3.0	0.0
1948	1949	303.5	0.0	0.0	0.0	0.0	0.0	64.0	117.3	38.1	69.1	0.0	15.0	0.0
1949	1950	467.9	0.0	0.0	0.0	0.0	27.2	182.4	110.5	110.0	28.2	9.7	0.0	0.0
1950	1951	319.5	0.0	0.0	7.6	27.9	37.8	18.3	80.0	57.2	24.9	61.2	4.6	0.0
1951	1952	761.2	0.0	0.0	0.0	9.7	33.8	167.4	286.3	37.8	159.8	66.5	0.0	0.0
1952	1953	425.7	0.0	0.0	0.0	2.5	97.0	184.2	56.6	6.9	25.7	52.8	0.0	0.0
1953	1954	460.2	0.0	0.0	0.0	0.0	45.2	0.0	152.7	134.1	110.0	18.3	0.0	0.0
1954	1955	459.7	0.0	0.0	0.0	0.0	74.7	56.4	96.0	48.0	63.2	94.7	26.7	0.0
1955	1956	742.7	0.0	0.0	0.0	0.0	6.4	287.8	331.2	33.5	0.0	61.0	22.9	0.0
1956	1957	407.7	0.0	0.0	0.0	0.0	0.0	0.0	176.0	122.2	29.7	50.8	29.0	0.0
1957	1958	899.4	0.0	0.0	0.0	40.1	2.8	84.8	116.8	246.1	278.1	117.6	13.0	0.0
1958	1959	290.1	0.0	0.0	2.5	0.0	0.0	5.6	42.2	189.0	0.0	50.8	0.0	0.0
1959	1960	442.5	0.0	0.0	8.4	0.0	0.0	66.3	128.5	176.8	8.9	53.6	0.0	0.0
1960	1961	225.3	0.0	0.0	0.0	0.0	151.4	12.2	40.6	0.0	18.0	1.8	1.3	0.0
1961	1962	731.3	0.0	0.0	2.3	0.0	111.8	41.1	66.5	412.0	97.0	0.0	0.5	0.0
1962	1963	381.3	0.0	0.0	0.0	11.7	0.5	10.7	93.2	134.9	70.9	55.6	1.8	2.0
1963	1964	309.4	0.0	3.0	21.8	6.4	93.0	0.8	77.0	1.0	89.7	11.2	1.8	3.8
1964	1965	603.5	0.0	0.5	0.0	18.3	50.8	265.2	24.6	10.4	67.3	166.4	0.0	0.0
1965	1966	372.1	0.0	0.0	0.0	0.0	242.6	28.7	69.1	27.4	4.3	0.0	0.0	0.0
1966	1967	418.6	0.0	0.0	1.3	0.0	43.7	80.0	134.1	9.4	24.1	126.0	0.0	0.0
1967	1968	398.3	0.0	0.0	0.0	0.0	118.6	29.2	34.0	59.9	143.0	13.5	0.0	0.0
1968	1969	705.4	0.0	0.0	0.0	35.6	26.7	49.0	361.7	189.7	12.7	30.0	0.0	0.0
1969	1970	277.4	0.0	0.0	0.0	2.0	58.4	5.1	105.2	67.6	39.1	0.0	0.0	0.0
1970	1971	417.6	0.0	0.0	0.0	0.8	162.8	150.1	29.2	30.0	16.0	15.2	13.5	0.0
1971	1972	227.3	0.0	0.0	0.0	0.0	7.9	189.0	20.8	5.6	0.0	3.6	0.0	0.5
1972	1973	537.0	0.0	0.0	0.0	5.3	94.2	33.3	166.1	186.7	51.3	0.0	0.0	0.0
1973	1974	422.9	0.0	0.0	6.1	23.4	52.3	44.7	204.5	81.8	10.2	0.0	0.0	0.0
1974	1975	380.0	0.0	0.0	0.0	16.5	5.8	136.7	17.3	87.9	83.6	32.3	0.0	0.0
1975	1976	174.5	0.0	0.0	0.0	9.1	9.4	1.5	0.0	88.4	30.0	21.6	0.8	13.7
1976	1977	302.5	0.0	1.5	61.7	0.0	11.9	24.1	92.5	4.8	33.0	0.0	72.4	0.5
1977	1978	1113.3	0.0	18.8	17.8	0.0	3.8	121.7	200.9	280.9	392.4	77.0	0.0	0.0
1978	1979	644.7	0.0	0.0	27.7	0.3	65.5	77.2	246.4	86.9	140.7	0.0	0.0	0.0
1979	1980	648.5	0.0	0.0	1.5	7.6	67.3	39.9	235.5	229.4	61.7	5.6	0.0	0.0
1980	1981	407.9	5.1	0.0	0.0	0.0	0.0	71.4	52.3	138.7	133.1	7.4	0.0	0.0
1981	1982	426.0	0.0	0.0	4.1	12.7	73.2	23.4	134.1	11.9	119.1	47.5	0.0	0.0
1982	1983	970.8	0.0	0.0	35.6	19.3	117.3	66.0	247.9	162.1	205.0	117.6	0.0	0.0
1983	1984	413.0	0.0	32.8	34.5	41.9	146.8	147.8	0.0	1.0	2.3	5.8	0.0	0.0
1984	1985	406.7	0.0	19.8	44.7	20.1	85.9	127.0	38.9	39.9	30.0	0.5	0.0	0.0
1985	1986	805.4	0.0	0.0	0.5	17.5	164.1	57.7	121.4	299.0	138.2	7.1	0.0	0.0
1986	1987	355.3	0.0	0.0	48.5	0.0	13.5	35.1	53.8	79.8	120.1	2.3	0.0	2.3
1987	1988	397.0	1.8	0.0	0.0	51.8	17.3	134.6	62.7	34.8	3.0	90.9	0.0	0.0
1988	1989	226.6	0.0	0.0	0.0	0.0	37.3	64.8	33.3	61.0	19.6	5.6	5.1	0.0
1989	1990	161.3	0.0	0.0	0.0	13.5	8.1	0.0	63.5	28.4	0.0	22.4	25.4	0.0
1990	1991	395.6	0.0	0.1	12.2	0.0	7.9	7.1	37.3	95.5	219.2	0.8	0.0	15.5
1991	1992	519.4	0.0	0.0	0.0	7.1	5.3	109.0	52.1	196.6	149.4	0.0	0.0	0.0
1992	1993	639.3	11.7	0.0	0.0	23.1	0.3	118.9	246.4	143.0	86.4	0.0	0.0	9.7
1993	1994	390.4	0.0	0.0	0.0	2.5	22.4	46.7	15.5	205.5	48.8	16.0	33.0	0.0
1994	1995	1146.3	0.0	0.0	6.6	0.0	45.7	40.6	777.7	21.3	229.1	4.6	9.9	10.7
1995	1996	395.2	0.0	0.0	0.0	2.5	0.0	66.8	72.1	170.9	47.0	31.0	4.8	0.0
1996	1997	593.1	0.0	0.0	0.0	35.1	64.3	226.1	267.7	0.0	0.0	0.0	0.0	0.0
1997	1998	1101.9	0.0	0.3	3.8	0.3	80.8	305.1	76.2	435.1	85.3	39.9	72.6	2.5

	Total	Jul	Aug	Sep	Oct	Nov	Dec	Jan	Feb	Mar	Apr	May	Jun
Mean	514.5	0.3	1.1	7.2	13.2	41.3	88.8	120.9	116.1	85.1	31.3	8.8	2.2
St Dev	234.1	1.4	4.5	15.7	21.8	48.3	85.5	126.3	100.2	83.4	40.7	18.8	8.7
Var	2155.4	0.1	0.8	9.7	18.7	92.0	288.1	629.9	399.3	276.9	66.0	14.1	3.0

monthly temperatures begin to decline, but mean maximum and extreme monthly maximum temperatures stay high due to a less persistent marine layer.

The Prisoners Harbor weather station location greatly affects its temperature regime. Located at an elevation of 122 m, the station sits on a north-facing coastal bluff overlooking the harbor (Figure 2). Station temperatures are moderated by nearness to the coast and are consistent throughout the year. The mean annual temperature for Prisoners Harbor is 16.1°C, just below that of Christy Airfield. The highest mean monthly temperature (19.1°C) was recorded in September. The extreme maximum temperature (34.8°C) was recorded in October. The lowest mean monthly temperature (13.6°C) was recorded in January and February. The extreme low temperature (5.5°C) was recorded in February. As with the Christy Airfield and Christy Pines stations, Prisoners Harbor weather station also exhibits a drop in mean monthly temperatures in June due to an increased marine layer. Interestingly, the central valley weather station shows no dip in mean monthly temperature in June owing to its interior position remote from the invading coastal marine layer.

Relative Humidity

Central valley relative humidity is mainly affected by the surrounding Pacific Ocean, but is also modified greatly by its inland valley location. Geographically surrounded by mountains, the central valley does not receive as much daily influence from marine intrusion, and as temperature rises humidity begins to decrease. The mean annual relative humidity of 72% is lower than any of the other stations (Figure 3). Humidity tends to drop slightly in April (68%) and in October/November (68 and 65%) but remains high in the intervening summer months. In June, humidity readings increase as the marine layer develops, creating early morning fog that burns off during the day. With the development of a Catalina Eddy, the thicker than normal marine layer allows fog to persist in the Central Valley for the entire day. In the late fall/early winter offshore winds develop bringing dry continental air to the island decreasing humidity. During periods of very strong offshore flow and high temperatures, relative humidity has reached minimum values of 3 to 4%.

Christy Airfield has the highest mean annual relative humidity (79%) of any weather station (Figure 3). Daily humidity remains high over the course of the year, except for October when mean monthly humidities drop to 67% associated with an increase in temperature and a change in wind direction as off-shore flow creates dryer conditions in this part of the island. During May through September, extreme minimum relative humidities remain high (35 and 51%) due to a deep persistent marine layer.

Christy Pines has a mean annual relative humidity of 75% (Figure 3). Humidities remain high through winter and peak in June with a mean monthly relative humidity of 92%, the highest monthly average of any weather station. In June mean monthly humidities never dropped below 49%, indicating a thick persistent marine layer. Near the end of

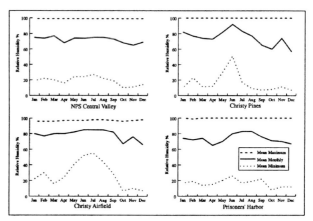

Figure 3. Mean monthly relative humidity comparison of four automated weather stations on Santa Cruz Island.

October humidities begin to fall as the marine layer breaks down due to increased offshore winds.

The mean annual relative humidity is 74% at Prisoners Harbor (Figure 3). Values of average relative humidity remain relatively constant throughout the year, and do not exhibit the drops in humidity seen at the Christy Airfield and Christy Pines stations during the winter. Summer humidities (June to September) remain high (80%) due to a persistent marine layer with the highest monthly mean relative humidities (83%) occurring in July and August with a range of 65 to 83%. The lowest mean monthly relative humidity (65%) was recorded in the month of April. Average monthly relative humidity values on Santa Cruz Island are high throughout the year at all stations. Values of maximum relative humidity are 99 to 100% for every month of the year. The greatest difference between the stations occurs in the summertime minimum values, which average about 10 to 12% at Prisoners Harbor and NPS Central Valley, but reach 48 to 50% at Christy Airfield and Christy Pines. These differences can be attributed to proximity to the coast and a prevailing west-northwest wind which brings moist marine air to Christy Airfield and Christy Pines throughout the summer.

Wind

Wind speed and direction within the central valley are strongly influenced by local topography. A windrose of average hourly wind direction for 1997 displays how the prevailing west-northwest wind is aligned parallel to the valley axis (Figure 4). A smaller easterly component of air flow results principally from cold air drainage within the central valley. Drainage down the axis of the central valley from east to west and input from nearby canyons helps to change wind direction from predominantly west to east in the early morning hours. Average wind speeds in the central valley are 4 to 6 m s^{-1}. Average hourly wind gusts ranging from 6 to 8 m s^{-1} are fairly common and are recorded from both the east and the west.

Winds at the Christy Airfield are predominantly from the west and west-northwest. Almost 84% of all winds

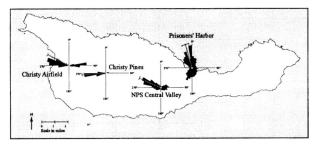

Figure 4. Average hourly wind direction in 1997 from four automated weather stations on Santa Cruz Island.

recorded flow from that direction. A smaller wind component comes from the east and east-southeast direction. The origin of this easterly component of flow is as yet unclear. It may result from downslope flow from the mountain peaks above the Christy Airfield and or from a contribution of strong Santa Ana winds. Average wind speeds at the Christy Airfield are between 4 and 6 m s^{-1} with gusts of up to 15 m s^{-1}. The strongest winds come from the east.

Wind speed and direction for the Christy Pines weather station are incomplete. In August of 1997, the wind speed sensor failed, leaving only values for wind direction. The wind speed and direction data for the Christy Pines are from January 1, 1997 to August 1, 1997. For this period, west winds predominated with values from the west, west-south-west, and west-northwest making up approximately 84% of all wind readings (Figure 4). Easterly winds made up a very smaller percentage of the total average, approximately 13%. Average wind speeds were between 4 and 6 m s^{-1}. Wind gusts of over 20 m s^{-1} were from the west, although most gusts greater than 16 m s^{-1} were from the east.

Wind speed and direction at Prisoners Harbor are highly modified by local topography. The Prisoners Harbor weather station recorded 50% of its total wind direction from the north and north-northwest as prevailing westerly winds are topographically modified to curl around the island. A smaller wind component is seen from the south, south-south-west and south-southeast. This wind from the south is mainly due to cold air drainage, occurring in the early morning hours. An easterly component of wind is also recorded approximately 12% of the time. Easterly air flows are due to both offshore flow and as frontal storms pass over the island. Average hourly wind speeds are between 4 and 6 m s^{-1}, with gusts of up to 21 m s^{-1}. Most high winds at Prisoners Harbor are seen during the passage of frontal storms over Santa Cruz Island.

Precipitation

Hand-recorded precipitation for the Main Ranch dates back to January 1904. This 94-year record was well maintained over the years and represents the longest precipitation record for any Channel Island (Table 1). The rainfall record was kept by the Caire Family, Stanton Family, and L. Laughrin. The rainfall patterns during the 94-year record at the Main Ranch are very similar to those for Santa Barbara (elev. 34 m), although rainfall totals at Santa Cruz Island

slightly exceed those at Santa Barbara. Santa Barbara's average rainfall total (431 mm) is nearly 85 mm less than that for Santa Cruz Island's Main Ranch station (515 mm). The greatest annual total (1426 mm) at the Main Ranch occurred in the 1940-1941 water year (July 1 to June 30), whereas Santa Barbara's greatest rainfall total (1194 mm) occurred in the 1997-1998 water year. The second-ranked largest precipitation total at Santa Barbara was 1148 mm for the 1940-1941 water year, 278 mm less than recorded at the Main Ranch. The Main Ranch's 1997-1998 water year total was its fourth greatest recorded total with 1102 mm. The lowest recorded rainfall total (161 mm) at the Main Ranch took place during the 1989-1990 water year and Santa Barbara's lowest rainfall total since 1904 was 162 mm in the 1923-1924 season. Santa Barbara's all-time lowest rainfall total was 114 mm in the 1876-1877 season, before records were kept on Santa Cruz Island (Ryan 1994). The greatest single monthly total for Santa Barbara was 615 mm in January of 1995 and in that same January, the Main Ranch recorded its greatest single month's precipitation total, 778 mm.

Rainfall totals for the Christy Airfield were recorded from January 1997 to August 1998. During the 1997-1998 water year Christy Airfield received 764 mm of precipitation (Figure 5). This was the lowest rainfall total from any weather station and is primarily due to its low elevation along the western coast of the island. The greatest monthly total was 333 mm, recorded in February of 1998. During the large two day storm of December 5 and 6, 1997, this station received 145 mm of rainfall in the first 24-hours and 170 mm total in 48-hours (Figure 6). This storm total was the lowest of all stations on the island.

For the 1997-1998 water year the Christy Pines station recorded the largest rainfall total (1082 mm) of any automated weather station (Figure 4). This water year total was just below that of the Main Ranch's 1102 mm total. The largest monthly rainfall total recorded at the Christy Pines was 469 mm in February of 1998. During the December 5 and 6, 1997 storm, this weather station recorded 217 mm of rainfall in 24-hours and 258 mm in 48-hours (Figure 6). Between 6 and 7 PM PST, this station recorded the greatest

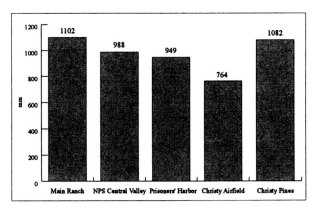

Figure 5. Santa Cruz Island 1997-1998 water year precipitation totals.

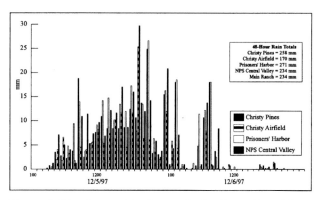

Figure 6. Hourly precipitation totals for Santa Cruz Island December 5 and 6, 1997.

hourly rainfall during the storm with 30 mm of recorded precipitation.

Prisoners Harbor precipitation record is slightly longer than Christy Airfield and Christy Pines, covering the period between June 1995 and August 1998. The 1995-1996 water year is invalid due to mechanical problems with the rain gauge. This problem was corrected for the 1996-1997 and 1997-1998 water years. During the 1997-1998 water year Prisoners Harbor received 949 mm of rainfall (Figure 4). The highest monthly total rainfall recorded (413 mm) occurred in February 1998. During the December 5 and 6, 1997 storm event, Prisoners Harbor received 205 mm of rainfall in the first 24-hours and 271 mm for the entire 48-hours period (Figure 6).

1997-1998 El Ñino Event

The 1997-1998 El Ñino event had a very significant impact on Santa Cruz Island. Besides the above average water year, Santa Cruz Island recorded its largest single day and two-day precipitation event in recorded history. The December 5 and 6 storm brought a record 170 to 271 mm of rain to parts of Santa Cruz Island (Figure 6). In the first 24-hours of the storm totals ranged from 145 mm at Christy Airfield, 217 mm at the Christy Pines, 176 mm at the National Park Service station, 227 mm at the Main Ranch, and 205 mm at Prisoners Harbor. The event began as an area of low pressure in the Gulf of Alaska. As the frontal storm moved toward the southern California coast, it began to intensify as it passed over the northeast Pacific Ocean. Early on December 5, the system began to tap moisture from the subtropical jet stream. This along with the typical slow down of frontal systems as they near the southern California coast allowed this storm to drop record moisture over the central and southern half of the island. Reports from the National Park Service Ranger at Scorpion Harbor detailed heavy rainfall, as much as 305 mm in the 48-hour event. This storm caused a large flash flood and debris flow through Scorpion Canyon and into the harbor. Buildings were moved off foundations, while vehicles and National Park Service equipment and data sheets were washed into the harbor.

Brumbaugh (1983) detailed significant storm events for Santa Cruz Island from 1898 to 1980. A modified version of Brumbaugh's table (Table 2) includes significant storm events from 1980 to 1998. Two more entries into the table were made from 1980 to 1998. The December 5, 1997 storm total of 227 mm would rank first over the 100 year precipitation record. The second entry from January 4, 1995 would be tied with two other storm events at 140 mm. This storm was ranked tenth although in that month of January 1995, the all-time maximum monthly total rainfall occurred on Santa Cruz Island with 777 mm (Table 1).

CONCLUSIONS

A preliminary analysis of the climate of Santa Cruz Island has been derived from four automated weather stations with records of between two and eight years and a 94-year manual rainfall record. The data suggest that there are notable microclimatic differences on the island which relate to distance from the coast, altitude, and position with respect to the east-west fault controlled the central valley. Additionally, it appears that the climate of Santa Cruz Island differs from mainland southern California coastal communities, with significantly higher relative humidities owing to the year-round influence of a marine layer, and rainfall totals that exceed those of the nearest neighboring mainland cities such as Santa Barbara.

Annual mean monthly temperatures on Santa Cruz Island vary according to altitude, nearness to the coast, and the depth and penetration of the marine layer. During summer, the marine inversion keeps coastal sites cool while the interior valley, protected from invading maritime air, warms rapidly. During winter strong westerly winds help dissipate the marine layer allowing temperatures to drop, especially in the interior valley.

The considerable thickness of the marine layer in the vicinity of Santa Cruz Island exerts a strong control on relative humidities, even at elevations of 400 m or more. All of the stations recorded mean maximum humidities of 99 to 100% during all months of the year, average relative humidity ranged from 65 to 83%, and mean minimums only reached very low values when strong offshore wind penetrated the island.

Recorded wind direction were strongly related to station position. The prevailing winds for the region are westerly, and this wind direction was clearly recorded at Christy Airport. These stations are located along the axis of the east-west trending central valley, which tends to topographically enhance wind flow. This control can be seen in the tendency of the secondary winds, related to cold air drainage and strong off-shore flow from the east. Prisoners Harbor, on the north coast, does not lie in the central valley, and its winds are principally from the north and south due to the prevailing wind being diverted around the island and cold air drainage.

Rainfall patterns on the island are similar to those recorded at Santa Barbara, but in general the totals are somewhat higher. The influence of island topography is shown in the somewhat higher rainfall totals at Christy Pines (elev. 419 m) with respect to the other stations.

Table 2. Extreme one-day rainfall on Santa Cruz Island, California 1904-1905 to 1980-1981, 1990-1991 to 1997-1998. Pre-1904 rainfall data are not from diaries, but from a loose note in the files at the Main Ranch. The note includes rainfall data from September 1898 to June 1900. It is not known whether the data represent a complete tally of that duration (Modified from Brumbaugh, 1983).

Rank	One-day (mm)	Year
1	227	1997
2	198	1956
3	178	1908
4	164	1941
5	163	1938
6	161	1962
7	158	1940
8	145	1979
9	141	1955
10	140	1926 1978 1995
13	130	1954
14	128	1899*
15	127	1968
16	122	1900*
17	120	1913
18	117	1964
19	114	1959
20	112	1907
21	110	1964
22	109	1937
23	104	1980
24	100	1958

The 1997-1998 El Ñino event brought record rainfall totals to Santa Cruz Island. The largest single day rainfall event was recorded on December 5, 1997. A devastating flood resulted, damaging equipment and property. With the addition of new weather stations in 1995 and 1996, this event was captured throughout the island and warrants further examination. Future weather stations are planned for Santa Cruz Island, which will help develop a more complete understanding of its many microclimates.

ACKNOWLEDGMENTS

The following persons and agencies contributed time, data, and equipment to the preparation of this report. Their assistance is greatly appreciated. Michael Swift, Mark Kuhlman, Greg Hargleroad, David Yoho, John Wall, Dr. Elliot McIntire, Dr. Amalie Orme, and Dr. Julie Laity of California State University Northridge; Santa Cruz Island Reserve, UCSB of the University of California Natural Reserve System; Gary Ryan, National Weather Service, Oxnard; Channel Islands National Park Service; the Nature Conservancy; and two anonymous reviewers.

LITERATURE CITED

Baynton, H. W., J. Bidwell, and D. W. Beran. 1965. The association of low-level inversions with surface wind and temperature at Point Arguello. Journal of Applied Meteorology 4:509-516.

Bosart, L. F. 1983. Analysis of a California Eddy event. Monthly Weather Review 111:1619-1633.

Brumbaugh, R. W. 1983. Hillslope gullying and related changes, Santa Cruz Island, California. University of California, Los Angeles (unpublished dissertation).

Clark, J. H. E. and S. R. Dembek. 1991. The Catalina Eddy event of July 1987: A coastally trapped mesoscale response to synoptic forcing. Monthly Weather Review 119:1714-1735.

Dorman, C. E. 1985. Evidence of Kelvin waves in California's marine layer and related eddy generation. Monthly Weather Review 113: 827-839.

Dorman, C. E. and C. D. Winant. 1995. Buoy observations of the atmosphere along the West Coast of the United States, 1981-1990. Journal of Geophysical Research 100(C8):16,029-16,044.

Kimura, J. C. 1974. Climate. Pages 2.1-2.70 in M. D. Daily, B. Hill, and N. Lansing, (eds.), Summary of Knowledge of the southern California Coastal Zone and Offshore Areas. Vol. 1, Physical Environment, Bureau of Land Management, Department of Interior. Contract 08550 CT4-1.

Mass, C. F. and M. D. Albright. 1989. Origin of the Catalina Eddy. Monthly Weather Review 117:2406-2436.

Nelson, C. S. 1977. Wind stress and wind stress curl over the California current. NOAA Technical Report NMFS SSRF-714, United States Department of Commerce.

Neiburger, M., D. S. Johnson, and C. Chien. 1961. Studies of the structure of the atmosphere over the eastern Pacific Ocean in summer. Vol. 1, No. 1, University of California Press, Berkeley and Los Angeles.

Rosenthal, J. 1972. Point Mugu Forecasters Handbook, Pacific Missile Range, Point Mugu, California. Technical Publication PMR-TP-72-1, p. 426.

Ryan, G. 1994. Climate of Santa Barbara, California. NOAA Technical Memorandum NWS WR-225, United States Department of Commerce.

Small, I. J. 1995. Santa Ana Winds and the Fire Outbreak of Fall 1993. NOAA Technical Memorandum NWS WR-230, United States Department of Commerce.

Thompson, W. T., S. D. Burk, and J. Rosenthal. 1996. An investigation of the Catalina Eddy. Monthly Weather Review 125(6):1135-1146.

Wakimoto, R. M. 1987. The Catalina Eddy and its effects on pollution over southern California. Monthly Weather Review 115:837-855.

NUMERICAL MODELING OF GUADALUPE ISLAND RESPONSE TO TSUNAMI ARRIVALS

Salvador F. Farreras and Jorge Reyes

Centro de Investigación Científica y Educación Superior de Ensenada (CICESE)
Apartado Postal 2732, Ensenada, Baja California 22800, Mexico, and
P.O. Box 434844, San Diego, CA 92143, USA
(52-61)-745050, FAX (52-61)-750574, E-mails: sfarrera@cicese.mx and jreyes@cicese.mx

ABSTRACT

Guadalupe Island, located off the coast of Baja California (Mexico), is considered as an eventual sea level reporting stations for a regional tsunami warning system. The knowledge of the tsunami response at the island can give an estimation in advance of the severity of the attack to be expected at neighboring mainland communities. The scattering of tsunami waves by the island is examined by solving the long wave equation through a time and space centered finite difference scheme. Relative amplitude and wave phase lag at several points along the island contour, for the most probable tsunami periods and incident directions to occur according to historical records, are computed. Maximum amplifications happen with short tsunami periods and close to energy convergence zones, where refraction is important. For large tsunami periods, reflection and diffraction become the dominant processes. The location under consideration to install a wave reporting station has adequate amplification characteristics for a tsunami warning system.

Keywords: Baja California, tsunami scattering, warning system.

INTRODUCTION

Several remote source tsunamis have affected the coastal communities of the Baja California peninsula in northwest Mexico (Farreras and Sanchez 1991). Guadalupe Island, lying outside the continental shelf, 250 km off the coast of Baja California (Figure 1) is capable to become a sea level reporting stations for a regional as well as the international Pacific Tsunami Warning System. The installation of a sea level pressure gauge, in the same place as the one that operated in the past, is presently in process.

Islands, far out from the continental shelves, provide a good option to obtain tsunami records in conditions near to those in the open ocean.

The objective of this study is to determine the tsunami amplitude and phase response along Guadalupe Island contour for several wave periods and incident directions; and obtain through this an estimation of the incoming tsunami wave parameters in the open ocean. This estimation can give information to neighboring mainland coastal

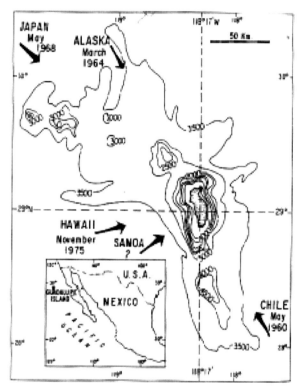

Figure 1. Guadalupe Island location, surrounding bathymetry, and approach direction of the five tsunami cases modeled in this study. Depths are in fathoms (one fathom = six feet).

communities on the arrival time and severity of the attack to be expected, before tsunami waves reach them.

METHODOLOGY

Reflection, refraction, shoaling, and diffraction in the local bathymetry and coastal configuration are the main physical processes occurring in the interaction of water waves with an island. About 25% of the tsunami energy is reflected at the continental shelf, while 100% do so at the arrival to the coast (Soloviev and Go 1974). Miyoshi (1983) states that refraction is the most important interaction process for a tsunami converging onto an island. Diffraction cause more harm to the coast when the size of the obstacle is comparable with the incident wave length (Dean and Dalrymple 1984). At the arrival to an island, tsunami waves may split into two, with one wave propagating around each side of the island, and both meeting at the sheltered region with a subsequent amplification in amplitude and destructive flow. This was the case in the 1992 Babi Island tsunami, as confirmed by numerical modeling and laboratory experiments (Yeh et al. 1994). Linear wave theory application to tsunami wave interaction with a continental shelf, although arguable (Voit 1987), has been successfully applied to the modeling of tsunami-island interactions by Houston (1978) and Tsuji (1985).

The linearized long wave equation in polar coordinates (r, θ) and time t is:

$$\frac{1}{g} \frac{\partial^2 \zeta}{\partial t^2} = \frac{1}{r} \frac{\partial}{\partial r} \left(rD \frac{\partial \zeta}{\partial r} \right) + \frac{D}{r^2} \frac{\partial^2 \zeta}{\partial \theta^2} \qquad (1)$$

where ζ is the free surface elevation, D is the mean water depth, and g is the gravitational acceleration. Bottom friction, surface wind stress, and Coriolis effect are neglected.

Zero component of radial flow $\frac{\partial \zeta}{\partial r} = 0$ and the radiation to infinity condition for the waves scattered outward $\frac{\partial \zeta_s}{\partial t} + (gD)^{1/2} \frac{\partial \zeta_s}{\partial r} \rightarrow 0$, are considered as inner and outer boundary conditions respectively.

To solve the equation, a Riemann's conformal mapping of the polar coordinate grid (r, θ) onto an image plane (ρ, β) where the orthogonal contours reproduce the real island shape at the unit circle, but approach a circular shape as the polar system radius is increased, is performed.

After the conformal mapping, the wave equation takes the form:

$$\frac{1}{gs^2} \frac{\partial^2 \zeta}{\partial t^2} = \rho \frac{\partial}{\partial \rho} \left(\rho D \frac{\partial \zeta}{\partial \beta} \right) + \frac{\partial}{\partial \beta} \left(D \frac{\partial \zeta}{\partial \beta} \right) \qquad (2)$$

where s is a scale factor.

This equation is solved numerically for monochromatic plane incident waves, $\zeta_I = e^{i(\kappa r \cos\theta - \omega t)}$ where κ is the wave number and ω is the angular frequency, by means of Vastano and Reid (1966) space-time centered finite difference algorithm. An integration time step of one second is used, to satisfy the stability criterian.

APPLICATION AND RESULTS

Five remote source tsunami arrival cases were modeled. Four of them correspond to real past events with the highest wave heights recorded in the Baja California coastal region according to Sanchez and Farreras (1992): 22 May 1960 from Chile, 28 March 1964 from Alaska, 16 May 1968 from Japan, and 29 November 1975 from Hawaii. The tsunami arriving from Hawaii was the only one recorded at Guadalupe Island, by the time the former sea level gauge station was in operation. The fifth case corresponds to a hypothetical arrival proceeding from Samoa. Directions of incidence for this five cases are shown in Figure 1.

For each approach direction, tsunami wave arrivals of 10, 15, 20, 25, 30, 35, and 40 minute periods were simulated. Amplitudes relative to the incident wave train and

phase lags referred to the far field wave timing at an azimuth 90° from the direction of the incident wave train, were obtained as results.

Relative amplitude distribution along contour azimuth positions for a 10 minute period tsunami arriving from Hawaii (Figure 2) shows:

a) for the variable depth real bathymetry, an amplification maximum in the sharp southwest corner where wave energy converges due to refraction; and

b) for a constant depth flat bottom, a typical symmetric reflection-diffraction response curve with one main maximum in the wave incidence direction and a secondary one 180° antipodal to the first.

The smoothness of the constant depth response curve, typical of an analytic solution for a simple geometry contour, indicates that Guadalupe Island is in the lower limit of object sizes that may significantly interact through diffraction with tsunami waves of such a period.

Isolines of relative amplitude and phase in a period-azimuth space, for tsunamis arriving from Japan (Figure 3), but similar to the other cases modeled, show:

a) an amplification maximum, due to reflection, for all periods at the azimuth of incidence;

b) another amplification maximum at the sharp southwest corner, where refraction is important, but only for less than 15 minute periods;

c) amplification decrease with period increase for all contour azimuthal locations; becoming almost 1.0 or less for periods higher than 35 minutes.

d) almost vertical phase isolines; an indication that this linear model is very little phase-dispersive: waves of different periods travel at about the same speed, without phase lags;

e) near-zero phase at the sharp southwest and northeast corners for periods higher than 15 minutes;

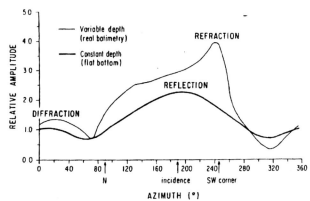

Figure 2. Relative amplitude distribution along contour azimuth positions for a ten minute period tsunami arriving from Hawaii.

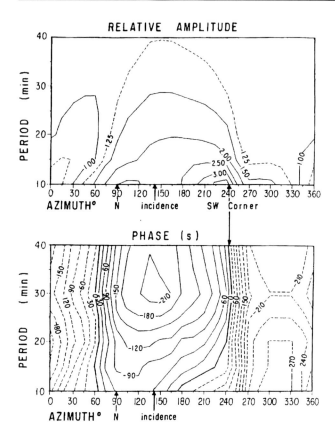

Figure 3. Amplitude and phase response along Guadalupe Island contour for tsunamis of several periods arriving from Japan (azimuth of incidence = 138°).

f) small azimuthal phase gradient in the incidence zone as a result of the wave front arrival almost parallel to the coastal contour; and

g) an increase of the above zone width, until the gradient almost disappears (horizontal isolines), with decreasing periods. This indicates that the wave front aligns in a larger lateral extension to the coastal contour (simultaneous arrival at all points) as refraction becomes more important.

The response at the southwest corner shows significant amplification for most of the periods considered (particularly the short ones) independently of the direction of incidence (Figure 4). This characteristic ensures enough sensitivity for tsunamis of the order of centimeter open ocean wave heights to be detected and recorded by instruments in this site. This location is also reasonably protected from storm wave action and is easily accessible as to become a permanent sea level and wave reporting station.

CONCLUSIONS

The linear model gives a suitable approximation of the tsunami response at Guadalupe Island, that can be used later on as an initial condition for an inland run-up non-linear simulation.

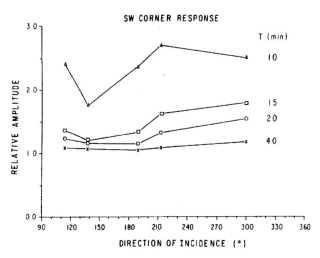

Figure 4. Amplitude response of Guadalupe Island Southwest corner for tsunami arrivals of several periods and directions of incidence.

Guadalupe Island size does not significantly affect the propagation of tsunami waves with periods greater than 35 minutes.

Maximum amplifications, due to refraction, occur for short periods near energy convergence zones.

Amplifications are smaller, and mainly due to diffraction and reflection, for long periods.

The southwest corner can be recommended as a permanent site for a sea level reporting station of regional or international tsunami warning systems because of its sensitivity to tsunami arrivals, its accessibility, and its reasonable storm wave protection.

LITERATURE CITED

Dean, R.A. and R. Dalrymple. 1984. Water Wave Mechanics for Engineers and Scientists. Prentice Hall Inc. New Jersey. 345 p.

Farreras, S.F. and A.J. Sanchez. 1991. The tsunami threat on the Mexican west coast: a historical analysis and recommendations for hazard mitigation. Natural Hazards 4(2 & 3):301-316.

Houston, J.R. 1978. Interaction of tsunamis with the Hawaiian islands calculated by a finite element numerical model. Journal of Physical Oceanography 8:93-102.

Miyoshi, H. 1983. Energy of the tsunami converging into an island. Pages 241-247 in Bernard, E. (ed.), Proceedings of the 1983 Tsunami Symposium. Pacific Marine Environmental Laboratory. National Oceanic and Atmospheric Administration. United States Department of Commerce, Seattle.

Sanchez, A.J. and S.F. Farreras. 1992. Catalog of tsunamis on the western coast of Mexico. World Data Center A for Solid Earth Geophysics. Publication SE-50. National Geophysical Data Center. NOAA. Boulder, Colorado. 79 p.

Soloviev, S.L. and Ch.N. Go. 1974. A Catalogue of Tsunamis on the Western Shore of the Pacific Ocean. Nauka Publishing House. Moskow. 310 p.

Tsuji, Y. 1985. Comparison of observed and numerically calculated heights of the 1983 Japan Sea tsunami. Pages 41-48 *in* Murty, T.S. and W.J. Rapatz (eds.), Proceedings of the International Tsunami Symposium. Institute of Ocean Sciences. Department of Fisheries and Oceans, Sidney.

Vastano, A.C. and R.O. Reid. 1966. A numerical study on the tsunami response at an island. A & M Project 471. Reference 66-26T. College Station: Department of Oceanography. Texas A & M University. 141 p.

Voit, S.S. 1987. Tsunamis. Annual Review of Fluid Mechanics 19:217-236.

Yeh, H., Liu, P., Briggs, M. and C. Synolakis. 1994. Propagation and amplification of tsunamis at coastal boundaries. Nature 372:353-355.

SEAFLOOR EARTHQUAKE MONITORING SYSTEM

Catherine M. Hoffman

Pacific OCS Region, U. S. Minerals Management Service,770 Paseo Camarillo, Camarillo, CA 91320
(805) 389-7575, FAX (805) 389-7592, E-mail: catherine.hoffman@mms.gov

ABSTRACT

Data on the response of seafloor sediments to earthquake-induced ground motion are scarce. To learn more about the response of seafloor sediments, the U.S. Minerals Management Service (MMS) installed a seafloor earthquake monitoring system (SEMS) network offshore southern California. The data gained will be used to improve safety standards relating to the structural aspects of offshore facilities. The SEMS is a network of three offshore seismic probes installed in locations of varying water depths. The probes were installed offshore Los Angeles County at Aera Energy LLC's Platform Eureka, Ventura County at Venoco Inc.'s, Platform Grace, and Santa Barbara County at Torch Operating Company's Platform Irene. The MMS and the California Division of Mines and Geology (DMG) have signed a joint agency work agreement for the maintenance and monitoring of the SEMS equipment. Data received from the SEMS will be incorporated into data from the DMG's onshore monitoring network and processed for public distribution to the engineering and scientific community. The DMG will be responsible for archiving all data received. Anyone can access the data from the SEMS by logging on to the DMG home page at:
www.consrv.ca.gov/dmg/csmip.

Keywords: Pacific OCS Region, earthquake, SEMS, DMG.

INTRODUCTION

Data on the response of seafloor sediments to earthquake induced ground motion are scarce. To learn more about the response of seafloor sediments, the U.S. Minerals Management Service (MMS) installed a seafloor earthquake monitoring system (SEMS) network offshore southern California. The data gained will be used to help improve safety standards relating to the structural aspects of offshore facilities. This SEMS is the only currently operating offshore seismic network in the United States.

The SEMS program is the result of recommendations provided by the Marine Board of the National Academy of Sciences to obtain data on seafloor seismic ground motions. In 1979, Sandia National Laboratory, under the sponsorship of the MMS and the U.S. Department of Energy, installed a series of prototype instruments known as SEMS. Since 1979, the MMS has installed four generations of SEMS equipment. The latest generation, SEMS IV, was installed in July 1995.

The SEMS IV is a network of three offshore seismic probes installed in locations of varying water depths. The probes were installed offshore Los Angeles County at Aera Energy LLC's Platform Eureka, Ventura County at Venoco Inc.'s Platform Grace and Santa Barbara County at Torch Operating Company's Platform Irene. The probes are imbedded three to seven feet into the sea floor approximately 400 feet from the platform and hardwired to seismic data recorders installed topside at the platform.

The SEMS IV area of coverage is extensive. A probe can record a magnitude 4.0 earthquake within a 25 mile radius and a magnitude 4.5 earthquake within a 65 mile radius. With 160 miles separating Platforms Irene and Eureka, the coverage for a moderately-sized earthquake in the southern California area is over 25,000 square miles.

The seismic probe was designed to protect the electronics under adverse deep water conditions and to minimize damage during the installation process. Each probe contains a three-axis magnetometer to calculate the probe's orientation after being embedded in the sea floor.

To install the probe, it was first attached to a vibrocorer/coretube assembly which was then slid into an installation cage. A crane was used to lower the equipment to the ocean floor with the help of an underwater Remotely Operated Vehicle (ROV) equipped with a camera. Once the cage was stable on the ocean floor, the vibrocorer was activated. After the probe was sufficiently embedded, the ROV used one of its robotic arms to release the probe from the coretube. The ROV backfilled the hole left behind by the coretube.

The SEMS IV instrumentation system was designed to measure three-axis acceleration. The seismic events are recorded by Quanterra Q680/LT-G computers. The probe and event recorder are powered directly from the platform power system, but backup battery power is also available.

On September 20, 1995 at 4:27 p.m., a magnitude 5.8 earthquake occurred in the Ridgecrest area. Though the earthquake's epicenter was 192 miles from Platform Irene, the earthquake registered loud and clear on its computer. In addition, the SEMS IV recorded the March 18, 1997 Barstow earthquake and several aftershocks to the 1994 Northridge earthquake.

The MMS and the California Division of Mines and Geology (DMG) have developed a joint agency work agreement for maintenance and monitoring of the SEMS IV equipment. Through this work agreement, the DMG will:

- Periodically monitor and test the SEMS IV to ensure that the instruments are operational.

- Perform onsite maintenance and inspection of the equipment once a year or as needed.

- Troubleshoot and repair the system as necessary to assure reliability.

The MMS will reimburse the DMG for any expenses incurred in the maintenance of the seismic equipment as well as provide the necessary software and technical information.

Data received from the SEMS will be incorporated into data from the DMG's onshore monitoring network and processed for public distribution to the engineering and scientific community. The DMG will be responsible for archiving all data received. The data from the SEMS IV can be accessed by logging on to th eDMG home page at: **www.consrv.ca.gov/dmg/csmip**.

SUMMARY OF THE MIOCENE IGNEOUS ROCKS OF THE CHANNEL ISLANDS, SOUTHERN CALIFORNIA

Peter W. Weigand[1] and Karen L. Savage[2]

[1]Department of Geological Sciences, California State University, Northridge, California 91330-8266
(818) 677-2564, FAX (818) 677-2820, E-mail: Peter.Weigand@CSUN.edu
[2] (818) 677-7098, E-mail: Karen.Savage@CSUN.edu

ABSTRACT

Middle Miocene igneous rocks, mainly volcanic, are found on all eight of southern California's Channel Islands. Activity began about 19 million years ago (Ma), became widespread by 17 Ma, and waned about 13 Ma. Andesite lava flows predominate on Anacapa Island. Santa Cruz Island has widespread lavas of basaltic-andesite to dacite in composition north of the cross-island fault and a thick sedimentary unit dominated by rhyodacitic debris south of the fault. Santa Rosa Island has a thick unit of basaltic debris and associated intrusions as well as a sedimentary unit containing conglomerates of volcanic debris. San Miguel Island has two volcanic units: an older unit of basaltic flows and sediments, and a younger unit of a felsic intrusion and associated flows and sediments. Santa Barbara Island is nearly entirely composed of basaltic to andesitic flows. On Santa Catalina Island is a diorite pluton and a volcanic sequence that ranges from basalt to rhyolite in composition. Volcanic rocks on San Clemente Island are dominated by andesite flows with minor rhyolite-dacite units. Igneous activity on San Nicolas Island is limited to several thin dikes of probable mafic composition. Widespread Miocene magmas in southern California were generated by decompression melting in response to extension related to the tectonic rotation of the Western Transverse Ranges block.

Keywords: Channel Islands, volcanics, Miocene.

INTRODUCTION

A burst of volcanic activity erupted throughout southern California during the middle of the Miocene Epoch mainly between about 17 and 13 Ma, resulting in about two dozen volcanic areas ranging from Point Arguello south to Rosarito Beach, Baja California (Weigand 1982; Dickenson 1998). Included in this igneous episode was activity on all eight of southern California's Channel Islands (Figure 1); coverage ranges from a maximum of 100% on Santa Barbara Island to a few dikes on San Nicolas Island. Forms of igneous rocks include lava flows, flow breccias, sedimentary units composed exclusively of volcanic material, dikes, and one plutonic intrusion (on Santa Catalina Island). The composition of the volcanic rocks ranges from basalt to rhyolite, with the most common being the intermediate

Figure 1. Map of the Channel Islands of southern California.

compositions basaltic-andesite and andesite. A summary of the age and petrology of the igneous suites on the islands is presented in Table 1. The suites on seven of the eight Channel Islands are summarized below.

This middle Miocene volcanism occurred during a period in which southern California experienced large amounts of rifting, clockwise rotation, and extension in and around the area of the Inner Borderland of Southern California (Crouch and Suppe 1993; Nicholson et al. 1994). Generation of magmas within this extensional environment has been interpreted as being the result of decompression melting of the mantle (Weigand et al. 1998; Dickinson 1998).

ANACAPA ISLAND

The geology of Anacapa Island has been summarized by Scholl (1960) and Norris (1995). The island is composed of a volcanic sequence that forms a gently north-dipping homocline. About 300 m of vesicular and porphyritic lava flows, breccia, agglomerate, and tuff are exposed, although neither the base nor top of the sequence are seen. Strata of San Onofre Breccia are interbedded with the volcanic rocks near their exposed base, implying a submarine origin for at least some of the volcanic rocks. Weigand (1993) found three

Table 1. Summary of Miocene Igneous Centers on the Channel Islands.

VOLCANIC CENTER	FORM	AGE RANGE (Ma)	ROCK TYPES	PETROLOGIC AFFINITY	$K_{57.5}$	$^{87}Sr/^{86}Sr$	ϵ_{Nd}	$\delta^{18}O$	REFS.
Anacapa Island	Ext	15.8-16.28(3)A	And 100%	Low-K CA	1.02 (3)	nd	nd	nd	1, 2
Santa Cruz Island Volcanics	Ext	16.1-16.5(2)K 16.33-17.12(5)A	BA 24% And 49% Dac 24% Rhy 3%	Low-K CA	0.98 (37)	0.7025-0.7032 (10)	nd	nd	3, 1, 2, 4, 5
Blanca Formation	Clasts	14.9-13.3(2)K	And 5% Dac 55% Rhy 40%	Low-K CA	0.98 (61)	0.7030-0.7040 (11)	nd	8.1 (2)	3, 6, 7
Santa Rosa Island Volcanics	Ext + Int	18.1-19.3(2)A	Bas 88% BA 12%	Low- to med-K CA	0.85 (8)	nd	nd	nd	1, 8
Beecher's Bay Formation	Clasts	15.8(1)	And 36% Dac 36% Rhy 27%	Low- to med-K CA	1.40 (11)	0.7029-0.7045(7)	3.4-6.1 (4)	nd	9
San Miguel Island Volcanics	Ext + Int	17.0-18.5(2)A	Bas 50% BA 8% Dac 17% Rhy 25%	Low- to med-K CA	na	nd	nd	nd	1, 8
Santa Barbara Island Volcanics	Ext	14.8-16.8(2)K 15.5(1)A	Bas 10% BA 30% And 60%	Low- to med-K CA	1.30 (10)	nd	nd	nd	10, 1, 8
Santa Catalina Island Volcanics	Ext	12.7-15.4(13)K 17.2(1)A	Bas 9% BA 26% And 46% Dac 14% Rhy 6%	Low- to med-K CA	0.94 (36)	0.7029-0.7034(2)	9.4 (1) 4.1-6.1(2)	nd	11, 1, 12, 13, 14
	Pluton	19.0(2)K	Diorite	nd	na	nd	nd	nd	11
San Clemente Island Volcanics	Ext	13.6-16.1(5)K	And 85% Dac 12% Rhy 3%	Med-K CA	1.23 (17)	0.7037-0.7045(3)	nd	6.8 (3)	3, 15, 16, 12, 17, 18
San Nicolas Island	Dikes	nd	nd	nd	nd	nd	nd	nd	19

Notes: Number in parentheses indicate number of samples for which data are available; Ext = extrusives; Int = intrusives, K = K-Ar dating, A = Ar-Ar dating, Bas = basalt, BA = basaltic andesite, And = andesite, Dac = dacite, Rhy = rhyolite, CA = calc-alkaline, $K_{57.5}$ = K_2O content of the suite at a value of 57.5% SiO_2; nd = not determined; na = not applicable.

REFERENCES:
1. Luyendyk et al. (1998)
2. Weigand (1993)
3. Turner (1970)
4. Higgins (1976)
5. Hurst (1983)
6. Savage and Weigand (1994)
7. Weigand, unpub. data
8. Weigand et al. (1998)
9. Chinn and Weigand (1994)
10. Howell (1976)
11. Vedder et al. (1979)
12. Weigand (1994)
13. Wood (1981)
14. Stewart et al. (1992)
15. Merrifield et al. (1971)
16. Olmstead (1958)
17. Johnson and O'Neil (1984)
18. Hawkins and Divis (1975)
19. Vedder and Norris (1963)

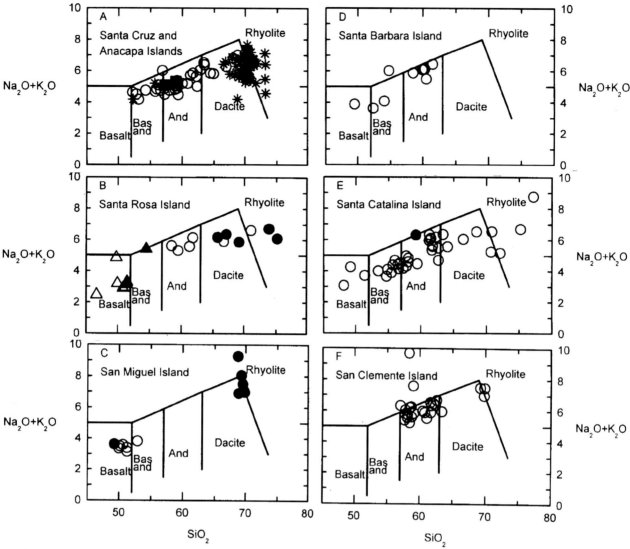

Figure 2. Classification diagram showing rock names (Le Bas et al. 1986). A. Santa Cruz and Anacapa Islands. Solid squares = Anacapa lavas, open circles = Santa Cruz Island Volcanics, stars = Blanca Formation clasts. B. Santa Rosa Island. Open triangles = Santa Rosa Island Volcanics intrusions, solid triangles = Santa Rosa Island Volcanics flows, open circles = clasts from the San Onofre breccia member, solid circles = clasts from members D and E of the Beecher's Bay Formation. C. San Miguel Island. Open circles = lower mafic unit, solid circles = upper felsic member. D. Santa Barbara Island. E. Santa Catalina Island. Open circles = Santa Catalina Island Volcanics, solid circle = diorite pluton. F. San Clemente Island.

analyzed samples to be andesitic, virtually identical in composition to andesites from the Santa Cruz Island Volcanics (Figure 2A). Luyendyk et al. (1998) obtained Ar-Ar dates on plagioclase separates from Anacapa lavas of 16.2±0.2 and 16.3±0.2 Ma.

SANTA CRUZ ISLAND

Santa Cruz Island, the largest of the northern Channel Islands, is cut by the east-west trending Santa Cruz Island fault. The northern half of the island is underlain mostly by Santa Cruz Island Volcanics and Monterey Formation, while the southern half consists of Jurassic metamorphic and plutonic rocks covered by a Tertiary sedimentary and volcaniclastic section.

Santa Cruz Island Volcanics

The Santa Cruz Island Volcanics exposed north of the Santa Cruz Island fault were named and subdivided into four members by Nolf and Nolf (1969). They form a north-dipping homocline composed of interbedded lava flows, flow breccias, and volcaniclastic rocks that have a cumulative thickness of 2,400 m and that are cut by numerous shallow intrusions at an inferred eruptive center near Devil's Peak. The formation overlies inferred San Onofre Breccia in the subsurface and is overlain by the Monterey Formation.

Nolf and Nolf (1969) and Crowe et al. (1976) summarized the stratigraphy and petrography of these volcanic rocks. The lowermost Griffith Canyon Member consists of flows and epiclastic volcanic breccias of basaltic and andesitic composition that were deposited in a subaerial environment. The overlying Stanton Ranch Member is composed of andesite flows, flow breccias, and subordinate tuff breccias erupted on the flanks of a volcanic edifice. The next younger Devil's Peak Member contains a variety of scoriaceous andesitic and dacitic flows, flow breccias, and reworked pyroclastic rocks apparently emplaced on the slopes of, and adjacent to, a volcanic center. The uppermost Prisoners Harbor Member is composed of andesitic and dacitic flows, flow breccias, and tuffaceous volcaniclastic beds, probably deposited in a submarine environment.

Chemical analyses by Crowe et al. (1976) and Weigand (1993) show that the volcanic rocks are polygenetic and range in composition from basaltic andesite to dacite (Figure 2A). These data largely confirm petrographic evidence showing the overall volcanic sequence to be mafic near the base (basalt and andesite), intermediate in composition in the middle members (largely andesite), and more felsic near the top (andesite and dacite).

Turner (1970) reported K-Ar age dates of 16.1 ± 0.9 Ma on a sample probably from the upper part of the Devil's Peak Member and 16.5 ± 0.8 Ma on a sample probably from the middle of the Prisoners Harbor Member (these and subsequent dates have been corrected to new IUGS constants). Crowe et al. (1976) reported dates of 16.0 ± 0.7 Ma and 19.9 ± 0.9 Ma on the same sample from a dike cutting the lower part of the Devil's Peak Member. The three younger dates are largely compatible with more recent Ar-Ar dates of 17.0 to 16.3 Ma (Luyendyk et al. 1998).

Volcanic Clasts from the Blanca Formation

The medial Miocene Blanca Formation crops out on the southern half of Santa Cruz Island. Exposures cover 20 km^2 and reach a maximum thickness of 1,400 m (Fisher and Charlton 1976). The Blanca locally overlies the Willows Plutonic Complex, the San Onofre Breccia, or the Rincon Formation. The top of the formation is nowhere exposed on land; it may continue offshore to the south (Vedder et al. 1986). The Blanca Formation consists of volcaniclastic conglomerates and breccias, epiclastic tuffaceous sandstone and siltstone interbedded with primary pyroclastic layers, and minor basaltic-andesite flows (McLean et al. 1976a). Weaver et al. (1969) divided the formation into three members — lower, middle, and upper — based on color, texture, and percentage of volcanic clasts. Deposition of the Blanca Formation is believed to have occurred in a nearshore marine environment, adjacent to an active volcanic source (Fisher and Charlton 1976).

Based on geochemical criteria, Savage and Weigand (1994) have shown that the majority of the clasts are classified as dacite and rhyolite (Figure 2A). In agreement with McLean et al. (1976b), Savage and Weigand (1994) concluded that the outcrop of volcaniclastic rocks overlying the San Onofre Breccia on the southwest side of the island is correlative with the Blanca Formation. Weaver et al. (1969) concluded that the source of the volcanic clasts of the Blanca Formation was the Santa Cruz Island Volcanics located north of the Santa Cruz Island fault, whereas Howell and McLean (1976) and Savage and Weigand (1994) presented

petrographic and geochemical evidence strongly suggesting that the Santa Cruz Island Volcanics were not the source; the volcanic center that served as the provenance for the clasts is currently unidentified. An andesite flow from the upper member of the Blanca Formation has been dated at 14.9 ± 0.8 Ma, and a dacite clast from the upper member has been dated at 13.3 ± 1.2 Ma, both by the K-Ar method (McLean et al. 1976a).

SANTA ROSA ISLAND

With an area of 218 km^2, Santa Rosa Island is the second largest of the Northern Channel Islands. The island is cut by the east-west trending Santa Rosa Island fault. North of the fault, well-developed Pleistocene terrace deposits overlie low-dipping, mid-Tertiary marine clastic and volcaniclastic units. South of the fault, the more rugged terrain is cut by deep canyons which expose older Tertiary sandstone and shale and middle Tertiary volcaniclastic strata cut by volcanic intrusions (Weaver and Nolf 1969).

Santa Rosa Island Volcanics

Volcanic rocks on Santa Rosa Island were first mapped by Kew (1927) as upper Miocene intrusions. Avila and Weaver (1969) recognized that the volcanic rocks consisted of intrusive, extrusive, and clastic components and named them the San Miguel Volcanics on the supposition that these volcanic rocks had their volcanic origin from nearby San Miguel Island to the west. Dibblee and Ehrenspeck (1998) proposed the name Santa Rosa Island Volcanics for this volcanic formation, which crops out in the central part of the island south of the Santa Rosa Island fault and on the central and western coasts north of this fault (Dibblee et al. 1998).

Chemical analyses from both lava flows and intrusions show that most are composed of basalt (Weigand et al. 1998; Figure 2B). Samples of flows are somewhat higher in SiO$_2$ than are samples of intrusions. A sample from an intrusion south of the fault has been dated at 18.1 ± 0.3 Ma by the Ar-Ar method on whole-rock material (Luyendyk et al. 1998). Intrusive activity persisted for some time because some of the bodies intrude the lower Monterey Shale of late Saucesian-Relizian age (ca. 16.5 to 15.5 Ma; Dibblee and Ehrenspeck 1998).

Volcanic Clasts from the Beecher's Bay Formation

Pebbles and cobbles of volcanic origin occur in three conglomeratic units which crop out along the northeastern and eastern coast of Santa Rosa Island. These conglomerates have been included in a variety of formations (see Chinn and Weigand 1994); we will follow the assignment of Dibblee et al. (1998). Nuccio and Wooley (1998) recommended that the unit be named the Beecher's Bay Formation and divided the formation into five informal units, designated A through E in ascending order. The lowermost blueschist-bearing unit A, exposed along the northwest shore of Carrington Point, has been named the San Onofre breccia facies of the Beecher's Bay Formation by Dibblee et al. (1998). These five units have been interpreted to represent various parts of a submarine fan complex (Nuccio and Wooley 1998).

Based on geochemical criteria, Chinn and Weigand (1994) showed the clasts from the San Onofre breccia facies to range in composition from andesite to dacite and the clasts from upper members D and E to range in composition from dacite to rhyolite (Figure 2B). Although only the San Onofre breccia member yielded andesite clasts, clasts from all three units sampled are very similar to each other with respect to trace elements (Chinn and Weigand 1994).

Although the formation as a whole is generally devoid of fossils, middle member C contains well-developed foraminiferal assemblages. Based on these assemblages and its stratigraphic position, the Beecher's Bay Formation is assigned a Relizian to middle-Luisian age (17 to 15 Ma; Avila 1968). A date of 15.80 ± 0.08 Ma was determined by the Ar-Ar method on plagioclase grains from a San Onofre andesite clast (Chinn and Weigand 1994). The same sample yielded two plagioclase grains that were significantly older (avg. = 24.4 Ma); these grains were presumably picked up from crustal rocks traversed by the ascending magma.

SAN MIGUEL ISLAND

San Miguel Island, the westernmost Channel Island, is composed of a sequence of sedimentary and volcanic strata that range in age from Upper Cretaceous to Miocene. These units are largely covered by Quaternary sands. Weaver and Doerner (1969) distinguished two members in the San Miguel Volcanics: 1) a lower member of basaltic flows and volcaniclastic strata which crop out on the southeastern third of the island, and 2) an upper member of massive dacite intrusions, flows, and clastic strata which crop out on the northern tip of the island around and south of Harris Point. The bimodality of the San Miguel Volcanics is largely confirmed by chemical composition. The lower member is primarily classified as basalt, while samples from the upper member straddle the dacite/rhyolite boundary; a single clast from the upper member is compositionally basalt (Weigand et al. 1998; Figure 2C). Several K-Ar dates have suggested that the San Miguel Volcanics are Oligocene in age (e.g. Crowe et al. 1976; Kamerling and Luyendyk 1985), in apparent conflict with paleontological evidence. However, a new Ar-Ar date of 17.7 ± 0.3 Ma on plagioclase from a basalt flow in the lower member (Luyendyk et al. 1998) is more geologically reasonable.

SANTA BARBARA ISLAND

Santa Barbara Island, the smallest of the Channel Islands, has had the least amount of geological study. Kemnitzer (1933) first mapped the island and showed it to consist nearly entirely of volcanic rocks whose Miocene age was established by a typical Luisian foraminiferal assemblage from intercalated shales (Kleinpell 1938). Vedder and Howell (1976) described a volcanic section more than 325 m in thickness that they divided into three general units. The

lower and thickest unit is composed of basalt or andesite flows, local flow breccia, and minor layered pyroclastic(?) material. Abundant pillow structures and vesicles suggest submarine eruption at shallow depth (Norris 1991). This unit is overlain by a thin, discontinuous unit of mudstone intercalated with lava flows, which in turn is overlain by a volcanic breccia that may in part be a hyaloclastite.

Weigand et al. (1998) sampled flows and volcanic clasts and found them to range in composition from basalt to andesite (Figure 2D); samples collected from the western side were uniformly andesite in composition. Howell (1976) reported K-Ar dates of 14.8 ± 1.8 and 16.8 ± 2.0 Ma on plagioclase separate from two andesite flows along the southeast part of the island. The average of these two dates is similar to the whole-rock Ar-Ar date of 15.5 ± 1.0 Ma reported by Luyendyk et al. (1998) on a basalt.

SANTA CATALINA ISLAND

Santa Catalina Island, the second largest Channel Island, is characterized by the widespread occurrence of Catalina Schist, a Mesozoic unit of exhumed oceanic crust. These rocks are cut by a Miocene intrusion and unconformably overlain in places by Miocene volcanic and sedimentary strata. Miocene igneous activity on Santa Catalina Island took two forms. A hornblende quartz diorite pluton intruded into Catalina Schist basement 19.5 ± 0.6 Ma (K-Ar; Vedder et al. 1979). This pluton covers an area of about 39 km^2 on the island and also crops out offshore over an additional area of about 7 km^2.

Unconformably overlying the schistose basement and diorite pluton is a formerly extensive sequence of volcanic and sedimentary rocks now limited to one broad area midway between Avalon and the Isthmus and several other small areas. Volcanic rocks now crop out over an area of about 32 km^2 on the island (Vedder et al. 1986). Surrounding much of the island is a unit of undifferentiated terrace deposits of late Miocene and Quaternary age; underlying this are additional exposures of Miocene volcanic rocks that cover about 190 km^2 (Vedder et al. 1986). Vedder et al. (1979) mapped in detail the volcanic and sedimentary sequence in the Fisherman's Cove, Cactus Peak-Cottonwood Canyon, and East End Quarry areas. The Fisherman's Cove sequence exceeds 150 m in thickness and is composed of a wide variety of fine-grained sedimentary rocks, volcanic and sedimentary breccias, extrusive flows and domes, and tabular intrusions. Wood (1981) showed the volcanic section in the Black Jack Peak-Whitley's Peak area to be composed of subaerially deposited lava flows, laharic breccias, and tabular and dome intrusions that exceed 400 m in thickness.

Chemical analyses (Vedder et al. 1979; Wood 1981; Weigand 1994) show the Black Jack Peak-Whitley's Peak volcanic section to be composed of a polygenetic suite that ranges from basalt to rhyolite in composition (Figure 2E). A single analyzed sample of the pluton plots near the andesite samples on this diagram. Based on 12 K-Ar measurements, Vedder et al. (1979) determined that volcanism on Santa

Catalina Island began about 14.7 Ma and extended until some time after 12.4 Ma. A single whole-rock Ar-Ar determination by Luyendyk et al. (1998) of 17.2 ± 0.6 Ma suggests that volcanism may have begun somewhat earlier.

SAN CLEMENTE ISLAND

San Clemente Island is the emerged portion of a structural block bounded on the northeast by the San Clemente fault that has a vertical displacement of at least 500 m (Junger 1976). The island consists of interbedded Miocene volcanic and sedimentary rocks, and is partly blanketed by Quaternary sedimentary rocks and unconsolidated sediments (Smith 1898; Olmsted 1958). Excluding the Quaternary cover, volcanic rocks crop out over an area of about 160 km² (Olmsted 1958). An additional 172 km² of volcanic rocks surround the island (Vedder et al. 1986).

Andesite flows and minor pyroclastic units that exceed 600 m in thickness dominate the bulk of San Clemente Island (Olmsted 1958). Dacite occurs as two or more distinct flows that overlie the andesite and that reach 70 m in thickness. Flows and minor tuffs of rhyolite up to 45 m in thickness also overlie the andesite flows; the rhyolite and dacite units are not in contact with each other. Merrifield et al. (1971) described the petrology of a core drilled at Eel Point, which is located about mid-island on the southwest coast. About 364 m of andesite were encountered, which are largely not exposed on the island.

Chemical analyses (Weigand 1994) confirm that the main volcanic unit is compositionally andesite, whereas samples from the upper dacite and rhyolite units are indistinguishable and plot on the dacite-rhyolite boundary (Figure 2F). Merrifield et al. (1971) reported a whole-rock K-Ar date determined from near the bottom of the Eel Point core of 16.1 ± 0.8 Ma and one from near the top of the core of 15.9 ± 0.7 Ma. They reported additional K-Ar ages on plagioclase separates of 15.4 ± 1 Ma from a subaerial andesite flow and 13.6 ± 0.4 Ma from a rhyolite collected near the top of the volcanic sequence. These dates are compatible with Luyendyk et al.'s (1998) whole-rock Ar-Ar dates which range from 16.0 to 14.5 Ma.

SAN NICOLAS ISLAND

San Nicholas Island consists of about 3,000 ft of Eocene sedimentary strata covered in places by Pleistocene marine terraces and wind-blown sand (Vedder and Norris 1963). Igneous activity on San Nicolas Island is limited to several dikes of possible basalt to andesite composition assumed to be middle Miocene in age (Vedder and Norris 1963).

DISCUSSION

The Miocene igneous suites on the Channel Islands exhibit geochemical characteristics that have traditionally been associated with igneous rocks produced above an active subduction zone (e.g., Thompson et al. 1984). However, it is now well established that subduction of the Farallon plate had ceased by the time and in the area that these igneous centers on the Channel Islands were active (Atwater 1989; Lonsdale 1991). Savage and Weigand (1997) have interpreted the generation of the middle Miocene Conejo Volcanics of the nearby Santa Monica Mountains, for which considerable major-oxide, trace-element, and isotopic data are available, in light of recent extensional tectonic models for southern California that involve large components of rifting, rotation, and extension in and around the areas currently occupied by the western Transverse Ranges and inner California Continental Borderland (Crouch and Suppe 1993; Nicholson et al. 1994). This model can explain the generation of all the Miocene igneous centers of coastal and offshore southern California, including the occurrences on the Channel Islands.

In short, Savage and Weigand (1997) proposed that generation of the Conejo magmas involved a two-stage process presented in a slightly modified form here. The first stage involved emplacement of oceanic lithosphere, including the subduction of accretionary sediments that became metamorphosed into Catalina Schist, beneath Western North America during subduction of the Farallon plate in Cretaceous and Paleogene time. The second stage involved the rifting and clockwise rotation of the western Transverse Ranges block caused by the capture of the partially subducted Monterey microplate by the Pacific plate at about 20 Ma. Continued rifting and rotation of the overlying continental crust in response to newly initiated transtensional Pacific plate motion of the captured microplate led to unroofing and exposure of the underlying Catalina Schist and to the attenuation and uplift of the underlying oceanic lithospheric and asthenospheric mantle. Decompression melting of this depleted mantle source produced primitive basaltic magmas that repeatedly intruded the overlying crust where they underwent fractional crystallization and assimilated Catalina Schist or isotopically similar material. Thus, the distinctive geochemical signatures in this suite were developed during magma evolution and interaction with previously subducted oceanic crust and were not derived from their primary source. These more evolved magmas erupted throughout what is now coastal and offshore southern California starting about 19 Ma and lasting until about 13 Ma in Channel Islands volcanic centers.

LITERATURE CITED

Atwater, T. 1989. Plate tectonic history of the northeast Pacific and western North America. Pages 21-72 in Winterer, E. L., D. M. Hussong, and R. W. Decker, (eds.), The Eastern Pacific Ocean and Hawaii. Boulder, Colorado, Geological Society of America, The Geology of North America, N.

Avila, F. A. 1968. Middle Tertiary stratigraphy of Santa Rosa Island, California [M.A. thesis]. Santa Barbara, University of California.

Avila, F. A. and D. W. Weaver. 1969. Mid-Tertiary stratigraphy, Santa Rosa Island. Pages 48-67 in Weaver, D. W., D. P. Doerner and B. Nolf (eds.), Geology of the Northern Channel Islands. Pacific Sections, American Association of Petroleum Geologists and Society of Economic Paleontologists and Mineralogists, Special Publication.

Chinn, B. D. and P. W. Weigand. 1994. Petrology and geochemistry of volcanic clasts from the Miocene Beecher's Bay Formation, Santa Rosa Island, California. Pages 255-265 in Halvorson, W. L. and G. J. Maender (eds.), The Fourth California Islands Symposium: Update on the Status of Resources. Santa Barbara Museum of Natural History, Santa Barbara, CA.

Crouch, J. K. and J. Suppe. 1993. Neogene tectonic evolution of the Los Angeles basin and inner borderland: A model for core complex-like crustal extension. Geological Society of America Bulletin 105:1415-1434.

Crowe, B. M., H. McLean, D. G. Howell and R. E. Higgins. 1976. Petrography and major element chemistry of the Santa Cruz Island volcanics. Pages 196-215 in Howell, D. G. (ed.), Aspects of the geologic history of the California Continental Borderland. Pacific Section American Association of Petroleum Geologists Miscellaneous Publication 24.

Dibblee, T. W., Jr. and H. E. Ehrenspeck. 1998. General geology of Santa Rosa Island. Pages 49-75 in Weigand, P. W. (ed.), Contributions to the geology of the northern Channel Islands, southern California. Pacific Section American Association of Petroleum Geologists, Miscellaneous Publication 45.

Dibblee, T. W., Jr., J. J. Woolley and H. E. Ehrenspeck. 1998. Geologic map of Santa Rosa Island, California. Dibblee Geological Foundation, Map #DF-67, scale 1:24,000. Santa Barbara, CA.

Dickinson, W. R. 1998. Tectonic implications of Cenozoic volcanism in coastal California. Geological Society of America 109:936-954.

Fisher, R. V. and D. W. Charlton. 1976. Mid-Miocene Blanca Formation, Santa Cruz Island, California. Pages 228-240 in Howell, D. G. (ed.), Aspects of the geologic history of the California Continental Borderland. Pacific Section American Association of Petroleum Geologists, Miscellaneous Publication 24.

Hawkins, J. W. and A. F. Divis. 1975. Petrology and geochemistry of mid-Miocene volcanism on San Clemente and Santa Catalina Islands and adjacent areas of the Southern California Borderland. Geological Society of America Abstracts with Programs 2:323-324.

Higgins, R. E. 1976. Major-element chemistry of the Cenozoic volcanic rocks in the Los Angeles basin and vicinity. Pages 216-227 in Howell, D. G. (ed.), Aspects of the geologic history of the California Continental Borderland. Pacific Section American Association of Petroleum Geologists Miscellaneous Publication 24.

Howell, D. G., 1976. A review of the estimates for the radiometric ages for the Relizian Stage of the Pacific coast. Pages 13-15 in Fritsche, A. E., TerBest Jr. and W. W.

Wornardt, (eds.), The Neogene symposium. Pacific Section Society of Economic Paleontologists and Mineralogists.

Howell, D. G. and H. McLean. 1976. Middle Miocene paleogeography, Santa Cruz and Santa Rosa Islands. Pages 266-293 in Howell, D. G. (ed.), Aspects of geologic history of the California Continental Borderland. Pacific Section American Association of Petroleum Geologists, Miscellaneous Publication 24.

Hurst, R. H., 1983. Volcanogenesis contemporaneous with mid-ocean ridge subduction and translation. Pages 197-213 in Augustithis, S. S. (ed.), The significance of trace elements in solving petrogenetic problems and controversies. Athens, Theophrastus Publications.

Johnson, C. M. and J. R. O'Neil. 1984. Triple junction magmatism: A geochemical study of Neogene volcanic rocks in western California. Earth and Planetary Science Letters 71:241-262.

Junger, A. 1976. Tectonics of the Southern California Borderland. Pages 486-498 in Howell, D. G. (ed.), Aspects of the geologic history of the California Continental Borderland. Pacific Section American Association of Petroleum Geologists Miscellaneous Publication 24.

Kamerling, M. J. and B. P. Luyendyk. 1985. Paleomagnetism and Neogene tectonics of the northern Channel Islands, California. Journal of Geophysical Research 90:12485-12502.

Kemnitzer, L E. 1933. The geology of Santa Barbara Island: [M.S. thesis]. Pasadena, California Institute of Technology, 45 p.

Kew, W. S. W. 1927. Geologic sketch of Santa Rosa Island, Santa Barbara County, California. Geological Society of America Bulletin 38:645-653.

Kleinpell, R. M. 1938. Miocene Stratigraphy of California. American Association of Petroleum Geologists, 450 p. Tulsa. OK.

Le Bas, M. J., R. W. Le Maitre, A. Streckeisen and B. Zanettin. 1986. A chemical classification of volcanic rocks based on the total alkali silica diagram. Journal of Petrology 27:745-750.

Lonsdale, P. 1991. Structural patterns of the Pacific floor offshore of Peninsular California. Pages 87-125 in Dauphin, J.P., and Simoneit, B.R., eds., The Gulf and Peninsular Province of the Californias. American Association of Petroleum Geologists Memoir 47.

Luyendyk, B. P., P. B. Gans and M. J. Kamerling. 1998. ^{40}Ar/^{39}Ar geochronology of Southern California Neogene volcanism. Pages 9-35 in Weigand, P. W. (ed.), Contributions to the geology of the northern Channel Islands, southern California. Pacific Section American Association of Petroleum Geologists Miscellaneous Publication 45.

McLean, H., B. M. Crowe and D. G. Howell. 1976a. Source of Blanca Formation volcaniclastic rocks and strike-slip faulting on Santa Cruz Island, California. Pages 294-308 in Howell, D. G. (ed.), Aspects of the geologic history of the California Continental Borderland. Pacific Section

American Association of Petroleum Geologists Miscellaneous Publication 24.

McLean, H., D. G. Howell and J. G. Vedder. 1976b. Miocene strata on Santa Cruz and Santa Rosa Islands — a reflection of tectonic events in the southern California borderland. Pages 241-253 *in* Howell, D. G. (ed.), Aspects of the geologic history of the California Continental Borderland. Pacific Section American Association of Petroleum Geologists Miscellaneous Publication 24.

Merrifield, P. M., D. L. Lamar and M. L. Stout. 1971. Geology of central San Clemente Island, California. Geological Society of America Bulletin 82:1989-1994.

Nicholson, C., C. Sorlien, T. Atwater, J. C. Crowell and B. P. Luyendyk. 1994. Microplate capture, rotation of the western Transverse Ranges, and initiation of the San Andreas transform as a low-angle fault system. Geology 22:491-495.

Nolf, B. and P. Nolf. 1969. Santa Cruz Island Volcanics. Pages 85-90 *in* Weaver, D. W., D. P. Doerner and B. Nolf (eds.), Geology of the Northern Channel Islands. Pacific Sections, American Association of Petroleum Geologists and Society of Economic Paleontologists and Mineralogists Special Publication.

Norris, R. M. 1991. A visit to Santa Barbara Island. California Geology, July:147-151.

Norris, R. M. 1995. Little Anacapa Island. California Geology, January/February:3-9.

Nuccio, R. M. and J. J. Wooley. 1998. Sedimentology of the Miocene Beecher's Bay Formation, Santa Rosa Island, California. Pages 91-101 *in* Weigand, P. W. (ed.), Contributions to the geology of the northern Channel Islands, southern California. Pacific Section American Association of Petroleum Geologists Miscellaneous Publication 45.

Olmsted, F. H. 1958. Geologic reconnaissance of San Clemente Island, California. U. S. Geological Survey Bulletin 1071-B:55-68.

Savage, K. L. and P. W. Weigand. 1994. Petrology and geochemistry of the volcanic clasts from the Miocene Blanca Formation, Santa Cruz Island, California. Pages 245-253 *in* Halvorson, W. L. and G. J. Maender (eds.), The fourth California Islands Symposium: Update on the status of resources. Santa Barbara Museum of Natural History, Santa Barbara, CA.

Savage, K. L. and P. W. Weigand. 1997. The petrogenesis of the of the mid-Miocene Conejo Volcanics, Western Santa Monica Mountains, California– calc-alkaline magmatism in an extensional environment. Geological Society of America, Abstracts with Program, Cordilleran Section 29: 62.

Scholl, D. W. 1960. Relationship of the insular shelf sediments to the sedimentary environments and geology of Anacapa Island, California. Journal of Sedimentary Petrology 30:123-139.

Smith, W. S. T. 1898. A geological sketch of San Clemente Island. U. S. Geological Survey 18th Annual Report 2:459-496.

Stewart, B. W., G. E. Bebout and M. Grove. 1992. Miocene magmatism in a transcurrent tectonic setting: Isotopic data from Santa Catalina Island. EOS Transactions of the American Geophysical Union 73:338.

Thompson, R. N., Morrison, M. A., Hendry, G. L., and Parks, S. J. 1984. An assessment of the relative roles of crust and mantle in magma genesis: An elemental approach. Philosophical Transactions of the Royal Society of London: Series A. 310:549-590.

Turner, D. L. 1970. Potassium-argon dating of Pacific Coast Foraminiferal Stages. Geological Society of America Special Paper 124:91-129.

Vedder, J. G. and R. M. Norris. 1963. Geology of San Nicolas Island California. U. S. Geological Survey Professional Paper 360, 65 p.

Vedder, J. G. and D. G. Howell. 1976. Neogene strata of the southern group of Channel Islands, California. Pages 47-52 *in* Howell, D. G. (ed.), Aspects of the geologic history of the California Continental Borderland. Pacific Section American Association of Petroleum Geologists Miscellaneous Publication 24.

Vedder, J. G., D. G. Howell and J. A. Forman. 1979. Miocene strata and their relation to other rocks, Santa Catalina California. Pages 239-257 *in* Armentrout, J. M., M. R. Cole and H. TerBest, Jr. (eds.), Cenozoic paleogeography of the Western United States. Pacific Section Society of Economic Paleontologists and Mineralogists, Pacific Coast Paleogeography Symposium 3.

Vedder, J. G., H. G. Greene, S. H. Clarke and M. P. Kennedy. 1986. Geologic map of the mid-southern California continental margin. *In* Greene, H. G. and M. P. Kennedy (eds.), Geologic map series of the California continental margin. California Division of Mines and Geology. Plate 2A, scale 1:250,000.

Weaver, D. W. and D. P. Doerner. 1969. Mid-Tertiary Stratigraphy, San Miguel Island. Pages 80-83 *in* Weaver, D. W., D. P. Doerner and B. Nolf (eds.), Geology of the Northern Channel Islands. Pacific Sections, American Association of Petroleum Geologists and Society of Economic Paleontologists and Mineralogists, Special Publication.

Weaver, D. W. and B. Nolf (directors and compilers). 1969. Geology of Santa Cruz Island (map). *In* Weaver, D. W., D. P. Doerner and B. Nolf (eds.), Geology of the Northern Channel Islands. Pacific Sections American Association of Petroleum Geologists and Society of Economic Paleontologists and Mineralogists Special Publication, scale: 1:24,000.

Weaver, D. W., G. Griggs, D. V. McClure and J. R. McKey. 1969. Volcaniclastic sequence, south-central Santa Cruz Island. Pages 85-90 *in* Weaver, D. W., D. P. Doerner and B. Nolf (eds.), Geology of the Northern Channel Islands. Pacific Sections, American Association of Petroleum Geologists and Society of Economic Paleontologists and Mineralogists, Special Publication.

Weigand, P. W. 1982. Middle Cenozoic volcanism of the western Transverse Ranges. Pages 170-188 *in* Fife, D. L. and J. A. Minch (eds.), Geology and mineral wealth of the California Transverse Ranges. Santa Ana, CA, South Coast Geological Society.

Weigand, P. W. 1993. Geochemistry and origin of middle Miocene volcanic rocks from Santa Cruz and Anacapa Islands, southern California Borderland. Pages 21-37 *in* Hochberg, F. G. (ed.), Recent advances in California island research: Santa Barbara Museum of Natural History, Santa Barbara, CA.

Weigand, P. W. 1994. Petrology and geochemistry of the Miocene volcanic rocks on Santa Catalina and San Clemente Islands, California. Pages 268-280 *in* Halvorson, W. L. and G. J. Maender (eds.), The fourth California Islands Symposium: Update on the status of resources. Santa Barbara Museum of Natural History, Santa Barbara, CA.

Weigand, P. W., K. L. Savage, T. Reid and B. D. Chinn. 1998. Composition of volcanic rocks on Santa Rosa, San Miguel, and Santa Barbara Islands, California. Pages 37-47 *in* Weigand, P. W. (ed.), Contributions to the geology of the northern Channel Islands, Southern California. Pacific Section American Association of Petroleum Geologists Miscellaneous Publication 45.

Wood, W. R. 1981. Geology, petrography, and geochemistry of the Santa Catalina Island volcanic rocks, Black Jack Peak to Whitley's Peak area [M. S. thesis]. Los Angeles, California State University, 146 p.

GEOLOGY OF SANTA ROSA ISLAND, CALIFORNIA

Thomas W. Dibblee, Jr.[1,2] and Helmut E. Ehrenspeck[2]

[1]Department of Geological Sciences, U.C. Santa Barbara, Santa Barbara, CA 93106
[2]Dibblee Geological Foundation, P.O. Box 60560, Santa Barbara, CA 93160
(805) 968-0481, E-mail: helmut98@earthlink.net

ABSTRACT

Santa Rosa Island consists of 220 km² of grass-covered hilly terrain, severely dissected by narrow canyons, eroded into mostly marine sedimentary formations of Eocene to middle Miocene age. Over much of the northern and western part of the island, these formations are beveled and covered by marine terraces, and a veneer of Pleistocene alluvium and wind-deposited dunes and drift sand.

The sedimentary sequence in ascending order is as follows: Eocene marine South Point Formation and Cozy Dell Shale; unconformably overlain by Oligocene-lower Miocene terrestrial Sespe Formation; conformably overlain by lower Miocene marine Vaqueros Sandstone and Rincon Claystone; conformably overlain by middle Miocene marine Monterey Shale containing the Santa Rosa Island Volcanics, a newly named sequence of marine volcaniclastic rocks; grading upward into middle Miocene marine Beechers Bay Formation of mostly tuffaceous sandstone, locally containing San Onofre Breccia, and minor volcanic conglomerate upsection. The exposed sequence aggregates roughly 2,000 m, with an additional 3,400 m of marine clastic rocks of Eocene to late Cretaceous age encountered in deep test drilling. The entire sequence up through the lower Monterey Shale is intruded by pods and sills of basalt-diabase.

The island is bisected by the east-west-striking Santa Rosa Island fault of left-slip movement, as indicated by deflected stream courses. Left slip of as much as 11 km is indicated by displaced rock units. A south-side-up component is evident from the generally higher and more rugged terrane south of the fault, and from exposure of the older formations only on that side of the fault.

North of the Santa Rosa Island fault, Miocene formations are folded along the Tecolote-Black Mountain anticline and subparallel Beechers Bay syncline farther north. South of the fault, the Miocene formations are compressed along the paired, northwest- to west-trending Soledad anticline and Pedregosa syncline, with adjacent minor subparallel faults. Complexly faulted and folded Eocene formations are exposed along the southwest and south coastal part of the island.

Keywords: Santa Rosa Island, Northern Channel Islands, Santa Barbara Channel, southern California, geology, structural geology, stratigraphy, geologic map, geologic history, physiography, Santa Rosa Island fault, tectonics.

INTRODUCTION

Previous Investigations

The earliest published geologic mapping investigation on Santa Rosa Island was by Kew (1927). During that time, major oil discoveries on the nearby mainland north of the Santa Barbara Channel spurred private exploration and geologic mapping on Santa Rosa Island by many oil companies to determine its oil potential (Daily 1998). One such geologic mapping investigation was by the lead author in 1938 largely on the north side of the island.

In the early 1960s, D. W. Weaver and others at the University of California at Santa Barbara (UCSB) conducted extensive geologic research on San Miguel, Santa Rosa, and Santa Cruz islands, resulting in a volume compiled by Weaver et al. (1969), which includes a detailed geologic map of Santa Rosa Island by Sonneman et al. (1969).

Many aspects of the geology of all the California Channel Islands were addressed in a volume edited by Howell (1976). The most recent collection of papers focusing on the geology of the Northern Channel Islands is that edited by Weigand (1998).

Purpose

The purpose of field investigations in 1996 and 1997 by Thomas W. Dibblee, Jr., John J. Woolley, and Helmut E. Ehrenspeck was to provide an updated geologic map (Dibblee et al. 1998) of Santa Rosa Island, similar to more than 80 full-color geologic quadrangles of coastal southern California published by the Dibblee Geological Foundation since 1986. A companion report on the geology of Santa Rosa Island (Dibblee and Ehrenspeck 1998) followed the publication of the map. This article and illustrations in this paper (Figures 1 through 4) are modified from that report.

PHYSIOGRAPHY

Santa Rosa Island, second largest of the four Northern Channel Islands, lies on an east-trending submerged platform extending eastward to the Santa Monica Mountains. Santa Rosa Island is slightly south of the Northern Channel Islands alignment and is diamond-shaped in outline. At 28 km long and up to 13 km wide, it is the widest of these islands, with an area of 217 km².

This island is a grass-covered hilly terrane dissected by narrow canyons and bordered on all but the eastern shoreline by steep wave-cut cliffs. Santa Rosa is bisected by the east-west-striking Santa Rosa Island fault (SRIF), which divides the island into two subequal halves of different physiography. The SRIF appears prominently on aerial photographs and topographic maps as a lineament, along which north-draining canyons from the south half of the island are deflected westward as they cross the fault (Figure 1).

Much of the north half of the island is sand-covered old marine terrace sloping gently northward from a dissected east-west trending ridge of bedrock hills elevated just north of the SRIF. The ridge reaches its high point of 396 m (1,298 ft) at Black Mountain. This ridge and adjacent terrace are dissected by narrow, steep-sided canyons, many of which drain northerly from the south half of the island.

Southern Santa Rosa Island is somewhat larger, higher, and more rugged, eroded to a terrane of ridges and drainage divides, with subdued crests of about 300 to 500 m elevation, separated by steep-sided, V-shaped canyons.

The main crest of the island strikes east-west from its east end almost to its west end, and is parallel to, and about 1.5 km south of, the SRIF. Near the center of the island, this crest reaches an inconspicuous high point of 479 m (1,574 ft) at Soledad Peak and 483 m (1,589 ft) at nearby Vail Peak (Figure 1).

GEOLOGIC SETTING

Santa Rosa Island and the other three Northern Channel Islands protrude from an east-west trending submerged platform about 125 km long, which continues eastward to the Santa Monica Mountains. Together, these features form the southern boundary of the western Transverse Ranges. The island exposes some 2,000 m of mostly marine sedimentary and volcaniclastic rocks of middle Miocene to Eocene age (Figure 2). A deep test well near its south coast penetrated an additional 3,400 m of marine sedimentary rock of Eocene, Paleocene, and late Cretaceous(?) age. Presumably, this thick stratified sequence overlies oceanic basement at a depth greater than 3,370 m below sea level.

On Santa Rosa Island, the Tertiary bedrock formations are generally tilted gently to the northeast, with subordinate folds of west to northwest-trending axial traces. The east-striking, near-vertical SRIF is the only major fault that completely transects this island; other faults are of local extent only.

North of the SRIF, only the Miocene part of the sedimentary sequence is exposed, and it is gently compressed into easterly trending folds. The sequence is broken by several minor faults parallel to the SRIF.

South of the SRIF, the entire Tertiary stratigraphic sequence is exposed. The oldest units crop out on the south coast and are overlain by progressively younger units to the

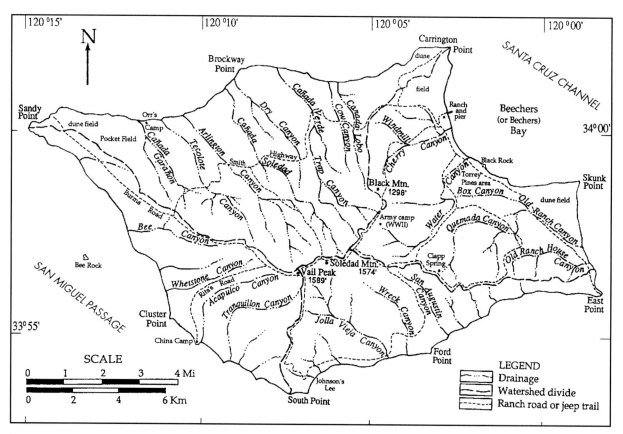

Figure 1. Drainage map of Santa Rosa Island, showing watershed divides, ranch roads, and major island locations. Note aligned canyons near the middle of the island which are deflected along the Santa Rosa Island fault.

northeastern coast. This sequence is compressed into a pair of subparallel southeast-trending folds. Near the south coast, the oldest exposed rocks, chiefly Eocene, are complexly disrupted by local faults of varying strikes.

ROCK UNITS

Pre-Cenozoic Crustal Basement Rocks

Crystalline basement rocks of pre-Cenozoic age are not exposed on Santa Rosa Island, but are deeply buried beneath a great thickness of Cenozoic sedimentary formations. The nearest pre-Cenozoic basement rocks are exposed on Santa Cruz Island and consist of fine-grained chlorite schist of probable Mesozoic age and diorite of late Mesozoic age (Weaver et al. 1969; Hill 1976).

Cenozoic Stratified Rock Sequence

Santa Rosa Island exposes mostly Tertiary stratified rocks (Figure 3). The oldest exposed rocks are of marine sedimentary origin, of Eocene age, and exposed near the south coast. Including an additional Eocene to Cretaceous (?) sequence known only from deep test drilling, over 3,350 m of these subsurface strata are present on this island (Figure 2).

Most of the island is underlain by sedimentary and volcaniclastic rocks of early to middle Miocene age. These rocks were deposited under subaerial to moderately deep marine conditions. As much as 2100 m of these Miocene rocks are exposed on this island and they represent the youngest consolidated strata on the island. Marine sedimentary rocks of Pliocene-Pleistocene age were deposited in local basins, but are not present on the Northern Channel Islands.

South Point Formation and Older Rocks (Eocene to Cretaceous(?) Age)

The oldest rock unit exposed on Santa Rosa Island is a marine sandstone unit named the South Point Formation by Weaver and Doerner (1969) for its exposures along the south coastal part of the island. Smaller outcrops also exist just south of the SRIF on western Santa Rosa Island (Dibblee et al. 1998). Only the upper 300 m of this formation are exposed on the island, but its total thickness of about 1,000 m is known from deep exploratory test holes on the island.

The South Point Formation is composed of hard, light gray, fine- to medium-grained, arkosic (feldspar-rich) sandstone in strata roughly 1 m thick, separated by thin partings of softer sandstone or gray, crumbly, micaceous shale. The sandstone weathers to a light brown color and, in places, contains brown, iron-rich concretions up to 1 m in diameter. The sandstone is devoid of molluscan fossils. Due to its hardness, the South Point Formation resists weathering and erosion.

Depositional Environment, Provenance and Age. The arkosic sandstones of the South Point Formation were derived from continental granitic basement terrane. A lack of

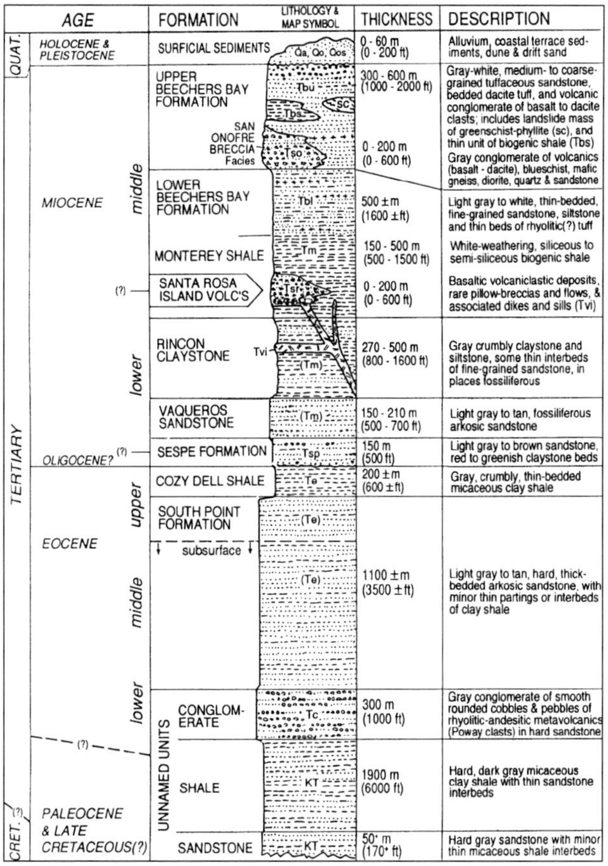

Figure 2. Stratigraphic column of Santa Rosa Island, using same formation symbols as in Figure 3.

molluscan remains suggests deposition in deep water, far from the shoreline. The massiveness and evenly fine-grained texture of the sandstone strata indicates deposition of sand-flow turbidites in a middle submarine fan environment. Crumpled bedding and other sedimentary structures indicate a paleoslope generally to the present-day north (Weaver and Doerner 1969).

Conglomerates in and below the South Point Formation (Figure 2) are composed of distinctive, smoothly rounded cobbles strikingly similar to the Eocene "Poway" conglomerates of the San Diego area. Over 30% of coarse sand grains within the South Point Formation have Poway-type compositions (Abbott et al. 1983).

Foraminiferal faunas in the South Point Formation are diagnostic of the Ulatisian and Narizian stages, or a middle Eocene age (Weaver and Do'erner 1969).

Cozy Dell Shale (Late Eocene Age)

Conformably overlying the South Point Formation is a thin, gray, marine shale unit, named by Weaver and Doerner (1969) as the Cozy Dell Shale for its similarities to the Cozy Dell Shale of the Santa Ynez Mountains. A complete section of this shale is exposed at several places along the south coastal part of the island, where it is up to 120 m thick. This unit is missing in the southwestern part of the island, where

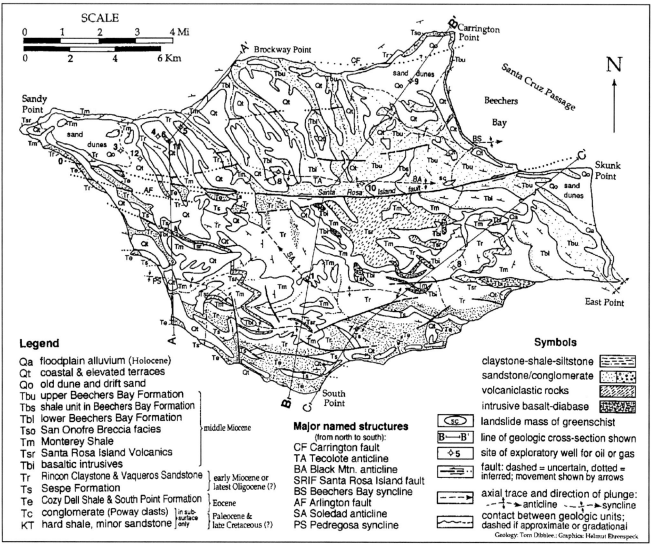

Figure 3. Generalized geologic map of Santa Rosa Island; for exploratory drill sites 0-12, see Dibblee et al. 1998.

the South Point Formation is disconformably overlain by the nonmarine Sespe Formation (Dibblee et al. 1998).

The Cozy Dell Shale ranges from highly fractured micaceous claystone to siltstone. It weathers brownish-gray at the surface and disintegrates so readily it is rarely exposed, except in canyon bottoms. It weathers to soft, clayey soil and forms a distinct topography of rounded grassy hills and slopes.

According to Weaver and Doerner (1969), the microfauna of the Cozy Dell Shale indicate a late Eocene age and suggest deposition under bathyal conditions.

Sespe Formation (Latest Oligocene(?)-Early Miocene Age)

Santa Rosa Island is the only Channel Island on which this terrestrial formation, so extensive on the mainland, exists. This formation is exposed only in the south part of the island and in fault slivers along the western SRIF (Figure 3).

The Sespe Formation is only about 150 m thick and thins eastward. It unconformably overlies the Cozy Dell Shale or South Point Formation with no visible discordance and is, in turn, overlain by the Vaqueros Sandstone, and in places, grades upward into it.

As described by Woolley (1978; 1998a), the Sespe Formation is mostly arkosic sandstone, silty mudstone, and granitic and volcanic conglomerate, with thin interbeds of green to red claystone. It is reddish and conglomeratic in exposures west of Johnson's Lee, but thins eastward and grades to a gray marine sandstone similar to the overlying Vaqueros Sandstone.

Depositional Environment, Provenance, and Age. The Sespe Formation was deposited as alluvium on a coastal floodplain when this area was elevated slightly above sea level by regional tectonic events (Dibblee 1982a, b; 1995) possibly coupled with worldwide sea level changes (Atwater 1998). Sediments were derived largely from a now-distant Mesozoic granitic and volcanic terrane of the Peninsular Ranges of the San Diego area (Woolley 1998a).

Sedimentary structures in the Sespe Formation indicate sediment transport to the present-day north (Weaver and Doerner 1969; Woolley 1998a). These data indicate that the Sespe of this island was not derived from the nearby mainland, but was linked, prior to regional tectonic rotation, to the Sespe Formation of the Santa Ana Mountains, now far distant.

Because the Sespe Formation interfingers both upward and laterally with the lower Miocene Vaqueros Sandstone, the Sespe is probably of early Miocene age, but could be as old as latest Oligocene.

Vaqueros Sandstone (Early Miocene Age)

The Vaqueros Sandstone is a shallow marine, locally fossiliferous sandstone that conformably overlies the Sespe Formation and underlies the Rincon Claystone. This unit is about 120 m in average thickness, which varies because the Vaqueros Sandstone interfingers with both the underlying Sespe and the overlying Rincon Claystone. In the southwestern part of the island, the Vaqueros thickens appreciably because the lower part of the Rincon Claystone interfingers westward into it. These two units are difficult to separate and therefore are shown undifferentiated on Figure 3.

The Vaqueros Sandstone is moderately lithified, light yellowish-gray, fine- to medium-grained, arkosic, weakly bedded to massive, and locally pebbly. Pebbles are compositionally similar to those in the Sespe.

Depositional Environment, Provenance, and Age.
The shallow marine Vaqueros Sandstone sequence marks the marine transgression, or flooding, over the Sespe floodplain. Current indicators show sediment transport was to the north (Woolley 1998a). Locally, the Vaqueros Sandstone contains abundant shallow marine fossils diagnostic of an early Miocene age (Avila and Weaver 1969).

The consistent transport directions and the predominantly sandy composition of the Vaqueros, Sespe, and South Point Formations indicate that these were derived from a common source terrane, namely the Peninsular Ranges region, and that Santa Rosa Island was part of the western Transverse Ranges crustal block, later to be horizontally rotated more than 90 degrees clockwise away from that region (Woolley 1998a).

Rincon Claystone (Early Miocene Age)

The Rincon Claystone directly overlies the Vaqueros Sandstone and is composed mostly of massive gray micaceous claystone, locally containing rust-colored dolomitic concretions. On Santa Rosa, this unit contains fine-grained blueschist detritus (Avila and Weaver 1969), unlike that on the nearby mainland.

Where exposed, it crumbles with ellipsoidal fracture and weathers to gray, adobe-like soil. Its grassy slopes are easily eroded and subject to landslides and soil slips.

This formation is exposed on both sides of the SRIF. To the north, it crops out extensively between Arlington and Garañon Canyons and near Carrington Point. To the south,

it is the most widely exposed formation on the island (Dibblee et al. 1998). The Rincon Claystone averages about 450 m in thickness, but, south of the SRIF, it thins westward by grading laterally into the Vaqueros Sandstone (Woolley 1978).

This formation contains some thick beds of fine-grained sandstone that appear to be interfingers from the Vaqueros Sandstone. Some of these strata contain abundant fossil oysters, indicating deposition in very shallow water. Other sandstone interbeds contain a diverse molluscan fauna characteristic of deeper-water, inner shelf deposition (Avila and Weaver 1969). The molluscan and foraminiferal assemblages both indicate an early Miocene age, mostly Saucesian stage (Weaver and Doerner 1969).

Monterey Shale (Early Middle Miocene Age)

A thin unit of cream-white, weathered, semi-siliceous to siliceous, biogenic shale conformably overlies the Rincon Claystone. This shale was formerly included in the Rincon Formation by Sonneman et al. (1969), but it is so similar in lithology and age to the lower Monterey Shale of the nearby mainland, that we assign it to the Monterey Shale. It ranges in thickness from about 90 to 200 m, but may be as thick as 250 m in the southwestern part of the island. This shale unit is somewhat more resistant to erosion than the underlying Rincon Claystone.

On both sides of the SRIF, the Monterey Shale includes a unit of volcanic rocks, the Santa Rosa Island Volcanics, near or at the base. The Monterey Shale directly below the volcanics contains a microfauna assigned to the late Saucesian stage, or "late early" Miocene age; the part above the volcanics contains a Relizian microfauna, of early middle Miocene age (Weaver and Doerner 1969).

The Monterey Shale represents biogenic deposition in a deep offshore basin isolated from most terrigenous sediment input.

Santa Rosa Island Volcanics (Early Middle Miocene Age)

Basaltic volcaniclastic rocks within the basal Monterey Shale on Santa Rosa Island were previously assigned to the San Miguel Volcanics by Weaver and Doerner (1969). However, the volcanics on Santa Rosa Island are not correlative with those of San Miguel Island because the latter include andesitic-dacitic rocks not found on Santa Rosa Island.

We have therefore renamed these entirely basaltic volcanic rocks for their namesake island and designated the type section as the thickest and most complete section exposed south of the SRIF; along the central divide, this section is located between the major eastward and northwestward drainages (Figure1) (Dibblee et al. 1998).

Extrusive Rocks.
The volcanic breccias exposed in the type area are most unusual and not seen elsewhere in southern California (Dibblee and Ehrenspeck 1998). They consist of gray-brown, crudely bedded strata composed entirely of basalt fragments embedded in basaltic rubble or sandstone. The presence of scattered oyster shells and occasional

pillow basalt fragments with chilled subvitreous margins indicate marine deposition.

This volcaniclastic unit was probably derived from flows shattered during contact with seawater, then transported, perhaps as debris flows into the deep marine environment of Monterey Shale deposition. This unit is up to 500 m thick near Soledad Mountain and exists within the lower Monterey Shale. Eastward along strike, and to the south and west, the Santa Rosa Island Volcanics thin to only a few tens of meters or less. The rapid thinning of this volcanic pile in most directions suggests that it was erupted and emplaced locally and is not a widespread unit.

Intrusive Rocks. Closely associated with the Santa Rosa Island Volcanics are scattered, shallow-intrusive feeder dikes, sills, and pods, as described by Dibblee and Ehrenspeck (1998). Most of these are intruded into the Rincon Claystone or lower Monterey Shale; a few dikes exist in the older formations. The largest intrusions are shown on the geologic map (Dibblee et al. 1998).

Age of Santa Rosa Island Volcanics. Two intrusions on Santa Rosa Island were dated at about 19 to 18 million years (Ma), or early Miocene age (Luyendyk et al. 1998). Volcanism must have persisted considerably beyond that time, because basaltic intrusions inject the lower Monterey Shale, of late Saucesian age (circa 18 to17 Ma), and the Santa Rosa Island Volcanics exist within the lower Monterey Shale.

Beechers Bay Formation (Middle Miocene Age)

On both sides of the SRIF, the Monterey Shale grades upward into a thick sequence of marine volcaniclastic rocks; the lower part is fine-grained, the upper part is mostly coarse-grained. The rocks range from tuffaceous shale-siltstone to volcanic conglomerate, with sandstone the predominant facies.

These clastic sediments are lithologically very different from the biogenic Monterey Shale, even though they are of similar age. Because these tuffaceous sediments are so unlike the biogenic siliceous Monterey Shale, Nuccio (1977) designated them as the Beechers Bay Formation, and we follow this designation.

On both sides of the SRIF, the clastic sedimentary series above the siliceous Monterey Shale is readily divisible into two parts. The lower part is thin bedded, gray to white, fine-grained sandstone-siltstone, roughly 500 m thick, which we designated as the lower Beechers Bay Formation. This unit grades upward into gray-white, coarse-grained, tuffaceous sandstones with local volcanic and "San Onofre" blueschist conglomerates, in total about 600 m thick (Figure 2). This part is designated as the upper Beechers Bay Formation (Dibblee et al. 1998). The entire sequence includes blueschist fragments and strata of white volcanic tuff throughout (Nuccio and Woolley 1998).

The entire Beechers Bay Formation, especially the upper part, includes complex and abrupt lateral facies variations in which fine-grained sediments grade laterally into coarse-grained sediments, and vice versa. These are interpreted to represent deposition in various parts of a growing submarine fan complex (Nuccio and Woolley 1998). Spectacular soft-sediment structures in both units indicate a consistent westerly sediment-transport direction from sources to the present-day east (Avila and Weaver 1969).

San Onofre Breccia Facies of Beechers Bay Formation. A highly unusual conglomeratic unit is exposed at the base of the upper Beechers Bay Formation near Carrington Point. It is up to 200 m thick and contains a diverse assemblage of volcanic, plutonic and metamorphic (blueschist) detritus (Figure 2). This unit was mapped by Sonneman et al. (1969) as the San Onofre Breccia, for its similarities to the type unit described near Oceanside, California. The age of the San Onofre Breccia facies on this island was uncertain until Chinn and Weigand (1994) obtained a radiometric date of circa 15.8 Ma, or early middle Miocene, from a dacite clast within that facies.

Upper Beechers Bay Formation. This unit is exposed along the north and northeast coasts of Santa Rosa Island on both sides of the SRIF, is roughly 600 m thick, and is composed mainly of gray-white volcaniclastic sandstone that coarsens upsection. It is prominently bedded with alternating hard and softer strata, of which the hard layers protrude where weathered.

Schist Landslide Mass. About 2 km east of Black Mountain, the upper Beechers Bay Formation encloses an unusual pod-like mass of rusty brown-weathered, brecciated rock, identified as chlorite-phyllite or chlorite schist (Kamerling 1994). The rock is very similar to the Santa Cruz Island Schist and, apparently, is a unique landslide mass within the Beechers Bay sandstone, emplaced from an unknown source.

Volcanic Conglomerates. The uppermost Beechers Bay Formation includes massive volcanic conglomerates, mostly andesite, dacite and rhyolite (Weigand et al.1998), pumiceous vitrophyre, and basalt. Spectacular exposures of these conglomerates occur at Black Rock, northeast of Water Canyon. At this location, the conglomeratic sediments appear to be mixed with, or locally injected by, basaltic lava.

Age and Provenance of Beechers Bay Formation. The radiometric age of about 15.8 Ma, early middle Miocene, obtained by Chinn and Weigand (1994) agrees with the Luisian microfaunal age, early middle Miocene, obtained by Avila and Weaver (1969).

Petrologic studies by Nuccio (1977) and Nuccio and Woolley (1998) indicate that this entire formation was derived from a then-nearby source area of active volcanism. The presence of blueschist fragments throughout the formation indicates that metamorphic oceanic basement was being exposed and eroded during that time. The upward coarsening of this formation indicates increasing relief of the volcanic source area.

Nuccio and Woolley (1998) concluded that the most likely volcanic source was in the vicinity of what is now Santa Catalina Island, where basaltic through dacitic volcanic rocks intrude and overlie Catalina blueschist basement. If this was the source area, the Santa Rosa Island area has since been shifted many kilometers northwestward with respect to that area.

Late Quaternary Sediments (Pleistocene to Recent Age)

Late Quaternary surficial deposits on Santa Rosa Island consist of alluvium that fills the flood plains of major canyons, older dissected alluvial deposits on wave-cut terraces, old inactive dune fields, and thin but extensive wind-deposited "drift" sand. These unconsolidated sediments were derived from the island itself, long after the older marine Tertiary formations of which it is composed were emerged and elevated in several stages during Pliocene-Pleistocene time, and are now eroded to low relief.

Landslides. Only moderate to large-sized landslides were mapped (Dibblee et al. 1998), and most of these exist in the Monterey Shale and Beechers Bay Formation, especially on steep slopes. An enormous number of small landslides or soil-slips on Santa Rosa Island could not be recorded at a map scale of 1:24000.

The most unusual landslide is the Lobo Canyon block slide (Dibblee et al. 1998), in which a 27-acre block of Beechers Bay Formation slid along a failed bedding plane into Lobo Canyon, as documented by Woolley (1994). The triggering event appears to have been the 1812 Santa Barbara Channel earthquake.

Alluvium. Surficial deposits mapped include two types: 1) alluvium that fills the bottoms and narrow flood plains of present drainages, and 2) widespread alluvial cover over the low, broad marine terraces (Figure 3) (Dibblee et al. 1998). Both types are gray-brown, reworked soil, sand and gravel, crudely bedded, and derived from the bedrock slopes. The stream-bottom alluvium typically is several meters thick and fills the lower parts of canyons to levels that vary with each canyon. The alluvial terrace material ranges from a few meters thick to locally in excess of 30 m. In many locations, the terrace alluvium yields disseminated bones of pygmy mammoth (*Mammuthus exilis*) (Agenbroad 1998).

In many canyons, the alluvial terrace is dissected by its main stream into a vertical-sided gully or barranca, from 3 to 30 m deep and similarly wide. Most of this island's barranca formation apparently occurred from the1840s to about 1900, coinciding with a period of overgrazing of the island by sheep. The earliest known photos of the island, taken around 1900, show the deep barrancas already in place, little different from today (Woolley 1998b).

Dunes and Drift Sand. The lower, wave-cut platforms of Santa Rosa Island are covered by a thin veneer of sand, now stabilized by vegetation. In late Pleistocene time, beach sand was widely eroded and redeposited as dune fields and drift sand. Locally, as at Carrington Point, extensive dune fields were formed (Figure 3), with sand up to 50 m thick. Partial to complete remains of pygmy mammoths have been found in dune sand (Woolley 1998b), including one near Carrington Point, dated at circa 12,800 years (Agenbroad 1998).

Wave-cut Platforms (Marine Terraces). Seven distinct terrace levels are recognized on Santa Rosa Island, more than on any of the other three Northern Channel Islands. They range in elevation from about 6 to 300 m (Orr 1960; Figure 9 in Vedder and Howell 1980). The most extensive platforms are the 6-m and the 15 to 20-m terraces, which we mapped, undifferentiated, around most of the island (Figure 3) (Dibblee et al. 1998). While some of these terraces are covered by drift sand or alluvium, others contain marine fossil remains. These have been used to infer late Pleistocene uplift rates for the island, and to extrapolate ages of older, higher terraces. If such interpretations are correct, the age of prominent 150-to180-m terrace remnants on the north side of Santa Rosa Island may be between 0.9 and1.1 Ma old (Colson et al. 1995).

GEOLOGIC STRUCTURE

Regional Structure of Northern Channel Islands Platform

Santa Rosa Island is a small elevated part of a large east-west trending submerged platform that includes all of the Northern Channel Islands. This platform is a broad, east-trending anticlinal uplift of a thick series of upper Mesozoic and Cenozoic sedimentary and volcanic rocks, deposited on a crustal basement platform of Mesozoic metamorphic and plutonic igneous rocks.

The sedimentary rocks on this platform are gently compressed into folds that trend generally west-northwest. This deformation is the local effect of regional crustal compression during the Pliocene to Recent Coast Range orogeny, which uplifted the platform from the submerged shelf that is now the southern California borderland.

The greatest amount of regional uplift on this platform during the Coast Range orogeny appears to have been along the Santa Cruz Island Fault (SCIF), and significantly less on the Santa Rosa Island fault (SRIF). Movement on both faults has been mainly left-slip. The SRIF is of lesser magnitude and appears to curve northeastward and die out under Santa Cruz Passage before reaching Santa Cruz Island (Junger 1976). To the west, it projects northwestward beyond the south side of San Miguel Island before it dies out (Junger 1979; Figure 1).

Structure of Santa Rosa Island

The generalized structure of Santa Rosa Island is shown on Figure 3 and on the geologic cross-sections of Figure 4. The SRIF bisects this island into a northern and southern structural block.

121

Northern Structural Block

The structure of the northern block, up to 6 km wide, is comparatively simple. At the surface, Miocene formations are regionally tilted north to northeastward away from the SRIF but, in large part, are anticlinally folded near the fault by the Tecolote-Black Mountain anticline. Westward, the narrow south flank of this anticline is faulted out within the SRIF zone. The anticline is structurally highest or "domed" in its western part, where it exposes the Rincon Claystone. To the east, successively higher strata of the Monterey Shale and Beechers Bay Formation are involved as this anticline plunges eastward through Black Mountain.

Farther north, the Miocene strata are weakly folded into the Beechers Bay syncline, which plunges easterly toward that bay (Figure 3). Eastward and offshore under Santa Cruz Passage, this syncline terminates in the Carrington Basin.

The weakly folded Miocene formations of the north block of Santa Rosa Island are broken by many minor high-angle faults of inferred left-slip movement (Sorlien et al. 1998) parallel and probably related to the east-striking SRIF. None of these faults are traceable for more than a few kilometers; they are exposed in some canyons but not on the intervening terraces. These faults, including the Carrington fault (Figure 3), predate the surficial cover, and none appear to be active.

Southern Structural Block

The structure of the southern block of Santa Rosa Island, as wide as 8 km onshore, is more complex. This block progressively exposes Eocene to Miocene formations northeastward as these formations dip generally in that direction. However, the formations are also folded along axes that trend generally west-northwest.

The most extensive fold is the Soledad anticline (Figure 3), which involves mostly Rincon Shale of the central part of this block. The fold axis trends northwestward, diagonal to the SRIF, across much of this block. Its northeast flank involves progressively younger Miocene formations that all dip northeast at low angles. Northwestward, the anticline is complexly involved with the SRIF zone, where it exposes slivers of the Vaqueros Sandstone to South Point Formations, both repeatedly faulted (Figure 4, cross-section A-A') (Dibblee et al. 1998; Figure 3).

The Soledad anticline is flanked on the southwest by the Pedregosa syncline, which is mostly within the Monterey

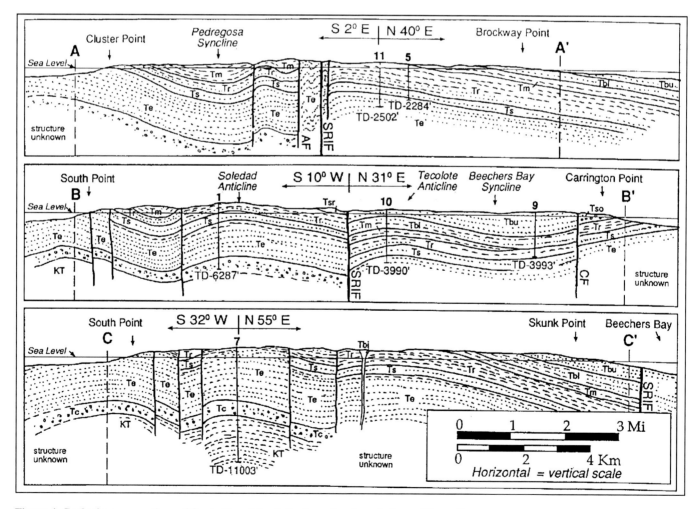

Figure 4. Geologic cross-sections of Santa Rosa Island; for legend and symbols, see Figure 3.

Shale and extends westward offshore. This syncline is off-set by a north-south fault (Figure 3).

The southernmost, coastal part of this block exposes the South Point, Cozy Dell, and Sespe Formations. In local areas, these formations are complexly folded but regionally dip northward at low to moderate angles. The high-angle faults that disrupt these rocks are of variable strikes, though generally parallel to the coastline.

Santa Rosa Island Fault

The Santa Rosa Island fault (SRIF) is one of the only two known major onshore faults of the Northern Channel Islands (Dibblee 1982a; b). It bisects the island in a nearly straight line with a slight northward curve to the west and east (Figure 3), and is readily apparent on aerial photos and topographic maps.

The SRIF is not exposed because it occupies a wide zone of gouge and crushed bedrock that is almost completely weathered to a thick cover of soil. No fresh exposures are seen, not even in the coastal terrace outcrops where it extends offshore. The SRIF is a single strand except along its western segment, where it is flanked by several minor parallel strands.

Left-slip movement on this fault during Pleistocene time is clearly evident from two physiographic aspects. First, the present shape of the island on a map suggests that the entire terrane north of the fault is shifted westward several kilometers with respect to the terrane south of it (Figures 1 and 3). Secondly, most canyons that drain northward across the fault from the generally higher terrane to the south are deflected westward, some more than 1 km (Figure 1).

The total cumulative left-slip displacement on the SRIF can be estimated from the Miocene formations laterally displaced by it. For example, the Santa Rosa Island Volcanics exposed at the island's west end, at Sandy Point, north of the SRIF, are displaced westward about 12 km from the same unit exposed south of the fault.

A minor vertical component of south-side-up displacement on the SRIF is apparent in its western part, where the older (Vaqueros to South Point) formations on the south side are juxtaposed against the younger (Rincon and Monterey) formations on the north side (Dibblee et al. 1998). South-side-up displacement is also evident from the island's physiography in that the terrane south of the SRIF is generally higher than that of the north side. Also, remnants of the highest (150 to 180 m) marine terrace appear to be tilted northward just north of that fault, suggestive of drag folding along the fault, south side up.

The SRIF is of Pleistocene age. Its inception was probably in Pliocene time, well after deposition of the Miocene Beechers Bay and older formations it involves. Its latest movements postdate the canyons deflected or offset by them. Most of the upper Pleistocene and Holocene alluvium on the western part of the island appears to be unbroken by the fault, with the possible exception of an exposure of terrace alluvium south of Arlington Canyon that suggests Holocene movement (Colson et al. 1995).

SUMMARY OF GEOLOGIC HISTORY

Late Cretaceous(?) to Early Tertiary Marine Deposition

Deposition of clastic sediments began in Cretaceous(?)-Paleocene time on a subsiding platform of oceanic basement or Franciscan rocks. Over 3500 m of sediments derived from a granitic terrane accumulated, with the South Point Formation deposited as a submarine fan, and the Cozy Dell Shale deposited in a bathyal or basin-plain environment.

Late Oligocene to Early Miocene Emergence, Uplift, and Resubmergence

In latest Oligocene-early Miocene time, the submerged region emerged slightly above sea level to form a coastal plain covered by a thin veneer of nonmarine, streamlaid sediments of the Sespe Formation. Nonmarine deposition was followed by renewed subsidence and the deposition of marine sands and clays of the Vaqueros Sandstone and Rincon Claystone on a rapidly subsiding shelf of shallow to moderate depth, succeeded by deposition of deep marine biogenic sediments of the Monterey Shale.

Onset of Horizontal Clockwise Rotation in Early Middle Miocene

Consistent northward sedimen-transport directions obtained from the above pre-middle Miocene clastic formations indicate that these units could not have originated from the Ventura basin to the north. Instead, these directions support a model of clockwise tectonic rotation of the western Transverse Ranges block of more than 90° since middle Miocene time, based on paleomagnetic data (Kamerling and Luyendyk 1985; Luyendyk 1991; Atwater 1998). Much of this rotation occurred between 18 and 14 Ma, during Monterey Shale deposition.

Early Middle Miocene Volcanism and Marine Deposition

Local basaltic intrusive and brief volcanic activity forming the Santa Rosa Island Volcanics began around 19 to 18 Ma, concurrent with the regional deposition of biogenic Monterey Shale on a deeply submerged shelf or basin.

Locally, biogenic deposits gave way to marine volcaniclastic deposits of the Beechers Bay Formation by middle Miocene time, about 16 Ma ago. These rocks were derived from nearby, active, andesitic-dacitic volcanism. Concurrently, blueschist and other basement rocks, eroded from a nearby source, were incorporated into the volcaniclastic sediments.

Pliocene-Early Coast Range Orogeny

By Pliocene time (circa 5 Ma), after most rotation of the western Transverse Ranges block had occurred, compressive deformation of the early Coast Range orogeny began the development and possible emergence of the

Channel Islands platform, including what is now the Santa Rosa Island area. Pliocene marine sediments accumulated in local basins but not on the Channel Islands platform (Vedder and Howell 1980). Mainland mountain ranges began to be elevated by regional compressive deformation.

Pleistocene-Late Coast Range Orogeny

By early Pleistocene time (circa 1.6 Ma), regional contraction caused by the late Coast Range orogeny accelerated uplift of mainland mountain ranges and renewed uplift of the north Channel Islands platform (Dibblee 1995). By mid-Pleistocene time, the Santa Rosa Island area was uplifted, largely on the SRIF, which developed around that time. Local tectonic uplift, coupled with fluctuating sea levels during middle to late Pleistocene time, created a flight of wave-cut terraces on Santa Rosa, the oldest and highest of which may exceed 1 Ma in age (Colson et al. 1995).

Late Pleistocene to Recent Events

During sea-level lowstands associated with Pleistocene glacial episodes, Santa Rosa Island combined with adjacent islands into Santarosae, an island landmass many times its present area (Junger and Johnson 1980; Vedder and Howell 1980). Sometime in late Pleistocene time, probably during a sea-level lowstand, mammoths arrived on Santa Rosa Island and began to evolve to pygmy mammoths (Agenbroad 1998; Thaler 1998). After severely stripping the island of vegetation, pygmy mammoths became extinct around 12 thousand (ka) years ago (Woolley 1998b).

Since the maximum late Pleistocene lowstand of 18 ka, the effects of a rapid sea level rise of at least 120 m, coupled with wave erosion, reduced Santa Rosa Island to its present size. Sand eroded from beaches by prevailing west-northwest winds was deposited in several dune fields; eolianites and drift sand covered its lower slopes and marine terraces (Woolley 1998b).

The rapid sea-level advance ceased about 6 ka (Vedder and Howell 1980). Continued tectonic uplift since late Pleistocene time has elevated this island to its present height. Much of this uplift has occurred along the SRIF, with at least one surface rupture recorded in Holocene time (Colson et al. 1995). Left slip along this fault has significantly displaced all major drainages that cross it.

In the 1800s, introduction of sheep resulted in several decades of sharply accelerated island-wide erosion, causing the incisement of deep barrancas and dissection of alluvial terraces (Woolley 1998b). Removal of the sheep by about 1900 has enabled the vegetative recovery of much of Santa Rosa Island.

ACKNOWLEDGMENTS

We wish to acknowledge field assistance by the following persons: William J. Faulkner (naturalist), Howard R. Level and Roupen L. Zakarian (volunteer geologists), all from Channel Islands National Park, Ventura; Peter W. Weigand, geologist, and Sandra L. Jewett, chemist, both of California State University, Northridge (CSUN); and Wendy Lou Bartlett, geologist, UCSB. Field trips were guided by John J. Woolley, geologist, and member of the Vail family of Vail and Vickers, owners of Santa Rosa Island and of its ranching operation for nearly a century. Publication funding for this map was provided by the Dibblee Geological Foundation and the Santa Cruz Island Foundation of Santa Barbara, California, including its Santa Rosa Island Chapter.

LITERATURE CITED

Abbott, P. L., R. R. Kies, W. R. Bachman, and C. J. Natenstadt. 1983. A tectonic slice of Eocene strata, northern part of California Continental Borderland. Pages 151-170 in La Rue, D. K. and R. J. Steel (eds.), Cenozoic Marine Sedimentation, Pacific Margin, U.S.A. Society of Economic Paleontologists and Mineralogists Special Publication.

Agenbroad, L. D. 1998. New pygmy mammoth (Mammuthus exilis) localities and radiocarbon dates from San Miguel, Santa Rosa, and Santa Cruz Islands, California. Pages 169-176 in Weigand, P. W. (ed.), Contributions to the geology of the Northern Channel Islands, southern California. American Association of Petroleum Geologists, Pacific Section, Miscellaneous Publication 45.

Atwater, T. M. 1998. Plate tectonic history of southern California with emphasis on the western Transverse Ranges and Santa Cruz Island. Pages 1-9 in Weigand, P. W. (ed.), Contributions to the geology of the Northern Channel Islands, southern California. American Association of Petroleum Geologists, Pacific Section, Miscellaneous Publication 45.

Avila, F. A. and D. W. Weaver. 1969. Mid-Tertiary stratigraphy, Santa Rosa Island. Pages 48-67 in Weaver, D. W., D. P. Doerner, and B. Nolf (eds.), Geology of the Northern Channel Islands (California). American Association of Petroleum Geologists and Society of Economic Paleontologists and Mineralogists, Pacific Sections, Special Publication 12.

Chinn, B. D. and P. W. Weigand. 1994. Petrology and geochemistry of volcanic clasts from the Miocene Beecher's Bay Formation, Santa Rosa Island, California. Pages 255-265 in Halvorson, W. L. and G. J. Maender (eds.), The Fourth California Islands Symposium: Update on the Status of Resources. Santa Barbara Museum of Natural History, Santa Barbara, CA.

Colson, K. B., T. K. Rockwell, K. M. Thorup, and G. L. Kennedy. 1995. Neotectonics of the left-lateral Santa Rosa Island fault, western Transverse Ranges, Southern California. Geological Society of America Cordilleran Section, 91st Annual Meeting, Abstracts with Program 7:5:11.

Daily, M. 1998. Santa Rosa Island geologic mapping and oil exploration, Page 2 (reverse side) on Geologic map of Santa Rosa Island, Santa Barbara County, California.

Dibblee Geological Foundation, Santa Barbara, California. Map DF-68.

Dibblee, T. W., Jr. 1982a. Regional geology of the Transverse Range Province of southern California. Pages 7-26 *in* Fife, D. L. and J. A. Minch (eds.), Geology and mineral wealth of the California Transverse Ranges, Mason Hill Volume. South Coast Geological Society, Santa Ana, California. Annual Symposium and Guidebook 10.

Dibblee, T. W., Jr. 1982b. Geology of the Channel Islands, southern California. Pages 27-40 *in* Fife, D. L. and J. A. Minch (eds.), Geology and mineral wealth of the California Transverse Ranges, Mason Hill Volume. South Coast Geological Society, Santa Ana, California. Annual Symposium and Guidebook 10.

Dibblee, T. W., Jr. 1995. Tectonic and depositional environment of the middle and upper Cenozoic sequences of the coastal southern California region. Pages 212-245 *in* Fritsche, A. E. (ed.), Cenozoic paleogeography of the western United States - II. Pacific Section, Society for Sedimentary Geology (SEPM) Book 75.

Dibblee, T. W., Jr. and H. E. Ehrenspeck. 1998. General geology of Santa Rosa Island. Pages 49-76 *in* Weigand, P. W. (ed.), Contributions to the geology of the Northern Channel Islands, southern California. American Association of Petroleum Geologists, Pacific Section, Miscellaneous Publication 45.

Dibblee, T. W., Jr., J. R. Woolley, and H. E. Ehrenspeck. 1998. Geologic map of Santa Rosa Island, Santa Barbara County, California. Dibblee Geological Foundation, Santa Barbara, California. Map DF-68. Scale 1:24,000.

Hill, D. J. 1976. Geology of the Jurassic basement rocks, Santa Cruz Island, California, and correlation with other Mesozoic basement terranes in California. Pages 16-46 *in* Howell, D. G. (ed.), Aspects of the geologic history of the California continental borderland. American Association of Petroleum Geologists, Pacific Section, Miscellaneous Publication 24.

Howell, D. G., (ed.). 1976. Aspects of the geologic history of the California continental borderland. American Association of Petroleum Geologists, Pacific Section, Miscellaneous Publication 24, 498 p.

Junger, A. 1976. Offshore structure between Santa Cruz and Santa Rosa Islands. Pages 418-426 *in* Howell, D. G. (ed.), Aspects of the geologic history of the California continental borderland. American Association of Petroleum Geologists, Pacific Section, Miscellaneous Publication 24.

Junger, A. 1979. Maps and seismic profiles showing geologic structure of the Northern Channel Islands platform, California continental borderland. United States Geological Survey, Miscellaneous Field Studies Map MF-991. Scale 1:250,000.

Junger, A. and D. L. Johnson. 1980. Was there a Quaternary land bridge to the Northern Channel Islands? Pages 33-39 *in* Power, D. M. (ed.), The California Islands: Proceedings of a multidisciplinary symposium. Santa Barbara Museum of Natural History.

Kamerling, M. J. 1994. Paleomagnetism and tectonics of the southern California continental borderland [Ph.D.dissertation]. University of California, Santa Barbara, 217 p.

Kamerling, M. J. and B. P. Luyendyk. 1985. Paleomagnetism and Neogene tectonics of the Northern Channel Islands, California. Journal of Geophysical Research 90:12,485-12,505.

Kew, W. S. W. 1927. Geologic sketch of Santa Rosa Island, Santa Barbara County, California. Geological Society of America Bulletin 38:645-653.

Luyendyk, B. P. 1991. A model for Neogene crustal rotations, transtension, and transpression in southern California. Geological Society of America Bulletin 103:1528-1536.

Luyendyk, B. P., P. Gans, and M. J. Kamerling. 1998. ^{40}Ar/^{39}Ar Geochronology of southern California Neogene volcanism. Pages 9-36 *in* Weigand, P. W. (ed.), Contributions to the geology of the Northern Channel Islands, southern California. American Association of Petroleum Geologists, Pacific Section, Miscellaneous Publication 45.

Nuccio, R. M. 1977. Sedimentology of the Beechers Bay Formation, Santa Rosa Island, California [M.A. thesis]. California State University, San Diego, 49p.

Nuccio, R. M. and J. J. Woolley. 1998. Sedimentology of the Beechers Bay Formation, Santa Rosa Island, California. Pages 91-102 *in* Weigand, P. W. (ed.), Contributions to the geology of the Northern Channel Islands, southern California. American Association of Petroleum Geologists, Pacific Section, Miscellaneous Publication 45.

Orr, P. C. 1960. Late Pleistocene marine terraces on Santa Rosa Island, California. Geological Society of America Bulletin 71:1113-1119.

Sonneman, H. (as modified and extended by D. W. Weaver, D. P. Doerner, and other anonymous authors) 1969. Geology of Santa Rosa Island. Map *in* Weaver, D. W., D. P. Doerner, and B. Nolf (eds.), Geology of the Northern Channel Islands (California). American Association of Petroleum Geologists and Society of Economic Paleontologists and Mineralogists, Pacific Sections, Special Publication 12. Map scale 1:24,000.

Sorlien, C. C., E. H. McWayne, M. J. Kamerling, and J. M. Galloway. 1998. Late Cenozoic faulting and progressive folding of northern Santa Rosa Island and southwestern Santa Barbara Channel, California. Pages 121-141 *in* Kunitomi, D. S., T. E. Hopps, and J. M. Galloway (eds.), Structure and petroleum geology, Santa Barbara Channel, California. American Association of Petroleum Geologists, Pacific Section, Miscellaneous Publication 46.

Thaler, P. F. 1998. Mammoth remains of the Channel Islands of California: A summary of geologic, biogeographic and evolutionary implications. Pages 161-167 *in* Weigand, P. W. (ed.), Contributions to the geology of the Northern Channel Islands, southern California. American Association of Petroleum Geologists, Pacific Section, Miscellaneous Publication 45.

Vedder, J. G. and D. G. Howell. 1980. Topographic evolution of the Southern California Borderland during late Cenozoic time. Pages 33-39 in Power, D. M. (ed.), The California Islands: Proceedings of a multidisciplinary symposium. Santa Barbara Museum of Natural History.

Weaver, D. W. and D. P. Doerner. 1969. Lower Tertiary stratigraphy of San Miguel and Santa Rosa Islands. Pages 30-47 in Weaver, D. W., D. P. Doerner, and B. Nolf (eds.), Geology of the Northern Channel Islands (California). American Association of Petroleum Geologists and Society of Economic Paleontologists and Mineralogists, Pacific Sections, Special Publication 12.

Weaver, D. W., D. P. Doerner, and B. Nolf (eds.). 1969. Geology of the Northern Channel Islands (California). American Association of Petroleum Geologists and Society of Economic Paleontologists and Mineralogists, Pacific Sections, Special Publication 12, 200 p., 3 geologic maps, scale 1:24,000.

Weigand, P. W. (ed.). 1998. Contributions to the geology of the Northern Channel Islands, southern California. American Association of Petroleum Geologists, Pacific Section, Miscellaneous Publication 45, 196 p.

Weigand, P. W., K. L Savage, B. D. Chinn, and T. Reid. 1998. Composition of volcanic rocks on Santa Rosa, San Miguel, and Santa Barbara Islands, California. Pages 37-48 in Weigand, P. W. (ed.), Contributions to the geology of the Northern Channel Islands, southern California. American Association of Petroleum Geologists, Pacific Section, Miscellaneous Publication 45.

Woolley, J. J. 1978. Sedimentology of the Tertiary Sespe and Vaqueros Formations, Santa Rosa Island, California [M. A. thesis]. California State University, San Diego, California, 72 p.

Woolley, J. J. 1994. Lobo Canyon Landslide: Santa Rosa Island, California. Pages 297-302 in Halvorson, W. L. and G. J. Maender (eds.), The Fourth California Islands Symposium: Update on the Status of Resources. Santa Barbara Museum of Natural History, Santa Barbara, CA.

Woolley, J. J. 1998a. Sedimentology of the Oligocene Sespe and Vaqueros Formations, Santa Rosa Island, California. Pages 77-90 in Weigand, P. W. (ed.), Contributions to the geology of the Northern Channel Islands, southern California. American Association of Petroleum Geologists, Pacific Section, Miscellaneous Publication 45.

Woolley, J. J. 1998b. Aspects of the Quaternary history of Santa Rosa Island, California. Pages 103-111 in Weigand, P. W. (ed.), Contributions to the geology of the Northern Channel Islands, southern California. American Association of Petroleum Geologists, Pacific Section, Miscellaneous, Publication 45.

SANTA ROSA ISLAND GEOLOGIC MAPPING AND OIL EXPLORATION

Marla Daily

Santa Cruz Island Foundation, 1010 Anacapa Street, Santa Barbara, CA 93101
(805) 963-4949, FAX (805) 963-9433, E-mail: scifmail@west.net

ABSTRACT

The story of oil exploration on Santa Rosa Island under Vail & Vickers ownership (1901 to 1986) covers the 43 year period from 1932 to 1975, and includes efforts by several companies, four of whom actually drilled: Standard Oil Company, Signal-Honolulu-Macco, J. R. Pemberton, and Mobil Oil Corporation. Despite repeated drillings in a variety of island locations, no significant oil was ever found. To obtain historical information, Vail & Vickers files were reviewed, and oral history interviews were conducted with Al and Russ Vail. In addition, surviving geologists and oil company employees were interviewed: Thomas W. Dibblee, Jr., Robert E. Anderson, Lloyd Edwards, William "Bill" E. Kennett, John A. Forman, and K. B. "Pete" Hall. In 1980, Santa Rosa Island became part of Channel Islands National Park. No further search for oil will be conducted on Santa Rosa Island.

Keywords: Santa Rosa Island, oil exploration, Vail & Vickers, drilling, geology.

INTRODUCTION

Santa Rosa Island is one of a chain of four islands (Anacapa, Santa Cruz, Santa Rosa and San Miguel) which makes up the westerly extension of the east-west trending Santa Monica mountains of the mainland. The islands are primarily composed of familiar sedimentary rocks with some interbedded volcanics much like those exposed on the mainland. However, basement rocks exposed on Santa Cruz Island are a rather exotic suite quite different from the granitics and metamorphics of the mainland basement. Like Santa Cruz Island, Santa Rosa Island is split by a major strike slip fault. On the low-relief northern one third of the island, Late Tertiary sediments and tuffaceous volcanics outcrop, with the major folding being a broad, gentle anticline. The more rugged, high-standing southern two thirds of the island exposes older, more resistant Lower Tertiary sandstones and shales overlain by red beds of the Sespe formation.

Just as the upturned Santa Ynez mountains form the north rampart of the Ventura/Santa Barbara sedimentary basin, so also do the Channel Islands define the south margin of this basin. For nearly 100 years, oil fields have been producing within this basin. It seemed possible to some exploration-minded oil companies that oil might be found along the south margin of the basin as it has been along the north edge.

The first formal geological exploration of Santa Rosa Island was conducted by William S. W. Kew (1890-1961), E. D. Lynton, and Paul Henderson in January of 1926. They had spent ten days on the island with permission of "Messrs. N. R. and Ed Vail," and had great assistance from the island foreman, C. W. Smith. A year later, Kew presented a paper, *Geological Sketch of Santa Rosa Island, Santa Barbara, County, California*, which he read before the Cordilleran Section of the Geologic Society of America on January 29, 1927. His work was subsequently published in the Bulletin of the Geological Society of America (Vol. 38, pp. 645-654), December 30, 1927). Kew noted his findings were published "with permission of Vail & Vickers and G. C. Gester, Chief Geologist of the Standard Oil Company of California."

Thomas Wilson Dibblee, Jr. (b. 1911) paid his first visit to Santa Rosa Island in September of 1928 during his high school years. He remembers vividly what happened on that trip:

> Mr. Ed Vail had invited my father to visit the island, and Dad took me along for the one-day trip. We left by boat from Santa Barbara, about 7:00 A.M. The boat trip took well over two hours, and when we got near the island the ocean got very rough, with large swells. We weathered the swells pretty well, but Mr. Vail's cocker spaniel got awfully sick. After we landed at the pier, we visited with Ed's brother, Russell, at the ranch house, and had lunch. Then I decided to go for a walk, as I have done all my life. It was great to explore this island, so new and unfamiliar to me. I walked and walked - all the way to Black Mountain. When I got there, I was worn out and fell asleep by a bush. After an hour or so, I walked back down to the ranch house. When I got there, the Vail brothers told me the boat could wait no longer, and had just left for Santa Barbara with my dad onboard! So there I was, stranded on the island with Russell and Ed Vail.
>
> They told me I was to accompany Mr. Russell Vail on their cattle boat, the *Vaquero*, already loaded with a herd of cattle that was being shipped overnight to San Pedro. The boat would be leaving shortly. So I embarked with Mr. Vail.

This slow trip was most interesting. The cattle down in the hold mooed and bawled constantly pretty much the entire trip. As the *Vaquero* lumbered along the south side of Santa Cruz Island, I stayed up on the deck and saw some pretty spectacular geology in the late afternoon sun - the huge white bluffs of volcanic ash layers, dipping toward the ocean, and further east, a thick section of Monterey Shale dipping into the coastal bluffs. I had just learned some geology on our Rancho San Julian earlier that same year, so seeing the island geology was really exciting. By the time we got to the east end of Santa Cruz Island it was getting dark, and time for dinner. The boat had a great cook. I remember he made corn muffins that tasted so good I could not stop eating them.

The boat finally arrived at San Pedro Harbor just before dawn the next morning. On the way to the harbor, the *Vaquero* somehow collided with a small yacht, which really stirred up the cattle and caused a lot of commotion all around, but I think no one was hurt. After the boat landed, Mr. Vail called my father and put me on a bus back to Santa Barbara. I had a very long day - at some inconvenience to the Vails; however, they never did bawl me out. And who would have known that almost exactly ten years later [1938], I would return to Santa Rosa Island to map its geology! (Thomas Wilson Dibblee, Jr., pers. comm., 1998).

Four years after Dibblee's premier island adventure, Standard Oil conducted the first exploration for oil on Santa Rosa Island.

The story of oil exploration on Santa Rosa Island covers a 43-year period (1932-1975), and includes efforts by several companies, four of whom actually drilled: Standard Oil Company, Signal-Honolulu-Macco, J. R. Pemberton, and Mobil Oil Corporation. Despite repeated drillings in a variety of locations, no significant oil was ever found.

STANDARD OIL COMPANY (1932-1933)

The Standard Oil Company exploration on Santa Rosa Island began in 1932 as reported in a local Santa Barbara paper:

Santa Rosa Island Oil Lease is Filed. Plans of the Standard Oil Company to extend the oil development activities, already launched upon Santa Cruz Island, to Santa Rosa Island as well, are indicated with the filing of a lease on Santa Rosa Island. The lease provides that drilling must be started before June 22 [1932]. The island has an area of 62,600 acres. The new Santa Rosa Island lease was signed by the Vickers Company, Margaret R. Vail, N. R. Vail, Mahlon Vail, Mary Vail Wilkinson, William Banning Vail, Edward N. Vail and Margaret Vail

Bell, as lessees. Negotiations were handled through the Security Title Insurance and Guarantee Company. [Santa Barbara Morning Press, 30 April 1932]

Standard Oil geologist, Carl St. John Bremner (1895-1944), surveyed the island by horseback and did the field mapping in preparation for his company's drilling. Before actual drilling operations could proceed however, first an infrastructure had to be provided for not only crew accommodations, but also for access on and around the rugged island. Supplies, construction materials and drilling equipment were off-loaded from Vail & Vickers boat, *Vaquero*, onto the pier located at Bechers Bay. In addition, an amphibious plane was used to fly crew and supplies from a bean field in Carpinteria to a field on Santa Rosa Island just east of the main ranch. Three wooden cabins were constructed on the flat field to the south and west of the pier head which accommodated up to 16 men. The first roads on the island were roads that Standard Oil built using a steam shovel. Dynamite blasting was necessary in areas on both Black Mountain and to the west of Scott's camp (Figures 1 and 2). Standard Oil Company only drilled one well, named Santa Rosa #1. It was drilled on Vail Peak to a total depth of 6,298 ft using a stationary rig. According to Al Vail, "they

Figure 1. Standard Oil Company erected the first well on Santa Rosa Island in 1932. The stationary rig drilled to a depth of 6,298 ft on Vail Peak.

Figure 2. Laura "Dusty" Vail, daughter of William Banning Vail, preparing blasting holes for the roadway construction to Vail Peak in 1932.

hit a lot of dust." The following year, in 1933, the well was capped and abandoned. The cabins and oil rig were removed by Standard Oil when they left the island, but today their road building efforts remain in use. Bremner also mapped Santa Cruz Island (1932) and San Miguel Island (1933), both of which were published (see references). His Santa Rosa Island work was considered proprietary, and hence not published. Bremner eventually left the service of Standard Oil to join the California-Ecuador Petroleum Company. He was killed in a plane crash in Peru on September 18, 1944.

RICHFIELD OIL COMPANY (1938)

Geologist Frank A. Morgan who had discovered the Elwood oil field in 1928, and Harold Hoots, chief geologist for the Union Oil Company, were well aware of the oil potential of Santa Rosa Island. In 1938, five years after Standard Oil Company pulled off the island, Morgan and Hoots arranged with Russell and Ed Vail to visit Santa Rosa on behalf of Richfield Oil Company. They included two local geologists who had been classmates at Stanford, Rodman K. Cross (1911-1970) and Thomas Dibblee, Jr., to help determine the island's oil potential. As Tom Dibblee remembered:

> When the four of us arrived, we rode horseback over the northern part of the island for a day or two to see the geology. After Morgan and Hoots

departed to their office suite in the black and gold Richfield building in downtown Los Angeles, Cross and I remained on the island for over two weeks in November 1938 to map the geology primarily north of the Santa Rosa Island fault, where the Vaqueros and Sespe sands that might contain oil are buried beneath the impervious Rincon Shale. It was thought there was a better chance of finding oil there than where Standard had drilled south of the fault. We also spent a day or two on the steep southeast side of the island to see the Vaqueros and Sespe sands wherever exposed. Rodman Cross and I spent most nights at the ranch house with Mr. Vail or his foreman, and we rode horseback each day to where we mapped the geology, usually one or two canyons a day, using aerial photographs to map on, as topographic base maps did not exist until years later. We camped a few nights on the western part of the island due to the long ride just to get back to that part to do field work. During our stay, the weather was surprisingly hot for that time of year, and in some of the canyons the temperatures ranged into the nineties. It was a strenuous effort, but when we returned to the mainland, we produced a geologic map of the part of the island we had mapped, showing what area would be most favorable for a test well. We found the best conditions to be in the vicinity of Tecolote and Garañon canyons, and at shallow depths. (Thomas Wilson Dibblee, Jr., pers. comm. 1998)

No lease resulted from these investigations, presumably because of existing heavy lease commitments by the company on the mainland. However, a few years later the island was leased by competitors that tested the area they had recommended, with negative results.

THE SUPERIOR OIL COMPANY (1947)

In 1947, William E. "Bill" Kennett (b. 1914) spent six weeks mapping the geology of Santa Rosa Island for The Superior Oil Company. (He mapped Santa Cruz and San Miguel islands as well). Permission for geological work on Santa Rosa Island was handled for Vail & Vickers by their friend and geologist, J.R. Pemberton. Pemberton warned Kennett: "the wind blows so hard out there that it takes three men to close a barbed wire gate." Undaunted, Kennett proceeded. In his private report to The Superior Oil Company, he noted that Standard Oil Company's well, Santa Rosa # 1, had been favorably located on one of the few major structures on the island. It had penetrated Early Miocene, Oligocene and a significant thickness of Eocene strata without shows of hydrocarbons. Kennett added that the most attractive untested closure of significant magnitude was in the northwestern part of the island where the northeasterly plunging Black Mountain anticline converged on the Santa Rosa Fault. The anticipated section would be similar to Standard's well, but may benefit from migration from the Channel. No test was proposed, although this area was later tested by Signal-Honolulu-Macco and Pemberton. At the time of Kennett's visit, he lived with the island's manager, Walter Lynch and his wife, Helen Kennett well remembered:

Our diet consisted mainly of beef, wild boar, fish, lobster and abalone. The midnight oil was burned many a night with Al Vail with our foursome playing cribbage. The losers got a smell of the cork while the winners took a snort. Scores began to even toward midnight. (William E. "Bill" Kennett, pers. comm., 1998)

Al Vail recalled Kennett was "the walkinest geologist ever born." (Al Vail, pers. comm., 1998)

SIGNAL-HONOLULU-MACCO (1948-1949)

Just after World War II, and fifteen years after Standard Oil Company drilled the island's first hole on Vail Peak, Signal-Honolulu-Macco [a partnership of Signal Oil & Gas Company, Honolulu Oil Corporation, and Macco Construction] entered into a lease agreement with Vail & Vickers to drill for oil. Honolulu Oil Company geologists Lowell E. Redwine (1911-1982) and Paul McGovney, and Signal Oil geologist Robert E. Anderson (b. 1920), stayed at the ranch house while they conducted field mapping and location preparation. Signal Oil & Gas was the partnership operator, and thus Anderson stayed on for the drillings as well. A total of three wells were drilled: Soledad #1, Garañon #3, and Tecolote #1. Although Signal-Honolulu-Macco was able to use the road previously constructed by Standard Oil as far as Soledad Mountain, this new partnership had to construct about four miles of road from Soledad Mountain northward to their drilling locations. During World War II, an Army encampment had been constructed on Santa Rosa Island and left abandoned after the war. Employees of Signal-Honolulu-Macco rehabilitated several of the barracks for their island operations. Vail & Vickers boat, *Vaquero*, had been commandeered for the war effort and not returned, and thus supplies for Signal-Honolulu-Macco had to be barged to the island by tow boat and beached at Water Canyon. Santa Barbara Aviation provided air service, and the Santa Fe Drilling Company brought an Ideco H-30 tilt-up rig to the island for the drilling operations. Soledad #1 was drilled to a depth of 3,772 ft before it was capped and abandoned in 1948. Garañon #3 was drilled to a depth of 3,360 ft before it was capped and abandoned in 1949. Tecolote #1 was drilled to a depth of 3,563 ft. Although it had a minor non-commercial showing of oil, it was capped and abandoned in 1949. At the time, oil was selling for $3 a barrel and this meager finding was judged uneconomic. Robert E. Anderson remembered:

As a rule, the drilling of a well was never shut down, not even for Christmas. In 1948, the companies got kind-hearted however, and shut down the drilling

on Christmas Eve day. The plan was to fly back and restart the day after Christmas. Someone jokingly asked me if it ever snowed on Santa Rosa Island. I laughed and said of course not. We all went home, and guess what? It snowed. The plane couldn't fly. So much for my weatherman's forecast. We couldn't get back to the island until almost New Years. That New Year's Day, we all enjoyed a 15-pound lobster caught by hand in a tide pool. (Robert E. Anderson, pers. comm., 1998)

Although Signal-Honolulu-Macco pulled off Santa Rosa Island in 1949, they retained their rights to use the island's surface for offshore operations until 1953. Today the island's Signal Road commemorates their efforts.

J. R. PEMBERTON (1949-1950)

Encouraged by the non-commercial showing of oil from Tecolote #1, and by Signal and Honolulu geologists, Vail and Vickers family members decided to form an in-house joint venture on the heels of the departure of Signal-Honolulu-Macco from Santa Rosa Island in 1949. John Roy "Bill" Pemberton (1884-1968), Vail family representative in oil matters, wrote:

This joint venture group intends to drill to the base of the Sespe formation at a location between 1500' and 3000' northeast of Tecolote #1 in hopes of finding a thickening down structure of the oil zone found in that well. The well will be under the supervision of Mr. Harold Hoots and myself. (John Roy "Bill" Pemberton, pers. comm., April 25, 1949)

Since Robert E. Anderson was so familiar with the island's geology, he was "loaned" by his employer, Signal Oil & Gas, to assist with the J. R. Pemberton venture. Signal Oil & Gas attorney, Sloan Flack, also invested in the syndicate. Louis H. Scott of Chino, California was hired as the drilling contractor. Three shallow holes were drilled: Tecolote #2 which ran to a depth of 2,284 ft, Tecolote #3, which ran to a depth of 1,585 ft, and a core hole located towards the island's west end. All proved dry and were capped in 1949 and 1950. During the Pemberton operations, Louis Scott and his crew stayed at the rehabilitated World War II barracks previously used by the Signal-Honolulu-Macco crew. Henceforth this island location has been known as Scott's Camp. All materials were barged and landed on the beach at Water Canyon.

K. B. HALL (1967-1971)

From 1967 through 1971, K. B. "Pete" Hall (b. 1916), as a consulting geologist with offshore and Channel Islands experience, represented Vail & Vickers in facilitating arrangements for geological investigations. During this time, several oil companies expressed an interest in oil and gas leasing, but none was consummated. "Tiger" Mike Davis out of Denver, used Hall to negotiate a lease on his behalf. Hall remembered:

> In 1969 and 1970, Bill Osborn, Exploration Services Company and myself negotiated a lease for Tiger Oil Company. No wells were drilled under this lease when it expired in 1971. I remember a sign on Santa Rosa Island which said *All our guests bring us happiness. Some on arrival, some on departure.* (K. B. "Pete" Hall, pers. comm., 1998)

MOBIL OIL CORPORATION (1971-1975)

Two decades after Pemberton's unsuccessful drilling venture on Santa Rosa Island, Mobil Oil Corporation developed an active interest in further island drilling. Thus far, a total of seven holes had been drilled, and only Tecolote #1 has shown any slim promise. Mobil's interest came hot on the heels of the now-famous Santa Barbara Oil Spill of 1969, which had served to heighten public awareness of environmental issues. As a result, loud concern was voiced that drilling would upset the island's ecological balance or disrupt archaeological sites. Mobil agreed to some of the most stringent environmental controls ever adapted for onshore drilling, and on October 14, 1971 they entered into a lease with Vail & Vickers. Terms of the agreement stated Mobil had to begin drilling no later than July 14, 1973.

> Each location was treated like an offshore drilling platform, and we took the same precautions that are normally required in the North Atlantic, the Pacific offshore and the Gulf of Mexico. The whole operation was sort of a test case. We had to reconfirm that an oil company could successfully drill in an environmentally hypersensitive area. (Mobil World, March 1975)

During the threat of the Cold War in the 1950's, the U. S. Air Force had built a large facility on the south side of the island at Johnson's Lee. It was manned from 1951 until 1963, and abandoned in 1965. Mobil Oil worked out of the abandoned facility, and barged their supplies to nearby Officer's Beach. By the early 1970s, no additional road building was required. Al Vail remembered, "Mobil had good equipment and it was a different ball game. It was a big operation. Most of them were flown out of Santa Barbara Aviation." (Al Vail, pers. comm., 1998)

Mobil maintained a 25-to-55-man crew on the island, all of whom had to adhere to strict rules. Hunting was forbidden and hiking was restricted. Smoking was limited to designated areas, and alcoholic beverages were banned. The men accepted the conditions in good grace, and apparently they found the operation something of a challenge. John Forman (b.1927) and Lloyd Edwards (b.1937) conducted preliminary field work. Using mapping by Weaver and Doerner et al (1969) together with Mobil surface mapping and two years of seismic exploration, they outlined Mobil's

drilling program. Geologists Lloyd Edwards, Jack Ells (b. 1946), Gene Hill and others sat the wildcats for Mobil. Within two years, six wells were drilled, all of them dry. The most notable well drilled was Santa Rosa #5 located in La Jolla Canyon. It was drilled on the crest of a large surface anticline to a depth of 11,003 ft-the deepest hole ever drilled on the island. It had tar shows at 3,090 ft, and gas shows from 10,849 to 10,851 ft. It effectively tested almost all of the Eocene section and bottomed in tight Cretaceous sandstones. Like all the other island wells ever drilled, it too was capped and abandoned. The last well drilled by Mobil was actually for Diamond Shamrock, named DS-SRI #1. Edwards remembered:

> That well was particularly discouraging because they lost about 1,000 ft of structural elevation, having moved only about 1,000 ft to the southwest. Obviously a large hidden fault lies between the DS-SRI #1 and Santa Rosa #9 in Tecolote Canyon. In spite of this, Jack Ells reports that the DS did have a five-foot Vaqueros oil sand. We really pounded every nail in the coffin on that island. It was over. (Lloyd Edwards, pers. comm., 1998)

In 1980, Santa Rosa Island became part of Channel Islands National Park. No further search for oil will be conducted on Santa Rosa Island.

LITERATURE CITED

Kew, W. S. W. 1927. Geological Sketch of Santa Rosa Island, Santa Barbara, County, California. Cordilleran Section of the Geologic Society of America, January 29, 1927.
Kew, W. S. W. 1927. Geologic Sketch of Santa Rosa Island, Santa Barbara County, California. Bulletin of the Geological Society of America 38:645-654.
Santa Barbara Morning Press, April 30, 1932.
Mobil World, March 1975, Mobil Oil Corporation.

SOURCES OF UNPUBLISHED MATERIALS

Anderson, Robert E. 2776 Club Drive, Los Angeles, CA 90064. Personal communication, 1998.
Dibblee, Jr., Thomas Wilson. 316 East Mission Street, Santa Barbara, CA 93105. Personal communication, 1998.
Edwards, Lloyd, 8022 South Albion Street, Littleton, CO 80122. Personal communication, 1998.
Hall, K. B. "Pete". 1303 Manzanita Drive, Santa Paula, CA 93060. Personal communication, 1998.
Kennett, William E. "Bill". 737 Sea Ranch Drive, Santa Barbara, CA 93109. Personal communication, 1998.
Pemberton, John Roy "Bill". Personal communication with Vail & Vickers, April 25, 1949.
Vail, Al. Vail & Vickers, 123 West Padre Street, Santa Barbara, CA 93101. Personal communication, 1998.

STRONTIUM ISOTOPE EVIDENCE FOR TIMING OF TERTIARY CRUSTAL EROSION SANTA CRUZ ISLAND

Martha Wulftange[1] and James Boles[2]

Department of Geological Sciences, University of California, Santa Barbara, CA 93106
(805) 893-3471, E-mail: [1]martha@magic.geol.ucsb.edu; [2]boles@magic.geol.ucsb.edu

ABSTRACT

Tertiary rocks on Santa Cruz Island record the erosion products of mid-crustal igneous rocks (Vaqueros Formation), blueschist-bearing subduction rocks (San Onofre Breccia), and products of active volcanism (Beechers Bay and Blanca Formations). The time span of deposition for the Oligocene-Miocene Vaqueros Formation through Miocene Beechers Bay-Blanca Formations, based on biochronology, is between 8 million years (Ma) and at least 17 Ma. This study measured strontium isotopic ratios in pectens and oysters from the Vaqueros and Blanca Formations and San Onofre Breccia. The ratios were correlated with the strontium sea water curve for an age estimate. Diagenetically unaltered samples were selected based on visual inspection, carbon and oxygen isotopic analysis, and x-ray diffraction (XRD). The strontium isotopic method yielded an age of 19 ± 1 Ma (early Miocene) for the upper Vaqueros Formation. Strontium ratio results from the San Onofre Breccia-Rincon Formation boundary indicate an age of 18.5 ± 1 Ma. The results from the basal Blanca Formation indicate an age of 19 ± 1 Ma, which is the same age as an unpublished result obtained on the basal Blanca Formation. The results of this study narrowly constrain the time span of deposition of the strata and indicate that volcanism, sedimentation, and inferred unroofing occurred almost synchronously at approximately 19 Ma.

Keywords: Santa Cruz Island, strontium isotopes, Vaqueros Formation, San Onofre Breccia, Blanca Formation, Transverse Ranges.

INTRODUCTION

Purpose

In this study, strontium isotope work was undertaken to determine the age of Oligocene-Miocene rocks of the Vaqueros, Rincon, Beechers Bay[1], and Blanca Formations and San Onofre Breccia in outcrops on the southwest part of Santa Cruz Island from Canada Posa Canyon to Laguna Canyon (Figure 1; Figure 2). This is the first study to use strontium isotopes to estimate the age of the strata on the southwest part of Santa Cruz Island. Previously, the formation ages were constrained solely by biochronology from

Figure 1. Location map showing sample areas, southwest Santa Cruz Island.

marine fossils (Bereskin and Edwards 1969). A comparison of their faunal ages with Correlation of Stratigraphic Units of North America (COSUNA) time charts (Lindberg 1984) indicates wide age ranges with overlapping boundaries during the late Saucesian and Relizian (Figure 3). Strontium isotope ratios of oysters and pectens were measured and compared to published strontium ratios of Tertiary sea water. The results constrain the formation's boundaries to narrower time intervals than those from the biostratigraphic studies. Based on our new understanding of the timing of deposition of the Miocene strata, we infer that there was rapid erosion (uplift?) of deep crustal rocks within the Transverse Range block during the Miocene.

Previous Work

The age and biostratigraphy of the sedimentary rock units on Santa Cruz Island have been broadly defined by paleontological work of Bereskin (1966) and Doerner

---

[1] The Beechers Bay was originally defined as a member of the Monterey Formation; but, due to its volcaniclastic character, we use the term "Beechers Bay Formation" (Howell and McLean 1976).

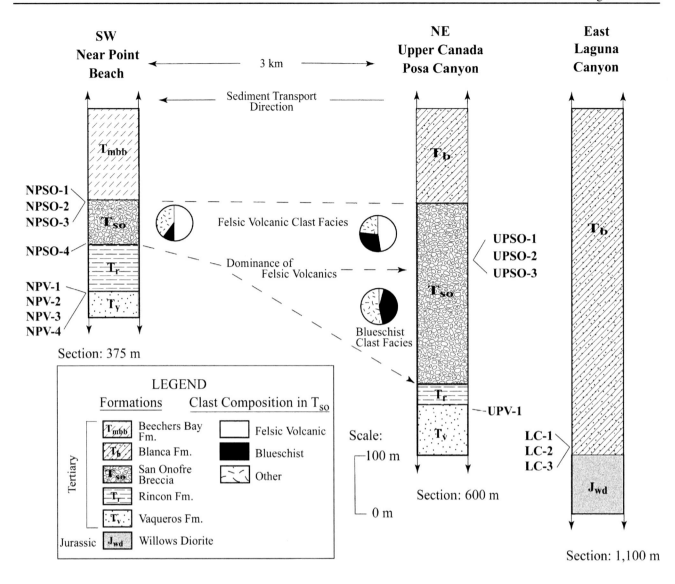

Figure 2. Stratigraphic columns of Miocene strata in Near Point Beach outcrops (distal facies), upper Canada Posa Canyon (proximal facies), and Laguna Canyon on Santa Cruz Island. The pie charts indicate the percentages of clast types in the San Onofre Breccia, (representative clast counts of greater than 100 pebble-size clasts in 1 m² grids) (Boles 1997). Sample locations are indicated in stratigraphic sections.

(1968), and are summarized in Weaver et al. (1969). Using the biostratigraphic time correlations from COSUNA (Lindberg 1984), we have estimated the biostratigraphic ages for the units (Figure 3) as follows: the Vaqueros as early Saucesian (~30 to 24 Ma), the Rincon as middle Saucesian to late Saucesian (~24 to 17.0 Ma), the San Onofre as late Saucesian to Relizian (~17.1 to 15.4 Ma), and the Beechers Bay-Blanca Formations as Relizian through Luisian, possibly Mohnian (~15.8 to 13 Ma). Based on these ages, deposition of the Vaqueros Formation through Beechers Bay-Blanca Formations represents a minimum time interval of 8 Ma to as much as at least 17 Ma. Our results suggest deposition occurred in a significantly shorter time interval.

Prior to this study, one fossil from the southwest corner of Santa Cruz Island was collected for strontium analysis. The fossil was collected at the Blanca-San Onofre boundary in upper Canada Posa Canyon. The $^{87}Sr/^{86}Sr$ value of

0.7086 correlates with an age of approximately 19 Ma, early Miocene (J. Schultz, UCSB, unpublished data). The biochronologic age suggested by the work of Bereskin and Edwards (1969) for the equivalent Beechers Bay-San Onofre boundary at Near Point Beach is 5 Ma older than the Blanca-San Onofre boundary determined by Schultz.

The age of the sparsely fossiliferous, volcaniclastic Blanca Formation is based on Potassium/Argon (K/Ar) dating. A volcanic clast from the middle member of the Blanca Formation yielded a K/Ar age of 13.3 ± 0.8 Ma, middle Miocene (McLean et al. 1976). An andesite flow from the upper member of the Blanca Formation yielded K/Ar ages of 14.9 ± 0.8 Ma (McLean et al. 1976). On the bases of these K/Ar dates, the age of the Blanca Formation is interpreted as late Saucesian to early Luisian.

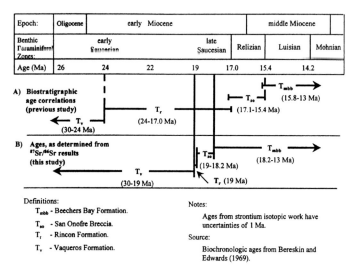

Definitions:

T_{mbb} - Beechers Bay Formation.

T_{so} - San Onofre Breccia.

T_r - Rincon Formation.

T_v - Vaqueros Formation.

Notes:

Ages from strontium isotopic work have uncertainties of 1 Ma.

Source:

Biochronologic ages from Bereskin and Edwards (1969).

Figure 3. Time chart comparing ages of stratigraphic units determined from A) previous studies, based on biochronology and B) this study, based on $^{87}Sr/^{86}Sr$ results.

STRATIGRAPHY AND SAMPLE COLLECTION

Representative stratigraphic sections of the Vaqueros Formation, Rincon Formation, San Onofre Breccia, Beechers Bay Formation, and Blanca Formation are exposed along a three-kilometer transect from upper Canada Posa Canyon southwest to Near Point Beach (Figure 2). Correlation of the stratigraphic units at Near Point Beach with those at upper Canada Posa Canyon indicates the thickness of the units decreases from northeast to southwest (the general direction of sediment transport). The section at Laguna Canyon is 1,100 meters (m) thick, the upper Canada Posa Canyon section is 600 m thick, and the Near Point Beach section is 375 m thick. Two outstanding differences between the Near Point Beach section and the upper Canada Posa Canyon section are: 1) the Rincon Formation is comparatively thinner in the upper Canada Posa Canyon section, and 2) the San Onofre Breccia at Near Point Beach is finer grained, thinner bedded, and has a higher volcanic/blueschist clast ratio compared to upper Canada Posa Canyon outcrops (Figure 2) (Boles 1997). The following summary of these formations is taken from Boles (1997); interpretations of depositional environments are those of Weaver and others (1969).

The Oligocene-Miocene Vaqueros Formation (disconformably overlying the Eocene Cozy Dell Shale) is a brown, thick-bedded, conglomerate overlain by brown sandstone. It is interpreted as having been deposited in an inner shelf to nonmarine environment, based on paleoecology and stratigraphic evidence. Marine fossil samples from the Vaqueros Formation were collected at Near Point Beach from the coarse sands and conglomerates within the upper 20 m of the stratigraphic section (Figure 2). The sample from upper Canada Posa Canyon was collected approximately 32 m below the Vaqueros-Rincon boundary.

The Rincon Formation and the San Onofre Breccia are Miocene in age. The Rincon Formation is a gray to brown, calcareous shale and mudstone. The depositional environment of the Rincon Formation at Near Point Beach is interpreted as middle to outer shelf (Bereskin and Edwards 1969).

The San Onofre Breccia is a bluish-gray conglomerate, sandstone, and mudstone. The upper Canada Posa Canyon section was deposited in a very shallow marine environment; whereas, the Near Point Beach section was deposited approximately 5 km in the direction of sediment transport. The samples collected from Near Point Beach are from the uppermost conglomerate of the San Onofre Breccia. The sample collected from the lower San Onofre Breccia at Near Point Beach is from the lowermost conglomerate above the Rincon Formation. The samples collected from upper Canada Posa Canyon are from approximately two-thirds up in the formation.

The Beechers Bay and Blanca Formations are time-equivalent Miocene units. The Beechers Bay Formation is a gray, thin-bedded siltstone to fine-grained volcaniclastic sandstone. The Blanca Formation is a light gray to buff, thick-bedded, volcaniclastic conglomerate, tuffaceous sandstone, and tuff. These strata were deposited on a relatively shallow shelf. The samples collected from the Blanca Formation are from the basal 5 m of the formation.

METHODS

We have compared strontium isotope ratios from marine shell tests with the time variations of $^{87}Sr/^{86}Sr$ values in sea water (Oslick et al. 1994). Oslick et al. (1994) data are based on comparing $^{87}Sr/^{86}Sr$ values of planktonic foraminifera to magnetostratigraphy that is constrained to about 40,000-yr variations. The $^{87}Sr/^{86}Sr$ value in sea water, currently 0.70906, is homogeneous because strontium has a long residence time in the ocean (about 5×10^6 yr), compared with the mixing time of the oceans (10^3 yr) (Faure 1997). The ratio of strontium in sea water has systematically increased in the past 30 Ma. Because oyster and pecten shells incorporate the same ratio of strontium in sea water into their shells, comparison of the ratio of strontium in the fossils to the strontium sea water curve yields age estimates. Recent resolution of the sea water curve (Oslick et al. 1994) permitted assignments of ages with a narrow range of uncertainty (± 1 Ma). The method described depends on selecting unaltered fossils that retain their original strontium isotopic ratio. Our selection criteria are described below.

Selection

Shell material was first selected by visual inspection. Criteria used to help select unaltered material included translucency, foliation of material, and retention of opalescence. Shell material lacking these qualities was avoided as it had a higher possibility of having undergone alteration of the original strontium isotopic ratio. Relatively large aliquots of powdered sample (0.4 grams) were prepared to ensure homogeneity for carbon, oxygen, and strontium isotopic analyses and x-ray diffraction (XRD).

Carbon and oxygen isotope values were used to determine if, and to what extent, the original $\delta^{18}O$ and $\delta^{13}C$ values of the shells were reset. Unaltered carbonate fossils should have $\delta^{18}O$ and $\delta^{13}C$ values close to 0 parts per million (‰) relative to the Cretaceous Peedee Formation standard (PDB). The $\delta^{13}C$ values of modern marine mollusks around the world vary within a small range of +4.2‰ to -1‰, and values have not appreciably changed since Cambrian times (Faure 1997). The $\delta^{18}O$ values are more variable throughout the oceans, and can be affected by ocean temperature (Faure 1997). Miocene waters had lower $\delta^{18}O$ values than today by approximately -1.5‰ (J. P. Kennett, pers. comm.). Because shells attain the same $\delta^{18}O$ values as the waters in which they form, values of -2‰ are reasonable for Miocene unaltered oysters. It is also possible that some of the oysters grew in brackish water, which would have a slightly negative $\delta^{18}O$ value. However, differences in temperature and salinity of the oceans during shell formation can cause unaltered shells to have values greater than 1‰ and less than -1‰. Based on the above, we considered samples with $\delta^{18}O$ and $\delta^{13}C$ values within ± 2.5‰ of 0‰ (PDB scale) to be unaltered and suitable for further analysis.

XRD analysis was conducted on a few samples to determine if the shells were pure calcite or had some impurities or alterations (such as clay, gypsum, dolomite, siderite, etc.) that could affect their strontium isotopic ratio. Analysis of five, randomly selected, apparently unaltered samples (based on visual and stable isotopic composition) indicated they were all pure calcite. The other remaining samples were not analyzed for their mineral composition because we believe visual inspection for impurities and oxygen and carbon isotopic analysis are more sensitive indicators of diagenetic alteration. Further analysis of the strontium concentration in the samples would have additionally helped in determining if diagenesis had occurred. Because oysters and pectens typically have greater than 1,000‰ strontium, a lower concentration could possibly indicate that strontium has been removed and the ratio likely reset.

Analytical Techniques

Unaltered samples were dissolved in dilute HCl (<0.2 M). After evaporation, residues were re-dissolved in 3 M HNO_3. Standard ion-exchange chromatography (Sr Spec resin, ElChrom Ind.'s Inc.) was employed to concentrate the strontium (G. Tilton, UCSB, unpublished data). Sr Spec resin is especially selective in separating calcium and other elements from strontium. Strontium concentrates were then analyzed on a Finnigan MAT 261 multicollector mass spectrometer at the Mattinson Laboratory in the Geological Sciences Department at the University of California, Santa Barbara (UCSB). Carbon and oxygen isotope values were determined using a VG mass spectrometer at the Kennett Laboratory in the Geological Sciences Department, UCSB. Samples with high $\delta^{13}C$ values (>2.5‰ and <-2.5‰) were deemed unacceptable, as the values likely indicate alteration.

RESULTS

Samples

Fifteen total samples of oysters and pectens were analyzed from Near Point Beach, upper Canada Posa Canyon, and Laguna Canyon (Figure 1; Figure 2). The complete stratigraphic sequence at Near Point Beach is exposed, which allowed us to obtain samples from the upper Vaqueros, lower San Onofre, and upper San Onofre (Figure 2). Eight samples analyzed were from this site. Four samples from the upper Vaqueros and middle San Onofre were also collected in upper Canada Posa Canyon. Three samples from the Blanca Formation were analyzed from upper Laguna Canyon. The stratigraphic locations of the analyzed samples are shown in Figure 2.

Carbon-Oxygen Results

Oxygen and carbon isotopic compositions were measured for thirteen of the fifteen samples. Three samples (LC-2, LC-3, and UPSO-2) had $\delta^{18}O$ and $\delta^{13}C$ values that approach or exceed -2.5‰ (Table 1), and are considered to be altered. Sample UPSO-2 appeared to be highly altered, as there was visible calcite growth between shell layers of the oyster. For comparison, sample UPSO-1, which was collected from the same location and did not appear altered, has $\delta^{18}O$ and $\delta^{13}C$ isotopic values within -2.5‰ of 0‰. The corrected carbon isotope results of sample UPSO-2 were below average (-6‰) compared with most other samples (-2‰). In addition, the strontium isotope ratios of UPSO-1 and UPSO-2 yielded different age results: 19.1 and 20.5 Ma respectively. These results support our selection criteria of using visual inspection and carbon and oxygen isotopes to gauge diagenetic alteration in the samples.

Strontium Results

The measured $^{87}Sr/^{86}Sr$ values are reported in Table 1 along with the analytical errors. The age reported in Table 1 was derived by comparing the $^{87}Sr/^{86}Sr$ value with the Miocene sea water curve of Oslick et al. (1994). In the study by Oslick et al. (1994), the Oligocene-Miocene data were fitted with two linear regression models. For the time period between 15.6 and 22.8 Ma (0.708789 to 0.708305) the determined slope was 0.000068 per Ma. Therefore, data were correlated to a trend line, t = -(1/0.000068)*x + 10,439, where t is the resulting age correlation, x is the $^{87}Sr/^{86}Sr$ isotopic result, and 10,439 is the y-intercept.

Uncertainties of strontium isotopic measurements are listed in Table 1. The largest uncertainty results in an age of ± 400,000 years. The analytical uncertainty of the correlated data from Oslick et al. (1994) is ± 1 Ma. Therefore, the uncertainty of ± 1 Ma given for all the age values is the estimated range of the data from Oslick et al. (1994).

Near Point Beach

The data of the Near Point Beach samples are presented in Figure 4. The $^{87}Sr/^{86}Sr$ results of the Vaqueros

Table 1. ^{87}Sr/^{86}Sr, carbon and oxygen isotopic analyses of oysters and pectens from Santa Cruz Island.

Location	Sample #	Age*[1] (Ma)	^{87}Sr/^{86}Sr*[2]	Standard Error*[3]	Sr Concentration		δ^{18}O PDB	δ^{13}C PDB
Near Point Beach								
Upper San Onofre	NPSO-1	18.2	0.708613	−0.000018			-1.200	-0.254
Breccia	NPSO-2	16.6	0.708721	−0.000020	810	Sr	n/a	n/a
	NPSO-3	16.5	0.708727	−0.000020	405	Sr	-2.078	-2.004
Lower San Onofre	NPSO-4	18.5	0.708593	−0.000015			-2.004	0.319
Breccia		18.6	0.708586	−0.000014				
Upper Vaqueros Fm.	NPV-1	18.9	0.708574	−0.000014			-1.893	-1.720
		18.4	0.708598	−0.000011				
	NPV-2	19	0.708563	−0.000015			-1.923	-2.094
	NPV-3	19.4	0.708535	−0.000016			-2.042	-2.060
	NPV-4	19.5	0.708526	−0.000027			-2.012	-1.422
		19.8	0.708509	−0.000023				
Upper Canada Posa Canyon								
San Onofre	UPSO-1	19.1	0.708554	−0.000017			-2.314	-2.300
Breccia	UPSO-2	20.5	0.708457	−0.000026			-1.607	-5.996
	UPSO-3	19	0.708559	−0.000012			n/a	n/a
Vaqueros Fm.	UPV-1	18.7	0.708581	−0.000024			-0.520	0.255
Laguna Canyon								
Blanca Fm.	LC-1	19.8	0.708508	−0.000017			-2.488	-2.123
	LC-2	-	0.705948	−0.000015	810 ppm Sr		-9.547	-15.273
	LC-3	nd	nd	nd			-1.155	-11.266
	987 Standards							
	2/20/98		0.710244	−0.000013				
	2/22/98		0.710224	−0.000013				
	2/23/98		0.710251	−0.000012				
	5/2/98		0.710259	−0.000015				
	5/3/98		0.710253	−0.000014				

Definitions:

δ^{13}C - Delta carbon 13

δ^{18}O - Delta oxygen 18

n/a - Not analyzed

nd - Not determined, the strontium concentration of the sample was too low to analyze

PDB - The PDB is the most widely used standard to determine the fractionation of carbon or oxygen isotopes. It is prepared from belemnites (Belemnitella americana) collected from the Cretaceous Peedee Formation.

- Parts per million

Notes:

*1 - Correlated age from Oslick et al. (1994).

*2 - Standards were run intermittently throughout analysis and the 987 reference sample data are within the commonly accepted value of 0.701250. Since the standard 987 data falls within the accepted value of 0.701250, the ^{87}Sr/^{86}Sr ratios are not adjusted.

*3 - Standard error of the mean: (2sigma)x10^{-6}

Comments:

Carbon and Oxygen Isotope analyses were from the Kennett Laboratory, Geology Dept., UCSB.

Samples UPSO-2, LC-2, and LC-3 may be altered, and their ^{87}Sr/^{86}Sr are suspect.

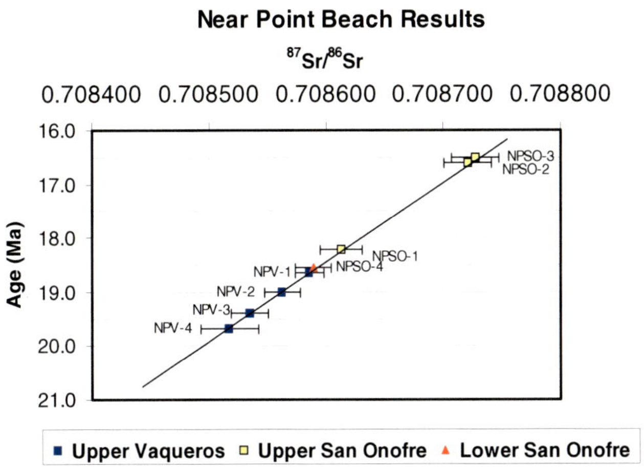

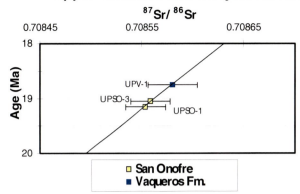

Near Point Beach Results

$^{87}Sr/^{86}Sr$

Figure 4. Graph showing results of Near Point Beach samples. Correlation of age with strontium isotopic ratios is based on Oslick et al. (1994).

Formation samples (NPV-1 through NPV-4) place their ages in the same relative order in which they were sampled from the stratigraphic column, indicating decreasing age (Figure 2) and confirming the validity of the strontium method. The data show that the boundary between the Rincon Formation and the upper Vaqueros Formation is 19 ± 1 Ma (early Miocene), at least 5 Ma younger than the 24 Ma age as suggested by biochronology of Bereskin and Edwards (1969). It is likely that this age of 19 ± 1 Ma approximates the age of the whole unit because the lower unit is comprised of thick-bedded conglomerate sequences that suggest rapid deposition.

One sample was analyzed from the lower San Onofre Breccia. The $^{87}Sr/^{86}Sr$ results of this sample indicated that the boundary between the lower San Onofre Breccia and the Rincon Formation is at 18.5 ± 1 Ma (early Miocene). Three samples were analyzed from the upper San Onofre. All three samples contained low amounts of strontium (<800‰). Results for sample NPSO-1 indicated an age of 18.2 ± 1 Ma. Two of these samples, NPSO-2 and NPSO-3, were spiked to check for strontium concentration in addition to the strontium isotopic values. The $^{87}Sr/^{86}Sr$ results for NPSO-2 and NPSO-3 correlated with ages of 16.6 Ma and 16.5 Ma, respectively. We believe that samples NPSO-2 and NPSO-3 have undergone some diagenetic alteration, due to the low concentration of strontium, (810‰ and 405‰, respectively). This would change the $^{87}Sr/^{86}Sr$ value; therefore, we believe the true depositional age of the upper San Onofre is closer to sample NPSO-1 at 18.2 ± 1 Ma (early Miocene).

Upper Canada Posa Canyon

The data for the San Onofre and Vaqueros samples from upper Canada Posa Canyon are shown on Figure 5. Strontium results of samples UPSO-1 and UPSO-3 from the middle San Onofre indicate an age of 19.1 ± 1 Ma and 19.0 ± 1 Ma, respectively (early Miocene). Results of sample UPV-1 from the top of the Vaqueros Formation correlate

Upper Canada Posa Canyon Results

$^{87}Sr/^{86}Sr$

Figure 5. Graph showing results of upper Canada Posa Canyon samples. Correlation of age with strontium isotopic ratios is based on Oslick et al. (1994).

with an age of 18.7 ± 1 Ma. Although the results may appear to be problematic in light of the relative stratigraphic positions of the units (i.e., 18.7 Ma Vaqueros sample stratigraphically below the 19.0 Ma San Onofre Breccia samples), they are not problematic if their uncertainties are considered (e.g., Vaqueros sample may be as old as 19.0 Ma and San Onofre Breccia samples may be as young as 18.7 Ma).

Laguna Canyon

The results from sample LC-1, from the basal Blanca Formation, show a $^{87}Sr/^{86}Sr$ value of 0.708508. This ratio correlates with previous work by Schultz (unpublished data), which resulted in a $^{87}Sr/^{86}Sr$ value of 0.70856 for a basal Blanca Formation sample from upper Canada Posa Canyon. This close agreement of the data indicates that the age of the base of the Blanca Formation is 19 ± 1 Ma (early Miocene).

DISCUSSION

The results of this study of southwest Santa Cruz Island constrain the time interval of deposition for the Oligocene-Miocene strata (Figure 3). The strontium results for Near Point Beach and upper Canada Posa Canyon indicate the age of the formation boundaries as follows: the Vaqueros-Rincon boundary is at 19 ± 1 Ma; the Rincon-San Onofre Breccia boundary is at 18.5 ± 1 Ma; and the San-Onofre Breccia-Beechers Bay boundary is at 18.2 ± 1 Ma (early Miocene).

Our results indicate the Vaqueros Formation and San Onofre Breccia depositional ages on the island are much closer then previously believed. This work shows that the time interval represented by the Rincon Formation is very short (less than 1 Ma) and that the deposition of the Vaqueros Formation and San Onofre Breccia were nearly synchronous events. In contrast, the age of the Vaqueros Formation in the western Transverse Ranges is 26 ± 2 Ma, based on strontium isotopic ratios (Rigsby 1989). Also, the San Onofre Breccia is believed to be 17-13 Ma in the San Diego area.

These strata on the mainland represent a much larger time interval than on Santa Cruz Island.

These results are important to the chronology of tectonic reconstruction of the region. Before the onset of rotation of the Transverse Ranges, Santa Cruz Island and San Diego were in close proximity (Figure 6). Evidence for this is seen in paleomagnetic records (Kamerling and Luyendyk 1985), and in the similarity of Eocene conglomerates in San Diego and on Santa Cruz Island (Abbott and Smith 1978). During the Miocene, the western Transverse Range block rifted, rotated, and translated northwestward with the Pacific plate (Atwater 1997). As a result, the region in its wake underwent extreme extension and crustal unroofing that became the inner California Continental Borderland (Nicholson et al. 1994). The tectonic rearrangement during the early Miocene in the area of San Diego caused uplift (shedding of clastic sediment of the Vaqueros Formation) and unroofing of high-pressure, low-temperature metamorphic rocks (blueschists and greenschists). The metamorphic rocks are observed in the San Onofre Breccia in San Diego, on the Coronado Islands, and on Santa Cruz Island (Stuart 1979). The Catalina Schist is believed to be a source rock for the San Onofre Breccia (Stuart 1979; Boles 1997). The timing of the inception of rifting of the Transverse Range block and subsequent unroofing of mid-crustal rocks can be inferred from the depositional age of the San Onofre Breccia. Crouch and Suppe (1993) infer uplift of the Catalina Schist from 22-25 Ma (early Miocene) and that it would take 3 Ma for it to be exposed[2]. During this time interval, strike-slip faults developed on the Pacific plate (within the Transverse Range block) through strain partitioning due to coupling of the Monterey plate with the Pacific plate (Nicholson et al. 1994). Perhaps at this time, the Transverse Range block began to break up, allowing for the deposition of the San Onofre Breccia to the west of present-day San Diego.

The results indicate the San Onofre Breccia on Santa Cruz Island was deposited rapidly and confirms it is the oldest part of the Formation, older then the Relizian-Luisian age (17.0-14.2 Ma) San Onofre Breccia in the San Diego area (Stuart 1979). This age relationship may indicate the source for the San Onofre Breccia on Santa Cruz Island was derived from an outboard sequence, and was uplifted 2-6 Ma earlier then the San Diego section which was derived from an inboard sequence (Figure 6A). This would concur with previous suggestions that the rifting occurred in a progressive arcuate fashion, based on the premise that the Vaqueros Formation and San Onofre Breccia are older on southwest Santa Cruz Island than on the mainland (Kamerling 1994). It is worth noting that the sediment transport direction for the San Onofre Breccia on Santa Cruz Island is

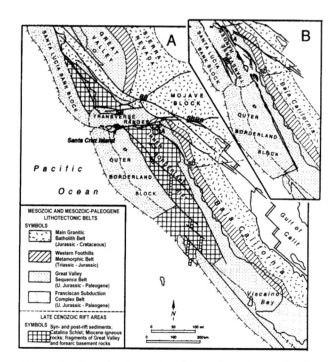

Figure 6. Map showing regional tectonic setting, indicating distribution of principal Mesozoic and Mesozoic-Paleogene lithotectonic belts (Atwater 1997; and Couch and Suppe 1993). A. Present configuration from central California to central Baja California, including inferred late Cenozoic rift areas (after Crouch and Suppe (1993)). Filled circles show the location of Santa Cruz Island. B. Likely mid-Cenozoic configuration of southwestern California and northern Baja California (after Crouch and Suppe (1993)). Split halves of filled circles show approximate reconstruction locations of northern and southern halves of Santa Cruz Island (Kamerling and Luyendyk (1985)). Cities located on map: SB, Santa Barbara; LA, Los Angeles; SD, San Diego. Tranpressional bends in the San Andreas fault: BB, "Big Bend"; SBMB, San Bernardino Mountain Bend.

opposite to that expected for a source from the inner borderland rift basin (Figure 6A).

Results indicate that volcanism, which was apparently related to extension, was active by 19 Ma (early Miocene). An age of 19 ± 1 Ma has been determined for volcanism on Santa Cruz Island (recorded by the Blanca Formation), and in San Diego (recorded by tholeiites on Coronado Islands (Lamb 1979)). Because blueschist detritus underlies and is interbedded with the volcanic rocks in both of these areas, we conclude that unroofing, erosion, and redeposition of the blueschist rocks were nearly synchronous with volcanism.

---

[2]It is assumed that the Catalina Schist was unroofed from mid-crustal depths of 10 to 15 km before being eroded. It is also assumed that the average rate of Neogene clockwise rotation was 5°-6°/Ma, and that the detachment surface had an eastern dip of approximately 35°.

SUMMARY AND CONCLUSIONS

In this study, fifteen megafossil samples from the Vaqueros and Blanca Formations and the San Onofre Breccia from Santa Cruz Island were analyzed to determine their strontium isotopic ratios. Strontium isotope analyses of the sampled rock units narrowly constrain the timing of deposition of blueschist and volcaniclastic detritus. The age of the top of the Vaqueros is 19 ± 1 Ma, 5 Ma younger than indicated by Bereskin and Edwards (1969) and 6 Ma younger than mainland rocks (Rigsby 1989). We are confident that these samples have undergone little or no alteration based on the carbon and oxygen isotopic results; also, the strontium ratio data from Near Point Beach place the samples in the same relationship as their position in the stratigraphic column.

The strontium isotope work suggests the basal San Onofre Breccia is 19 ± 1 Ma, more than 2 Ma older than in San Diego. The age of the boundary between the San Onofre Breccia and Beechers Bay Formation, determined from this study (18.2 ± 1 Ma), correlates with previous strontium data indicating an age of approximately 19 Ma (J. Schultz, unpublished data). Previous work (Bereskin and Edwards 1969) suggested the age of the San Onofre Breccia was late Saucesian to Relizian (17.0 to 15.4 Ma). The $^{87}Sr/^{86}Sr$ results suggest that the 300-m San Onofre Breccia conglomerate was deposited in approximately 1 Ma.

The onset of volcanism, which is indicative of rifting, and recorded by tholeiites in San Diego (Lamb 1979) and by the Blanca Formation on Santa Cruz Island (this study), was 19 ± 1 Ma. The results of the study indicate volcanism, sedimentation, and inferred unroofing occurred almost synchronously at approximately 19 Ma.

ACKNOWLEDGMENTS

We would like to thank Erin Lutrick for her assistance with the XRD work and for her assistance with the carbon and oxygen data. We would like to thank Jan Schultz, Dr. George Tilton, and, especially, Julie Bryce for assistance with the strontium isotope work. Use of Santa Cruz Island Reserve was facilitated by Dr. Lyndal Laughrin, who was of great assistance. Also, we would like to thank Karen Thompson in the UCSB Kennett Laboratory for analyzing for the carbon and oxygen isotopic ratios. This project was supported by a grant from the UCSB Faculty Mentorship Program.

LITERATURE CITED

Abbott, P. L. and T. E. Smith. 1978. Trace element comparisons of clasts in Eocene conglomerates, southwestern California and northwestern Mexico. Journal of Geology 86:753-762.

Atwater, T. M. 1997. Plate tectonic history of southern California with emphasis on the western Transverse Ranges and Santa Cruz Island. Pages 50-58 *in* Boles, J. R. and W. Landry (eds.), Santa Cruz Island, Geology Field Trip Guide. San Diego Association of Geologists, Annual Field Trip, October, 1997.

Bereskin, S. R. 1966. Miocene Biostratigraphy of Southwestern Santa Cruz Island, California (Master's thesis): University of California, Santa Barbara, CA.

Bereskin, S. R. and L. N. Edwards. 1969. Mid-Tertiary stratigraphy, southwestern Santa Cruz Island. Pages 68-79 *in* Weaver, D. W., D. P. Doerner, and B. Nolf (eds.), Geology of Northern Channel Islands (California). American Association of Petroleum Geologists, Pacific Section, Special Publication.

Boles, J. R. 1997. Geologic introduction and lithologic units. Pages 3-18 *in* Boles, J. R., and W. Landry (eds.), Santa Cruz Island, Geology Field Trip Guide. San Diego Association of Geologists, Annual Field Trip, October, 1997.

Crouch, J. K. and J. Suppe. 1993. Late Cenozoic tectonic evolution of the Los Angeles basin and inner California borderland: A model for core complex-like crustal extension. Geological Society of America Bulletin 105(11):1415-1434.

Doerner, D. P. 1968. Lower Tertiary Biostratigraphy of Santa Cruz Island (Master's thesis): University of California, Santa Barbara, CA.

Faure, G. 1997. Principles of Isotope Geology. John Wiley and Sons, New York, NY.

Howell, D. G. and H. McLean. 1976. Middle Miocene paleogeography, Santa Cruz and Santa Rosa Islands. Pages 266-293 *in* Howell, D. G. (ed.), Aspects of Geologic History of the California Continental Borderland. American Association of Petroleum Geologists, Pacific Section, Miscellaneous Publication 24.

Kamerling, M. J. 1994. Paleomagnetism and Tectonics of the Southern California Continental Borderland (Ph.D. dissertation): University of California, Santa Barbara, Santa Barbara, CA. 217 p.

Kamerling, M. J. and B. P. Luyendyk. 1985. Paleomagnetism and Neogene tectonics of the northern Channel Islands, California: Journal of Geophysical Research. 90:12485-12502.

Lamb, T. N. 1979. Geology of Coronado Islands, Baja California. Pages 119-138 *in* Stuart, C. J. (ed.), Miocene Lithofacies and Depositional Environments, Coastal Southern California and northwestern Baja California. Society of Economic Paleontologists and Mineralogists, Pacific Section, 138 p.

Lindberg, F. A. 1984. Correlation of Stratigraphic Units of North America (COSUNA), Southern California Region. American Association of Petroleum Geologists, Miscellaneous Publication.

McLean, H., D. G. Howell, and J. G. Vedder. 1976. Miocene strata on Santa Cruz and Santa Rosa Islands - A reflection of tectonic events. Pages 241-255 *in* Howell, D. G. (ed.), Aspects of Geologic History of the California Continental Borderland. American Association of Petroleum Geologists, Pacific Section, Miscellaneous Publication 24.

Nicholson, C., C. C. Sorlien, T. Atwater, J. C. Crowell, and B. P. Luyendyk. 1994. Microplate capture, rotation of the western Transverse Ranges, and initiation of the San Andreas transform as a low angle fault system. Geology 22:491-495.

Oslick, J. S., K. G. Miller, and M. D. Feigenson. 1994. Oligocene-Miocene strontium isotopes: stratigraphic revisions and correlations to an inferred glacioeustatic record. Paleoceanography 9(3):427-443.

Rigsby, C. A. 1989. Depostional Environments, Paleogeography, and Tectonic Implications of the Oligocene-Early Miocene Vaqueros Formation in the Western Transverse Ranges of California (Ph..D. dissertation): University of California, Santa Cruz, Santa Cruz, CA. 144 pp.

Stuart, C. J. 1979. Lithofacies and origin of the San Onofre Breccia, coastal California. Pages 25-42 *in* Stuart, C. J. (ed.), Miocene Lithofacies and Depositional Environments, Coastal Southern California and Northwestern Baja California. Society of Economic Paleontologists and Mineralogists, Pacific Section, 138 p.

Weaver, D. W. 1969. Mid-Tertiary stratigraphy, southwestern Santa Cruz Island. Pages 68-79 *in* Weaver, D. W., D. P. Doerner, and B. Nolf (eds.), Geology of Northern Channel Islands (California). American Association of Petroleum Geologists, Pacific Section, Special Publication, 200 p.

Weaver, D. W., D. P. Doerner, and B. Nolf (eds.). 1969. Geology of Northern Channel Islands (California). American Association of Petroleum Geologists, Pacific Section, Special Publication, 200 p.

SOURCES OF UNPUBLISHED MATERIALS

Kennett, J. P. University of California, Santa Barbara, Department of Geological Sciences, CA 93106.

Schultz, J. Santa Barbara City College, Department of Earth and Planetary Sciences, CA 93109.

Tilton, G. University of California, Santa Barbara, Department of Geological Sciences, CA 93106.

COASTAL BLUFF VEGETATION CHANGE OVER 25 YEARS ON SANTA CRUZ ISLAND

Nancy J. Vivrette

Santa Barbara Botanic Garden, 1212 Mission Canyon Road, Santa Barbara, CA 93105
(805) 682-4726, FAX (805) 563-0352, E-mail: bhaller@sbbg.org

ABSTRACT

Distribution of coastal bluff vegetation was monitored by continuous line transect over a 25 year period on Fraser Point, Santa Cruz Island. Introduced annual species (such as *Mesembryanthemum crystallinum* L.) were abundant after periods of disturbance and or drought. Native annual species (such as *Lasthenia californica* Lindley.) were abundant after periods of high late autumn and winter rainfall. *Dudleya nesiotica* (Moran) Moran, a rare island endemic, persisted in the same section of the transect over the entire course of the study. The introduced perennial *Atriplex semibaccata* R.Br. was selectively removed by pig rooting. The native perennial *Frankenia salina* (Molina) I. M. Johnston expanded its range after pig rooting. Once a species occupied a site, it usually continued to occupy that site due to high levels of seed deposition or vegetative reproduction until unusual meteorological events triggered its replacement. Rapid replacements of one annual species by another, occasionally in one season, were preceded by meteorological events which suppressed one species and favored the other. Summer rainfall accompanied by high temperatures followed by warm fall rains favored germination of *Mesembryanthemum* and simultaneously inhibited germination of *Lasthenia*. Rainless summers followed by cold fall rains favored *Lasthenia* germination and inhibited *Mesembryanthemum* germination. Establishment of vegetation patterns, or shifts in those patterns, are rare events triggered by unusual weather.

Keywords: Vegetation change, coastal bluff, *Mesembryanthemum crystallinum* L., *Lasthenia californica* Lindley, germination, dormancy, establishment, maintenance.

RESEARCH NOTE

This study documents change in the distribution of annual and perennial plant species on a coastal bluff over a 25 year period. The distribution patterns were documented annually using a 250 m continuous line transect on Fraser Point, Santa Cruz Island, Santa Barbara County, California. The investigation was designed to identify the processes which lead to the establishment of a vegetation pattern and the maintenance of that pattern over time. During the course of the study, it became clear that establishment and maintenance of a pattern are not controlled by the same environmental or biotic conditions. Establishment of a new vegetative pattern was observed several times during the course of this investigation. Establishment events are rare and typically occur in response to extreme or unusual weather conditions. Loss of dominance by one species and replacement by another is the basis of the establishment of a vegetation pattern. Such replacement occurs in annual plants when the germination requirements for one species are met while germination is simultaneously inhibited for the previously dominant species. Once it is established, maintenance of a vegetation pattern usually continues for several to many years. Gradual replacement of one species by another (succession) was not observed in this vegetation. Each species responded to the meteorological and biotic conditions in a unique way. Groups of species did not respond simultaneously to changes in environmental conditions.

Maintenance of a vegetation pattern is controlled by several factors. In the annual species, a large seed bank in the soil can promote continued dominance by the species that produced it. Soil samples in the upper centimeter underneath *Mesembryanthemum crystallinum* L. (Nomenclature according to Junak et al. (1995) can consist of 90% seed of this species by weight. This large bank of long-lived seeds (at least 25 years), allows the species to reestablish whenever conditions are favorable. Germination of the non-native *Mesembryanthemum* is favored by any form of disturbance which reduces standing biomass: grazing, trails, roads, drought. Fire not only removes biomass, it also breaks dormancy in seeds with hard or semi-hard seedcoats, such as the seed of *Mesembryanthemum*. Areas in Baja California, Mexico, which are dry farmed and then burned, may develop continuous cover of *Mesembryanthemum crystallinum*. Dominance by *Mesembryanthemum* is maintained in part by the release of salt from the dried dead plants into the soil beneath them (Vivrette and Muller 1977). Heavy rains will leach this accumulated salt and under the right conditions, allow other species to germinate and grow in areas previously occupied by *Mesembryanthemum*. *Mesembryanthemum* seed also must be leached by fresh water before it will germinate (Vivrette 1980). After leaching, it germinates best at warm temperatures (20 to 30°C). Since leaching can occur throughout the rainy season, there can be several waves of germination throughout the fall and spring.

The native *Lasthenia californica* Lindley germinates best under cool conditions (5 to 15°C). *Lasthenia* can germinate over a broad range of soil salinities (Vivrette 1980). If the seed is exposed to warm, moist conditions (summer rain followed by high temperatures), a strong secondary dormancy is initiated. The seed is then less likely to germinate in subsequent rains, regardless of the temperature. This enforced dormancy may increase the longevity of the seed in the field. Under constant dry, cool conditions in the laboratory, the seed of *Lasthenia* is short lived (1 to 2 years). In the field, *Lasthenia* seed can remain viable up to 10 years. *Lasthenia* will replace *Mesembryanthemum* when there is no summer rain, and the first rains in the fall are cool. Once there is a standing biomass of *Lasthenia*, *Mesembryanthemum* is less likely to germinate and is unable to grow in the low light conditions. *Mesembryanthemum* will replace *Lasthenia* when a salt-leaching summer rain is followed by warm fall rains, standing biomass is low and there are bare areas of soil exposed, especially after a drought or disturbance.

The distribution of perennials changes more slowly. *Salicornia subterminalis* Parish was reduced after a series of freezing nights. The introduced perennial *Atriplex semibaccata* R.Br. was selectively removed by pig rooting. The upper parts of the plant were pushed aside, and the roots were eaten. The disturbance caused by the pigs unearthed many *Frankenia salina* (Molina) I. M. Johnston stems. New plants grew from these stems, expanding the coverage by this species. The rare island endemic, *Dudleya nesiotica* (Moran) Moran, persisted in the same area for the entire course of the study. The individual plants were larger or smaller depending on the rainfall, but the position of the *Dudleya* patches along the transect remained the same. This suggests that there may be some site-specific condition which favors *Dudleya*.

Establishment of a new vegetation pattern is an unusual event controlled by weather conditions. Once established, a vegetation pattern usually is maintained for several to many years.

LITERATURE CITED

Junak, S., T. Ayers, R. Scott, D. Wilken, and D. Young. 1995. A Flora of Santa Cruz Island. Santa Barbara Botanic Garden. 397p.

Vivrette, N. J. and C. H. Muller. 1977. Mechanism of invasion and dominance of coastal grassland by *Mesembryanthemum crystallinum*. Ecological Monographs. 47:301-318.

Vivrette, N. J. 1980. Zonation of coastal plant species and their correlation with salt levels in the soil. Pages 207-213 *in* Power, D. M. (ed.), The California Islands: Proceedings of a Multidisciplinary Symposium. Santa Barbara Museum of Natural History, Santa Barbara, CA.

MAPPING GRADATIONS AMONG VEGETATION COMMUNITIES ON SANTA CRUZ ISLAND WITH FIELD AND REMOTE SENSING DATA

Michelle Cobb and Leal A. K. Mertes

Department of Geography, University of California, Santa Barbara, CA, 93106-3060
(805) 893-7017, FAX (805) 893-3146, Email: leal@geog.ucsb.edu; mlcobb@yahoo.com

ABSTRACT

Vegetation changes on Santa Cruz Island, especially those due to changes in grazing impacts, have made it useful to prepare a new vegetation map that is complementary to maps such as reported by Minnich (1980). Through the combination of field and remote sensing data of Santa Cruz Island, vegetation maps that emphasize both distinct vegetation communities and gradations among them were produced. The stratified random sampling scheme for field plots resulted in a data set detailing species dominance in significant vegetation communities. TWINSPAN (two-way indicator species analysis) was used to produce a classification of the 93 field samples yielding eight major classes that were interpreted to represent: grassland, coastal sage scrub, fennel-invaded, mixed coastal sage scrub/grassland, mixed oak woodland/island chaparral, island chaparral, Bishop pine forest, and oak woodland. The 'mixed' classes represent the intergrading of vegetation associations described by Junak et al. (1995). These field data were used to assess classification accuracy for maps depicting locations and extent of the community types produced from a Bayesian and a map-guided classifier based on a Landsat image for October 1993. Spectral mixture analysis was used to map the gradations within and between the vegetation communities.

Keywords: Spectral mixture analysis, map-guided classification, Bayesian classification.

INTRODUCTION

Santa Cruz Island is one of the four Northern California Channel Islands, a westward extension of the Santa Monica Mountains. Santa Cruz Island is the largest of the eight California Channel Islands with an area of 249 km². It is located approximately 40 km off of the coast of southern California and is separated from the mainland by the Santa Barbara Channel (Figure 1). With the most rugged topography of the northern islands, Santa Cruz Island displays remarkable physiognomic diversity. Santa Cruz Island supports the widest variety of indigenous flora (420 species) of any of the Channel Islands, including seven endemic species (Raven 1967). Philbrick and Haller (1977) described ten plant communities: southern beach and dune, coastal bluff, coastal-sage scrub, valley and foothill grassland, island chaparral, southern coastal oak woodland, island woodland, Bishop pine forest, coastal marsh and southern riparian woodland. Minnich (1980) reported that oak-woodland, grassland, chaparral, and coastal sage scrub covered 89% of the island. Jones et al. (1993) reported percent cover of 11 vegetation classes derived from a digitized vegetation map based on 1:24,000 color infrared (CIR) aerial photographs: grasses (52.5%), chaparral (18.4%), barren (9.7%), riparian (7.2%), coastal sage scrub (5.1%), oaks (4.1%), pines (1.5%), island oak (0.7%), island ironwoods (0.4%), woody exotics (0.3%), and coastal bluff (0.1%). Junak et al. (1995) described 16 plant associations: southern beach and

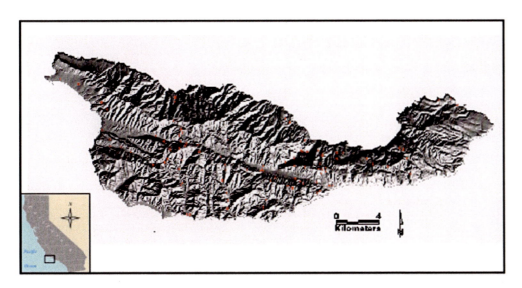

Figure 1. Shaded relief image using the sun angle and azimuth of the satellite at the time of data capture and a DEM. Plot locations are indicated by red markers.

dune, valley and foothill grassland, coastal-bluff scrub, coastal-sage scrub, coyote-brush scrub, island chaparral, island woodland, southern coastal oak woodland, Bishop pine forest, intertidal and subtidal marine, coastal marsh and estuary, freshwater seeps and springs, vernal ponds, riparian herbaceous vegetation, mule-fat scrub, southern riparian woodland.

As a result of decades of extensive overgrazing by feral sheep and cattle, the island suffered severe environmental degradation (Brumbaugh 1980; Minnich 1980; Hobbs 1980; Van Vuren and Coblentz 1987). Due to this damage, The Nature Conservancy (TNC), proprietor of the western 90% of Santa Cruz Island, removed approximately 38,000 sheep and 20,000 cattle during the 1980s (Schuyler 1993). The objectives of this program were to "preserve, protect, and restore the natural systems, flora and fauna of the island" (Klinger et al. 1994: 341). Unfortunately, one result of these control efforts was the accelerated invasion of exotic species, especially fennel (*Foeniculum vulgare*), into many of the island's plant communities (Beatty and Licari 1992). TNC not only continues restoration of native floral communities, but also works to control the expansion of invasive exotic plant species (Brenton and Klinger 1994).

Given Santa Cruz Island's ecological diversity and TNC's current management philosophy to promote restoration, the island is a virtual mecca for many types of research. Much of this research relies on basic ecological descriptors for the island, including topography, geology, hydrology, and climate. Information on the island's vegetation cover, which results from the synthesis of ecological factors, is often fundamental to many research projects. Surprisingly, no contemporary or field-verified vegetation cover map of the island exists. The most recent vegetation map utilized by some researchers was published by R. Minnich in 1980. This classification was derived from 1:22,000 CIR photography acquired during July 1970, a period of intense grazing by feral sheep (Van Vuren 1981). The classification was not comprehensively verified in the field; instead "... the primary role of fieldwork was the characterization of photographic data" (Minnich 1980: 124). Using laboratory and field techniques, the physiognomic vegetation classes were identified based on crown structure, height, spread, and other morphological characteristics using aerial photographic interpretation. As experienced by Minnich and other researchers, the island's large size and rugged terrain limits the use of traditional field techniques for land-cover mapping. If the spatial scale is appropriate, remotely sensed imagery can efficiently analyze a large area for vegetation cover. However, simultaneous collection of traditional field, or ground-verified, habitat data is crucial to the calibration of the remotely sensed imagery. Using geographic information systems technology, the remote sensing and field data can be entered into a database using software designed to input, store, manipulate, analyze, and output spatial information. In this case, the various pertinent themes of data, such as satellite imagery, locations of field plots, attributes of the field plots and elevation contours, can be combined and/or compared with each other in order to perform the desired spatial analysis.

One of the major obstacles encountered when attempting to describe the type, location, and size of areas of similar land-cover is that geographical information is imprecise, meaning that the boundaries between different phenomena are fuzzy or there is heterogeneity within a class (Jensen 1996). Satellite imagery contains pixels with mixtures of land-cover categories that are not easily classified or labeled. The mixtures are not strictly limited to land-cover but also represent topographic variation. Shading of or shadows in a pixel will dramatically affect the reflectance measured by the satellite. However, the typical approach to classification is to determine to which class a pixel belongs. This type of classification uses a hard classification algorithm which is based on classical set theory that requires precisely defined boundaries for which an element either is or is not a member of a given set (Jensen 1996). It is understandable to want to be able to label an entity as one thing or another; such as a tree that is a pine, oak, cottonwood, or cypress. Yet, in the case of a pixel in a satellite image, the entity is a portion of the earth that is covered by a variety of types of natural and human-made substances. Fuzzy set theory provides a tool for dealing with the real-world issues of land-cover mapping. Fuzzy set theory allows a given pixel to have percentages or portions of membership in different classes, such as soil, shade, and vegetation.

The objective of this paper is to present the results of three classification algorithms to determine the most appropriate method, or a combination of methods, to employ in land-cover mapping of rugged terrain. Maps depicting locations and extent of the primary community types were generated from two hard classification methods: Bayesian (Jensen 1986) and an iterative, map-guided (Stoms et al. 1998). Spectral mixture analysis (Smith et al. 1990; Adams et al. 1994; Mertes et al. 1995) was used to map the intergrading of the communities as expressed in the TWINSPAN results.

METHODS

Field Data Collection

During the fall of 1993 through the spring of 1994, 93 vegetation plots were established using a stratified-random sampling scheme (Figure 1). Nine vegetation cover classes were surveyed island-wide, including the eight physiognomic types mapped by Minnich (1980): grassland, island chaparral, coastal sage scrub, woodlands, Bishop pine forest, riparian, barren, and woody exotics. The vegetation cover class of fennel grassland was also included due to the recent invasion of *Foeniculum vulgare* into many of the shrub communities (Beatty and Licari 1992). The island's vegetation types were first stratified using interpretations of 1991 CIR photos (scale 1:24,000). Then field plots were randomly located within the identified stratified stands. The plots measured 60 by 60 m in order to include sufficient areal coverage for ground verification of remotely sensed imagery with a spatial resolution of 30 by 30 m. Each plot's location was recorded on the 1991 CIR photos and the following attributes were measured in the field: 1) slope and aspect, 2) dominant species, 3) percent cover of dominant species, 4) percent cover of litter, exposed litter and soil, and 5) soil color. The flora referenced during field data collection was The Jepson Manual: Higher plants of California (Hickman 1993). The emphasis of this paper will be on the presence/absence and percent cover of dominant species. For further details on the field data collected, refer to Cobb (1999).

Field Data Analysis

All of the field data were entered into a spreadsheet in preparation for both integration into the Geographical Information System (GIS) database and the species and sample ordination analysis. The locations of the plots, represented as points in the database, were screen-digitized using USGS digital data (Digital Line Graph files of hydrography and hypsography) to transfer their locations from 1991 CIR photos into the GIS database. The attributes of the plots were imported into the GIS, appended to the field plot location data layer. Elevation values were calculated by overlaying the points on a Triangulated Irregular Network (TIN) of Santa Cruz Island. The TIN was derived from a mosaic of USGS Digital Elevation Models (DEM) which have a spatial resolution of 30 m by 30 m. Next, the attributes were exported from the GIS database and formatted for import into a FORTRAN based vegetation analysis program, TWINSPAN.

Hill (1979) describes TWINSPAN as a two-way indicator species analysis used to produce a classification of the field samples in two definitions of space (species in species space and species in sample space) using both frequency and presence/absence data. TWINSPAN is a polythetic divisive classification technique that analyzes the presence/absence data of dominant species within each sample (or plot). The program employs a two-way ordination technique that groups species with other similar species and the same with the samples. Among the results listed are the differential species which are those that have distinct ecological preferences and can be used to identify particular environmental conditions. TWINSPAN is designed to construct ordered two-way tables identifying the differential species using reciprocal averaging of samples. The program performed a dichotomized ordination analysis of the samples and qualitatively identifies the differential species on each side of a crude dichotomy. Using these differential species, the ordination was further divided to achieve a user-defined level of dichotomy. Although indicator species analysis is not the focus of TWINSPAN, indicator ordination or a simplified ordination based upon differential species was performed. The main result of TWINSPAN is a table of the samples classified into groups, or classes, to which labels are attached. The number of these classes depends on the number of iterations requested by the user. In this case, data for 85 plots were analyzed (the riparian, barren and woody exotic plots were removed for the final analysis because they were

extreme outliers) with three iterations within TWINSPAN, and eight final classes resulted.

Image Analysis

A Landsat 5 Thematic Mapper (TM) scene of central California dated October 20, 1993, was selected based on the absence of cloud cover and coincidence with collection of field data. Elements of an image processing software package, Image Processing Workbench (Frew 1990) and spatial analysis tools embedded in ARC/INFO®, a GIS software package (Environmental Systems Research Institute, Redlands, California) were employed to generate a landcover map of Santa Cruz Island. Following pre-processing of the image, three classification methods were applied to the data: 1) Bayesian classification, 2) map-guided classification, and 3) spectral mixture analysis. Then two post-processing procedures were performed to complete the three classifications. Lastly, the accuracy of the three methods was assessed using both a quantitative and a qualitative approach.

Image pre-processing begins with geometric rectification, the process by which the "geometry of an image area is made planimetric" (Jensen 1986:103). First, the image coordinates were translated to real-world coordinates using 20 ground control points and United States Geological Survey (USGS) Digital Line Graph files as the basemap. Next, intensity interpolation was performed to calculate each pixel's digital number (DN) at the new spatial location. The nearest-neighbor interpolation method, where the DN of the pixel closest to the original pixel location is assigned to the pixel at its new spatial location, was chosen because this method does not alter the original DNs (Jensen 1986). Lastly, the images were corrected for atmospheric effects through the minimum DN subtraction method to account for path radiance (Jensen 1986).

The Bayesian classification is a supervised method based on maximum likelihood statistics that yields a hard classification. Using the field data, training sites were identified and used as input to the statistical portion of the supervised classification process (Richards 1986). These sites provided sample DNs, or relative values of reflectance, on which the classification was based. The statistics generated from the training sites set the rules for the maximum likelihood classes. To determine the best bands, or wavelengths, of the satellite imagery for use in the classification, a divergence operation was performed (Jensen 1986). Given the six possible bands, the four most informative bands (TM bands 3, 4, 5 and 7) were chosen for the analysis. The Bayesian classification method analyzes covariance values, user-defined a priori probabilities as weights for each class, and chi-square values as classification thresholds (Jensen 1986). This approach weeds out atypical values and highlights previously unidentified spectral classes, which otherwise would simply have been assigned to the 'most similar class' in a standard Boolean classification (Jensen 1986).

The map-guided classification (MGC) method was developed by the Institute for Computational Earth System Science at the University of California at Santa Barbara

(Stoms et al. 1998). MGC is an iterative procedure consisting of two steps using functions within the GRID module of ARC/INFO®. The first step is to perform unsupervised clustering on the image with ISOCLUSTER. Next, the MLCLASSIFY function assigns unclassified pixels to the clusters determined with ISOCLUSTER. MGC requires an input map to be used as training data. As described in Stoms et al. (1998:14):

> "The information classes in the input map are compared with the spectral clusters, and the spectral cluster with the highest level of association (i.e., the highest ratio of pixels in a cluster and information class combination relative to the sum of pixels in the cluster in all classes) is assigned to its corresponding information class. The algorithm then removes pixels in that spectral cluster from the data set and repeats the two-step procedure with the remaining data. Processing continues iteratively until all pixels have been assigned to [a class] that best matches their spectral signature or until a stopping rule is invoked."

In this case, the training sites used in the Bayesian classification were used as the input map data and the program performed 17 iterations.

Given the natural tendency of vegetation classes to lack distinct borders, vegetation communities commonly mix or overlap resulting in gradients. Based on the theory that pixels tend to be inherently heterogeneous, standard classification techniques do not accurately represent reality (Jensen 1986). The fact that pixels contain varying proportions of vegetation, soil, and topography complicates attempts to assign pixels into predefined vegetation community classes. Spectral mixture analysis (SMA) is based on defining endmembers that are represented by spectral data for a homogeneous pixel of, for example, vegetation, shade, and soil (Smith et al. 1990; Mertes et al. 1993; Adams et al. 1994). From the results of the mixing model with the image spectral endmembers, the amount that each image endmember contributed to the composition of each pixel was computed as a fraction value. The fraction images were combined and the patterns of fraction combinations were interpreted to represent the different vegetation categories. Using additive color combinations as a guide, the final SMA map retains information on both the locations of distinct classes as well as the gradations among them.

A traditional approach to the assessment of image classification accuracy is the quantitative comparison of test site data to the classified values in terms of correct or incorrect. This assessment is typically expressed by calculating the mapping accuracy (MA). The MA is the percentage of the number of pixels classified correctly over the summation of the number of pixels classified correctly and classified incorrectly by both errors of commission and omission (Jensen 1986; Richards 1986):

$$MA = \left(\left(\frac{\text{correct}}{(\text{correct} + \text{omission} + \text{commission})} \right) * 100 \right)$$

The data from the training and test sites were used to calculate the MA for the hard classification methods. In an attempt to evaluate the accuracy of the hard classifications within a descriptive context, a fuzzy sets approach was applied to the 93 field samples' observed vegetation class versus their assigned values from the hard classification methods. Fuzzy accuracy assessment "recognizes the inherent ambiguity, or fuzziness, of land-cover classes" (Stoms et al. 1998:835). This method replaces the traditional labels of correct or incorrect categories with "linguistic values" (Gopal and Woodcock 1994:183), such as, absolutely right, good answer, reasonable or acceptable, understandable but wrong, and absolutely wrong (Gopal and Woodcock 1994; Stoms et al. 1998).

Lastly, the total areal coverage for each vegetation community was calculated for the Bayesian and MGC vegetation maps. To calculate correctly the coverage area of a given land-cover class from the image data, it is necessary to account for the difference between the apparent pixel area (1141 m²) versus the true area as it varies with slope. Therefore, for each vegetation category total true area (TTA) was calculated according to:

$$TTA = \left(\left(\frac{\text{width of pixel}}{\cos(\text{slope of pixel})} \right)^2 * (\text{number of pixels in class}) \right)$$

RESULTS

Field Data Results

The field data analysis using TWINSPAN resulted in eight major classes which were interpreted as representing the following communities: grassland, mixed coastal sage scrub, fennel-invaded, mixed coastal sage scrub/grassland, mixed oak woodland/island chaparral communities, island chaparral, Bishop pine forest, and oak woodland (Table 1). The classes labeled as 'mixed' appear to represent intergrades described by Junak et al. (1995). The dominant species associated with each vegetation community type are listed in Table 2.

The following discussion includes a description of each TWINSPAN class and the logic behind the labeling process. Class 000 was labeled grassland, as all 12 samples in the group were field plots of grassland. There were no indicator species for this class; however, the preferential species included: *Atriplex spp., Brassica nigra, Bromus mollis, Dichelostemma capitatum, Erodium spp., Lamarckia spp.,* and *Foeniculum vulgare.* Class 001 was labeled mixed coastal sage scrub/grassland, as the majority of the samples

Table 1. TWINSPAN groupings and fuzzy accuracy assessment values for field plots. Abbreviations for the vegetation type: CH = island chaparral, CS = coastal sage scrub, F = fennel-invaded, G = grassland, OW = oak woodland, and P = Bishop pine forest. The fuzzy accuracy assessment (FAA) values translate as follows: 1 = absolutely right, 2 = good answer, 3 = reasonable, 4 = understandable, but wrong, and 5 = absolutely wrong.

Plot Name	Bayesian Class	Bayesian FAA	MGC Class	MGC FAA	TWINSPAN Class	TWINSPAN Description
CH-01	CH	1	CH	1	101	island chaparral
CH-02	CH	1	CH	1	101	island chaparral
CH-03	P	4	CH	1	101	island chaparral
CH-04	CH	1	CH	1	101	island chaparral
CH-05	OW	2	CH	1	100	mixed oak woodland/chaparral
CH-06	OW	3	CH	1	101	island chaparral
CH-07	CH	1	P	4	101	island chaparral
CH-08	CH	1	CH	1	101	island chaparral
CH-09	OW	3	OW	3	101	island chaparral
CH-10	CH	1	P	5	100	mixed oak woodland/chaparral
CH-11	P	5	CH	1	100	mixed oak woodland/chaparral
CH-12	CS	5	G	5	100	mixed oak woodland/chaparral
CH-13	P	4	P	4	101	island chaparral
CH-14	CH	1	CH	1	100	mixed oak woodland/chaparral
CH-15	CH	1	CH	1	110	Bishop pine forest
CS-01	CS	1	OW	5	10	fennel-invaded
CS-02	G	2	G	2	11	mixed coastal sage
CS-03	CH	5	CS	1	10	fennel-invaded
CS-04	G	2	G	2	1	mixed coastal sage/grassland
CS-05	G	2	G	2	11	mixed coastal sage/grassland
CS-06	CH	5	F	3	1	mixed coastal sage/grassland
CS-07	OW	4	none	5	1	mixed coastal sage/grassland
CS-08	CS	1	OW	4	1	mixed coastal sage/grassland
CS-09	CS	1	G	2	10	fennel-invaded
CS-10	G	2	G	2	11	mixed coastal sage
CS-11	6	3	F	3	11	mixed coastal sage
CS-12	OW	4	F	3	11	mixed coastal sage
CS-13	G	2	G	2	11	mixed coastal sage
CS-14	CH	5	CH	5	11	mixed coastal sage
F-01	6	1	F	1	11	mixed coastal sage
F-02	6	1	G	2	10	fennel-invaded
F-03	6	1	F	1	10	fennel-invaded
F-04	none	5	G	1	10	fennel-invaded
F-05	CH	5	CH	5	10	fennel-invaded
F-06	none	5	CH	5	10	fennel-invaded
F-07	CH	5	F	1	10	fennel-invaded
F-08	G	2	G	2	10	fennel-invaded
F-09	CH	5	F	1	10	fennel-invaded
G-01	none	5	CS	2	0	grasslands
G-02	CS	2	OW	4	10	fennel-invaded
G-03	G	1	G	1	10	fennel-invaded
G-05	CH	5	CH	5	11	mixed coastal sage
G-06	OW	4	F	2	0	grasslands
G-07	P	4	P	4	0	grasslands

Table 1. Continued.

Plot Name	Bayesian Class	Bayesian FAA	MGC Class	MGC FAA	TWINSPAN Class	TWINSPAN Description
G-08	OW	4	CS	2	0	grasslands
G-09	G	1	F	2	0	grasslands
G-10	none	5	G	1	11	mixed coastal sage
G-11	CH	5	F	2	10	fennel-invaded
G-12	OW	2	CH	5	1	mixed coastal sage/grassland
G-13	G	1	G	1	0	grasslands
G-14	CS	2	OW	4	0	grasslands
G-15	CS	2	CS	2	0	grasslands
G-16	CH	5	CH	5	0	grasslands
G-17	CH	5	CS	2	1	mixed coastal sage/grassland
G-18	none	5	G	1	0	grasslands
G-19	G	1	G	1	0	grasslands
G-20	none	5	OW	4	0	grasslands
OW-01	CH	4	P	5	111	oak woodland
OW-02	OW	1	CH	4	111	oak woodland
OW-03	CH	2	OW	1	100	mixed oak woodland/chaparral
OW-04	6	4	OW	1	1	mixed coastal sage
OW-05	CH	2	CH	2	101	island chaparral
OW-06	none	5	OW	1	100	mixed oak woodland/chaparral
OW-07	CH	2	CH	2	100	mixed oak woodland/chaparral
OW-08	CH	2	CH	2	100	mixed oak woodland/chaparral
OW-09	G	4	G	4	10	fennel-invaded
OW-10	P	5	CH	5	10	fennel-invaded
OW-11	CH	3	CH	3	11	mixed coastal sage
OW-12	CH	3	CH	3	111	oak woodland
OW-13	CH	3	CH	3	111	oak woodland
OW-14	CS	4	OW	1	100	mixed oak woodland/chaparral
OW-15	CS	3	OW	1	1	mixed coastal sage
OW-16	CH	2	CH	2	100	mixed oak woodland/chaparral
OW-17	CS	5	OW	1	111	oak woodland
P-01	OW	5	OW	5	110	Bishop pine forest
P-02	CS	5	OW	5	110	Bishop pine forest
P-03	CH	3	CH	3	110	Bishop pine forest
P-04	CH	3	P	1	110	Bishop pine forest
P-05	CH	3	CH	3	110	Bishop pine forest
P-06	CH	3	CH	3	110	Bishop pine forest
P-07	CH	3	CH	3	110	Bishop pine forest
P-08	P	1	P	1	110	Bishop pine forest
P-09	none	5	OW	5	110	Bishop pine forest
P-10	none	5	OW	5	110	Bishop pine forest
P-11	OW	5	none	5	110	Bishop pine forest

were identified as coastal sage scrub in the field. This group of samples consists of four coastal sage scrub, three grassland, and two oak woodland plots. Class 001 had two indicator species that helped to distinguish it from Class 000: *Bromus rubens* and *Quercus agrifolia*. These two species are typically dominant species of grassland and oak woodlands plots, respectively (Junak et al. 1995). The preferential species included *Artemisia californica, Baccharis pilularis, Bromus rubens, Eriogonum arborescens, Gnaphalium spp., Lotus scoparius, Opuntia spp., Quercus agrifolia,* and *Rhus integrifolia.* Species that held no preference for either class were: *Avena spp., Bromus diandrus, Lolium spp., Nassella spp.,* and *Hordeum spp.* Class 010 was labeled fennel-invaded due to the overwhelming number of samples in the group that were identified in the field as fennel grasslands. This class consisted of eight

Table 2. Dominant species typically found in each community type and the related TWINSPAN code(s) for each community type.

Grassland   000 and 001

Atriplex semibaccata	*Brassica nigra*
Avena spp.	*Bromus diandrus*
Baccharis glutinosa	*Bromus mollis*
Baccharis pilularis	*Lolium* spp.

Oak woodland   111 and 100

Adenostoma fasciculatum	*Heteromeles arbutifolia*
Arctostaphylos spp.	*Quercus agrifolia*
Ceanothus arboreus	*Quercus dumosa*
Cercocarpus betuloides	

Island chaparral   101 and 100

Adenostoma fasciculatum	*Heteromeles arbutifolia*
Arctostaphylos spp.	*Quercus agrifolia*
Ceanothus arboreus	*Quercus dumosa*
Ceanothus megacarpus	*Rhus integrifolia*
Cercocarpus betuloides	*Rhus ovata*
Eriogonum arborescens	

Coastal Sage Scrub   001 and 011

Artemisia californica	*Eriogonum arborescens*
Avena spp.	*Eriogonum grande*
Baccharis pilularis	*Haplopappus squarrosus*
Bromus diandrus	*Lotus scoparius*
Bromus mollis	*Rhus integrifolia*
Encelia californica	*Salvia* spp.

Bishop Pine Forest   110

Arctostaphylos spp.	*Quercus agrifolia*
Pinus muricata	

Fennel-invaded   010

Artemisia californica	*Bromus mollis*
Avena spp.	*Eriogonum arborescens*
Baccharis pilularis	*Eriogonum grande*
Bromus diandrus	*Foeniculum vulgare*

Riparian   not included in the analysis

Avena spp.	*Eriogonum grande*
Baccharis glutinosa	*Hordeum californica*
Baccharis pilularis	*Mimulus* spp.
Eriogonum arborescens	*Salix* spp.

Woody Exotics   not included in the analysis

Eucalyptus globulus

---

fennel grassland, three coastal sage scrub, three grassland, and two oak woodland plots. Along with *Foeniculum vulgare*, the indicator species for the class included *Eriogonum grande*, *Hordeum spp.*, and *Artemisia californica*, which are either typical dominant species of grassland or coastal sage scrub associations (Junak et al. 1995). The preferential species included: *Baccharis pilularis, Bromus mollis, Eriogonum grande, Hordeum spp.*, and *Marrubium vulgare*. Class 011 was labeled mixed coastal sage scrub, as the 11 samples were a mixture of seven coastal sage scrub, two grassland, one oak woodland, and one

fennel grassland. The indicator species were *Artemisia californica* and *Eriogonum arborescens*, which Junak et al. (1995) identify as dominant species of coastal sage scrub. The preferential species included *Artemisia californica, Eriogonum arborescens, Quercus dumosa*, and *Rhus integrifolia*. Species that held no preference for either class were *Avena spp.* and *Bromus diandrus*. Class 100 was labeled mixed oak woodland/island chaparral, as the 11 plots were almost evenly split between the two classes (six oak woodland and five island chaparral). Two species of *Bromus* were indicator species: *Bromus mollis* and *Bromus diandrus*. The occurrence of these grasses is indicative of oak woodlands' understory; however, this is not true of typical chaparral plots, which tend to lack any understory (Holland and Keil 1990). Preferential species in this mixed oak woodland/chaparral class included: *Avena spp., Bromus diandrus, Bromus mollis, Ceanothus arboreus, Quercus agrifolia*, and *Rhus integrifolia*. Class 101 was labeled island chaparral, as the ten plots were dominated by nine plots identified as island chaparral in the field and with one oak woodland plot. This class did not have any indicator species; however, the preferential species included: *Ceanothus arborescens, Dodecatheon clevelandii, Eriogonum grande, Erodium spp., Hordeum spp., Pinus muricata*, and *Solanum spp.*. Species that held no preference for either class were: *Adenostoma fasciculatum, Arctostaphylos spp., Bromus rubens, Cercocarpus betuloides, Gnaphalium spp., Heteromeles arbutifolia, Lotus scoparius, Mimulus spp.*, and *Quercus dumosa*. Class 110 was labeled Bishop pine forest, as all 11 pine forest field plots fell into this group, along with one chaparral plot. *Pinus muricata* and *Mimulus spp.* were the indicator species while the preferential species included: *Arctostaphylos spp., Baccharis pilularis, Ceanothus arboreus, Comarostaphylis diversifolia, Lotus scoparius, Mimulus spp., Pinus muricata* and *Rhus integrifolia*. Class 111 was labeled oak woodland, as all samples were identified as oak woodland plots in the field. There were no indicator species; however, the preferential species included: *Bromus diandrus, Claytonia perfoliata, Encelia californica, Foeniculum vulgare, Marah macrocarpus, Marrubium vulgare*, and *Solanum spp.* The non-preferential species were *Heteromeles arborescens* and Quercus agrifolia.

Image Analysis Results

The eight vegetation classes from the TWINSPAN results were used as a guide in the analysis of the remote sensing data. The Bayesian (Figure 2a) and map-guided (Figure 2b) classification methodologies produced maps depicting the locations and extent of primary community types. Table 3 contains the error or confusion matrices for the classification results which were used to calculate the MA for the Bayesian and the map-guided classifications, respectively. The MA for the Bayesian method was 65.3% for training sites and 15.7% for test sites. The MA for the map-guided classification was 40.9% for training sites and 31.5% for test sites.

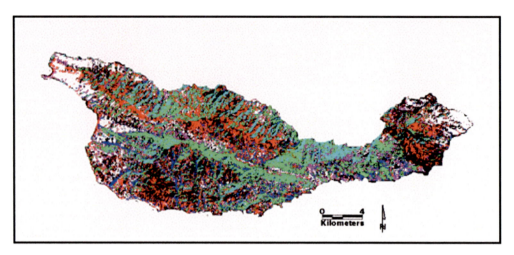

Figure 2a. Bayesian classification results (white = grassland, red = oak woodland, green = Island chaparral, blue = coastal sage scrub, cyan = Bishop pine forest, magenta = fennel-invaded).

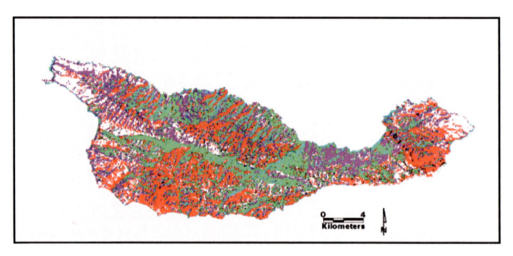

Figure 2b. Map-guided classification results (white = grassland, red = oak woodland, green = Island chaparral, blue = coastal sage scrub, cyan = Bishop pine forest, magenta = fennel-invaded).

agrifolia). Another example is coastal sage scrub plot CS-11 which was classified as fennel-invaded by both classifiers and as mixed coastal sage/grassland by the TWINSPAN analysis; thus, the label of reasonable was assigned due to the degree of mixing these two vegetation communities. Eleven plots (13%) were labeled 'understandable, but wrong' (FAA value 4) for the Bayesian method and 9 plots (11%) for MGC. Plot OW-14 was assigned a FAA value of 4, as it was classified as a mixed oak woodland/chaparral plot by TWINSPAN and as coastal sage scrub by the Bayesian method. Although some oak woodland plots were analyzed by TWINSPAN to 'mix' with coastal sage scrub, the species within this plot were not indicative of the mixed coastal sage class. Hence, the Bayesian classification of coastal sage scrub for this plot was understandable, but not correct. Twenty-six plots (34%), nine (11%) of which were unable to be classified in the Bayesian method, were labeled 'absolutely wrong,' representing values completely inconsistent with field observations. Within the same category there were seventeen plots (20%), two (2%) of which were unclassified in the map-guided classification. Thus, 54% of the field plots were at least partially consistent (i.e., 'absolutely right', 'good answer', or 'reasonable') for the Bayesian classification method and 69% for MGC.

In order to analyze the results of the hard classifications methods, 85 of the field samples were analyzed using the fuzzy accuracy assessment (FAA) method (Table 1). Forty-one percent of the plots were in the 'best' class category (i.e., 'absolutely right' or 'good answer'; FAA values 1 and 2, respectively) for the Bayesian method compared to 56% for MGC. These plots were completely consistent with the results from the image classification schemes and the TWINSPAN analysis. For example, an island chaparral plot (CH-05) was classified as oak woodland in the Bayesian method and in the TWINSPAN mixed oak woodland/chaparral class; thus, it was assigned a FAA value of 2 or 'good answer'. Another 14% were categorized as 'reasonable' (FAA value 3) values for the Bayesian method compared to 13% for the MGC method. Examples for this category are two Bishop pine forest plots (P-06 and P-07) that were classified as island chaparral by both methods; however, field data document the presence of dominant species which frequently occur in both the island chaparral and Bishop pine forest communities (i.e., *Arctostaphylos spp.* and *Quercus*

Even though the accuracies as assessed by both classical and fuzzy methods appear to be low, it is of interest to compare the total true area covered by each vegetation class of the two hard classification methods. Of the reported total area for Santa Cruz Island (249 km²), the Bayesian classification yielded the following percent cover results: grassland = 16.7% (41.7 km²), oak woodland = 23.9% (59.4 km²), island chaparral = 21.8% (54.2 km²), coastal sage scrub = 7.8% (19.4 km²), Bishop pine forest = 12.0% (29.8 km²), and fennel-invaded = 5.6% (14.0 km²). In comparison, the MGC yielded the following percent cover results: grassland = 16.7% (41.6 km²), oak woodland = 18.2% (45.4 km²), island chaparral = 24.3% (60.5 km²), coastal sage scrub

Table 3. Confusion matrices for Bayesian and map-guided classifications.

Bayesian	Class 1	Class 2	Class 3	Class 4	Class 5	Class 6	Total	Correct %	Omission %	Commission %	MA %
Grassland	**266.0**	7.0	0.0	4.0	0.0	0.0	277.0	96.0	4.0	13.7	84.4
Oak Woodland	8.0	**27.0**	26.0	8.0	3.0	3.0	84.0	32.1	67.9	48.8	21.6
Training Island Chaparral	2.0	25.0	**293.0**	8.0	13.0	13.0	369.0	79.4	20.6	17.3	67.7
Sites Coastal Sage Scrub	13.0	6.0	4.0	**73.0**	0.0	1.0	103.0	70.9	29.1	22.3	57.9
Bishop Pine Forest	0.0	2.0	30.0	0.0	**142.0**	2.0	180.0	78.9	21.1	8.9	72.4
Fennel-invaded	15.0	1.0	4.0	3.0	0.0	**52.0**	92.0	56.5	43.5	20.7	46.8
								77.2	**22.8**	**18.2**	**65.3**

Bayesian	Class 1	Class 2	Class 3	Class 4	Class 5	Class 6	Total	Correct %	Omission %	Commission %	MA %
Grassland	**29.0**	16.0	0.0	0.0	1.0	9.0	96.0	30.2	69.8	35.4	84.4
Oak Woodland	2.0	**12.0**	74.0	0.0	13.0	7.0	112.0	10.7	89.3	42.9	21.6
Test Island Chaparral	0.0	2.0	**129.0**	1.0	66.0	0.0	201.0	64.2	35.8	160.2	67.7
Sites Coastal Sage Scrub	27.0	27.0	6.0	**36.0**	0.0	2.0	128.0	28.1	71.9	2.3	57.9
Bishop Pine Forest	0.0	1.0	205.0	2.0	**3.0**	0.0	220.0	1.4	98.6	67.3	72.4
Fennel-invaded	5.0	2.0	37.0	0.0	68.0	**26.0**	169.0	15.4	84.6	10.7	46.8
								25.4	**74.6**	**61.9**	**15.7**

Map-guided	Class 1	Class 2	Class 3	Class 4	Class 5	Class 6	Total	Correct %	Omission %	Commission %	MA %
Grassland	**245.0**	15.0	1.0	2.0	0.0	14.0	277.0	88.4	20.2	11.6	73.6
Oak Woodland	8.0	**14.0**	23.0	17.0	8.0	10.0	84.0	16.7	122.6	83.3	7.5
Training Island Chaparral	6.0	13.0	**263.0**	4.0	50.0	17.0	369.0	71.3	33.1	28.7	53.6
Sites Coastal Sage Scrub	18.0	73.0	3.0	**1.0**	0.0	5.0	103.0	1.0	23.3	99.0	0.8
Bishop Pine Forest	0.0	1.0	90.0	1.0	**68.0**	20.0	180.0	37.8	39.4	62.2	27.1
Fennel-invaded	24.0	1.0	5.0	0.0	13.0	**42.0**	92.0	45.7	71.7	54.3	26.6
								57.3	**40.0**	**42.7**	**40.9**

Map-guided	Class 1	Class 2	Class 3	Class 4	Class 5	Class 6	Total	Correct %	Omission %	Commission %	MA %
Grassland	**29.0**	16.0	0.0	0.0	1.0	9.0	96.0	72.9	44.8	25.0	51.1
Oak Woodland	2.0	**12.0**	74.0	0.0	13.0	7.0	112.0	1.8	71.4	92.0	1.1
Test Island Chaparral	0.0	2.0	**129.0**	1.0	66.0	0.0	201.0	77.6	118.4	20.4	35.9
Sites Coastal Sage Scrub	27.0	27.0	6.0	**36.0**	0.0	2.0	128.0	3.1	8.6	89.8	3.1
Bishop Pine Forest	0.0	1.0	205.0	2.0	**3.0**	0.0	220.0	35.9	20.5	59.5	31.0
Fennel-invaded	5.0	2.0	37.0	0.0	68.0	**26.0**	169.0	68.6	28.4	30.2	54.0
								46.1	**74.6**	**50.2**	**31.5**

= 4.5% (11.2 km²), Bishop pine forest = 5.1% (12.7 km²), and fennel-invaded = 15.1% (37.5 km²).

Due to the low accuracies and inconsistencies between the Bayesian classification and MGC and to portray the TWINSPAN results spatially, spectral mixture analysis was used as an alternative method to map the intergrading of the communities. Figure 3 is a ternary plot of a field sample for each TWINSPAN class within the context of the mixing model fractions. Interpretation of the ternary plot requires consideration of how the components (soil, vegetation, and shade) would physically mix in the landscape. Although island chaparral is more open compared to the mainland communities (Holland and Keil 1990; Junak et al. 1995), for the sake of explanation we refer to the characteristics of typical chaparral. Chaparral has a dense, complex crown resulting in a high level of self shading while the dense canopy cover prevents an aerial view of soil. The reasonable fraction combination for typical chaparral would be 0.0 soil, 0.5

vegetation, and 0.5 shade. In the case of island chaparral, the fraction combination was approximately 0.1 soil, 0.5 vegetation, and 0.4 shade. In contrast, during the fall season the grasslands are dominated by senesced or dry grass and characteristically have effectively no self-shading. The spectral signature of senesced or non-photosynthetic vegetation is similar to barren areas (e.g., Jensen 1986: 159, Figure 7-31). Therefore, the fraction combination for the grassland plot is approximately 1.0 soil, 0.0 vegetation, and 0.0 shade. To aid in the interpretation of both Figure 3 and the vegetation map shown in Figure 4, the mixing of the fractions can also be interpreted with respect to the mixing of additive primary colors (i.e., red = 100% bright soil, green = 100% healthy vegetation, and blue = 100% deep shade). For example, the dark green-blue color (mixture of vegetation and shade) representing an island chaparral plot is in sharp contrast to the red color (100% soil) of the grasslands and barren areas.

DISCUSSION AND CONCLUSIONS

Through the combination of field and remote sensing data of Santa Cruz Island, vegetation maps that emphasize both distinct vegetation communities and gradations among them were produced. TWINSPAN (two-way indicator species analysis) was used to produce a classification of 93 field samples yielding eight major classes that are interpreted to represent: grassland, coastal sage scrub, fennel-invaded, mixed coastal sage scrub/grassland, mixed oak woodland/ island chaparral, island chaparral, Bishop pine forest, and oak woodland. These field data were used to assess classification accuracy for maps depicting locations and extent of the primary community types produced from a Bayesian and an iterative clustering classifier. Spectral mixture analysis was used to map the gradations within and between the vegetation communities on the island.

Results from both hard classification approaches were similar to the 89% cover of the dominant communities (oak-woodland, grassland, chaparral, and coastal sage scrub)

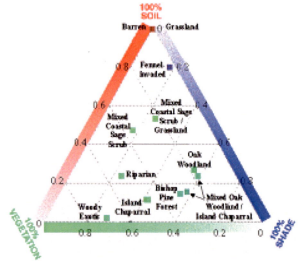

Figure 3. Ternary plot of fraction images from spectral mixture analysis.

reported by Minnich (1980). Combining the areal extent of the grassland, coastal sage scrub, fennel-invaded, coastal sage scrub, oak woodland, island chaparral and Bishop pine forest communities, the Bayesian classification yielded 88% cover and the map-guided classification yielded 84% cover. The low accuracies and inconsistent areal extents of the Bayesian and map-guided classification methods are not surprising in that a hard classification algorithm is based on classical set theory requiring pixels to be assigned to one or another class and these assignments are typically evaluated on a correct/incorrect basis. In addition, remote sensing data is not typically homogenous and the lack of distinct boundaries among vegetation communities only increases the difficulty of accurately mapping land-cover.

It is not entirely surprising that a fuzzy accuracy assessment of the Bayesian and map-guided methods yielded only slightly improved results. However, the spectral mixture analysis, with the assumption of heterogeneous data, proves to be much more conducive to mapping naturally occurring phenomena. In terms of practical use of the SMA map in the field, an understanding of the premise of the method must be attained.

The following is a discussion of the eight TWINSPAN classes with respect to the SMA results. The TWINSPAN and SMA results were generally analogous for the grassland, fennel-invaded and coastal sage scrub field data. In fact, in the case of the coastal sage scrub classes, the SMA results proved to be more useful than those of TWINSPAN. Beginning with the grassland class, as one would expect from image data collected during the fall season, the grassland plot had little or no shade and was absent of healthy vegetation, and therefore yields a reddish-orange color on the SMA map. In terms of the TWINSPAN analysis, this is a relatively distinctive class from the other vegetation communities aside from barren areas. In the case of the fennel-invaded sample plot, the purple-bluish color from the SMA map corresponds well with the TWINSPAN results as the class has a distinct fraction combination (approximately 0.8 soil, 0.0 vegetation, 0.2 shade) from the other classes. Fennel (*Foeniculum vulgare*) flowers during the months of February through June and is a perennial herb measuring 1 to 2 m tall (Junak et al. 1995:80) resulting in a lack of healthy vegetation in fall and a modest degree of self-shading. The coastal sage scrub and mixed coastal sage scrub/grassland classes are yellowish-green colors on the SMA map. As yellow results from the additive mixture of red and green (Paine 1981:228, Plate 1), this yellowish-green color indicates a

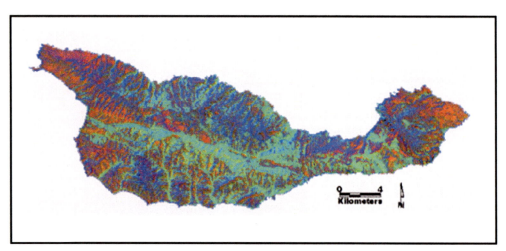

Figure 4. Color composite image of the soil (red), vegetation (green) and shade (blue) fraction images from the spectral mixture analysis.

higher fraction of healthy vegetation (0.3) along with the high fraction of soil (0.5) present in the grassland sample and some shade (0.2). Perhaps due to the fact that the TWINSPAN analysis is limited to the input data of presence/absence and relative dominance of species within the field plots, samples labeled as coastal sage scrub in the field were not easily distinguished from the grassland and fennel-invaded plots. However, the ternary plot illustrates the ability to identify the differences between grassland, fennel-invaded and coastal sage scrub communities through SMA.

As indicated by the mixed results from the TWINSPAN analysis of the oak woodland, island chaparral and Bishop pine forest field data, the SMA results were more subtle than for the grassland, fennel-invaded and coastal sage scrub classes. Although the fraction combinations for the woody classes are relatively distinguishable, their colors from the SMA map are similar, which creates difficulty in visual interpretation. In general, the variations in the amount of shade and vegetation for each of the classes coincide with field observations. For example, the fraction combination of 0.3 soil, 0.2 vegetation and 0.5 shade for the oak woodland class is consistent with a community which contains open space (soil), sparse vegetation and typically occurring on "north-facing slopes, [in] ravines, and [in] narrow canyons" (Junak et al. 1995:20) which explains the high fraction of shade. In the case of the island chaparral, the fraction combination of 0.1 soil, 0.5 vegetation and 0.4 shade is consistent with a more open woodland than mainland chaparral (Holland and Keil 1990) occurring on north-facing slopes. As the Bishop pine forest populations are recovering from the effects of grazing of feral sheep, one of the three populations on the island (Pelican Bay) is described as "primarily open, with scattered groves of mature pine" (Wehtje 1994:331) and another (Christy Pines) has a rich understory consisting of species such as *Adenostoma fasciculatum*, *Arctostaphylos insularis*, *Ceanothus arboreus*, which are dominants of the island chaparral community. Thus, the fraction combination of 0.15 soil, 0.3 vegetation and 0.55 shade can be construed as consistent with the Christy Pines population, but not as much with the more open, Pelican Bay population. Hence, we see the mixtures of the communities in the TWINSPAN results and the similarities in their colors on the SMA map.

In conclusion, although the SMA map does not yield measurements of areal extent for each vegetation community on the island, it does serve as a guide to the type of land-cover likely to be found at any location. Through the analysis of combinations of proportions of soil, vegetation and shade pixel by pixel, the distinct and subtle differences amongst and between the various vegetation communities are illuminated.

ACKNOWLEDGMENTS

Funding for this research was provided by the University of California Natural Reserve System and a California Space Grant fellowship to M. L. Cobb. For their valuable support and guidance, we thank Lyndal Laughrin and the staff of the University of California Natural Reserve System, Steve Junak of the Santa Barbara Botanic Garden, and Rob Klinger of The Nature Conservancy. Lastly, our sincere thanks for the tireless encouragement and assistance of Kevin Crooks.

LITERATURE CITED

Adams, J. B., D. E., Sabol, V. Kapos, R. F. Almeida, D. A. Roberts, M. O. Smith and A. R. Gillespie. 1994. Classification of multispectral images based on fractions of endmembers: Application to land-cover change in the Brazilian Amazon. Remote Sensing of Environment 52:137-154.

Beatty, S. W. and D. L. Licari. 1992. Invasion of fennel (*Foeniculum vulgare*) into shrub communities on Santa Cruz Island, CA. Madroño 39:54-66.

Brenton, B. and R. Klinger. 1994. Modeling the expansion and control of fennel (*Foeniculum vulgare*) on the Channel Islands. Pages 497-504 *in* Halvorson, W. and G. Maender (eds.), The Fourth California Islands Symposium: Update on the Status of Resources. Santa Barbara Museum of Natural History, Santa Barbara, CA.

Brumbaugh, R. W. 1980. Recent geomorphic and vegetation dynamics on Santa Cruz Island, California. Pages 139-158 *in* Power, D. M. (ed.), The California Islands: Proceedings of a Multidisciplinary Symposium. Santa Barbara Museum of Natural History, Santa Barbara, CA.

Cobb, J. L. 1999. Mapping gradients on Santa Cruz Island, California from remotely sensed and ground sample data. Masters Thesis. University of California, Santa Barbara, CA.

Frew, J. E., Jr. 1990. The Image Processing Workbench. Ph.D. dissertation. University of California, Santa Barbara, CA.

Gopal, S. and C. Woodcock. 1994. Theory and methods for accuracy assessment of thematic maps using fuzzy sets. Photogrammetric Engineering & Remote Sensing 60:181-188.

Hickman, J. C. (Ed.). 1993. The Jepson Manual: Higher Plants of California. University of California Press. Berkeley and Los Angeles, CA.

Hill, M. O. 1979. TWINSPAN, a FORTRAN Program for Arranging Multivariate Data in Ordered Two-way Table by Classification of Individuals and Attributes. Cornell University. Ithaca, NY.

Hobbs, E. 1980. Effects of grazing on the northern populations of *Pinus muricata* on Santa Cruz Island, California. Pages 159-166 *in* Power, D. M. (ed.), The California Islands: Proceedings of a Multidisciplinary Symposium. Santa Barbara Museum of Natural History, Santa Barbara, CA.

Holland, V. L. and D. J. Keil. 1990. California Vegetation. California Polytechnic State University, San Luis Obispo, CA.

Jensen, J. R. 1986. Introductory Digital Image Processing: A Remote Sensing Perspective. Prentice-Hall. NJ.

Jensen, J. R. 1996. Introductory Digital Image Processing: A Remote Sensing Perspective, 2nd Edition. Prentice-Hall. NJ.

Jones, J. A., S. A. Junak and R. J. Paul. 1993. Progress in mapping vegetation on Santa Cruz Island and preliminary analysis of relationships with environmental factors. Pages 97-104 in Hochberg, F. G. (ed.), Third California Islands Symposium: Recent Advances in California Islands Research. Santa Barbara Museum of Natural History, Santa Barbara, CA.

Junak, S., T. Ayers, R. Scott, D. Wilken and D. Young. 1995. A Flora of Santa Cruz Island. Santa Barbara Botanic Garden and California Native Plant Society. Santa Barbara, CA.

Klinger, R., P. Schuyler and J. Sterner. 1994. Vegetation response to the removal of feral sheep from Santa Cruz Island. Pages 341-350 in Halvorson, W. and G. Maender (eds.), The Fourth California Islands Symposium: Update on the Status of Resources. Santa Barbara Museum of Natural History, Santa Barbara, CA.

Mertes, L. A. K., M. O. Smith and J. B. Adams. 1993. Estimating suspended sediment concentrations in surface waters of the Amazon River Wetlands from Landsat Images. Remote Sensing of Environment 43:281-301.

Mertes, L. A. K., D. L. Daniel, J. M. Melack, B. Nelson, L. A. Martinelli and B. R. Forsberg. 1995. Spatial patterns of hydrology, geomorphology, and vegetation on the floodplain of the Amazon River in Brazil. Geomorphology 13: 215-232.

Minnich, R. A. 1980. Vegetation of Santa Cruz and Santa Catalina Islands, Pages 123-138 in Power, D. M. (ed.), The California Islands: proceedings of a Multidisciplinary Symposium. Santa Barbara Museum of Natural History, Santa Barbara, CA.

Paine, David P. 1981. Aerial Photography and Image Interpretation for Resource Management. John Wiley and Sons, NY.

Philbrick, R. N. and J. R. Haller. 1977. The southern California Islands. Pages 893-906 in Barbour, M. G. and J. Major (ed.), Terrestrial Vegetation of California. John Wiley and Sons, NY.

Raven, P. H. 1967. The floristics of the California Islands. Pages 57-67 in Philbrick, R. N. (ed.), Proceedings of the Symposium on the Biology of the California Islands. Santa Barbara Botanic Garden, Santa Barbara, CA.

Richards, J. A. 1986. Remote Sensing Digital Image Analysis. Springer-Verlag, Berlin.

Schuyler, P. 1993. Control of feral sheep on Santa Cruz Island. Pages 443-452 in Hochberg, F. G. (ed.), Third California Islands Symposium: Recent Advances in California Islands Research. Santa Barbara Museum of Natural History, Santa Barbara, CA.

Smith, M. O., S. L. Ustin, J. B. Adams and A. R. Gillespie. 1990. Vegetation in deserts: I. A regional measure of abundance from multispectral images. Remote Sensing of Environment 31:1-26.

Stoms, D. M., M. J. Bueno, F. W. Davis, K. M. Cassidy, K. L. Driese and J. S. Kagan. 1998. Map-guided classification of regional land-cover with multi-temporal AVHRR data. Photogrammetric Engineering & Remote Sensing 64: 831-838.

Van Vuren, D. 1981. The feral sheep on Santa Cruz Island: Status, impacts, and management recommendations. Report to The Nature Conservancy, Arlington, VA.

Van Vuren, D. and B. E. Coblentz. 1987. Some ecological effects of feral sheep on Santa Cruz Island, California, USA. Biological Conservation 41:253-268.

Wehtje, W. 1994. Response of a bishop pine (Pinus muricata) population to removal of feral sheep on Santa Cruz Island, California. Pages 331-340 in Halvorson, W. and G. Maender (eds.), The Fourth California Islands Symposium: Update on the Status of Resources. Santa Barbara Museum of Natural History, Santa Barbara, CA.

ISLAND JEPSONIA (*JEPSONIA MALVIFOLIA*) DEMOGRAPHY ON SANTA ROSA AND SANTA CRUZ ISLANDS, CALIFORNIA

Katherine A. Chess[1], Kathryn McEachern[1], and Dieter H. Wilken[2]

[1]U. S. Geological Survey – Biological Resources Division, Western Ecological Research Center, Channel Islands Field Station, 1901 Spinnaker Dr., Ventura, CA 93001
(805) 658-5753, FAX (805) 658-5798, E-mail: kathryn_mceachern@usgs.gov
[2]Santa Barbara Botanic Garden, 1212 Mission Canyon Rd., Santa Barbara, CA 93105
(805) 682-4726, ext.124, FAX (805) 563-0352, E-mail: wilken@lifesci.lscf.ucsb.edu.

RESEARCH NOTE

The California Channel Islands have a long history of grazing by introduced herbivores. Consequently, the population dynamics of island plants reflect the cumulative effects of historic and current trampling, browsing, grazing, and disturbance by these exotic herbivores. Island jepsonia (*Jepsonia malvifolia*) (Greene) was classified in the Catagory-2 Federal status while that designation existed, because of apparent population declines related to herbivore habitat use. It is a perennial herb in the Saxifrage family with a distribution on Guadalupe Island (Baja California) and all California Channel Islands except Anacapa, Santa Barbara, and San Miguel (Munz 1963, 1974; Ornduff 1969, 1970; Junak et al. 1995). It occurs on coastal bluffs and north-facing slopes in association with chaparral, coastal scrub, oak woodland, and pine forest (Munz 1974; Elvander 1993; Junak, et al. 1995). Island jepsonia plants develop leaves from a fleshy underground corm in the winter and spring months, but they flower when the leaves are dormant during fall and early winter. This species has two morphological flower types designated pin (short anthers and an exserted stigma) or thrum (exserted anthers and a short stigma).

Historic and current records for island jepsonia indicated populations were rare and apparently declining on the islands. The corm of island jepsonia is a food source likely favored by pigs. If this species is particularly threatened by pigs, populations should be recovering on Santa Rosa Island, where feral pigs were eliminated in 1992. In contrast, Santa Cruz Island populations should reflect the demographic effects of continuing pig predation. We initiated this research to compare population performance on the two islands, to evaluate populations in contrasting habitats on Santa Rosa Island, and to evaluate factors associated with population decline. Little was known about island jepsonia distribution on Santa Rosa Island, so mapping surveys were conducted there to document the range of habitats occupied by island jepsonia during the 1995 flowering season when the plants were easiest to see. Known locations (Junak pers. comm. 1995) were visited on Santa Cruz Island. Santa Rosa Island surveys found island jepsonia to be widely distributed in island chaparral and adjacent grasslands, and occasionally on canyon walls. On Santa Cruz, island jepsonia occurs primarily in grassy openings in island chaparral.

Permanent demography plots were established on Santa Rosa and Santa Cruz Islands in fall 1995 (McEachern et al. 1997). Six sites were selected for sampling on Santa Rosa and three on Santa Cruz. On Santa Rosa, two replicate sites were selected within each of the three major habitats occupied by island jepsonia. At each site, three plots were subjectively located in spots with at least five flowering plants per 50 x 50 cm plot; objectives were to sample at least 15 flowering plants per site. Since the number of sites was limited and island jepsonia plants were less dense on Santa Cruz than on Santa Rosa, three to eight plots were installed at each of three chaparral opening sites to ensure adequate sample size. Plant species frequency and vegetation cover data were collected in randomly placed belt transects during spring 1996, to characterize the community at each study site. The three community types sampled on Santa Rosa Island were mixed chaparral dominated by prostrate *Adenostoma fasciculatum* and *Quercus pacifica*; grassland dominated by exotic annual species of *Avena*, *Vulpia* and *Bromus*; and canyon walls dominated by various native shrubs and herbs, including *Dodecatheon clevelandii* ssp. *insulare*, with significant coverage of cryptobiotic crust. On Santa Cruz, exotic annual grasses (*Avena*, *Vulpia*, *Gastridium*, and *Bromus*) and other herbaceous species dominated the openings in *Arctostaphylos insularis*/*Quercus pacifica* chaparral.

Demographic data were collected during late fall for flowering plants, starting in November of 1995, and late winter for vegetative plants, starting February of 1996. Plants were mapped in permanent plots on a 1 x 1 cm grid system and remapped and measured annually to determine growth patterns, reproductive output and mortality. Flowering data collected included number of inflorescences per plant, number of flowers per inflorescence, inflorescence height, and morphological type of inflorescence (pin or thrum). Vegetative data collected were number of leaves, and length and width of leaves for calculating size indices for all established plants. Seedlings were counted, measured, and tallied in each

10 cm x 10 cm square within the plot to assess seedling recruitment. Seedlings surviving into the following year were mapped to the nearest 1cm and percent seedling survival was calculated each year. Mean numbers of plants per plot were calculated by life stage classes (vegetative and reproductive plants; small, non-reproductive, apparently one- or two-year old plants; seedlings; and flowering plants). Trends in population size were evaluated by plotting changes in numbers of vegetative plants counted in spring 1996, 1997 and 1998.

Populations on Santa Rosa Island are growing through recruitment of new plants from seed, with the highest population growth rates in grasslands. Excluding seedlings, the grassland community (n=6 plots) increased nearly 250% over three years, growing from a mean density of 26.8 ± 14.0 plants per plot in 1996 to 36.0 ± 17.9 in 1997 and 62.0 ± 42.3 in 1998. The mean number of plants per plot averaged over three years was 41.6. In the chaparral community (n=6 plots), established plant density increased nearly 40%. There were an average of 17.2 ± 5.9 plants per plot in 1996, 23.7 ± 8.1 in 1997 and 23.7 ± 7.2 in 1998, for a mean plot density over the three years of 21.4. The canyon sites averaged 25.8 ± 16.0 plants per plot in 1996 and 40.8 ± 25.4 in 1997. Vegetative plant data were not collected in canyons for spring 1998, so additional population growth cannot be reported. The mean number of plants per plot averaged over the two years was 33.3. For all life stages there is high variability in mean plant density among plots within sites for each sample year.

Results from Santa Cruz Island populations are mixed, even though the island jepsonia habitats are similar. Two of the three sites show a decreasing trend in population size. The third site, near the Christy pines, seems to be growing slightly, mainly through the appearance of established plants that were dormant in 1996, and recruitment in 1997 and 1998. Island jepsonia mortality is variable among sites on Santa Cruz Island. Pig predation is a major source of plant mortality at the two Santa Cruz Island sites with declining sample population sizes. At these two sites, pig rooting was observed in or near plots every season. Spring 1996 data indicate that pig rooting killed 67% of flowering plants present the previous fall in plots at these two sites. Pig predation continued, and in fall 1997, more plots were installed to increase sample size. Recruitment at these sites has been consistently low to nonexistent. The Christy pines site was affected to a much lesser extent by pig rooting until 1998, and is the site where recruitment occurred. Apparently pigs did not frequent this area nearly as much as the sites closer to the Main Ranch and Central Valley from 1995 to 1998 when the pig population was declining (Klinger unpublished data). The pig population increased during 1998, probably due to high rainfall and resulting increased food availability. During December 1998, and February 1999 sampling, pig rooting was recorded in or near all plots at the Christy pines site.

Overall, on Santa Cruz Island, the number of plants in plots increased between 1996 and 1997, but then decreased slightly between 1997 and 1998. The mean number of vegetative plants per plot, excluding seedlings, was 2.6 ± 2.5 (n=16 plots) in 1996, 4.2 ± 3.8 (n=16 plots) in 1997 and 4.0 ± 4.1(n=19 plots) in 1998 for an average of 3.6 plants per plot across three years. The large 1996-1997 increase was mainly driven by the appearance of small dormant individuals and seedlings at the Christy study site. Even though new reproductive and vegetative plants were observed in some plots over years, the overall proportion of plants that flower each year has decreased. During fall of 1995, a total of 57 flowering plants were sampled in plots. In 1996, only 10 flowering plants were present in plots, followed by only 9 in 1997 and 15 in 1998.

Some general trends are apparent as a result of this study. A majority of plants do not flower annually, and flowering is not always followed by vegetative growth. High recruitment and lowered mortality appears correlated with high rainfall in both the small and large plant size classes on both islands. On Santa Rosa Island, *Jepsonia* populations are growing with differential recovery rates in different plant communities. Populations on Santa Cruz Island are variable, with two sites showing signs of population decline, due largely to feral pig activity that kills plants and lowers seed production, while one site showed signs of slow growth until 1999. The elimination of feral pigs from Santa Rosa Island has apparently benefited island jepsonia, and possibly other fleshy-rooted species as well. Eradication of pigs from Santa Cruz Island could reverse the declining trends seen there, if the eradication is done before corm and seed banks are thoroughly depleted.

LITERATURE CITED

Elvander, P. 1993. Saxifragaceae. Pages 1002-1011 *in* Hickman, J. (ed.), The Jepson Manual: Higher Plants of California. University of California Press, Berkeley, CA.

Junak, S., T. Ayers, R. Scott, D. Wilken, and D. Young. 1995. A flora of Santa Cruz Island. Santa Barbara Botanic Garden and the California Native Plant Society.

Munz, P. 1963. A California Flora. University of California Press, Berkeley, CA.

Munz, P. 1974. A flora of southern California. University of California Press, Berkeley, CA.

Ornduff, R. 1969. Ecology, morphology, and systematics of *Jepsonia* (Saxifragaceae). Brittonia 21: 286-296.

Ornduff, R. 1970. Heteromorphic incompatibility in *Jepsonia malvifolia*. Bulletin of the Torrey Botanical Club 97: 258-261.

SOURCES OF UNPUBLISHED MATERIALS

Junak, S., Santa Barbara Botanic Garden, 1212 Mission Canyon Rd., Santa Barbara, CA 93105. Personal Communication 1995.

McEachern, A. K., D. H. Wilken and K. A. Chess. 1997. Inventory and Monitoring of California Islands Candidate Plant Taxa. Unpublished report by U.S. Geological Survey, Biological Resources Division, Channel Islands Field Station, Ventura, CA.

Klinger, R., The Nature Conservancy, 213 Stearns Wharf, Santa Barbara, CA 93101. Unpublished 1999.

SOFT-LEAVED PAINTBRUSH (*CASTILLEJA MOLLIS*) DEMOGRAPHY ON SANTA ROSA ISLAND, CHANNEL ISLANDS, CALIFORNIA

Kathryn McEachern and Katherine A. Chess

U.S. Geological Survey- Biological Resources Division, Western Ecological Research Center
Channel Islands Field Station, 1901 Spinnaker Drive, Ventura, CA 93001
(805) 658-5753, FAX (805) 658-5798, E-mail: kathryn_mceachern@usgs.gov

RESEARCH NOTE

Castilleja mollis (Pennell) (soft leaved paintbrush) is a green semi-parasitic subshrub in the Scrophulariaceae, listed as endangered by the federal government in 1997 (U.S. Fish and Wildlife Service 1997). It was thought to be distributed along the mainland coast in San Luis Obispo County and on Santa Rosa and San Miguel islands (Hoover 1970; Munz 1973). However, it is now recognized as a taxon restricted to Santa Rosa Island (Ingram 1990; Heckard et al. 1991), where it is found in two isolated populations occupying coastal dune scrub along the northern shores of the island. It grows in close proximity to a near relative, *C. affinis* ssp. *affinis*, at both locations, and hybrids form between the two taxa (Ingram 1990). Historic records indicated a broader range for *C. mollis* on the island, but herbarium specimens show that these were actually *C. affinis* ssp. *affinis* locations (Ingram 1990). *C. mollis* was collected from San Miguel Island in the 1930s, but no specimens were found in subsequent surveys (Junak, pers. comm. 1994) or as part of this research, and it is believed extirpated from that island (U.S. Fish and Wildlife Service 1997). Both Santa Rosa Island populations were open to access by cattle, deer and elk until June 1998, when the cattle were removed from the island. Stem breakage from ungulate trampling has been cited as a threat to *C. mollis* by botanists for many years (Ingram 1990), and it was a major factor in the federal listing decision (U.S. Fish and Wildlife Service 1997).

This research provides basic information on *Castilleja mollis* ecology, distribution, and abundance and establishes a long-term monitoring program for both populations on Santa Rosa Island. Systematic, island-wide *C. mollis* surveys were made in 1994, along with pilot sampling in nonpermanent randomly located plots to determine density, damage, hybridization potential, and host plant and community associations. Permanent demography plots were sampled annually in the summers of 1995 to 1998.

In April and May 1994, historic locations and potential *C. mollis* habitats were surveyed on foot. Plants were mapped as they were found, voucher specimens were collected and stored at the Santa Barbara Botanic Garden, population boundaries were mapped, and numbers of plants within boundaries were estimated. A very large *C. mollis* population occurs intermittently along about 4 km of the northwestern shore of Santa Rosa Island between Jaw Gulch and Sandy Point. More than 1,000 individuals occur there in sandy openings or on thin sandy soils over limestone terrace deposits in scattered groups of ten to several hundred individuals. Estimates indicated that several hundred plants existed on the sandy north- and northwest-facing bluffs of Carrington Point, in narrow bands where vegetation has less than about 60% cover and trailing disturbance from cattle, deer, and elk is minimal. This population apparently hybridizes with *C. affinis* ssp. *affinis*, which is most common on the uppermost slopes of the bluff.

In June 1994, six 25 x 4-m plots were randomly sampled at each population to better quantify *C. mollis* abundance and condition. Numbers of plants and broken stems were counted for estimates of plant density and damage levels, floral and leaf characters were measured to estimate the spatial distribution of possible hybridization with *C. affinis* ssp. *affinis*, distances to nearest neighbors were measured to determine potential host plants, and community composition was recorded. A total of 1,002 plants was counted in the twelve plots. The mean number of plants/m² on Carrington Point was 0.51 ± 0.38 (standard deviation), and 1.16 ± 0.75 at Jaw Gulch. Broken stems averaged 55% of all stems in plots at Carrington Point, and 44% at Jaw Gulch. Floral and leaf measurements indicated that hybridization may be occurring where *C. mollis* grows in close contact with *C. affinis* ssp. *affinis*. The two taxa are in closest proximity along the upper elevation of the northwest-facing bluff slopes at Carrington Point, and on the slopes above the terrace between Jaw Gulch and Sandy Point. By far the most frequent nearest perennial plant neighbor to *C. mollis* , and its most likely host, was *Isocoma menziesii*. The plant community at both sites is a degraded, fragmented dune scrub dominated by prostrate *I. menziesii*, with scattered *Astragalus miguelensis*, *Atriplex californica*, and *Erigeron glaucus*. Patches of *Distichilis spicata* and *Bromus diandrus* occur with annual grasses and herbs in openings among the shrubs. At Jaw Gulch, the community also includes substantial cover of *Eriogonum grande* var. *rubescens* and *Mesembryanthemum crystallinum*. Both mapping surveys and plot censuses indicated that ungulate trailing was common in the population boundaries. Deer scat was seen most frequently at

Carrington Point, while elk scat was more frequent at Jaw Gulch. Cattle used both areas and were present during all of the 1994 field work.

Nine permanent, randomly located, 5 x 5-m demography plots were installed June to August 1995. Three pairs of plots were located at Carrington Point, each pair consisting of an upslope and a downslope plot. Three plots were established on the nearly level marine terraces west of Jaw Gulch. For plot location, the occupied habitat was subdivided into thirds along the east-west length of the population, and plot locations were randomly chosen within each third. The upslope/downslope plot pairs at Carrington Point were designed to track performance of plants that may be influenced by *C. affinis* ssp. *affinis*, versus those that should be less affected. Because the main terrace *C. mollis* occurrence at Jaw Gulch did not appear influenced by *C. affinis* ssp. *affinis*, paired plots were not established there. All plants, or ramets, within plots were mapped and tagged. Numbers of live stems were counted on each tagged plant, and the numbers of broken and browsed stems were counted. Stems were tallied as browsed only when it was clearly apparent that browsing had occurred. Numbers of inflorescences were recorded for each stem. For five randomly chosen inflorescences per plot, numbers of flowers and phenological stages were recorded. Insect damage to stems and inflorescences was recorded, as were any other unusual plant characteristics. The plots were resampled in the summers of 1996, 1997, and 1998. Each plot was searched for seedlings and new vegetative plants annually, all plants previously mapped were relocated and measured or recorded as dead, and general habitat conditions and species present were noted. Data were summarized by plot and averaged independently for each population.

C. mollis generally grows by the production of branches from a woody caudex that forms at or just below the soil surface. More rarely, groups of stems appear to emerge from deep roots that are commingled with those of *I. menziesii*. Generally, this caudex or stem grouping is within or at the edge of an *I. menziesii* plant mat, and the *C. mollis* branches grow within the *I. menziesii* canopy. Branches of *C. mollis* can range from one centimeter to nearly a meter in length, are brittle and woody, and can persist for several years if undisturbed. Plants are mapped and tagged at the caudex or where a tight group of stems emerges from the ground unassociated with a caudex. Plants are tagged as new in the plot only when they have this central, branching tendency. The longest branches sometimes run along the ground surface and appear to re-emerge from duff at the soil surface up to several decimeters from the caudex. When this happens, these branches are traced to their origin to determine to which tagged plant they belong. A total of 437 plants, or ramets, have been tagged in the demography study from its inception in 1995 through 1998: 277 at Carrington Point (n=6 plots) and 160 at Jaw Gulch (n=3 plots). Both measurements of plant size (number of stems and length of longest stem), as well as the annual plant mapping, indicate that plants vary greatly in size and shape from year to year.

Populations tend to be dominated by small established plants at both sites, by both measures of plant size. Mean density of plants in plots is generally lower at Carrington Point (1.04 plants/m² over the four years) than at Jaw Gulch (1.24 plants/m²). Less than half of the plants form inflorescences each year.

There has been very high turnover of plants in plots at both sites during the study. In 1998, only about half of the plants previously mapped in plots were still there. Plant loss has ranged from none to more than half of the plants present in the plot the previous year. However, this loss is nearly replaced by the formation of new vegetative plants, or ramets, each year. Establishment of plants from seed virtually did not occur 1995 to 1997. In 1998, there was a flush of seedling recruitment in the westernmost pair of plots at Carrington Point, and several other plots had one or two seedlings. At Carrington Point, the net result of this pattern of turnover has been fluctuation about a mean of 22 plants per plot 1995 through 1997, with an increase to nearly 36 plants per plot in response to the recruitment episode. At Carrington Point, the numbers of plants in plots ranged from 20.3 ± 13.8 to 23.3 ± 16.5 from 1995 through 1997 (n=6 plots), while mean plant density rose to 36.3 ± 28.2 in 1998. At Jaw Gulch, the average plant density was highest in 1995, at 37.3 ± 8.7 plants per plot (n=3 plots); it declined to 21.3 ± 11.1 in 1996, and rose to 32.6 ± 11.8 in 1998.

Scraping of the ground surface by deer and elk during the fall and winter rutting season was a significant source of mortality in some plots in some years at both sites, killing from zero to more than 40% of plants in the affected plots. The caudex is uprooted and killed, *I. menziesii* plants are also lost, and patches of bare ground ranging up to a meter or more in diameter are created by this activity. Deer were active at Carrington Point, while elk prints and scat were associated with the damage at Jaw Gulch. Damage appears to be higher at Jaw Gulch than at Carrington Point. Other causes of plant mortality are not obvious. From 1995 to 1998, the mean percent of plants at each site with broken and ungulate-browsed stems has ranged from slightly less than one-third to about two-thirds of all plants present. Generally, stem breakage results in the loss of entire inflorescences. Additionally, a majority of plants exhibit some insect feeding damage to leaves or inflorescenses. When it occurs on inflorescences, insect damage generally results in the loss of several individual flowers rather than entire inflorescences.

Recruitment from seed generally occurs annually in other Pacific coastal *Castilleja* species (Weatherwax, pers. comm. 1997). This research shows that for 1995 to 1998, plants or ramets lost from the *C. mollis* sample populations have been replaced mainly by vegetative reproduction. Without the small flush of seedlings that occurred in 1998, the Carrington Point population would be seen as fluctuating for the short-term about a low mean plant density, while the Jaw Gulch population appeared to declining slightly. A continued lack of *C. mollis* recruitment from seed could result in population declines when vegetative plant mortality is high and sustained. Stem breakage by trampling, browsing and insect damage can all reduce seed set with cumulative negative effects on population growth potential over many years. Mortality of established plants from the deer and elk scraping activity can further reduce reproductive output from an established population.

C. mollis has apparently maintained a presence in the face of generally high plant loss through vegetative resprouting and the formation of new caudices that persist for one to several years. Sexual reproduction has contributed very little to population turnover during the course of this study. Given the apparent importance of vegetative reproduction for short-term population maintenance, conservation measures should focus for the short-term on preservation and restoration of community structure to ensure vegetative growth and improve the longevity of existing plants. To ensure persistence over the long term, conservation management should seek to reduce and eliminate ungulate damage to plants that reduces the annual seed rain, prevents the development of a seed bank, and creates conditions unfavorable for seedling regeneration. The conservation goal should be to restore the balance of both vegetative and sexual *C. mollis* reproduction within dune scrub communities that can support long-lived individuals of both *C. mollis* and its host plants.

Keywords: California Channel Islands, Santa Rosa Island, *Castilleja mollis*, soft-leaved paintbrush, endangered, demography, disturbance, ungulates.

LITERATURE CITED

Heckard, L., S. Ingram, and T. Chuang. 1991. Status and distribution of *Castilleja mollis*. Madroño 38:141-142.

Hoover, R. F. 1970. Flora of San Luis Obispo County. University of California Press, Los Angeles, CA.

Ingram, S. W. 1990. An examination of *Castilleja mollis* and its distribution. Report prepared for The Nature Conservancy, Nipomo Dunes Preserve, Central Coast and Valley Office, San Luis Obispo, CA.

Munz, P. 1973. A California Flora. University of California Press, Berkeley, CA.

U.S. Fish and Wildlife Service. 1997. Final rule for 13 plant taxa from the northern Channel Islands, California. Federal Register, Vol. 62, No. 147.

SOURCES OF UNPUBLISHED MATERIALS

Junak, S. 1994. Santa Barbara Botanic Garden, 1212 Mission Canyon Road, Santa Barbara, CA 93105. Personal Communication.

Weatherwax, M. 1997. The Jepson Herbarium, 1001 Valley Life Sciences Building #2465, University of California, Berkeley, CA 94720. Personal Communication.

THE CURIOUS CASE OF THE SANTA ROSA ISLAND PEDESTALS

John Cloud[1] and Robert S. Taylor[2]

[1] Geography Department, University of California, Santa Barbara, CA 93106
(805) 893-3663, FAX (805) 893-7782, E-mail: cloud9@geog.ucsb.edu
[2] Geography Department, University of California, Santa Barbara, CA 93106
(805) 893-7044, FAX (805) 893-7782, E-mail: rtaylor@geog.ucsb.edu

ABSTRACT

We examined a series of erosionally isolated pedestals on Santa Rosa Island that constitute natural grazing exclosures. The sites are widely separated, but occur on geologically similar marine terrace formations. Vegetation on the pedestals was markedly richer in native shrubs and other perennials and was more complex in structure than vegetation on comparable adjacent geomorphic surfaces not isolated from grazing and browsing, which were dominated by Eurasian grasses and ruderal forbs. The pedestals offered varying degrees of ungulate exclusion, possibly over different time periods. Vegetation on the pedestals was once probably representative of that seen across their respective terraces at the time they became isolated. Current differences in vegetation composition and structure on and off the pedestals apparently reflect cumulative impacts of nonnative ungulates on marine terrace vegetation since pedestal isolation. The pedestals provide some indication of the regenerative ability of native shrub species after removal or diminution of grazing and browsing. More detailed quantitative surveys of vegetation on and off the pedestals would be useful in predicting future vegetation responses to the removal of all nonnative ungulates.

Keywords: Santa Rosa Island, erosional geomorphology, ungulates, coastal sage scrub, Eurasian grasses, ruderal forbs, vegetation monitoring, vegetation change, disturbance.

INTRODUCTION

Eurasian flora and fauna were introduced to the California islands so long ago, and their impacts have been so pervasive, that it is difficult to project pre-contact vegetation cover and community composition confidently. At the same time, the proceeding or imminent removal of most or all Eurasian herbivores from many of the islands invites speculation about the changes in vegetation composition and cover that will occur with the animals' departure. Santa Rosa Island contains a set of refugia, areas from which Eurasian ungulates have been excluded, to varying degrees and for various lengths of time. We suggest that examination of these refugia and their surroundings can provide insight into both pre-contact vegetation conditions, and also the future changes in vegetation that may occur after non-native ungulate

removal. There are three potential classes of refugia on Santa Rosa Island. The first is explicitly fenced enclosures and exclosures on the island. Extant exclosures date back perhaps 30 years at most, and most of the older exclosures are of limited value to projections of vegetation change for the great uplands majority of the island's area, because the earliest exclosures were established in riparian zones. The second class of refugia is aquatically isolated islets adjacent to the island. Moran (1998) examined the biota of goat-free islets of Guadalupe Island to speculate about pre-contact flora of the main island. Unfortunately, there are no equivalent islets with soil established adjacent to either Santa Rosa Island or any of the other California islands. The third class of refugia is topographically determined. At one end of a spectrum are vertical refugia (i.e., cliffs), a traditional predilection of botanists. Cliffs exclude herbivores, but their vegetation composition can be projected to other parts of the landscape only with difficulty. At the other end of the spectrum are horizontal refugia—flat or gently sloping sections of terrain isolated by catastrophic erosion surrounding them. Horizontal refugia are still problematic, as we will discuss, but we suggest that their close examination may prove quite fruitful to many issues of island vegetation dynamics.

METHODOLOGY

A reconnaissance of the island in 1997 by Cloud had disclosed a curious pedestal of gently sloping soil, entirely surrounded by profoundly eroded badlands, on a slope east of the mouth of Jolla Vieja creek on the south side of the island. The pedestal flora was visually completely distinct from that of adjacent slopes beyond the badlands, being covered with profuse perennial shrubs and sage scrub. Anecdotal accounts from other island specialists indicated there were other pedestals scattered about the island in widely separated locations, which led to the proposal to investigate the pedestal refugia in some detail. The authors and Lauren Johnson, then a botanist in Channel Islands National Park, made an initial reconnaissance of Santa Rosa Island pedestals June 21-23, 1998. We located three pedestals (Figure 1) and searched for but were unable to locate a fourth pedestal identified by Dr. Elizabeth Painter and Dr. Dieter Wilkin.

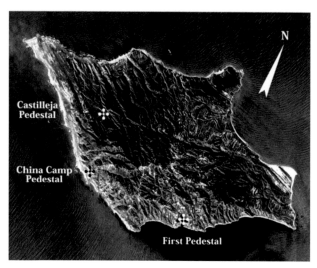

Figure 1. A now declassified Corona reconnaissance satellite photograph of Santa Rosa Island, taken March 17, 1966, with the approximate positions of First Pedestal, China Pedestal, and Castilleja Pedestal noted.

At each of the three pedestals, we determined their position by averaging GPS single-receiver geo-positions, measured the height, length, area, slope, aspect, and general context of each pedestal, and photographed the pedestals and their surroundings extensively. We conducted a census of all vascular plant species found on each pedestal, collecting voucher specimens for subsequent identification as necessary. We characterized the geological context of each pedestal by reference to the geologic map of Santa Rosa Island (Dibblee et al. 1998) in consultation with geologist Helmut Ehrenspeck.

RESULTS

Table 1 contains physical descriptions and geomorphological characteristics of the pedestals. Tables 2, 3, and 4 contain the species inventories for each pedestal, using taxonomy from Junak et al. (1995 and 1997).

We found all three pedestals to be qualitatively quite distinct in biota from adjacent non-isolated areas of similar soil type and general aspect. The pedestals were variably difficult for large mammals (including us) to access. They probably vary significantly in their histories of relative inaccessibility, although these factors are difficult to quantify.

First Pedestal is located south of and below a section of the road from Jolla Vieja east to Wreck Canyon. The pedestal is actually the largest and most vegetatively diverse of a complex of pedestaled surfaces formed by catastrophic badlands erosion of Quaternary alluvium (Qam) deposited on an island marine terrace, underlaid by South Point Sandstone formation (Tsp) (Table 1; Dibblee et al. 1998). The pedestal was covered with perennial shrubs, principally *Artemisia californica*, *Lotus dendroideus dendroideus*, and *Rhus integrifolia*, with 5 to 10 % absolute cover by the grass

Nassella pulchra. A single large *Coreopsis gigantea* was clinging to the eroding edge of the pedestal (Table 2). In contrast, the adjacent slopes of the same alluvium beyond the isolating badlands were covered primarily by *Avena* and *Bromus* grass species.

We accessed the pedestal by traversing the upland neck of dried alluvium connecting the pedestal to higher sections of the badlands. Access is problematical during the dry season, and probably impossible for large mammals during the rainy season. We surmise that cows have been excluded from the pedestal for some time, and that deer and elk are currently excluded. The pedestal had a well-defined series of small mammal trails and bedding areas—and a severed head of a striped skunk. We observed island foxes in the immediate vicinity of the badlands.

China Camp Pedestal is actually an intermediately isolated sloping bench of Quaternary alluvium (Qam) overlaying Sespe Formation marine clastics (Ts) located between China Camp and Cluster Point on the south-west coast of the island. (Table 1; Dibblee et al. 1998). The pedestal is triangularly shaped, like a slice of pie, bounded by the convergence of two first-order deeply incised gullies that meet in a "V" at the lower tip of the pedestal. The upper end of the pedestal is bounded by cliffs mounting up the hill slope behind the pedestal. The pedestal surface is about 100 m long and perhaps 40 m wide at its widest point. The pedestal vegetation was visually distinctive at any distance due to high cover by perennial shrubs, (principally *Artemisia californica*) relative to the topographically similar slopes beyond the bounding gullies. Adjacent areas contained a larger proportion of Eurasian annual grasses and forbs, and much lower shrub cover (Table 3). An examination of cow trails on and around the pedestal indicated that large mammals were not completely excluded from access, but that access was more difficult and considerably more infrequent than on adjacent slopes. On the pedestal, annual grass cover was highest and shrub cover lowest in areas where cow pies and elk scat and trails indicated some ungulate access. In areas of high shrub cover, we saw no evidence of ungulates.

Castilleja Pedestal is the largest of another series of pedestals and grazing refugia, located on Pocket Field north of the Arlington Fault and immediately north of and below the Smith Highway on the northern slope of the island (Table 1). Castilleja Pedestal and the other refugia are older Quaternary dune and drift sands (Qos) thickly deposited on marine terraces, possibly on South Point Sandstone (Tsp) (Dibblee et al. 1998). Like the other pedestals, the vegetation is markedly richer in perennial shrubs, particularly *Artemisia californica*, but it also contained a high coverage of *Castilleja* sp. (as yet unidentified) that was visually quite apparent from a distance (Table 4). Many shrubs on the pedestal appeared mature or senescent, with many of them extending over the uppermost 2 to 3 m of the pedestal face. We found a distinct, well developed cryptogramic crust on some areas of the pedestal. There were deer and elk footprints in the bottoms of the gullies on both sides and *Heteromeles arbutifolia* with severe browse lines in the gully,

Table 1. Physical descriptions of pedestals on Santa Rosa Island.

Provisional Name	First Pedestal	China Camp Pedestal	Castilleja Pedestal
UTM (zone10S) easting	770,767	761,526	760,719
UTM (zone10S) northing	3,756,423	3,757,613	3,762,314
elevation (meters)	50	25	205
aspect	SE	SW	N
length (meters)	30	100	70
width (meters)	max 7, mean 4	max 40, mean 20	4-12
approximate area (m²)	120	2000	500
approximate slope	20%	15-25%	25%
substrate	Quaternary alluvium (Qam) deposited on the coastal marine terrace, underlaid by South Point Sandstone formation (Tsp).	Toe of a slope of Sespe Formation marine clastics (Ts).	Older Quaternary dune and drift sands (Qos) thickly deposited on marine terraces, possibly on South Point Sandstone (Tsp).
isolating features	Gullies in erosional badlands	Two converging gullies, with a cliff on the upslope side.	Gullies in erosional badlands
recent ungulate signs?	None	Yes, cowpies, elk scat, trails at the extreme downslope end. A few cowpies in the NW corner.	None

Table 2. Plants found on First Pedestal.

Species	life form	absolute cover [a]
Artemisia californica	shrub	50%
Atriplex semibaccata	subshrub	-
Avena barbata	annual grass	-
Baccharis pilularis consanguinea	shrub	1%
Bromus hordeaceus	annual grass	-
Bromus madritensis rubens	annual grass	-
Coreopsis gigantea	shrub/ succulent	-
Gastridium ventricosum	annual grass	-
Gnaphalium bicolor	forb	-
Hazardia squarrosa v. grindelioides	shrub	-
Isocoma menziesii (v. sedoides?)	subshrub	-
Lotus dendroideus dendroideus	subshrub	15%
Nassella pulchra	perennial bunchgrass	5-10%
Opuntia littoralis littoralis	succulent	-
Pellaea andromedifolia	fern	-
Rhus integrifolia	shrub	5%
Cover by shrubs and subshrubs		80%
Total cover (including annuals)		>95%

[a] Visual estimates of absolute cover for dominant species only.

Table 3. Plants found on China Camp Pedestal.

Species	life form	absolute cover [a]
Achnatherum diegoense	perennial bunchgrass	-
Amblyopappus pusillus	forb	-
Artemisia californica	shrub	$\leq 80\%$
Astragalus (trichopodus s. lonchus?)	subshrub	-
Atriplex semibaccata	subshrub	-
Avena barbata	annual grass	-
Baccharis pilularis consanguinea	shrub	-
Bromus diandrus	annual grass	-
Bromus hordeaceus	annual grass	-
Bromus madritensis rubens	annual grass	-
Centauria melitensis	forb	-
Daucus pusillus	forb	-
Distichlis spicata	perennial grass	-
Hordeum murinum leporinum	annual grass	-
Isomeris arborea	shrub	-
Layia platyglossa	forb	-
Lupinus succulentus	forb	-
Malacothrix saxatilis v. implicata	perennial herb	-
Malva parviflora	forb	-
Medicago polymorpha	forb	-
Melilotus indicus	forb	-
Mesembryanthemum nodiflorum	succulent	-
Nassella pulchra	perennial bunchgrass	-
Sonchus oleraceus	forb	-
Cover by shrubs and subshrubs		$\leq 80\%$
Total cover (including annuals)		$\geq 95\%$

[a] Visual estimates of absolute cover for dominant species only. Annual cover greatest low on slope. Shrub cover greatest midslope.

but we found no obvious evidence of browsing or scat on the pedestal. Access to the pedestal was at least as difficult at to First Pedestal and involved scrambling on all fours along the neck connecting the pedestal to the land beyond the badlands erosion.

Drs. Elizabeth Painter and Dieter Wilkin have observed a fourth pedestal (UTM zone 10S, easting 764,060, northing 3,762,400) in the western fork of Dry Canyon, but we were unable to locate it as we returned to camp at dusk.

DISCUSSION

Our examination of the Santa Rosa Island pedestals weaves together three strands of ecological investigation: speculation about broad suites of changes in xeric western American vegetation communities attendant on the introduction of Eurasian flora and fauna (Stoddart 1941; Hull and Hull 1974; Vale 1975); the possible applications of topographically isolated horizontal refugia in research on ungulates and vegetation change, including erosionally isolated mesas (Driskoll 1964) and kipukas isolated by lava flows (Tisdale et al. 1965); and the investigation of vegetation changes following ungulate removal (Harniss and West 1973).

The three pedestals we examined differed significantly in vegetation structure and species composition from adjacent areas beyond the isolating eroding gullies and badlands around them. Although the pedestals are several miles apart in three of the four major watershed segments of the island, we were initially surprised to note how geomorphologically similar the pedestals appeared. Each is a summit of thick Quaternary alluvium deposited on much more resistant marine sandstone and marine clastics, located at the toe of steeper slopes. In hindsight, these geological conditions are necessary for the formation of pedestals—if there were not steeper upland slopes to erode around them in incised gullies, ungulate access would not be restricted. Likewise, if the easily eroded marine sediment layer overlaying the resistant strata beneath were not thick, the resultant pedestals would be short, offering less impediment to animal access.

Table 4. Plants found on Castilleja Pedestal.

Species	life form
Achillea millefolium	perennial herb
Artemisia californica	shrub
Atriplex semibaccata	subshrub
Avena barbata	annual grass
Baccharis pilularis consanguinea	shrub
Bromus diandrus	annual grass
Bromus hordeaceus	annual grass
Bromus madritensis rubens	annual grass
Cardionema ramosissimum	perennial herb
Carpobrotus chilensis	succulent
Castilleja (affinis s. affinis?)	perennial herb
Centaurium davyi	forb
Cirsium sp.	forb
Daucus pusillus	forb
Gnaphalium (californicum?)	forb
Hazardia squarrosa v. grindelioides	shrub
Hemizonia fasciculata	forb
Melilotus indicus	forb
Mesembryanthemum crystallinum	succulent
Microseris sp.	forb
Polypogon monspeliensis	annual grass
Sisyrinchium bellum	perennial herb
Spergularia macrotheca macrotheca	forb
Vulpia myuros v. hirsuta	annual grass

Shrub cover variable, from 50-70% in some areas to <5% in other areas. Annual grass cover approaches 100% in between shrubs, + 30-90% overall.

This means that the processes of vegetation change we infer from the pedestals may be most applicable to other areas with similarly deep alluvial substrates on the island.

We note that the pedestals appear to have become isolated from ungulate access as a result of recent and continuing erosion. The pedestals appear to have undergone a community composition shift from the Eurasian annual grasses still predominant on surrounding soils beyond the isolating badlands, to predominantly sage scrub and perennial shrubs. We propose that this is re-establishment of sage scrub on the pedestals, rather than preservation of remnants of some earlier pristine community. It is clear that the pedestal surfaces were once easily accessible gentle slopes that were subsequently isolated by episodes of catastrophic erosion. We cannot determine how long the isolating processes took. It is likely, however, that the gullies isolating the pedestals started after intensive grazing began on the island in the 1850s, which correlates with massive deposition of eroded sediments on the island lowlands beginning about that time (Cole and Liu 1994). We surmise that the soil surfaces comprising the pedestals were once undifferentiated from their surroundings. Hence the future pedestal surfaces were once

probably impacted by grazing in a manner similar to the surrounding areas. Therefore their current vegetation composition represents change from previously more disturbed conditions. Although we did not discover any truly rare species on the pedestals (every botanist's dream on that denuded island) neither did we encounter any explosions of invasive exotic species. We note further that all these pedestals are located within one hundred meters of island roads, suggesting that investigations further afield may reveal more pedestals.

The pedestals of Santa Rosa Island are a unique and temporary resource. It is possible that the principal era of recent erosion on the island was initiated by sheep and occurred during their era (Woolley 1998), but we saw abundant evidence that the pedestals are still eroding rapidly. Erosional processes triggered or accelerated by ungulates can continue even after the animals have been removed (Trimble and Mendel 1995). As sheep, pigs, and now cows have been removed from the island, and the removal of horses, elk, and deer is imminent, we propose establishing permanent vegetation transects across each of the pedestals, including sections of adjacent lands along the transect lines beyond their isolating badlands. Lauren Johnson has already established a point intercept transect at midslope on China Camp Pedestal. Interpreting the pedestals' histories is difficult, but it is quite possible that the pedestals represent the longest time series of ungulate exclosures on nearly flat terrain in existence on Santa Rosa Island.

LITERATURE CITED

Cole, K. L. and Geng-Wu Liu. 1994. Holocene paleoecology of an estuary on Santa Rosa Island, California. Quaternary Research 41:326-335.

Dibblee, T. W., Jr., J. J. Woolley, and H. E. Ehrenspeck. 1998. Geologic Map of Santa Rosa Island, Santa Barbara County, California. Dibblee Geologic Foundation.

Driscoll, R. S. 1964. A relict area in the central Oregon juniper zone. Ecology 45:345-353.

Harniss, R. O. and N. E. West. 1973. Vegetation patterns of the National Reactor Testing Station, SE Idaho. Northwest Science 47: 30-45.

Hull, A. C. and M. K. Hull. 1974. Presettlement vegetation of Cache Valley, Utah and Idaho. Journal of Range Management 27:27-43.

Junak, S., S. Chaney, R. Philbrick, and R. Clark. 1995. A checklist of vascular plants of Channel Islands National Park. Second Edition. Southwest Parks and Monuments Association, Tucson, AZ.

Junak, S., S. Chaney, R. Philbrick, and R. Clark. 1997. A checklist of vascular plants of Channel Islands Natiional Park. Second Edition. Southwest arks and Monuments Association, Tucson, AZ.

Moran, R. 1998. Guadalupe Island and its flora. Fremontia, 26:3-11.

Stoddart, L. A. 1941. The Palouse grassland association in northern Utah. Ecology 22:158-167.

Tisdale, E. W., M. Hironaka, and M. A. Fosberg. 1965. An area of pristine vegetation in Craters of the Moon National Monument. Ecology 46:349-352.

Trimble, S. W. and A. C. Mendel. 1995. The cow as a geomorphic agent—a critical review. Geomorphology 13:233-253.

Vale, T. R. 1975. Presettlement vegetation in the Sagebrush-grass area of the Intermountain West. Journal of Range Management 28:32-45.

Woolley, J. J. 1998. Aspects of the Quaternary geology of Santa Rosa Island, California. Pages 2147-2152 *in* Weigand, P. W. (ed.), Contributions to the geology of the Northern Channel Islands, Southern California. Geological Society of America Bulletin 81.

THE RELATIONSHIP OF BISHOP PINE CONE MORPHOLOGY TO SEROTINY ON SANTA CRUZ ISLAND, CALIFORNIA

Steven M. Ostoja[1] and Robert C. Klinger[2,3]

[1]Department of Biological Science, California Polytechnic State University, San Luis Obispo, CA 93407
(805) 756-2788, E-mail:sostoja@polymail.calpoly.edu
[2]The Nature Conservancy, 213 Stearns Wharf, Santa Barbara, CA 93101, (805) 962-9111
[3] Current Address: Section of Evolution & Ecology, University of California, Davis, CA 95616
(530) 752-1092, E-Mail: rcklinger@ucdavis.edu

ABSTRACT

We tested the effect of increasing temperature on the serotiny of Bishop pine cones collected from three stands on Santa Cruz Island. We hypothesized that cone adaptations to the historic fire regime would be more important than adaptations to local site conditions or morphological variation, and that patterns of serotiny between the stands would be similar. Fifty cones from each stand were tested at five different temperatures (30°, 80°, 130°, 180°, 230°C). The number of open scales/cone was related positively to temperature, but there was no significant difference in the percentage of scales opening at temperatures greater than 130°C. Morphological differences in the cones existed between the stands, but there was no significant difference between the stands in the percentage of scales opening at the different temperatures. At intermediate temperatures (130° and 180°C), the percentage of open scales/cone was positively related to cone size, but negatively related to the number of scales/cone. These results indicate that local adaptations are not directly influencing serotiny patterns in the island's Bishop pines, and that variations in fire behavior can lead to potentially different patterns of postfire regeneration.

Keywords: Bishop pine, fire, Santa Cruz Island, serotiny.

INTRODUCTION

Bishop pines and other closely related species are characterized by cones sealed by a resinous coating, which melts when exposed to sufficient heat, resulting in the release of mature seeds. Because of this reproductive strategy, and because these species occur in maritime and insular regions dominated by chaparral and scrub communities, it is assumed that they are adapted to historical periodic fires and may even require fire for successful regeneration (Vogl 1973; Zedler 1986). It is also assumed that the level of serotiny in closed cone pines should mainly depend on the fire regime (Holland and Keil 1995), but other factors such as local environmental conditions or morphological traits may influence serotiny as well (Perry and Lotan 1979; Borchert 1985). For Bishop pine as a species, as well as other closely related pines (Monterey pine *Pinus radiata*, knobcone pine *Pinus* *attenuata*, and pygmy pine *Pinus contorta bolanderi*), an understanding of the degree of serotiny and the relative influence of different factors on serotiny becomes an important element in understanding the ecology of this species.

Stands of Bishop pine on Santa Cruz Island occur in different edaphic and local climatic conditions, possess different morphological characteristics, and have recent differences in the levels and types of disturbance. A general policy of fire suppression during the ranching era of the nineteenth and twentieth centuries prevented the spread of any large fires on the island, and differential grazing impacts by feral sheep have severely reduced fuel loads in some stands and not others (Hobbs 1980; Carroll et al. 1993; Wehtje 1994). Recently, two of the islands three stands of pines have suffered from a wood engraver beetle population increase (*Ips* sp.), which has led to an accumulation of dense, continuous fuel loads within these stands. Linhart et al. (1967) reported morphological variations in cones between the stands, and Hobbs (1980) noted differences among soils and local climate. These local ecological differences could result in cones from different stands opening at different temperatures as a result of varying fire intensities (Gauthier et al. 1996) and potentially different responses to fire by the cones as a result of morphology.

In the long-term absence of fire, a stand of trees may become senescent as individual trees lose vigor and produce fewer and fewer new cones. Observations we made in the stands over the last eight years indicated that cones were opening and seedling regeneration was occurring in all three despite the absence of fire, but how this compared to potential regeneration following a fire was unknown. In addition, the form of the response of the cones opening at different temperatures was unknown. Several possibilities exist, including a direct linear response with increasing temperature; a linear response up to a threshold temperature (beyond which relatively few scales opened); or a stepwise response to multiple ranges of temperatures, where the percentage of scales that opened remained constant within each range.

The goal of this study was to identify the response of Bishop pine cones to varying temperatures, determine whether this pattern was characteristic of the different stands, and relate morphological characteristics of the cones to the patterns we observed in the scales opening. We hypothesized that if morphology or local environmental conditions had modified the response of the cones to the historic fire regime, then we would expect to see different patterns of scales opening between the different stands or among cones of different sizes. Alternatively, if adaptations to the historic fire regime were more important than adaptations to local conditions, then we did not expect to see differences between stands in the proportion of open scales at different temperatures.

From a conservation and management perspective, determination of the relative degree of serotiny between the different populations helps in the development of appropriate fire management plans for the species and the communities they occur in. This understanding includes the prediction of how different populations can be expected to regenerate in response to specific climatic and disturbance events. If the response of Bishop pine cones to varying fire effects is determined, then steps may be taken to more completely understand the fire ecology within this ecosystem where the natural fire regime has been altered.

STUDY LOCATION

A general description of Santa Cruz Island is given in Junak et al. (1995). There are three separate stands of Bishop Pines on Santa Cruz, commonly referred to as the east (or Chinese Harbor), north (or Pelican Bay), and west (Christy) stands (Linhart et al. 1967). The three stands occur in different soil types and differ considerably in floristic structure and composition, but all are on sites exposed to maritime influences and occur where fog is common in the summer (Minnich 1980).

The east stand occurs on the north and south maritime facing slopes in the isthmus of the island. The stand is divided into two subsections; a north facing zone overlooking Chinese Harbor and a south-facing zone overlooking Yellowbanks (also known as Los Pinos del Sur). The elevation ranges from 100 to 300 m. Soils in both zones are derived from the Monterey Shale Formation, and tend to be shallow and relatively well drained. Bishop pines are not uniformly distributed in the stand, but are scattered in relatively discrete patches. The stand has a dense layer of shrubs, including *Quercus parvula, Q. pacifica, Arctostaphylos viridissima, Adenostema fasciculatum, Lotus dendroideus, Mimulus longiflorus,* and *M. flemingii.* Herbaceous species are relatively uncommon in most parts of the stand, and the organic litter layer is deep and relatively uniform in extent.

The north stand occurs from Twin Harbors to Prisoners Harbor, but pine trees reach their greatest density in the Pelican Bay region, roughly midway between the other two harbors. Trees in this area occur in a relatively uniform distribution, but become more scattered towards Prisoners Harbor. The elevation ranges from 50 to 250 m. Soils are derived from basalt formations, and tend to be very shallow and rocky. Much of the physiognomy is a result of 100 years

of overgrazing by feral sheep (Hobbs 1980; Wehtje 1984). The north stand is more open than the east or west stands; the shrub layer is relatively low and open, and comprised predominantly of *Arctostaphylos tomentosa, M. flemingii, Q. pacifica,* and *Q. parvula.* Ground cover is mainly bare ground, with relatively little herbaceous cover or organic litter.

The west stand occurs from Centinela pass to Cañada Christy and Sierra Blanca ridge, with the densest concentration of trees occurring towards the upper parts of Cañada Cervada and Cañada Sauces. The trees tend to occur relatively uniformly throughout the stand, although discrete clumps of trees occur on the outer parts. The elevation ranges from 100 to 500 m. The soils are highly variable in depth, and are derived from three different geologic formations: Willows diorite, Blanca volcanics, and Santa Cruz Island schist. The west stand is the most diverse of the three in floristic composition and structure. There are relatively few shrubs in parts of the stand where soils are shallow and well drained, but in most parts the shrub layer is extremely tall and dense and the litter layer is deep. Species richness is high, and includes *Q. pacifica, Q. parvula, Heteromeles arbutifolia, Cercocarpus betuloides, Ceanothus arboreus, M. longiflorus, Arctostaphylos glauca, A. tomentosa, L.dendroideus,* and *Adenostema fasciculatum.* Herbaceous species include *Lilium humboldtii, Dichelostemma capitatum, Calochortus albus, Silene laciniata,* and *Sanicula hoffmannii.*

METHODS

We collected 150 cones in the summer of 1995 and stored them in paper bags in a cooler at 5°C. Five cones were randomly selected from each of ten trees in each stand. Trees were selected to be relatively uniform in age and size class. Because prior classification of pines into two species on Santa Cruz has been rejected (Linhart et al. 1967; Junak et al. 1995), and because cones with characteristics of the two varieties can occur on the same tree (R. Klinger, pers. obs.), we did not attempt to stratify the cones by forma.

From each cone the maximum length, width at widest point, weight, and the number of scales were recorded. Scales were counted on a randomly selected quarter of each cone. One of the five cones from each tree was randomly selected for exposure to a different temperature setting ranging from 30°C to 230°C in 50° increments (30°, 80°, 130°, 180°, or 230°). Any cone selected for any specific heat treatment which had any degree of scale separation was not included in the analysis (n=4).

In a laboratory oven each randomly selected cone was subjected to a specific temperature setting for a period of 25 minutes. To account for temperature fluctuations, the oven was preheated for the desired setting for 30 minutes prior to cones going into the oven chamber. To insure accurate temperature readings, three laboratory thermometers were also used both during the duration of the preheating period and during duration of each actual run. At the end of each run the cones where removed and set out at room temperature for a period of 20 minutes. We felt this was representative of the period of time when a fire has passed, yet cone response is not complete. Each cone was then reweighed, inverted to remove the seeds, and open scales counted. Only scales that were thought to be sufficiently open for seed displacement were considered open scales.

For each cone we calculated the percentage of scales that opened, then tested differences between stands and temperatures with a 2-way ANOVA with one nested factor (trees within stands). We used a Tukey test for post-hoc comparisons. We tested differences between stands in cone size (height) and the number of scales/cone with a MANOVA with the same nested factor as in the 2-way ANOVA. All cones were included in the analysis. We tested the relationship between the percentage scales open/cone and the size and number of scales/cone with multiple linear regression analysis. We tested this relationship for temperatures >30°C because very few scales opened at this temperature. Each temperature was analyzed separately.

Prior to accepting the results of any statistical test, we performed a residual analysis to test assumptions underlying parametric ANOVA. The number of scales/cone was square root transformed for the MANOVA test. Two cones were identified as outliers in the 2-way ANOVA and omitted from the analysis. We dropped one outlier from the 130° analysis, two from the 180° analysis, and one from the 230° analysis in the multiple regression tests. Cases with missing data (scales already opened) were also omitted from the analyses.

RESULTS

We computed a Pearson correlation matrix to assess redundancy among the variables we measured for each cone (Table 1). Height, width, and weight were strongly correlated with each other, therefore we selected height and the number of scales as the variables we would use in statistical tests. We selected height because the data had a more normal distribution than width and weight.

There was a significant relationship between temperature and the percentage of open scales/cone (F=327.08, df=4,102, p=0.000). Cones tested at 30°C had significantly fewer open scales than all other temperatures; <1% of the scales opened at this temperature. Cones tested at 80°C had significantly fewer open scales than the three higher temperatures, but there was no significant difference between 130°, 180°, and 230° (Figure 1). There was no significant difference in the percentage of scales opening between the different stands (F=0.71, df=2,102, p=0.49) or in an interaction between stands and temperature (F=1.15, df=8,102, p=0.34).

There was a significant difference in cone size and the number of scales/cone between the three stands (Wilks Lambda=0.286, F=51.68, df=4,238 p=0.000). There was no significant difference in the number of scales/cone between the north and east stands (F=0.099, df=1,120, p=0.754), but

cones from the north stand were 27% larger than cones in the east stand (F=4.24, df=1,120, p=0.042). Cones from the west stand were significantly larger and had significantly more scales than cones in either of the other stands (Wilks Lambda=0.296, F=141.83, df=2,119, p=0.000). Cones from the west stand were 33% larger and had 35% more scales than the other two stands (Figure 2).

There was no significant relationship between cone size or the number of scales/cone and the percentage of open scales/cone for the 80° and the 230° tests. There was a significant positive correlation between cone size and the percentage of open scales/cone and a significant negative correlation with the number of scales/cone and the percentage of open scales/cone for 130° and 180° (Table 2).

Table 1. Pearson correlation coefficient matrix between four variables measured on Bishop pine cones from Santa Cruz Island, CA.

	Height	Width	Weight	Scales
Height	1.000			
Width	0.813	1.000		
Weight	0.840	0.895	1.000	
Scales	0.541	0.594	0.626	1.000

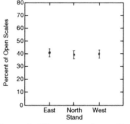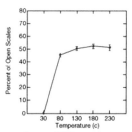

Figure 1. The percentage of scales opening on Bishop pine cones as a function of temperature and stands from which cones were collected. Santa Cruz Island, California, 1995.

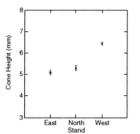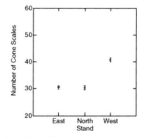

Figure 2. Relationship between the size of Bishop pine cones and the number of scales/cone among three stands on Santa Cruz Island, California.

Table 2. Multiple linear regression tests of the relationship between percent open scales and the height and number of scales/cone from Bishop pines on Santa Cruz Island, CA.

Effect	Coefficient	95% C.I.		t	p
		Lower	Upper		
80°					
Constant	37.46	20.07	54.85	4.42	0
Height	1.7	-1.54	4.93	1.07	0.292
Scales	-0.05	-0.52	0.42	-0.23	0.823

R=0.213, Adjusted R^2 = 0.00

130°					
Constant	39.72	24.15	55.28	5.25	0
Height	5.69	2.75	8.63	3.98	0
Scales	-0.62	-1.05	-0.19	-2.95	0.007

R=0.627, Adjusted R^2 = 0.347

180°					
Constant	53.72	35.3	72.26	5.99	0
Height	4.87	1.02	8.72	2.6	0.015
Scales	-0.87	-1.39	-0.35	-3.46	0.002

R=0.578, Adjusted R^2 = 0.281

230°					
Constant	71.41	52.04	90.77	7.63	0
Height	-1.12	-5.63	3.39	-0.51	0.612
Scales	-0.36	-0.98	-0.27	-1.18	0.25

R=0.399, Adjusted R^2 = 0.086

DISCUSSION

The results of this study suggest that a serotiny threshold of 80° to 130°C exists for Bishop pines in all three stands on Santa Cruz Island. This similar cone response in all the stands probably indicates the importance of adaptation to a historic fire regime, with local environmental factors having relatively little influence on the response. Studies done on jack pine in the Great Lakes region of North America indicate that adaptations to historic fire regimes (or, alternatively, adaptations over large geographic scales) may be more facultative than obligatory, and populations which are relatively close geographically but occur in sites with different fire regimes can evolve different levels of serotiny (Gauthier et al. 1996). The most likely reasons we do not observe this on Santa Cruz Island is that variations in local factors are not important enough, or have not existed long enough, to override the more important influence of similar temperature and moisture patterns which occur in the maritime areas across the island.

Although Bishop pine cones will open at ambient temperatures, this fraction is very small compared to the proportion opening at higher temperatures. However, increasing temperatures beyond 130°C does not result in a greater proportion of scales opening, indicating that hotter fires may not necessarily benefit seedling regeneration any more than a relatively cool fire would. It is even possible that a hotter fire could result in lower seedling germination if shed seeds were burnt directly in the flame, scorched in the hot ash bed, or rendered inviable if nutrients were volatalized.

Our results show that the cones in the west stand are larger and have more scales than in the eastern or northern stands, which is consistent with the findings of Linhart et al. (1967). This size difference is most likely a function of abiotic factors providing a better habitat, including greater amounts of fog, lower wind velocity and richer soil with greater water holding capacity (Hobbs 1980). As a result, the trees can probably put more resource allocation into reproduction than physiological maintenance.

The influence of cone size on serotiny only at intermediate temperatures may be an interaction between physical mechanisms and evolutionary adaptations. At lower temperatures, there is not enough heat to physically make most cones open, while at high temperatures there is so much heat that opening in all cones will be at a maximum, regardless of size. But in the intermediate temperature ranges, it may be an evolutionary advantage to have larger cones open and release greater absolute amounts of seed than small ones. Larger cones have a relatively lower number of scales open than smaller ones, which probably is related to the surface area of the cone that is exposed to heat. But in terms of absolute numbers, more seeds will be released from the larger cones, thereby increasing the number of seeds that could survive to germinate and become established in the burn area. If this hypothesis were true, it would imply that different patterns of seedling regeneration would occur in each of the stands as either a function of varying fire intensity or as a result of differential morphology following fires of intermediate intensity.

It has been suggested that without fires, closed cone conifers may be at risk of succumbing to parasites and be replaced by other species (Holland and Keil 1995). Because Bishop pines will reproduce without fire, this scenario would probably only happen under extreme conditions. However, it is clear that reproduction in Bishop pines is greater at higher temperatures, and since the community they occur in is characterized by species with fire adaptations (Carroll et al. 1993), it would appear as if some degree of burning within the stands would not have any severe detrimental effect on the species or the community. However, allowing fires to occur in the Bishop pine stands should be approached cautiously. Because of suppression practices over the last 150 years, fuel loads in the western stand are very high and a fire would exhibit extreme behavior. The north stand is recovering from overgrazing by feral sheep, and regeneration is relatively high. Seedlings and saplings are relatively young and could be killed by a fire, therefore fire in this stand is probably inappropriate for another 10 to 25 years. In addition, pine stands have a greater proportion of native species than most other vegetation communities on Santa Cruz, and consideration must be given to what types of nonnative fire following species would colonize the stands after a burn. A high proportion of nonnative species did not invade a prescribed burn in the east pine stand in 1994 (R. Klinger, unpublished data), however this may not be the case in the other stands.

Although we have determined serotiny characteristics of Bishop pines on the island, a great deal of ecological work needs to be done to increase our understanding of factors determining reproductive patterns of the species and community attributes of the stands. Systematically broadening the scope of our knowledge of Bishop pines and the island pine community can contribute substantially to the understanding of ecological and evolutionary adaptations to fire in this and other maritime and insular closed cone conifer forests.

ACKNOWLEDGMENTS

We thank Rashell Ralston for collecting the cones, and technicians in the Biology Department at Cal Poly San Luis Obispo for designing and constructing the oven we used in the temperature trials. Comments from two anonymous reviewers improved the quality of the manuscript.

LITERATURE CITED

Borchert, M. 1985. Serotiny and cone-habit variation in populations of *Pinus coulteri* (Pinaceae) in the southern Coast Ranges of California. Madroño 32:29-48.

Carroll, M. C., L. L. Laughrin, and A. Bromfield. 1993. Fire on the California islands: does it play a role in chaparral and closed cone pine forest habitats. Pages 73-88 *in* Hochberg, F. G. (ed.), The Third California Islands Symposium: Recent Advances in Research on the California Islands. Santa Barbara Museum of Natural History, Santa Barbara, CA.

Gauthier, S., Y. Bergeron, and J. P. Simon. 1996. Effects of fire regime on the serotiny level of jack pine. Journal of Ecology 84:539-548.

Hobbs, E. 1980. Effects of grazing on the northern populations of *Pinus muricata* on Santa Cruz Island, California. Pages 159-166 *in* Power, D. M. (ed.), The California Islands: Proceedings of a Multidisciplinary Symposium. Santa Barbara Museum Of Natural History, Santa Barbara, CA.

Holland, V. L. and D. J. Keil. 1995. California Vegetation. Kendall/Hunt, Dubuque, IA.

Junak, S., T. Ayers, R. Scott, D. Wilken, and D. Young. 1995. A Flora of Santa Cruz Island. Santa Barbara Botanic Garden, Santa Barbara, CA.

Linhart, Y. B., B. Burr, and M. T. Conkle. 1967. The closed cone pines of the Northern Channel Islands. Pages 151-178 *in* Philbrick, R.N. (ed.), Proceedings of the Symposium on the Biology of the California Islands. Santa Barbara Botanic Garden, Santa Barbara, CA.

Minnich, R. 1980. Vegetation of Santa Cruz and Santa Catalina Islands. Pages 123-128 *in* Power, D. M. (ed.), 1980. The California Islands: Proceedings of a Multidisciplinary Symposium. Santa Barbara Museum of Natural History, Santa Barbara, CA.

Perry, D. A. and J. E. Lotan. 1979. A model of fire selection for serotiny in Lodgepole pine. Evolution 33:958-968.

Vogl, R. J. 1973. Ecology of knobcone pine in the Santa Ana Mountains. Ecological Monographs 43:125-43.

Vogl, R. J., W. P. Armstrong, K. L. White, and K. L. Cole. 1977. The closed cone pines and cypress. Pages 295-358 *in* Barbour, M. G. and J. Major (eds.), Terrestrial Vegetation of California, John Wiley and Sons. New York, NY.

Wehtje, W. 1994. Response of a Bishop pine (*Pinus muricata*) population to removal of feral sheep on Santa Cruz Island, California. Pages 331-340 *in* Halvorson, W. L. and G. Maender (eds.) The Fourth California Islands Symposium: Update on the Status of Resources. Santa Barbara Botanic Garden, Santa Barbara, CA.

Zedler, P. H. 1986. Closed-cone conifers of the chaparral. Fremontia 14:14-17.

SOURCES OF UNPUBLISHED MATERIALS

Klinger, R. C., Ecologist. The Nature Conservancy, Santa Cruz Island Preserve, 213 Stearns Wharf, Santa Barbara, CA. 93101. (805) 962-9111. [Present Address: Section of Evolution & Ecology, University of CA, Davis, CA 95616, (530) 752-1092, rcklinger@ucdavis.edu]. Observations on pine cone morphology, data on prescribed burn in east stand of Bishop pines.

REGENERATION OF BISHOP PINE (*PINUS MURICATA*) IN THE ABSENCE AND PRESENCE OF FIRE: A CASE STUDY FROM SANTA CRUZ ISLAND, CALIFORNIA

Hartmut S. Walter and Leila A. Taha

Department of Geography, University of California, Los Angeles
P. O. Box 951524, Los Angeles, CA 90095-1524
(310) 825-3116, FAX (310) 206-5976, E-mail: walter@geog.ucla.edu

ABSTRACT

Remnant stands of overaged Bishop pine (*Pinus muricata*) on Santa Cruz Island suffered catastrophic mortality rates during the pronounced California drought episode of 1986-1991. This pine is generally characterized as a fire-obligate species. Natural fires are, however, quite exceptional on the Channel Islands, and the life span of Bishop pines does not exceed 60 to 80 years. How then has this population persisted over centuries and millennia? We established circular census plots of 0.1 acre in size surrounding tall pine snags in three pine patches. We counted all seedlings and saplings and recorded their ages. The results showed that the dying and dead pine stands were substantially regenerating in the absence of any wildfire. An out-of-control prescribed fire — fanned by Santa Ana winds— burned most of the eastern pine patch in December 1994; it provided a rare opportunity to evaluate the impact of the fire factor on this pine population. This event consumed most living and dead biomass above the surface. The hypothesis of a resilient 'pyrofugal' species is proposed that evades post-Pleistocene fire regimes in landscapes where natural wildfires are rare.

Keywords: Bishop pine, *Pinus muricata*, closed cone pines, Santa Cruz Island, fire ecology, island biogeography.

INTRODUCTION

The Bishop pine (*Pinus muricata*) is a member of a small set of closed cone pines that are generally considered to be fire-dependent for regeneration and long-term persistence. In this paper we report and discuss data on the natural regeneration on Bishop pines on Santa Cruz Island, the largest of the California Channel Islands, where natural wildfires have been exceedingly rare in historic time. Based on anecdotal qualitative information from brief visits of Bishop pine stands on the island, we developed the following research hypothesis: Bishop pines of Santa Cruz Island do not require periodic fire events for seed germination and stand regeneration. Our specific objectives were to seek answers to the following questions:

1. How much stand regeneration occurs with and without the presence of wildfires?

2. What are the mechanisms of seed availability, dispersal, and germination in the Bishop pine?

3. What is the role of fire in the evolution and ecology of coastal pine species?

CLOSED CONE PINES AND FIRE

In closed cone pines the cones do not open and release their seeds right after maturation; instead the cones are serotinous or 'late-opening' and retain the seeds in the tree canopy or inside the cone for many years. Viable seed was taken from cones of lodgepole pine (*P. contorta* var. *latifolia*) 75 years after cone maturation (Agee 1993:133). The high ambient temperatures of a fire burning through the crown of a serotinous pine melts the resin seal of the closed cones, and "they open soon after" (Agee 1993:134). In the introduction to their review of California closed cone pine and cypress taxa Vogl et al. (1977:295) state: "The major species are intimately related to fire, characterized by a closed-cone habit or by serotinous cones, whereby the ovulate cones remain sealed after maturity, usually accumulating on the tree until opened by fire." In California, there are three principal species with closed cone characteristics, knobcone pine (*P. attenuata*), Monterey pine (*P. radiata*), and Bishop pine (*P. muricata*).

Knobcone pines occur in California on apparently infertile, acid, and dry substrates that may also contain toxic elements; such substrates limit and reduce the growth and presence of other plant species. Stands of this pine generally occur where they are exposed to marine air; the substrate (often serpentinite) has a high water-retaining capacity. Cones of this pine remain unopened and attached to the trunk, usually for the life of the tree. Detached cones and those on fallen branches and pine snags also remain closed. "Only rarely do the heavy, wooden cones open without fire. Reproduction is also absent in decadent stands where the majority of trees are senescent or dying" (Vogl et al.

1977:330). Fire-opened cones shed their seeds to the ash-covered surface; the seedbed is rich in minerals and offers high insolation. The trees have a short life span of around 50 years, rarely 100 years. Fire frequency is 33 to 50 years due to favorable fuel conditions, relatively dry sites, and the proximity of other fire type communities.

Monterey pines occur naturally within 8 km of the coast of central California, from sea level to 300 m. There is no clear understanding of the physical or biotic factors limiting this highly successful commercial timber tree to its restricted range. The cones remain on the trees for years, but open and close several times during this period, producing a light seed rain that results in small numbers of pine seedlings. In one study, the latter were thin, small, and had sparse needles (Vogl et al. 1977). By contrast, strong and healthy seedlings were found after a recent surface burn. Fires that produce optimum conditions for reproduction "are not as often the catastrophic types common to the other species, but are more frequently surface fires in which parent trees survive" (Vogl et al. 1977:347).

The Bishop pine occurs in California from Humboldt County in the north to Santa Barbara County, and on Santa Cruz and Santa Rosa islands; in Baja California, it is found in two isolated stands on Cedros Island and near San Vicente. This pine is morphologically more variable than other pines; it exists in maritime climates along the coast and up to 400 m above sea level. Frequent fogs and fog drip provide additional moisture to the pines in the often extremely long dry late spring, summer, and fall season. Vogl et al. (1977:337) surmise that this pine "has survived climatic changes since the Pleistocene times because of reduced plant competition on the poor, acid, and often swampy soils, ... and possible high water tables." Stands of Bishop pine are "characteristically even-aged, originating after fire.... On rare occasions, old cones open on hot days. ...A fire-free period of 80+ year (yr) would also allow trees to succumb to diseases and die without reproducing....Fire appears to be a critical factor in the continuance of *P. muricata*..." (Vogl et al. 1977:337-338).

In their concluding paragraphs, the authors make a strong case for the necessity of fire for the long-term persistence of the closed cone pines: "Since most of these conifers are obligate fire types, fire cannot be eliminated or replaced by any other process....If fire is not reintroduced, these groves and forests will eventually be eliminated...The continuance of these conifers, however, can be assured only by ecological management, which will have to include the reintroduction of fire" (Vogl et al. 1977:349-350).

In summary, the expert assessment of these and other closed cone conifers emphasizes the importance of fire for stand continuance and survival of the species. Reproduction and regeneration without an accompanying fire event is seen as uncommon or rare processes and leading to the development of weak pine seedlings.

PINES AND FIRE ON THE CHANNEL ISLANDS

The effect of fire on the vegetation and pines of the Channel Islands has been investigated by several authors. Hobbs studied the regeneration of all three populations of Bishop pine on Santa Cruz Island in 1977-1978 (Hobbs 1980). She established study sites and counted the number of seedlings in each. No seedlings were found in the sheep-grazed northern population, but pine seedlings were recorded in every sheep-free study site located in the western and eastern pine stands. She questioned the existence of an obligate fire factor by concluding: "Moreover, the fact that abundant regeneration was recorded in the other two populations dismisses the question of whether fire is a necessary agent for opening the cones and distributing seed" (Hobbs 1980:165).

A more detailed mapping of the northern pine population was carried out by W. Wehtje in 1990. Between 1981 and 1988 over 37,000 feral sheep were removed from the central and western part of Santa Cruz Island, and the general area of the northern pine stand was essentially sheep-free by 1985 (Wehtje 1994). Some 65% of the pine seedlings recorded in 1990 were 5 yr or younger. Many of them had recolonized grassy and bare surfaces that had been free of pines as a result of a massive 4800 ha fire that occurred in September. 1931 (Hobbs 1980; Carroll et al. 1993), and of serious overgrazing. A small lightning-caused fire in 1987 burned 1.4 ha of the northern study area. Wehtje examined the remaining evidence of this fire as well as charcoal from the earlier fire. Both fires killed many pines, in 1987 "even when only scorched"; he concluded that "Bishop pine appears to be very sensitive to fire damage" (Wehtje 1994:339).

Contrary, therefore, to the almost uniformly positive assessment of the fire factor by many authors, and the pleading for the "reintroduction" of fire by Vogl et al. (1977:350) in the ecological management of close cone forests, the evidence from the two Santa Cruz Island studies does not support the need for fire in Bishop pine persistence and regeneration.

Other research has documented the rarity of lightning-caused fire on the Channel Islands; only three such events have occurred in recorded history compared to some 44 accidental and intentional fires (Carroll et al. 1993). Post-fire analysis of plant succession and richness on Santa Catalina Island shows vigorous resprouting and germination of native island shrubs, trees, and herbs. Germination experiments of both mainland and island chaparral shrubs revealed interesting differences, however. Significant numbers of island seeds exhibited higher germination in unburned control sites than their mainland counterparts. This may reflect an adaptation of island taxa to a lower fire frequency and greater time intervals between fires favoring between-fire seedling establishment (Carroll et al. 1993). No pines were included in these studies.

Bishop pines were found as macrofossils in deposits on Santa Cruz Island dated 14,000 BP. "Abundant" charcoal in Holocene deposits of this island may be have resulted from natural prehistoric fires (Junak et al.1995:35) or from accidental or intentional fires caused by native Americans who were a part of this island ecosystem for the past 7,000 to 10,000 years. We are not aware of any study containing detailed prehistoric fire intensity and frequency data for Santa Cruz Island; thus we are left wondering whether there were large fires every 500 years or so, whether the frequency alternated depending on fluctuating climatic cycles and/or the need or carelessness of Native Americans fishing and harvesting marine resources on the island.

The three disjunct stands or populations of Bishop pine (Figure 1) consisted of overaged trees as well as many young saplings and seedlings in the late 1980s. The severe California drought of 1986-1991 in conjunction with a severe bark beetle infestation killed off nearly every tall pine in the denser stands. By 1994, the island landscape had lost the familiar green pine forest patches and gained instead two rather unsightly stands of dead trees in the western and eastern part of the island (Photo 1). In the northern pine patch, however, mature trees grew in isolated clusters; they died as well but their snags did not dominate the landscape due to the presence of evergreen oak and ironwood trees as well as many pine saplings.

In May 1994, we heard rumors of a plan for a prescribed fire in the eastern pine patch. We had looked forward to observe the regeneration process of all pine patches without fire and sheep-grazing; based on the existing database from detailed field-based studies (Hobbs 1980; Wehtje 1994) and abundant qualitative evidence of widespread pine germination (Photo 2) and recolonization, little if any rationale existed for staging an intentional fire event. This provided the stimulus for our research.

Photo 1. Senescent stand of Bishop pine (*Pinus muricata*); western patch, 19 September 1994.

Photo 2. Pine seedling under snag; western patch, 19 September 1994.

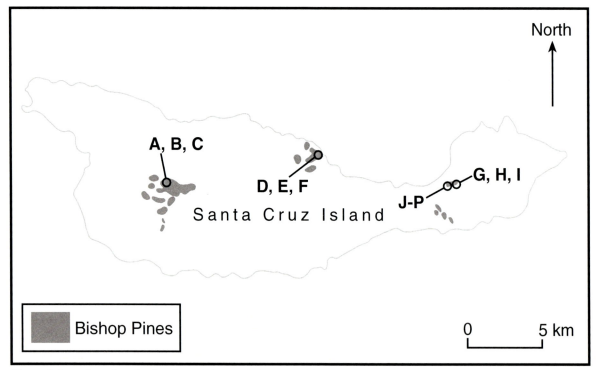

Figure 1. Location of study plots in the Bishop pine stands of Santa Cruz Island. Simplified map from Wehtje (1994).

STUDY SITES AND METHODOLOGY

In September 1994 we established study plots for a quantitative survey of pine regeneration in the northern and eastern pine patches but not in the western patch. On 7 December 1994, a prescribed burn of part of the eastern pine patch was conducted by the Nature Conservancy and the National Park Service. Unfortunately, a strong Santa Ana wind developed the following night, re-igniting the fire and creating a firestorm that burned nearly the entire eastern patch, including our study plots. In June 1998, all study plots were revisited and new plots censused in the western patch as well as in the post-fire habitat of the eastern patch (Figure 1).

Census of Pine Seedlings

Our research goal was not to establish an accurate figure of seedling density for the entire patch; we wanted to document the natural regeneration potential of mature and senescent Bishop pines. Three study plots were established in each pine patch (plots A -I). At random, we selected the trunk of a large dead pine as the center of each study plot and delineated a circular area around it of 0.1 acre in size. A random selection of study sites irrespective of the presence of snags was avoided for two reasons: 1) there was a scarcity of tall snags with potentially thousands of cones, and 2) we wanted, wherever possible, to establish the origin of any pine seedling counted. In some instances, other snags were nearby, however, and their cones and seeds may also have dispersed into the study plot.

We measured the circumference of each pine at breast height (dBH); we counted every live, diseased, or dead pine seedling standing in a plot. Each pine was aged according to the number of annual whorls present. This method of aging was generally simple and accurate; in rare cases, however, Bishop pines may grow two whorls per year creating an overestimate of age by at most one or two years. We determined site characteristics for each pine seedling's germination site as either bare ground (or grass cover), under snag (beneath pine trunk or downed branches), or under tree/shrub (oak tree/shrub, manzanita, and others).

In 1998, we established seven new study sites (J-P) in the burned section of the eastern patch. No tall pines had survived the fire and we selected at random any standing stem indicating the former presence of a mature pine.

Longer-term Observations of Pine Regeneration

The senior author has photographed and recorded portions of the island's pine patches since 1972. In particular, he became interested in the fate of two solitary pine trees growing out of the stony and denuded ridge of the Sierra Blanca to the SW of the western patch. Their demise and seed release and subsequent growth of young pines was followed with great interest from 1990 to 1999.

Cone Opening, Seed Release, and Germination

We made observations on the presence of open and closed cones on the ground and on branches and trunks of live and dead pines (Photos 3 and 4). In addition, the senior author collected three dozen cones of various sizes, from dead and live branches of pines from the eastern and western patches. Three of the cones had opened by circa 40% at the time of collection from a snag. The others were closed and often covered with lichen.

The cones were put in a plastic bag, sealed, and hidden from the sun and other heat sources. They were then put in a large plastic salad bowl and positioned on a backyard table in West Los Angeles where they were fully exposed to the normal midday and afternoon sun and ambient temperatures. Every few days the bowl was checked for newly opened cones, and all released seeds were collected and stored in small stamp envelopes.

A dozen of the released seeds were placed in standard pine germination tubes, filled with half garden and half potting soil, on 15 November 1998; the tubes were left on a garden table in West Los Angeles and watered twice per week through March 1999. An additional 72 seeds were placed in potting soil on 1 February 1999.

Photo 3. A Bishop pine snag with thousands of closed pine cones, 19 September 1994.

Photo 4. Close-up of a cluster of mature spiky 'razorback' closed cones of dead Bishop pine, 19 September 1994.

RESULTS

All study plots contained pine seedlings in the absence of fire (Photos 5 through 8). In 1994, study plots D-I had a total of 312 live seedlings (max. 187, min. 7/plot) on 0.6 acre of pine-occupied surface (Table 1); this equals 520 seedlings/acre or 1,484 seedlings/ha. The parent trees of these seedlings measured between 72 and 220 cm in circumference. Larger snags had more seedlings around them. Some snags still had closed cones on their branches.

The western pine patch (plots A-C) was censused four years later. It contained more seedlings than the other patches, but 223 out of 334 seedlings were 4 yr or younger; only an average number of 36.7 seedlings/plot were 5 yr or older. We assume that some members of the 5+ yr cohorts perished between 1994 and 1998; still, the general magnitude of pine seedlings appears to have been similar to that of the other plots in 1994.

Figures 2 and 3 show the age distribution of Bishop pine seedlings. Germination and survival rates were highest in the years of 1993 and 1994. The oldest seedlings go back to 1975 in the western patch, 1981 in the northern patch, and 1985 in the eastern patch.

Most seedlings were growing on bare ground or in a low grass cover (Table 2) but a sizable number of seedlings had germinated and survived beneath the canopy of shrubs or live trees belonging to manzanita (*Arctostaphylos* sp.), oak (*Quercus* sp.), or other non-coniferous plants (Figure 4). The lowest germination and survival was recorded for seedlings located under the parental tree's trunk and cone-laden branches (Table 2).

Photo 7. Dead pines dominate the island landscape; eastern patch, 20 September 1994.

Photo 5. Pine snags and seedlings west of Pelican Bay; northern patch, 21 September 1994.

Photo 6. Dead pines and oak trees, and pine saplings near Pelican Bay; northern patch, 8 August 1991.

Photo 8. Small pine seedlings on bare surface of trail leading through the eastern patch, 20 September 1994.

Table 1. Live Bishop pine seedlings on Santa Cruz Island (1994, 1998).

Age	A	B	C	D	E	F	G	H	I	Total
1	21	11	10	55	1	4	11	8	3	124
2	0	26	10	64	2	3	15	6	2	128
3	4	46	10	31	1	7	9	6	1	115
4	11	53	21	15	3	1	6	1	0	111
5	6	24	20	5	5	1	3	0	0	64
6	2	6	4	3	4	0	0	0	1	20
7	3	5	7	3	5	0	0	1	0	24
8	2	0	4	2	1	1	0	0	0	10
9	3	0	2	2	2	0	0	0	0	9
10	3	1	2	4	1	0	1	0	0	12
11	4	1	0	0	2	0	0	0	0	7
12	0	0	2	0	4	0	0	0	0	6
13	1	0	2	2	0	0	0	0	0	5
14	1	0	0	1	3	0	0	0	0	5
15	0	0	0	0	0	0	0	0	0	0
16	0	0	0	0	0	0	0	0	0	0
17	1	0	1	0	0	0	0	0	0	2
18	1	0	0	0	0	0	0	0	0	1
19	1	0	1	0	0	0	0	0	0	2
24	1	0	0	0	0	0	0	0	0	1
Total	65	173	96	187	34	17	45	22	7	646

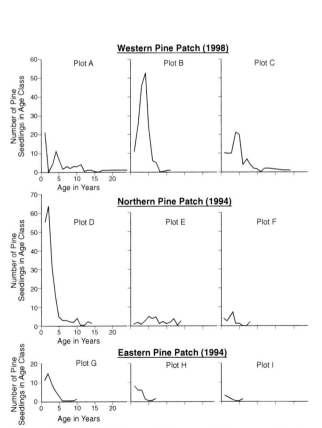

Figure 2. Number of pine seedlings counted per age class in nine study plots.

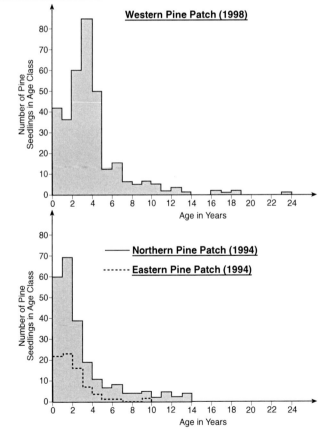

Figure 3. Cumulative total number of pine seedlings counted in the western, northern and eastern pine patch. Note that the western patch was censused four years later than the others.

Table 2. Location of live pine seedlings/saplings.

Plot	Plot Type			Total
	Bare Ground	Under Snag	Under Live Shrub/Tree	
A	43	8	14	65
B	84	42	47	173
C	59	22	15	96
D	177	3	7	187
E	31	0	3	34
F	16	0	1	17
G	18	13	14	45
H	9	7	6	22
I	2	3	2	7
Total	439	98	109	646
%	68%	15%	17%	100%

Figure 4. Typical microhabitats for the germination and growth of pine seedlings on Santa Cruz Island: 1) bare surface or grass, 2) under shrubs and trees, 3) under snags and dead branches, and 4) in rock cracks.

The seven study plots on the burned eastern pine patch had a total of nine pine seedlings: three plots had no seedlings at all; the others had 1 (5 yr), 1 (3 yr), 3 (3, 4, 5 yr), and 4 (3, 4, 4, 5) seedlings. The 1994 wildfire had burned everything with the exception of the central lower stems of some of the biggest trees (Photos 9 and 10). Branches, twigs, and all cones on the ground and in the tree canopy of snags and all non-pine vegetation had burned up. On 25 June 1998, the island's plant community was in an early stage of fire recovery. Three oak species were resprouting strongly, *Arctostaphylos* seedlings were abundant, and there were annual and perennial wildflowers and grasses everywhere. But there were practically no pine seedlings. A somewhat tentative re-census of the 1994 study plots (the exact boundaries were

unclear as the parent tree snags had disappeared) revealed no surviving pine seedlings.

The examination of pine snags in unburned sections of the island showed that the trees were heavily loaded with cones. More of the latter were opened the longer the tree had been dead. The ridge pines of the Sierra Blanca had been dead at least 5 to 10 years by 1992. They still held unopened cones, but on the steep east-facing slope beneath them, the seeds of these parent trees had already established a new grove of dozens of young pines 5-10 yr old.

A total of 25 mature cones (gray and brown colored) were among those collected from the ground or cut from branches of dead Bishop pines on 23 and 25 June 1998. In the ambient warm summer climate of West Los Angeles (max. daily temperatures 24 to 33°C.) several half-opened cones began to open completely within a few days and to release their seeds. After just 30 days 217 seeds had fallen out, an additional 495 in the next 30 days, and another 224 by 3 October 1998, when all cones had released all their seeds. No force or artificial heat source was used to open any of the cones. A total of 936 seeds were counted (37.4 seeds/cone).

Photo 9. Same trail as on Photo 8 leading through post-fire successional landscape of eastern patch. Note the few charred remains of former pine stand, 25 June 1998.

Photo 10. Successional habitat four growing seasons after wildfire event with *Quercus*, *Arctostaphylos*, *Mimulus*, and *Lotus* shrubs; eastern pine patch near China Harbor, 25 June 1998.

Germination trials of these seeds are still under way. The first of 12 seeds placed in small soil-filled tubes on 15 November 1998 germinated 60 days later and was a healthy-looking, 2.5 cm tall seedling on 22 January 1999; the second seedling emerged on 9 February 1999. Five seeds from the second batch of 72 seeds had germinated by 30 March 1999. All seedlings had a vigorous appearance.

DISCUSSION

Our results confirm and consolidate the earlier findings of Hobbs (1980) and Wehtje (1994) about the natural regeneration of Bishop pines on Santa Cruz Island: in the absence of feral sheep and cattle, thousands of seeds have germinated and pine saplings have begun to replace the now dead former canopy trees. In 1994, most of the new growth was concentrated in the western and northern patches (Tables 1 and 2); the eastern patch had relatively few pine seedlings because of constant browsing from a few dozen sheep that were still using this area in 1994. Several seedlings in this patch showed signs of sheep damage.

Overall, the young pines looked healthy and survived as would be expected. Many saplings survived the extreme climatic variations of extreme drought years (1986-1991) followed by erratic months of high and low rainfall in the subsequent years until 1998. Under optimal conditions of climate, sun exposure, and surface nutrients, an open pine grove of 25 mature dead pines/ha might produce more than 5,000 seedlings/ha in the 1 to 10 year range. Plot B and plot D are examples of this high regeneration capacity of Bishop pines on Santa Cruz Island after the removal of feral herbivores (sheep, cattle, and most hogs).

These examples of successful regeneration occurred in the absence of fire. Clearly, a hike through the western and northern pine grove today shows the validity of Hobbs' statement that fire is not a necessary agent for regeneration (Hobbs 1980). The thousands of opened cones on pine snags and the groves of pine saplings downhill from isolated groves or solitary trees (as observed on the Sierra Blanca Ridge) are evidence of the normal function of the island's weather factors in accomplishing cone opening, seed release and seed germination and survival.

The observation of the process of cone opening under normal ambient temperatures showed that detached cones may open within days or weeks. A cone that rolls into a crack of dark volcanic rocks (common in the northern pine stand) may experience a surface temperature during a normal, slightly misty summer day (measured on 8 August 1991 by H. S. Walter) that is too hot for the human touch speeding up the drying of cone resin and subsequent opening. Cones on trees are cooled by wind and cooler air temperatures and may need longer to dry up and open. It is therefore likely that trees growing in the relatively coolest, windiest, and foggiest locations should hold on to their closed cones the longest. This explains the long persistence of the isolated pine snags on the Sierra Blanca and can be used to

develop a model of the generation change in these Bishop pines (Figure 5).

The parent tree dies as a result of disturbance or senescence but releases its many, many seeds from a huge number of cones gradually over a number of years, perhaps decades. This is part of the 'evader' strategy of plant response to disturbance (Agee 1993:135) that includes "species with relatively long-lived propagules that are stored in the soil or canopy." This has the advantage that seeds from a dead tree become available for germination in subsequent years and seasons under different climatic and other environmental conditions some of which more optimal than others for germination and growth. Figure 5 models a 75-year cycle of generational turnover.

Admittedly, the aftermath of the 1994 wildfire on the eastern patch is a singular case study. It consumed all biomass above the surface, but casual inspection of the burn site revealed no lasting damage to any major vegetation element except Bishop pine (Photos 9 and 10). Oak shrubs, manzanita bushes, and many other plants were 1 to 2 m high and vigorously growing. All live and dead pines were destroyed within the fire's perimeter, including 100,000s of cones and millions of seeds. A very tiny fraction of both of the latter survived. This effect of a true wildfire event corresponds closely, however, to the response of all closed cone pines to catastrophic fires (Vogl et al. 1977; Agee 1993; Wehtje

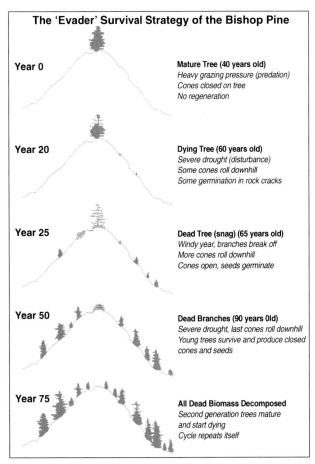

Figure 5. Model of the Bishop pine's natural regeneration cycle in the absence of wildfire.

1994). What seems important to us is the fact that these pines are sensitive to any hot fire. Since the majority of fires in the chaparral and oak-covered slopes of coastal California are usually quite hot — infrequent as they naturally occur — they are likely to kill live and dead pine as well as most cones and seeds. Clearly then, the Bishop pine cannot be called a fire-adapted or -obligate species.

Table 3 shows the probable response of Bishop pines to three different fire-related regimes: no fire, surface fire, and hot crown fire. The latter might spare some cones on green maturing trees with lower fuel loads but would be disastrous at all other times. Benefits to a pine stand accrue only from two regimes. 1) A low burning surface fire would save and open cones in the canopy of young and mature forests; this would cause massive seed release and germination. A recent (1995?) mainland fire near Lompoc may be a case study for this regime type: the burn area was covered with thousands of Bishop pine seedlings in 1998 (D. Kraus, pers. comm.). The resulting forest stand would be even-aged. Older (senescent) forests, however, would lose most of their seeds as trees disintegrate and more and more branches lie close to the surface, exposing them to the flames. 2) The no-fire-regime scenario would also replace the forest, but gradually over perhaps half a tree generation. Succeeding generations of forests would always be uneven-aged, which in our understanding of ecological processes would give them a survival advantage vis-à-vis susceptibility to disease and parasite organisms.

Fire is, of course, a positive factor for germination because the seedbed is enriched by nutrients that may otherwise be unavailable to a pine seed. But that is true for most seeds. Seed scarification by fire is not necessary for germination in the Bishop pine as shown by the spontaneous regeneration on our study plots and by the successful germination of fresh seeds collected from initially closed cones. Fire also reduces ground cover, eliminates potential competitors for water and other resources, and provides maximum exposure to sunlight (Spurr and Barnes 1980). Pines are excellent pioneer species and do very well on overgrazed lands. On Santa Cruz Island, we recorded far more seedlings growing on bare surfaces than under or in the midst of snags and/or live shrubs and trees (Table 2). The probability of a low-intensity surface fire providing these conditions for pine regeneration is, however, extremely low where dead pine fuel and seeds are near ground level. This is usually the case in mature and senescent stands.

Closed cone pines are considered relicts from the Pleistocene (Vogl et al. 1977). They persist in coastal landscapes that do not offer the dry and fire-prone interior environments of the continent. Instead of classifying them as fire-requiring species whose ecological management "will have to include the reintroduction of fire" might it not be closer to reality to classify them as 'pyrofugal' species? Their current habitats, the relatively low plant cover surrounding them, and their maritime climate preferences (low lightning and fire frequency) indicate their survival only in the relatively fire-safest environments of California's brush- and woodlands. They are resilient (Westman 1986) in this Mediterranean-type landscape system because of their fire-evading reproductive strategy. This hypothesis is backed by our observations from Santa Cruz Island. It would be interesting to test its validity beyond the Channel Islands through a study of the natural regeneration of fire-free stands of Bishop and other closed cone conifers in continental settings.

Table 3. Bishop pine stand regeneration and fire.

Pine Age	Fire Factor		
	No Fire	Low Surface Fire	Hot Crown Fire
Pine Stand Young 1 - 20 Years	All cones closed	Some cones survive	All cones consumed
Maturing 20 - 50 Years	All cones closed	Canopy cones survive and seeds germinate	Some cones survive to open and seeds geminate
Senescent > 50 Years	Some cones open and seeds germinate	Canopy cones survive and seeds germinate	Few cones and seedlings survive. Minor regeneration
Dead Stand	Gradual cone opening and full regeneration	Low regeneration. Most cones and seeds consumed by fire	No regeneration. All cones and seedlings consumed by fire

ACKNOWLEDGMENTS

We thank the Natural Reserve System of the University of California for their long-term support of our research and teaching on Santa Cruz Island. We appreciate the field assistance of a number of UCLA students, particularly Caitlin A. Dempsey and Claudia Büll. The paper benefited from the helpful comments of an anonymous reviewer. The Academic Senate of UCLA provided minor financial support for the long-term island studies of the senior author.

LITERATURE CITED

Agee, J. K. 1993. Fire ecology of Pacific Northwest forests. Island Press. Washington, DC.

Carroll, M. C., L. L. Laughrin and A. C. Bromfield. 1993. Fire on the California Islands: does it play a role in chaparral and closed cone pine forest habitats? Pages 73-88 in Hochberg, F. G. (ed.), Third California Islands Symposium: Recent Advances in Research on the California Islands. Santa Barbara Museum of Natural History, Santa Barbara, CA.

Hobbs, E. 1980. Effects of grazing on the northern population of Pinus muricata on Santa Cruz Island, California.

Pages 159-165 *in* Power, D. M. (ed.), The California Islands: Proceedings of a Multidisciplinary Symposium. Santa Barbara Museum of Natural History, Santa Barbara, CA.

Junak, S., T. Ayers, R. Scott, D. Wilken, and D. Young. 1995. A Flora of Santa Cruz Island. Santa Barbara Botanic Garden. Santa Barbara, CA.

Spurr, S. H. and B. V. Barnes. 1980. Forest Ecology, 3rd edition. John Wiley & Sons. New York, NY.

Vogl, R. J., W. P. Armstrong, K. L. White and K. L. Cole. 1977. The closed-cone pines and cypress. Pages 295-358 *in* Barbour, M. G. and J. Major (eds.), Terrestrial Vegetation of California. John Wiley & Sons, New York, NY.

Westman, W. 1986. Resilience: concepts and measures. Pages 5-19 *in* Dell, B., A. J. M. Hopkins and B. B. Lamont (eds.), Resilience in Mediterranean-type Ecosystems. Dr. W. Junk Publishers, Dordrecht.

Wehtje, W. 1994. Response of a Bishop pine (*Pinus muricata*) population to removal of feral sheep on Santa Cruz Island, California. Pages 331-340 *in* Halvorson, W. L. and G. J. Maender (eds.), The Fourth California Islands Symposium: Update on the Status of Resources. Santa Barbara Museum of Natural History, Santa Barbara, CA.

SOURCE OF UNPUBLISHED MATERIALS

Kraus, D. 69 E. Lewis Street, Ventura, CA.

NATIVE SHRUB RECOVERY IN NONNATIVE ANNUAL GRASSLANDS, CALIFORNIA CHANNEL ISLANDS

Patricia M. Corry[1] and A. Kathryn McEachern[2]

[1]1820 Flowerree St., Helena, MT 59601 (406) 449-7133
[2]U.S. Geological Survey-Biological Resources Division, Western Ecological Research Center
Channel Islands Field Station, 1901 Spinnaker Drive, Ventura, CA 93001
(805) 658-5753, FAX (805) 658-5798, E-mail: kathryn_mceachern@usgs.gov

RESEARCH NOTE

Grazing by introduced herbivores on the California Channel Islands converted much of the native Mediterranean scrub to grasslands dominated by a few Eurasian annual genera (Dunkle 1950; Philbrick 1979; Cole and Liu 1994). Remaining native woody communities are fragmented, and many are reduced to isolated patches on steep slopes and ravines. Introduced herbivores are being removed from the islands, and restoration of native flora and fauna is a common management goal. Management agencies would benefit from an ability to predict where native plant community recovery is most likely to require active intervention and what type of intervention is most effective.

Studies of disturbed Mediterranean systems invaded by nonnative annual grasses show variable recovery of native species following release from grazing (Kirkpatrick and Hutchinson 1980; Hobbs 1983; Eliason and Allen 1997). Why native shrub species successfully invade some annual grasslands while other shrub-grass boundaries remain static is not well understood. Philbrick (1979), Hobbs (1983), and others suggest that soil texture and water-holding capacity are factors, noting the apparent affinity of annual grasslands for deep, clayey soils and of native shrubs for coarse-grained substrates. Halvorson et al. (1997, unpublished data) found native shrub cover on San Nicolas Island correlated with sandy, low nutrient, and low cation exchange capacity (CEC) soils while annual grasslands are on high clay, nutrient, and CEC soils. However, correlations were less significant at sites on other islands where soil texture is less variable.

We investigated biological and physical factors to characterize change across the shrubland-grassland boundary, and determine if biological or physical gradients exist which may affect the success of native shrub invasion into grassland. We were also interested in the extent to which native shrub cover influences native plant biodiversity. Five study sites where shrublands grade into grasslands were selected on four Channel Islands. Shrub communities at the sites are dominated by *Isocoma menziesii* on San Nicolas and San Miguel Islands and by *Lycium californicum* on Santa Barbara Island. The two sites on Santa Rosa Island include *Adenostoma fasciculatum* chaparral and

Artemisia californica scrub. Grasslands at the sites are dominated by annual species of *Avena*, *Bromus* and *Vulpia*.

Three replicate sets of five equally-spaced, 30-m transects were established parallel to the shrubland-grassland boundary at each site, spanning the transition from shrubland to grassland. Slope, aspect, substrate characteristics and line-intercept relative cover were recorded for each transect. Shrub density and demography data, mean litter depth, and soil unconfined compressive strength (estimated by pocket penetrometer) were collected from five randomly located 2 m^2 plots on each transect. Soil samples were collected from the shrubland, grassland, and center transects of each 5-transect replicate set. Samples were analyzed for grain size distribution, moisture retention, pH, electrical conductivity, nutrients, organic matter, major ions, exchangeable cations, CEC, and sodium adsorption ratio. Relative cover, species richness, and Shannon-Wiener diversity indices were calculated for each transect. Cover and physical data were ordinated using nonmetric multidimensional scaling, and Pearson's correlations were calculated between dominant species cover and physical data. Data were analyzed to show whether patterns of change in biological and physical factors were correlated across the gradient, and whether correlations were consistent from site to site.

Results show that species richness and diversity generally decrease from shrubland to grassland at all sites. The decline in richness is greatest among native species but also occurs in nonnative species. Native shrub recruitment varies dramatically among the study sites. Physical data explain few of the differences in species cover and shrub density among sites. Litter cover, litter depth, and soil compressive strength increase across the gradient from shrubland to grassland, showing the most consistent correlations with changes in species cover of any physical factors. Soil chemistry shows some within-site trends across the gradient. However, trends are inconsistent and sometimes contradictory among sites. Attempts to promote native plant restoration through soil amendments would require site-specific evaluation.

Species reproductive strategies and community structure could explain the differences in shrub recovery among the sites. Recruitment of shrubs into grassland is occurring at the two *I. menziesii*-dominated sites, where the dominant and subdominant shrubs form an open canopy and are composites with abundant, wind-dispersed seeds. Little or no recruitment is evident at the *L. californicum* and *A. fasciculatum* sites, where the dominant species form prostrate, nearly closed canopies and have fruits with limited dispersal ability. Results suggest that community structure and reproductive strategies and growth habits of the dominant shrubs should be primary considerations in prioritizing and planning native shrub community restoration.

LITERATURE CITED

Cole, K. L. and G. W. Liu. 1994. Holocene paleoecology of an estuary on Santa Rosa Island, California. Quaternary Research 41:326-335.

Dunkle, M. 1950. Plant ecology of the Channel Islands of California. Allan Hancock Pacific Expeditions 13 (3):247-386. University of Southern California Press, Los Angeles.

Eliason, S. A. and E. B. Allen. 1997. Exotic grass competition in suppressing native shrubland re-establishment. Restoration Ecology 5 (3):245-255.

Hobbs, E. 1983. Factors controlling the form and location of the boundary between coastal sage scrub and grassland in southern California. Ph.D. dissertation, University of California at Los Angeles.

Kirkpatrick, J. B. and C. F. Hutchinson. 1980. The environmental relationships of California coastal sage scrub and some of its component communities and species. Journal of Biogeography 7:23-38.

Philbrick, R. 1979. Vegetation. Pages 5.58-5.59 *in* D. M. Power (ed.), Natural Resources Study of the Channel Islands National Monument, California. Santa Barbara Museum of Natural History, Santa Barbara, California.

SOURCES OF UNPUBLISHED MATERIALS

Halvorson, W. L., J. Belnap and K. McEachern. 1997. San Nicolas Island restoration and monitoring: final report to Pt. Mugu Naval Air Weapons Station. Unpublished report by U.S. Geological Survey, Cooperative Studies Unit, University of Arizona, Tucson.

FENNEL *(FOENICULUM VULGARE)* MANAGEMENT AND NATIVE SPECIES ENHANCEMENT ON SANTA CRUZ ISLAND, CALIFORNIA

Wesley I. Colvin III[1] and Stephen R. Gliessman[2]

Department of Environmental Studies, University of California, Santa Cruz, CA 95064
[1](831) 459-5818; [2](831) 459-4051, FAX (831) 459-2867, E-mail: gliess@zzyx.ucsc.edu

ABSTRACT

Fennel *(Foeniculum vulgare)* an invasive, perennial herb known from Santa Cruz Island, California, underwent a population explosion for many years during the past decade after the removal of feral and domestic animals. Potentially occurring in large monocultural stands over three meters in height, fennel heavily impacted native and endemic plant species. An eight-year study showed that digging fennel out of the ground was the most effective eradication tool. Herbicide application was also effective, but this required periodic reapplication for this effectiveness to be maintained. Unfortunately for native plant species, both removal methods were often followed by the invasion of other exotic plant species that continued to inhibit native plant species. Recovery of native species is greatest with a 30 to 40% reduction in fennel cover. When fennel was cut in early May and the resulting litter was removed, native perennial species averaged over sixty percent of the total nonfennel perennial abundance with a mean richness of three species from 1993 to 1998. This management strategy encouraged natural successional processes towards the historical predisturbance native shrub and tree vegetation, and it discouraged a successional shift towards an exotic annual grassland.

Keywords: Santa Cruz Island, California, fennel, Foeniculum vulgare, exotic species, eradication, native species enhancement, and restoration.

INTRODUCTION

Regions possessing Mediterranean-type climates are most heavily impacted by introduction of invasive nonnative species that are encouraged by the settlement and development activities of humans (Mooney 1988). Island ecosystems are especially vulnerable to these invasions because the largely-endemic species assemblages lack defenses sufficient to ward off invaders (Vitousek 1988). The biota of Santa Cruz Island, California, has been subjected to these selective forces for at least seven thousand years, with the last 150 years most likely exerting the greatest selective pressure (Junak et al. 1995). This pressure is the result of the interaction of four introduced species whose life histories have had the largest ecosystem-level impacts: pigs, sheep, cattle, and fennel.

Fennel has been on Santa Cruz Island for more than a century (Brenton and Klinger 1994). Pigs and sheep were introduced to the island in the 1850s and formed substantial feral populations that became the likely avenues of fennel introduction (Beatty and Licari 1992). Greene (1887) reported that fennel was well established on hillsides near Prisoners Harbor in 1888. Cattle ranching and roads were the probable vectors of dispersal over the past 100 years (Beatty and Licari 1992).

In 1978, The Nature Conservancy acquired a conservation easement on the western 90% of Santa Cruz Island and became the sole owner of this parcel in 1987 (Junak et al. 1995). Between 1981 and 1987, The Nature Conservancy eliminated more than 36,000 feral sheep from this portion of the island and then removed approximately 1,500 head of cattle in 1988 (Brenton and Klinger 1994). With this elimination of all large grazing herbivores and the end of a five-year drought in 1991, fennel underwent a rapid and substantial expansion of its range to dominate approximately 10% of the island's area (Brenton and Klinger 1994). The thickest patches of fennel were located where grazing animals once created the most disturbance: holding areas, watering holes, and the flatlands throughout the central valley of the island (Dash and Gliessman 1994).

Fennel is an erect perennial herb of the family Apiaceae. The leaves have sheathing bases and become pinnately dissected two to four times with thread-like pinnae. The stems are smooth and exude a white, powdery coating. The plant reaches average heights from one to two meters but has been observed at heights over three meters (W. Colvin, pers. obs. 1996). It blooms from February (Junak et al. 1995) through September (W. Colvin, pers. obs. 1996). Fennel thrives on well-drained, loamy soil, and occurs across a broad life zone between the temperatures of 4 to 27°C, annual precipitation of 300 to 2600 mm, and soil pH between 4.8 and 8.3 (Simon 1984).

Several researchers have reported allelopathic potential for fennel. Allelopathic compounds are secondary plant chemicals with the potential for phytotoxicity. Chaturvedi and Muralia (1975) were the first to investigate the allelopathic potential of plants in the family Apiaceae using a rapid bioassay technique. They found that fennel seed extracts produced the strongest inhibitory effects on growth and germination against cumin *(Cuminum cyminum)*, followed by carum *(Carum copticum)*, carrot *(Daucus carota* L.*)*, and coriander *(Coriandrum sativum* L.*)*. Aoki (1990) found that fennel leaf extracts inhibited the germination and growth of rye *(Secale cereale)*, radish *(Raphanus sativa* "red pak"*)*, and lettuce *(Lactuca sativa* Burpee's "Green Ice Loosehead"*)* in laboratory bioassays and had the same effect on rye and lettuce in greenhouse studies. Granath (1992) was the first to investigate the allelopathic potential of fennel leaf extracts on seeds collected from Santa Cruz Island. For non-native grasses, it was found that fennel leaf extracts stimulated growth of wild oat *(Avena fatua)*, decreased growth of ripgut grass *(Bromus diandrus)* and soft chess *(Bromus hordeaceus)*, and left the growth of barley *(Hordeum murinum* ssp. *leporinum)* unchanged. Germination remained unchanged for all species except soft chess, which exhibited a decline as fennel leaf extract concentrations increased. Regarding native species, Colvin (1996) found that fennel leaf extracts suppressed the growth of beach evening primrose *(Camissonia cheiranthifolia)*, germination of mountain garland *(Clarkia unguiculata)*, and germination and growth of California poppy *(Eschscholzia californica)*, white baby lupine *(Lupinus nanus)*, and desert bluebells *(Phacelia campanularia)*. Fennel appears to inhibit its own germination and growth as well (Colvin 1996).

MATERIALS AND METHODS

Dash and Gliessman (1994) outlined the initial protocol for this field study. No changes have occurred to that protocol in the interim; however, the focus of the project has changed in two ways. Based on the findings of Dash (1993), a program of native species enhancement onto the study site was instituted in September 1995. Seeds of native perennials were collected on the island and broadcast by hand into the southern halves of each treatment area within the four replicates. The northern halves of each treatment were left unenhanced as intra-plot controls (Figure 1). Perennial species richness and abundance were tallied and comparisons between native and exotic species determined between treatments as well as any differences in recruitment between the enhanced and unenhanced portions of the treatments. Observations by Colvin (1996) prompted the construction of a fence in February 1998 around the study site to exclude feral pigs from introducing further experimental biases into future results.

Site Description

The experiment occurred on the north-facing slope of the Central Valley floor south of the Santa Cruz Island Fault and north of the South Ridge Road. It was approximately 0.5 km east of the University of California Field Station. The experimental treatments were randomly assigned to six plots within rows referred to as blocks and replicated four times (Figure 1). It was bounded by the Valley Road to the north and in proximity to the eucalyptus grove at Camino de la Casa to the east.

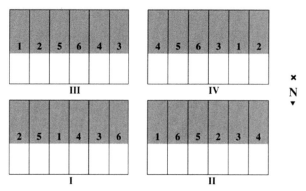

The size of each treatment measures 5.4 x 15.4 meters

TREATMENTS:

1. Control - leave fennel untouched
2. Cut and leave cuttings - leave fennel on the surface as mulch
3. Cut and remove cuttings - remove plant material from treatment
4. Dig - dig out root system and remove from plot
5. Herbicide - fennel cut and stems sprayed only from 1990 to 1992
6. Cut and remove cuttings twice - repeat treatment Spring and Summer

Figure 1. Randomized fennel treatments assigned to the experimental field plots on Santa Cruz Island from May 1990 to September 1998 (adapted from Dash and Gliessman, 1994). Each treatment was replicated four times. Shaded areas were enhanced by hand broadcasting native seed collected on the island. Unshaded areas were left alone as intra-plot controls.

RESULTS

When fennel was left alone, fennel coverage averaged over 90% within the study plots for eight years (Figure 2). When it was dug out of the ground, there was no fennel cover after five years. All three of the cut fennel manipulations maintained an average fennel coverage between 60 and 70% for eight years regardless of whether the resulting litter was removed. When the herbicide Roundup® was applied from 1990 to 1992, fennel coverage was lowest after two years and returned to that of the various cutting manipulations after eight years.

Annual nonfennel biomass reached a peak in 1993 for all treatments (Figure 3). Biomass was greatest where herbicide was applied, followed by cutting fennel twice per year and removing the resulting litter. In 1993, the control possessed the lowest quantity of nonfennel annual biomass while the cut, cut and remove, and dig manipulations possessed moderate quantities. By 1998, total annual nonfennel biomass decreased below 100 g/m² in all treatments. When fennel was left alone, the quantity of annual nonfennel biomass remained lowest. The percentage of nonnative species in the total annual nonfennel density approached 100% across all treatments from 1991 to 1997, except for the control treatment in 1997 where it approached 80% (Table 1).

Perennial nonfennel abundance reached a peak across all treatments after six years (Figure 4). In 1998, all three of the cut fennel manipulations achieved a mean abundance of 120 individuals per plot regardless of whether the resulting litter was removed. Digging fennel out of the ground resulted in a mean abundance of over 80 individuals per plot.

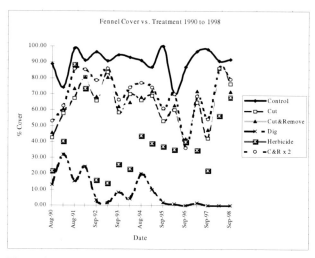

Figure 2. Percent cover of fennel within the experimental plots on Santa Cruz Island from 1990 to 1998.

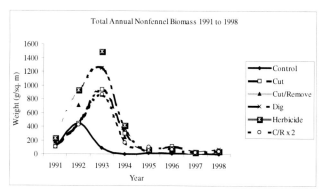

Figure 3. Total annual nonfennel biomass (g/m²) within the experimental plots on Santa Cruz Island from 1991 to 1998.

Table 1. The percentage of exotic annual species within the total nonfennel annual density in the study plots on Santa Cruz Island, CA from 1991 to 1997.

	1991	1992	1993	1994	1995	1996	1997
Control	100%	100%	99%	100%	100%	99%	80%
Cut	100%	100%	100%	100%	97%	99%	99%
Cut and remove	100%	98%	99%	99%	98%	100%	98%
Dig	98%	100%	100%	100%	100%	100%	99%
Herbicide	100%	99%	100%	100%	100%	100%	100%
Cut and remove twice	100%	99%	100%	99%	100%	99%	95%

Herbicide application resulted in a mean abundance of over 60 individuals per plot. When untreated, mean perennial abundance never exceeded one individual per square meter. The percentage of native perennials within the total nonfennel perennial abundance was greatest when fennel was cut and the litter removed in May, followed by cutting fennel and removing the litter twice per year from 1993 to 1998 (Table 2). The percentage of native perennials rarely exceeded 10% when fennel was dug out of the ground

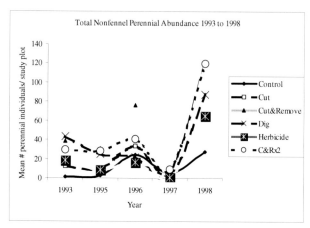

Figure 4. The mean number of perennial individuals within the experimental plots on Santa Cruz Island in the total nonfennel perennial abundance from 1993 to 1998.

Table 2. The percentage of native perennials within the total nonfennel perennial abundance in the study plots on Santa Cruz Island, CA from 1993 to 1998.

	1993	1995	1996	1997	1998
Control	20%	80%	89%	36%	63%
Cut	16%	38%	78%	40%	49%
Cut and remove	55%	69%	82%	50%	50%
Dig	4%	4%	13%	75%	3%
Herbicide	14%	21%	65%	0%	61%
Cut and remove twice	52%	53%	64%	89%	54%

during the same time frame. When fennel was untreated, cut, or treated with an herbicide, the percentage of native perennials was highly variable from 1993 to 1998. Native perennial richness was greatest with a mean of four species when fennel was cut and left on the ground from 1993 to 1998 (Table 3). With a mean of three species, native perennial richness was equal for the other treatments during the same time frame. When fennel was left alone or dug out of the ground, native perennial richness was lowest with a mean of two species. No noticeable differences existed in native species abundance or richness between the enhanced and unenhanced portions of the plots.

Table 3. Native perennial species richess (s) within the study plots on Santa Cruz Island, CA from 1993 to 1998.

	1993	1995	1996	1997	1998
Control	1	2	3	2	2
Cut	3	3	5	4	3
Cut and remove	3	4	3	1	3
Dig	2	3	3	1	2
Herbicide	4	3	4	0	4
Cut and remove twice	4	3	4	1	3

DISCUSSION

Any management strategy that seeks to remove fennel from Santa Cruz Island should include restoration of total ecosystem relationships to fennel-affected areas so that natural successional processes encourage the recruitment of native species rather than introduced ones. Santa Cruz Island ecosystem preservation has been a focus of efforts by The Nature Conservancy to protect remnants of California's natural heritage (VanVuren and Coblentz 1989). The predisturbance plant communities associated with our study's location were probably chaparral and oak woodland (Minnich 1980). Fennel and nonfennel biomass indices from the past eight years must be examined so that an effective management policy can be developed.

After eight years, fennel coverage remained unchanged on average in the untreated study plots. The most successful method of fennel eradication from the study plots was by digging plants out of the ground and removing the resulting litter. Herbicide application was the second most successful technique of eradication but required periodic reapplication. Whereas, all three of the variations in cutting fennel and either leaving or removing the resulting litter produced moderate rates of fennel decline. Trends in nonfennel biomass must be examined to determine which fennel removal technique encourages the greatest recovery of native species. The quickest method to eradicate fennel may not be the most desirable management objective if other invasive exotic species replace it, yellow star thistle *(Centaurea solstitialis)* for example (W. Colvin, pers. obs. 1996).

One hundred years of grazing by domestic and feral animals have left a preponderance of exotic annual and perennial seeds in the seed bank. The allelopathic potential of fennel appears to suppress the germination and recruitment of both native and exotic, annual and perennial, plant species based on the results of both laboratory bioassays and the field study plots. A reduction in fennel coverage appears to release these seeds from the direct interference of allelopathic fennel compounds and allow other plant species to increase in abundance, richness, and diversity. Although annual nonfennel biomass remained below 150 g/m² across all treatments over the past four years, exotic annual plant species dominated native annual plant species throughout the entire course of this study. These species, primarily associated with European grasslands, were not part of the predisturbance condition of the site. For this reason, increasing the recruitment of native perennials over exotic perennials should be a primary goal of any fennel eradication policy. This was achieved when fennel was cut and the litter removed in May. When this method was used, native perennial plants comprised over sixty percent on average of the total nonfennel perennial abundance with a mean richness of three native species in the field study plots from 1993 to 1998. This occurred regardless of whether the enhancement of the southern halves of each treatment with native seed was effective. It was expected that enhancement of the southern halves of each treatment with native seed would further promote native perennial recruitment; however, the results of the past three years remain inconclusive.

It is suspected that the rooting activities of the feral pig *(Sus scrofa)* nullified any benefits the native species enhancement protocol instituted in 1995 may have produced. Damage to ecosystem structure and function by feral pig feeding activities on Santa Cruz Island is well documented (VanVuren 1984; Peart et al. 1994). Since 1994, the feral pig population appears to have increased. This coincides with the dramatic decrease in annual nonfennel biomass observed throughout all six plot manipulations over the past four years. Although statistical correlation between these two phenomena was not attempted, the study site contained large quantities of pig scat and established game trails by 1996 that were not present in 1994 (S. Gliessman, pers. comm. 1996). For this reason, a fence was constructed around the study site in 1998.

Biological control of fennel populations by introducing known pathogens has never been proposed. Several pathogens have been identified for fennel around the world. In India, the fungi *Fusarium solani* (Gupta and Srivastava 1978), *Ramularia foeniculi* (Lakra 1993), and *Sclerotinia sclerotiorum* (Sehgal and Agrawat 1971) have been identified as the causal agents of fennel soft rot. In Italy, bacterial soft rot of fennel is caused by *Erwinia carotova* (Mazzuchi and Dalli 1974) and fungal soft rot by *Phomopsis foeniculi* (Evidente et al. 1994). California is known to contain three reported fennel pathogens. Koike et al. (1992) reported the fungus *Cercosporidium punctum* as the causal agent of fennel rot in Monterey County, and it is known to occur in Santa Barbara and Santa Cruz Counties as well. Recently, the bacterium *Pseudomonas syringae* was implicated in causing a foliar disease of fennel (Koike et al. 1993). In the Salinas Valley, fennel has been used as a rotation crop with lettuce where fennel stem rot caused by the fungus *Sclerotinia minor* was first reported (Koike 1994). Although precedent exists for the successful introduction of biocontrols to manage other exotic species introductions to Santa Cruz Island (Wenner and Thorp 1994), research must be performed before any of these fennel pathogens can be introduced as biocontrol agents to make certain that they will not switch to other hosts in the family Apiaceae that are native to the island.

Ecological invasion by exotic species is a pandemic phenomenon that has caused ecological as well as economic havoc to private and public lands (Schneider 1994). Native plant species on the California Channel Islands have been negatively impacted by the exotic species introductions caused from human activities and the continuous disturbance caused by introduced animals (Junak 1996). On Santa Cruz Island, California, exotic species represent twenty six percent of the island's total plant species (Junak et al. 1995). Eradication of one exotic species, however minimal the effort, is another human activity that has the potential to create the disturbance required for the successful invasion and recruitment of more exotic plant species where only one problem existed previously. In southern California where restoration did not occur to shrublands disturbed by anthropogenic activities as long as seventy-one years earlier, exotic annual species dominated disturbed sites with the few native perennial colonizers atypical of the late successional plant communities in the surrounding area (Allen et al. 1995). When restoration followed disturbance, they found exotic annuals were still prevalent, but native perennials established from seed and recovered best adjacent to native shrub vegetation.

Prioritization and coordination objectives for the removal of exotic species are necessary for successful implementation of these protocols to occur (Vitousek 1988; Westman 1990; Hiebert and Stubbendiek 1993; Leppla 1996). The management of Santa Cruz Island's natural resources is now under the jurisdiction of several public and private conservation and preservation agencies and entities. Cooperation between organizations is essential in this conglomeration of parties affected by exotic species introductions. Fennel and feral animals do not observe the jurisdictional boundaries of these management groups. Eradication goals and restoration objectives must be adaptable and flexible to deal with new types of situations. The foraging activities of feral pigs negatively impact the recovery and restoration of native plant species in fennel affected areas and further facilitates invasion by exotic plant species. The removal of feral animals on Santa Cruz Island must occur before native plant restoration is attempted. Fennel eradication and native plant restoration techniques developed for use in the Central Valley may not be appropriate or suitable for use on the North Slope or Cañada Christy areas of the island. Fennel and ranching coexisted on this island for over a century. All ranching operations ceased on the island in 1988. The study of fennel eradication is approaching a decade. It may take at least this amount of time or greater before an eradication strategy is fully implemented and restoration objectives are realized. Therefore, the protocol adopted must be cost effective. It will utilize a minimal amount of human resources over time while maximizing the recovery of native species using ecological seral succession.

ACKNOWLEDGMENTS

We would like to thank all of the individuals who have participated in Natural History Field Quarter from 1995 to 1998, including those people affiliated/related to these participants, for their invaluable volunteer assistance. Without the help of these individuals, totaling close to one hundred people, the data collection and treatment manipulations required for this project could not have been accomplished. There are also several individuals not necessarily affiliated with Natural History Field Quarter that deserve mention. Those persons are: Emily Althoen; Jerry Brownrigg; Marla Daily; Jeff Howarth; Lyndal Laughrin; Megan Lulow; Teresa MacKenzie; Laura, Max, and Serafina Ruiz; Sara Weiner-Boone; and Hopi Wilder. We would like to thank Charles Leavell, Tom Morris, and Allan Schoenherr for editorial review as well as the staff at MBC Applied Environmental Sciences. The Department of Environmental Studies and the Alfred E. Heller Chair in Agroecology at the University of California, Santa Cruz provided funds for this project. Finally, the following agencies and entities deserve credit for their assistance: the National Park Service, The Nature Conservancy, the Santa Cruz Island Foundation, and the United States Navy.

LITERATURE CITED

Allen, E., C. Davis, and B. Heindl. 1995. Trajectories of succession and restoration of southern California shrublands after anthopogenic disturbance. American Journal of Botany 82:33.

Beatty, S. and D. Licari. 1992. Invasion of fennel (*Foeniculum vulgare*) into shrub communities on Santa Cruz Island, CA. Madroño 39:54-66.

Brenton, B. and R. Klinger. 1994. Modeling the expansion of fennel (*Foeniculum vulgare*) on the Channel Islands. Pages 497-504 *in* Halvorson, W., and G. Meander, (eds.), The Fourth Channel Islands Symposium: Update on the Status of Resources. Santa Barbara Museum of Natural History: Santa Barbara, CA.

Chaturvedi, S. and R. Muralia. 1975. Germination inhibitors in some Umbellifer seeds. Annals of Botany 39:1125-1129.

Dash, B. and S. Gliessman. 1994. Nonnative species eradication and native species enhancement: Fennel on Santa Cruz Island. Pages 505-512 *in* Halvorson, W., and G. Meander, (eds.), The Fourth Channel Islands Symposium: Update on the Status of Resources. Santa Barbara Museum of Natural History: Santa Barbara, CA.

Evidente, A., R. Lanzetta, M. Abouzeid, M. Corsaro, L. Mugnai, and G. Surico. 1994. Foeniculoxin, a new phytotoxic geranylhydroquinone from *Phomopsis foeniculi*. Tetrahedron 34:10371-10378.

Greene, E. 1887. Studies in the botany of California and parts adjacent. VI. Notes on the botany of Santa Cruz Island. Bulletin of the California Academy of Sciences 2:377-418.

Gupta, J. and V. Srivastava. 1978. A new rot of fennel caused by *Fusarium solani*. Indian Journal of Mycology and Plant Pathology 8:206.

Heibert, R. and J. Stubbendiek. 1993. Handbook for ranking exotic plants for management and control. Natural resources report; NPS/NRMWRO/NRR-93/08. United States Department of the Interior, National Park Service, Natural Resources Publication Office, Denver, CO.

Junak, S. 1996. Non-native plants on the California Channel Islands: an overview of their proliferation and impacts. American Journal of Botany 83:165.

Junak, S., T. Ayers, R. Scott, D. Wilken, and D. Young. 1995. A Flora of Santa Cruz Island. Santa Barbara Botanic Garden, Santa Barbara, CA.

Koike, S., E. Butler, and A. Greathead. 1992. Occurrence

of *Cercosporidium punctum* of fennel in California. Plant Disease 76:539.

Koike, S., R. Gilbertson, and E. Little. 1993. A new bacterial disease of fennel in California. Plant Disease 77:319.

Koike, S. 1994. First report of stem rot of fennel in the United States caused by *Sclerotinia minor*. Plant Disease 78:754

Lakra, B. 1993. Epidemiology and management of Ramularia blight of fennel *(Foeniculum vulgare)*. Indian Journal of Mycology and Plant Pathology 23:70-77.

Leppla, N. 1996. Environmentally friendly methods for reducing the damage caused by exotic weeds in natural habitats: Conflicts of interest, safegaurds and national policy. Castanea 61:214-225.

Mazzuchi, U., and A. Dalli. 1974. Bacterial soft rot of fennel *(Foeniculum vulgare* var. *dulce* Mill.*)* Phytopathologia Mediterranea 13:113 -116.

Minnich, R. 1980. Vegetation of Santa Cruz and Santa Catalina Islands. Pages 123-137 *in* Power, D. M. (ed.), The California Islands: Proceedings of a Multidisciplinary Symposium. Santa Barbara Museum of Natural History, Santa Barbara, CA.

Mooney, H. 1988. Lessons from Mediterranean-climate regions. Pages 181-189 *in* Wilson, E. O. (ed.), Biodiversity. National Academy Press.

Peart, D., D. Patten, and S. Lohr. 1994. Feral pig disturbance and woody species seedling regeneration and abundance beneath coast live oaks *(Quercus agrifolia)* on Santa Cruz Island, California. Pages 313-322 *in* Halvorson, W., and G. Meander, (eds.), The Fourth Channel Islands Symposium: Update on the Status of Resources. Santa Barbara Museum of Natural History: Santa Barbara, CA.

Schneider, D. 1994. Slow-motion explosion: the exponential spread of exotic species. Whole Earth Review 83:100-105.

Sehgal, S., and J. Agrawat. 1971. Drooping of fennel *(Foeniculum vulgare)* due to *Sclerotinia sclerotiorum*. Indian Phytopathology 24:608-609.

Simon, J. 1984. Herbs: an indexed bibliography, 1971-1980. Archon Books, Hamden, CT.

VanVuren, D. 1984. Diurnal activity and habitat use by feral pigs on Santa Cruz Island, California. California Fish and Game 70:140-144.

VanVuren, D., and B. Coblentz. 1989. Population characteristics of feral sheep on Santa Cruz Island. Journal of Wildlife Management 53:306-313.

Vitousek, P. 1988. Diversity and biological invasions of oceanic islands. Pages 181-189 *in* Wilson, E. O. (ed.), Biodiversity. National Academy Press.

Wenner, A. and R. Thorp. 1994. Removal of feral honey bee *(Apis mellifera)* colonies from Santa Cruz Island. Pages 513-522 *in* Halvorson, W., and G. Meander, (eds.), The Fourth Channel Islands Symposium: Update on the Status of Resources. Santa Barbara Museum of Natural History: Santa Barbara, CA.

Westman, W. 1990. Park management of exotic plant species-problems and issues. Conservation Biology 4:251-260.

SOURCES OF UNPUBLISHED MATERIALS

Aoki, M. E. 1990. Fennel on Santa Cruz Island. Senior Thesis. Board of Environmental Studies, University of California, Santa Cruz, CA 95064.

Colvin, W. I., III. 1223 W. Woodcrest, Fullerton, CA 92833. Personal Observation 1996.

Colvin, W. I., III. 1996. Fennel *(Foeniculum vulgare)* Removal from Santa Cruz Island, California: Managing Successional Processes to Favor Native over Nonnative Species-further studies in methodology, native species enhancement, allelopathy, and potential biocontrols. Senior Thesis. Board of Environmental Studies, University of California, Santa Cruz, CA 95064.

Dash, B. 1993. Exotic Species Eradication and Native Species Enhancement: FENNEL *(Foeniculum vulgare* Mill.) on Santa Cruz Island. Senior Thesis. Board of Environmental Studies, University of California, Santa Cruz, CA 95064.

Gliessman, S. Department of Environmental Studies, University of California, Santa Cruz, CA 95064. Personal Communication 1996.

Granath, T. 1992. Fennel on Santa Cruz Island....Year II. Senior Thesis. Board of Environmental Studies, University of California, Santa Cruz, CA 95064.

COMPOSITION AND STRUCTURE OF A GRASSLAND COMMUNITY FOLLOWING PRESCRIBED BURNS ON SANTA CRUZ ISLAND

Robert C. Klinger[1] and Ishmael Messer[2]

[1]The Nature Conservancy, 213 Stearns Wharf, Santa Barbara, CA 93101
(805) 962-9111, E-mail: rckscip@aol.com
Present Address: Section of Evolution and Ecology, University of California, Davis, CA 95616
(530) 752-1092, E-mail: rcklinger@ucdavis.edu
[2]Channel Islands National Park, 1901 Spinnaker Drive, Ventura, CA 93002
(805) 375-0902, E-mail: Ish_Messer@nps.gov

ABSTRACT

A series of three prescribed burns varying in size from 270 to 490 hectares was done in grasslands on Santa Cruz Island between 1993 and 1995. The two main goals of the burns were to begin an evaluation of the effect of fire as an ecological process in the island's communities, and to determine if fire can be used as a restoration tool to enhance native plant species distribution and abundance in grasslands on Santa Cruz Island. Although total species richness and diversity tended not to change systematically as a result of burning, the postburn composition of the burned areas was significantly different from that of preburned conditions and unburned controls (matched to each burned plot by year). The response to burning varied between different vegetation guilds and within the different burn areas. Burned and unburned plots were dominated by alien grasses in all years, while the guild that tended to show the greatest positive response to the burns were annual forbs. By the third year postburn, the burned plots were beginning to return to a composition similar to preburn conditions. The richness and abundance of native species tended to either increase or remain unchanged as a result of the burning.

Keywords: Diversity, grasslands, fire, prescribed burns, Santa Cruz Island.

INTRODUCTION

Grasslands in California have undergone dramatic changes in composition and distribution over the last 200 years. Community composition has been severely altered by heavy grazing from domestic livestock and the introduction of alien plant species, leading to a conversion from communities dominated by native perennial bunchgrasses and forbs to ones comprised predominantly of alien annual grasses and forbs (Heady 1977; Bartolome et al. 1986; Mack 1989). Removing grazing pressure does not lead to a return of native perennial bunchgrasses or a reduction in abundance of alien grasses, so alien herbaceous species persist in grasslands throughout the state (White 1967; Bartolome and Gemmill 1981; Baker 1989). Compounding the problems of drastically altered grazing regimes and the influx of alien species has been the reduction in extent of native grasslands. Beginning in the middle to late twentieth century, the amount of natural grassland area in the state has been reduced by urbanization and agriculture. As a result of the combination of conversion from perennial to annual grassland and habitat loss, remnant patches of native perennial grassland usually exist now as small, isolated fragments.

Grassland communities on the California islands underwent a similar conversion as a result of severe overgrazing from feral and domestic livestock (Minnich 1980; Junak et al. 1995). The islands remain relatively undeveloped and loss of habitat has not been a serious problem, but alien herbaceous species dominate grassland communities, resulting in the distribution and abundance of native herbaceous species becoming more restricted than alien species (Klinger 1998). Programs to remove feral and domestic animals have been undertaken by most of the organizations managing the islands (Schuyler 1993; Halvorson 1994; Keegan et al. 1994), with the primary goal of enhancing and/or restoring the composition, structure and function of the natural communities. However, based on the patterns observed on the mainland, these removal programs will in all likelihood be only a first step in a much longer management process, and other types of programs will need to be tested and evaluated before an effective restoration protocol can be designed (Klinger et al. 1994; Laughrin et al. 1994).

Prescribed burning has been suggested as a potential tool for restoring native species to grassland communities and has been tested in several areas of California (Parsons and Stohlgren 1989; Dyer et al. 1996). The results of these experiments have been mixed; in the foothills of the Sierra Nevada the biomass of alien annual grass was reduced and the biomass of both alien and native forbs increased following three successive burns (fall or spring), but these effects were transient and were not sustained beyond the burning treatments (Parsons and Stohlgren 1989). At the Jepson Prairie, Dyer et al. (1996) found that recruitment of *Nasella pulchra* was relatively high in burned areas but was also highly dependent on variations in annual climatic conditions.

The historic role of fire on the structure and composition of plant communities on the California islands is poorly understood. Although it is generally accepted that fire was an important component of the islands' natural systems, and plant species on the islands have similar adaptations to fire as those on the mainland (Carroll et al. 1993), information is lacking on the historic fire regime. We know fire was suppressed over the last 150 years, both by human choice and lack of extensive fuels because of the severe overgrazing which had occurred, but we know little about aboriginal burning on the islands and less about naturally occurring fires. From a contemporary perspective, it is likely that fires on the islands will grow more frequent. They will be a result of a continuing increase in the extent and density of fuels, natural and accidental ignition (Carroll et al. 1993), prescribed burning and reduced suppression efforts (Wells 1991).

The contemporary role of fire has two aspects then: the first as a naturally occurring process in an ecological regime drastically different from historic ones, and the second as a restoration tool. These aspects are not necessarily exclusive, but must be evaluated by different criteria. It is recognized that the invasion of alien species can alter disturbance regimes (Mack and D'Antonio 1998), leading to different patterns of succession and composition in the disturbed communities. As more and more areas become impacted and altered by nonnative plants and animals, scientists and land mangers are trying to understand ecological processes from both an historical and contemporary perspective relative to these invasions. It is believed that by understanding the historic relationship of communities and their disturbance regimes, effective management tools can be developed for preserving the biological integrity of natural systems. Few truly natural systems exist any more, and for agencies responsible for the management of natural communities and their resources, determining what the outcomes will be of a natural process within the context of communities severely altered in composition and structure is an important undertaking.

In this study we used prescribed burning as a way of evaluating the role of fire on the structure, diversity, and composition of grasslands on Santa Cruz Island, and to evaluate the effectiveness of prescribed burning for creating conditions beneficial to native species in these communities. We chose to conduct the study in grasslands because of their extensive distribution on the islands, because alien species have had the greatest relative impact in these as opposed to other communities, and because the light, flashy fuels make grasslands the most likely areas for a fire to either start or be carried across an extensive part of the island.

STUDY AREA

The project was conducted in grasslands on the southwest side of Santa Cruz Island. A detailed description of the island is given in Junak et al. (1995). Soils in the southwest grasslands are derived mainly from shale and silt deposits and are cut with deep gullies as a result of locally severe erosion. Three relatively broad watercourses drain the area; Poso, Alegria, and Sauces creeks. The elevation ranges from 0 to 350 m, with the topography characterized by relatively steep hills (30 to 80% slope) dissected by numerous small drainages.

The two primary plant communities which occurred in the study area were grasslands and coastal scrub. Grasslands comprised over 80% of the area and were dominated by alien grasses (*Lolium multiflorum, Avena barbata, A. fatua, Bromus diandrus, B. mollis, B. rubens, Vulpia myuros*), with an interspersion of native shrubs (*Artemisia californica, Baccharis pilularis, Hazardia squarrosus, Rhus integrifolia*). Coastal scrub was dominated by native shrubs, alien grasses, and a combination of native and alien forbs (*Atriplex semibaccata, Dichelostemma capitatum, Erodium spp., Sanicula arguta, Sisyrinchium bellum*). Relatively small patches of native grass (*Nasella pulchra*) occurred throughout the grasslands and coastal scrub communities.

METHODS

The study was conducted from the spring of 1993 to the spring of 1998. We selected three contiguous treatment areas of varying size and configuration to be burned and an adjacent unburned area to be a control (Table 1). One of the three treatment areas was burned each fall (early November to early December) from 1993 to 1995.

We monitored the effect of fire on herbaceous and woody species by sampling in the spring preceding each burn and then each spring for three years after. We collected data in 10 burned and 10 control grassland plots (matched by year) for each of the treatments. The data included estimates of species richness, cover of herbaceous and woody species, and density of woody species. We also recorded the aspect, slope (degrees), and elevation for each plot.

We estimated cover with the point-intercept method (Bonham 1989) and followed sampling protocols used by Channel Islands National Park (Halvorson et al. 1988). A 30-m-long tape was extended along a randomly selected compass bearing, and every 3 cm along the tape a thin metal rod was vertically lowered and the species of plant which it intercepted was recorded. The height of the tallest species intercepted by the point was also recorded. We made a list

Table 1. Sizes and timing of prescribed burns for three treatments and one control area in grasslands on the southwest side of Santa Cruz Island, California.

Area	Size (Ha)	Burn Date
Control	160	Unburned
Poso	340	Nov-93
Alegria	270	Dec-94
Sauces	490	Nov-95

of all species occurring in a 2-m-wide belt (one meter on either side of the tape) along the tape, and counted the number of shrubs and trees rooted within the 2-m-wide belt. Shrubs were recorded if they were more than half rooted within the belt, and each species was recorded as either a seedling (no lignification of the main stem) or adult.

Vegetation species were grouped into eight different guilds (Table 2), and we calculated four different estimates of abundance for each guild. These included absolute and relative percent cover, and the mean number and percentage of species/plot. We did not analyze the mean number and percentage of species/plot for native annual grass and alien perennial forbs because there were too few species for a meaningful test (n=3 and 2, respectively).

We calculated three indices of alpha diversity (local or within plot diversity) for burned and unburned areas using the program BIODIV (Baev and Penev 1995). Species richness (S) was measured as the presence of all species within the 30 x 2 m belt. Species diversity using abundance estimates (% absolute cover) was calculated with Hills N2 (N2), while species evenness was estimated using Molinari's index (E). We selected these indices based on their biological interpretability and recommendations made by Magurran (1988) and Alatalo (1981).

We estimated beta diversity (differential diversity between plots, habitats, or treatments) with Whittaker's beta, calculated as gamma diversity (total species within a treatment condition/within plot diversity S) (Shmida and Wilson 1985). Gamma diversity for each of the six treatment and control conditions was estimated as the total number of species summed across the preburn and three postburn seasons.

We used canonical correspondence analysis (CANOCO) (ter Braak 1995) to determine the influence of various environmental variables on species composition in the different treatment conditions. Variables used to test against the ordination scores included the percent bare ground and litter, slope (degrees), aspect (calculated as degrees from true north), elevation, and whether a plot was burned or not. We broke the analyses into four separate years: preburn and each of the three postburn years. Because rainfall varied between years we included each year as a covariate in the ordination, thereby adjusting the scores and holding the effect of precipitation constant. All species were included in the analysis, but we downweighted rare ones (ter Braak 1995). Monte Carlo simulation tests were used to test for the significance of the ordination scores for the first canonical axis and the entire ordination (ter Braak 1995).

We performed analysis of variance with repeated measures (RmANOVA) to test whether the diversity indices, cover estimates, and number and percentage of species in each guild differed among burned condition (burned vs. unburned), the year a particular area was burned (burn area), and the number of years postburn (the repeated factor). The analyses were partitioned into between subjects and within subjects groups. Each measure of diversity and abundance was tested separately. We used scatterplots and normal probability plots to evaluate residuals from the univariate tests for determining whether the assumptions of normality, linearity, equal variances and no outliers were valid. To avoid problems with violations of the sphericity assumption of RmANOVA, we used the Huynh-Feldt epsilon adjustment of the univariate F-statistics and Wilks Lambda for the multivariate tests to determine the significance of the analyses. Cover values and percentage of species in each guild were arcsin transformed, and the mean number of species/plot in each guild was square root transformed. All statistical analyses were done using the GLM procedure of SYSTAT (Wilkinson 1990). Statistical tests were considered significant if $p < 0.05$, and marginally significant if $0.05 < p < 0.10$.

RESULTS

There was a significant between-subjects interaction among burned/unburned condition and burn area (F=4.55, df=2,54, p=0.01) for total species richness (S). There was no significant difference in S among burn conditions in Poso and Sauces, but S was significantly greater in burned than unburned plots for all postburn years in Alegria (Wilks Lambda=0.72, F=2.29, df=8,102, p=0.03). There was a significant within-subjects interaction between the year postburn and the burn area (F=5.13, df=6,162, p=0.000). Species richness decreased significantly in Sauces, increased significantly in Alegria, and did not change significantly in Poso (Figure 1A).

Species diversity (N2) varied significantly between the three burn areas for between-subjects cases (F=3.86, df=2,54, p=0.03). N2 was significantly lower in Sauces than in Poso or Alegria (Wilks Lambda=0.656, F=6.679, df=4,51, p=0.000), and significantly greater in Alegria than Poso (Wilks Lambda=0.562, F=9.923, df=4,51, p=0.000). There was a significant within-subjects interaction in burn condition, burn area and the year post burn (F=2.15, df=6,162, p=0.05). There was no significant difference in N2 between burned and unburned plots for preburn conditions in Poso

Table 2. Vegetation guilds and the number of species/guild in grassland burn areas on the southwest side of Santa Cruz Island, California, 1993 to 1998.

Guild	Number of Species
Native Annual Forbs	51
Native Perennial Forbs	31
Native Annual Grass	3
Native Perennial Grass	5
Alien Annual Forbs	23
Alien Perennial Forbs	2
Alien Annual Grass	13
Shrubs**	12
Total	150

** There was only one species of alien shrub (*Marrubium vulgare*), so it was lumped with the others.

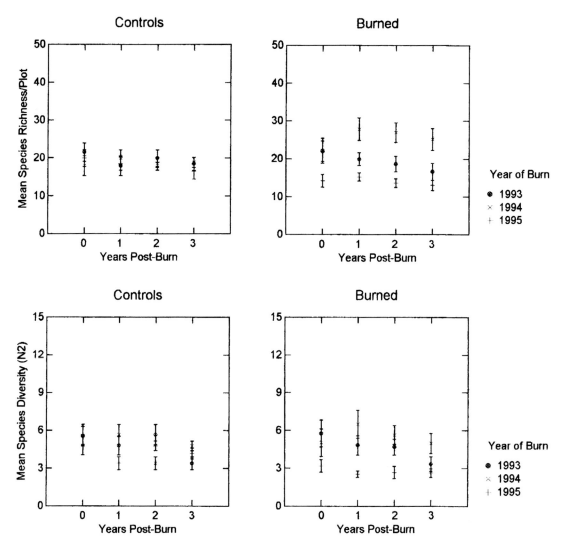

Figure 1A. Patterns of species richness and diversity in burned and unburned grasslands on Santa Cruz Island, California, 1993 to 1998.

and Alegria, but N2 was significantly lower in burned than unburned plots in Sauces. For postburn conditions, there was no significant difference in N2 between burned and unburned plots during any year in Poso. In Alegria, N2 was significantly greater in burned plots than unburned ones in the second year postburn. N2 was significantly lower in burned than unburned plots in Sauces during all years except the first postburn. There was an overall linear decrease in N2 between 1993 and 1998, regardless of burn condition or burn area (F=13.22, df=1,54, p=0.001) (Figure 1A).

There was a significant within-subjects interaction between burn area and the year postburn for beta diversity (F=3.984, df=6,162, p=0.003). Beta diversity showed a significant linear increase in Poso and a significant linear decrease in Alegria, and did not change significantly in Sauces (F=4.819, df=1,54, p=0.012) (Figure 1B). There were no significant between-subject differences in beta diversity among any of the burn condition or burn area combinations.

There was no significant difference in species evenness (E) among any of the burn condition or burn area combinations (F=0.79, df=3,162, p=0.50) (Figure 1B).

Three canonical axes could be interpreted in each of the four CANOCO ordinations. The three axes accounted for 76 to 83% of the variance between species composition and the environmental variables, and between 13 to 15% of the variability in the species abundance's (Table 3). All Monte Carlo tests for both the first canonical axis and the overall ordination were significant.

Species composition shifted dramatically as a result of burning, and this effect was most pronounced in the first year postburn (Table 3). In the preburn conditions, species composition was influenced most by the physical nature of the plots, specifically the aspect, elevation, and slope (Table 3). Before each burn, there was no distinct separation of plots or in species in different vegetation guilds (Figure 2A). In the first year postburn, species composition was

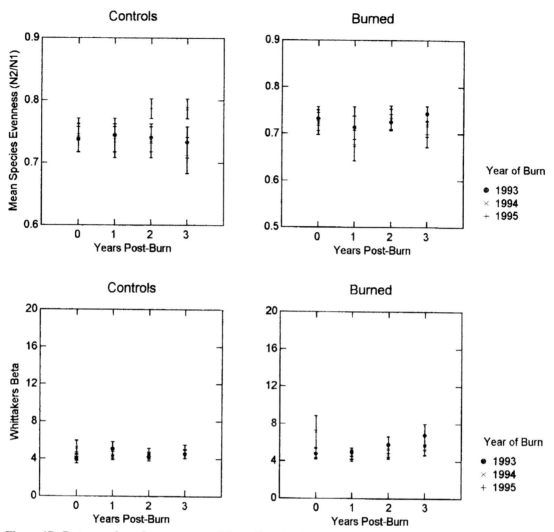

Figure 1B. Patterns of species evenness and beta diversity in burned and unburned grasslands on Santa Cruz Island, California, 1993 to 1998.

determined primarily by the burn condition of a plot. There was a distinct separation of burned and unburned plots, and there was a strong association in the distribution and abundance of most of the native forb species with burn plots (Figure 2B). This pattern continued into the second year postburn, although the association was not as strong as in the first year postburn. The correlation of burning with the first canonical axes dropped from 0.83 to 0.45, and species composition differences between burned and unburned plots were not as distinct (Figure 2C). By the third year postburn, the distinction in species composition had further weakened, and the correlation with species composition was more strongly influenced by the aspect of a plot than with burning (Table 3 and Figure 2D).

Alien grass and forb species were the dominant components of species richness and cover in all years and conditions (Figure 3). Over 60% of the species were comprised of members of these two groups. Alien annual grass

comprised 69 to 71% of the relative cover in unburned areas and 63 to 70% in burned plots, while alien forbs comprised 14 to 16% in unburned areas and 13 to 21% in burned areas. Native forbs comprised 14 to 15% of the species in unburned plots and 19 to 25% in burned plots, while relative cover ranged from 1 to 3% in unburned plots and 3 to 6% in burned plots. The percent of native grass species ranged between 7 to 9% in unburned plots and 6 to 7% in unburned plots, while relative cover ranged from 8 to 11% in unburned plots and 6 to 10% in burned plots. Shrubs comprised 10% of the species in unburned plots and 5% in burned plots. The relative cover of shrubs ranged from 3 to 5% in unburned plots and 1.5 to 5% in burned plots.

Prior to burning, there was no significant difference between burned and unburned plots for the mean number and percentage of native annual forbs (F=0.51, df=2,54, p=0.60). Following burning there was a significantly greater number and percentage in burned than unburned areas

Table 3. Variable loadings and percent of variance accounted for three axis derived by canonical correspondence analysis of 150 plant species in burned and unburned grasslands on the southwest side of Santa Cruz Island, California, 1993 to 1998.

Variable	Species Axis 1	Species Axis 2	Species Axis 3	Environmental Axis 1	Environmental Axis 2	Environmental Axis 3	Summary	Axes 1	Axes 2	Axes 3
Preburn Conditions										
Bare Ground (%)	-0.018	0.652	0.159	-0.023	0.953	0.228	Eigen Value	0.120	0.069	0.060
Litter (%)	0.394	0.146	-0.093	0.489	0.213	-0.134	*Species/Environment Correlation	0.806	0.685	0.698
Burned	0.217	0.086	-0.605	0.269	0.125	-0.866	*Cumulative % Variance Species	7.2	11.4	15.0
Aspect	-0.629	0.093	-0.200	-0.781	0.136	-0.287	Species/Environmental	39.8	62.7	82.7
Slope	-0.353	0.123	0.133	-0.438	0.180	0.190				
Elevation	-0.437	-0.019	0.418	-0.542	-0.028	0.599				
1st Year Postburn										
Bare Ground (%)	0.393	-0.076	0.148	0.454	-0.094	0.267	Eigen Value	0.128	0.107	0.058
Litter (%)	0.031	0.536	0.263	0.036	0.667	0.475	*Species/Environment Correlation	0.866	0.804	0.553
Burned	0.826	-0.139	0.035	0.954	-0.173	0.064	*Cumulative % Variance Species	6.6	12.1	15.1
Aspect	-0.281	-0.516	0.297	-0.324	-0.642	0.537	Species/Environmental	33.5	61.5	76.6
Slope	-0.277	-0.262	-0.119	-0.320	-0.326	-0.216				
Elevation	-0.535	-0.110	0.120	-0.617	-0.137	0.217				
2nd Year Postburn										
Bare Ground (%)	0.152	-0.095	0.273	0.227	-0.128	0.419	Eigen Value	0.109	0.106	0.076
Litter (%)	0.097	-0.167	0.507	0.146	-0.226	0.778	*Species/Environment Correlation	0.663	0.737	0.652
Burned	0.450	0.352	-0.271	0.679	0.478	-0.416	*Cumulative % Variance Species	4.9	9.6	13.0
Aspect	0.225	-0.642	-0.137	0.339	-0.871	-0.210	Species/Environmental	29.0	57.2	77.4
Slope	-0.275	-0.243	-0.055	-0.415	-0.329	-0.084				
Elevation	-0.281	-0.346	0.131	-0.424	-0.469	0.201				
3rd Year Postburn										
Bare Ground (%)	0.237	0.350	0.120	0.337	0.571	0.219	Eigen Value	0.152	0.086	0.062
Litter (%)	0.023	0.136	0.348	0.033	0.222	0.636	*Species/Environment Correlation	0.703	0.614	0.547
Burned	-0.319	0.384	-0.222	-0.454	0.626	-0.405	*Cumulative % Variance Species	6.9	10.7	13.5
Aspect	0.646	-0.022	-0.161	0.919	-0.036	-0.295	Species/Environmental	38.6	60.5	76.2
Slope	0.044	-0.062	-0.106	0.063	-0.101	-0.194				
Elevation	0.139	-0.137	-0.107	0.197	-0.223	-0.195				

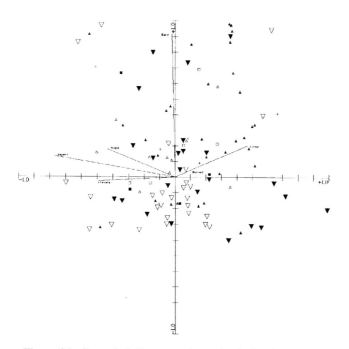

Figure 2A. Canonical Correspondence Analysis triplot of site and species scores for grassland plots on Santa Cruz Island, California. Symbols: large upside-down dark triangles=burned plots; large upside-down open triangles=unburned plots; small dark triangles=native forbs; small open triangles=alien forbs; small dark squares=native grass; small open squares=alien grass; crosses=shrubs. Data are for preburned conditions.

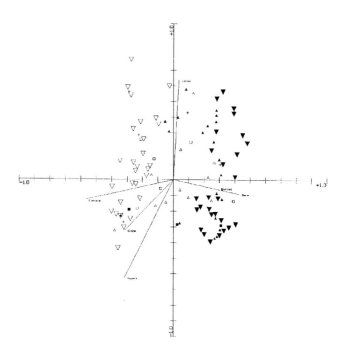

Figure 2B. Canonical Correspondence Analysis triplot of site and species scores for grassland plots on Santa Cruz Island, California. Symbols: large upside-down dark triangles=burned plots; large upside-down open triangles=unburned plots; small dark triangles=native forbs; small open triangles=alien forbs; small dark squares=native grass; small open squares=alien grass; crosses=shrubs. Data are for the first year postburn.

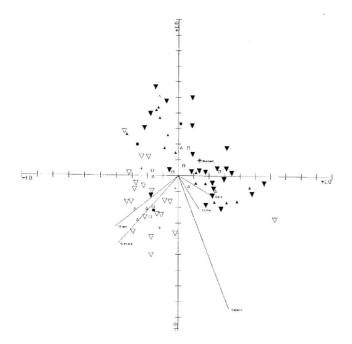

Figure 2C. Canonical Correspondence Analysis triplot of site and species scores for grassland plots on Santa Cruz Island, California. Symbols: large upside-down dark triangles=burned plots; large upside-down open triangles=unburned plots; small dark triangles=native forbs; small open triangles=alien forbs; small dark squares=native grass; small open squares=alien grass; crosses=shrubs. Data are for the second year postburn.

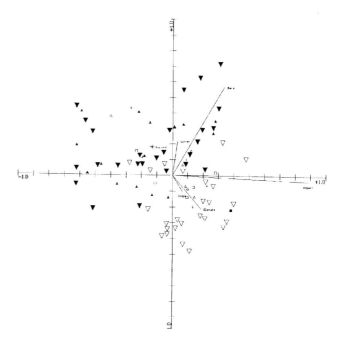

Figure 2D. Canonical Correspondence Analysis triplot of site and species scores for grassland plots on Santa Cruz Island, California. Symbols: large upside-down dark triangles=burned plots; large upside-down open triangles=unburned plots; small dark triangles=native forbs; small open triangles=alien forbs; small dark squares=native grass; small open squares=alien grass; crosses=shrubs. Data are for the third year postburn.

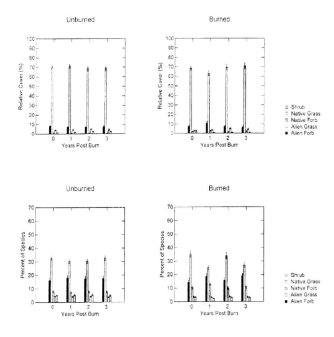

Figure 3. Relative percent cover and species composition for different vegetation classes in burned and unburned grasslands on Santa Cruz Island, California, 1993 to 1998.

(F=3.25, df=8,102, p=0.001). This pattern varied by the burn year and the year postburn (F=2.63, df=6,147, p=0.02), but the overall effect was a net increase, especially in the first year postburn. There was no significant difference between burned and unburned plots for absolute or relative cover in the preburn conditions, but cover was 3 to 4 times greater in burned than unburned areas in the first and third years postburn (Wilks Lambda=0.75, F=3.76, df=4,46, p=0.01).

The mean number of native perennial forb species differed significantly between burn condition and burn area for the between-subjects analysis (F=3.23, df=2,54, p=0.05). There was no significant difference between burned and unburned plots in Poso and Sauces, but there were significantly more in burned than unburned plots in Alegria (Wilks Lambda=0.82, F=2.75, df=4,51, p=0.04). The mean number of native perennial forb species varied significantly between the different burn years and the year post burn (F=2.40, df=6,162, p=0.03) for the within-subjects analysis. Consistent with the between-subjects analysis, there was no significant difference between burned and unburned plots in Poso and Sauces, but there was significantly more in burned than unburned plots in Alegria for all years. There was no significant change in the mean percentage of native perennial forb species in any condition.

There was a significant between-subjects interaction among burn condition and burn area for both absolute and relative cover of native perennial forbs (F=5.86, df=2,52, p=0.01), and also a significant within-subjects interaction between burn area and the year postburn for absolute and relative cover (F=2.75, df=6,159, p=0.02). There was no significant difference among the different conditions prior

to burning, but after burning the burned plots in Alegria had significantly greater absolute and relative cover in all years than did unburned plots (Wilks Lambda=0.67, F=2.79, df=8,100, p=0.01).

The mean percent absolute and relative cover of native annual grass decreased significantly in all burn areas (F=8.41, df=3,93, p=0.001), but there was no difference in the pattern as a result of being burned or unburned (F=0.19, df=1,31, p=0.66). The mean percent absolute and relative cover of native perennial grass increased significantly in all burn areas and burn conditions (F=3.26, df=3,159, p=0.02).

There was a significant within-subjects interaction between burn condition, burn year, and the year postburn for the mean percentage of native perennial grass species (F=3.36, df=6,159, p=0.001). Their percentage increased significantly in burned plots in Poso and Sauces and in unburned plots in Alegria, but did not change significantly for burned plots in Alegria or unburned plots in Sauces. They initially decreased between preburn and the first year postburn in unburned plots in Poso, but then increased significantly in the last two postburn areas. In contrast, there was a significant between-subjects interaction between burn condition and burn area for the mean number of native grass species (F=3.45, df=23,54, p=0.04). This result is difficult to clearly interpret however, because the initial mean number of species was significantly higher in burned than unburned plots in Alegria, and in unburned than burned plots in Sauces (Wilks Lambda=0.72, F=2.28, df=8,102, p=0.03).

The mean number of alien annual forb species varied significantly among burn areas (F=3.07, df=2,54, p=0.05) but not by burn condition (F=0.29, df=1,54, p=0.59). There was a significant between-subjects interaction for the mean percent of alien annual forbs between burn condition and burn area (F=4.92, df=2,54, p=0.01); there was no significant difference between burned and unburned plots in Poso and Sauces, but the burned plots in Alegria had a significantly lower percentage than unburned plots. Absolute cover of alien annual forbs varied between years, burn area, and burned and unburned plots (F=4.03, df=6,162, p=0.000). There was no significant difference in the preburn plots in Poso and Alegria, but absolute cover was significantly greater in unburned plots in Sauces (F=5.36, df=1,54, p=0.001). In the first year postburn, burned plots had significantly greater absolute cover in Poso and Sauces, while burned plots in Poso and Alegria had significantly greater cover in the second year postburn. There was no significant difference in the third year postburn. The pattern for relative cover was the same as for absolute cover.

There was no significant difference in the percent absolute cover of alien perennial forbs in preburn plots (F=0.06, df=1,54, p=0.81), but unburned plots had significantly greater cover in the first year postburn (F=36.12, df=1,54, p=0.000). There was no significant difference in the second or third years postburn (F=2.37, df=1,54, p=0.13). The pattern for relative cover was the same as for absolute cover.

The mean number and percent of alien grass species varied among burned/unburned condition, burn area, and the postburn year (F=3.65, df=6,162, p=0.000). There was no significant difference among burned and unburned plots in any of the burn areas in the preburn years, or in any of the postburn years in Poso. In Alegria, there were significantly fewer species in unburned plots in the second year postburn, but fewer in burned plots in the third year postburn (Wilks Lambda=0.65, F=7.01, df=4,51, p=0.01). There were significantly more species in unburned plots in Sauces in the first and third years postburn (Wilks Lambda=0.80, F=3.19, df=4,51, p=0.02). The percent absolute and relative cover of alien grass varied among burned condition, burn area, and burn year (F=2.81, df=6,162, p=0.01). In Poso, there was no significant difference between burned and unburned plots in any of the burn years. There was no significant difference among burn conditions or burn areas for the preburn or third postburn years in Alegria and Sauces. Cover was significantly greater in unburned plots the first year postburn in Alegria, but was significantly greater in burned plots the second year postburn in both Alegria and Sauces areas.

The mean number and percent of shrub species varied among burned condition, burn area, and burn year (F=3.54, df=6,162, p=0.000). There were no significant differences among burned and unburned plots in any year for Poso and Alegria. In Sauces, there were significantly more species in unburned plots in the preburn and first two years postburn. The percent absolute and relative cover of shrubs varied among years between burned and unburned plots (F=12.04, df=6,126, p=0.000). There was significantly greater shrub cover in burned plots in the preburn years (F=4.35, df=1,42, p=0.04), but there was no significant difference between burned and unburned plots in the postburn years. The density of shrubs varied significantly between the different burn areas and years, but there was no significant difference in total shrub density or the density of seedlings or adults among burned and unburned plots.

DISCUSSION

From an ecological perspective, single fires appear to have only a temporary effect on structural aspects of grasslands on Santa Cruz Island. There were differences between burned and unburned conditions for some of the variables we measured, but in general, effects were dependent mainly on conditions intrinsic to the different areas. These differences were often inconsistent among years, treatments, and burn area as well. This outcome is similar to what Dyer et al. (1996) found at Jepson Prairie in northern California, where the regeneration of native bunch grass was as dependent on environmental variation as it was on burning or grazing treatments.

The effect of fire on diversity, structure, and composition was relatively brief and most pronounced in the first year postburn, and, to a lesser extent, the second year postburn. Species richness, alpha diversity, and beta diversity all varied after the burn, but in no distinct pattern; each area that was burned had a response different from the other areas. These differences appear to be related to site

characteristics, although it is very possible that other factors such as rainfall patterns, weather during the fire, and fire intensity could be major influences as well.

Burning had little effect on the structure of the communities; alien grasses dominated the cover in all conditions, and although shrub cover in burned plots was reduced relative to preburn conditions, shrub density did not change in any significant way. Although it may seem contradictory for shrub density not to change while cover decreases, this is because the dominant shrub species occurring in the burned areas on Santa Cruz Island have the ability to resprout. So, although cover is reduced because leaves and stems are burned back, relatively few of the shrubs die and density remains about the same.

Some studies indicate postfire vegetation changes occur in a brief period of time (Holland 1986) and are characterized mainly by species already occurring within the burn area. Relative abundances can change, but the basic suite of species does not, a pattern called "autosuccessional" (Hane 1971). Our data support these hypotheses, and it is unlikely that diversity patterns would change in any systematic way under these conditions. Furthermore, because alien grasses produce rich seed banks, it is unlikely that a single fire would deplete these, and studies in grasslands throughout California have shown that alien grass continues to remain the most abundant group of plants after a burn (Parsons and Stohlgren 1989; Dyer and Rice 1997).

The most noticeable change brought on by fire was in species composition. Canonical correspondence analysis clearly indicated that burning has at least short-term effects on composition and can override site-specific factors that are the main determinants of composition in the absence of fire. The change in composition was not limited to individual species; some guilds, especially annual forbs, responded in consistent ways to the burns. Parsons and Stohlgren (1989) reported a similar pattern in grasslands in the foothills of the Sierra Nevada, and this pattern has been well-recognized for years in other Mediterranean climate communities (Trabaud 1994).

Fire ecologists have become increasingly aware that many factors interact to influence fire effects on species composition. These include the season a burn occurs, fire behavior (intensity, rate of spread, severity), the spatial and temporal scales associated with the fire regime, landscape level processes, and historical land use (Naveh 1994; Whelan 1995). In our study, topography was the primary determinant of species composition in unburned conditions, and it influenced species composition even in recently burned areas. The topographic influence was secondary to fire effects in the first two postburn years; however, by the third year after burning, fire effects were being masked by topographic characteristics. Different guilds showed different temporal patterns for species richness and abundance in the burned areas, but by the third year postburn virtually all guilds were essentially at the same relative levels as in unburned areas. Differences in annual rainfall likely had a weak effect on some guilds, and other factors for which we did not collect data (e.g., physical and chemical soil properties) undoubtedly did as well. Historically, all of the areas had different levels of grazing by feral sheep and livestock, which has had a notable influence on the relative amounts of bare ground between sites. Each of these factors will directly and indirectly influence fire effects by modifying fire behavior at local scales (intensity and duration), site scales (intensity, duration, extent, type), and landscape scales (intensity, duration, extent, type, seasonality, frequency). They also add complexity to evaluating fire effects, because different groups of species will show variable responses according to when, where and what types of data are being collected.

From a restoration perspective, single fires on Santa Cruz will have relatively little effect in enhancing grassland communities for native species. This appears to be characteristic of most grasslands in California where species composition has been drastically altered by grazing and the abundance of alien annual grasses (Dyer 1993; Dyer and Rice 1997). Although alien species continued to dominate burned areas in our study, the prescribed burns were an encouraging initial step in creating ecological conditions beneficial to native species. Most groups of native species either increased or remained the same in abundance, and alien species did not increase in abundance. However, it is clear it will be necessary to significantly modify species composition at both local and site scales before native species can begin to reach levels of abundance comparable to that of alien species (Dyer and Rice 1997).

Developing a prescribed burning regime that is beneficial to native species will take years of experimentation and evaluation at different scales. As Whelan (1995) points out, if conservation of biodiversity is the primary management goal, trying to determine and mimic a historical fire regime may be inappropriate. The ecosystem on Santa Cruz Island that the historic fire regime occurred in has been significantly altered, and it is unrealistic to expect the system to respond in the same way as it did in the past. It is more important to try and determine which components of a fire regime can be manipulated to benefit the most native species, and determine the range of environmental conditions that these can then be applied (Kilgore 1973).

Because our study only involved single burns done in the fall, making generalizations about fire effects on the islands would be premature. We encourage the use of small scale experiments to test differential effects of burning with variable seasons, frequency, and return interval, then applying these findings to relatively large areas where the influence of larger landscape level factors (topography, climate, environmental patchiness; fire duration, extent, intensity) on the management prescription can be evaluated. We also encourage incorporating different time scales to studies on fire in the California islands; individual projects should span several years, and evaluation of different burn studies should be done over several decades.

ACKNOWLEDGMENTS

We thank the California Department of Forestry and Bobby Ouellette from Alan Hancock College Fire Technology Program for providing crews and equipment to conduct the burns. Channel Islands National Park provided transportation to the island and logistical support. Lyndal Laughrin graciously made facilities and vehicles at the University of California Natural Reserve Station available for housing, meals, and transportation. Robin Wills, Jennifer Gibson, Oren Pollak, Tony Nelson, Mark Sanderson, Trish Smith, Ethan Aumack, Emily Hebard, Brian Kitzerow, Rick Young and Shirley Bailey of The Nature Conservancy helped in all aspects of planning, burning, support, and data collection. Numerous volunteers cut miles of fireline, helped collect data, or provided logistical support, especially Mark DiMaggio and Ken Ward with their students from Paso Robles High School; Joe Yuska and his students from Lewis and Clark College; and David Allen, Wendy Hatch, Rik Katzmaier, Shirley Imsand, Diane Lipkin, Tom Maxwell, Christopher and Mary-Louise Mueller, Marie Ofria, Tim Richards, Bill Turpin, and Jonathan Wheately. Robin Wills and two anonymous reviewers provided insightful editorial comments. Extra special thanks to John Conti, without whose quiet, patient and consistently high-quality efforts this project could not have been completed.

LITERATURE CITED

Alatalo, R. V. 1981. Problems in the measurement of evenness in ecology. Oikos 37:199-204.

Baev, P. V., and L. D. Penev. 1995. BIODIV: Program for calculating biological diversity parameters, similarity, niche overlap, and cluster analysis. Pensoft, Sofia, Bulgaria.

Baker, H. G. 1989. Patterns of plant invasion in North America. Pages 44-57 in Mooney, H. A. and J. A. Drake (eds.), Ecology of Biological Invasions of North America and Hawaii. Springer-Verlag, New York, NY.

Bartolome, J. W. and B. Gemmill. 1981. The ecological status of *Stipa pulchra* (Poaceae) in California. Madroño 28:172-184.

Bartolome, J. W., S. E. Klukkert, and W. J. Barry. 1986. Opal phytoliths as evidence for displacement of native Californian grassland. Madroño 33:217-222.

Bonham, C. D. 1989. Measurements for Terrestrial Vegetation. John Wiley & Sons, New York, NY.

Carroll, M. C., L. L. Laughrin, and A. Bromfield. 1993. Fire on the California islands: does it play a role in chaparral and closed cone pine forest habitats. Pages 73-88 in Hochberg, F. G. (ed.), The Third California Islands Symposium: Recent Advances in Research on the California Islands. Santa Barbara Museum of Natural History, Santa Barbara, CA.

Dyer, A. R. and K. J. Rice. 1997. Intraspecific and diffuse competition: the response of *Nasella pulchra* in a California grassland. Ecological Applications 7:484-492.

Dyer, A. R., H. C. Fossum, and J. W. Menke. 1996. Emergence and survival of *Nassella pulchra* in a California grassland. Madroño 43:316-333.

Halvorson, W. L. 1994. Ecosystem restoration on the Channel Islands. Pages 567-571 *in* Halvorson, W. L. and G. J. Maender (eds.), The Fourth California Islands Symposium: Update on the Status of Resources. Santa Barbara Museum of Natural History, Santa Barbara, CA.

Halvorson, W. L., S. D. Viers, R. A. Clark, and D. D. Borgias. 1988. Terrestrial vegetation monitoring handbook. Channel Islands National Park, Ventura, CA.

Hane, T. L. 1971. Succession after fire in the chaparral of southern California. Ecological Monographs 41:27-52.

Heady, H. F. 1977. Valley grassland. Pages 491-533 *in* Barbour, M. G. and J. Major (eds.), Terrestrial Vegetation of California. John Wiley and Sons, New York, NY.

Holland, P. G. 1986. Mallee vegetation:steady state or successional. Australian Geographer 17:113-120.

Junak, S., T. Ayers, R. Scott, D. Wilken, and D. Young. 1995. A Flora of Santa Cruz Island. Santa Barbara Botanic Garden, Santa Barbara, CA. 397 pp.

Keegan, D. R. B. E. Coblentz, and C. S. Winchell. 1994. Ecology of feral goats eradicated on San Clemente Island, California. Pages 323-330 *in* Halvorson, W. L. and G. J. Maender (eds.), The Fourth California Islands Symposium: Update on the Status of Resources. Santa Barbara Museum of Natural History, Santa Barbara, CA.

Kilgore, B. M. 1973. The ecological role of fire in Sierran conifer forests: its application to National Park management. Quaternary Research 3: 496-513.

Klinger, R. C. 1998. Santa Cruz Island monitoring program. Volume 1: Vegetation communities 1991-95 report. The Nature Conservancy, Santa Barbara, CA. 59 pp.

Klinger, R. C., P. Schuyler and J. D. Sterner. 1994. Vegetation response to the removal of feral sheep from Santa Cruz Island. Pages 341-350 *in* Halvorson, W. L. and G. J. Maender (eds.), The Fourth California Islands Symposium: Update on the Status of Resources. Santa Barbara Museum of Natural History, Santa Barbara, CA.

Laughrin, L. L., M. Carroll, A. Bromfield, and J. Carroll. 1994. Trends in vegetation changes with removal of feral animal grazing pressures on Santa Catalina Island. Pages 523-530 *in* Halvorson, W. L. and G. J. Maender (eds.), The Fourth California Islands Symposium: Update on the Status of Resources. Santa Barbara Museum of Natural History, Santa Barbara, CA.

Mack, R. A. 1989. Temperate grasslands vulnerable to plant invasion: characteristics and consequences. Pages 155-179 *in* Drake, J. A., H. A. Mooney, F. DiCastri, R. H. Groves, F. J. Kruger, M. Rejmanek, and M. Williamson (eds.), Biological Invasions: a Global Perspective. John Wiley and Sons, New York, NY.

Mack, M. C. and C. M. D'Antonio. 1998. Impacts of biological invasions on disturbance regimes. Trends in Ecology and Evolution 13: 195-198.

Magurran, A. E. 1988. Ecological Diversity and its Measurement. Cambridge University Press, Cambridge, UK. 179 pp.

Minnich, R. A. 1980. Vegetation of Santa Cruz and Santa Catalina Islands. Pages 123-138 *in* Power, D. M. (ed.), The California Islands: Proceedings of a Multidisciplinary Symposium. Santa Barbara Museum Of Natural History, Santa Barbara, CA.

Naveh, Z. 1994. The role of fire and its management in the conservation of Mediterranean ecosystems and landscapes. Pages 163-186 *in* Moreno, J. M. and W. C. Oechel (eds.), The Role of Fire in Mediterrranean-type Ecosystems. Springer-Verlag, New York, NY.

Parsons, D. J. and T. J. Stohlgren. 1989. Effects of varying fire regimes on annual grasslands in the southern Sierra Nevada of California. Madroño 36:154-168.

Schuyler, P. 1993. Control of feral sheep (*Ovis aries*) on Santa Cruz Island, California. Pages 443-452 *in* Hochberg, F. G. (ed.), The Third California Islands Symposium: Recent Advances in Research on the California Islands. Santa Barbara Museum of Natural History, Santa Barbara, CA.

Shmida, A. and M. V. Wilson. 1985. Biological determinants of species diversity. Journal of Biogeography 12:1-20.

ter Braak, C. J. F. 1995. Ordination. Chapter 5 *in* Jongman, R. H. G., C. J. F. ter Braak, and O. F. R. Van Tongeren (eds.), Data Analysis in Community and Landscape Ecology. Cambridge University Press, Cambridge, UK.

Trabaud, L. 1994. Postfire plant community dynamics in the Mediterranean Basin. Pages 1-15 *in* Moreno, J. M. and W. C. Oechel (eds.), The Role of Fire in Mediterranean-type Ecosystems. Springer-Verlag, New York, NY.

Wells, M. L. 1991. Santa Cruz Island fire management plan. Report to The Nature Conservancy, Santa Cruz Island Preserve. The Nature Conservancy, Santa Barbara, CA.

Whelan, R. J. 1995. The Ecology of Fire. Cambridge University Press, Cambridge, UK. 346 pp.

White, K. L. 1967. Native bunchgrass (*Stipa pulchra*) on Hastings Reservation, California. Ecology 48:949-955.

Wilkinson, L. 1990. SYSTAT:the System for Statistics. SYSTAT, Evanston, IL.

ANALYSIS OF VASCULAR PLANT SPECIES DIVERSITY OF THE PACIFIC COAST ISLANDS OF ALTA AND BAJA CALIFORNIA

Thomas A. Oberbauer

Department of Planning and Land Use, County of San Diego
5201 Ruffin Road, Suite B-5, San Diego, CA 92123
(619) 694-3700, FAX (619) 694-2555, E-mail:TOBERBPL@co.san-diego.ca.us

ABSTRACT

Each of the Pacific coast islands of southern California and Baja California is unique with its own particular attributes. They vary greatly in size and distance from the mainland. Traditional analysis of island species diversity is based on the relationship between area and the number of species. However the widely different topography, climatic conditions, and geology also have a very strong influence of the diversity of plant species. The islands are also home to a large number of species which are endemic to one or more of the islands, and not found on the mainland. The existence of these plants in the flora of the islands is the result of biogeographical effects. Many of the endemic species were once common on the mainland as evidenced by fossils. Certain genera of plants, particularly *Dudleya, Cryptantha, Galium, Malva, Malacothrix, Phacelia, Quercus, Arctostaphylos, Lotus, Hemizonia*, and *Eschscholtzia* are well represented in the endemic flora. Unfortunately, most of the islands have been subjected to serious environmental damage from long periods of vegetation destruction by feral herbivores. Recent successes in feral animal removal provides hope, but there is still a need for the removal of rabbits from Todos Santos, and San Benito, and goats from Los Coronados and Guadalupe where they have caused the extinction of plants and bird species.

Keywords: Coronado Islands, Guadalupe Island, Cedros Island, California Islands, Baja California, Mexico, flora, vegetation, botany, feral animals.

INTRODUCTION

The California Channel Islands of both southern California and Baja California, including some in the state of Baja California Sur, create an island archipelago of unique and diverse features. The archipelago extends six degrees of latitude from near 28°N latitude to 34°N latitude. The islands range in size from rocks less than 0.5 km^2 to 348 km^2. These islands vary greatly in distance from the mainland, ranging from as close as 6 km to 252 km. Each island has distinct topography, ranging upwards to 1,298 m in elevation, though most are much lower. An additional physical feature that affects the diversity of species on these islands is that they are within the southern end of a Mediterranean climatic regime typified by rainfall in winter, though the amount and percentage of summer rainfall on these islands increases near the lower latitudes. Mediterranean climates are known to sustain vascular plant species diversity (Wilson 1992).

The diversity of the flora of these islands is a manifestation of all of these factors. The whole archipelago supports approximately 920 native taxa, 174 of which are endemics (including 12 which are thought to be extinct), on a total of 1,517 km^2. This is roughly one-seventh the area of San Diego County which supports approximately 2,000 species with around 25 endemics (Beauchamp 1986).

MATERIALS AND METHODS

Evaluation of Factors that Affect Diversity in the Pacific Coast Islands of Alta and Baja California

The physical attributes including distance from the mainland, area, elevation, and approximate rainfall were compared with the total number of native species and number of endemics for each of the islands. In addition, an analysis evaluated the percentage of shared species between each of the islands. Sources for this information are listed at the end of the sections for each group of islands.

Each of the islands contains a number of elements that affect the number of species present. Due to geographic relationships, the Alta California Islands have often been divided into a northern and southern group. The northern group are mostly trending in a linear, east-west pattern, parallel to the Transverse Ranges of California, while the southern group are scattered in a north-south direction, with varied distances from the mainland.

Table 1 summarizes the attributes of the islands. See Philbrick (1967) for a map of the islands. Table 2 lists some of the physical characteristics of the islands as well as major conservation problems to be discussed later. These tables provide a summary of the diversity of the geologic formations that make up the islands, their climates, elevation and distances from the mainland. The tables are intended to demonstrate the individuality of each of the islands.

Oberbauer, T. A.

Table 1. Attributes of California Pacific Islands.

Island	Area (km^2)	No. Plants/ (Endemics)	Plants/area	Elev. (m)	Rainfall	Distance to Mainland
Cedros	348	224 (19)	0.64	1194	63-200 mm	23 km
Guadalupe	249	156 (34)	0.69	1298	100-300 mm	252 km
Santa Cruz	244	480 (6)	1.95	660	400-560 mm	30 km
Santa Rosa	217	387 (5)	1.70	480	300-430 mm	44 km
Santa Catalina	194	427 (8)	2.15	631	250-400 mm	32 km
San Clemente	145	272 (14)	1.79	589	150-300 mm	79 km
San Nicolas	58	139 (3)	1.97	277	250 mm	98 km
San Miguel	37	198 (1)	4.62	262	340 mm	42 km
Natividad	7.2	63 (0)	7.22	148	63 mm	7 km
San Benito	6.4	42 (4)	6.50	20	63 mm	66 km
Anacapa	2.9	191 (2)	57.24	284	325 mm	20 km
Santa Barbara	2.6	88 (3)	27.69	193	300 mm	61 km
Los Coronados	2.5	96 (3)	38.00	190	180 mm	13 km
San Martin	2.3	80 (1)	28.26	146	130 mm	5 km
Todos Santos	1.2	108 (0)	71.67	100	130 mm	6 km
San Geronimo	0.4	4 (0)	10.00	40	80 mm	9 km

Islands listed in order of area. Island area and distance to mainland from Philbrick (1967), elevations for California Islands from the USGS topographic maps. Elevations for Baja California islands from Bostic, 1975, and nautical charts. Number of endemics and number of plants from California islands from Raven (1963), Foreman (1967), Thorne (1967), Philbrick (1972), Wallace (1985), Junak et al. (1995), for Baja California Islands from Oberbauer (1993 and 1999), Junak and Philbrick (1994a, 1994b, 1999a, and 1999b), and Moran (1996). Rainfall data from Hastings (1964) and Hastings and Humphrey (1969) as well as estimates from personal observation.

California Islands — Northern Group

The northern group of islands consists of San Miguel, Santa Rosa, Santa Cruz, and Anacapa islands. This group contains two of the larger islands, and the islands with the highest seasonal rainfall of all of the California Channel Islands. All of the islands in this northern group are included in the Channel Islands National Park.

For many years, the status of these islands relative to connections to the mainland was unclear. During the Pleistocene pluvial periods when the sea level was 140 m lower than present (Vedder and Howell 1980), it is now generally accepted that the northern group, though connected together, were still separated from the mainland by a relatively narrow channel. Fossil pygmy mammoths have been found on Santa Rosa and San Nicolas islands (Thorne 1969), and a display in the Channel Islands National Park visitor center depicts the Santa Rosa Island fossil site. This indicates that they were not beyond the dispersal abilities of large, non-amphibious mammals. See Wallace (1985), Clark et al. (1990), Skinner and Pavlick (1994), Wehtje (1994), and Junak et al. (1995) for more specific information about these islands.

California Islands — Southern Group

The southern group of the California Channel Islands consists of Santa Barbara, San Nicolas, Santa Catalina, and San Clemente islands. Geographically, these islands are not as closely allied to one another as are the Northern Channel Islands. While the northern group consists of a regular chain of islands in an east-west line, the southern group islands are scattered in divergent locations. None of these islands have been connected to the mainland, though Santa Barbara and San Nicolas islands were probably submerged during the dry interglacial periods (Philbrick 1972; Vedder and Howell 1980). For more specific details of these islands, see also Raven (1963), Foreman (1967), Thorne (1967), Davis (1980), Philbrick (1980), Westec Services (1978), Wallace (1985), Clark and Halverson (1990), and Oberbauer (1994).

Baja California Islands

The Baja California Islands consist of Islas Los Coronados, Todo Santos, San Martin, San Geronimo, San Benito, Cedros, Natividad, and Guadalupe islands. They extend more than 500 km down the coast of the northern

202

Table 2. Physical conditions of islands and their conservation problems.

Island	Geological Characteristics	Major Vegetation	Conservation Issues
San Miguel	Sandstones	CU, CHP, CSS, G	Revegetation of areas eroded by past feral animals. Protected by National Park.
Santa Rosa	Sandstones, metamorphosed	DU, CHP, CSS, G, OW, CF, LY	Revegetation of areas grazed by cattle, deer, and elk. Designated part of National Park.
Santa Cruz	Sandstones, mudstones, metamorphosed	DU, CHP, CSS, G, OW, CF, LY, RIP	Natural revegetation of areas overgrazed sheep and pigs. Proected by Nature Conservancy and National Park.
Anacapa	Indurated sedimentary, mudstones	CHP, CSS, G, MS	Some revegetation. Protected by National Park.
Santa Barbara	Indurated sedimentary	CSS, G, MS	Natural revegetation of areas formerly impacted by rabbits. Protected by National Park.
San Nicolas	Sandstones	DU, CSS, G, MS, RIP	Natural revegetation of areas grazed by sheep and remove feral cats.
Santa Catalina	Metamorphic, volcanic, sedimentary	CHP, CSS, G, MS, OW, LY, RIP	Control of feral pigs, goats, and bison. Protected by private conservancy.
San Clemente	Volcanic, sedimentary	DU, CHP, CS, G, MS, LY	Under Navy ownership and efforts are underway to restore natural habitats.
Los Coronados	Mudstones and indurated sandstones	MS, CSS, B	Control of feral animals. Protection of important bird colonies.
Todos Santos	Metamorphosed volcanics	DU, MS	Control of feral animals. Contains bird colonies.
San Martin	volcanic	DU, MS	Prevention of introduction of feral animals and weedy plants. Historically contained important bird colonies.
San Geronimo	Sedimentary	Mostly B	Prevention of introduction of weedy plants.
Natividad	Sedimentary, metamorphosed sediments	LD	Control of off road vehicles, expansion of village. Contains important bird colonies.
Cedros	Sedimentary, metamorphosed sediments	DU, CHP, CSS, G, MS, CF, UD, LD, SB, B, J	Control of feral cats, potential introduction of feral animals, recurring fires.
San Benito	Sedimentary, metamorphosed	LD, B	Continued control of feral animals. Contains important bird colonies.
Guadalupe	Volcanic	(CHP), (CSS), G, MS, CF, (OW), LD, B, P, J	Control of feral goats, cats, and dogs.

LEGEND: DU=dune; CHP=chaparral; CSS=coastal sage scrub; G=grassland; MS=maritime sage scrub; CF=coniferous forest; OW=oak woodland; LY=Lyonothamnus/Prunus woodland; UD=upper desert scrub; LD=lower desert scrub; SB=sea-bluff succulent; B=naturally barren; RIP=riparian; J=junipers; P=palms. Parentheses denotes communities that are extirpated.

half of Baja California. They are more varied than the islands of Alta California. Several of the groups, Los Coronados, Todo Santos, and San Benito, consist of more than one island. Each group has different geologic origins ranging from volcanic to metamorphic marine sediments and each has relatively distinct vegetation communities. Most support forms of maritime desert scrub or maritime succulent scrub with differences in the dominant species although Cedros and Guadalupe islands support or supported

northern coniferous forest communities as well as patches of chaparral and coastal sage scrub.

With the publication of the proceedings from this symposium, published species lists exist for all of the islands except San Geronimo Island. Species list references for the Baja California Islands include Oberbauer (1993), Junak and Philbrick (1994a, 1994b, 1999a and b, this volume), Moran (1996), and Oberbauer (1999, this volume). For more information on the physical and natural history of each of the islands please see Blake (1961), Cohen et al. (1963), Hastings (1964), Hastings and Humphrey (1969), Bostic (1975), Axelrod (1977), Batiza (1977), Wiggins (1980), Moran (1983 and 1996), Kilmer (1984), Lamb (1992), Oberbauer (1992), and Hickman (1993).

RESULTS

Plant Species Diversity

The relationship between the area of an island and the number of species which inhabit it is a well-known concept as is the fact that distance from the mainland correlates with the number of endemic species which are restricted to that island (MacArthur and Wilson 1967). Raven (1969) assessed the floras of the California Channel Islands in terms of their conformance to a mathematical model that predicts that the number of species of any group of organisms increases in approximate logarithmic manner in relation to the area of sampling. Such analysis assumes some degree of uniformity between the islands in order to predict with any accuracy, the number of vascular plant species that are likely to inhabit them. As is described in Tables 1 and 2, except for a few of the northern California islands, both the California and Baja California Islands lack uniformity of major features.

Figure 1 graphs the log of the number of species against the log of the area of the island. Figure 2 graphs the island area with the number of endemics. The diversity of species present and the number that are endemic are actually the result of a combination of all of the attributes of an area, be it island surrounded by ocean or mountain surrounded by lowland. Figure 3 shows that the number of endemics is related both to distance from the mainland and the area of the island.

Among other factors that affect the diversity of species and the number of endemics, the topography of an island is extremely significant. The topography also has influenced the length of time that an island has been exposed above sea level. Several of the lower islands, Santa Barbara, San Nicolas, and San Geronimo, would have been completely submerged during the interglacial and xerothermal period. This could have an effect on lowering the diversity, though in the case of the Santa Barbara and San Nicolas islands, this effect appears to be slight. An island like Cedros would have a much lower diversity if it were simply a table-land rather than a mountainous island with rolling dunes, deep canyons, and high cliffs. Another factor that seems to have a direct bearing on the number of species in the Channel Islands of California and Baja California is the average rainfall. Figure 4, which depicts the simple total species/area relationship, shows the island groups falling along two linear relationships. The northern islands generally have more total plant species, regardless of their size. The more xeric southern islands with major areas which generally receive less than 200 mm rainfall have a lower diversity of species overall. This probably reflects conditions on the adjacent

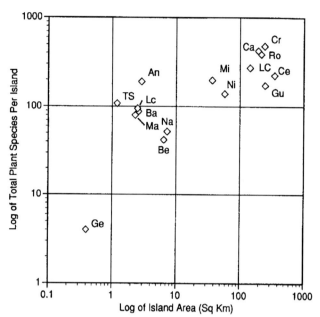

Figure 1. Log of total species of plants per island versus log of island area.

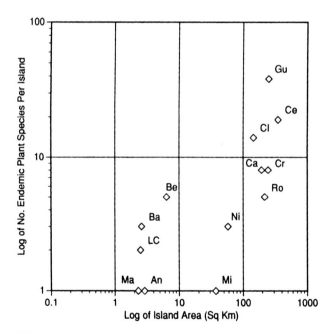

Figure 2. Log of endemic plant species per island versus log of island area.

mainland. A lower number of species likely occurs per area in Baja California than occurs in southern California, hence, fewer mainland species are available to disperse to the islands.

It is of use to compare these relationships with the relationships of the islands in the Gulf of California (Sea of Cortez) where the climate is more uniform in at least in the northern half of the Peninsula where, the average annual rainfall is approximately 50 to 75 mm. Cody et al. (1983, Figure 4.6a) created plant species-area plots for islands in the Sea of Cortez and the California Channel Islands.

Similar to the graph depicted in Figure 6, the drier Sea of Cortez Islands have an overall diversity than the more mesic California Channel Islands. In the Sea of Cortez, the area to numbers of species would be predicted to be more regular due to the greater uniformity in the climate as well as the closer proximity of all of the islands to the mainland (Cody et al. 1983; Moran 1983). The uniformity of the linear species area relationship depicted by Cody et al. (1983) is a reflection of this.

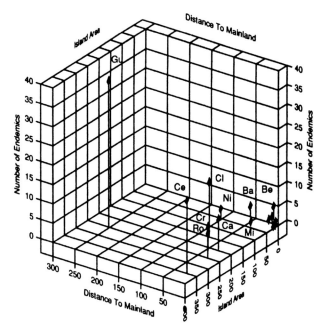

Figure 3. Three-dimensional graph depicting the relationship between number of endemics, area of the islands, and distances from the mainland.

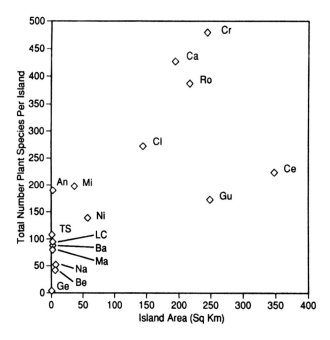

Figure 4. Total number of plant species versus island area.

Relationships of floras of the islands

Several of the islands are very close in their floral affinities. Table 3 lists the percentage overlap in native flora for all of the islands. This is a simple percentage relationship and not a Sorensen index for diversity because the size of the islands and size of the floras have a major influence on the percent overlap. Obviously, smaller islands have larger percentages of their floras shared with larger islands than the larger islands share with the smaller islands.

There are a number of key points that can be assessed with these figures. First, the northern islands have a close relationship with several shared insular endemics (Attachment 1) and a high percentage of shared species, but not as close as one might expect. Anacapa shares 82%, Santa Rosa shares 81%, and San Miguel shares 75% with Santa Cruz Island. It may seem surprising that Santa Cruz Island, which has a large flora and diverse topography, does not contain all the species of the adjacent Anacapa and Santa Rosa islands. This demonstrates the individual differences between each of the islands.

In the northern islands, Santa Cruz Island contains the most species and other islands share the most with it indicating the importance of its flora. In the southern group, the other islands share the most species with Santa Catalina. San Clemente, its closest neighbor shares 77%, not as high a percentage as one might expect given their close proximity to one another. San Martin, Los Coronados, Cedros, and Guadalupe islands respectively share 64%, 78%, 39% and 55% with Santa Catalina Island.

Other islands share many species with Cedros Island. In the very south, San Benito and Natividad islands share 70% and 67% respectively with Cedros Island. San Martin, Todos Santos, and Los Coronados islands share 50%, 45%, and 46% with Cedros Island.

The relationship between Guadalupe and the other islands is also noteworthy. Fifty-five percent of Guadalupe's plants occur on Santa Catalina Island, and 49% occur on San Clemente Island. Although 30% of the species that occur on Cedros also occur on Santa Cruz, 47% of the species that occur on Guadalupe also occur on Santa Cruz. Unexpectedly only 28% of the species on Guadalupe also occur on Cedros even though Cedros is much nearer to Guadalupe than Guadalupe is to Santa Cruz. A number of plants on Guadalupe do not occur on any of the other islands but are found farther north in central California. This may be due to the cool north-south flowing California current and may also be affected by the paleogeologic history which will be discussed further below.

As one might expect, there is a low relationship between the very southern islands — San Benito and Natividad — and the Alta California Channel Islands. It is noteworthy that San Benito and Natividad islands share a higher percentage with Catalina and San Clemente islands than they do with Todos Santos and Los Coronados islands. In reverse, the northern islands share a small percentage of their floras with the relatively small floras of the southern Baja

California islands because of the more desert-like conditions in the south as well as the distance separating them.

The individual nature of the islands is further indicated by the fact that relatively few species occur on all or nearly all of them (Attachment 1). These species include *Opuntia prolifera, Aphanisma blitoides, Oligomeris linifolea, Phyllospadix scouleri, Phyllospadix torreyana, Eschscholzia ramosa*, and *Lepidium oblongum* var. *insulare*.

Furthermore, the endemic species that are confined to individual islands in the northern group also provides an indication of the unique nature of each of the islands (Attachment 2). Of particular note are the endemics confined to the small islands such as Santa Barbara, Los Coronados, San Martin and San Benitos.

Table 3. Percentage overlap between floras of the islands of California and Baja California. Numbers in columns represent the percentage of the flora of the island listed in the heading for a row that is also found on the island.

Island which is basis for comparison	Percentage of compared island's native flora which also occurs on island listed below.															
	Mi	Ro	Cr	An	Ba	Ni	Ca	Cl	Le	To	Ma	Ge	Be	Na	Ce	Gu
San Miguel (Mi)	-	76	75	48	20	35	58	46	18	21	13	0.5	2.0	2.5	19	22
Santa Rosa (Ro)	39	-	81	38	13	21	61	42	14	15	9.5	0.5	2.6	2.6	14	19
Santa Cruz (Cr)	31	65	-	32	11	17	63	38	13	14	9	0.4	2.5	2.5	14	17
Anacapa (An)	50	77	82	-	28	34	70	59	31	31	20	1.6	7.4	6.8	31	28
Santa Barbara (Ba)	45	58	64	61	-	52	70	70	41	42	28	3.4	14	14	36	45
San Nicolas (Ni)	50	58	60	46	33	-	60	58	19	20	17	2.1	7.2	8	23	27
Santa Catalina (Ca)	27	55	71	31	14	20	-	49	17	19	12	0.7	4.0	4.2	20	22
San Clemente (Cl)	33	59	68	41	23	30	77	-	23	25	17	1.1	6.2	6.2	24	31
Los Coronados (Lc)	38	58	64	61	38	28	78	66	-	67	37	3.2	16	16	46	36
Todo Santos (To)	39	55	64	54	34	26	74	63	59	-	40	1.9	13	15	45	39
San Martin (Ma)	33	46	55	48	31	30	64	59	44	54	-	2.5	17	21	50	29
San Geronimo (Ge)	25	50	50	75	75	75	75	75	75	50	50	-	75	75	100	50
San Benito (Be)	9.5	24	2.8	33	28	24	40	40	36	33	33	7.1	-	57	70	33
Natividad (Na)	9.6	19	23	25	23	21	35	33	29	31	33	5.8	46	-	67	27
Cedros (Ce)	17	24	31	26	14	14	39	30	20	22	18	1.8	13	16	-	22
Guadalupe (Gu)	25	43	47	31	23	22	55	49	20	24	13	1.2	8.1	8.1	28	-

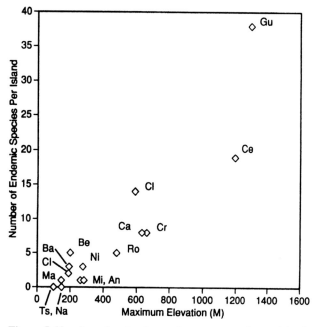

Figure 5. Number of endemic species versus maximum island elevation.

Paleogeographic History

Dunkle (1950), Stebbins and Major (1965), Axelrod (1977), Raven and Axelrod (1978), and Philbrick (1980) discussed the paleobiological history of the plants that inhabit the islands, particularly the endemics. The consensus is that the majority of the endemics are relicts from previous times when they occurred on the mainland as well as the islands. One striking example is *Lyonothamnus floribundus* fossils of which have been found on the mainland into Nevada (Axelrod 1977). Several of the species that are near-endemics may also be relictual. For many years, *Crossosoma californica* was thought to be endemic to San Clemente, Santa Catalina and Guadalupe islands. However, it was also found on the mainland on the Palos Verdes Peninsula in Los Angeles County (Hickman 1993). *Chaetopappa lyoni* was thought to be a Santa Catalina endemic until it was found on the Palos Verdes Peninsula (Philbrick 1980), which itself was an island during the xerothermal period when the sea level was higher due to polar ice melt. *Prunus ilicifolia* ssp. *lyonii* appears on a number of the California islands and is also found in deep canyons in central Baja California. A similar distribution exists for *Salvia brandegei*, which occurs on Santa Rosa Island and near the coast in north-central Baja California.

It is thought that one of the reasons that species persist on islands is that island climates, even those that receive relatively low rainfall, are very equitable (Carlquist 1974). The moderating influence of the ocean limits the temperature extremes. The cool, moist air that results from the condensation over the cold water of the California current produces fog on any land mass that is high enough to raise an obstruction to air flow. Because of this fog, Cedros and Guadalupe islands are able to support remnant pine forest and chaparral communities even with little rainfall. Other factors that allow many species to endure on islands include the absence of herbivores and possibly less competition from more wide-ranging species for microhabitats.

On the other hand, a few of the endemic groups appear to be relatively new species. "New" species are usually members of widespread genera with great diversity, especially annuals, and which have many species adapted to specific conditions (Stebbins and Major 1965). The *Cryptanthas* endemic to Guadalupe, San Clemente, Catalina, and San Nicolas islands may represent more recent species as well as the *Malacothrix*, *Phacelias*, and *Gilias* that are found in various forms on several of the islands. Most of these are annuals or short-lived perennials.

One of the most interesting genera on all of the islands and many of the adjacent mainland bluffs and headlands, is the genus *Dudleya*. They are highly diversified and appear to be either extremely adaptable to particular locations or were very diverse at one time on the mainland and later found refuge on the islands and coastal bluffs. Island species in this genus range from small, narrow-leaved species to large, succulent, almost woody plants.

The genus *Hemizonia* is also well represented on the islands, particularly the perennial species. On the mainland, the perennial species are quite restricted, but on the islands *H. greeneana*, *H. palmeri*, and others are woody endemics. In general, woody perennials are considered to be more primitive than their annual relatives (Stebbins and Major, 1965). It appears that the perennial species of *Hemizonias* are older and survive on islands and other coastal headlands where the even temperatures have allowed them to remain.

DISCUSSION

Effects of Man

All of the islands have been subjected to human effects, mostly indirectly through feral herbivores. The California islands have recently been the subject of feral animal eradication programs to eliminate goats and pigs and mule deer on San Clemente, sheep on Santa Cruz and San Nicolas, burros on San Miguel, and rabbits on Santa Barbara. There have been efforts to reduce goats, deer, and bison on Santa Catalina (See Table 2). The recovery effects have been remarkable.

The Baja California islands have also suffered from feral animals. The impact from goats to Guadalupe Island has been tragic. Unless they are eradicated, the remaining species will become extinct as six of the endemics already have. South Los Coronados Island now has goats, which have impacted the *Malva occidentalis*. Rabbits were introduced to Todos Santos Island in the 1970s. Both burros and rabbits were introduced to West San Benito Island in the late 1980s. Fortunately, Cedros Island is mostly intact and its indigenous (endemic) deer even survive. In addition to the feral herbivores, which denude the islands of endemic vegetation, introductions of feral cats and rodents have contributed to the extinction of endemic birds and to the reduction in populations of ground and burrow nesting birds. Very recently, there have been efforts to reduce feral animals on Baja California islands through the Island Conservation and Ecology Group based in Santa Cruz, California, and Guerrero Negro, Baja California. They have carried out feral animal eradication programs on the Todos Santos and San Benito islands.

As land and resource managers in addition to being concerned citizens, it is vital that we work toward the removal of the feral animals from the islands. The ecosystems of entire islands are being destroyed, in particular with the recent introductions. It would be a great accomplishment to remove feral animals from all of these islands, especially Guadalupe.

ACKNOWLEDGMENTS

The author would like to thank Reid Moran, Jon Rebman, and Steve Junak for information on the species that exist on particular islands. Thanks are also extended to the anonymous reviewers of the draft. Special thanks are for Michael U. Evans for generating the three-dimensional graphs. José Delgadillo is also to be thanked for coordinating the first botanical symposium on Baja California in April of 1996 which was the inspiration for this paper.

LITERATURE CITED

Axelrod, D. I. 1977. Outline of history of California vegetation. Pages 139-193 *in* Barbour, M. G. and J. Major (eds.), Terrestrial Vegetation of California. John Wiley and Sons, New York, NY.

Batiza, R. 1977. Petrology and density of Guadalupe Island: an alkalic seamount on a fossil ridge crest. Geology 5:760-764.

Beauchamp, R. M. 1986. A Flora of San Diego County, California. Sweetwater River Press, National City, CA.

Blake, S. F. 1961. Edward Palmer's visit to Guadalupe Island, Mexico in 1875. Madroño 16:1-4.

Bostic, D. L. 1975. A Natural History Guide to the Pacific Coast and North Central Baja California and Adjacent Islands. Biological Education Expeditions. Vista, CA.

Carlquist, S. 1974. Island Biology. Columbia University Press, New York, NY. 660 p.

Channel Islands National Park. 1987. A checklist of vascular plants of Channel Islands National Park. Channel Islands National Park, Santa Barbara Botanic Garden and SW Parks and Monument Association, Tucson, AZ.

Clark, R., W. Halvorson, A. Saurdo, and K. Danielsen. 1990. Plant communities of Santa Rosa Island, Channel Islands National Park. Technical Report No. 42. Cooperative National Park Resources Studies Unit. University of California, Davis, CA.

Clark, R. and W. Halvorson. 1990. Endangered and rare plants of Santa Barbara Island, Channel Islands National Park. Technical Report No. 37. Cooperative National Park Resources Studies Unit. University of California, Davis, CA.

Cody, M., R. Moran and H. Thompson. 1983. The plants. Pages 49-97 in Case, T.J., and M. L. Cody (eds.), Island Biogeography in the Sea of Cortez. University of California Press, Berkeley and Los Angeles, CA.

Cohen, L., K. C. Condie, L. J. Kuest Jr., G. S. Mackenzie, F. H. Meister, P. Pushkar, and Alan M. Stueber. 1963. Geology of the San Benito Islands, Baja California, Mexico. Geological Society of America Bulletin 74:1355-1370.

Davis, W. S. 1980. Distribution of *Malacothrix* (Asteraceae) on the California Islands and the origin of endemic insular species. Pages 227-234 in Power, D. M. (ed.) The California Islands: Proceedings of a Multidisciplinary Symposium. Santa Barbara Museum of Natural History, Santa Barbara, CA.

Dunkle, M. B. 1950. Plant ecology of the Channel Islands of California. Publication of the Allan Hancock Pacific Expedition 13:247-386.

Foreman, R. E. 1967. Observations on the flora and ecology of San Nicolas Island. U.S. Naval Radiological Defense Laboratory TR-67-8, San Francisco, CA.

Hastings, J. R. 1964. Climatological data for Baja California. University of Arizona Institute of Atmospheric Physics, Technical Reports on the meteorology and climatology of arid regions. No. 14:1-132.

Hastings, J. R., and R. Humphrey. 1969. Climatological data for Baja California. University of Arizona Institute of Atmospheric Physics, Technical Reports on meteorology and climatology of arid regions. No. 18:1-96.

Hickman, J. C. (ed.) 1993. The Jepson Manual. Higher Plants of California. University of California Press, Berkeley and Los Angeles, CA.

Junak, S. A. and R. Philbrick. 1994a. The vascular plants of Todos Santos Island, Baja California, Mexico. Pages 407-428 in Halvorson, W. L. and G. J. Meander (eds.), Fourth California Islands Symposium: Update on the Status of Resources. Santa Barbara Museum of Natural History, Santa Barbara, CA.

Junak, S. A. and R. Philbrick. 1994b. The flowering plants of San Martin Island, Baja California, Mexico. Pages 429-447 in Halvorson, W. L. and G. J. Meander (eds.), Fourth California Islands Symposium: Update on the Status of Resources. Santa Barbara Museum of Natural History, Santa Barbara, CA.

Junak, S. A. and R. Philbrick, 1999a. The flowering plants of San Benito Island, Baja California, Mexico. Pages 235 to 236 in Browne, D. R., K. L. Mitchell, and H. W. Chaney, (eds.), Proceedings of the Fifth California Islands Symposium, 29 March to 1 April 1999. Santa Barbara Museum of Natural History, Santa Barbara, CA. Sponsored by the U.S. Minerals Management Service, Pacific OCS Region, 770 Paseo Camarillo, Camarillo, CA 93010. OCS Study No. 99-0038.

Junak, S. A. and R. Philbrick, 1999b. The flowering plants of Isla Natividad, Baja California, Mexico. Pages 224 to 234 in Browne, D. R., K. L. Mitchell, and H. W. Chaney, (eds.), Proceedings of the Fifth California Islands Symposium, 29 March to 1 April 1999. Santa Barbara Museum of Natural History, Santa Barbara, CA. Sponsored by the U.S. Minerals Management Service, Pacific OCS Region, 770 Paseo Camarillo, Camarillo, CA 93010. OCS Study No. 99-0038.

Junak, S. A., T. Ayers, R. Scott, D. Wilken, and D. Young. 1995. A flora of Santa Cruz Island. Santa Barbara Botanic Garden and California Native Plant Society, Santa Barbara, CA.

Kilmer, F. H. 1984. Geology of Cedros Island, Baja California, Mexico. Frank Kilmer, Department of Geology, Humboldt State University, Arcata, CA.

Lamb, T. N. 1992. Geology of the Coronado Islands. Pages 32-83 in Perry, L. (ed.), Natural History of the Coronado Islands, Baja California, Mexico (Revisited 1992). San Diego Association of Geologists, San Diego, CA.

MacArthur, R. H. and E. O. Wilson. 1967. The Theory of Island Biogeography. Princeton University Press, Princeton, NJ.

Moran, R. 1983. Vascular plants of the Gulf Islands. Pages 348-381 in Case, T. J., and M. L. Cody (eds.), Island Biogeography in the Sea of Cortez. University of California Press, Berkeley and Los Angeles, CA. Appendix 4.1.

Moran, R. 1996. The flora of Guadalupe Island, Mexico. Memoirs of the California Academy of Sciences 19:1-190.

Oberbauer, T. A. 1992. Vegetation of Islas Los Coronados. Pages 16-22 in Perry, L. (ed.), Natural History of the Coronado Islands, Baja California, Mexico (Revisited 1992). San Diego Association of Geologists, San Diego, CA.

Oberbauer, T. A. 1993. Floristic analysis of vegetation communities on Isla de Cedros, Baja California, Mexico. Pages 115-131 in Hochberg, F. G. (ed.), Third California Island Symposium: Recent Advances in Research on the California Islands. Santa Barbara Museum of Natural History, Santa Barbara, CA.

Oberbauer, T. A. 1994. San Clemente Island revisited. Fremontia 22:11-13.

Oberbauer, T. A. 1999. Vegetation and flora of Islas Los Coronados, Baja California, Mexico. Pages 212 to 223 in Browne, D. R., K. L. Mitchell, and H. W. Chaney, (eds.), Proceedings of the Fifth California Islands Symposium, 29 March to 1 April 1999. Santa Barbara Museum of Natural History, Santa Barbara, CA. Sponsored by the U.S. Minerals Management Service, Pacific OCS Region, 770 Paseo Camarillo, Camarillo, CA 93010. OCS Study No. 99-0038.

Philbrick, R. N. (ed.) 1967. Proceedings of the Symposium on the Biology of the California Islands. Santa Barbara Botanic Garden, Santa Barbara, CA.

Philbrick, R. N. 1972. The plants of Santa Barbara Island, California. Madroño 21:329-393.

Philbrick, R. N. 1980. Distribution and evolution of endemic plants of the California Islands. Pages 173-187 in Power, D. M. (ed.), The California Islands: Proceedings of a Multidisciplinary Symposium. Santa Barbara Museum of Natural History, Santa Barbara CA.

Raven, P. H. 1963. A flora of San Clemente Island, CA. Aliso 5:289-347.

Raven, P. H. 1967. The floristics of the California Islands. Pages 57-67 in Philbrick, R. N. (ed.), Proceedings of the Symposium on the Biology of the California Islands. Santa Barbara Museum of Natural History, Santa Barbara, California.

Raven, P. H. and D. I. Axelrod. 1978. Origins and relationships of the California flora. University of California Pub. Bot. 72:1-134.

Skinner, M. W. and B. M. Pavlick. 1994. California Native Plant Society's Inventory of Rare and Endangered Vascular Plants of California. California Native Plant Society Special Publication No. 1, Fifth Edition.

Stebbins, G. L. and J. Major. 1965. Endemism and speciation in the California flora. Ecological Monographs. 35:1-35.

Thorne, R. F. 1967. A flora of Santa Catalina Island, CA. Aliso 6:1-77.

Thorne, R. F. 1969. The California Islands. Annals of the Missouri Botanical Gardens 56:391-408.

Vedder, J. G. and D. G. Howell. 1980. Topographic evolution of the southern California borderland during late Cenozoic time. Pages 7-71 in Power, D. M. (ed.), The California Islands: Proceedings of a Multidisciplinary Symposium. Santa Barbara Museum of Natural History, Santa Barbara, CA.

Wallace, G. D. 1985. Vascular plants of the Channel Islands of Southern California and Guadalupe Island, Baja California, Mexico. Contributions in Science No. 365. Natural History Museum of Los Angeles County.

Wehtje, W. 1994. Response of bishop pine (Pinus muricata) population to the removal of feral sheep on Santa Cruz Island, California. Pages 331-340 in Halvorson, W. L. and G. J. Meander (eds.), Fourth California Islands Symposium: Update on the Status of Resources. Santa Barbara Museum of Natural History, Santa Barbara, CA.

Westec Services. 1978. Survey of archaeological and biological resources of San Nicolas Island. Westec Services, San Diego. Manuscript on file at Ogden Environmental, San Diego, CA.

ATTACHMENT 1: PLANTS FOUND ON MULTIPLE ISLANDS BUT NOT THE MAINLAND.

Agave sebastana CE, NA, BE
Arabis hoffmannii RO*, CR
Arctostaphylos tomentosa ssp. *insulicola* RO, CR
Arctostaphylos tomentosa ssp. *subcordata* RO, CR
Artemisia nesiotica NI, BA, CL
Astragalus miguelensis MI, RO, CR, AN, CL
Astragalus traskiae NI, BA
Berberis pinnata ssp. *insularis* RO, CR, AN
Calystegia macrostegia ssp. *amplissima* NI, BA, CL
Calystegia macrostegia ssp. *macrostegia* MI, RO, CR, AN, CA, GU, MA
Castilleja lanata ssp. *hololeuca* MI, RO, CR, AN
Castilleja mollis RO, MI
Ceanothus arboreus RO, CR, CA
Ceanothus megacarpus ssp. *insularis* MI*, RO, CR, AN, CA, CL
Cryptantha traskiae NI, CL
Dendromecon harfordii var. *harfordii* RO, CR
Dendromecon harfordii var. *rhamnoides* CA, CL
Dissanthelium californicum CA*, CL*, GU*
Dudleya albiflora CE, NA, ES
Dudleya candelabrum MI, RO, CR
Dudleya greenei MI, RO, CR, CA
Eriogonum arborescens RO, CR, AN
Eriogonum grande ssp. *grande* AN, CL, CA, CR
Eriogonum grande ssp. *rubescens* MI, RO, CR, AN
Eriophyllum nevinii BA, CA, CL
Erysimum insulare ssp. *insulare* MI, RO, CR, *AN*
Eschscholzia ramosa MI, RO, CR, NI, BA, CA, CL, GU, TO, LC, MA, BE, CE, NA
Ferocactus chrysacanthus CE, BE
Galium angustifolium ssp. *foliosum* RO, CR, AN
Galium buxifolium MI, CR
Galium californicum ssp. *miguelense* MI, RO
Galium nuttallii ssp. *insulare* RO, CR, CA
Galvesia speciosa BA*, CL, CA, GU
Gilia nevinii RO, CR, AN, NI*, BA, CA, CL, GU
Hazardia canus CL, GU
Hazardia detonsa RO, CR, AN
Helianthemum greenei MI*, RO, CR, CA
Hemizonia clementina AN, NI, BA, CA, CL
Heuchera maxima RO, CR, AN
Jepsonia malvifolia RO, CR, NI, CA, CL, GU
Malva assurgentiflora ssp. *assurgentiflora* MI, RO, NI
Malva assurgentiflora ssp. *glabra* CA, CL
Malva occidentalis LC, GU
Malva pacifica BE, GE, CE
Linanthus pygmaeus ssp. *pygmaeus* CL, GU
Lomatium insulare NI, CL, GU
Lotus argophyllus ssp. *argenteus* NI, BA, CA, CL, GU
Lotus dendroideus var. *dendroideus* RO, CR, AN, CA
Lupinus guadalupensis CL, GU
Lycium brevipes var. *hassei* CA*, CL*
Lyonothamnus floribundus ssp. *aslpenifolius* RO, CR, CL

Attachment 1: Cont'd.

Malacothrix foliosa AN, BA, NI, CL, LC
Malacothrix indecora MI*, *CR*
Malacothrix saxatilis var. *implicata* MI, RO, CR, AN, NI
Malacothrix squalida CR, AN
Mammillaria pondii CE, NA
Mentzelia hirsutissima var. *nesiotes* CE, NA, BE
Mimulus flemingii RO, CR, AN, CL
Mimulus latifolius CR, GU
Phacelia cedrosensis CE, NA
Phacelia insularis var. *insularis* MI, RO
Phacelia floribunda CL, GU
Phacelia lyonii CA, CL
Quercus X *macdonaldii* RO, CR, CA
Quercus pacifica RO, CR, CA
Quercus tomentella RO, CR, AN, CA, CL, GU
Rhamnus pirifolia MI*, RO, CR, CA, CL, GU
Scrophularia villosa RO, CA, CL, GU
Senecio lyonii CA, CL, MA, GU
Sibara filifolia CR*, CA*, CL
Solanum clokeyi RO, CR
Solanum wallacei CA, GU
Trifolium gracilentum var. *palmeri* NI, BA, CA, CL, GU

ATTACHMENT 2: SPECIES ENDEMIC TO ONE ISLAND

SANTA ROSA
    Arctostaphylos confertiflora
    Dudleya blochmanae ssp. *insularis*
    Dudleya sp. nova
    Gilia tenuiflora ssp. *hoffmannii*
    Pinus torreyana ssp. *insularis*
SANTA CRUZ
    Arctostaphylus insularis
    Arctostaphylus viridissima
    Dudleya nesiotica
    Lotus argophyllus ssp. *niveus*
    Malacothamnus fasciculatus var. *nesioticus*
    Ribes thacherianum
    Thysanocarpus laciniatus var. *conchuliferus*
ANACAPA
    Malacothrix foliosa ssp. *crispifolia*
    Malacothrix junakii
SAN NICOLAS
    Eriogonum grande ssp. *timorum*
    Lycium verrucosum*
    Malacothrix foliosa ssp. *polycephela*
    Phacelia cinerea*
SANTA BARBARA
    Dudleya traskiae
    Eriogonum giganteum ssp. *compactum*
    Malacothrix foliosa ssp. *philbrickii*
    Platystemon californica ssp. *ciliata*
SANTA CATALINA
    Arctostaphylus catalinae
    Cercocarpus traskiae

    Dudleya hassei
    Eriodictyon traskiae ssp. *traskiae*
    Eriogonum giganteum ssp. *giganteum*
    Galium catalinense ssp. *catainense*
    Lyonothamnus floribundus ssp. *floribundus*
    Mimulus traskiae*
SAN CLEMENTE
    Astragalus nevinii
    Brodiaea kinkiense
    Camissonia guadalupensis ssp. *clementina*
    Castilleja grisea
    Delphinium variegatum ssp. *kinkiense*
    Delphinium variegatum ssp. *thornei*
    Eriogonum giganteum ssp. *formosum*
    Galium catalinense ssp. *acrispum*
    Lithophragma maxima
    Lotus argophyllus ssp. *adsurgens*
    Lotus dendroideus var. *traskiae*
    Malacothamnus clementina
    Stephanomeria blairii
    Tritelia clementina
GUADALUPE
    Baeropsis guadalupensis
    Brahea edulis
    Camissonia guadalupensis ssp. *guadalupensis*
    Castilleja fruticosa
    Castilleja guadalupensis*
    Cistanthe guadalupensis
    Cryptantha foliosa
    Cupressus guadalupensis ssp. *guadalupensis*
    Dudleya guadalupensis
    Dudleya virens ssp. *extima*
    Eriogonum zapatoense
    Erysimum moranii
    Eschscholzia elegans
    Eschscholzia palmeri
    Galium angulosum
    Githopsis diffusa var. *guadalupensis*
    Hemizonia frutescens
    Hemizonia greeneana ssp. *greeneana*
    Hemizonia palmeri
    Hesperelaea palmeri*
    Lavatera lindsayi
    Lupinus niveus
    Marah guadalupensis
    Perityle incana
    Phacelia phyllomanica
    Pinus radiata var. *binata*
    Pogogyne tenuiflora*
    Satureja palmeri*
    Senecio palmeri
    Sphaeralcea palmeri
    Sphaeralcea sulpherea
    Stephanomeria guadalupensis
    Triteleia guadalupensis
    Guadalupe unique forms

Arctostaphylos sp. extinct*
Unidentifiable plant without fruit, now extinct
SAN MARTIN
   Chenopodium flabellifolium
LOS CORONADOS
   Dudleya candida
   Galium coronadoense
   Malacothrix insularis
SAN BENITOS
   Cryptantha patula
   Dudleya linearis
   Hemizonia streetsii
   Mammilaria neopalmeri
   San Benito unique form
   Senecio benedictus

CEDROS
   Cryptantha maritima ssp. *cedrosensis*
   Dudleya cedrosensis
   Dudleya pachyphyta
   Eriogonum molle
   Harfordia macroptera var. *fruticosa*
   Leptodactylon veatchii
   Lotus cedrosensis
   Mammillaria goodridgei var. *goodridgei*
   Mammillaria goodridgei var. *rectispina*
   Monardella thymifolia
   Penstemon cedrosensis
   Pinus radiata var. *cedrosensis*
   Senecio cedrosensis
   Verbesina hastata
   Xylonagra arborea var. *arborea*
   Xylonagra arborea var. *wigginsiae*

VEGETATION AND FLORA OF ISLAS LOS CORONADOS BAJA CALIFORNIA, MEXICO

Thomas A. Oberbauer

Department of Planning and Land Use, County of San Diego
5201 Ruffin Road, Suite B-5, San Diego, CA 92123
(619) 694-3700, FAX (619) 694-2555, E-mail:TOBERBPL@co.san-diego.ca.us

ABSTRACT

Islas Los Coronados are a group of four small islands in Mexico, near the International Border with the United States. Together, they comprise approximately 2.5 km^2 and lie 13 km from the mainland (See Figures 1 and 2). Vegetation is Maritime Succulent Scrub dominated by *Encelia californica, Euphorbia misera, Hazardia berberidis, Atriplex canescens, Bergerocactus emoryi, Opuntia littoralis,* and *Lycium californicum.* Middle Rock and Middle Island also have barren areas covered with bird guano. On South Island, the north facing slope supports Coastal Sage Scrub. Botanically, the South Island is the most diverse, containing a number of insular endemics including *Eschscholzia ramosa, Malva occidentalis,* and *Malacothrix foliosa.* The *Malva* is noteworthy since it is also found on Isla Guadalupe about 350 km to the south. Islas Los Coronados support three endemics, *Galium coronadoense* and *Malacothrix insularis,* which have only been found on the South Island, and *Dudleya candida,* which has been found on all four of the islands. Unfortunately, the South Island has a small herd of goats that has had an effect in reducing the areas of shrubs, including the *Malva.*

Keywords: Coronado Islands, Islas Los Coronados, North Coronado Island, South Coronado Island, Middle Coronado Island, California Islands, Baja California, Mexico, flora, vegetation, botany, feral animals.

INTRODUCTION

The vegetation of Islas Los Coronados falls within Thorne's (1976) classification of Maritime Sage Scrub and Holland's (1986) Maritime Succulent Scrub (Oberbauer 1992). The flora reflects this vegetation. However, each of the islands in the four-island group has different vegetation and floral characteristics due to differences in size, topography, soils, and disturbance, both natural and the result of human influence.

Two historical accounts exist of the vegetation of Islas Los Coronados. Bartlett (1854) described the South Island as "entirely destitute of trees. A few small shrubs are seen; and wherever there is soil, it is covered with grass and a great abundance of wildflowers...like patches of orange, purple and yellow when seen from the water." Greene (1885)

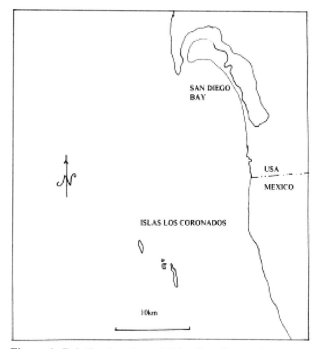

Figure 1. Relative location of Islas Los Coronados to the shoreline.

made a number of collections of plants on the north end of the island and discussed the dry condition of the season in which he landed on the island.

Islas Los Coronados have been visited by a number of collectors dating back to Bartlett (1854), but also Greene (1885). Others who made plant collections include Pond in 1889, Wiggins in 1949, Blakely, who made several visits during the 1960s, Philbrick who made collections during the 1960s and 1970s with Ricker and Benedict, and especially Reid Moran who made collections from the 1950s, 1960s, and 1970s. There have also been a number of incidental collectors including Frank Stephens, Charles Shaw, Frank Gander and A. J. Stover. With the exception of Reid Moran, most of the collectors landed on the South Island and spent only short visits there. Greene's and Pond's collections are housed in the Greene Herbarium at the University of Notre Dame. Blakely, Philbrick and Ricker, and Philbrick and Benedict collections are at the Santa Barbara Botanic Garden. Most Reid Moran collections, the author's collections, and collections by the remainder of those

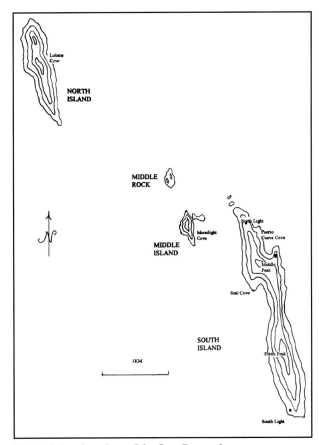

Figure 2. Landmarks on Islas Los Coronados.

mentioned above are at the San Diego Museum of Natural History.

MATERIALS AND METHODS

Field surveys were conducted on the islands from boats as well as land. The islands were surveyed and circumnavigated by boat in November 1978 and 1979, and May and July of 1990, August 1992 and June 1993. Landing occurred on the South Island, including a traverse down the west side on foot, in November of 1978 and 1979. In May of 1989 and June of 1993, the area north of Middle Peak was explored. In April of 1991, the entire reachable portion of the island was surveyed on foot following exceptional February and March rains. Landing occurred on the North Island in May and June of 1989 with an overnight stay and thorough survey in March 1990. Middle Rock was visited in May of 1989, May and July of 1990, and spring of 1991, with two overnight stays. Middle island was visited on land and thoroughly explored in August 1990. All plant species were noted during each of these visits and an emphasis was placed on collecting specimens of the native species. Examinations were made of the plant collections at the San Diego Museum of Natural History and the Santa Barbara Botanic Garden. In addition, written inquiries were made to the University of Notre Dame and the National Museum of Natural History at the Smithsonian Institution. Furthermore,

information on collections from the genus *Malacothrix* was provided by William S. Davis of the University of Louisville. Collected specimens were identified using Munz (1974), Wiggins (1980), and Hickman (1993). The vegetation analysis is comprised mostly of descriptive evaluations with notations of the distribution and relative abundance of the dominant species that comprise the vegetation.

RESULTS

Vegetation Description

North Coronado Island

The vegetation on Islas Los Coronados reflects the relatively dry maritime climate, similar to the southern end of Point Loma where the average rainfall has been measured between 6 and 7 inches on the lower slopes (Lynch 1931). North Coronado Island is large enough to contain various microhabitats for plants. The southeastern slopes and northern end of the island are a series of rocky cliffs of durable red sandstone. The vegetation of the rocky cliffs is composed of *Coreopsis maritima*, *Perityle emoryi*, *Stephanomeria diegensis*, *Dudleya candida*, *Lycium californicum*, *Mirabilis californica*, and *Opuntia littoralis*. In some locations, the *Dudleya* forms mats up to a few meters across. Populations of *Mammillaria dioica* and *Bergerocactus emoryi* occur on the island, but they are rare.

An amphitheater-shaped talus slope exists on the northeastern portion of North Coronado Island. This slope supports a combination of introduced and native disturbance oriented plants including *Sonchus* sp., *Malva parviflora*, *Stellaria media*, *Bromus carinatus*, *Hordeum* sp., *Lamarckia aurea* and *Mesembryanthemum crystallinum*. *Coreopsis maritima* occurs in a few large patches here.

The basic vegetation on the central ridge of the island, where soil development has occurred, consists of *Atriplex canescens*, *Hazardia berberidus*, *Encelia californica*, *Opuntia prolifera*, *Opuntia littoralis*, *Marah macrocarpus*, and *Lycium californicum*. In addition, there are significant portions of the upper ridge of the island that are covered with solid patches of *Atriplex canescens*. In the southern third of the island, a terrace is nearly barren except for *Mesembryanthemum crystallinum*.

The upper portions of the northern end and the terrace area of the North Island are major nesting colony sites for the western gull. Large areas of the southeastern slopes of the island were until recently major nesting sites for the California brown pelican. The combination of heavy concentrations of guano and physical disturbance for nest locations has prevented much vegetation growth with the exception of disturbance-and salt-tolerant plants such as *Mesembryanthemum* and *Hordeum*.

Middle Rock

Physically, the island consists of a guano-washed rock hill on the south side, and a smaller ridge on the north side with a small amphitheater-like depression between them. The island is composed of relatively infertile sandstone and mudstone. The vegetation on Middle Rock is generally very sparse, with the majority of the island nearly barren. On the western side of the rock hill, a few patches of the rocky slope vegetation similar to that on the North Island include *Coreopsis, Dudleya, Opuntia prolifera, O. littoralis,* and *Stephanomeria diegensis.* A few individuals of *Lycium californicum* also occur in these areas. These patches occur where a veneer of soil has accumulated over the solid rock base. In some locations, the lower edges of the soil are sloughing down slope, gradually reducing the area habitable by vegetation.

The inner basin area of the island contains deeper soil materials, dominated by a sparse growth of *Suaeda californica.* The introduced *Chenopodium murale* is one of the most common plants on this island, but it does not form continuous cover. *Malva parviflora* and *Hordeum leporinum* are common in the soft soils in the inner basin and a few specimens of *Salsola iberica* occur there. It is noteworthy that a moderate sized *Rhus integrifolia* occurred on the island until 1987 or 1988, its skeleton remaining in the upper part of the inner basin.

Middle Island

The Middle Island is topographically a steep hill with a peninsular-like structure on the northeast side which forms a protected cove referred to as Moonlight Cove. The island is constructed of extensively weathered and unstable material that gives way in handfuls or slope-sized masses.

The barren nature of this island is probably a combination of the unstable substrates and heavy use by breeding and roosting sea birds. The east side is a heavily eroding and slumping area that supports a very sparse vegetation with scattered *Atriplex canescens, Suaeda californica, Chenopodium murale, Salsola iberica,* and *Atriplex californica.* The majority of plants occur as isolated individuals in a hard packed guano surface. This is particularly true of the *Hazardia berberidus* shrubs on the northern edge of the ridge-like spine, and small clusters of *Suaeda californica* and *Encelia californica* high on the west slope of the island. In contrast to these sparsely growing species, *Mesembryanthemum crystallinum* grows in large patches on the steep north slope following favorable rains.

The only area of vegetation growth in the form of a community occurs on the southwest, windward slope of the island. There grows a patch of *Lycium californicum, Mammillaria dioica, Euphorbia misera, Mirabilis californica, Dudleya candida, Bergerocactus emoryi,* and *Opuntia prolifera.* Since the North Island pelican colony relocated to Middle Island in the late 1980s, this area, which is on the outer edge of the colony, has become disturbed.

Eriogonum fasculatum and *Encelia californica* occur as very sparse individuals on some short, east facing cliffs near the top of the southern portion of the island. The extreme southern tip of the island is a rocky ridge with both *Opuntia littoralis* and *O. prolifera,* and *Stephanomeria*

diegensis on the predominantly rock slopes. *Marah macrocarpus* also occurs here.

South Island

The South Island is the largest and highest of the Los Coronados group and it has a greater number of plant species than the others. The major topographic factors that exist there are Puerto Cueva Cove located about one quarter the way down on the east side, Middle Peak with an elevation of approximately 180 m located about one third the way down the island, Seal Cove on the west side, and South Peak with an elevation of approximately 160 m.

Major factors of disturbance on South Island have been the military outpost consisting of a half dozen structures above Puerto Cueva Cove and an old casino. The old casino was built during the U. S. Prohibition era for gambling and consumption of alcoholic beverages. However it was destroyed in heavy winds and storms of January of 1988. Several trails cross the northern end of the island and extend to the southern end serving the navigational light.

In Puerto Cueva Cove, a few burros have been traditionally kept to carry materials to the navigational lights at the northern and southern ends of the island, however since the mid 1980s these animals have been augmented by several dozen goats. The goats have caused a noticeable adverse effect on the vegetation. As on the other islands, breeding colonies of birds have affected the vegetation on the southern end. Natural erosion of steep, unstable surfaces has left barren the nearly vertical slopes around Puerto Cueva Cove and Seal Cove and portions of the southern end of the island. There are also large sandstone outcrops that in one place on the eastern side form a "chute" that extends from the upper slopes of the island to near sea level.

On the upper slopes of the island, particularly in the northern end, the scrub community is dominated by *Encelia californica, Euphorbia misera, Hazardia berberidus, Rhus integrifolia, Bergerocactus emoryi, Opuntia littoralis,* and *Lycium californicum.* On the extreme northern end near the lighthouse, the vegetation takes on the aspect of Coastal Sage Scrub with dominants of *Artemisia californica, Rhus integrifolia, Eriogonum fasciculatum,* and a patch of *Heteromeles arbutifolia.* This is the only location on the island where the *Erigonium fasciculatum, Heteromeles arbutifolia,* and *Baccharis sarothroides* grow. The endemic *Galium coronadoense* and *Galium angustifolium* also occur near the north end, on the east facing slope, west of Puerto Cueva Cove.

As one moves southward on the island, the diversity of shrubs decreases somewhat. The *Encelia, Euphorbia misera, Lycium, Opuntia littoralis,* and *O. prolifera* extend the entire length of the island, but with a lower density on the southern end than in the more northerly locations. In the more southerly locations, *Suaeda californica, Atriplex canescens, Chenopodium californicum, C. murale, Cleome isomeris* and *Oligomeris linifolia* are major components of the vegetative cover. *Mesembryanthemum crystallinum* is common in the vegetation over the entire island, especially in disturbed areas such as along trails. It is of interest that it provides shelter for the commonly occurring endemic rattlesnake, *Crotalus viridus caliginus. Erodium cicutarium* and *Lamarckia aurea* are also widespread on the island, though most prevalent in areas that are disturbed by trails.

In partially shaded, rocky areas, such as the east facing slopes south of the military buildings, *Marah macrocarpus, Antirrhinum nutallianum, Eucrypta chrysanthemifolia* and *Pholistoma racemosum* grow in a lush cover. The sandstone outcrops that occur down the east side of the island have large patches and clusters of *Dudleyas*, particularly *D. candida* and *D. anomala*. The cobblestone cliffs around the cove are covered with *Cleome* and *Dudleya candida*.

The slopes of Middle Peak support a vegetative cover of low growing perrenials and annuals. Dominants here include *Mammillaria dioica, Lepidium oblongum insulare, Calandrinia maritima, Lycium californicum, Eschscholzia ramosa, Cryptantha intermedia* and *C. maritima*.

About two thirds of the way down the island grows the *Malva occidentalis* which is elsewhere found only on the outer islet of Isla Guadalupe. It formed dense thickets in the late 1970s with shrubs up to a meter in height. In 1991 after years of drought and probable impacts from goats, the only *Malvas* found were small seedlings or resprouting plants no more than a few inches high.

In some areas, the *Hazardia berberidus* forms nearly pure stands, particularly the slope above Puerto Cueva Cove on the north portion of the island. However, in the late 1980s and early 1990s, the drought and goat herd reduced the importance of this shrub. During the heavy rains of March 1991, this area was revegetated by a carpet of native wildflowers including extensive areas of *Collinsia heterophylla, Linaria canadensis, Lasthenia coronaria, Claytonia perfoliata, Astragalus trichopodus* ssp. *leucopsis, Delphinium parryi*, and *Eschscholzia californica*. From the water, the views of this area were identical to those described by Bartlett (1854) nearly 145 years ago.

Floristics

The islands support three endemics, *Dudleya candida, Malacothrix insularis*, and *Galium coronadoense*, and three insular endemics, *Eschscholtzia ramosa, Malva occidentalis*, and *Malacothrix foliosa*. There are a total of 96 native species including 11 monocots and 18 members of the Asteraceae. An additional 30 introduced species are present. Since the earliest explorers documented the vegetation on South Coronado Island, there have been subtle changes. Greene, in 1885, listed two species, *Gilia capitata* and *Lotus scoparius* that have not been found for many years, though they were considered common during his times. The collection of the *Aesculus parryi* by Pond is of special note since it has not been found this far north on the adjacent mainland and can apparently no longer be found on these islands. It is also noteworthy that new weedy species have been introduced, some by humans and some — such as the *Myoporum* and *Lycopersicon* on the North Island — by western gulls

that have ingested fruits and seeds from restaurants and ornamental plants on the mainland.

DISCUSSION

Over the years, there have been numerous proposals for development on these islands. They have also been traditionally visited by egg collectors and fishermen. Furthermore, the presence of goats on the south island is particularly disturbing as they devour the vegetation and cause the reduction of native species. However, as was illustrated by comparison of the appearance of the south island in 1854 by Bartlett to that of the spring of 1991, there is still a relatively intact flora that must be protected. For a complete catalogue of the vascular flora, see the Attachment.

ACKNOWLEDGMENTS

The author gratefully acknowledges William T. Everett, for arranging transportation to the islands on a number of private boats, the owners of the boats, and the San Diego Association of Geologists who provided access on several occasions. People who have assisted in the research on the islands include Reid Moran, who made the greatest number of collections; R. Mitchel Beauchamp; Jon Rebman; Geoffrey Levin; and Steve Junak who provided access to collections and data at the Santa Barbara Botanic Garden and in his own files.

LITERATURE CITED

Bartlett, J. 1854. Personal Narrative of exploration and incidents in Texas, New Mexico, California. Appleton, NY.

Greene, E. 1885. Botany of the Coronado Islands. Western American Scientist 1(10):69-71.

Hickman, J. C. (ed.) 1993. The Jepson Manual: Higher plants of California. University of California Press, Berkeley, CA.

Holland, R. F. 1986. Preliminary description of the terrestrial natural communities of California. State of California Department of Fish and Game. 156 p.

Lynch, H. B. 1931. Rainfall and stream runoff in Southern California since 1769. Metropolitan Water District of Southern California. 17 pp plus appendices.

Munz, P. A. 1974. A Flora of Southern California. University California Press, Los Angeles, CA.

Oberbauer, T. A. 1992. Vegetation of Islas Los Coronados. Pages 16-22 *in* Perry, L. (ed.), Natural History of the Coronado Islands, Baja California (revised 1992). San Diego Association of Geologists.

Thorne, R. F. 1976. The vascular plant communities of California. Pages 1-31 *in* Latting, J. (ed.), Plant Communities of Southern California. California Native Plant Society Special Publication No. 2.

Wiggins, I. L. 1980. Flora of Baja California. Stanford University Press, Stanford, CA.

ATTACHMENT

Vascular Plants of Islas Los Coronados

Non-Flowering Plants

Polypodiaceae

Pellaea andromedaefolia (Kaulf.) Fee S North facing slope above PC Cove and NE slope of South Island, 6-21-60, *RM 8301* (SD); 4-21-91 *T0 SLC91-09* (SD).

Polypodium californicum Kaulf. Reported by Greene, 1885. S North end of island, 3-14-64, *Blakley 6445*; 3-19-66, *Blakley 6616*; 3-19-66 *Philbrick B66-262*; center of island, 5-7-76 *RM 23101*. All at SBBG.

Angiosperms

Aizoaceae

*Carpobrotus chilensis (Molina) N.E.Br. Reported by Greene, 1885. N Southeast of lighthouse, 3-20-66 and 3-15-64, *Blakley 6743, 6481*. S Near shore on northeast side, 3-14-70 *Philbrick & Ricker B70-25* (All at SBBG).

*Mesembryanthemum crystallinum (L.) Rothm. N Forms extensive cover of steep slopes, 6-10-89 TO obs. MR In small patches in basin area, 6-12-90, *TO MRLC90-02* (SD). MI In a few large patches on the north slope 8-26-90. S Forms a major part of the cover, especially in the disturbed areas, 4-21-91, TO obs.

*Mesembryanthemum nodiflorum (L.) Rothm. S In drier and more disturbed areas than *G. crystallinum*, 4-21-91, TO obs.

Anacardiaceae

Rhus integrifolia (Nutt.) Brew. & Wats. S Scattered on the N third of the island on NE, 4-21-91, TO obs. MR One dead snag, 6-12-90, TO obs. MI Southern ridge, 8-26-1990, *TO MRLC90-10* (SD).

Apiaceae

Apiastrum angustifolium Nutt. S Central portion of the island on the west side trail, 4-21-1991, *TO SLC91-24* (SD).

Daucus pusillus Michx. Reported by Greene, 1885. S Southwest part of island, 3-14-70, *Philbrick & Ricker B70-16* (SBBG).

Asteraceae

Amblyopappus pusillus H. & A. S Open disturbed areas along trails over the island, 5-7-76, *RM 23132*; 4-21-1991, *TO SLC91-23* (both at SD).

Artemisia californica Less. S Scattered over N 2/3 of island, pruned by goats and drought, 4-21-1991, *TO SLC91-30* (SD).

Baccharis sarothroides Gray S N end one plant observed in midst of impenetrable cactus patch, 4-21-91, TO obs.

Coreopsis maritima (Nutt.) Hook. F. N In colorful patches over the island, 3-24-90, *TO NLC90-07*. MR Upper ridge and in rock crevices, 6-12-1990, *TO MRLC90-03*. S Central portion, 5-7-76, *RM 23144*; 4-21-1991, *TO SLC91-13* (All at SD).
Encelia californica Nutt. Very common on both N and S islands. N 3-25-90, *TO NLC90-06*; S 5-7-76, *RM 23108*. MI Top of ridge on barren west side, 8-26-90, *TO MILC90-04* (All at SD).

Eriophyllum confertiflorum (DC.) A. Gray S N slope above PC cove, 5-7-76, *RM 23116* ; 4-21-1991, *TO SLC91-02* (Both at SD).

Gnaphalium microcephalum Nutt. S 6-14-37 *Stover*.

Gnaphalium ramosissimum Nutt. **S** On northern end, 4-21-91, obs. TO.

Hazardia berberidus (A. Gray) E. Greene **N** Over major portion of island, 3-24-90, *TO NLC90-04* (SD). **S** In stands over island, large patch on north slope above PC cove, 6-4-1889, *Pond* (Greene Herbarium). **MI** Scattered individuals on barren north slope, 8-26-1990, *TO MILC90-09* (SD).

Lasthenia chrysostoma (F. & M.) **S** 5-16-1885, *Greene* (Greene Herbarium) and observed 4-21-91 near highest part of island, TO.

Lasthenia coronaria (Nutt.) Ornduff **S** Extensive patches on north slope above PC cove and scattered to S peak, 3-19-66, *Blakley 6624* (SBBG); 3-14-70, *Philbrick & Ricker B70-15* (SBBG); 5-7-76, *RM 23125* (SD); 4-21-91, *TO SLC91-37* (SD).

Malacothrix foliosa A. Gray **S** Central portion of the island, 5-12-1895 *A.W. Anthony* (UC); 5-30-26 *W.M. Pierce 98743* (POM); 6-10-26 *M.E. Jones* (POM); 4-21-91, *TO SLC91-33* (SD).

Malacothrix insularis Greene. Endemic. **S** Abundant, 5-16-1885, *Greene*, including type (CAS, UC, DS, US). Also 5-30-26, *W.M. Pierce 98743* (POM); and from one colony of ca. 100 on steep west slope in southern part of island, not seen elsewhere, 5-8-76, *RM 23158* (SD).

Malacothrix similis W. Davis & Raven. **S** Ridge north of PC cove, northern portion of island, 3-19-66, *Philbrick B66-280* (SBBG).

Perityle emoryi Torrey **N** Over entire island, 3-15-64, *Blakley 6490* (SBBG); 3-25-90, *TO NLC90-05*. **S** Lower dry slopes over whole island, 3-20-66, *Philbrick B66-243* (SBBG); 5-7-76, *RM 23135* (SD).

Rafinesquia californica Nutt. **S** NE slope on north end, 6-1-63, *RM 21056* (SD); on NE slope on north end in locations along west side of island, 4-21-91, *TO SLC91-16, SLC91-14* (SD).

Sonchus oleraceus L. **MR** In basin area, 3-3-70, *RM 16786*. **N** Scattered locations, 4-25-77, *RM 23977* (SD). **S** Mostly near military camp, 5-7-76, *RM 23112* (SD).

Sonchus tenerrimus L. 5-8-76, *RM 23162* (SD).

Stephanomeria diegensis Gottlieb **N** Grew in extensive stands over island July 1990, 3-15-64, Blakley 6488; 3-19-66, *Philbrick* B66-222 (SBBG); 6-10-89, *TO NLC89-07* (SD). **MI** Obs. 8-26-90, TO on S end. **MR** 6-12-90, *TO MRLC90-04* (SD).

Uropappus lindleyi (DC.) Nutt. [*Microseris linearifolia* (DC.) Sch.-Bip.] Reported by Greene 1885 .

Boraginaceae

Cryptantha intermedia (A. Gray) Greene **S**, Scattered in openings over N 2/3 of island, 5-16-1885, *Greene* (GREENE); 5-7-76, *RM 23129* (SD); 4-21-91, *TO SLC91-26* (SD).

Cryptantha maritima Greene **S** SW slope of middle peak, 3-19-66, *Blakley 6675* (SBBG); 4-21-91 *TO SLC91-19* (SD).

Brassicaceae

Descurainia pinnata (Walt.) Britt. ssp. *glabra* (Woot.& Stand.) Detling **S** Around south peak, 4-21-91, *TO SLC91-39* (SD).
Lepidium oblongum Small var. *insulare* C.L. Hitchc. **S** On SW slope of middle peak and along trail near south peak, 3-19-66 *Blakley 6649* (SBBG); island ridge, 4-21-91, *TO SLC91-39, SLC91-22*

Sisimbrium irio L. **S** A few scattered along trail to S light house, 4-21-91, *TO SLC91-43* (SD).

Cactaceae

Bergerocactus emoryi (Engelm.) Britton & Rose **N** In patches, 2-20-58, *RM 6557* (SD). **S** Over island, mostly west side, 5-7-1976, *RM 23137* (SD). **MI** One patch on SW side, 8-26-90, TO obs.

Mammillaria dioica K. Brandegee **N** A few locations on upper ridge, 3-20-66, *Blakley 6732* (SBBG). **S** Scattered length of island, mostly on spine, 3-14-64, 3-19-66, *Blakley 6644* and *6476* (SBBG). **MI** Southwest slope, 8-26-90, *TO obs.*

Opuntia littoralis (Engelm.) Ckll. var. *littoralis* **N** Dominant member of vegetation, 6-10-89, TO obs. **MR** on SW ridge, 6-12-90, *TO MRLC 90-05* (SD). **S** Dominant form of vegetation, 10-19-13, *SB Parish 8834*; 5-26-47, *George Lindsay* (SD). **MI** SW side, 8-26-90, TO obs.

Opuntia oricola Philbrick **S** Reported by Beauchamp.

Opuntia prolifera Engelm. **N** Above Fish camp, 3-20-66, Blakeley 6741 (SBBG). **S** Common, 4-21-91, TO obs. **MI** SW slope, 8-26-90, TO obs. **MR** 6-12-90, *TO obs.*

Capparaceae

Cleome isomeris Greene **S** On cliff slopes within PC cove and lower slopes on S end, 3-19-66, *Blakely 6706* (SBBG); 2-8-69, *Philbrick and Benedict B69-13* (SBBG); 5-7-76 *RM 23143* (SD).

Caryophyllaceae

*Silene gallica L. **S** N slope above PC cove, 5-7-76, *RM 23100* (SD).

Silene laciniata Cav. ssp. *major* Hitchc. & Maguire **S** N slope above PC cove, 6-21-60, *RM 8308* et al. (SD); 6-2-71 *RM 18460* (SD).

*Spergularia villosa (Pers.) Camb. **S** Along trail to landing below military camp, 6-10-89, *TO NLC 89-02*; 3-24-90 *NLC 90-03* (SD).

*Stellaria media (L.) Vill. **N** E slope above landing , 6-10-89, TO obs. **S** A patch above military camp near flat pad, 4-21-91, *TO SLC91-21* (SD).

Chenopodiaceae

Aphanisma blitoides Nutt. **S** One quarter mile north of southern light, 3-14-64, *Blakley 6464* (SBBG).

Atriplex californica Moq. **N** In scattered patches, 4-23-16, *Stephens* (SD), **MR** Dominant vegetation in basin, 3-3-70, *RM 16788* (SD). **S** Lower slopes around island, 5-7-76, *RM 23145* (SD); 4-21-91, *TO SLC 91-29* (SD).

Atriplex canescens (Pursh) Nutt. ssp. *canescens* **N** Dominant vegetation on southern 2/3 of island, 5-20-58, *RM 6558* (SD). **S** Most common on southern ridge and slopes, 2-20-66, *Blakley 6716*; 2-8-69 *Philbrick & Benedict B69-9*; 5-8-76, *RM 23159* (SD).

*Atriplex semibaccata R. Br. **S** Along trails, 3-19-66, *Blakley 6656* (SBBG). **MI** East slope, 7-9-58, *RM 6811*(SD).

Atriplex serenana var. *davidsonii* (Standl.) Munz **S** Middle of island, 3-14-64, Blakley 6447 (SBBG).

Atriplex pacifica Nelson **S** Southwest slope of island, 5-7-76, *RM 23133*.
Chenopodium californicum (S. Wats.) S. Wats. **S** Very common, 5-7-76, *RM 23108* (SD). **N** Very common, 5-3-70, *RM et al. 16798* (SD); 6-10-89, *TO NLC89-05* (SD).

*Chenopodium murale L. **N** 6-10-89, *TO NLC89-06* (SD). **MR** Obs. 6-12-90 TO, **S** Very common, 5-7-76, *RM 23111* (SD).

Salsola iberica Sennen & Pau **N** Mostly on ridge top and paths, 3-25-90, *TO NLC90-08* (SD). **MR** Mostly in basin, 6-12-90, TO obs, **S** In a few locations along trails, 5-7-76, *RM 23134* (SD). **MI** In trough area on upper island, 8-26-90, TO obs.

Suaeda californica S. Wats. **MR** Dominant in basin, 3-3-70, RM 16785; 6-12-90, TO NLC90-08 (SD). **MI** E slope 7-9-58, *RM 6807*; 8-26-90, *TO MILC90-03* (SD). **S** Along southern, lower slopes, 6-14-37 *Stover.*

Convolvulaceae

Calystegia macrostegia ssp. *longiloba* Brummit **S** Western side of island, 3-14-64, *Blakley 6446* (SBBG); 5-7-76, *RM 23115* (SD).

Dichondra occidentalis House **S** South to south peak, 2-8-69 *Philbrick and Benedict B66-281* (SBBG).

Crassulaceae

Crassula connata (Ruiz & Pav.) A.Berger **S** Above PC cove , 3-19-66, *Blakley 6620* (SBBG); 3-19-66, *Philbrick B66-284*; 3-14-70, *Philbrick & Ricker B70-21* (SBBG); 4-21-91, *TO SLC91-25* (SD).

Dudleya anomala (Davidson) Moran **S** Common on E slope of island, 7-10-73, *Philbrick B69-12* (SBBG); 6-21-60, *RM 8307* (SD).

Dudleya attenuata ssp. *orcuttii* (Rose) Moran **S** North end ridge, 6-20-59, *RM 7504*; 6-21-60, *RM 8308* (SD).

Dudleya candida Britton Endemic. **N** Green and chalky, 3-25-90, *TO NLC90-10* (SD). **S** 7-28-28, *Kessler "Isotype"*; 6-14-37, *A. J. Stover* (SD). **MR** 6-12-90, *TO MRLC90-09* (SD). **MI** 8-26-90, *TO MILC90-06* (SD).

Dudleya lanceolata (Nutt.) Britton & Rose **S** Slope above cove, 6-20-59, RM 7505 (SD).

Dudleya x *semiteres* (Rose) Moran **S** RM field notes 6-20-59.

Cucurbitaceae

Marah macrocarpus (Greene) Greene **N** Relatively common, 3-25-90, obs. TO. **S** Very common over island, 1-4-1889, *Greene* (GREENE); 5-7-76, *RM 23118* (SD). **MI** One at S end, 8-26-90, *TO MILC90-08* (SD).

Euphorbiaceae

Euphorbia misera Benth. **S** Dominant, 5-7-76, *RM 23114* (SD). **MI** On SW slope, 8-26-90, *TO MILC90-11* (SD).

Fabaceae

Astragalus trichopodus ssp. *leucopsis* (T. & G.) Thorne **S** Patches above PC cove, 7-26-1948, *Charles Shaw* (SD); 6-30-68, *RM*; 5-7-76, *RM 23104* (SD).

Lotus scoparius (Nutt.) Ottley Reported by Greene, 1885.

Lupinus succulentus Dougl. **S** Along E side trail past middle peak and west side of middle portion, 4-21-91, *TO SLC91-34* (SD).

Medicago polymorpha L. **N** 3-25-90, TO obs. **S** 4-21-91, *TO SLC91-34* (SD).

Trifolium tridentatum Lindl. **S** On slope above PC cove, 4-21-91, *TO SLC91-36* (SD).

Geraniaceae

Erodium cicutarium (L.) L'Her. **S** Very common over island, 5-7-76, *RM 23110* (SD).

Erodium botrys (Cav.)Bertol **S** Above Puerto Cueva cove, 4-21-91, obs. TO.

Erodium moschatum (L.)L'Her. **S** North slope, 5-7-76, *RM 23113* (SD).

Hipocastanaceae

Aesculus parryi A.Gray **S** Collected 6-4-1889 by *Pond HG#06931#25927* (GREENE). Apparently no longer extant.

Hydrophyllaceae

Eucrypta chrysanthemifolia (Benth.) Greene **S** Shaded areas NE and SW side, 3-19-66, *Blakley 6650* (SBBG), 3-19-66 (SBBG); *Philbrick B66-310* (SBBG); 5-7-76, *RM 23128*, 4-21-91, *TO SLC91-42* (SD).

Phacelia distans Benth. **S** SW side along trail, 5-8-76, *RM 23154* (SBBG); 3-14-64, 3-19-66, *Blakley 6451, 6641* (SBBG); 4-21-91, *TO SLC91-40* (DS).

Phacelia ixodes Kellogg **S** North of Hotel cove, N end and along SW side trail, 5-7-76, *RM 23142* (SD).

Pholistoma auritum (Lindl.) Lilga Reported by Greene, 1885.

Pholistoma racemosum (Nutt.) Constance **S** SE side above PC cove, 5-7-76, *RM 23150*; 4-21-91, *TO SLC91-07* (SD).

Malvaceae

Malva occidentalis (S. Wats) M.F. Ray **S** Much reduced in 1991 along SW side of island and top of south peak, 5-16-1885, *Greene* (GREENE), 4-22-70, RM 17481; 5-8-76 RM 23156,23157 (SD) others.

Malva parviflora L. **N** 3-25-90 obs. TO common along trails and open places. **MR** In basin, 6-12-90, *TO MRLC90-10* (SD). **S** common along trails, 5-7-76, *RM 23109* (SD).

Myoporum laetum Forst. f. Ngaio. **N** Top of N ridge, carried by gulls, 3-25-90, obs. TO. **S** Planted near military camp, 5-7-76, *RM 23149* (SD).   .

Nyctaginaceae

Mirabilis californica A. Gray **N** Common in shrubs and rocks, 3-25-90, *TO NLC90-11* (SD). **MI** On southwestern slope, 8-26-90, *TO MILC90-05* (SD). **S** Common length of island, 5-7-76, *RM 23120* (SD).

Papaveraceae

Eschscholzia californica Cham. var. *peninsularis* (Greene) Munz **S** Growing in colorful patches on slopes around PC cove, 3-14-64, *Blakley 6417* and 3-19-66, *6680* (SBBG); 4-21-91, *TO SLC91-04* (SD) .

Eschscholzia ramosa Greene **S** Very common middle 1/3 of island, 2-26-49, *Wiggins 11989* ; 6-21-60, *RM 8303*; 5-7-76, *23136, 23147* et al.; 4-21-91, *TO SLC91-28* (all SD).

Stylomecon heterophylla (Benth.) G. Taylor **S** On NE side of middle peak, 3-19-66, *Blakley 6627* (SBBG); 4-21-91, *TO SLC91-44* (SD).

Polemoniaceae

Gilia capitata ssp. *abrotanifolia* (Nutt.) V. Grant. Reported by Greene, 1885.
Linanthus dianthiflorus (Benth.) Greene **S** Slope above PC cove and saddle at middle of island, 3-19-66, *Blakley 6621* (SBBG); 5-7-76, *RM 23130* (SD); 4-21-91, *TO SLC91-17* (SD).

Polygonaceae

Eriogonum fasciculatum Benth. **S** On north end only, 5-7-76, *RM 23148* (SD). **MI** A few clusters on E slopes of upper central portion, 8-26-90, *TO MILC90-01* (SD).

Pterostegia drymarioides F.&M. **S** On shaded SW side, 4-21-91, *TO SLC91-15* (SD).

Portulacaceae

Calandrinia maritima Nutt. **S** On slopes of middle peak to central saddle, 4-21-91, *TO SLC91-39* (SD).

Claytonia perfoliata Willd. ssp. mexicana (Rydb.) J.M.Miller & K.L.Chambers. **S** On north slope above PC cove, 3-19-66, *Blakley 6679* (SBBG); 2-8-69, *Philbrick & Benedict B69-19* (SBBG); 4-21-91, *TO SLC91-03* (SD).

Ranunculaceae

Clematis pauciflora Nutt. Reported by Greene, 1885. **S** Occasional over island, 3-19-66, *Blakley 6665* (SBBG); 5-7-76, *RM 23119* (SD).

Delphinium parryi A. Gray. **S** Slope above PC cove, 3-19-66, *Blakley 6683* (SBBG); 5-7-76, *RM et al.23124* (SD);, 4-21-91, *TO SLC91-08* (SD).

Resedaceae

Oligomeris linifolia (Vah.) J.F. Macbr. **S** Common south of middle peak on open slopes, 3-19-66, *Blakley 6670*; 5-7-76, *RM 23161* (SD); 4-21-91, *TO SLC91-31* (SD). **MI** 7-9-58, *RM 6808* (SBBG).

Rosaceae

Heteromeles arbutifolia (Lindl.) Roem. **S** SE slope NW of PC cove, 6-2-71, *RM 8464* (SD).

Rubiaceae

Galium angustifolium Nutt. **S** NE slope above PC cove; dioeceous, 3-14-64, *Blakley 6432* (SBBG); 5-9-76, *RM 23151* (SD).

Galium coronadoense Dempster Endemic. **S** NE slope above PC cove, polygamous, 6-21-60, *RM 8317* (SD); 6-2-71, *RM 18454, 18455, 18456, 18463* (SD); 5-7-76, *RM 23123* (SD).

Saxifragaceae

Jepsonia parryi (Torr.) Small. **S** Rare on rocky clay N slope, south of N light house, 3-14-64, *Blakley 6437* (SBBG).

Scrophulariaceae

Antirrhinum nuttallianum forma *pusillum* (Brandegee) Munz. **S** Common over island, 6-14-37, *F. Gander*; 5-7-76, *RM 23141*; 4-21-91, *TO SLC91-20* (SD). **N** In steep drainage NE side, 6-10-89, *TO NLC89-03* (SD).

Collinsia heterophylla Buist. **S** N slope above PC cove in 1991, 4-21-91, *TO SLC91-10* (SD).

Linaria texana Scheele **S** In large patches on slopes above PC cove in 1991, 5-7-76, *RM 23140*; 4-21-91, *TO SLC91-41* (SD).

Solanaceae

Lycium californicum Nutt. **N** Over lower slopes of island, 3-25-90, *TO NLC90-09*. **MR** 6-12-90, *TO MRLC90-01*. **MI** 8-26-90, *TO MILC90-02*. **S** Mostly over W and lower slopes of island , 5-8-76, *RM 23160*; 4-21-91, *TO SLC91-27* (all SD).

Nicotiana clevelandii A. Gray. **N** 5-20-58, *RM 6543* (SD).

Solanum nodiflorum Jacq. **N** In rocks near N end, 3-20-58 *RM 6544*; 6-10-89, *TO NLC89-01.*

Lycopersicon esculentum* Mill. **N On upper ridges, seeds carried by gulls, 6-10-89, *TO NLC89-04* (SD).

Urticaceae

Parietaria floridana Nutt. **S** On NE slope S of PC cove, 4-21-91, *TO SLC91-06* (SD).
Urtica urens* L. **N Above landing area, 3-25-90, *TO NLC90-12* (SD).

Monocots

Amaryllidaceae

Dichelostemma pulchellum (Salisb.) Heller **N** One patch seen, 5-20-58, *RM 6547* (SD). **S** Very common much of upper part of island, 2-26-49, *Wiggins 11994* (SD); 5-8-76, *RM 23153* (SD); 4-21-91, *TO SLC91-11* (SD).

Liliaceae

Calochortus splendens Dougl. **S** Occasional northern third of island, 5-7-76, *RM 23105*; 4-21-91, *TO SLC91-35* (both SD).

Orchidaceae

Piperia cooperi (S. Watson) Rydb. **S** Only one in burned area, 6-21-60, *RM 8311* (SD).

Poaceae

Agrostis pallens Trin. [*diegoensis* Vasey] **S** 1-21-60, *RM 8312* (SD).

Avena barbata* Brot. **S NW of PC cove, 5-7-76, *RM 23098* (SD).

 Avena fatua* L. **S Much of island, 4-21-91, obs. TO.

Bromus carinatus H. & A. **N** Common above landing, 3-20-58, *RM 6551*, 3-3-70, *RM 16795*; 4-25-77, *RM 23976*; 3-24-90, *TO NLC90-13* (all SD).

Bromus mollis* L. **S NW of PC cove, 4-21-91 obs. TO.

Bromus rubens* L. **S Above PC cove, 5-7-76, RM 23106 (SD).

Cynodon dactylon* (L.) Pers. **S 6-14-37, *Stover* (SD)

Distichlis spicata (L.) Greene. **S** Above PC cove, 4-21-91, obs. TO.

Hordeum murinum* ssp. *glaucum* (Steud.) Tzvelev. **N Common in gull disturbed areas, 3-25-90, *TO NLC90-02* (SD). **MR** In basin, 6-12-90, obs. TO. **S** On slopes above PC cove, 5-8-76, *RM 23146* (SD).

Hordeum murinum* ssp. *leporinum* (Link) Arcang. **S Near military structures, 3-25-90, *TO NLC90-01* (SD).

Lamarckia aurea* (L.) Moench. **N Above landing, 6-10-89 obs. TO. **S** Very common and widespread, especially along trails, 5-7-76, RM 23102 (SD).

Leymus condensatus (Presl.) Love. Reported by Greene, 1885. **S** top of narrow isthmus between N. and S. points of island and near north light, 3-19-66, *Blakley 6632, 6686* (SBBG); on north east slope, 5-8-76, *RM 23131* (SD).

Melica imperfecta Trin. **N** 4-1-34, *Alderson.* **S** On NE side and middle saddle, 3-14-64, Blakley 6428 (SBBG).

Muhlenbergia microsperma (DC.) Kunth. **S** S slope of middle peak and south peak, 3-14-64, *Blakley 6438* (SBBG); 4-21-91, *TO SLC91-12, SLC91-18* (SD).

Stipa pulchra Hitchc. **S** NW of PC cove, 3-14-64, *Blakley 6471* (SBBG); 3-19-66, *Philbrick B66-267, B66-310* (SBBG); 5-7-76, *RM 23122* (SD).

*Vulpia myuros var. *hirsuta* Hack. Reported by Greene, 1885. **S** NW slope, 5-8-76, RM 23121 (SD).

Zosteraceae

Phyllospadix scouleri Hook. **MR** Near east side of island, 3-3-70, *RM 16793* (SD).

Abbreviations: N = North Island, **MR** = Middle Rock and **MI** = Middle Island, **S** = South Island; RM = Reid Moran, TO = Thomas Oberbauer, obs.=observed, PC cove = Puerto Cueva cove.

Species Included in Other Draft Lists but not Verified: *Chaenactis glabriuscula, Hazardia orcuttii, Isocoma venetus, Malacothrix coulteri, Opuntia hybrid occidentalis,* and *Trifolium palmeri.*

FLOWERING PLANTS OF NATIVIDAD ISLAND, BAJA CALIFORNIA, MEXICO

Steven A. Junak[1] and Ralph Philbrick[2]

[1]Santa Barbara Botanic Garden, 1212 Mission Canyon Road, Santa Barbara, CA 93105
(805) 682-4726 ext. 105, Fax (805) 563-0352, E-mail: sjunak@sbbg.org
[2]29 San Marcos Trout Club, Santa Barbara, CA 93105, (805) 967-0875

ABSTRACT

Natividad Island, situated 7 km off Punta Eugenia, Baja California, Mexico has an area of 7.2 km². Maritime desert scrub vegetation, dominated by drought-resistant shrubs and cacti, covers most of the island. Spectacular displays of native annuals, like *Chaenactis lacera* and *Coreocarpus involutus*, can be seen in years with adequate rainfall. Disturbed areas on the south end of the island are periodically dominated by nonnative plant taxa like *Chenopodium murale*, *Malva parviflora*, and *Mesembryanthemum crystallinum*. A total of 77 native and naturalized vascular plant taxa have now been documented for the island, representing 31 families and 63 genera. The five largest plant families represented in the island's flora are Asteraceae, Brassicaceae, Cactaceae, Chenopodiaceae, and Fabaceae. Five plant taxa endemic to the California Islands have been found there, although one has presumably been introduced. At least one additional taxon known from the island (an *Astragalus*) may be a California Island endemic, but needs further study. Although the island is included in Mexico's Vizcaíno Biosphere Reserve, activities associated with a small town (e.g., off-road motor vehicle use and recent introductions of goats and sheep) represent serious threats to the terrestrial ecosystem. Significant terrestrial resources that need protection include nesting colonies of black-vented shearwaters and populations of endemic land snails and deer mice.

Keywords: Natividad Island, Isla Natívidad, California Islands, Baja California, Mexico, endemic plants, flora, vegetation, botanical exploration, feral animals.

INTRODUCTION

Natividad Island, a natural area that is part of Mexico's Vizcaíno Biosphere Reserve, is known for its rugged coastline, dramatic landscapes, nesting seabird populations, and endemic plants and animals. For at least 100 years, the biota on this island has been subjected to damage caused by feral animals, including cats, goats, and sheep. Sensitive terrestrial resources of Natividad Island include breeding populations of Brandt's and double-crested cormorants, brown pelicans, osprey, peregrine falcons, western gulls, and over 90% of the world population of black-vented shearwaters (Donlan et al. 1999, this volume). There is also an endemic subspecies of deer mouse (Huey 1964) and a land snail that is endemic to Natividad and Cedros islands (Smith et al. 1990). Human visitation and activity has increased dramatically during the last decade, raising the demand for information about the island's flora and the potential for nonnative plant introductions. We hope to promote further scientific investigations on this picturesque island by providing here 1) an introduction to its geography and vegetation, 2) a short history of botanical exploration, 3) a description of historical changes in the vegetation and flora, and 4) an annotated checklist of the flowering plants.

PHYSICAL ENVIRONMENT

Eight islands lie off the west coast of Baja California between the United States/Mexico border and Punta Eugenia, which is located about 575 km (357 mi) south of the international border. Ranging in size from 0.4 to 348 km² (0.2 to 134 mi²), seven of the islands are on the continental shelf, and six of them lie within 23 km (14 mi) of the coastline. Situated near the edge of the continental shelf, the San Benito Islands are 66 km (41 mi) from the nearest point on the mainland but only 27 km (17 mi) from neighboring Cedros Island. Guadalupe is an oceanic island situated 252 km (157 mi) off the Baja California coast.

Natividad Island, with its center near latitude 27° 53' N and longitude 115° 11' W, is located about 556 km (345 mi) south of the border between the United States and Mexico. Situated between Cedros Island and the tip of Punta Eugenia, it is about 7 km (5 mi) from the adjacent mainland. The island's axis is oriented in a northwest-southeast direction (see Figure 1). It has a total area of 7.2 km² (2.8 mi²) and is about 6.0 km (3.75 mi) long. Its width varies from about 0.8 km (0.5 mi) at its northwestern end to about 2.4 km (1.5 mi) near the southeastern end (Nelson 1921). A central spine with several rounded peaks reaches a maximum elevation of 149 m (490 ft). Several canyons are present, especially on the east side of the central ridge. Although the coastline is mostly rocky, there are sandy beaches on both sides of the island near its southeastern end.

Even though there are no natural sources of fresh water on the island, about 400 permanent residents live in a

Figure 1. Aerial view of Natividad Island, looking northwest along main axis (photo taken by S. Junak on 14 March 1995).

small town at the southern end of the island (Donlan et al. 1999, this volume). Most of the residents are fishermen who harvest abalone and lobster seasonally and belong to a cooperative (Buzos y Pescadores) based at Bahía Tortugas on the Vizcaíno peninsula. A desalination plant produces fresh water and generators supply electricity for the village. An unsurfaced airstrip is located just east of the village, where regular flights from Ensenada and Guerrero Negro provide rapid access by air. Small boats can land on a cobble beach at a small cove near the village. There arc motorized vehicles on the island and a road system provides access to all but the northern reaches, including a lighthouse on the island's spine. A trail system provides access to the north end of the island. Natividad has become a popular destination for surfers from the United States. A southern California company offers fly-in trips to the island and accommodations in the village.

In recent years, human impacts on the island have increased dramatically. The majority of the island's roads were built in the early 1990s and off-road vehicle activity has damaged sensitive breeding populations of black-vented shearwaters and populations of native plants (S. Junak, pers. obs.).

Weather records are not available for Natividad Island, but the climate can be estimated from a station on neighboring Cedros Island and two stations on the adjacent mainland. Limited precipitation and temperature records, for 4 to 6 year spans, are available for Isla Cedros (latitude 28° 04' N, longitude 115° 14' W, elevation 500 m), Vizcaíno (27° 58' N, 114° 07' W, elevation n.a.), and Bahía Tortugas (27° 43' N, 114° 56' W, elevation 5 m) (Hastings 1964). All of these stations have an arid climate, with mean annual precipitation amounts ranging from 65.1 to 121.3 mm (2.6 to 4.8 in). About 95 to 96% of the precipitation at these three sites falls in the fall and winter, between the months of September and March. December, January, and February are usually the wettest months.

Rainfall on Natividad and on neighboring Cedros Island is generally very sporadic and long periods of drought are the norm. Between 1 January 1945 and 31 December 1947, personnel at the weather station on Cedros Island recorded precipitation on only 20 days (5 rainy days in 1945,

6 in 1946, and 9 in 1947) (Osorio Tafall 1948). Although the winter months are usually the wettest, no rain at all fell on Cedros Island between 6 June 1945 and 12 August 1946! Heavy rainstorms associated with tropical cyclones can drop significant amounts of moisture in the late summer or early fall. Such a storm dropped 36.5 mm (1.4 in) of rain on 28 September 1946 (Osorio Tafall 1948).

Mean annual temperatures at the three weather station sites listed above range from 19.0 to 20.6°C (66.2 to 69.1°F). Typically, the coolest months are January and February, with mean monthly temperatures at the three stations ranging from 15.3 to 17.6°C (59.5 to 63.7°F) for January and from 16.4 to 17.3°C (61.5 to 63.1°F) for February. August and September are typically the warmest months, with mean monthly temperatures ranging from 23.2 to 25.1°C (73.8 to 77.2°F) for August and from 22.8 to 25.5°C (73.0 to 77.9°F) for September.

HISTORY OF BOTANICAL EXPLORATION

Although botanists visited neighboring Cedros Island as early as 1859 (Nelson 1921) and the San Benito Islands in 1875 (Junak and Philbrick 1999, this volume), the first botanical collections on Natividad Island were not made until 1897. In the spring of that year, field biologist and ornithologist Alfred W. Anthony and a number of other scientists visited most of the islands off the west coast of Baja California on Anthony's schooner *Wahlberg* (Brandegee 1900; Moran 1952). Anthony and Townshend S. Brandegee of the University of California at Berkeley both collected plants on Natividad Island on 10 April 1897. Brandegee (1900) reported 36 native and three nonnative plant taxa for the island.

During the first quarter of the twentieth century, two expeditions sponsored by the California Academy of Sciences stopped at Natividad, but only a few botanical specimens have been preserved. The first of these trips was in the spring of 1903, when the Academy organized a journey aboard the schooner *Mary Sachs*. F. E. Barkelew reportedly collected botanical specimens, but they were apparently destroyed by the San Francisco fire in April 1906 (Nelson 1921).

The schooner *Academy* stopped at Natividad in mid-July 1905, while en route to the Galapagos Islands on another expedition sponsored by the California Academy of Sciences (Slevin 1931). The botanist on this voyage, Alban Stewart, collected a few specimens from the island on July 19th.

A 43-year lull in botanical collecting activities on Natividad was broken in 1948, when Reid Moran and George Lindsay collected a few specimens there on April 28th of that year (Moran and Lindsay 1949). Moran later became curator of botany at the San Diego Museum of Natural History. Lindsay became director of the San Diego Museum of Natural History and then the California Academy of Sciences (Mitich 1989). Moran returned to the island on 21 April 1963, while on an expedition aboard the yacht *Gringa*.

He landed there again on 24 June 1968, while on an expedition aboard the *Stella Polaris* sponsored by the Smithsonian Institution.

During the 1970s, '80s, and '90s, only a few trips were made to the island. Michael Benedict of the Santa Barbara Botanic Garden collected there on 7 March 1971. R. Mitchel Beauchamp of San Diego made collections there on 10 April 1971. Ralph Philbrick and Michael Benedict explored most of the island and collected plants on 23-25 March 1974. Philbrick returned to the island on 12-13 July 1983, accompanied by Marla Daily and Steve Junak. Daily and Junak collected there again on 31 March 1987, and Junak returned on 14-17 March 1995, during a very wet season.

In summary, we know of only 11 botanists who have collected specimens on Natividad Island, during 11 separate trips. Undoubtedly additional botanists, especially from Mexico, have also visited the island but we have not seen their collections. To our knowledge, the island has not been systematically surveyed and collections have only been made during the months of March (3 trips), April (5 trips), June (1 trip), and July (2 trips). Additional exploration is needed to completely document the flora.

HISTORICAL CHANGES IN THE VEGETATION AND FLORA

The island's vegetation has been disturbed by a century or more of human activities and by introduced animals. The first botanist to visit Natividad, T. S. Brandegee, noted the effects of introduced goats on succulent plants (especially *Dudleya*) and reported three nonnative plant taxa (*Chenopodium murale*, *Mesembryanthemum crystallinum*, and *Sonchus tenerrimus*). He described the situation on the island (Brandegee 1900):

"There is no fresh water upon it, so that a resident band of goats must often satisfy their thirst by eating succulent plants, and have already nearly exterminated the Cotyledons [live-forever or *Dudleya*]. There are no trees, but a few small bushes of *Veatchia* [elephant tree or *Pachycormus*] are found and a dozen specimens of *Cereus pringlei* [cardon or *Pachycereus*], ten to fifteen feet high, are scattered about. The vegetation is scant and the general appearance of the island is barren. Most of the plants grow also upon Cedros, and these, with a few belonging to San Bartolome Bay, constitute its entire flora, for there is not an endemic species. The rainfall of the season had been even less than that of the southern end of Cedros, consequently the annuals were small and few in number, and the collection not as large as it would have been at a more favorable time."

Since subsequent visitors in the early 1900s (e.g., Thayer and Bangs 1907; Nelson 1921; Hanna 1925) did not mention goats in their accounts of the island, it is possible that the band of goats described by Brandegee did not

persist. At least one of the nonnative plants reported by Brandegee was soon common on the island. Nelson (1921) commented that: "The ice plant (*Mesembryanthemum*) is the most abundant plant and carpets much of the island." Howell (1932) noted that there was a "Japanese abalone camp" at the south end of the island in August 1932 but did not go ashore to collect plants.

Additional nonnative plants were not reported for the island until the 1960s, when two additional taxa (*Mesembryathemum nodiflorum* and *Portulaca oleracea*) were found. Most of the nonnative plants now known from the island were not seen there until after 1970 (see Table 1).

Nonnative animals seen on the island in March 1974 included feral cats, a burro, tame pigeons, and a caged rabbit (R. Philbrick, pers. obs.). In March 1987, a small band of about 10 goats was seen near the northwestern end of the

Table 1. Dates of first known records of nonnative plants on Natividad Island.

Plant	Date of first known record*
Chenopodium murale	1897
Mesembryanthemum crystallinum	1897
Sonchus tenerrimus	1897
Mesembryanthemum nodiflorum	1963
Portulaca oleracea	1968
Zea mays	1974
Cakile maritima	1987
Malva parviflora	1987
Sisymbrium irio	1987
Sonchus oleraceus	1987
Eragrostis pectinacea	1995
Malva pacifica	1995
Pelargonium hortorum	1995
Phalaris minor	1995

*See text and appendix for additional information.

island (S. Junak, pers. obs.). In March 1995, two dogs were seen near the village and about 10 goats and three sheep were seen near the summit on the island (S. Junak, pers. obs.). By 1997, about 40 goats and 15 sheep were present on the island, along with an introduced antelope squirrel and feral cats (Donlan et al. 1999, this volume).

Through the cooperative efforts of the Island Conservation and Ecology Group and the Vizcaíno Biosphere Reserve, all of the goats and sheep were removed to a farm near Ensenada in 1997 (Donlan et al.1999, this volume). Feral cat removal was begun in 1998; only a few apparently remain on the island at present. The antelope squirrels also remain on the island.

Most of the plants seen by Brandegee in 1897 are still present on the island. California mustard (*Guillenia lasiophylla*) has not been seen in recent years. Coulter's saltscale (*Atriplex coulteri*) was reported by Brandegee but no voucher specimen has been found. Brandegee may have actually seen one of the other annual *Atriplex* species known from the island.

For decades, crystalline iceplant (*Mesembryanthemum crystallinum*) has been the most abundant of the nonnative plants on the island. In 1995, it was the dominant species on coastal flats around the perimeter of the island. In that year, the small-flowered iceplant (*Mesembryanthemum nodiflorum*) was also widespread around the island's perimeter. Nettle-leaf goosefoot (*Chenopodium murale*) was abundant and widespread in disturbed areas throughout the island. Slender sow-thistle (*Sonchus tenerrimus*) was common throughout the island. Cheeseweed (*Malva parviflora*) was occasional but widespread. The other plant taxa that have been introduced to the island occur in scattered populations and do not dominate large areas.

In summary, nonnative plants and animals have had significant effects on the terrestrial ecosystem of Natividad Island for decades. Thanks to the recent efforts of the Island Conservation and Ecology Group, officials of the Vizcaíno Biosphere Reserve, leaders of the fishing cooperative, and the island's residents have begun the process of removing nonnative animals. The native plants of Natividad Island will undoubtedly benefit from these efforts. However, the problems caused by nonnative plants remain and will probably intensify if more areas of the island are disturbed by human activities.

VEGETATION

The terrestrial vegetation on Natividad Island is generally characterized by low-growing, drought-resistant shrubs and stem succulents with open spaces between them. In years with adequate rainfall, annual plants occupy many of these open spaces for a month or more. In some areas, however, dense stands of chollas (*Opuntia* spp.) form almost impenetrable thickets.

The dominant plant community is maritime desert scrub. This vegetation type consists almost entirely of low perennials, with no trees and few shrubs taller than one meter. The tallest plants on the islands are cardón (*Pachycereus pringlei*) and coastal agave (*Agave sebastiana*). Dominant perennial species in the maritime desert scrub include the shrubs and suffrutescent perennials *Atriplex julacea, Encelia palmeri, Euphorbia misera, Frankenia palmeri, Lycium* spp., *Suaeda moquinii, Viguiera lanata,* and the cacti *Echinocereus maritimus, Ferocactus fordii* var. *grandiflorus, Mammillaria hutchinsoniana* and an undescribed *Opuntia* species. *Pachycereus pringlei* occurs as scattered individuals that tower above the surrounding vegetation. *Opuntia cholla* forms dense thickets in the central highlands. The succulent *Dudleya albiflora* also occurs in dense populations in the central highlands. The cover of the perennial

species is not continuous, and short-lived or ephemeral taxa dominate some areas. Large numbers of winter annuals, including *Chaenactis lacera, Coreocarpus involutus, Eschscholzia ramosa,* and *Plantago ovata* occur in some of the open sites between the larger plants after adequate rainfall.

Rocky canyon walls in the northern and central portions of the island support a rich mixture of native plants, including the dominants listed above and other shrubs like *Pachycormus discolor* var. *veatchiana, Pithecellobium confine,* and *Simmondsia chinensis.* The shrubs *Bebbia juncea* and *Sphaeralcea fulva* are common in some canyon bottoms. Native annuals like *Aphanisma blitoides, Eschscholzia ramosa,* and *Perityle emoryi* can be abundant in canyon bottoms in wet years.

Beaches and other sandy areas near the eastern shore support patches of coastal strand vegetation. Dominant species here include *Astragalus magdalenae* var. *magdalenae, Atriplex leucophylla, Cakile maritima, Frankenia palmeri,* and *Suaeda moquinii.* In rocky intertidal and subtidal habitats around the margin of the island, *Phyllospadix scouleri* occurs in a surf-grass community.

Introduced annuals are common along trails, roads, and in areas that have been disturbed by seabird activity. *Mesembryanthemum crystallinum* and *M. nodiflorum* cover large areas around the island's perimeter, as does *Chenopodium murale. Malva parviflora* occurs in scattered patches throughout the island.

FLORA

The documented flora of Natividad Island includes 77 vascular plant taxa representing 31 families and 63 genera (see Appendix). Two additional plant taxa (*Abutilon californicum* and *Atriplex coulteri*) have been reported in the literature but no voucher specimens have been found to date, so they are not included in the statistics given here. The largest families are the Asteraceae (10 taxa), Chenopodiaceae (8 taxa), Cactaceae (7 taxa), Fabaceae (6 taxa), Brassicaceae (5 taxa), Malvaceae (4 taxa), and Solanaceae (4 taxa). The largest genus is *Atriplex*, which is represented on Natividad by five native species. Genera represented by two taxa include *Astragalus, Chamaesyce, Lepidium, Lycium, Mesembryanthemum, Opuntia, Phacelia,* and *Sonchus.* The fact that Natividad has a substantially larger flora than the San Benito Islands is probably correlated with its closer proximity to other land masses, its larger size, and greater diversity of habitats.

Native and Endemic Plant Taxa

A total of 63 plant taxa presumed to be native have been documented for Natividad Island to date. Plant families with the highest number of native taxa include Asteraceae (8 taxa), Cactaceae (7 taxa), Chenopodiaceae (7 taxa), Fabaceae (6 taxa), and Solanaceae (4 taxa). With five native species on the island, *Atriplex* is the largest genus.

Astragalus, Chamaesyce, Lepidium, Lycium, Opuntia, and *Phacelia* are each represented by two native taxa.

About 40% of the native plant taxa found on Natividad are endemic to Baja California, including six of the island's seven cacti. Many taxa found on the island are restricted to the Vizcaíno Desert region or nearly so. At least five of the island's plant taxa are restricted to the California Islands or offshore rocks and are not found on the adjacent mainland. Three taxa (*Cochemia pondii, Mentzelia hirsutissima* var. *nesiotes,* and an undescribed species of *Opuntia*) are found only on Natividad and neighboring islands. Another insular endemic (*Eschscholzia ramosa*) is more widespread but has not been found on the mainland. One additional taxon (*Astragalus* aff. *gambelianus*) may also be endemic to Cedros and Natividad islands, but its relationship with other taxa on the mainland needs further study.

Over 50% of the native plant taxa known from Natividad Island have not been found on the San Benito Islands. This may be partially attributed to the latter's geographic isolation and limited topographic diversity. On the other hand, the San Benitos have certainly been more thoroughly collected than has Natividad Island.

Nonnative Plant Taxa

At least 14 plant taxa in eight families and 11 genera have been introduced to Natividad, primarily since the 1960s (see Table 1). These introductions represent about 18% of the island's total flora. By comparison, known percentages of nonnative plants on the other islands off the west coast of Baja California range from about 17% on the San Benito Islands to about 50% on San Geronimo Island. Eight of the island's nonnative plants originated in Europe, one originated as a domestic plant in eastern Mexico (i.e., *Zea mays*), three are native to South Africa, one is native to North America (i.e., *Eragrostis pectinacea*), and one is native to several Baja California islands but has apparently been introduced by humans on Natividad (i.e., *Malva pacifica*). Three plant families (Aizoaceae, Geraniaceae, and Poaceae) are represented on Natividad solely by nonnative taxa. Several families (Aizoaceae, Asteraceae, Brassicaceae, and Malvaceae) are each represented by two nonnative taxa. Genera represented by two nonnative taxa include *Mesembryanthemum* and *Sonchus*. On Natividad, 12 of the introduced plant taxa are herbaceous annuals, one is a subshrub, and one is a shrub.

At least two additional plants may have been introduced to Natividad. *Plantago ovata,* presumed at this point to be native to Natividad, is also known from all of the California Channel Islands and from Guadalupe, San Benito, and Cedros islands. Although it was among the first plants reported for Natividad (as *Plantago patagonica*), this *Plantago* may be a very early introduction from the Mediterranean area of Europe (Dempster 1993). *Datura discolor* is presently presumed to be native to Natividad, but may have been introduced by human activites.

ACKNOWLEDGMENTS

The authors gratefully acknowledge the help of Michael Benedict, Marla Daily, Wayne Ferren, Paul Fryxell, Reid Moran, and Jon Rebman, who kindly shared their botanical observations and/or information on their collections from Natividad Island. Josh Donlan and Brad Keitt shared information on recent changes on the island. We thank the curators and staff of the following herbaria for their hospitality and for loaning selected specimens: California Academy of Sciences, Rancho Santa Ana Botanic Garden, San Diego Natural History Museum, and University of California at Berkeley. We would also like to thank the Mexican government for allowing access to their islands, the residents of Natividad Island for their hospitality, and Captain Kirk Connally for organizing trips to the island under the auspices of Terra Marine Research and Education. Funding for most of our field trips was provided by the Santa Barbara Botanic Garden. Steve Junak thanks his companions Jon Janoff, Gail Milliken, and Charles J. Rennie, III for an exciting and memorable trip to the island in 1995.

LITERATURE CITED

Abrams, L. 1923-1960. Illustrated Flora of the Pacific states: Washington, Oregon, and California. Stanford University Press, Stanford, CA. 4 volumes. 2771 pp.

Beauchamp, R. M. 1986. A Flora of San Diego County, California. Sweetwater River Press, National City, CA. 241 pp.

Brandegee, T. S. 1900. Voyage of the *Wahlberg.* Zoe 5 (2):19-28.

Brummitt, R. K. and C. E. Powell (eds.) 1992. Authors of Plant Names. Royal Botanic Gardens, Kew, Great Britain. 732 pp.

Coyle, J. and N. C. Roberts. 1975. A Field Guide to the Common and Interesting Plants of Baja California. Natural History Publishing Company, La Jolla, CA. 206 pp.

Dempster, L. T. 1993. Plantaginaceae. Pages 820-821 *in* Hickman, J. C. (ed.), The Jepson Manual: Higher Plants of California. University of California Press, Berkeley, Los Angeles, and London.

Donlan, C. J., B. R. Tershy, B. S. Keitt, J. A. Sanchez, B. Wood, A. Weinstein, D. A. Croll, and M. A. Hermosillo. 1999. Island conservation action in northwest Mexico. Pages 330 to 338 *in* Browne, D. R., K. L. Mitchell, and H. W. Chaney (eds.), Proceedings of the Fifth California Islands Symposium. 29 March to 1 April 1999. Santa Barbara Museum of Natural History, Santa Barbara, CA. Sponsored by the U.S. Minerals Management Service, Pacific OCS Region, 770 Paseo Camarillo, Camarillo, CA 93010. OCS Study No. 99-0038.

Hanna, G. D. 1925. Expedition to Guadalupe Island, Mexico, in 1922. Proceedings of the California Academy of Sciences (Fourth Series) 14:217-275.

Hastings, J. R. 1964. Climatological data for Baja California. Technical Reports on the Meteorology and Climatology of Arid Regions 14. Institute of Atmospheric Physics, University of Arizona, Tucson, AZ. 132 pp.

Hickman, J.C. (ed.) 1993. The Jepson Manual: Higher Plants of California. University of California Press, Berkeley, Los Angeles, and London. 1400 pp.

Holmgren, P. K., N. H. Holmgren, and L C. Barnett. 1990. Index Herbariorum, Part I: The herbaria of the world. Eighth edition. Regnum Vegetabile 120:1-693. New York Botanical Garden, Bronx, NY.

Huey, L. M. 1964. The mammals of Baja California, Mexico. Transactions of the San Diego Society of Natural History 13:85-168.

Junak, S. and R. Philbrick. 1999. Flowering plants of the San Benito Islands, Baja California, México. Pages 235 to 246 in Browne, D. R., K. L. Mitchell, and H. W. Chaney (eds.), Proceedings of the Fifth California Islands Symposium. 29 March to 1 April 1999. Santa Barbara Museum of Natural History, Santa Barbara, CA. Sponsored by the U.S. Minerals Management Service, Pacific OCS Region, 770 Paseo Camarillo, Camarillo, CA 93010. OCS Study No. 99-0038.

Martínez, M. 1979. Catálogo de Nombres Vulgares y Científicos de Plantas Mexicanas. Fondo de Cultura Económica, México, D.F.

Mitich, L. W. 1989. George E. Lindsay, explorer and plantsman: Part 2. Cactus and Succulent Journal 61:17-21.

Moran, R. 1952. The Mexican itineraries of T. S. Brandegee. Madroño 11:221-252.

Moran, R. and G. Lindsay. 1949. Desert islands of Baja California. Desert Plant Life 21:125-128.

Nelson, E. W. 1921. Lower California and its natural resources. Memoirs of the National Academy of Sciences 16:1-194.

Osorio Tafall, B. F. 1948. La Isla de Cedros, Baja California. Boletín de la Sociedad Mexicana de Geografía y Estadística 66:317-402.

Slevin, J. R. 1931. Log of the Schooner Academy on a voyage of scientific research to the Galapagos Islands, 1905-1906. Occasional Papers of the California Academy of Sciences Number 17. 162 pp.

Smith, A. G., W. B. Miller, C. C. Christensen, and B. Roth. 1990. Land mollusca of Baja California, Mexico. Proceedings of the California Academy of Sciences 47:95-158.

Thayer, J. E. and O. Bangs. 1907. Birds collected by W. W. Brown, Jr. on Cerros [sic], San Benito, and Natividad islands in the spring of 1906, with notes on the biota of the islands. Condor 9:77-81.

Wiggins, I .L. 1980. Flora of Baja California. Stanford University Press, Stanford, CA. 1025 pp.

SOURCES OF UNPUBLISHED MATERIALS

Hale, G. O. 1941. A survey of the vegetation of Cedros Island, Mexico. Unpublished M. A. thesis, University of California, Los Angeles, CA. 96 pp.

Howell, J. T. 1932. Field notes for 17 August 1932. Unpublished manuscript on file at California Academy of Sciences, San Francisco, CA.

APPENDIX

ANNOTATED CATALOG OF THE FLOWERING PLANTS OF NATIVIDAD ISLAND

Plants listed in this table are arranged alphabetically by family within two major plant groups (dicotyledonous and mono cotyledonous flowering plants). Taxa presumed to be introduced to Baja California and/or Natividad Island by human activities are preceded by an asterisk (*). The list does not include plant taxa that have been planted at the village unless they are surviving without cultivation in other parts of the island. Unsubstantiated reports (reports for which no voucher specimen has been found) are enclosed in braces (i.e., { }).

For most taxa, nomenclature follows Wiggins (1980) or Hickman (1993). Abbreviations of author names have been mostly standardized according to Brummitt and Powell (1992). Selected synonyms are shown in brackets (i.e., [ ]). Common names are mostly according to Abrams (1923-1960) and Hickman (1993), with a few additions from Beauchamp (1986), Coyle and Roberts (1975), and Martínez (1979).

Abundance ratings (rare, scarce, occasional, common, and abundant) and distribution descriptions are based on observations of the authors during years with average rainfall. Many of the annuals will not even be present during dry years. Dates of first known collection or report from the island are included for nonnative taxa.

Up to three voucher specimens are cited for each taxon. These are arranged chronologically by date of collection. T. S. Brandegee's collections are listed with the date shown on the original labels (i.e., 10 Mar 1897, 10 Apr 1897, or 10 Apr 1889), but he apparently was only on Natividad Island on 9-10 April 1897 (Moran 1952). Specimens without date of collection are cited as "n.d."; those collections without collector's number are listed as "s.n.". Specimens are deposited at the Santa Barbara Botanic Garden (SBBG) unless otherwise noted. Abbreviations for herbaria are those used in Holmgren et al. (1990). Herbarium accession numbers are cited only if there is no collector number.

Dicotyledonous Flowering Plants

Aizoaceae (Iceplant Family)

Mesembryanthemum crystallinum L. CRYSTALLINE ICEPLANT Abundant; disturbed flats and slopes throughout island, but especially in central and southern portions. First noted on the island in 1897 (Brandegee 1900).

7 Mar 1971, *Benedict s.n.* (SBBG 43818); 23 Mar 1974, *Philbrick & Benedict B74-49.*

Mesembryanthemum nodiflorum L. SMALL-FLOWERED ICEPLANT Occasional; disturbed flats around perimeter. First collected in 1963, but already well established at that time.

21 Apr 1963, *Moran 10789* (SD); 7 Mar 1971, *Benedict s.n.* (SBBG 43873); 26 Mar 1974, *Philbrick B74-101.*

Anacardiaceae (Sumac Family)

Pachycormus discolor var. *veatchiana* (Kellogg) Gentry [*Veatchia cedrosensis* A.Gray, *V. discolor* var. *v.* I.M.Johnst.] ELEPHANT TREE or TOROTE Rare; canyons in central portion of island. Endemic to Baja California.

25 Mar 1974, *Philbrick & Benedict B74-80*; 25 Mar 1974, *Philbrick & Benedict B74-81*; 31 Mar 1987, *Junak 3284.*

Asteraceae (Sunflower Family)

Amblyopappus pusillus Hook. & Arn. PINEAPPLE WEED Common; slopes and flats, mostly around perimeter.

23 Mar 1974, *Philbrick & Benedict B74-4.*

Ambrosia chenopodifolia (Benth.) W.W.Payne [*Franseria c.* Benth.] SAN DIEGO BUR-SAGE Occasional; flats at upper elevations.

24 Mar 1974, *Philbrick & Benedict B74-56*; 13 Jul 1983, *Junak 1891*; 15 Mar 1995, *Junak 5888.*

Bebbia juncea (Benth.) Greene var. *juncea* SWEETBUSH Scarce; both sides of island, primarily in arroyos.

10 Apr 1897, *Brandegee s.n.* (UC 91015); 21 Apr 1963, *Moran 10802* (DS,SD,UC); 15 Mar 1995, *Junak 5887.*

Chaenactis lacera Greene CUTLEAF PINCUSHION Common; scattered locations throughout island, especially in arroyos and on coastal flats. Endemic to Baja California.

10 Apr 1897, *Brandegee s.n.* (DS 228009); 31 Mar 1987, *Junak 3276.*

Coreocarpus involutus Greene [*Leptosyne i.* Greene] Abundant; open sites throughout island. Endemic to Baja California.

10 Mar 1897, *Brandegee s.n.* (UC 89271); 21 Apr 1963, *Moran 10791* (SD,UC); 14 Mar 1995, *Junak 5868.*

Encelia palmeri Vasey & Rose PALMER'S BUSH SUNFLOWER Common; northern and central portions of island, especially on west side of ridge. Endemic to Baja California.

24 Jun 1968, *Moran 15134* (SD,UC); 31 Mar 1987, *Junak 3270.*

Perityle emoryi Torr. [*P.grayi* Rose] EMORY'S ROCK DAISY Occasional; flats and arroyos throughout island.

10 Mar 1897, *Brandegee s.n.* (UC 90622); 23 Mar 1974, *Philbrick & Benedict B74-1*; 14 Mar 1995, *Junak 5861.*

*Sonchus oleraceus L. COMMON SOW-THISTLE Scarce; along road near lighthouse and community dumpsite. First noted at village in 1987.

16 Mar 1995, *Junak 5921.*

*Sonchus tenerrimus L. SLENDER SOW-THISTLE Common; slopes, flats, and arroyos throughout island. First collected in 1897.

10 Apr 1897, *Brandegee s.n.* (UC 92392); 25 Mar 1974, *Philbrick & Benedict B74-88*; 14 Mar 1995, *Junak 5862.*

Viguiera lanata (Kellogg) A.Gray VIZCAINO SUNFLOWER Common; slopes throughout island. Endemic to Baja California.

10 Apr 1897, *Brandegee s.n.* (UC 89798); 24 Jun 1968, *Moran 15138* (UC).

Boraginaceae (Borage Family)

Cryptantha maritima (Greene) Greene var. *maritima* [*Krynitzkia m.* Greene] GUADALUPE ISLAND CRYPTANTHA Occasional; open sites throughout island.

10 Apr 1897, *Brandegee s.n.* (UC 78553); 31 Mar 1987, *Junak 3260*; 16 Mar 1995, *Junak 5917.*

Brassicaceae (Mustard Family)

*Cakile maritima Scop. SEA ROCKET Occasional; beaches and coastal flats at southeastern end of island. First collected on the island in 1987.

30 Mar 1987, *Junak 3253*; 14 Mar 1995, *Junak 5859.*

Guillenia lasiophylla (Hook. & Arn.) Greene [*Caulanthus l.* (Hook. & Arn.) Payson] CALIFORNIA MUSTARD Rare; not seen recently.

10 Apr 1897, *Brandegee s.n.* (UC 117304).

Lepidium lasiocarpum var. *latifolium* C.L.Hitchc. Common; flats and arroyos in scattered locations throughout island.

14 Mar 1995, *Junak 5864* (RSA,SBBG).

Lepidium oblongum var. *insulare* C.L.Hitchc. LENTEJILLA Occasional; flats and arroyos in northern portion of island.
10 Apr 1897, *Brandegee s.n.* (UC 117601); 15 Mar 1995, *Junak 5902.*

*Sisymbrium irio L. LONDON ROCKET Occasional; open sites in scattered locations throughout island. First noted at the village in 1987.
15 Mar 1995, *Junak 5890*; 15 Mar 1995, *Junak 5907.*

Cactaceae (Cactus Family)

Cochemia pondii (Greene) Walton [*Mammillaria p.* Greene] BIZNAGITA Occasional; open sites scattered at upper elevations. Endemic to Cedros and Natividad islands.
23 Mar 1974, *Philbrick & Benedict B74-31.*

Echinocereus maritimus (M.E.Jones) K.Schum. COASTAL MOUND CACTUS Common; slopes and flats in scattered locations at upper elevations. Endemic to Baja California.
23 Mar 1974, *Philbrick & Benedict B74-32*; 15 Mar 1995, *Junak 5884.*

Ferocactus fordii (Orcutt) Britton & Rose var. *grandiflorus* G.E.Linds. VIZCAINO BARREL CACTUS Common; slopes and flats in scattered locations at upper elevations. Endemic to Baja California.
23 Mar 1974, *Philbrick & Benedict B74-9*; 15 Mar 1995, *Junak 5886.*

Mammillaria hutchinsoniana (Gates) Boed. VIEJITA Occasional; open sites in scattered locations throughout island. Endemic to Baja California.
28 Apr 1948, *Lindsay 572* (CAS); 24 Jun 1968, *Moran 15131* (SD); 23 Mar 1974, *Philbrick & Benedict B74-8.*

Opuntia sp. nova CEDROS ISLAND CHOLLA Common; rocky slopes and flats throughout island. Endemic to San Benito, Cedros, and Natividad islands.
23 Mar 1974, *Philbrick & Benedict B74-33.*

Opuntia cholla Weber CHOLLA PELONA Common; rocky slopes and flats at upper elevations in central portion of island. Endemic to Baja California.
23 Mar 1974, *Philbrick & Benedict B74-34.*

Pachycereus pringlei (S.Watson) Britton & Rose [*Cereus p.* S.Watson] CARDON or CARDON PELON Occasional; scattered locations at upper elevations, mostly on west side of ridge.
23 Mar 1974, *Philbrick & Benedict B74-21.*

Chenopodiaceae (Goosefoot Family)

Aphanisma blitoides Moq. APHANISMA Common; flats and arroyos in scattered locations throughout island.
10 Apr 1897, *Brandegee s.n.* (UC 116498); 21Apr 1963, *Moran 10799* (SD); 23 Mar 1974, *Philbrick & Benedict B74-25.*

Atriplex barclayana (Benth.) D.Dietr. SALADILLO Scarce; coastal flats on northeast side of island.
24 Jun 1968, *Moran 15130* (RSA).

{*Atriplex coulteri* (Moq.) D.Dietr. Reported for the island by Brandegee (1900); no specimen has been found.}

Atriplex aff. *davidsonii* Standl. DAVIDSON'S SALTSCALE Occasional; scattered locations at upper elevations.
31 Mar 1987, *Junak 3272*; 15 Mar 1995, *Junak 5906.*

Atriplex julacea S.Watson Abundant; throughout island. Endemic to Baja California.
Mar-Jun 1897, *Anthony 365* (DS,UC); 21 Apr 1963, *Moran 10786* (SD); 10 Apr 1971, *Beauchamp 2176* (SD).

Atriplex leucophylla (Moq.) D.Dietr. SEA SCALE Rare; beach at southeast end of island.
26 Mar 1974, *Philbrick & Benedict B74-102*; 16 Mar 1995, *Junak 5928.*

Atriplex pacifica A.Nelson SOUTH COAST SALTSCALE Occasional; disturbed sites in scattered locations at upper elevations.
7 Mar 1971, *Benedict s.n.* (SBBG 43876); 31 Mar 1987, *Junak 3255*; 31 Mar 1987, *Junak 3256.*

*Chenopodium murale L. NETTLE-LEAF GOOSEFOOT Abundant; disturbed sites throughout island. First noted on the island in 1897 (Brandegee 1900).
24 Jun 1968, *Moran 15129* (SD); 23 Mar 1974, *Philbrick & Benedict B74-48.*

Suaeda moquinii (Torr.) Greene BUSH SEEPWEED Common; flats throughout island.
21 Apr 1963, *Moran 10784* (SD); 7 Mar 1971, *Benedict s.n.* (SBBG 43874); 23 Mar 1974, *Philbrick & Benedict B74-15.*

Crassulaceae (Stonecrop Family)

Dudleya albiflora Rose LIVE-FOREVER or SIEMPREVIVA Common; slopes and flats at upper elevations. Endemic to Baja California.
21 Apr 1963, *Moran 10794* (SD); 12 Jul 1983, *Junak 1878.*

Cucurbitaceae (Gourd Family)

Echinopepon minimus (Kellogg) S.Watson   Occasional; canyon bottoms, slopes, and flats in northern and central portions of island. Endemic to Baja California.
24 Mar 1974, *Philbrick & Benedict B74-69*; 25 Mar 1974, *Philbrick & Benedict B74-91*; 31 Mar 1987, *Junak 3275*.

Cuscutaceae (Dodder Family)

Cuscuta californica Hook. & Arn.   DODDER or WITCH'S HAIR   Scarce; saddle on north side of summit. Parasitic on annual species of *Astragalus* and *Lotus* on Natividad Island.
15 Mar 1995, *Junak 5914*.

Euphorbiaceae (Spurge Family)

Chamaesyce bartolomaei Millsp. [*Euphorbia b.* Greene]   GOLONDRINA   Occasional; mostly on flats in central portion of island. Endemic to Baja California.
21 Apr 1963, *Moran 10795* (SD,UC); 10 Apr 1971, *Beauchamp 2181* (SD).
Chamaesyce polycarpa Millsp. var. *polycarpa* [*Euphorbia p.* Benth. var. *p.*]   GOLONDRINA   Scarce; flats in central portion of island.
21 Apr 1963, *Moran 10795 1/2* (SD); 24 Mar 1974, *Philbrick & Benedict B74-52*.
Euphorbia misera Benth.   CLIFF SPURGE   Common; rocky slopes and flats throughout island, especially at higher elevations.
23 Mar 1974, *Philbrick & Benedict B74-41*.

Fabaceae (Pea Family)

Astragalus aff. *gambelianus* E.Sheld.   GAMBEL'S DWARF LOCOWEED   Occasional; open sites at higher elevations in central portion of island. Specimens from Natividad and Cedros islands appear to represent an undescribed form; they need further study.
25 Mar 1974, *Philbrick & Benedict B74-75*; 15 Mar 1995, *Junak 5913*.
Astragalus magdalenae Greene var. *magdalenae*   Occasional; sandy sites near the coast, especially in southern portion of island.
21 Apr 1963, *Moran 10787* (SD); 10 Apr 1971, *Beauchamp 2186* (SD).
Astragalus nuttallianus var. *cedrosensis* M.E.Jones   Occasional; open sites at higher elevations in central portion of island.
15 Mar 1995, *Junak 5911*; 15 Mar 1995, *Junak 5919*.
Lotus salsuginosus subsp. *brevivexillus* Ottley [*Hosackia maritima* Nutt.]   COASTAL LOTUS   Occasional; open sites at higher elevations, primarily in central portion of island.
15 Mar 1995, *Junak 5910*; 16 Mar 1995, *Junak 5922*.
Phaseolus filiformis Benth.   Scarce; slopes on west side of main ridge.
25 Mar 1974, *Philbrick & Benedict B74-77*; 13 Jul 1983, *Junak 1892*; 16 Mar 1995, *Junak 5925*.
Pithecellobium confine Standl.   PALO FIERRO or EJOTON   Rare; upper elevations in central portion of island. Endemic to Baja California.
24 Jun 1968, *Moran 15141* (SD); 25 Mar 1974, *Philbrick & Benedict B74-79*.

Frankeniaceae (Frankenia Family)

Frankenia palmeri (Molina) I.M.Johnst.   PALMER'S FRANKENIA or YERBA REUMA   Occasional; flats at upper elevations and on coastal flats at northeast end of island.
7 Mar 1971, *Benedict s.n.* (SBBG 43875); 23 Mar 1974, *Philbrick & Benedict B74-40*; 15 Mar 1995, *Junak 5899*.

Geraniaceae (Geranium Family)

*Pelargonium x *hortorum* L.H.Bailey   GARDEN GERANIUM   Rare; disturbed coastal flats on east side of island. First collected in 1995.
15 Mar 1995, *Junak 5892*.

Hydrophyllaceae (Waterleaf Family)

Phacelia cedrosensis Rose   CEDROS ISLAND PHACELIA   Occasional; scattered locations in central portion of island. Endemic to Baja California.
10 Apr 1897, *Brandegee s.n.* (UC 107529); 25 Mar 1974, *Philbrick & Benedict B74-85*; 15 Mar 1995, *Junak 5880*.
Phacelia ixodes Kellogg   COSTA BAJA PHACELIA or ISLAND MISERY   Scarce; northern and central portions of island. Endemic to Baja California. This plant should be avoided as it can cause severe contact dermatitis in humans.
24 Jun 1968, *Moran 15139* (SD,UC); 24 Mar 1974, *Philbrick & Benedict B74-63*; 31 Mar 1987, *Junak 3280*.

Pholistoma racemosum (Nutt.) Constance Rare; central portion of island.
> 24 Mar 1974, *Philbrick & Benedict B74-64.*

Loasaceae (Stick-leaf Family)

Mentzelia hirsutissima var. *nesiotes* I.M.Johnst. NATIVIDAD ISLAND BLAZING STAR Occasional; arroyos, rocky slopes, and flats in central portion of island. Endemic to San Benito, Cedros, and Natividad islands.
> 10 Apr 1899, *Brandegee s.n.* (UC 205872); 13 Jul 1983, *Junak 1893*; 14 Mar 1995, *Junak 5874.*

Malvaceae (Mallow Family)

{*Abutilon californicum* Benth. Reported for the island (as *A. lemmonii* S.Watson) by Hale (1941); no specimen has been found.}

Eremalche exilis (A.Gray) Greene [*Malvastrum e.* A.Gray] Occasional; open flats and disturbed sites in scattered locations throughout island; locally abundant in hills at north end of island.
> Apr 1897, *Brandegee s.n.* (UC 174768); 25 Mar 1974, *Philbrick & Benedict B74-90*; 15 Mar 1995, *Junak 5889.*

Malva pacifica M.F.Ray [*Lavatera venosa* S.Watson] SAN BENITO ISLAND BUSH MALLOW Rare; southeast end of island, in small swale at southeast end of airstrip. Native populations are endemic to San Gerónimo Island, the San Benito Islands, and an islet at the mouth of Bahía Tortugas; probably introduced on Natividad, Cedros, and Asunción islands. First collected on Natividad Island in 1995.
> 16 Mar 1995, *Junak 5915.*

Malva parviflora L. CHEESEWEED Occasional; disturbed sites throughout island. First noted in the village in 1987.
> 17 Mar 1995, *Junak 5933.*

Sphaeralcea fulva Greene DESERT MALLOW Common; canyons in northern portion of the island, on both sides of the main ridge. Endemic to Baja California.
> 24 Jun 1968, *Moran 15136* (SD); 24 Mar 1974, *Philbrick & Benedict B74-65*; 15 Mar 1995, *Junak 5898.*

Nyctaginaceae (Four-O'Clock Family)

Abronia maritima S.Watson STICKY SAND-VERBENA Scarce; sandy sites at southern end of island.
> 23 Mar 1974, *Philbrick & Benedict B74-13*; 16 Mar 1995, *Junak 5916.*

Mirabilis californica A.Gray WISHBONE BUSH Common; slopes in scattered locations.
> 23 Mar 1974, *Philbrick & Benedict B74-6*; 24 Mar 1974, *Philbrick & Benedict B74-58*; 31 Mar 1987, *Junak 3281.*

Onagraceae (Evening Primrose Family)

Camissonia crassifolia (Greene) Raven Scarce; sandy sites on west side of island. Endemic to Baja California.
> 24 Mar 1974, *Philbrick & Benedict B74-50*; 26 Mar 1974, *Philbrick & Benedict B74-96*; 17 Mar 1995, *Junak 5929.*

Papaveraceae (Poppy Family)

Eschscholzia ramosa Greene ISLAND POPPY Common; arroyos and flats in scattered locations. Endemic to Santa Rosa, Santa Cruz, Santa Barbara, San Nicolas, Santa Catalina, San Clemente, Los Coronados, Todos Santos, San MartÍn, Guadalupe, San Benito, Cedros, and Natividad islands.
> 10 Apr 1897, *Brandegee s.n.* (UC 142900); 23 Mar 1974, *Philbrick & Benedict B74-24*; 14 Mar 1995, *Junak 5865.*

Plantaginaceae (Plantain Family)

Plantago ovata Forssk. [*P. insularis* Eastw.] Common; open sites in scattered locations throughout island. May not be native to the island.
> 10 Apr 1897, *Brandegee s.n.* (UC 102770); 31 Mar 1987, *Junak 3262.*

Polygonaceae (Buckwheat Family)

Eriogonum pondii Greene var. *pondii* POND'S BUCKWHEAT Occasional; rocky slopes on west side of main ridge, in central portion of island. Endemic to Baja California.
> 21 Apr 1963, *Moran 10803* (GH,SBBG,SD,US); 24 Mar 1974, *Philbrick & Benedict B74-59*; 16 Mar 1995, *Junak 5923.*

Portulacaceae (Purslane Family)

Calandrinia maritima Nutt. SEA KISSES or SEASIDE CALANDRINIA Occasional; rocky slopes in central and southern portions of island.
> 23 Mar 1974, *Philbrick & Benedict B74-43*; 13 Jul 1983, *Junak 1889*; 17 Mar 1995, *Junak 5930.*

Portulaca oleracea L. PURSLANE Scarce; rocky slopes on west side of main ridge, in central portion of island. First collected in 1968.

24 Jun 1968, *Moran 15143* (SD).

Resedaceae (Mignonette Family)

Oligomeris linifolia Vahl [*O. subulata* Webb] OLIGOMERIS Occasional; rocky slopes in central portion of island.

21 Apr 1963, *Moran 10790* (SD,UC); 31 Mar 1987, *Junak 3257*; 14 Mar 1995, *Junak 5858*.

Scrophulariaceae (Figwort Family)

Antirrhinum watsonii Vasey & Rose [*A. kingii* var. *w.* (Vasey & Rose) Munz, *Sairocarpus w.* Vasey & Rose) D.A. Sutton] WATSON'S SNAPDRAGON Scarce; arroyos and flats, primarily on east side of main ridge.

13 Jul 1983, *Junak 1895*; 15 Mar 1995, *Junak 5879*; 15 Mar 1995, *Junak 5896*.

Simmondsiaceae (Jojoba Family)

Simmondsia chinensis (Link) C.Schneider JOJOBA or GOAT-NUT Rare; rock face in canyon in northeastern portion of island.

31 Mar 1987, *Junak 3282*.

Solanaceae (Nightshade Family)

Datura discolor Bernh. JIMSON WEED Scarce; scattered locations in northern and central portions of island. May not be native to the island; first collected in 1963.

21 Apr 1963, *Moran 10800* (SD); 10 Apr 1971, *Beauchamp 2184* (SD).

Lycium brevipes Benth. var. *brevipes* FRUTILLA Common; scattered locations throughout island.

17 Mar 1995, *Junak 5932*.

Lycium californicum Nutt. CALIFORNIA BOXTHORN Occasional; hilltop near north end of island.

24 Jun 1968, *Moran 15135* (SD,UC).

Nicotiana clevelandii A.Gray CLEVELAND'S TOBACCO Common; scattered locations throughout island.

10 Apr 1897, *Brandegee s.n.* (UC 103919); 21 Apr 1963, *Moran 10792* (SD); 31 Mar 1987, *Junak 3274*.

Zygophyllaceae (Caltrop Family)

Fagonia laevis Standl. FAGONIA Occasional; open sites on ridgetops near lighthouse.

23 Mar 1974, *Philbrick B74-38*; 14 Mar 1995, *Junak 5873*.

Monocotyledonous Flowering Plants

Agavaceae (Agave Family)

Agave sebastiana Greene [*A. shawii* var. *sebastiana* (Greene) Gentry] COASTAL AGAVE or MESCAL Occasional; scattered locations throughout island. Endemic to Baja California.

24 Jun 1968, *Moran 15142* (SD); 25 Mar 1974, *Philbrick & Benedict B74-74*; 13 Jul 1983, *Junak 1899*.

Poaceae (Grass Family)

*Eragrostis pectinacea (Michx.) Nees LOVEGRASS Rare; along trail at top of coastal bluffs on west central side of island. Probably not native on the island; first collected in 1995.

16 Mar 1995, *Junak 5927*.

*Phalaris minor Retz. MEDITERRANEAN CANARY GRASS Rare; disturbed flats on ridgetop north of lighthouse. First collected in 1995.

16 Mar 1995, *Junak 5920*.

*Zea mays L. CORN Rare; along trail just south of lighthouse. Probably will not persist or become naturalized. Known from a single collection of volunteer seedlings in 1974.

24 Mar 1974, *Philbrick & Benedict B74-72*.

Zosteraceae (Eel-Grass Family)

Phyllospadix scouleri Hook. SURF-GRASS Occasional; rocky intertidal and subtidal habitats around perimeter of island.

21 Apr 1963, *Moran 10783* (SD).

FLOWERING PLANTS OF THE SAN BENITO ISLANDS, BAJA CALIFORNIA, MEXICO

Steven A. Junak[1] and Ralph Philbrick[2]

[1]Santa Barbara Botanic Garden, 1212 Mission Canyon Road, Santa Barbara, CA 93105
(805) 682-4726 ext. 105, FAX (805) 563-0352, E-mail: sjunak@sbbg.org
[2]29 San Marcos Trout Club, Santa Barbara, CA 93105, (805) 967-0875

ABSTRACT

The San Benito Islands, comprising three islets with a combined area of just over 5 km², are located about 480 km south of the border between the United States and Mexico. They lie at the edge of the continental shelf, about 27 km west of Cedros Island and 66 km from the Baja California peninsula. A total of 51 native and naturalized plant taxa, representing 24 families and 42 genera, have been documented for the three islets. At least three of them are endemic to the San Benito Islands (*Dudleya linearis*, *Hemizonia streetsii*, and *Mammillaria neopalmeri*), while six others are restricted to two or more of the California Islands. Maritime desert scrub vegetation covers most of the landscape and annual wildflowers (like the endemic *Hemizonia*) can be extremely abundant in years with adequate rainfall. Of the nine nonnative plant taxa that have been found on the San Benitos, only two annual iceplants (*Mesembryanthemum crystallinum* and *M. nodiflorum*) are abundant. The terrestrial ecosystem has been degraded by nonnative herbivores for at least 50 years, but recent conservation actions have nearly put an end to destructive browsing. Introduced rabbits are still decimating native plant populations on the eastern islet, but have now been removed from the western and middle islets.

Keywords: San Benito Island, San Benito Islands, Isla San Benito, California Islands, Baja California, Mexico, endemic plants, flora, vegetation, botanical exploration, feral animals.

INTRODUCTION

The San Benito Islands are natural areas known for their rugged coastline, dramatic landscapes, nesting seabird populations, endemic plants and animals, and rocky beaches teeming with elephant seals and sea lions. Insects thought to be endemic to the San Benitos include a scorpion (*Vaejovis baueri*) (Williams 1980) and at least two tenebrionid beetles (*Helops benitensis* and *Stibia williamsi*) (Blaisdell 1943). An endemic land snail (*Xerarionta pandorae*) is known only from the San Benito Islands (Smith et al. 1990). Endemic subspecies of Leach's storm-petrel (*Oceanodroma leucorrhoa chapmani*), rock wren (*Salpinctes obsoletus tenuirostratus*), savannah sparrow (*Passerculus sandwichensis sanctorum*), and house finch (*Carpodacus mexicanus mcgregori*) have been described from the islands, although the McGregor house finch is now presumed to be extinct (Jehl 1971; Boswall 1978). An endemic subspecies of side-blotched lizard (*Uta stansburiana*) has also been reported from the San Benitos (Bostic 1975). At least three vascular plant taxa are endemic to the San Benitos (*Dudleya linearis*, *Hemizonia streetsii*, and *Mammillaria neopalmeri*) and six others are restricted to two or more of the California Islands.

For at least 50 years, the biota on these islands has been subjected to damage caused by feral animals, including burros, cats, and goats. Rabbits have been introduced during the last decade, threatening several endemic plant taxa. Human visitation has also increased during the last two decades, raising both the demand for information about the island's flora and the potential for nonnative plant introductions. We hope to promote further scientific investigations on this picturesque group of islands by providing here 1) an introduction to their geography and vegetation, 2) a short history of botanical exploration, 3) a description of historical changes in the vegetation and flora, and 4) an annotated checklist of the flowering plants.

PHYSICAL ENVIRONMENT

Eight islands lie off the west coast of Baja California between the United States/Mexico border and Punta Eugenia, located about 575 km (357 mi) south of the international border. Ranging in size from 0.4 to 348 km² (0.2 to 134 mi²), seven of the islands are on the continental shelf, and six of them lie within 23 km (14 mi) of the coastline. Situated near the edge of the continental shelf, the San Benito Islands are 66 km (41 mi) from the nearest point on the mainland but only 27 km (17 mi) from neighboring Cedros Island. Guadalupe is an oceanic island 252 km (157 mi) off the Baja California coast.

The San Benito Islands, centered near latitude 28° 18' 30" N and longitude 115° 34' 00" W, are situated about 480 km (300 mi) south of the border between the United States and Mexico. The San Benitos are three islets, named West San Benito (also known as San Benito Occidental or Benito del Oeste), Middle San Benito (San Benito Central or Benito del Centro), and East San Benito (San Benito Oriental or

Benito del Este). According to a recent survey (Carrasco 1978), the three islets have a combined area of 5.03 km² (1.94 mi²). It should be noted that this figure differs from earlier measurements of 6.4 km² (Philbrick 1967). Their coastline is rocky, but with several cobble beaches (see Figure 1). There are no permanent sources of fresh water on any of the islets.

West San Benito, the largest islet, has an area of about 3.46 km² (1.34 mi²) and is about 2.85 km (1.77 mi) long and 2.40 km (1.49 mi) wide at its widest point (Carrasco 1978). It has the most topographic diversity of the island group and is about 216 m (708 ft) high. The central part is elevated and relatively flat in several areas, with the high point just west of the middle. The central highlands are surrounded by elevated marine terraces. Several canyons on the north and south sides of the highlands provide moister habitats than the open slopes for plant life and provide some protection from strong winds.

A community of fishermen lives in a village at the southeastern end of the west islet, where there is a small cove and cobble beach protected from north and west swells. Up to 70 people live there for a part of the year (Donlan et al. 1999, this volume). These fishermen, who belong to a cooperative based at the cannery village on neighboring Cedros Island, harvest abalone and lobster seasonally. Fresh water, groceries, and supplies are delivered by boat. A trail system gives access to the north side of the islet and connects the village and two navigation lights on the northwestern and southern sides of the islet.

Middle San Benito lies just northeast of West San Benito, separated by a channel only 1.5 to 4.5 fathoms (9 to 27 ft) deep. Between Middle and East San Benito is Canal de Peck, 12 to 25 fathoms (72 to 150 ft) deep. Middle San Benito, the smallest islet, has an area of 0.53 km² (0.20 mi²) and is about 1.40 km (0.87 mi) long, and 0.80 km (0.50 mi) wide at its widest point (Carrasco 1978). This islet is mostly flat and has the least topographic diversity, gradually rising to a high point of about 25 m (82 ft) near the eastern end. Middle San Benito has no human inhabitants.

While the long axes of West and Middle San Benito run east and west, East San Benito has a north-south orientation. East San Benito, with an area of 1.04 km² (0.40 mi²), is about 2.40 km (1.49 mi) long and 1.50 km (0.93 mi) wide at its widest point (Carrasco 1978). Four conspicuous buttes, the tallest reaching an elevation of about 138 m (453 ft), dominate the topography, with a few smaller hills scattered around them. Coastal terraces surround the buttes and hills and form most of the perimeter of the island. East Benito has no human residents.

The geology of the San Benito Islands was studied by Van West (1958) and by Cohen et al. (1963). These islands are of considerable interest to geologists because they are near the interface between the oceanic and continental crusts. The islands consist of a folded and sheared synclinal sequence of graywacke, chert, basalt, altered basalt and carbonate, serpentinite, and glaucophane rocks of Jurassic age. Cohen et al. (1963) reported that the association of rocks

Figure 1. View of Middle and East San Benito from the highlands of West San Benito Island (photo taken by S. Junak on 27 February 1997).

found on the San Benitos is closely related to the Franciscan rocks of California.

No weather records are available for the San Benito Islands, but the climate can be estimated from a station on neighboring Cedros Island and two on the adjacent mainland. Limited precipitation and temperature records, for 4 to 6 year spans, are available for a site near the village on Isla Cedros (latitude 28° 04' N, longitude 115° 14' W, elevation 500 m), Vizcaino (27° 58' N, 114° 07' W, elevation n.a.), and Bahia Tortugas (27° 43' N, 114° 56' W, elevation 5 m) (Hastings 1964). All these stations have an arid climate, with mean annual precipitation ranging from 65.1 to 121.3 mm (2.6 to 4.8 in). About 95 to 96% of the precipitation falls in the fall and winter, between September and March. December, January, and February are usually the wettest months.

Rainfall on the San Benitos and on neighboring Cedros Island is generally very sporadic with long periods of drought. Between 1 January 1945 and 31 December 1947, personnel at the weather station on Cedros Island recorded rain on only 20 days (5 days in 1945, 6 in 1946, and 9 in 1947) (Osorio Tafall 1948). Although the winter months are usually the wettest, no rain at all fell on Cedros Island between 6 June 1945 and 12 August 1946! Heavy rainstorms associated with tropical cyclones can drop significant amounts of moisture in the late summer or early fall. Such a storm dropped 36.5 mm (1.4 in) of rain on Cedros Island on 28 September 1946 (Osorio Tafall 1948). A water spout destroyed most of the village on West San Benito in early 1992 (S. Vogel, pers. comm. 1993).

Mean annual temperatures at these three weather stations range from 19.0 to 20.6°C (66.2-69.1°F). Typically, the coolest months are January and February, with mean monthly temperatures ranging from 15.3 to 17.6°C (59.5 to 63.7°F) for January and from 16.4 to 17.3°C (61.5 to 63.1°F) for February. August and September are typically the warmest months, with mean monthly temperatures ranging from 23.2 to 25.1°C (73.8 to 77.2°F) for August and from 22.8 to 25.5°C (73.0 to 77.9°F) for September.

HISTORY OF BOTANICAL EXPLORATION

Thomas H. Streets, on the U.S. Navy surveying expedition of the North Pacific between 1873 and 1875, collected the first known botanical specimens from the San Benito Islands in December 1875. San Benito Island tarweed (*Hemizonia streetsii*) and San Benito Island bush mallow (*Lavatera venosa,* now known as *Malva pacifica*) were described from his collections. Streets apparently collected specimens of other plants as well, including island poppy (*Eschscholzia ramosa*).

Charles F. Pond, a U.S. Navy Lieutenant serving on the U.S.S. *Ranger* during a survey of Baja California's coastline and islands, made the next botanical collections on the San Benitos. His discoveries on the island were reported by Edward L. Greene of the University of California at Berkeley (Greene 1889). According to Greene, Pond visited West San Benito several times between December 1888 and February 1889 and also landed on East San Benito. Pond collected additional plant specimens on Los Coronados, San Martin, Cedros, and Asuncion islands between December 1888 and June 1889 (Nelson 1921, Notre Dame-Greene Herbarium 1987).

Edward F. Palmer visited West San Benito on 25 March 1889, while collecting plants for the U.S. Department of Agriculture (McVaugh 1956). He also visited Los Coronados, Guadalupe, and Cedros islands in 1888 and 1889. Palmer's observations and collections from the Mexican islands were published by George Vasey and Joseph N. Rose (1890) of the U.S. Department of Agriculture. The only nonnative plant observed by the early collectors on the San Benitos (Pond and Palmer) was crystalline iceplant (*Mesembryanthemum crystallinum*).

In 1896, field biologist and ornithologist Alfred W. Anthony chartered a schooner and explored the west coast of Baja California (Nelson 1921). During this voyage, he collected plants on the San Benito Islands sometime between July and October 1896.

In the spring of 1897, A. W. Anthony and a number of other scientists visited most of the islands off the west coast of Baja California on Anthony's schooner *Wahlberg* (Brandegee 1900; Moran 1952). Anthony and Townshend S. Brandegee of the University of California at Berkeley both collected plants on the San Benito Islands during the last week of March. Brandegee (1900) reported 14 plant taxa that had not previously been documented for the island, including the nonnative slender sow thistle (*Sonchus tenerrimus*).

During the first quarter of the twentieth century, two expeditions sponsored by the California Academy of Sciences stopped at the San Benitos, but only a few botanical specimens have been preserved. The first of these trips was in the spring of 1903, when the Academy organized a journey aboard the schooner *Mary Sachs*. F. E. Barkelew reportedly collected botanical specimens from the San Benito Islands, but they were apparently destroyed by the San Francisco fire in April 1906 (Nelson 1921).

The schooner *Academy* stopped at the San Benito Islands in mid-July 1905, while en route to the Galapagos Islands on another expedition sponsored by the California Academy of Sciences (Slevin 1931). The scientific party visited West San Benito on 14 July and landed on both Middle and East San Benito on 15 July. Additional trips were made to both West and East San Benito on 17 July. The botanist on this voyage, Alban Stewart, collected a few specimens from the San Benitos, including San Benito Island tarweed (*Hemizonia streetsii*).

Joseph N. Rose, of the U.S. National Museum and Carnegie Institution of Washington, collected on the San Benito Islands on 9 March 1911. He was aboard the *Albatross* expedition to Baja California, which was sponsored by the American Museum of Natural History.

P. J. Rempel of the University of Southern California collected terrestrial plants on West San Benito Island in mid-July 1937. He was on an expedition aboard the *Velero III* sponsored by the Allan Hancock Foundation (Fraser 1943; Gentry 1949). Rempel collected small-flowered iceplant (*Mesembryanthemum nodiflorum*), apparently the third nonnative plant species to establish populations on the San Benitos. Rempel also collected plants on Cedros Island during the same voyage.

During the 1940s, '50s, and '60s, Reid Moran and George Lindsay were the primary collectors on the San Benitos. Their first trip to West San Benito was on 18-20 April 1948 (Moran and Lindsay 1949). Moran later became curator of botany at the San Diego Museum of Natural History. Lindsay collected plants on the San Benitos on 5-6 February 1950; he subsequently became director of the San Diego Museum of Natural History and then the California Academy of Sciences (Mitch 1989). Moran returned to West San Benito on 24 May 1952 during an expedition to the Gulf of California aboard the *Orca* (Lindsay 1952) and collected plants from all three San Benito Islands on 18-19 April 1963, while on an expedition aboard the yacht *Gringa*. Darley F. Howe and entomologist C. F. Harbison of the San Diego Natural History Museum visited West San Benito on 8-9 November 1966. While she was a graduate student at San Jose State College, Joyce MacFall Roderick collected a few specimens on West Benito in December 1966 (Roderick and Roderick 1967).

During the 1970s, Reid Moran was the most frequent botanical visitor to the San Benitos. He visited West and East San Benito on 19-20 April 1970, on a return trip from Guadalupe Island. Moran made additional trips to the San Benitos on 25 May 1971 (middle islet), 24 January 1972 (west islet), 26 March 1973 (west islet), 25 March 1974 (west islet), and 12 May 1979 (west islet). Other collectors on West San Benito during this decade included R. Mitchel Beauchamp of San Diego (on 8 February and 4 April 1971, and on 28 February 1972), Gilbert A. Voss of the Quail Botanical Gardens (on 13 February 1972), Edward F. Anderson of Whitman College (on 8 January 1973), Mark Hoefs of the Wrigley Botanical Garden (on 19 January 1975), and James Henrickson of California State University at Los

Angeles (on 19 January 1975). Beauchamp also collected on East San Benito on 28 February 1972. Ralph Philbrick collected plants from West Benito on 20 January 1975 and Michael Benedict visited the same islet on February 23rd of the same year; both were collecting specimens for the Santa Barbara Botanic Garden. Christopher Davidson of the Los Angeles County Museum of Natural History collected plants on West San Benito on 19 February 1977; Elizabeth McClintock of the California Academy of Sciences and Wilda Ross collected there on 19 February 1978.

During the 1980s, botanists from Rancho Santa Ana and Santa Barbara botanic gardens made several trips to the San Benitos. Ralph Philbrick and Peter Schuyler of the Santa Barbara Botanic Garden landed on the east islet on 4-5 July 1983, while Marla Daily and Steve Junak collected plants on West San Benito. Robert F. Thorne, of Rancho Santa Ana Botanic Garden, visited the west islet on 31 January 1985 and on 16 February 1986. Steve Junak collected on the east islet on 28-29 March 1987 and returned to West San Benito on March 29th, along with Marla Daily. Other collectors on West San Benito during the 1980s included Thomas Oberbauer of San Diego (on 17 February 1981 and 11 January 1983).

In the 1990s, Steve Junak made several additional trips to West San Benito, on 12 March 1991, 15 March 1993, 3 March 1996, 27 February 1997, and 27 February 1998. He also visited East San Benito on 2 March 1996, along with several other botanists from southern California. Patricia West of Flagstaff, Arizona collected a number of voucher specimens on West and East San Benito on 3-14 December 1997.

In summary, at least 30 botanists have collected specimens during more than 40 trips to the San Benito Islands. Undoubtedly additional botanists, especially from Mexico, have also visited the islands, but we have not seen their collections.

HISTORICAL CHANGES IN THE VEGETATION AND FLORA

The island's vegetation has been disturbed by decades of human activities and by introduced herbivores, including burros, goats, and, most recently, rabbits. No herbivores were noted by early visitors to the islands (e.g., Brandegee 1900; Thayer and Bangs 1907; Hanna 1925). By 1918, there was a lobster camp on West San Benito, and a Japanese abalone camp was there in 1922 (Hanna 1925). Cats had apparently been introduced by early residents or visitors and were having a significant effect on nesting sea birds by 1922 (Hanna 1925).

Several shrubs (*Mirabilis californica*, *Trixis angustifolia*, and *Viguiera lanata*) reported by Greene (1889) have not been seen by subsequent visitors. *Dudleya albiflora* was apparently collected by Alban Stewart in 1905, but has not been seen since. These native plants may have been extirpated on the San Benitos by introduced herbivores.

By the time that Moran and Lindsay visited the islands in 1948, burros and goats had been introduced to West San Benito and were eating some of the plants, including the endemic San Benito Island bush mallow (*Lavatera venosa* or *Malva pacifica*) and San Benito Island live-for-ever (*Dudleya linearis*). Moran (1948) reported that *Lavatera* was then "uncommon on the island because of burros and goats." Lindsay (1950) stated that "... *Lavatera* is found on all three of the San Benito Islands, but is most common on Middle Benito, where it has not been destroyed by goats." Moran and Lindsay (1951:78-80) reported "wild goats and two or three burros" and stated that "at the time of our visit, it [*Lavatera*] was scarcely to be found on the main island; like its cousin of the California islands, it seems to be a favorite of browsing animals and hence is now nearly confined to the rocks offshore." They found only a few living plants of *Dudleya linearis* on the western islet and observed that "... many dead caudices showed that it had been quite common until recently. Apparently the burros ... and goats are rapidly exterminating the *Dudleya*." Moran (1951:191) reported that "In 1948, there were few living plants of *Dudleya linearis* on the west island of the San Benito group, and only three were found in flower. Many dead caudices showed that this plant had recently been more common. Apparently burros like to exterminate it. However, on the east island, where burros are absent, I found no plants at all of *Dudleya*."

No goats were seen on the San Benitos Islands by Philbrick or Junak during any of their visits between 1975 and 1992. Burros, however, were seen many times during the same time period, usually in small bands of three to six animals. Boswall (1978) saw four dogs, nine burros, and one goat during a three-week stay on West San Benito in 1975. In the early 1990s, rabbits were introduced and goats were re-introduced to West San Benito. According to residents on West San Benito, there were a few rabbits there in 1993, about 20 goats that had been there for about six months, and 8 to 10 burros (Pers. comm. to S. Junak, March 1993). By 1995, the rabbits and goats were having a marked effect on some plants of West San Benito, especially the endemic live-forever (*Dudleya linearis*) (S. Vogel, pers. comm. 1995). By March 1996, live dudleyas were extremely rare on the islet; numerous dead caudices were seen in several canyons on the north side (S. Junak, pers. obs.).

Rabbits were also introduced to East San Benito sometime before the spring of 1996. They were common there in March 1996; it was an extremely dry year on the island and the rabbits were eating the bark of cliff spurge (*Euphorbia misera*) which has a caustic milky juice (S. Junak, pers. obs.).

Thanks to the cooperative efforts of the Island Conservation and Ecology Group and the Mexican Office of National Protected Areas, rabbit and goat removal began on West San Benito in early 1998 (Donlan et al.1999, this volume). Over a seven-month period, over 400 rabbits were removed from West San Benito by hunting and/or trapping. About 15 rabbits were also removed from Middle San Benito during the same time period (Donlan et al. 1999, this volume). West and Middle San Benito are now reportedly free of rabbits and goats; rabbits remain on East San Benito however. Burros remain on West Benito, where they are used to transport supplies to the lighthouses on the island, but they have been corralled and imported food is now provided for them (Donlan et al. 1999, this volume).

At least nine nonnative plant taxa have been introduced onto the San Benitos, most of them since the 1970s (see Table 1). Annual iceplants (*Mesembryanthemum crystallinum* and *M. nodiflorum*) are currently the most abundant of the introduced plants. At present, the other plant taxa that have been introduced to the islands grow in scattered populations and do not dominate large areas.

In summary, a continued presence of herbivores on all three islets would undoubtedly have had deleterious effects on the unique plant life of the San Benitos. Goats have decimated the flora of Guadalupe Island (Moran 1996), while sheep and rabbits nearly drove the endemic *Dudleya* on Santa Barbara Island to extinction (Philbrick 1972; Moran 1978). The recent conservation actions on West and Middle Benito may have saved several unique plants from extinction. At times, the abundance and distribution of some endemic plant species, notably the San Benito Island bush mallow (*Malva pacifica*) and San Benito Island live-forever (*Dudleya linearis*), have been drastically affected by introduced herbivores. Several native shrubs that were reported in the late 1890s have not been seen in recent years and may have disappeared from the San Benitos because of herbivores.

VEGETATION

The terrestrial vegetation on the San Benito Islands is characterized by low-growing, widely spaced, drought-resistant shrubs and stem succulents with large open spaces between them. In years with adequate rainfall, annual plants occupy many of these open spaces for a month or more.

The dominant plant community is maritime desert scrub. This vegetation type consists almost entirely of low perennials, with no trees and few shrubs taller than one meter. The tallest plants on the islands are coastal agave (*Agave sebastiana*), which is abundant and conspicuous on slopes, and old man cactus (*Lophocereus schottii*), which grows only in an isolated colony on East San Benito. Dominant perennial species in the maritime cactus scrub include the shrubs and suffrutescent perennials *Agave sebastiana, Euphorbia misera, Frankenia palmeri, Lycium brevipes, L. californicum, Malva pacifica, Suaeda moquinii,* and the cacti *Mammillaria neopalmeri* and *Opuntia* sp. nova. The cover of the perennial species is not continuous, and short-lived or ephemeral taxa dominate some areas. Large numbers of winter annuals, including *Calandrinia maritima, Cryptantha* spp., *Eschscholzia ramosa, Hemizonia streetsii,* and *Perityle emoryi,* grow in open sites between the larger plants after rainstorms. A perennial herb with a subterranean corm (*Dichelostemma capitatum*) is locally common but is active only while soil moisture is high.

Table 1. Dates of first known records of nonnative plants on the San Benito Islands.

Plant	Date of first known record*
Mesembryanthemum crystallinum	1889
Sonchus tenerrimus	1897
Mesembryanthemum nodiflorum	1937
Malva parviflora	1970
Chenapodium murale	1972
Melilotus indicus	1979
Cakile maritima	1993
Datura discolor	1997
Erodium moschatum	1998

*See text and appendix for additional information.

Canyons on the north side of West San Benito support a rich mixture of native plants, some of which are found only on north-facing slopes. In years with adequate rainfall, *Malva pacifica* is extremely abundant and is a conspicuous dominant. Rocky canyon walls support populations of *Agave sebastiana, Dudleya linearis, Encelia asperifolia, Euphorbia misera, Phacelia ixodes, Petalonyx linearis,* and *Senecio cedrosensis.* Native annuals like *Aphanisma blitoides, Cryptantha maritima, Cryptantha patula, Eschscholzia ramosa,* and *Perityle emoryi* can be abundant in canyon bottoms in wet years.

Sandy and gravelly areas near the shore, especially on the north side of West San Benito, support small patches of depauperate coastal strand vegetation. Dominant species here include *Atriplex barclayana, Cakile maritima, Frankenia palmeri,* and *Suaeda moquinii. Frankenia* and *Suaeda* dominate large areas of alkaline flats around the perimeter of the islands, along with *Mesembryanthemum crystallinum* and *M. nodiflorum.* In rocky intertidal and subtidal habitats around the margin of the island, *Phyllospadix scouleri* and *P. torreyi* grow in a surf-grass community.

Introduced annuals are common along trails used by burros and humans and in areas disturbed by seabird activity. *Mesembryanthemum crystallinum* and *M. nodiflorum* cover large areas around the island's perimeter, while *Chenopodium murale* and *Malva parviflora* grow in scattered patches.

FLORA

The documented flora of the San Benito Islands includes 51 vascular plant taxa representing 24 families and 42 genera (see Appendix). Four additional plant taxa (*Errazurizia benthamii, Mirabilis californica, Trixis angustifolia,* and *Viguiera lanata*) have been reported in the literature but no voucher specimens have been found to date, so they are not included in the statistics given here. The largest families are the Asteraceae (seven taxa), Chenopodiaceae (five taxa), and Cactaceae (four taxa). Genera represented by two taxa include *Atriplex, Cryptantha, Lepidium, Lycium, Mesembryanthemum,* and *Phyllospadix*.

Native and Endemic Plant Taxa

A total of 42 plant taxa presumed to be native have been documented for the San Benito Islands to date. Plant families with the highest number of native taxa are Asteraceae (six taxa), Cactaceae (four taxa), and Chenopodiaceae (four taxa). The genera *Atriplex, Cryptantha, Lepidium, Lycium,* and *Phyllospadix* are each represented by two native taxa.

Many of the native plant taxa found on the San Benitos are endemic to Baja California. At least nine of them are restricted to the California Islands or offshore rocks and are not found on the adjacent mainland. Three plant taxa are known only from the San Benito Islands (*Dudleya linearis, Hemizonia streetsii,* and *Mammillaria neopalmeri*). Four taxa (*Ferocactus chrysacanthus, Mentzelia hirsutissima* var. *nesiotes, Opuntia* sp. nova, and *Senecio cedrosensis*) are found only on the San Benitos and neighboring islands. Two other insular endemics (*Eschscholzia ramosa* and *Malva pacifica*) are more widespread but are not found on the mainland. One additional taxon (*Cryptantha patula*) may also be endemic to the San Benito Islands, but its relationship with other species on the Baja California mainland needs further study.

Nonnative Plant Taxa

At least nine plant taxa in eight families and eight genera have been introduced to the San Benitos, primarily since the 1970s (see Table 1). These introductions represent about 17% of the island's total flora. By comparison, known percentages of nonnative plants on the other islands off the west coast of Baja California range from about 18% (Natividad Island) to about 50% (San Geronimo Island). Six of the island's nonnative plants originated in Europe and two taxa are native to South Africa. The only plant family represented on the San Benitos solely by nonnative taxa is the Aizoaceae. The Aizoaceae is also the only family with more than one introduced taxon, namely two species of *Mesembryanthemum*. On the San Benitos, all of the introduced plant taxa are annual plants. Conspicuously absent from these desert islands are the invasive European grasses found on many of the other islands off the west coast of Baja California.

One additional plant may have been introduced to the San Benitos. *Plantago ovata*, presumed at this point to be native to the San Benitos, is also known from all of the California Channel Islands and from Guadalupe, Cedros, and Natividad islands. Although it was among the first plants reported for the San Benitos, this *Plantago* may be a very early introduction from the Mediterranean area of Europe (Dempster 1993).

ACKNOWLEDGMENTS

The authors gratefully acknowledge the help of Michael Benedict, Marla Daily, Josh Donlan, Wayne Ferrren, Judy Gibson, Mark Hoefs, Reid Moran, Jon Rebman, Bob Thorne, Steve Vogel, Gil Voss, and Patty West, who kindly shared their observations and/or information on collections from the San Benito Islands. Reid Moran and an anonymous reviewer made many useful comments on earlier versions of this paper. We thank the curators and staff of the following institutions for their hospitality and for loaning selected specimens: California Academy of Sciences, Harvard University, New York Botanical Garden, Notre Dame University, Rancho Santa Ana Botanic Garden, San Diego Natural History Museum, Smithsonian Institution, and University of California at Berkeley. We thank Scott Miller for information on endemic insects. We would also like to thank the Mexican government for allowing access to their islands and the residents of West San Benito Island for their warm hospitality. Funding for field trips was provided by the Santa Barbara Botanic Garden.

LITERATURE CITED

Abrams, L. 1923-1960. Illustrated Flora of the Pacific states: Washington, Oregon, and California. Stanford. University Press, Stanford, CA. 4 volumes. 2771 pp.

Beauchamp, R. M. 1986. A Flora of San Diego County, California. Sweetwater River Press, National City, CA. 241 pp.

Blaisdell, F. E. 1943. Contributions toward a knowledge of the insect fauna of Lower California, Number 7. Coleoptera: Tenebrionidae. Proceedings of the California Academy of Sciences (Fourth Series) 24:171-288.

Bostic, D .L. 1975. A Natural History Guide to the Pacific Coast of North Central Baja California and Adjacent Islands. Biological Educational Expeditions, Vista, CA. 184 pp.

Boswall, J. 1978. The birds of the San Benito Islands, Lower California, Mexico. Bristol Ornithology 11:23-32.

Brandegee, T S. 1900. Voyage of the *Wahlberg*. Zoe 5(2):19-28.

Britton, N. L. and J. N. Rose. 1919. The Cactaceae. Publication 248, Volume 1. Carnegie Institution of Washington, Washington, DC. 236 pp.

Brummitt, R. K. and C. E. Powell (eds.) 1992. Authors of Plant Names. Royal Botanic Gardens, Kew, Great Britain. 732 pp.

Carrasco, M. F. 1978. Las Islas de Baja California. Comisión Agraria Mixta, Mexicali, México. 121 pp.

Cohen, L. H., K. C. Condie, L. J. Kuest, Jr., G .S. MacKenzie, F. H. Meister, P. Pushkar, and A. M. Stueber. 1963. Geology of the San Benito Islands, Baja California, Mexico. Geological Society of America Bulletin 74:1355-1370.

Coyle, J. and N. C. Roberts. 1975. A Field Guide to the Common and Interesting Plants of Baja California. Natural History Publishing Company, La Jolla, CA. 206 pp.

Dempster, L. T. 1993. Plantaginaceae. Pages 820-821 *in* Hickman, J. C. (ed.), The Jepson Manual: Higher Plants of California. University of California Press, Berkeley, Los Angeles, and London.

Donlan, C. J., B. R. Tershy, B. S. Keitt, J. A. Sanchez, B. Wood, A. Weinstein, D. A. Croll, and M. A. Hermosillo. 1999. Island conservation action in northwest Mèxico. Pages 330 to 338 *in* Browne, D. R., K. L. Mitchell, and H. W. Chaney (eds.), Proceedings of the Fifth California Islands Symposium. 29 March to 1 April 1999. Santa Barbara Museum of Natural History, Santa Barbara, CA. Sponsored by the U.S. Minerals Management Service, Pacific OCS Region, 770 Paseo Camarillo, Camarillo, CA 93010. OCS Study No. 99-0038.

Fraser, C. M. 1943. General account of the scientific work of the *Velero III* in the eastern Pacific, 1931-1941. Part I. Historical introduction, *Velero III*, personnel. Allan Hancock Pacific Expeditions 1(1):1-48.

Gentry, H. S. 1949. Land plants collected by the *Velero III,* Allan Hancock Pacific Expeditions 1937-1941. Allan Hancock Pacific Expeditions 13(2):1-245.

Greene, E. L. 1889. The vegetation of the San Benito Islands and a list of plants. Pittonia 1:261-266.

Hanna, G. D. 1925. Expedition to Guadalupe Island, Mexico, in 1922. Proceedings of the California Academy of Sciences (Fourth Series) 14:217-275.

Hastings, J. R. 1964. Climatological data for Baja California. Technical Reports on the Meteorology and Climatology of Arid Regions 14. University of Arizona, Tucson, AZ. 132 pp.

Hickman, J. C. (ed.) 1993. The Jepson Manual: Higher Plants of California. University of California Press, Berkeley, Los Angeles, and London. 1400 pp.

Holmgren, P. K., N. H. Holmgren, and L C. Barnett. 1990. Index Herbariorum, Part I: The herbaria of the world. Eighth edition. Regnum Vegetabile 120:1-693.

Jehl, J. R. 1971. The status of *Carpodacus mcgregori.* Condor 73:375-376.

Lindsay, G. 1952. The Sefton Foundation-Stanford University expedition to the Gulf of California in 1952. Belvedere Scientific Fund.

Lindsay, G. 1996. The Taxonomy and Ecology of the Genus *Ferocactus.* Tireless Termite Press, San Diego, CA. 444 pp.

Martínez, M. 1979. Catálogo de Nombres Vulgares y Científicos de Plantas Mexicanas. Fondo de Cultura Económica, México, D.F.

McVaugh, R. 1956. Edward Palmer, Plant Explorer of the American West. University of Oklahoma Press, Norman. 430 pp.

Mitich, L. W. 1989. George E. Lindsay, explorer and plantsman: Part 2. Cactus and Succulent Journal 61:17-21.

Moran, R. 1952. The Mexican itineraries of T. S. Brandegee. Madroño 11:221-252.

Moran, R. 1996. The flora of Guadalupe Island, Mexico. Memoirs of the California Academy of Sciences 19:1-190.

Moran, R. 1978. Resurrection of *Dudleya traskiae.* Fremontia 5(4):37-38.

Moran, R. and G. Lindsay. 1949. Desert islands of Baja California. Desert Plant Life 22:125-128.

Moran, R. and G. Lindsay. 1951. San Benito Islands. Desert Plant Life 23:78-83.

Nelson, E. W. 1921. Lower California and its natural resources. Memoirs of the National Academy of Sciences 16:1-194.

Osorio Tafall, B. F. 1948. La Isla de Cedros, Baja California. Boletín de la Sociedad Mexicana de Geografía y Estadística 66:317-402.

Philbrick, R. 1967. Introduction. Pages 3-8 *in* Philbrick, R. (ed.), Proceedings of the Symposium on the Biology of the California Islands. Santa Barbara Botanic Garden, Santa Barbara, CA.

Philbrick, R. 1972. The plants of Santa Barbara Island, California. Madroño 21:329-393.

Roderick, D. and J. M. Roderick. 1967. Destination: San Benito Islands. Pacific Discovery 20(6):1-9.

Slevin, J. R. 1931. Log of the Schooner *Academy* on a voyage of scientific research to the Galapagos Islands, 1905-1906. Occasional Papers of the California Academy of Sciences 17:1-162.

Smith, A. G., W. B. Miller, C. C. Christensen, and B. Roth. 1990. Land mollusca of Baja California, Mexico. Proceedings of the California Academy of Sciences (Fourth Series) 47:95-158.

Thayer, J. E. and O. Bangs. 1907. Birds collected by W. W. Brown, Jr. on Cerros [sic], San Benito, and Natividad islands in the spring of 1906, with notes on the biota of the islands. Condor 9:77-81.

Vasey, G. and J. N. Rose. 1890. List of plants collected by Dr. Edward Palmer in 1889. Contributions from the U.S. National Herbarium 1:9-28

Wiggins, I. L. 1940. Taxonomic notes on the genus *Dalea* Juss. and related genera as represented in the Sonoran Desert. Contributions of the Dudley Herbarium 3:41-64.

Wiggins, I .L. 1980. Flora of Baja California. Stanford University Press, Stanford, CA. 1025 pp.

Williams, S. C. 1980. Scorpions of Baja California, Mexico, and adjacent islands. Occasional Papers of the California Academy of Sciences 135:1-127.

SOURCES OF UNPUBLISHED MATERIALS

Lindsay, G. 1950. Label data for herbarium specimen collected on Middle San Benito Island on 5 Feb 1950 (*Lindsay 1823*) deposited at University of California, Berkeley, CA.

Moran, R. 1948. Label data for herbarium specimen collected on West San Benito Island on 18 Apr 1948 (*Moran 2948*) deposited at University of California, Berkeley, CA.

Moran, R. 1951. A revision of *Dudleya* (Crassulaceae). Unpublished Ph.D. dissertation, University of California, Berkeley, CA. 295 pp.

Notre Dame-Greene Herbarium. 1987. Computer database printout of 212 botanical specimens collected by Charles F. Pond in Lower California and deposited in the Notre Dame-Greene Herbarium, University of Notre Dame, Notre Dame, Indiana. Unpublished manuscript on file, Santa Barbara Botanic Garden, CA.

Rebman, J. San Diego Natural History Museum, Balboa Park, San Diego, California 92112. Personal communication to S. Junak in 1997.

Van West, O. 1958. Geology of the San Benito Islands and the southwest part of Cedros Island, Baja California, Mexico. Unpublished M.A. thesis, Claremont Graduate School, Claremont, CA. 78 pp.

Vogel, S. Cabrillo Marine Aquarium, 3720 Stephen White Drive, San Pedro, California 90731. Personal communications to S. Junak in 1993 and 1995.

APPENDIX

ANNOTATED CATALOG OF THE FLOWERING PLANTS OF THE SAN BENITO ISLANDS

Plants listed in this table are arranged alphabetically by family within two major plant groups (dicotyledonous and monocotyledonous flowering plants). Taxa presumed to be introduced to Baja California and/or the San Benito Islands by human activities are preceded by an asterisk (*). The list does not include plant taxa that have been planted at the village unless they are surviving without cultivation in other parts of the islands. Unsubstantiated reports (reports for which no voucher specimen has been found) are enclosed in braces (i.e., { }).

For most taxa, nomenclature follows Wiggins (1980) or Hickman (1993). Abbreviations of author names have been mostly standardized according to Brummitt and Powell (1992). Selected synonyms are shown in brackets (i.e., [ ]). Common names are mostly according to Abrams (1923-1960) and Hickman (1993), with a few additions from Beauchamp (1986), Coyle and Roberts (1975), and Martinez (1979).

Abundance ratings (rare, scarce, occasional, common, and abundant) and distribution descriptions are based on observations of the authors. Dates of first known collection or report from the San Benitos are included for nonnative taxa.

Up to five voucher specimens are cited for each taxon. These are arranged first by islet (i.e., WSBe for West San Benito Island, MSBe for Middle Island, and ESBe for East Island) and then chronologically by date of collection. Labels on some early voucher specimens did not include precise locality information; these are cited as SBe (for San Benito Island). Specimens without date of collection are cited as "n.d."; those collections without collector's number are listed as "s.n.". Abbreviations for herbaria are those used in Holmgren et al. (1990). Herbarium accession numbers are cited only if there is no collector number.

Dicotyledonous Flowering Plants

Aizoaceae (Iceplant Family)

Mesembryanthemum crystallinum L. CRYSTALLINE ICEPLANT Common; disturbed flats and slopes on west and east islets. First reported by Greene (1889). Palmer reported that this taxon was "very plentiful" on the west islet (Vasey and Rose 1890).
WSBe, 19 Jan 1975, *Henrickson 14514a* (RSA-POM); WSBe, 31 Jan 1985, *Thorne 58467* (RSA-POM).

Mesembryanthemum nodiflorum L. SLENDER-LEAVED ICEPLANT, SMALL-FLOWERED ICEPLANT Common; disturbed flats on all islets. First collected on the west islet in 1937.
WSBe, 14-15 Jul 1937, *Rempel 369* (RSA-POM); WSBe, 14-15 Jul 1937, *Rempel 371* (RSA-POM); WSBe, 18 Apr 1948, *Moran 2949* (UC); WSBe, 19 Jan 1975, *Henrickson 14514b* (RSA-POM).

Asteraceae (Sunflower Family)

Amblyopappus pusillus Hook. & Arn. PINEAPPLE WEED Occasional; slope and flats, especially around perimeters, on all islets.
SBe, 9 Mar 1911, *Rose 16052* (GH, NY); WSBe, 7 Feb 1972, *Beauchamp 3178* (SD); ESBe, 6 Feb 1950, *Lindsay 1832* (UC).

Encelia asperifolia (S.F.Blake) Clark & Kyhos [*E. californica* var. *asperifolia* S.F.Blake] BUSH SUNFLOWER Scarce; slopes and canyon walls on west islet.
SBe, 27 Mar 1897, *Brandegee s.n.* (UC 135059); WSBe, 9 Nov 1966, *Howe s.n.* (SD 67083); WSBe, 31 Jan 1985, *Thorne 58475* (RSA-POM, UC).

Hemizonia streetsii A.Gray SAN BENITO ISLAND TARWEED Common; slopes and flats of all islets. Can be very abundant in years with sufficient rainfall. Endemic to the San Benito Islands.
   SBe, 25 Mar 1889, *Palmer 720* (CAS, NY); WSBe, 24 May 1952, *Moran 4189* (DS); MSBe, 19 Apr 1963, *Moran 10754* (SD, UC); ESBe, 20 Apr 1970, *Moran 17443* (SD).

Perityle californica Benth. Scarce; flats and arroyos on north side of west islet.
   WSBe, 25 Mar 1974, *Moran 21169* (SD); WSBe, 13 Feb 1972, *Voss 1211* (SD); WSBe, 29 Mar 1987, *Junak 3235* (SBBG).

Perityle emoryi Torr. [*P.grayi* Rose] EMORY'S ROCK DAISY Common; flats and arroyos on all islets.
   SBe, Feb 1889, *Pond s.n.* (ND-G 061166); WSBe, 8 Jan 1973, *Anderson 3218* (RSA-POM); MSBe, 5 Feb 1950, *Lindsay 1825* (SD, UC).

Senecio cedrosensis Greene CEDROS ISLAND RAGWORT Occasional; rocky canyon walls on north side of west islet. Endemic to West San Benito and Cedros islands. Foliage on plants from West San Benito is strongly scented while plants on Cedros are unscented; the San Benito population needs further study and may represent an undescribed taxon.
   WSBe, 24 Jan 1972, *Moran 19060* (SD); WSBe, 26 Mar 1973, *Moran 20314* (SD); WSBe, 23 Feb 1975, *Benedict s.n.* (SBBG 53386).

Sonchus tenerrimus L. SLENDER SOW-THISTLE Occasional; slopes, flats, and arroyos on west islet. First reported for the island by Brandegee (1900).
   WSBe, 7 Feb 1972, *Beauchamp 3174* (SD); WSBe, 25 Mar 1974, *Moran 21170* (SD); WSBe, 16 Feb 1986, *Thorne 61507* (RSA-POM).

{*Trixis californica* Kellogg Reported (as *T. angustifolia* A.Gray) for west islet by Greene (1889); no specimen has been found.}

{*Viguiera lanata* (Kellogg) A.Gray Reported for west islet by Greene (1889); no specimen has been found.}

Boraginaceae (Borage Family)

Cryptantha maritima (Greene) Greene var. *maritima* [*Krynitzkia m.* Greene] GUADALUPE ISLAND CRYPTANTHA Common; flats and arroyos on north side of west islet.
   SBe, 28 Apr 1897, *Brandegee s.n.* (NY, UC 78552); WSBe, 26 Mar 1973, *Moran 20312* (RSA-POM, SD); WSBe, 15 Mar 1993, *Junak 5305* (SBBG).

Cryptantha patula Greene SAN BENITO ISLAND CRYPTANTHA Scarce; flats and arroyos on north side of west islet. Only seen in wet years. May be endemic to the San Benito Islands; the relationship of this taxon with *C. pondii* needs further study.
   SBe, 1889, *Pond s.n.* (ND-G 001388); SBe, 27 Mar 1897, *Brandegee s.n.* (UC 78590); WSBe, 15 Mar 1993, *Junak 5308* (NY,RSA,SBBG,UC); WSBe, 15 Mar 1993, *Junak 5321* (RSA,SBBG,SD,US).

Brassicaceae (Mustard Family)

Cakile maritima Scop. SEA ROCKET Scarce; beaches at northeastern side of west islet. First collected on the island in 1993.
   WSBe, 15 Mar 1993, *Junak 5312* (SBBG); WSBe, 27 Feb 1998, *Junak 6272* (SBBG).

Lepidium lasiocarpum var. *latifolium* C.L.Hitchc. Occasional; flats and arroyos on west islet.
   SBe, n.d., *Brandegee s.n.* (UC 117600).

Lepidium oblongum var. *insulare* C.L.Hitchc. LENTEJILLA Occasional; flats and arroyos on all islets.
   SBe, 27 Mar 1897, *Brandegee s.n.* (UC 117594); SBe, Mar-Jun 1897, *Anthony 275* (DS, SD); ESBe, 20 Apr 1970, *Moran 17446* (SD).

Cactaceae (Cactus Family)

Ferocactus chrysacanthus (Orcutt) Britton &.Rose CEDROS ISLAND BARREL CACTUS Rare; rocky slopes at upper elevations on west islet. Endemic to West San Benito and Cedros islands (Lindsay 1996).
   WSBe, 9 Feb 1986, *Thorne 61505* (RSA-POM).

Lophocereus schottii (Engelm.) Britton & Rose var. *schottii* OLD MAN CACTUS or GARAMBULLO Rare; localized colony on flats of east islet.
   ESBe, 19 Apr 1963, *Moran 10755* (SD).

Mammillaria neopalmeri Craig SAN BENITO ISLAND MAMMILLARIA Occasional; rocky flats on all islets. Can be locally abundant. Endemic to the San Benito Islands.
   SBe, Mar-Jun 1897, *Anthony 278* (DS); WSBe, 20 Jan 1975, *Philbrick B75-26* (SBBG).

Opuntia sp. nova CEDROS ISLAND CHOLLA Common; rocky slopes and flats on all islets. An undescribed taxon which is apparently endemic to San Benito, Cedros, and Natividad islands (J. Rebman, personal communication, 1997). Sterile specimens of this taxon were collected as early as 1911 (Britton and Rose 1919; Moran and Lindsay 1951) but no flowers have been collected to date. Some plants on East Benito may represent yet another undescribed taxon (Moran and Lindsay 1951).

WSBe, 9 Mar 1911, *Rose 16043* (US); WSBe, 20 Jan 1975, *Philbrick B75-34* (SBBG).

Chenopodiaceae (Goosefoot Family)

Aphanisma blitoides Moq. APHANISMA Occasional; flats and arroyos on west and east islets.

SBe, Jul-Oct 1896, *Anthony s.n.* (UC 116501); WSBe, 18 Apr 1963, *Moran 10745* (SD); ESBe, 20 Apr 1970, *Moran 17450* (SD).

Atriplex barclayana (Benth.) D.Dietr. [*A. b.* subsp. *dilatata* (Greene) H.M.Hall & Clem.] SALADILLO Occasional; coastal flats on all islets; locally common on north side of west islet.

SBe, Mar-Jun 1897, *Anthony 269* (UC); WSBe, 8 Feb 1971, *Beauchamp 1532* (RSA-POM).

{*Atriplex coulteri* (Moq.) D.Dietr. Reported for the island by Brandegee (1900); all specimens seen appear to be *A.* aff. *davidsonii.*}

Atriplex aff. *davidsonii* Standl. DAVIDSON'S SALTSCALE Scarce; flats on west islet.

SBe, Mar-Jun 1897, *Anthony 277* (CAS, RSA-POM); WSBe, 24 May 1952, *Moran 4194* (DS).

*Chenopodium murale L. NETTLE-LEAF GOOSEFOOT Common; disturbed flats near village on west islet and on east islet. First collected on the island in 1972.

WSBe, 24 Jan 1972, *Moran 19062* (SD); WSBe, 31 Jan 1985, *Thorne 58476* (RSA-POM).

Suaeda moquinii (Torr.) Greene BUSH SEEPWEED Common; coastal flats on all islets.

SBe, 1889, *Pond s.n.* (ND-G 015455); WSBe, 18 Apr 1963, *Moran 10739* (SD); ESBe, 20 Apr 1970, *Moran 17452* (SD).

Crassulaceae (Stonecrop Family)

Crassula connata (Ruiz & Pavon) A. Berger [*C. erecta* (Hook. & Arn.) A. Berger] PYGMY WEED Rare; coastal flats near village on west islet.

WSBe, 15 Mar 1993, *Junak 5306* (SBBG).

Dudleya albiflora ROSE LIVE-FOREVER or SIEMPREVIVA Rare; apparently known only from a collection made in 1905. The specimen cited below may have been mislabelled as to location. This dudleya has not been seen on the San Benitos by other collectors, but it is common on Cedros and Natividad, the next islands visited by Stewart.

SBe, 14 Jul 1905, *Stewart s.n.* (CAS 136281).

Dudleya linearis (Greene) Britton & Rose SAN BENITO ISLAND LIVE-FOREVER Scarce; canyon walls and slopes on north side of west islet. Endemic to West San Benito Island.

SBe, 1889, *Pond s.n.* (ND-G 020620); WSBe, 18 Apr 1963, *Moran 10744* (SD).

Cuscutaceae (Dodder Family)

Cuscuta californica Hook. & Arn. DODDER or WITCH'S HAIR Occasional; north shore of west islet. Parasitic on *Frankenia palmeri* and several annual species on San Benito.

WSBe, 26 Mar 1973, *Moran 20315* (RSA-POM, SD); WSBe, 19 Feb 1977, *Davidson 5455* (RSA-POM, SD).

Euphorbiaceae (Spurge Family)

Euphorbia misera Benth. CLIFF SPURGE Common; rocky slopes and flats on west and east islets. E. L. Greene applied the name *Euphorbia benedicta* to plants from the San Benito islands; they may indeed represent a distinct taxon and need further study.

SBe, Jul-Oct 1896, *Anthony 20* (NY); SBe, 9 Mar 1911, *Rose 16050* (NY); WSBe, 9 Mar 1971, *Benedict s.n.* (SBBG 48227); ESBe, 6 Feb 1950, *Lindsay 1827* (UC).

Fabaceae (Pea Family)

{*Errazurizia benthamii* (Brandegee) I.M.Johnst. Reported for San Benito Island by Wiggins (1940); no specimen has been found.}

Lotus salsuginosus subsp. *brevivexillus* Ottley [*Hosackia maritima* Nutt.] COASTAL LOTUS Occasional; flats on west islet.

SBe, 28 Mar 1897, *Brandegee s.n.* (UC 80939); WSBe, 26 Mar 1973, *Moran 20318* (SD).

*Melilotus indicus (L.) All. YELLOW SWEET CLOVER Rare; known from a single collection made in 1979 near village on west islet.

WSBe, 12 May 1979, *Moran 27230* (SD).

Phaseolus filiformis Benth. Scarce; north side of west islet.

SBe, 28 Mar 1897, *Brandegee s.n.* (UC 82395); WSBe, 31 Jan 1985, *Thorne 58474* (RSA-POM).

Frankeniaceae (Frankenia Family)

Frankenia palmeri (Molina) I.M.Johnst. [*F. grandifolia* Cham. & Schltdl.] PALMER'S FRANKENIA or YERBA REUMA
Common; lower slopes and flats around perimeters of all islets.
WSBe, 9 Mar 1971, *Benedict s.n.* (SBBG 48233); WSBe, 20 Jan 1975, *Philbrick B75-25* (SBBG).

Geraniaceae (Geranium Family)

Erodium moschatum (L.) L'Her. WHITESTEM FILAREE Rare; disturbed flats near village on west islet. First collected in 1998.
WSBe, 27 Feb 1998, *Junak 6283* (SBBG).

Hydrophyllaceae (Waterleaf Family)

Phacelia ixodes Kellogg COSTA BAJA PHACELIA or ISLAND MISERY Occasional; rocky n-facing slopes, primarily in canyons, on north side of west islet. This plant should be avoided as it can cause severe contact dermatitis in humans.
SBe, Jul-Oct 1896, *Anthony s.n.* (UC 107389); WSBe, 6 Feb 1950, *Lindsay 1833* (UC); WSBe, 12 May 1979, *Moran 27237* (SD).

Loasaceae (Stick-leaf Family)

Mentzelia hirsutissima var. *nesiotes* I.M.Johnst. NATIVIDAD ISLAND BLAZING STAR Rare; rocky slopes and flats of west islet. Endemic to San Benito, Cedros, and Natividad islands.
SBe, 28 Mar 1897, *Brandegee s.n.* (UC 138558).
Petalonyx linearis Greene Occasional; rocky canyon walls, arroyos, and slopes on west islet.
SBe, Jul-Oct 1896, *Anthony 31* (SBBG); WSBe, 8 Feb 1971, *Beauchamp 1535* (SD); WSBe, 4 Apr 1971, *Beauchamp 2093* (SD).

Malvaceae (Mallow Family)

Eremalche exilis (A.Gray) Greene [*Malvastrum e.* A.Gray] Rare; not seen recently.
SBe, Mar 1897, *Brandegee s.n.* (UC 174088).
Malva pacifica M.F.Ray [*Lavatera venosa* S.Watson] SAN BENITO ISLAND BUSH MALLOW Common; arroyos, slopes,and flats throughout west islet; scattered on flats of middle and east islets. Native populations are endemic to San Geronimo Island, the San Benito Islands, and an islet at the mouth of Bahia Tortugas; probably introduced on Cedros, Natividad, and Asuncion islands.
SBe, 27 Mar 1897, *Brandegee s.n.* (UC 109034, 109040); WSBe, 25 Mar 1974, *Moran 21173* (SD, UC); MSBe, 5 Feb 1950, *Lindsay 1823* (UC); MSBe, 25 May 1971, *Moran 18399* (SD); ESBe, 20 Apr 1970, *Moran 17442* (SD).
Malva parviflora L. CHEESEWEED Occasional; disturbed flats near lighthouse and village on west islet. First collected on the island in 1970.
WSBe, 19 Apr 1970, *Moran 17435* (SD); WSBe, 20 Jan 1975, *Philbrick B75-30* (SBBG); WSBe, 9 Feb 1986, *Thorne 61517* (RSA-POM).

Nyctaginaceae (Four-O'Clock Family)

{*Mirabilis californica* A.Gray Reported for west islet by Greene (1889); no specimen has been found.}

Papaveraceae (Poppy Family)

Eschscholzia ramosa Greene [*E. crassula* Greene] ISLAND POPPY Common; arroyos and flats on west and east islets. Endemic to Santa Rosa, Santa Cruz, Santa Barbara, San Nicolas, Santa Catalina, San Clemente, Los Coronados, Todos Santos, San Martin, Guadalupe, San Benito, Cedros, and Natividad islands.
SBe, Dec 1875, *Streets s.n.* (GH); SBe, 25 Mar 1889, *Palmer 909* (CAS); WSBe, 20 Apr 1948, *Moran 2953* (GH); ESBe, 6 Feb 1950, *Lindsay 1829* (UC).

Plantaginaceae (Plantain Family)

Plantago ovata Forssk. [*P. insularis* Eastw.] Occasional; flats on west and east islets. May be introduced.
SBe, Feb 1889, *Pond s.n.* (ND-G 050700); SBe, 27 Mar 1897, *Brandegee s.n.* (UC 102793).

Portulacaceae (Purslane Family)

Calandrinia maritima Nutt. SEA KISSES or SEASIDE CALANDRINIA Common in arroyos and on flats of west islet; scarce on flats of east islet.
WSBe, 7 Feb 1972, *Beauchamp 3179* (SD); ESBe, 20 Apr 1970, *Moran 17448* (SD).

Resedaceae (Mignonette Family)

Oligomeris linifolia Vahl OLIGOMERIS Common; coastal slopes and flats on west and east islets.
SBe, Mar-Jun 1897, *Anthony 272* (SD); WSBe, 7 Feb 1972, *Beauchamp 3169* (SD); ESBe, 20 Apr 1970, *Moran 17447* (SD).

Scrophulariaceae (Figwort Family)

Antirrhinum watsonii Vasey & Rose [*A. kingii* var. *w.* (Vasey & Rose) Munz, *Sairocarpus w.* Vasey & Rose) D.A. Sutton]
WATSON'S SNAPDRAGON Scarce; arroyos and flats of west and east islets.
WSBe, 26 Mar 1973, *Moran 20317* (SD); WSBe, 12 May 1979, *Moran 27235* (SD).

Solanaceae (Nightshade Family)

*Datura discolor Bernh. JIMSON WEED Rare; disturbed flats near village on west islet. Probably introduced; first collected at village garbage dump in 1997.
WSBe, 5 Dec 1997, *West 13* (SBBG); WSBe, 27 Feb 1998, *Junak 6282* (SBBG).

Lycium brevipes Benth. var. *brevipes* FRUTILLA Common; flats on all islets.
WSBe, 12 May 1979, *Moran 27239* (SD).

Lycium californicum Nutt. CALIFORNIA BOXTHORN Occasional on flats of west islet; common on flats of east islet.
SBe, 28 Mar 1897, *Brandegee s.n.* (UC 103835); WSBe, 12 May 1979, *Moran 27238* (SD); ESBe, 20 Apr 1970, *Moran 17445* (SD).

Monocotyledonous Flowering Plants

Agavaceae (Agave Family)

Agave sebastiana Greene [*A. shawii* var. *sebastiana* (Greene) Gentry] COASTAL AGAVE or MESCAL Abundant; slopes of west and east islets.
SBe, Mar-Jun 1897, *Anthony 264* (DS, US); WSBe, 8 Nov 1966, *Howe & Harbison s.n.* (SBBG 55151); WSBe, 9 Mar 1971, *Benedict s.n.* (SBBG 43885); WSBe, 20 Jan 1975, *Philbrick B75-31* (SBBG).

Alliaceae (Onion Family)

Dichelostemma capitatum (Benth.) A.W.Wood [*D. pulchellum* (Salisb.) A.A. Heller] BLUE DICKS Locally common near lighthouse and along north shore of west islet; occasional elsewhere on west and east islets.
WSBe, 11 Jan 1889, *Pond s.n.* (ND-G 000246).

Zosteraceae (Eel-Grass Family)

Phyllospadix scouleri Hook. SURF-GRASS Common; rocky intertidal and subtidal habitats along north shores of west and middle islets.
WSBe, 18 Apr 1963, *Moran 10742* (SD); WSBe, 19 Apr 1970, *Moran 17440* (RSA-POM, SD); MSBe, 25 May 1971, *Moran 18400* (RSA-POM).

Phyllospadix torreyi S.Watson SURF-GRASS Occasional; rocky intertidal and subtidal habitats along west shore of west islet.
WSBe, 31 Jan 1985, *Thorne 58485* (RSA-POM).

STREAM FAUNA OF SANTA CRUZ ISLAND

Laura J. Furlong[1] and Adrian M. Wenner[2]

[1]Westmont College, 955 La Paz Road, Santa Barbara, CA 93108
(805) 688-6175, FAX (805) 565-7035, E-mail: furlong@westmont.edu
[2]University of California, Santa Barbara, CA 93106
(805) 963-8508, FAX (805) 893-8062, E-mail: wenner@lifesci.ucsb.edu

ABSTRACT

Records indicate that entomologists have collected insects from the California islands since the late 1800s. Despite over 100 years of entomological collection on the islands, several aquatic insect groups remain poorly described. This study represents the first intensive collection of California Channel Island aquatic insects. Samples taken from seven Santa Cruz Island streams from 1990 to 1997 yielded 39 taxa previously undescribed from the California islands and 47 new records for Santa Cruz Island. Compared to the nearby mainland, Santa Cruz Island streams support a depauperate fauna. Of the 161 total taxa (generic level) listed for Santa Cruz Island and the nearby mainland, only 94 occur on the island. The assemblage of taxa on Santa Cruz Island does not represent a random subset of the total. Aquatic flies (Diptera) and beetles (Coleoptera) are over-represented on the island, while caddisflies (Trichoptera) and stoneflies (Plecoptera) are under-represented. This disharmonic island assemblage may result from differences in the dispersal and colonization abilities of aquatic insect taxa. In addition, the depauperate nature of riparian vegetation on Santa Cruz Island might exclude aquatic groups relying heavily upon allochthonous stream input.

Keywords: Aquatic insects, stream fauna, biogeography, disharmony, dispersal, Santa Cruz Island.

INTRODUCTION

A basic knowledge of the system under consideration is an essential component to ecological, evolutionary, and biogeographical research. In particular, taxonomic surveys provide essential baseline information used for monitoring, management, and conservation purposes. This is especially true for undescribed systems and/or areas of great ecological concern, such as the Northern Channel Islands. With multiple agencies involved in management and restoration projects on the islands, the availability of baseline data is essential for the documentation of the success of these programs. Although adequate taxonomic documentation exists for some island animal groups, others are poorly known. Information for several insect groups is minimal or completely lacking (Miller 1985). In particular, aquatic insect groups have received scant attention on the California

islands. Monitoring aquatic macroinvertebrates could be of great value in management and restoration programs, especially if combined with data regarding watershed recovery from grazing and/or exotic plant and animal removal. A primary goal of this study is to provide baseline knowledge of aquatic insect assemblages for Santa Cruz Island streams.

In addition, this research compares the stream insect assemblage of Santa Cruz Island with those found in nearby mainland streams. Islands, especially oceanic islands, typically support non-random subsets of organisms found in source areas. Carlquist (1974) and Pielou (1979) proposed that this phenomenon results from the differential dispersal and colonization abilities of organisms. Species with good dispersal and/or colonization abilities (such as bats and/or strand plants) are often over-represented on islands compared to the mainland (Carlquist 1974), whereas those with poor dispersal ability across oceans (such as freshwater fishes and large mammals) are under-represented. Therefore, island biotas are characteristically disharmonic, "containing only a small proportion of the basic adaptive types found in surrounding source regions" (MacArthur and Wilson 1967). This phenomenon is more easily observed on distant oceanic islands but evident on the California islands as well. Savage (1967) noted that the California island herpetofaunas "are depauperate and composed of vagile forms." In reference to land vertebrates, Wenner and Johnson (1980) noted that the assemblages present on the Northern Channel Islands do not represent a random assortment, but are "the sorts of animals one might associate with an Indian culture or which could have rafted to the islands."

As discussed by Wenner and Johnson (1980), species with poor dispersal and colonization abilities may also become established on an island through random events. Though freshwater species rarely disperse across salt water, most stream insects possess winged adult forms allowing for aerial transport. It is also possible that these organisms may raft to islands on debris originating from stream banks. The presence of aquatic insects on distant oceanic islands, such as the Hawaiian Archipelago, is evidence that some aquatic groups are capable of long distance dispersal (Howarth and Polhemus 1991).

Once a colonizing species reaches an island, appropriate habitat and adequate resources must be available for the organism to become established (Carlquist 1974). There-fore, the relative ecological poverty of some islands may also contribute to the depauperate nature of their biotas. These and other factors combine to produce a biota that may have a very different composition than that of the mainland. The depauperate nature of islands makes them particularly interesting for general ecological studies, because the sys-tems are often simplified versions of those on the mainland.

This project explores three aspects of the Santa Cruz Island stream fauna. First, the study provides baseline infor-mation regarding the stream insect assemblage on Santa Cruz. Second, it examines to what degree mainland stream insects are represented on Santa Cruz Island. Third, this work investigates whether the island stream insect assemblage appears to be a random subset of mainland assemblages or represents a disharmonic assemblage.

MATERIALS AND METHODS

Collections were taken from several locations on Santa Cruz Island (34° 04' 39" N to 33° 57' 33" N, 119° 55' 44" W to 119° 31' 10" W), the largest and most topographically diverse of the California islands. The surface of Santa Cruz Island is divided by a number of watersheds varying in size from less than 1 km² to nearly 35 km². Several streams flow year around, fed by emergent groundwater. However, most drainages sustain flow only following storm events. The majority of island collections were taken from the following watersheds: Black Point, Coches, Horquetta, Laguna, Pris-oners, Sauces, and Willows (Figure 1). The watershed area

of these streams varies from 1.09 km² (Black Point) to 34.66 km²(Prisoners). In addition to collections taken directly from island streams, adults forms of stream insects were collected utilizing a black light at the Santa Cruz Island field station. Mainland collections were taken from three coastal Santa Barbara County streams: Rattlesnake-Mission Creek (34° 27' 30" N, 119° 41' 30" W), Refugio Creek (34° 30' 00" N, 120° 3' 30" W), and Jalama Creek (34° 32' 30" N, 120° 27' 30" W). Detailed information regarding island and main-land collection sites may be found in Furlong (1999).

To maximize opportunities for obtaining the greatest number of taxa, collections from both island and mainland streams took place during all seasons. Island collections were conducted from 1990 to 1997; mainland samples were taken during 1997. The number of sampling sites per stream ranged from three to five. Both pool and riffle habitats were sampled at each site (for detailed site descriptions see Furlong 1999). In all, this sampling effort included over 75 collection dates with over 800 samples taken. As suggested by Elliott (1979), we employed standardized kick samples over a given area (1 m) for a given amount of time (30 seconds) to obtain semi-quantitative samples of benthic taxa. In addition, stan-dardized net sweeps (five sweeps of 1 m each) were used to collect surface taxa. All collections were taken with a 300 micron mesh dip net. Occasionally, insects were collected by hand-picking with forceps. Insects collected in this study will be vouchered at the Santa Barbara Museum of Natural History.

Collections from the Los Angeles County Museum of Natural History, Santa Barbara Museum of Natural History,

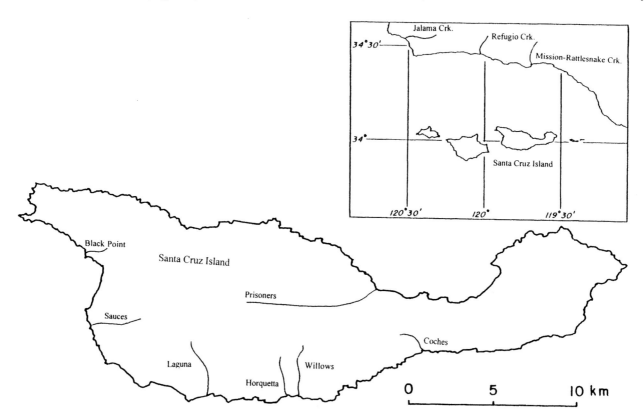

Figure 1. Location of mainland and Santa Cruz Island streams used for aquatic insect collection.

California Academy of Sciences, and Santa Cruz Island Reserve were examined to verify identifications and supplement the inventory of mainland and island taxa. Additionally, California Channel Island insect records provided by Scott Miller (Bishop Museum) were utilized to draft a more complete account of Santa Cruz Island aquatic insects (Miller, pers. comm. 1996). Unpublished records of *Mesocapnia projecta* (Plecoptera) were provided by Richard Bauman (pers. comm. 1999). Published lists of mainland stream taxa provided additional information regarding the richness of mainland streams (Wenner and Busath 1977; Cooper et al. 1986). Island and mainland taxa were compared at the generic level to account for possible errors and differences in species-level identifications. Taxa identified to family level only were counted as one genus in mainland-island comparisons.

To determine if island taxa represent a random subset of total taxa, the Kolmogorov-Smirnov goodness of fit Dmax was calculated for the observed distribution of island taxa within Orders compared to the expected distribution (Zar 1984). The expected distribution was determined by calculating the percent of total taxa found on the island (at the generic level, excluding Chironomidae due to insufficient identification). The total number of taxa per insect Order was multiplied by this figure to obtain the expected number of island taxa per Order.

RESULTS

General Collection

This collection effort yielded many taxa previously undescribed for Santa Cruz Island (for full list of stream taxa see Furlong 1999). In all, 90 taxa were collected from island streams. In addition, 6 taxa were identified from our terrestrial collections and previously unidentified museum/reserve collections. Of these 96 taxa, 47 represent new records for Santa Cruz Island and 39 represent new records for the California Channel Islands (not including Chironomidae, Table 1). Several of these new records consist of identifications at greater levels of taxonomic resolution. This collection effort did not account for 52 aquatic or semi-aquatic taxa listed for Santa Cruz Island (Miller, pers. comm. 1996).

Several non-insect macroinvertebrates also were collected during this study. These include flatworms (*Dugesia*, Phylum Platyhelminthes), horsehair worms (Phylum Nematomorpha), bivalve molluscs (possibly Family Sphaeriidae), and the gastropod *Physa*. In addition, several non-insect arthropod taxa were encountered: water mites (Class Arachnida), seed shrimp (Class Ostracoda), copepods (Class Copepoda), and the amphipod *Hyallela azteca* (Saussure). The only vertebrate taxa occupying island streams were tadpoles of the Pacific tree frog (*Hyla regilla* Baird & Girard). Freshwater fishes do not occur in Santa Cruz Island streams.

Mainland vs. Santa Cruz Island

Mainland and island collections and records yielded a total of 161 taxa at the generic level (Furlong 1999). Dipterans exhibited the greatest overall richness, accounting for approximately 31% of all taxa (Table 2). The proportion of island stream taxa composed of dipterans, at 40%, was higher than that for the mainland, at 29%. The same pattern was observed in the richness of coleopteran taxa. Beetles, with a total of 20.5% of the total taxa, comprised a greater proportion of the island taxa (25%) compared to that found in the mainland assemblage (19%). Taxa in the Order Plecoptera contributed the least to island richness at 1%, while contributing more than 7% to the mainland assemblage (Table 2).

Of the total 161 taxa (generic level), 145 (90%) occurred in mainland streams and 94 (58%) in island streams. The greatest disparity in richness emerged within the orders Plecoptera and Trichoptera. Mainland records contained 11 and 22 taxa within the orders Plecoptera and Trichoptera, respectively (Table 2). However, only one stonefly and eight caddisfly taxa were collected from Santa Cruz Island streams. An additional 27 families of aquatic insects found in nearby mainland streams did not appear in samples from Santa Cruz Island. In contrast, three families recorded for Santa Cruz Island were absent in mainland records.

For most insect orders, the number of island taxa observed approximated the number expected (at the generic level, Figure 2). However, the expected number of taxa was much higher than observed for the orders Trichoptera (13 expected, 8 observed) and Plecoptera (6 expected, 1 observed). The number of dipteran and coleopteran taxa observed exceeded the expected number of taxa (Diptera: 29 expected, 37 observed; Coleoptera: 19 expected, 23 observed). The Kolmogorov-Smirnov goodness of fit Dmax calculated for overall observed versus expected richness within orders was significant ($Dmax_{n\,8,\,k\,92} = 12$) at the 0.05 level.

DISCUSSION

Faunal Survey

The limited scope of this collection effort, relative to the size of the island, yielded a considerable amount of new information regarding Santa Cruz Island stream fauna (Table 1). In all this study contributes 47 new records of Santa Cruz Island insects, of these 39 are new records for the California Channel Islands. A total of 52 aquatic and semi-aquatic insects recorded for Santa Cruz Island were not collected during this effort; however, many of these taxa occupy environments not encompassed by this study (intertidal, standing water, damp soil) and others were identified to a higher level of taxonomic resolution than employed in this effort. It is likely that more aquatic insects could be recorded for Santa Cruz Island if additional streams are sampled. Rearing studies and collections of terrestrial adult stages also would increase the degree of taxonomic resolution of several aquatic insects collected during this study.

Table 1. New records of aquatic insect taxa from Santa Cruz Island. This list was compiled from stream collections, terrestrial adult collections, unpublished records, and museum specimens. Excluding Chironomidae, this effort adds 47 records of insect taxa for Santa Cruz Island and 39 records for the California Channel Islands.

Taxa:	Taxa:	Taxa:
Ephemeroptera	Trichoptera (continued)	Diptera (continued)
Baetidae	Sericostomatidea	Simuliidae (pupa used for
* *Baetis bicaudatus*	* *Gumaga sp.*	species identification)
* *B. tricaudatus*	Coleoptera	* *Simulium aureum*
* *Callibaetis pictus*	Gyrinidae	* *S. latipes*
* *Centroptilum sp.*	*Gyrinus plicifer*	* *S. piperi*
Caenidae	Haliplidae	* *S. virgatum*
* *Caenis sp.*	*Peltodytes simplex*	Chironomidae
Odonata	Dytiscidae	(tentative identifications)
Aeshnidae	*Agabinus glabrellus*	Tanypodinae
* *Anax walsinghami*	* *A. sculpturellus*	* *Ablabesmyia sp.*
Libellulidae	*Agabus discors*	* *Pentaneura sp.*
* *Paltothemis lineatipes*	*Hydroporus vilis*	* *Procladius sp.*
* *Pantala flavescens*	* *Hydrovatus brevipes*	Orthocladiinae
Sympetrum corruptum	*Rhantus gutticollis*	* *Cricotopus sp.*
* *Tramea sp.*	Hydroscaphidae	* *Eukiefferiella sp.*
Coenagrionidae	* *Hydroscapha natans*	* *Orthocladius sp.*
* *Argia sedula*	Hydrophilidae	Chironminnae
Plecoptera	* *Anacaena signaticollis*	*Chironomus sp.*
Capniidae	*Berosus punctatissimus*	* *Kiefferulius sp.*
* *Mesocapnia projecta*	* *Helochares normatus*	* *Rheotanytarsus sp.*
Hemiptera	* *Hydrobius fuscipes*	Dixidae
Notonectidae	* *Hydrophilus triangularis*	* *Dixa (Dixa) sp.*
* *Notonecta hoffmanni*	Hydraenidae	* *D. (Meringodixa) sp.*
Megaloptera	* *Ochthebius interruptus*	* *D. (Paradixa) sp.*
Corydalidae	* Scirtidae	Tabanidae
* *Protochauliodes simplus*	Elmidae	* *Chrysops sp.*
Trichoptera	* *Ordobrevia nubifera*	Sciomyzidae
Philopotamidae	Diptera	
* *Wormaldia sp.*	Tipulidae	
Hydroptilidae	* *Dicranota sp.*	
* *Hydroptila sp.*	* *Hexatoma sp.*	
* *Ochrotrichia sp.*	Psychodidae	
Lepidostomatidae	* *Maruina sp.*	
* *Lepidostoma sp.*		

* New record for California Channel Islands

Depauperate Nature of Santa Cruz Island Biota

Though Santa Cruz Island is only 30 km from the mainland and has 16 ecologically diverse plant communities (Junak et al. 1995), its fauna is notably depauperate. Santa Cruz Island supports only 45% of the herpetofauna found in comparable habitats in Ventura County (Savage 1967) and 12% of land mammal species (excluding bats) observed on the coastal mainland (van Bloeker 1967; Wenner and Johnson 1980). With respect to breeding land birds, 39 species occur on the island, compared with 160 species breeding in comparable mainland habitats (Diamond and Jones 1980).

The richness of Santa Cruz Island insects varies by group. The 37 Orthoptera taxa, probably the most thoroughly studied of all island insect orders, comprise only 53% of those collected from the Santa Monica Mountains (Rentz and Weissman 1982; Weissman 1985). In a survey comparing the Santa Cruz Island Lepidoptera fauna with that of the Big Creek Reserve (Monterey, California) only 543 taxa were found on the island compared with 901 species at Big Creek (Powell 1994). The results of surveys by Rust et al. (1985)

Table 2. Number and percent taxa per Order from records and collections of mainland Santa Barbara County coastal streams and Santa Cruz Island streams.

Order	Total Taxa Generic Level		Mainland Taxa Generic Level		Island Taxa Generic Level	
	Total Taxa per Order	% of Total Taxa	Taxa per Order	% of Taxa per Order	Taxa per Order	% of Taxa per order
Ephemeroptera	11	6.8	11	7.6	5	5.4
Odonata	17	10.6	16	11.1	10	10.9
Plecoptera	11	6.8	11	7.6	1	1.1
Hemiptera	12	7.5	11	7.6	6	6.5
Megaloptera	3	1.9	3	2.1	2	2.2
Trichoptera	22	13.7	22	15.3	8	8.7
Lepidoptera	2	1.2	1	0.7	2	2.2
Coleoptera	33	20.5	28	19.4	23	25.0
Diptera	50	31.1	42	29.2	37	40.2
Total Taxa	161	100.0	145	100.0	94	100.0

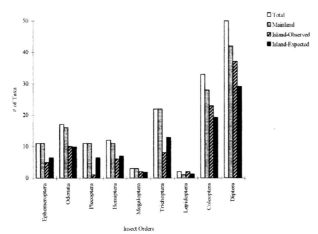

Figure 2. Comparison of total, mainland, and island richness of stream taxa per Order. Overall, Santa Cruz Island stream taxa account for 58% of the total taxa (at the generic level). Expected island richness per Order was estimated as 58% of total taxa per Order.

and Thorp et al. (1994) reveal that the Santa Cruz Island bee fauna accounts for only 19% (105 species) of mainland taxa (an estimated 520). This value appears low compared to Orthoptera and Lepidoptera figures, but Thorp et al. (1994) suggest that island figures "considerably underestimate" the actual number of bee species.

The number of stream insect taxa recorded for Santa Cruz Island accounts for approximately 58% of the total number of island and mainland stream insects (Table 2). Island Plecoptera exhibit very low richness compared with the mainland and with other island insect groups, with the island supporting only 9%, or one out of eleven mainland taxa. Trichoptera taxa also exhibit low richness compared to the mainland. Island representation within the groups Ephemeroptera, Odonata, and Hemiptera (aquatic) compares

well with that of island orthopterans and terrestrial lepidopterans. Compared to other insect groups, aquatic beetles, flies, and megalopterans commonly occurred on the island.

Overwater dispersal may be difficult for freshwater organisms; however, very few island aquatic insects are strictly aquatic. The majority possess a winged and/or terrestrial adult stage. Some aquatic forms disperse readily, with odonates and aquatic members of the orders Hemiptera, Coleoptera, and Diptera occurring on the Hawaiian Islands (Howarth and Polhemus 1991). Ephemeroptera and Trichoptera occur as far as 300 km from the mainland in the Atlantic (Malmqvist 1993). On South Pacific islands one can find those forms 600 to 700 km from possible sources (Winterbourn 1980). Plecopterans have been collected from the subantarctic islands Snares, Aukland, and Campbell (approximately 100 to 600 km south of New Zealand). However, these stoneflies consist of taxa with terrestrial nymphs and apterous adults closely related to New Zealand species and may not have dispersed overwater (Winterbourn 1980).

Records indicate that aquatic insects have crossed distances much greater than the Santa Barbara Channel (30 km). In addition, the distance to the Northern Channel Islands was even less in the past. During periods of low sea level, the lowest occurring approximately 17,000 to 18,000 years ago, the Northern Channel Islands formed the island Santarosae (e.g., Vedder and Howell 1980). The width of the Santa Barbara Channel at that time was only 6 km (Wenner and Johnson 1980). The expanded island area, combined with the reduced overwater dispersal distance, increased the probability of immigration would occur from the mainland and that island populations would establish and expand.

Given the overwater dispersal capabilities of aquatic insects and the relatively narrow barrier to dispersal presented by the Santa Barbara Channel, one might realize that other factors could contribute to the low richness of Santa Cruz Island aquatic insects. Also, it is necessary to interpret the above data in light of the difficulties associated with island-mainland comparisons. Ecological poverty may limit the number of organisms that occur on an island (Mac Arthur and Wilson 1967). For example, immigrating animals may encounter a depauperate flora or lack of specific prey taxa. In addition, island organisms may experience increased rates of extinction due to small population sizes, low genetic variability, and/or introduction of exotic species (Carlquist 1974). Island biotas may also "appear" depauperate due to sampling bias. Often, island organisms are not as well known or as thoroughly studied as their mainland counterparts. Contrasting island richness with larger areas of the mainland introduces an additional source of bias. In spite of the difficulties inherent in comparing the richness of mainland and island biotas, such comparisons continue to interest researchers.

Junak et al. (1995) noted that the Santa Cruz Island flora appears "harmonic and balanced compared to regional floras of comparable size on the adjacent mainland, with a few conspicuous exceptions." Among those "exceptions" is the absence or limited distributions of several species that dominate mainland riparian woodlands. Alder (*Alnus rhombifolia* Nutt.), sycamore (*Plantanus racemosa* Nutt.), and California-bay (*Umbellaria californica* Hook. & Arn.) do not, with the exception of a few introduced sycamores, occur on the island (Junak et al. 1995). Riparian woodlands supporting cottonwood (*Populus* spp.) occur in a few isolated island drainages, primarily on the inaccessible north side of the island, in Cottonwood Canyon, and in a few south draining watersheds (Junak et al. 1995; Furlong, pers. obs. 1995). Willows (*Salix* spp.) and mulefat (*Baccharis salicifolia* DC.) dominate the majority of Santa Cruz Island riparian corridors. Mainland insect groups relying heavily upon alder, sycamore, and cottonwood leaves as a food sources would be unable to establish on Santa Cruz Island.

Once organisms reach an island and become established, their populations face the possibility of extinction due to such factors as low genetic variability (Carlquist 1974) and relatively small population sizes (Pielou 1979). These factors also contribute to the depauperate nature of island biotas. In reference to Santa Cruz Island, insects may have crossed the Santa Barbara Channel repeatedly, as birds have (Diamond and Jones 1980). Those immigrants would therefore contribute to the island gene pool, reducing the risk of extinction for island populations. Research comparing the genetic variability of aquatic insect taxa from the mainland and island could determine whether genetic restriction may contribute to the low richness of some island aquatic groups.

Small habitat areas support smaller populations, which in turn become more susceptible to extinction (MacArthur and Wilson 1967). The habitat size of Santa Cruz Island has not been static. During the Pleistocene, eustatic sea level fluctuations resulted in numerous expansions and contractions in the surface area of the Northern Channel Islands, as well as changes in the width of the Santa Barbara Channel

(Vedder and Howell 1980). During periods of high sea level, the probability of island extinctions increased as island surface area decreased and distances from source populations increased. In addition to island-wide extinctions, localized extinction events may also occur on Santa Cruz Island. Winter storm events often result in stream scour. These events might result in occasional extinction of aquatic insect populations restricted to streams experiencing frequent winter scour.

Through various activities, man also contributes to island extinctions (Carlquist 1974; Marshall 1988). The introduction of sheep, cattle, and pigs in the mid 1880s decimated the native plant communities, with up to 48 plant species lost from Santa Cruz Island (Peart et al. 1994). Introduced grasses gradually replaced the native flora in heavily grazed areas (Junak et al. 1995). In addition to the loss of native plant cover, grazing and activities of feral pigs resulted in increased erosion. Sheep and cattle grazing on most of Santa Cruz Island ended in 1988, but feral pigs continue to impact island communities. Though not documented on Santa Cruz Island, the activities of the grazing animals and pigs may well have degraded riparian habitats and may to some extent contribute to the depauperate nature of the stream fauna. However, portions of the three mainland streams may be more impacted by human activities (urban development, farming, grazing) than those on the island.

The richness of island biotas may be underestimated due to sampling bias. Islands are relatively inaccessible. Therefore, studies of island biotas may not be conducted as frequently or thoroughly as those of mainland sites. In addition, mainland surveys may encompass a greater range of habitats and a larger area. Together, these factors contribute to a mainland bias in taxonomic richness. In this study, we tried to avoid these biases, taking island samples over the course of seven years from seven streams. Mainland collections came from three streams over the course of six months. Additional mainland lists included these same streams, with one exception. The Wenner and Busath (1977) list included samples from Cold Spring and San Jose creeks. However, samples from these streams added no additional taxa to the mainland records.

The sources used for the mainland list do not appear to represent a greater sampling effort compared with the effort expended to develop the Santa Cruz Island list. The Wenner and Busath (1977) list was developed from 60 samples. Cooper et al. (1986) constructed their list from approximately four years of seasonal sampling. Our mainland list was produced from approximately 90 samples. The Santa Cruz Island list represents a seven-year effort with over 700 samples processed.

A possible bias could result due to the relative distance between mainland streams. The distances between Jalama and Refugio creeks and between Rattlesnake-Mission and Refugio are approximately 30 km. Jalama and Rattlesnake-Mission creeks are separated by approximately 60 km. The island, by contrast, is only 38 km in length. In addition, the size of the Jalama watershed is much larger than any watershed on Santa Cruz Island.

In all, it appears that the depauperate nature of Santa Cruz Island aquatic insect taxa may not be due solely to difficulties associated with overwater dispersal. One must also consider the potential roles of the poverty of island riparian vegetation and island extinction rates. In addition, the greater area over which the mainland samples were taken may introduce a mainland sampling bias.

Disharmony of Santa Cruz Island Biota

Differential dispersal abilities and ecological tolerances result in disharmonic island biotas, dominated by species with "positive adaptations for long-distance dispersal and for establishment" (Carlquist 1974). The determination of dispersal ability (to islands) can be assessed by determining a propagule's ability to stay suspended in air, its tolerance to cold, desiccation and salt water, its ability to float, its reproductive characteristics, and its ecological requirements. The work of Carlquist (1974) contributes much to our understanding of the dispersal abilities of plants. However, other than comparing the attributes of animals with those above features, the determination of the dispersal abilities of animals is somewhat circular. Those animals that have dispersed far are considered good dispersers.

Santa Cruz Island, as Santarosae Island, has been separated from the mainland by as little as 6 km. In spite of this relatively narrow barrier to dispersal, portions of its fauna appear disharmonious. For example, only 12% of mainland mammals are found on the island, compared with 45% of the herpetofauna. According to records compiled by Darlington (1957) and Carlquist (1974), maximum known dispersal distances of reptiles (lizards - 3,200 km, snakes - 960 km) and amphibians (800 km) generally exceed that of land mammals (rodents - 960 km, small non-rodents - 322 km, large mammals 40 km). Compared with the higher percentage of herpetofauna, the overall low proportion of mammals and complete absence of large mammals on Santa Cruz Island, leads to the inference that this lack of balance results from differential dispersal abilities. Given that the Northern Channel Islands have supported and continue to support sizable populations of introduced large mammals and have supported mammoth populations in the past (e.g., Wenner and Johnson 1980), it is doubtful that ecological poverty precludes the establishment of large native mammals on these islands.

The distribution of aquatic insect within orders also appears disharmonic when compared to the mainland distribution. The expected (based on proportions of total taxa within orders) and observed distributions of taxa within insect orders differ significantly. The numbers of observed Coleoptera and Diptera taxa exceeded the expected (Figure 2). In addition, these groups account for a greater percent of island aquatic taxa compared with the mainland (Table 2). Taxa in the orders Plecoptera and Trichoptera exhibit opposite trends (Figure 2; Table 2). Aquatic coleopterans and dipterans occur on islands as distant as Hawaii (3,200 km

distant; Howarth and Polhemus 1991) and aquatic dipterans occupy ecologically poor islands such as Surtsey (a recent volcanic island; Lindroth et al. 1973) and Macquarie (a subantarctic island; Marchant and Lillywhite 1994). In contrast, trichopterans do not occur on distant oceanic islands such as Hawaii, but have been collected from numerous islands in the South Pacific (Winterbourn 1980). However, many of these islands are considered continental (Carlquist 1974). Plecoptera are rarely collected from islands more distant than Santa Cruz Island (e.g., Winterbourn 1980; Malmqvist et al. 1993).

These observations appear to support the concept that aquatic beetles and flies disperse more readily and caddisflies and stoneflies disperse less readily to islands than other aquatic insect groups.

Aerial and shipboard trapping also contribute to our knowledge of aquatic insect dispersal capabilities. A shipboard trapping program supported by the Bishop Museum from 1957 to 1966 included cruises in the Pacific, Atlantic, Antarctic and Indian Oceans. Insects collected during that program included 11 aquatic Diptera families, 6 aquatic Hemiptera families, 5 aquatic Coleoptera families, 2+ families of odonates, one family of ephemeropterans, and 2 unidentified trichopterans (Holzapfel and Harrell 1968; Holzapfel and Perkins 1969). The these families are a subset of those collected during this study and listed for other islands. The Bishop Museum also conducted an aerial trapping program over the Pacific Ocean from 1966 to 1969 (Holzapfel 1978). These collections were taken at altitudes up to 2,745 m; however no insects were recovered above 1,525 m. The majority of trapped insects (93 of 101 specimens) were recovered from samples taken soon after take-offs and landings. The only aquatic taxa recovered by these efforts were flies (Chironomidae). A single chironomid was collected at high altitudes.

Because distance data was not published with the aerial and shipboard trapping results, one cannot make assumptions regarding dispersal distances. However, several groups found on Santa Cruz Island and more distant islands were recovered by the aerial and shipboard trapping efforts. Conversely, with few exceptions, these efforts did not recover many groups that were not recorded from Santa Cruz and other islands.

If published dispersal distances and trapping efforts truly represent the differential dispersal capabilities of aquatic groups, then these differences may contribute to the unbalanced nature of Santa Cruz Island's aquatic insects. Coleopterans and dipterans exhibit the ability to disperse farther than other orders. These groups are over-represented on Santa Cruz Island compared to the mainland. In contrast, Plecoptera and Trichoptera do not appear to possess the dispersal capabilities observed in other aquatic orders. Plecoptera and Trichoptera rarely occur on Santa Cruz Island compared to the mainland. However, one must consider the possible effects of ecological poverty on these under-represented groups.

The depauperate nature of riparian vegetation might exclude functional groups (shredders) that feed upon sycamore, alder, and cottonwood leaves. Shredding taxa account for a large proportion of mainland plecopteran (73%) and trichopteran (41%) taxa. Of shredder taxa, only one of the eight Plecoptera and two of nine Trichoptera occur on Santa Cruz Island. Mainland trichopterans in the collector guild are well represented on Santa Cruz Island (five of seven taxa). This anecdotal observation indicates that the depauperate nature of Santa Cruz Island's riparian vegetation may also play a role in the lower than expected richness of island Plecoptera and Trichoptera.

The stage is now set for further studies of Channel Island aquatic insect ecology and biogeography. Studies of stream taxa on other islands and comparisons of richness between islands would be of interest. Using aquatic insects as biomonitors of watershed recovery might be an additional focus of island research.

ACKNOWLEDGMENTS

Partial funding for this project was provided by the Mildred E. Mathias Student Research Grant. We thank the numerous volunteers who assisted with sample collection. In particular, we thank Cara Murphy and Jamie Furlong. We also thank Lyndal Laughrin and Brian Guererro of the UC Natural Reserve System for their assistance with island travel arrangements, Scott Miller and Richard Bauman for providing unpublished records of island insect occurrences, and Peter Allan for his help with figure preparations.

LITERATURE CITED

Carlquist, S. J. 1974. Island Biology. Columbia University Press. New York, NY.

Cooper, S. D., T. L. Dudley and N. Hemphill. 1986. The biology of chaparral streams in Southern California. Pages 139-151 in Devries, J. (ed.), Proceedings of the Chaparral Ecosystems Research Conference. Water Resources Center Report 62.

Darlington, P. J. 1957. Zoogeography: The Geographical Distribution of Animals. John Wiley and Sons, Inc. New York, NY.

Diamond, J. M. and H. L. Jones. 1980. Breeding land birds of the Channel Islands. Pages 507-612 in Power, D. M. (ed.), The California Channel Islands: Proceedings of a Multidisciplinary Symposium. Santa Barbara Museum of Natural History. Santa Barbara, CA.

Elliott, J. M. 1979. Statistical Analysis of Samples of Benthic Invertebrates. Freshwater Biological Association Scientific Publication No. 25.

Furlong, L. J. 1999. Biogeography and ecology of Santa Cruz Island Streams. Ph.D. Dissertation, University of California, Santa Barbara, CA.

Holzapfel, E. P. and J. C. Harrell. 1968. Transoceanic dispersal studies of insects. Pacific Insects 10(1):115-153.

Holzapfel, E. P. and B. D. Perkins. 1969. Trapping of airborne insects on ships in the Pacific, Part 7. Pacific Insects 11(2):455-476.

Holzapfel, E. P. 1978. Transoceanic airplane sampling for organisms and particles. Pacific Insects 18(3-4):169-189.

Howarth, F. G. and D. A. Polhemus. 1991. A review of the Hawaiian stream insect fauna. Pages 40-50 in New directions in research, management and conservation of Hawaiian freshwater stream ecosystems. Proceedings of the 1990 Symposium on Freshwater Stream Biology and Fisheries Management. State of Hawaii, Department of land and Natural Resources. Honolulu, HI.

Junak. S., T. Ayers, R. Scott, D. Wilken, and D. Young. 1995. A Flora of Santa Cruz Island. Santa Barbara Botanic Garden. Santa Barbara, CA.

Lindroth, C. H., H Andersson, H. Bödvarsson, and S. H. Richter. Surtsey, Iceland. 1973. The development of a new fauna, 1963-1970. Terrestrial Invertebrates. Entomologia Sandinavica Supplementum, 5.

Marchant, R. and P. Lillywhite. 1994. Survey of stream invertebrate communities on Macquarie Island. Australian Journal of Marine and Freshwater Research 45(4):471-474.

MacArthur, R. H. and E. O. Wilson. 1967. The Theory of Island Biogeography. Princeton University Press, Princeton, NJ.

Malmqvist, B., A. N. Nilsson, M. Baez, P. D. Armitage, and J. Blackburn. 1993. Stream macroinvertebrate communities in the island of Tenerife. Archiv für Hydrobiologie 128(2):209-235.

Marshall, L. G. 1988. Extinction. Pages 219-254 in Myers, A. A. and P. S. Giller (eds.), Analytical Biogeography: an Integrated Approach to the Study of Animal and Plant Distributions. Chapman and Hall. New York, NY.

Miller, S. E. 1985. The California Channel Islands - past, present and future: an entomological perspective. Pages 3-27 in Menke, A. S. and D. R. Miller (eds.), Entomology of the California Channel Islands: Proceedings of the First Symposium. Santa Barbara Museum of Natural History. Santa Barbara, CA.

Peart, D., D. T. Patten, and S. L. Lohr. 1994. Feral pig disturbance and woody species seedling regeneration and abundance beneath Coast Live Oaks (Quercus agrifolia) on Santa Cruz Island, California. Pages 313-322 in Halvorson, W. L. and G. J. Maender (eds.), The Fourth California Islands Symposium: Update on the Status of Resources. Santa Barbara Museum of Natural History. Santa Barbara, CA.

Pielou, E. C. 1979. Biogeography. John Wiley and Sons, Inc. New York, NY.

Powell, J. A. 1994. Biogeography of Lepidoptera on the California Channel Islands. Pages 449-464 in Halvorson, W. L. and G. J. Maender (eds.), The Fourth California Islands Symposium: Update on the Status of Resources. Santa Barbara Museum of Natural History. Santa Barbara, CA.

Rentz, D. C. F. and D. B. Weissman. 1982. Faunal affinities, systematics, and bionomics of the Orthoptera of the California Channel Islands. University of California Publications in Entomology 94:1-240.

Rust, R. W., A. S. Menke, and D. R. Miller. 1985. A biogeographic comparison of the bees, sphecid wasps, and mealybugs of the California Channel Islands (Hymenoptera, Homoptera). Pages 29-59 in Menke, A. S. and D. R. Miller (eds.), Entomology of the California Channel Islands: Proceedings of the First Symposium. Santa Barbara Museum of Natural History. Santa Barbara, CA.

Savage, J. M. 1967. Evolution of the insular herpetofaunas. Pages 219-227 in Philbrick, R. N. (ed.), Proceedings of the Symposium on the Biology of the California Islands. Santa Barbara Botanic Garden. Santa Barbara, CA.

Thorp, R. W., A. M. Wenner, and J. F. Barthell. 1994. Flowers visited by honey bees and native bees on Santa Cruz Island. Pages 351-365 in Halvorson, W. L. and G. J. Maender (eds.) The Fourth California Islands Symposium: Update on the Status of Resources. Santa Barbara Museum of Natural History. Santa Barbara, CA.

van Bloeker, J. C. 1967. The land mammals of the Southern California Islands. Pages 245-263 in Philbrick, R. N. (ed.), Proceedings of the Symposium on the Biology of the California Islands. Santa Barbara Botanic Garden. Santa Barbara, CA.

Vedder, J. G. and D. G. Howell. 1980. Topographic evolution of the Southern California Borderland during late Cenozoic time. Pages 7-31 in Power, D. M. (ed.), The California Channel Islands: Proceedings of a Multidisciplinary Symposium. Santa Barbara Museum of Natural History. Santa Barbara, CA.

Weissman, D. B. 1985. Zoogeography of the Channel Island Orthoptera. Pages 61-68 in Menke, A. S. and D. R. Miller (eds.), Entomology of the California Channel Islands: Proceedings of the First Symposium. Santa Barbara Museum of Natural History. Santa Barbara, CA.

Wenner, A. M. and A. L. Busath for R. P. Howmiller (posthum.). 1977. Species differences in breakdown of tree leaves in streams - significance for composition of stream communities. Report No. 39, California Water Resources Center. University of California, Davis. Davis, CA.

Wenner, A. M. and D. L. Johnson. 1980. Land vertebrates on the California Channel Islands: sweepstakes or bridges? Pages 497-530 in Power, D. M. (ed.), The California Channel Islands: Proceedings of a Multidisciplinary Symposium. Santa Barbara Museum of Natural History. Santa Barbara, CA.

Winterbourn, M. J. 1980. The freshwater insects of Australasia and their affinities. Palaeogeography, Palaeoclimatology, Palaeoecology 3(1908):235-249.

Zar, J. H. 1984. Biostatistical Analysis, 2nd ed. Prentice-Hall. Engelwood Cliffs, NJ.

SOURCES OF UNPUBLISHED MATERIALS

Bauman, R.W., M. L. Bean Life Science Museum, Brigham Young University, Provo, UT, 84602.

Furlong, L. J., Westmont College, 955 La Paz, Santa Barbara, CA 93108. Personal Observation 1995.

Miller, S. E., International Centre of Insect Physiology and Ecology, Box 30772, Niarobi, Kenya. Personal Communication 1996.

REMOVAL OF EUROPEAN HONEY BEES FROM THE SANTA CRUZ ISLAND ECOSYSTEM

Adrian M. Wenner[1], Robbin W. Thorp[2], and John F. Barthell[3]

[1]University of California, Santa Barbara, CA 93106
(805) 963-8508, FAX (805) 893-8062, E-mail: wenner@lifesci.ucsb.edu
[2] University of California, Davis, CA 95616
(530) 752-0482, FAX (530) 752-1537, E-mail: rwthorp@ucdavis.edu
[3] University of Central Oklahoma, Edmond, OK 73034
(405) 974-5779, FAX (405) 330-3824, E-mail: jbarthell@ucok.edu

[1]Corresponding author, current mailing address: 967 Garcia Road, Santa Barbara, CA 93103

ABSTRACT

In 1988, we began to remove European honey bee colonies from Santa Cruz Island, California, in order to restore native bee populations and pollination systems in the Channel Islands National Park. Of the five islands in the Park, only Santa Cruz Island had honey bees, introduced more than 120 years ago. Initially, we located colonies by improved beehunt techniques and began to eliminate colonies on the eastern half of the island at the end of the third season. We also recorded swarms trapped in decoy hives and in cavities formerly occupied by colonies, eventually tallying nearly 300 colonies on the 25,000 hectare island. Midway in the program, drastic changes in the ecology (e.g., cattle removal, spread of exotic weeds, abundant rainfall) led us to employ a biological control agent to eliminate the remaining colonies. In December 1993, January 1994, and February 1994, we loaded a total of 85 mites (*Varroa jacobsoni*, parasitic only on bees of the genus *Apis*) onto foraging bees at a few sites on the eastern half of the island. Colony mortality remained unchanged in 1994 and 1995 but escalated in 1996 and 1997. All 117 of the routinely monitored feral colonies had perished by January 1998.

Keywords: Feral honey bees, *Apis mellifera*, native bees, ecosystem restoration, exotic weeds, biological control, *Varroa jacobsoni*, Santa Cruz Island.

INTRODUCTION

An earlier contribution in this series (Wenner and Thorp 1994) provided comprehensive coverage of the rationale, goals, scope, and progress to date in our long-term feral honey bee (*Apis mellifera* L.) removal project on Santa Cruz Island. The question addressed at that time: Will removing an introduced insect species change habitat quality for native plants and pollinators and also restore and/or increase species diversity and abundance?

That earlier report placed the study into ecological perspective, reviewed foraging behavior and the role of honey bees in ecosystems, outlined the seasonal sequence for nectar and pollen production by native and introduced plants, and summarized the distribution, abundance, and mortality of feral honey bee colonies as of that time. That report also contained a summary of results from studies of plant visitation by insects; honey bee removal on the east half of Santa Cruz Island had altered the relative insect representation on plant species under study in favor of native forms (Figures 2 and 3 in Wenner and Thorp 1994).

By the end of the first five years of this project, several events forced a change in approach. In particular, after removal of most sheep and cattle, exotic weeds (a primary food resource for the exotic honey bees) dramatically increased in island coverage. In addition, the long-term series of drought years had ended. Those two factors combined provided a vastly increased food supply for honey bee colonies, enhancing colony replication via swarming.

Unexpectedly, and a factor in line with our goals, another development impinged on our project, as outlined briefly in the Wenner and Thorp (1994) report. Some honey bee colonies in Florida and Wisconsin had perished due to a parasitic mite (*Varroa jacobsoni;* Oudemans 1904) infestation the very month (October, 1987) that we received approval to initiate this project.

That voracious, blood-sucking mite had crossed over from parasitization of the Asian honey bee (*Apis cerana* F.) to the European honey bee (*A. mellifera*) three decades earlier in central Asia (e.g., Mobus and de Bruyn 1993) and became rapidly and unwittingly transported around the world by beekeepers and bee researchers. Within only a decade after first discovery in the United States, varroa mites occurred in all of the mainland states and Alaska (Wenner and Bushing 1996). Colony mortality was recorded in Ventura County, California as early as October 1989.

We recognized the inevitability of invasion of Santa Cruz Island by varroa mites and pre-empted that eventuality with a deliberate use of those mites as a biological control agent against the European honey bee, in line with our original goal to eliminate those exotic bees from the island. Fortunately, varroa mites fit all nine criteria insisted upon by The Nature Conservancy before release of biological control agents into their preserves (Randall et al. 1994, unpublished and updated list). Of greatest importance, perhaps, is the fact that this mite species is "highly specialized to survive and reproduce on its honey bee host" (De Jong 1990:205). Any eventuality of an adverse crossover to a native bee species thus seemed highly unlikely.

This report covers progress on the honey bee removal portion of our long-term pollination/bee visitation study, with special emphasis on the efficacy of the varroa mite as a biological control agent in the Santa Cruz Island ecosystem.

MATERIALS AND METHODS

Locating and Monitoring Honey Bee Colonies

Throughout this project we found and plotted locations of European honey bee colonies on topographic maps. At the end of the second year (Fall 1990), colony extermination began on the eastern half of the island. In most cases, colonies were anesthetized with methyl chloroform (i.e., 1-1-1 trichloroethene) and then suffocated by closing off all entrances to the colony. Colonies in fractured rock crevices, etc. often required two or more attempts.

Eventually, we also had approximately 150 swarm hives (e.g., Schmidt and Thoenes 1990) in place throughout the island, with fresh swarm attraction/settling lures inserted into most of them each winter. As logistics permitted, we checked as many as possible several times each season for the presence of new swarms. If located on the eastern half of the island, the new swarms so caught were routinely killed until the spring of 1994 — at the time our biological control program began.

We also occasionally checked most cavities (time permitting) that had formerly held colonies, several times each season, to ascertain if they had been re-occupied. Again, if on the eastern half of the island, we killed new colonies until the spring of 1994. That inspection activity collectively amounted to hundreds of visits to swarm hives and former cavities during the first 11 years of this project.

Varroa Introduction and Monitoring

In December of 1993, and in January and February of 1994, we attached a total of 85 varroa mites (*Varroa jacobsoni*) to foraging worker honey bees — but only at select sites on the eastern half of the island. We extracted those mites from drone brood obtained from a single colony in an apiary located at the University of California, Santa Barbara.

The innoculation process involved placing a mite in a mason jar along with a foraging worker bee collected from a flower. After the mite could no longer be seen in the jar, we allowed the worker bee to return to its colony. Most mites were released in the Prisoners and Coches Prietos drainages, with a smaller total number placed on foraging honey

bees near the U.S. Navy facility. From that time on, we did not kill bee colonies anywhere on the island but instead waited for colony demise by natural mite spread.

We know from the literature that only a small percentage of the mites introduced would have been viable (e.g., Martin and Kemp 1997); hence, the innoculum of 85 mites would have amounted to a very few dozen viable mites.

In addition, we established three standard beekeeping wooden monitoring hives in Prisoners, Islay, and Laguna drainages (with island colonies obtained from swarm hives) to enable us to better assess mite reproduction and spread. Initially, we introduced ten mites directly into the Prisoners stream hive; later, we introduced some of their offspring to the hive in Islay Canyon. The Laguna hive later gained its infestation by natural mite spread.

Each established beekeeping hive had a removable tray inserted below the brood combs. By inspecting such trays during each island visit we could ascertain the degree of varroa mite infestation (e.g., Martin and Kemp 1997). In addition, we could insert a miticide strip into the hive and examine the mite drop after a few hours.

RESULTS

In the 11-year period (through the 1998 season), we found or captured a total of 292 honey bee colonies (Table 1). During the first four drought years, existing colonies produced only a few swarms. Once the drought broke (1991-1992), our attention necessarily became focused increasingly on checking known colonies, monitoring the installed swarm hives for occupancy, and examining cavities where colonies had been killed earlier. Extensive elimination of colonies on the east half of the island continued for the next two seasons (1992 and 1993; Figure 1).

Table 1. Total number of feral honey bee colonies dealt with on Santa Cruz Island during an eleven year period.

Season	Rainfall (Prior Winter) inches	mm	Original Colonies Found	Swarms Caught	Total Colonies
1988	15.6	396	27	0	27
1989	8.9	226	35	0	35
1990	6.4	163	28	0	28
1991	15.6	396	27	9	36
1992	20.4	518	11	27	38
1993	25.2	640	7	46	53
1994	15.4	391	2	22	24
1995	45.1	1146	2	38	40
1996	15.6	396	0	11	11
1997	23.4	594	0	0	0
1998	43.3	1100	0	0	0
Totals			139	153	292

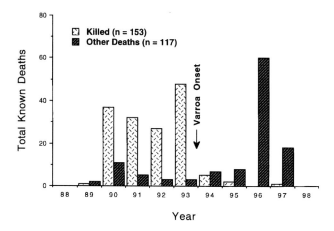

Figure 1. Total mortality of monitored feral honey bee colonies on Santa Cruz Island during an 11-year period. Deliberate elimination of colonies on the eastern half of the island continued until the onset of a varroa mite infestation (winter of 1993-1994). After a two-year period, mites eliminated the remaining monitored colonies.

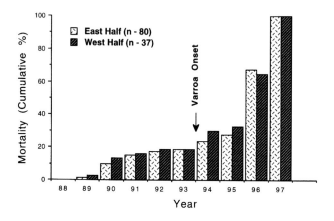

Figure 2. Cumulative mortality of monitored feral colonies on the two halves of Santa Cruz Island, aside from those colonies deliberately eliminated (as in Figure 1). By the end of 1997, all monitored colonies had perished.

As indicated in Wenner and Thorp (1994), we killed no colonies until the third season. By the end of the 1993 season, we had methodically eliminated virtually all known colonies on the eastern half of the island (Figure 1 herein; Table 5 of Wenner and Thorp 1994). The plentiful rains of the 1992-1993 winter, however, resulted in an excessive swarm rate (Table 1), forcing us to turn to use of the varroa mite as a biological control (Materials and Methods section).

Beginning in 1994 (after mite release), we increased the inspection rate of colonies, swarm hives, and vacated cavities in order to record swarm incidence and mortality — both natural mortality and that due to varroa mite infestation. During the entire 1994 and 1995 seasons, natural colony mortality remained at the same level observed in earlier years (Figure 1).

We detected no colony mortality in those two seasons that could be attributed to varroa mite infestation. As an example, a total of 16 such examinations of the Prisoners stream monitoring hive during a more than two-year period after inoculation revealed no visible adverse effect of mite infestation during that time. Beginning in early 1996, however, colony demise escalated; the colonies in hives and most remaining monitored Santa Cruz Island honey bee colonies collapsed that year (Figures 1 and 2).

The initial presence of mites only on the eastern half of the island permitted us to assess how rapidly those mites would cause colony collapse on the western half of the island as well. That demise, in fact, occurred almost as rapidly as on the eastern half of the island (Figure 2). By the end of the 1996 season, some colonies in the Laguna and Pozo drainages (southwest portion of the island) had already perished.

By January 1998, all monitored honey bee colonies were dead (Figure 2). However, on visits later in 1998 we found an occasional honey bee (at most one per minute) foraging midday on yellow star thistle plants (*Centaurea solstitialis* L.) between the main ranch buildings and the Portezuela region, as well as very few foragers visiting horehound (*Marrubium vulgare* L.) at the entrance to the east pine forest.

By contrast, the steady hum of European honey bees that pervaded all parts of the island a dozen years ago no longer exists. Now, foraging honey bees on Santa Cruz Island are vastly outnumbered by native bees on the island (e.g., preliminary results in Thorp et al. 1999).

By employing beelining techniques (Wenner et al. 1992) in September 1998, we determined that at least two colonies still persisted in the central portion of the island. The approximate locations: in the upper reaches of Cañada de la Mina and Gallina Canyon. All colonies surrounding those locations had perished from mite infestation in the 1996 and 1997 seasons.

DISCUSSION

Schmitz and Simberloff wrote:

"The Nature Conservancy, which operates the largest private U.S. reserve system, views non-indigenous plants and animals as the greatest threats to the species and communities its reserves protect. It can ill afford the increasing time and resources that introduced-species problems cost, and the progress it makes on its own properties is almost always threatened by reinvasion from surrounding lands." (Schmitz and Simberloff 1977:36).

While one can readily appreciate the damage to an ecosystem occasioned by introduced pigs, sheep, or weeds, the adverse effects of an exotic insect species usually go unnoticed. We began our honey bee removal project more than a decade ago with the above considerations in mind.

In contrast to conditions on the mainland, removal of honey bees from Santa Cruz Island would unlikely be followed by "reinvasion from surrounding lands." For example, Santa Rosa Island — located less than 10 km away — has apparently never had honey bees, despite the fact that honey bees have been present on Santa Cruz Island for more than a century (Wenner and Thorp 1993).

In fact, it was the relative ecological diversity of flower-visiting insects on Santa Rosa Island — compared to what one could have observed previously on Santa Cruz Island plants — that inspired us to launch this project (Wenner and Thorp 1994). In contrast to observations on Santa Rosa Island, exotic (European) honey bees dominated flower-visitation on Santa Cruz Island when we began our study, a circumstance that posed a special challenge as an ecological study.

Whereas native bees thrive in certain seasons, honey bee colonies exist year-round, partly by virtue of the fact that they store honey and pollen and can survive adverse conditions by relying on those stores. In good rainfall years, honey bees — by foraging primarily on exotic plant species — likely provide no appreciable competition with native bees.

During drought years, on the other hand, honey bees may no longer have adequate nectar and pollen input from the locally ill-adapted foreign weed sources. As an ultimate generalist forager (e.g., Thorp et al. 1994), the honey bee can instead exploit emergent pollen and nectar sources of drought-resistant native plants normally visited only by native bee species. Once that exploitation of extraordinary food supplies occurs, competition between honey bees and native bees would become intense. Native species may likely fail to complete their life cycles in most parts of the island once such adverse conditions arise.

We thus have a phenomenon of episodic competition through time (that is, through a many year period), rather than a competition at all times (as treated in most ecological theory, but see Wiens 1977). The casual observer can easily miss the severity of honey bee competition as it relates to native bee survival. This study thus began on the assumption of a potential long-term impact of honey bee competition on native bee populations.

Initially, the methodology we employed to find (Wenner et al. 1992) and remove colonies during the first few years of our European honey bee elimination project served us well. By the end of the 1993 season, few colonies remained on the eastern half of Santa Cruz Island. At that same time, however, unforeseen changes in the island ecology (as outlined in the Introduction) occurred and stimulated us to exploit the varroa mite as a biological control agent.

Within three years after introduction, the varroa mite had effectively brought the honey bee population under control and rendered that exotic species ineffective in competition with native bee species.Our find of a two-year latency period after innoculation and before colony collapse apparently represents a first. Worldwide, beekeepers and bee

researchers have been caught by surprise when colonies collapsed — without knowing when varroa mites first arrived in their area. Will the varroa mites completely eliminate the honey bee colonies on Santa Cruz Island? A very few colonies still functioned during the 1998 season. However, we know that a swarm sometimes leaves an infested colony just before its collapse and survives for another year or two before it, in turn, succumbs to mite infestation.

Earlier assessments, based mainly on data from 1993 to 1995 when the effects of varroa mite introductions were first felt in California (e.g., Kraus and Page 1995; Thorp 1996), suggested that feral honey bee swarms in California did not survive more than one year after leaving parent colonies. However, on the nearby mainland (unpublished documentation during 1998 in the city of Santa Barbara, Cronshaw 1998) and elsewhere in California (R. Thorp, pers. obs. 1998) feral honey bee colonies have apparently experienced a resurgence in survival time more recently.

Will feral honey bee colonies on Santa Cruz Island undergo a resurgence from the few colonies that still exist there? That remains to be seen — conditions on the island differ in important ways from those on the mainland. In particular, swarms on the mainland can emit from managed colonies kept alive by miticide inserts and can re-occupy existing cavities depopulated earlier by varroa mite infestations. Santa Cruz Island, by comparison, harbors no such managed colonies.

Is one of the few remaining colonies on Santa Cruz Island resistant to the mites? That is highly unlikely, since an allozyme study (R. Page, pers. comm. 1990) revealed that the island honey bees, isolated for more than a century, had little or no genetic variability and constituted a clone of sorts.

On the other hand, if continued survival did occur, a truly resistant colony could prove a boon to beekeepers, since no such strain has been found in the world to date. Surveys taken during the 1999 season should reveal whether honey bee colonies still remain on Santa Cruz Island or whether a total eradication has been achieved.

ACKNOWLEDGMENTS

We thank the late Dr. Carey Stanton for permission to proceed with the project in October, 1987, as well as Al and Russ Vail for providing access and logistic support during visits to Santa Rosa Island. Thanks also go to Dr. Lyndal Laughrin and Brian Guererro of the University of California's Natural Reserve System for their steady support through the years. Scores of volunteers, including Joe Alcock, John Bishop, Dan Meade, and Chris Spohrer, assisted us during the decade. Dr. Barry Schuyler and the United States Navy provided valuable transportation to and from the island. Justin Schmidt and Steven Thoenes of the United States Department of Agriculture in Tucson, Arizona provided swarm hives and fresh lures each season. The National Science Foundation, The Nature Conservancy, the College of Creative Studies at the University of California, Santa Barbara, and Faculty Research Funds from the University of California at the Santa Barbara and Davis campuses provided partial funding.

LITERATURE CITED

De Jong, D. 1990. Mites: Varroa and other parasites of brood. Pages 200-218 *in* Morse, R. A. and R. Nowogrodzki (eds.), Honey Bee Pests, Predators, and Diseases, Second Edition. Cornell University Press, Ithaca, NY.

Kraus, B. and R. E. Page, Jr. 1995. Effect of *Varroa jacobsoni* (Mesostigmata: Varroidae) on feral *Apis mellifera* (Hymenoptera: Apidae) in California. Environmental Entomology 24:1473-1480.

Martin, S. J. and D. Kemp. 1997. Average number of reproductive cycles performed by *Varroa jacobsoni* in honey bee (*Apis mellifera*) colonies. Journal of Apicultural Research 36:113-123.

Mobus, B. and C. de Bruyn. 1993. The New Varroa Handbook. Northern Bee Books, Scout Bottom Farm, Mytholmroyd, Britain.

Schmidt, J. O. and S. C. Thoenes. 1990. The efficiency of swarm traps: What percent of swarms are captured and at what distance from the hive. American Bee Journal 130:811.

Schmitz, D. C. and D. Simberloff. 1997. Biological invasions: a growing threat. Issues in Science and Technology 13:33-40.

Thorp, R. W. 1996. Resource overlap among native and introduced bees in California. Pages 143-151 *in* Matheson, A., S. L. Buchmann, C. O'Toole, P. Westrich, and I. H. Williams (eds.), The Conservation of Bees. Linnean Society Symposium Series No. 18. Academic Press, New York, NY.

Thorp, R. W., A. M. Wenner, and J. F. Barthell. 1994. Flowers visited by honey bees and native bees on Santa Cruz Island. Pages 351-365 *in* Halvorson, W. L. and G. J. Meander (eds.), Fourth California Islands Symposium: Update on the Status of Resources. Santa Barbara Museum of Natural History, Santa Barbara, CA.

Wenner, A. M., J. E. Alcock, and D. E. Meade. 1992. Efficient hunting of feral colonies. Bee Science 2:64-70.

Wenner, A. M. and W. W. Bushing. 1996. *Varroa* mite spread in the United States. Bee Culture 124:341-343.

Wenner, A. M. and R. W. Thorp. 1993. The honey bees of Santa Cruz Island. Bee Culture 121:272-275.

Wenner, A. M. and R. W. Thorp. 1994. Removal of feral honey bee (*Apis mellifera*) colonies from Santa Cruz Island. Pages 513-522 *in* Halvorson, W. L. and G. J. Meander (eds.), Fourth California Islands Symposium: Update on the Status of Resources. Santa Barbara Museum of Natural History, Santa Barbara, CA.

Wiens, J. A. 1977. On competition and variable environments. American Scientist. 65:590-597.

SOURCES OF UNPUBLISHED MATERIALS

Cronshaw, P. 612 Tabor Lane, Montecito, CA 93108. Unpublished documentation on honey bee swarms in Santa Barbara, CA 1998.

Page, R. Department of Entomology, University of California, Davis, CA 95616. Personal Communication 1990.

Randall, J. M., Borgias, D., Serpa, L., and Turner, C. Policy on Intentional Release of Non-indigenous Biocontrol Agents on Preserves Owned or Managed by The Nature Conservancy. The Nature Conservancy, 201 Mission Street, Fourth Floor, San Francisco, CA 94105. Unpublished document updated on 14 February 1994.

Thorp, R. W. Department of Entomology, University of California, Davis, CA 95616. Personal Observation 1998.

POLLEN AND NECTAR RESOURCE OVERLAP AMONG BEES ON SANTA CRUZ ISLAND

Robbin W. Thorp,[1] **Adrian M. Wenner,**[2] **and John F. Barthell**[3]

[1]Dept. of Entomology, University of California, Davis, CA 95616
(530) 752-0482, FAX (530) 752-1537, E-mail: rwthorp@ucdavis.edu
[2]Dept. of Ecology, Evolution, and Marine Biology, University of California, Santa Barbara, CA 93106 (805) 963-8508, FAX
(805) 893-8062, E-mail: wenner@lifesci.ucsb.edu
[3]Dept. of Biology, University of Central Oklahoma, Edmond, OK 73034
(405) 974-5779, FAX (405) 974-3824, E-mail: jbarthell@ucok.edu

ABSTRACT

In 1988, we initiated studies on the potential impact of introduced feral European honey bees on native bees and pollination of flowering plants on Santa Cruz Island. Honey bees tend to forage most frequently on introduced flowering plants. Their food resource use overlaps primarily with generalist native bees. Results obtained provide a baseline to determine effects of removing honey bees on restoration of native bees and pollination systems. Removal of honey bees from this isolated ecosystem is nearly complete and is predicted to: 1) increase food availability for native bees; 2) reduce seed set of some introduced flowering plants; and 3) have little or no negative effect on seed production of most native plants, including rare and endemic species. Long-term monitoring of native bee populations and experiments on plant reproduction are being used to test these predictions. Complications include: 1) recent invasion and spread of an alien leafcutting bee that may become the important pollinator of yellow star-thistle; 2) some alien plants may be important food resources for some native bees; 3) removal of grazing animals; 4) extreme rainfall fluctuations from prolonged drought to El Niño induced wet; and 5) dramatic increases in some weeds, especially fennel.

Keywords: Honey bee, *Apis mellifera*, leafcutting bee, *Megachile apicalis*, native bees, resource overlap, pollination, bee diversity, ecosystem restoration, Santa Cruz Island.

INTRODUCTION

The honey bee, *Apis mellifera* L., and its many subspecies and races are native to much of Europe, Africa, and parts of Asia. It has been purposefully introduced from Europe to most of the world. In most countries where it has been introduced, concerns have been expressed by some that the honey bee may compete with native bees and other flower-visiting organisms for pollen and nectar resources, may interfere with effective pollination of native flora, may cause abnormal hybridization in some plants, and may compete with birds and mammals for nest cavities (Pyke and Balzer 1985; Willis et al. 1990; Paton 1993; Sugden et al.

1996; Butz Huryn 1997). Some tests have added and removed honey bee colonies and measured all bees before, during, and after these perturbations (Schaffer et al. 1979, 1983; Pyke and Balzer 1985). These perturbation experiments were limited to short-term measures and did not address potential long-term reproductive effects. Few studies have dealt with effects on reproductive biology of potential competitors (Roubik 1978, 1980, 1982, 1983, 1989, 1996a, 1996b; Roubik et al. 1986; Sugden and Pyke 1991; Paton 1993).

Santa Cruz Island provides a potential study site for testing long-term effects of removal of honey bees. It is far enough from the mainland (ca. 25 miles) to prohibit reestablishment on their own without aid of human transport. The bee fauna is relatively well known (Rust et al. 1985; Thorp et al. 1994). Procedures for removal of honey bees are discussed by Wenner and Thorp (1994) and Wenner et al. (1999, this volume). Background information on the biodiversity, resource use, and overlap of resource use between honey bees and other bees on Santa Cruz Island are discussed by Thorp et al. (1994). This paper updates results of our studies since 1993.

This paper represents the second part of the Santa Cruz Island bee saga. Wenner addressed the first part, the removal of European honey bees (Wenner and Thorp 1994; Wenner et al. 1999, this volume). The removal of honey bees from Santa Cruz Island is nearly complete (Wenner et al. 1999, this volume). This second part of the study considers the impact of honey bee removal on native bees and pollination systems of native and exotic flowering plants. In 1988, when Wenner and coworkers started dealing with the problem of European honey bee removal, we also initiated collection of baseline data on biodiversity of bees, flower visitation, and overlap in use of pollen and nectar resources between native and introduced bees (Thorp et al. 1994).

MATERIALS AND METHODS

Sampling of bees to determine faunal diversity, floral resource use and overlap, and reproductive biology included the use of various "low technology" tools. The same was true for our gathering of data on visitation patterns, guilds of bee visitors, and their relative abundances at flowers. Aerial insect net collections and visual observations of bees at flowers provided the main sources of data. The latter included walking transects and stationary, timed counts at various flowers.

Trap-nests helped determine the reproduction of species of the guild of cavity-nesting bees (Thorp et al. 1992). This guild of bees was selected for ease of monitoring and comparison with similar data being gathered at several mainland sites in central California in another project being conducted in cooperation with Gordon Frankie, University of California, Berkeley (Thorp et al. 1992; Thorp 1996).

We have also collected some data on diversity of bees and their floral resource use from Santa Rosa Island. These data provide a baseline for comparison with the fauna and flora of an adjacent island off the coast of southern California that has never had honey bees.

Additions to the baseline data in Rust et al. (1985) and Thorp et al. (1994) are in Tables 1 through 4.

RESULTS

Since our initial publication (Thorp et al. 1994), we have accumulated additional records that can be added to Tables 1 and 3, and Appendices 1 through 3 of that paper. We have found an additional nine species of bees on the island (Table 1), all natives. We also add 13 more flowering plants used as food sources by honey bees (Table 2). Native bees visit a total of 11 of those 13 flowering plant species and share pollen and nectar resources of these plants with honey bees (Table 3). We also observed native bees visiting

flowers of *Eucalyptus globulus* Labill and *Raphanus sativus* L., especially *Andrena prunorum* Cockerell on wild radish.

Among the endemic plants visited by honey bees, we have additional records of other bee visitors to *Lyonothamnus floribundus* A. Gray: *Andrena* sp., *Augochlorella pomoniella* Cockerell, *Ceratina acantha* Provancher, *Colletes* sp., *Hylaeus* sp., and *Protosmia rubifloris* (Cockerell). The overall guild of flower visitors also includes small wasps and beetles, especially tumble flower beetles (Mordellidae).

Additional plants monitored, but not visited by honey bees include: natives *Artemisia californica* Less. (coastal sagebrush), *Comarostaphylos diversifolia* (Parry) Greene (summer holly), *Helianthemum scoparium* Nutt. (common rush-rose), and *Sisyrinchium bellum* S. Watson (blue-eyed grass); endemics *Malacothamnus fasciculatus* (Torr. & A. Gray) Greene var. *nesioticus* (B. L. Rob.) Kearney (Santa Cruz Island bush mallow) and *Rhamnus pirifolia* Greene (island redberry); and alien: *Malva parvifolia* L. (cheeseweed). An endemic species of special interest that is not visited by honey bees is the Santa Cruz Island bush mallow, *Malacothamnus*. The guild of bee visitors observed at flowers of this plant include: *Augochlorella pomoniella*, *Bombus edwardsii* Cresson, *Ceratina acantha*, *Diadasia nitidifrons* Cockerell, *Dialictus* sp., *Halictus* (*Seladonia*) sp., *Lasioglossum channelense* McGinley, and *Osmia* sp., with most frequent visitation by *Ceratina* females and *Lasioglossum* males.

The introduced leafcutting bee, *Megachile* (*Eutricharaea*) *apicalis* Spinola has expanded its range on the island (Figure 1). During the drought years from 1988 through 1991, it seemed limited to the area of the University of California (UC) Field Station and Islay Canyon. In 1992,

Table 1. New species records and additions to biogeographic relationships and floral host specializations of bees found on Santa Cruz Island for 1994 to 1998[1].

Species	Distribution[2]	Flower Hosts
Andrenidae		
Andrena (Diandrena) gnaphalii (Cockerell)	SoCA	ligulate Asteraceae
Halictidae		
Halictus farinosus Smith	W USA	generalist
Lasioglossum titusi (Crawford)	Pac Coast	Asteraceae
Megachilidae		
Callanthidium illustre (Cresson)	W NA	generalist
Ashmeadiella opuntiae (Cockerell)	W NA	Cactaceae
Megachile angelarum Cockerell	W NA	generalist
Coelioxys octodentata Say	NA	generalist
Anthophoridae		
Diadasia nigrifrons (Cresson)	W USA	*Sidalcea*
Diadasia nitidifrons Cockerell	W USA	*Malacothamnus*[3]

[1] Additions to Tables 1 to 3 in Thorp et al. 1994.

[2] From Hurd 1979.

[3] On the mainland it occurs mostly on *Sphaeralcea*, but also known to visit *Malacothamnus*.

Table 2. Additional records of flowers visited by honey bees on Santa Cruz Island for 1994 to 1998.

Flowers	Status[4]	Preferred by *Apis*	for[5]	Visited by non-*Apis* bees
Eriophyllum confertiflorum (golden yarrow)[2]	N	N	+	+
Hedera helix (English ivy)	I	PN	+	-
Hirschfeldia incana (sort-podded mustard)[3]	I	PN	+++	+
Lathyrus vestitus (wild pea)[2]	N	N	+	+
Lupinus albifrons (silver lupine)[2]	N	P	+	+
Melilotus indicus (yellow sweet clover)[2]	I	N	+	+
Persea americana (avocado)	I	N	+	+
Raphanus sativus (wild radish)[2]	I	PN	+++	+
Rhus ovata (sugar bush)	N	PN	+	+
Rosmarinus officinalis (Rosemary)	I	N	+++	-
Stephanomeria exigua coronaria (milk-aster)	N	PN	+	+
Veronica anagalis-aquatica (water speedwell)[2]	I	PN	+	+
Wisteria sp. (wisteria)	I	N	+	+

[1] Additions to Appendix 1 in Thorp et al. 1999.

[2] Plant species formerly listed in Appendix 3 in Thorp et al. 1994 as not visited by *Apis*.

[3] Some records reported in Thorp et al. 1994 under *Brassica* sp. probably belong here.

[4] Status abbreviations: N = native; I = introduced.

[5] Used by *Apis* for: N = nectar; P = pollen; PN = both pollen and nectar.

it was found in the lower half of the Navy Road and by 1993 it had been found at the Chapel at the Main Ranch and as far west as Cascada. By 1994, it had reached the lower portion of Portezuela. By September 1996, it was found at Prisoners Harbor and to the west at the bottom of Centinela Grade. By October 1997, its range extended from the Main Ranch Airstrip to the Pozo drainage in the southwest of the island. This expansion has been in conjunction with the presence of its principle food host, yellow star-thistle, *Centaurea solstitialis* L. However we have also found females visiting flower heads of *C. mellitensis* L. to a lesser extent. In addition, we have records of one male each on *Marrubium*, *Silybum*, and *Grindelia*.

Cavity nesting species of bees that have occupied our trap-nests include: *Anthidium maculosum* Cresson, *Ashmeadiella opuntiae* (Cockerell), and *Megachile apicalis*. The most frequent occupations have been by *Anthidium*. In addition native spider wasps of the genus *Trypoxylon* and eumenid wasps of the genus *Euodynerus* compete with bees for nest holes. The European earwig, *Forficula auricularia* L., also competes with cavity-nesting bees and wasps for tunnels, especially in wet years.

Nest sites of numerous ground nesting species of bees have been located including: *Colletes* sp., *Andrena* (*Hesperandrena*) spp., *A.* (*Diandrena*) spp., *A.* (*Onagrandrena*) *oenotherae* Timberlake, *A.* (*Plastandrena*) *prunorum*, *A.* (*Tylandrena*) *subaustralis* Cockerell, *Agapostemon texanus* Cresson, *Anthophora edwardsii* Cresson, *Habropoda depressa* Fowler, and *H. miserabilis* (Cresson). We have also encountered the cuckoo bee,

Melecta separata callura (Cockerell), and the nocturnal mutillid wasp, *Sphaeropthalma* sp. in association with nests of *Anthophora edwardsii*. One of us (AMW) found a huge nest site of *Andrena prunorum* in April 1998. Investigations into the nest biology of this bee were conducted in April and July by RWT. This bee is apparently bivoltine with overlapping generations, since both eggs and pupae were found in nests in April. Eggs to overwintering post-defecating larvae were found in July.

On 21 March 1994, AMW and assistants collected bees mostly on *Brassica* on the eastern end of Santa Cruz Island. These collections produced no honey bees, but yielded a total of 298 individuals belonging to 13 genera and over 20 species of native bees.

Counts of bees at flowers show that *Apis* declined sharply in conjunction with the heavy mortality caused by varroa mites (see Wenner et al. 1999, this volume). In the past one could be sure to see large numbers of honey bees at the more preferred flowers. During the past two years we have had to hunt diligently to find sites still supporting foraging honey bees. One of us (AMW) made collections in early September 1997 on four plant species (mustard, yellow star-thistle, coastal goldenbush, and island buckwheat) and early January 1998 on manzanita. In September 1997 a total of eight honey bees were found on mustard (four at two sites), and on yellow star-thistle (four at one site) while all four plant species yielded 8 genera, 11 species and 94 individuals (27 males, 57 females) of native bees. A survey of bees visiting manzanita in January 1998 (the same transect surveyed in January 1992) produced no honey bees, but did

Table 3. Additions to food resource sharing: flowers visited by honey bees and new records for the guilds of other bees that visit them on Santa Cruz Island for 1994 to 1998.[1]

Eriophyllum confertiflorum (golden yarrow)
   Augochlorella pomoniella, Colletes sp., *Megachile* sp., *Melissodes* sp.

Eucalyptus globulus (blue gum)[2]
   Agapostemon texanus, Dialictus sp. 1, *Dialictus* sp. 2.

Hirschfeldia incana (short-podded mustard)
   Augochlorella pomoniella, Colletes sp., *Ceratina acantha, Melissodes* sp., *Triepeolus* sp.

Lupinus albifrons (silver lupine)
   Anthidium maculosum, Anthophora edwardsii, Bombus edwardsii, Diadasia bituberculata, Habropoda depressa, Megachile brevis, M. coquilletti, Synhalonia sp.

Melilotus indicus (yellow sweet clover)
   Andrena sp.

Persea americana (advocado)
   Andrena prunorum, Ceratina acantha, Evylaeus sp., *Halictus (Seladonia)* sp., *Hylaeus* sp.

Raphanus sativus (wild radish)
   Agapostemon texanus, Andrena prunorum, Andrena spp., *Anthophora edwardsii, Augochlorella pomoniella, Bombus edwardsii, Ceratina acantha, Dialictus* sp., *Evylaeus* sp., *Halictus (Seladonia)* sp., *Hylaeus* sp, *Lasioglossum channelense, Melecta separata callura, Nomada* sp, *Synhalonia* sp.

Rhus ovata (sugar bush)
   Agpostemon texanus, Andrena cerulea, Andrena spp., *Bombus edwardsii, Evylaeus* sp., *Habropoda depressa, Hylaeus* sp., *Nomada* sp., *Protosmia rubifloris.*

Stephanomeria exigua coronaria (milk-aster)
   Augochlorella pomoniella.

Veronica anagalis-aquatica (water speedwell)
   Ceratina acantha.

Wisteria sp. (wisteria)
   Bombus edwardsii.

[1]Additions to Appendix 2 in Thorp et al. 1994.
[2]On Appendix 1 list of flowers used by Apis in Thorp et al. 1994, but no other bees known as visitors at this time.

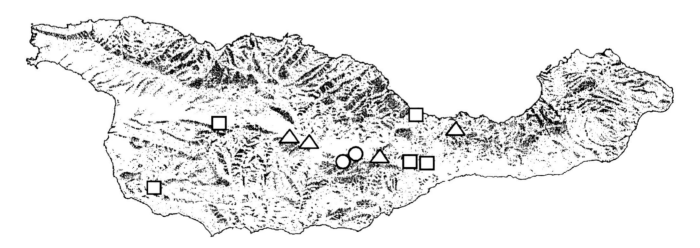

Figure 1. Santa Cruz Island: distribution of the introduced leafcutting bee, *Megachile apicalis,* since its first detection in 1988. Circles = 1988-1994; triangles = 1996; squares = 1997-1998.

yield native bees of 4 genera, 5 species and 18 individuals (6 males, 12 females). At the few remaining sites in the Central Valley where honey bees still forage we made a number of transect counts through yellow star-thistle in July 1998 (Table 4). In addition, we found three honey bees at the eastern Pine Forest in 10 minutes with three observers = 0.03 bees/observer minute and two honey bees in 35 minutes with one observer in lower Portezuela = 0.06 bees/observer minute druing our search from the eastern sheep fence to Christy Ranch in July 1998. Counts at yellow star-thistle in September 1998 produced a total of 83 bees in 41 minutes, only five were honey bees. There was also a diverse guild of non-bee visitors on yellow star-thistle in September 1998 including Lepidoptera (*Vanessa*, *Papilio*, *Pieris*, Hesperiidae, *Celerio lineata* (Fabricius), and Noctuidae); Diptera (*Eristalis*, Syrphidae, Bombyliidae), and Hymenoptera (*Bembix*).

Oligolectic bees often occur in association with plants rarely or never visited by *Apis* and may be their most important pollinators. Those bees include *Diadasia biturberculata* (Cresson) on *Calystegia*, *Diadasia nigrifrons* (Cresson) on

occurs at a mainland site, Mount Diablo State Park (RWT unpublished observation).

We found 13 more flowering plants used for food sources by honey bees since 1993 (Table 2). Five of these are natives; the other eight are introduced plants. Of the 13 additional species visited by honey bees, the most favored are introduced plants, including one for nectar only. Three of those introduced plants (*Hedera*, *Rosmarinus*, and *Wisteria*) do not appear in the Flora of Santa Cruz Island (Junak et al. 1995) because they have not escaped from plantings in association with the Main Ranch and the UC Field Station. Four of the native plant species are also visited by native bees and are only sparingly utilized by honey bees. The introduced wild radish is heavily visited by native bees, especially *Andrena prunorum*.

In an earlier paper (Thorp et al. 1994), we reported finding *Apis* on 57 of 154 (37%) flowering plants examined. In that paper introduced flowering species comprised about 35% of our honey bee visitation records, and most of the highly "preferred" floral resources were introduced species. With our new data these percentage figures increase

Table 4. Honey bee abundance on yellow star-thistle (*Centaurea solstitialis*) in the Central Valley of Santa Cruz Island in July 1998.

Day	Location	No. of *Apis*	Observation Period (min)	No. of Observers	No. of *Apis* per observed min.
20	E of Main Ranch	3	20	2	0.07
20	E of Main Ranch	3	20	2	0.07
20	Chapel	5	5	2	0.5
20	Main Ranch to Field Station	0	5	2	0
22	W of Sherwood E plot 1	17	20	2	0.43
22	W of Sherwood E plot 2	23	20	3	0.38
22	W of Sherwood E plot	7	20	3	0.12

Sidalcea, *D. nitidifrons* on *Malacothamnus*, *D. rinconis* Cockerell on *Opuntia*, *Andrena* (*Diandrena*) spp. on *Lasthenia*, *A.* (*Hesperandrena*) spp. on *Lasthenia*, and *A.* (*Onagrandrena*) *oenotherae* on *Camissonia*.

SUMMARY AND DISCUSSION

Rust et al. (1985) published lists of bees known from the Channel Islands that included 84 species from Santa Cruz Island. We provided additions to these records (Thorp et al. 1994), raising the total number of bees reported for Santa Cruz Island to 105. Since 1993, we found an additional nine species of native bees on the island (Table 1). *Ashmeadiella* was reared from a trap-nest, *Callanthidium* and *Chalicodoma* are also known to nest in preexisting cavities, and *Coelioxys* is a cuckoo bee that lays its eggs in nests of *Megachile*. The other five species nest in the ground. Four of the species are pollen specialists (oligolectic bees). *Diadasia nitidifrons*, a pollen specialist on Malvaceae, was found visiting the endemic bush mallow, *Malacothamnus*, an association that also

slightly. Honey bees visited flowers of 70 of 168 (41.7%) of the flowering plants examined. Of those 70, 40.0% (28) are introduced species. Those 28 include most of the flowers on which we most frequently encounter foraging honey bees and overlap with native bees.

We continue to test our initial predictions that removal of honey bees from Santa Cruz Island should: 1) increase food availability for native bees, 2) reduce seed set of some introduced weedy flowering plants, and 3) have little or no negative impact on seed production of most native plants, including rare and endemic species (Thorp et al. 1994). Our approach is to use long-term monitoring of honey bee and native bee populations. Experiments on plant reproduction are being used or will be used to test these predictions (see Barthell et al. 1999, this volume).

In 1992, we monitored a transect along the South Ridge Road to determine the numbers of honey bees versus native bees visiting flowers of manzanita (Wenner and Thorp 1994). In January 1998, honey bees were absent along this transect due to depredations by varroa mites. The manzanita supported a diverse assemblage of native bees. Their numbers were low, but this was probably due to the El Niño weather pattern that caused delays of two to four weeks in emergence of many native bees and other insects throughout California.

With the recent sharp decline in honey bees on the island (Wenner et al. 1999, this volume), foraging pressure on overlapping resource plants decreased, especially on introduced weeds. In September 1998 on yellow star-thistle, honey bees represented only 6% in contrast to 97% in July 1994 (Barthell et al. 1999, this volume). Nectar feeders other than bees were also frequently seen on yellow star-thistle, especially Lepidoptera and Diptera. Thus a more diverse total guild of flower feeders visits yellow star-thistle than indicated by our list of the guild of bees (Thorp et al. 1994).

Reduction in seed set after removal of honey bees may not occur as predicted for some other exotic weeds since they are also frequently visited by diverse guilds of native bees. Examples may include Asteraceae: *Centaurea solstitialis*, *Cichorium intybus* L., and *Silybum marianum* (L.) Gaertn.; Brassicaceae: *Raphanus sativus*, *Brassica* spp. and *Cakile maritima* Scop.; Fabaceae: *Lotus corniculatus* L.; and Lamiaceae: *Marrubium vulgare* L.. We have found that *Apis* contribute signigficantly to reproduction of yellow star-thistle, especially on the mainland and may have been responsible for its initial rapid spread (Barthell et al. 1994, 1995). However, the introduced leafcutting bee, *Megachile apicalis* continues to expand its range on Santa Cruz Island (Figure 1) and may perpetuate and enhance the reproduction of yellow star-thistle in the absence of the honey bee.

This is supported by many of our observations to date. Most of the native plants that honey bees seem to prefer also have diverse guilds of native bees or may be primarily pollinated by other insects (Thorp et al. 1994). *Asclepias fascicularis* Decne in A.DC. is frequently visited by a variety of wasps. *Baccharis salicifolia* (Ruiz & Pav.) Pers. (as *glutinosa* Pers.) has a diverse guild of bee visitors and is often visited by flies and other insects. *Prunus* and *Toxicodendron* are visited by numerous small native bees although the generic diversity is not great. *Heteromeles* frequently receives visits by a diverse assemblage of bees, and *Salvia* is heavily visited by numerous large bees.

Native gumplant, *Grindelia camporum* Greene, and yellow star-thistle have similar guilds of bee visitors (Thorp et al. 1994), but gumplant received a low preference rating for honey bee visits. We find that native bees are far more frequent visitors than honey bees to gumplant (Barthell et al. 1999, this volume). We have not found honey bees visiting the endemic *Malacothamnus*. Honey bees are mostly rare visitors compared to native bees and other insects at flowers of other island endemics: *Dudleya nesiotica* (Moran) Moran, *Lyonothamnus*, and *Malacothrix* (Thorp et al. 1994). Thus, removal of honey bees from the island will not likely have any detrimental impact on the reproduction of these species.

Many oligolectic (pollen specialist) bees tend to be dominant visitors to their host plants and are likely to be their most important pollinators. Honey bees rarely visit flowers of those plants on Santa Cruz Island. We recorded honey bees only rarely from *Calystegia* and not at all from *Camissonia*, *Lasthenia*, *Malacothamnus*, *Opuntia*, and *Sidalcea*.

This research project provides an unique opportunity to test effects of removal of *Apis* that is not feasible in most mainland sites. However, Santa Cruz Island has undergone many changes since just before and during the tenure of our studies (Thorp 1996). The effects of many of these, especially in combination, may overwhelm our abilities to sort out predicted changes that may be attributed to honey bee removal. Such changes include: 1) removal of sheep (by about 1987) and most of the cattle (by 1988); 2) weather-prolonged drought (1987-1990); 3) subsequent unusual spring rain patterns in 1990-1992 (1991 March miracle and 1992 February rains) followed by above normal rains during the 1992-1993, 1994-1995, and 1997-1998 seasons; 3) dramatic fluctuations in feral pig populations (e.g., crash in 1990 and 1991); 4) dramatic increases in coverage by introduced weeds, especially fennel since 1992 due to release from grazing animals and enhanced by rains after drought; and 5) introduction (1988) and spread of the exotic, cavity-nesting, leafcutting bee, *Megachile apicalis*.

ACKNOWLEDGMENTS

Partial funding for continuation of this project has been provided by the Department of Entomology, University of California, Davis, and the College of Creative Studies, University of California, Santa Barbara (UCSB). We thank the UCSB Natural Reserve System, especially Lyndal Laughrin and Brian Geurerro, and The Nature Conservancy for access to the island and for logistical support. We also thank the many volunteers including: L. M. Polakoff, M. Kinsey, C. Spohrer, K. Schick, Yaacov Lensky and his wife Miriam for field assistance. We thank Rob Klinger and Dieter Wilken for help in locating populations of *Malacothamnus*. Steve Junak, Dieter Wilken, and other botanists who identified plants for us. We also appreciate the intellectual stimulation provided by many colleagues housed at the U.C. Field Station during our visits to the island.

LITERATURE CITED

Barthell, J. F., J. M. Randall, R. W. Thorp, and A. M. Wenner. 1994. Invader assisted invasion: pollination of yellow star-thistle by feral honey bees in island and mainland ecosystems. Supplement to the Bulletin of the Ecological Society of America 75(2):10. [Abstract]

Barthell, J. F., R. W. Thorp, and A. M. Wenner. 1995. Invaders preferring invaders: the case of yellow star-thistle, gum-weed and feral honey bees on Santa Cruz Island. Supplement to the Bulletin of the Ecological Society of America 76(2):15. [Abstract].

Barthell, J. F., R. W. Thorp, A. M. Wenner, and J. M. Randall. 1999. Yellow star-thistle, gumplant, and feral honey bees on Santa Cruz Island: a case of invaders assisting invaders. Pages 269 to 273 *in* Browne, D. R., K. L. Mitchell, and H. W. Chaney, (eds.), Proceedings of the Fifth California Islands Symposium, 29 March to 1 April 1999. Santa Barbara Museum of Natural History, Santa Barbara, CA. Sponsored by the U. S. Minerals Management Service, Pacific OCS Region, 770 Paseo Camarillo, Camarillo, CA 93010. OCS Study No. 99-0038.

Butz Huryn, V. 1997. Ecological impacts of introduced honey bees. Quarterly Review of Biology. 72(3):275-297.

Hurd, P. D. 1979. Superfamily Apoidea. Pages 1741-2209 *in* Krombein, K. V., P. D. Hurd, Jr., D. R. Smith, and B. D. Burks (eds.), Catalog of Hymenoptera in America North of Mexico. Smithsonian Institution Press, Washington, DC, Vol. 2.

Junak, S., T. Ayers, R. Scott, D. Wilken, and D. Young. 1995. A flora of Santa Cruz Island. Santa Barbara Botanical Garden, Santa Barbara, CA. 397 pp.

Paton, D. C. 1993. Honeybees in the Australian environment: does *Apis mellifera* disrupt or benefit native biota? Bioscience 43:95-103.

Pyke, G. H. and L. Balzer. 1985. The effects of the introduced honey-bee on Australian native bees. New South Wales National Parks Wildlife Service, Occasional Papers, Number 7.

Roubik, D. W. 1978. Competitive interactions between neotropical pollinators and Africanized honey bees. Science 201:1030-1032.

Roubik, D. W. 1980. Foraging behavior of competing Africanized honeybees and stingless bees. Ecology 61:836-845.

Roubik, D. W. 1982. Ecological impact of Africanized honeybees on native neotropical pollinators. Pages 233-247 *in* P. Jaisson, (ed.), Social Insects in the Tropics. Paris: Université Paris-Nord.

Roubik, D. W. 1983. Experimental community studies: time-series tests of competition between African and neotropical bees. Ecology 64:971-978.

Roubik, D. W. 1989. Ecology and Natural History of Tropical Bees. New York: Cambridge University Press. 514 pp.

Roubik, D. W. 1991. Aspects of Africanized honey bee ecology in tropical America. Pages 259-281 *in* Spivak, M., D. J. C. Fletcher, and M. D. Breed, (eds.), The "African" honey bee. Westview Press. Boulder, CO. 435 pp.

Roubik, D. W. 1996a. Measuring the meaning of honey bees. Pages 163-172 *in* Matheson, A., S. L. Buchmann, C. O'Toole, P. Westrich, and I. H. Williams (eds.), The Conservation of Bees. Linnean Society Symposium Series No. 18. London: Academic Press. 252 pp.

Roubik, D. W. 1996b. African honey bees as exotic pollinators in French Guiana. Pages 173-182 *in* Matheson, A., S. L. Buchmann, C. O'Toole, P. Westrich, and I. H. Williams (eds.), The Conservation of Bees. Linnean Society

Symposium Series No. 18. London: Academic Press. 252 pp.

Roubik, D. W., J. E. Moreno, C. Vergara, and D. Wittman. 1986. Sporadic food competition with the African honey bee: projected impact on neotropical social bees. Journal of Tropical Ecology. 2:97-111.

Rust, R., A. Menke, and D. Miller. 1985. A biogeographic comparison of the bees, sphecid wasps, and mealy bugs of the California Channel Islands (Hymenoptera, Homoptera). Pages 29-59 *in* A. S. Menke and D. R. Miller (eds.), Entomology of the California Channel Islands, Proceedings of the First Symposium. Santa Barbara 178 pp.

Schaffer, W. M., D. B. Jensen, D. E. Hobbs, J. Gurevitch, J. R. Todd, M. Valentine Schaffer. 1979. Competition, foraging energetics, and the cost of sociality in three species of bees. Ecology 60:976-987.

Schaffer, W. M., D. W. Zeh, S. L. Buchmann, S. Kleinhaus, M. Valentine Schaffer. 1983. Competition for nectar between introduced honey bees and native North American bees and ants. Ecology 64:564-577.

Sugden, E. A. and G. H. Pyke. 1991. Effects of honey bees on colonies of *Exoneura asimillima*, an Australian native bee. Australian Journal of Ecology. 16:171-181.

Sugden, E. A., R. W. Thorp, and S. L. Buchmann. 1996. Honey bee-native bee competition: focal point for environmental change and agricultural response in Australia. Bee World 77(1):26-44.

Thorp, R. W. 1996. Resource overlap among native and introduced bees in California. Pages 143-151 *in* Matheson, A., S. L. Buchmann, C. O'Toole, P. Westrich, and I. H. Williams (eds.), The Conservation of Bees. Linnean Society Symposium Series No. 18. London: Academic Press. 252 pp.

Thorp, R. W., G. W. Frankie, J. Barthell, D. Gordon, L. Newstrom, T. Griswold, J. Schmidt, and S. Thoenes. 1992. Ecological research...Long-term studies to gauge effects of invading bees. California Agriculture 46(1):20-23. (Jan. 1992).

Thorp, R. W., A. M. Wenner, and J. F. Barthell. 1994. Flowers visited by honey bees and native bees on Santa Cruz Island. Pages 351-365 *in* Halvorson, W. L. and G. J. Maender (eds.), The Fourth California Islands Symposium: Update on the Status of Resources. Santa Barbara Museum of Natural History, Santa Barbara, CA.

Wenner, A. M. and R. W. Thorp. 1994. Removal of feral honey bee (*Apis mellifera*) colonies from Santa Cruz Island. Pages 513-522 *in* Halvorson, W. L. and G. J. Maender (eds.), The Fourth California Islands Symposium: Update on the Status of Resources. Santa Barbara Museum of Natural History, Santa Barbara, CA.

Wenner, A. M., R. W. Thorpe, and J. F. Barthell. 1999. Removal of European honey bees from the Santa Cruz Island ecosystem. Pages 256 to 260 *in* Browne, D. R., K. L. Mitchell, and H. W. Chaney, (eds.), Proceedings of the Fifth California Islands Symposium, 29 March to 1 April 1999. Santa Barbara Museum of Natural History,

Santa Barbara, CA. Sponsored by the U. S. Minerals Management Service, Pacific OCS Region, 770 Paseo Camarillo, Camarillo, CA 93010. OCS Study No. 99-0038.

Wills, R. T., M. N. Lyons, and D. T. Bell. 1990. The European honey bee in Western Australian kwongan: foraging preferences and some implications for management. Proceedings of the Ecological Society of Australia. 16:167-176.

YELLOW STAR-THISTLE, GUMPLANT, AND FERAL HONEY BEES ON SANTA CRUZ ISLAND: A CASE OF INVADERS ASSISTING INVADERS

John F. Barthell[1], Robbin W. Thorp[2], Adrian M. Wenner[3], and John M. Randall[4]

[1]Dept. of Biology, University of Central Oklahoma, Edmond, OK 73034
(405) 974-5779, FAX (405) 974-3824, E-mail: jbarthell@ucok.edu
[2]Dept. of Entomology, University of California, Davis, CA 95616
(530) 752-0482, FAX (530) 752-1537, E-mail: rwthorp@ucdavis.edu
[3]Dept. of Ecology, Evolution and Marine Biology, University of California, Santa Barbara, CA 93106
(805) 963-8508, FAX (805) 893-8062, E-mail: wenner@lifesci.ucsb.edu
[4]The Nature Conservancy, Wildland Weeds Management and Research, Department of Vegetable Crops,
University of California, Davis, CA 95616
(530) 754-8890, FAX (916) 752-4604, E-mail: jarandall@ucdavis.edu

ABSTRACT

Feral honey bees have populated Santa Cruz Island (SCI) for over a century; this circumstance has produced an ideal setting for testing the hypothesis that honey bees promote the reproductive success of introduced weeds on the island. Fully one quarter of the vascular plant species on SCI are introduced, many of them well-established in the island's Central Valley. To test our hypothesis we compared the native gumplant, *Grindelia camporum*, and the introduced yellow star-thistle, *Centaurea solstitialis*, for their attractiveness to honey bees and native bee species. Overall, numbers of honey bees observed at yellow star-thistle exceeded those of native bees by a ratio of at least 33 to 1 while native bee numbers exceeded those of honey bees at gumplant by at least 46 to 1. We also employed an exclusion experiment with three mesh bag treatments to separate the effects of honey bees and selected native pollinator groups on seed head development. Seed head weights obtained from plots of gumplant and yellow star-thistle demonstrate that, when honey bees were fully excluded (while allowing native bee visitation), average seed head weight of yellow star-thistle significantly declined while that of gumplant did not.

Keywords: *Apis mellifera*, *Centaurea solstitialis*, *Grindelia camporum*, honey bees, invasions, Santa Cruz Island.

INTRODUCTION

Feral honey bees (*Apis mellifera* L.) were introduced to the eastern United States over 250 years ago (Crosby 1986). As their westward migration (assisted by man) ensued, honey bees established thriving, feral populations. During the 1830s, Washington Irving (1956) noted an episode of "bee-hunting" in what is now Oklahoma, a practice common among Native Americans who had considered the bees an omen of advancing settlers. By 1853, colonies had been transported to and established in California (Watkins 1968) and have since adapted so well to the north-south length of the state as to reflect clines in both morphology and allozymes (Daly et al. 1991; Nielsen et al. 1994). Only recently, with the invasion of the ectoparasitic varroa mite, have feral honey bee populations begun to show a decline (Kraus and Page 1995). Despite the highly successful occupation of our native ecosystems by honey bees, their effects on native organisms have received little attention and experimental studies of their interactions with plant and native pollinator populations in North America are generally lacking in the literature (but see Butz Huryn 1997).

In the late 1980s, two of us (Robbin W. Thorp and Adrian M. Wenner) began investigating honey bee effects on Santa Cruz Island (SCI) with the ultimate goal of removing honey bees from the island (Wenner and Thorp 1994; Wenner et al. 1999, this volume). SCI is a relatively isolated island locale (several kilometers from the mainland) that has apparently supported feral honey bees for a century or more. This setting therefore provides an ideal venue for a classical "removal" study from which one can infer the historical consequences of the honey bee's presence there. In anticipation of the eventual removal of the honey bees from SCI, we began to design experimental exclusion studies that assess honey bee effects on plants.

With over 26% of the vascular plant species on Santa Cruz Island being nonnative (Junak et al. 1995), we hypothesized a relationship between honey bees and the high densities of introduced plant species, a relationship that may be mutualistic in nature. One such species is yellow star-thistle (*Centaurea solstitialis* L.) a European invader that now covers innumerable acres of land in the northwestern United States (Maddox and Mayfield 1985). In an earlier study (Barthell et al. unpublished manuscript-a) we examined the relationship between honey bee densities and seed set levels in this species. In the current study, however, we opted to compare the role of honey bees in the pollination of both yellow star-thistle and the native gumplant species, *Grindelia camporum* E. Greene, to test the hypothesis that the introduced species benefits more from honey bee pollination than the native species.

MATERIALS AND METHODS

Santa Cruz Island

Santa Cruz Island (SCI) is located off the southern California coast south of Santa Barbara. It is the largest of the eight Channel Islands, occupying 25,000 hectares. Its recent history (since 1800s) included heavy agricultural usage, including a vineyard and, most recently, a cattle ranch. In 1965 the University of California began managing aspects of research on the island and in 1987 The Nature Conservancy purchased the western 90% of the island and began managing it as a nature preserve. The National Park Service, which now owns the eastern 10% of the island, assists in its management. Despite its protected state, the Central Valley of the island still bears the remnants of its agricultural use, including considerable densities of introduced weed species (e.g., fennel, mustard, horehound, and yellow star-thistle).

The study was conducted among four study plots on the island (two per study plant species). Two of these were located in the Central Valley, one (containing gumplant) near the University of California Field Station and a second one (containing yellow star-thistle) alongside the main road just east of a large grove of eucalyptus trees dubbed "Sherwood Forest" by local researchers. The other two plots were located near the western edge of the Central Valley. One of these (containing yellow star-thistle) was alongside an abandoned section of road a short walking distance from the "Cascada" region (noted for its year-round spring). The remaining "Portezuela" plot was located at the top of the Portezuela grade (western edge of the Central Valley) and contained gumplant.

Monitoring Visitation

Twenty study plants were selected along a transect within each plot (about a meter separating plants). Flowers on the previously selected study plants in each plot were monitored for visitors simultaneously during four separate half-hour time periods on 12 July, 1994: 09:00-09:30, 12:00-12:30, 15:00-15:30, and 18:00-18:30. During each period, visiting bees were censused on the designated study plants during a 2.5 min walk along each transect, recording the number and types of visitors among the 20 study plants. This walk was reversed back to the starting point during another 2.5 min period. This process was repeated five additional times (producing a 30 min monitoring period).

Seed Head Weights

Four treatments were used in the study. The control was a flower bud without any obstruction to potential visitors while the remaining three used a mesh exclosure that prevented visitation by varying degrees. Exclosures were constructed from 20 cm-diameter circles of nylon mesh fitted with draw-strings. The largest mesh exclosure treatment contained 5 mm diameter openings which excluded large pollinators such as certain anthophorid bee species and bumble bees. A medium mesh treatment (3 mm openings) excluded honey bees but allowed visitation by small-bodied native pollinators (e.g., halictid bees). Finally, a fine diameter mesh (1 mm openings) excluded all bees.

The treatments were assigned by dividing each study plant into four quadrants, denoted as NE, SE, SW and NW. A single flower bud (of comparable developmental stage) was identified in each quadrant and marked with an identification tag. Treatments were randomly assigned to the selected buds. Since many flower heads were damaged during the study, alternate buds were sometimes selected to replace them.

All flower buds were allowed to develop and senesce before the flower heads were enclosed with a fine mesh bagging material that prevented the loss of any seeds. Fully senesced seed heads were later removed and stored in plastic bags.

In the laboratory, senesced seed heads were cut from their stems and weighed. The dense, viable seeds in successfully pollinated plants were assumed to contribute mostly to seed head weight, an assumption successfully employed in at least one other study on an unrelated plant species (Barthell and Knops 1997).

RESULTS

Visitation

Visitation data presented in Table 1 demonstrate that the two yellow star-thistle plots were predominantly visited by honey bees. At the Sherwood plot, for example, honey bees out-numbered native bees by a ratio of 34 to 1, while at the Cascada plot the ratio was 33 to 1. Native bees were mostly species in the family Halictidae (five observations) and the Anthophoridae (seven observations), with only one megachilid bee observed.

In contrast to study plots of yellow star-thistle, gumplant plots were seldom visited by honey bees (Table 1). The ratio of honey bees to native bees at the Field Station plot was 1 to 46 with no honey bee visitation at the Portezuela plot. The dominant native visitors were in the families Halictidae (61 total observations) and Anthophoridae (92 total observations).

Seed Head Weights

Treatment effects were observed for both yellow star-thistle (P = .0002; F = 7.243; df = 3) and gumplant (P = .0001; F = 9.815; df = 3) plot pairs according to a 2-way ANOVA. However, the yellow star-thistle plot at Cascada was so severely damaged from the chewing and tearing of treatment bags by the Channel Islands fox that we consider the analysis of data from that plot inconclusive. Only four control exclosure bags remained for analysis while many other bagged heads (though not completely removed from the plant) were compromised in their development. A comparison of the two yellow star-thistle plots in this study reveals the extent of this discrepency (Table 2).

Mean separation tests reveal that yellow star-thistle seed weights were significantly different between the large and medium mesh exclosure treatments (Fisher PLSD = .033) in the Sherwood yellow star-thistle plot (Table 2). There was no difference between these treatments, however, for the gumplant plots at the Field Station and Portezuela (Fisher PLSD = .109 and .122, respectively).

DISCUSSION

During simultaneous monitoring periods reported for this study, numbers of honey bees observed at yellow star-thistle far exceeded those of native bees and, conversely, native bees were far more abundant than honey bees at gumplant patches. These results are consistent with subsequent seed head weight patterns indicating that (for the study plots that escaped fox intrusion) yellow star-thistle seed heads from control and large-mesh treatments were significantly greater than the honey bee-excluding medium-mesh treatment in the Sherwood plot. No significant differences between these same treatments were observed in either gumplant plot. We find the results of the Cascada plot (containing yellow star-thistle) inconclusive given the high level of treatment damage caused by the Channel Islands fox, otherwise known as "demonic intrusion" (Hurlbert 1984). Our previous yellow star-thistle

study that examined the same treatments in both island and mainland ecosystems but which used numbers and ratios of viable and non-viable seeds corroborate the results of the Sherwood plot (Barthell et al. unpublished manuscript-a). The visitation patterns described here for honey bees at yellow star-thistle are corroborated by Maddox et al. (1996) in California. Guilds of bees previously identified visiting our two plant species on SCI show considerable overlap, but honey bees seem to prefer yellow star-thistle (Thorp at al. 1994).

Although further comparisons are required (and are forthcoming), honey bees appear to demonstrate a propensity for visitation to and pollination of introduced European weeds such as yellow star-thistle. The disproportionate visitation (and resulting pollination) by honey bees to this introduced species demonstrates a discernible link between plant reproductive success and this widespread and long-term invasive pollinator. It is also realistic to consider the relationship between honey bees and yellow star-thistle, in the context of ecological invasion, as a "mutualism." The importance of such species interactions, when both interacting species benefit, are frequently underestimated in ecology (Bronstein 1994) and deserve special consideration in our understanding of invasion mechanisms.

Does the mutualistic interaction of honey bees with yellow star-thistle translate to range expansion for yellow star-thistle? Information from our study does not address this question directly. However, historical evidence indicates that

Table 1. Total numbers of bees (according to family) observed visiting each of four study plots on Santa Cruz Island (12 July 1994).

Taxa	Yellow Star-Thistle Plots		Gumplant Plots	
	Sherwood	Cascada	Field Station	Portezuela
Apidae (*Apis*)	135 (97)	300 (97)	2 (2)	0 (0)
Megachilidae	0 (0)	1 (<1)	2 (2)	5 (7)
Halictidae	1 (1)	4 (1)	26 (28)	35 (51)
Anthophoridae	3 (2)	4 (1)	63 (68)	29 (42)
Totals	139 (100)	309 (100)	93 (100)	69 (100)

Table 2. Mean ± S E and sample size (n) from seed head weights for study plots of yellow star-thistle and gumplant study plants according to four treatment categories.[1]

Study Plot	No Mesh	Large Mesh	Medium Mesh	Small Mesh
Star-thistle Plot I "Sherwood"	0.29 – 0.013 (19)[a]	0.28 – 0.013 (19)[a]	0.23 – 0.011 (17)[b]	0.21 – 0.009 (15)[c]
Star-thistle Plot II[2] "Cascada"	0.31 – 0.012 (15)[a]	0.31 – 0.011 (17)[a]	0.28 – 0.014 (16)[a]	0.28 – 0.013 (4)[a]
Gumplant Plot I "Field Station"	0.67 – 0.047 (20)[a]	0.61 – 0.028 (20)[a,b]	0.60 – 0.045 (20)[a,b]	0.42 – 0.030 (15)[b]
Gumplant Plot II "Portezuela"	0.65 – 0.042 (18)[a]	0.55 – 0.056 (13)[a]	0.57 – 0.040 (17)[a]	0.46 – 0.028 (18)[b]

[1] Protected Fisher's LSD results are denoted by letters; values followed by different letters (superscript) are significantly different from others in the same row.

[2] This plot received extensive damage by Channel Island foxes, particularly the small mesh treatment plants.

such a scenario is at least possible, as it appears that yellow star-thistle was introduced to the western United States (seeds of which appeared in building materials of homes) before the introduction of honey bees in the mid 1800s (Hendry and Bellue 1936). The later introduction of commercial hives and subsequent spread of feral honey bee populations in the state may, ultimately, have promoted the spread of yellow star-thistle.

Surprisingly few studies have endeavored to examine the extent of impact by honey bees on the native and introduced flora of North America. A recent review of the subject by Butz Huryn (1997) suggests that most evidence to date demonstrates visitor abundance shifts at flowers (perhaps an indication of interference competition) without direct linkage to the reproductive fate of native pollinators or plants. Roubik (1983), for example, did not find such evidence when measuring resource stores of native stingless bees in South America during invasion of the region by African honey bees. Many such studies may be limited, however, by the ability to adequately measure the variables in question. Frankie et al. (1998), for example, predict such difficulties in measuring invasion effects of honey bees in a study that monitored abundances of solitary, cavity nesting bees in California. However, under the right experimental circumstances, similar methods were used to detect other invader effects on solitary bees (Barthell et al. 1998). Indeed, as the number of invasive species increases within our native ecosystems, more efforts should be made to measure their effects before their negative consequences require us to learn about them *ex post facto*.

Elton (1958) concluded a certain inevitability to invasions, suggesting that invading species expand their ranges among continents just as diffusing particles expand in solution. Only recently have ecologists begun to examine the details of invasion mechanisms (e.g., Vivrette and Muller 1977; Vitousek and Walker 1989) which suggest that invasions, though not necessarily predictable in their onset, can eventually be understood in terms of the interactions of invaders with their new environments. One means by which invaders can exploit new environments is through a reunion with past ecological associates. The results of this study suggest that such an association exists between European-originating honey bees and yellow star-thistle populations in the western United States. Such associations are not likely to be uncommon. On SCI and elsewhere in California, for example, there is evidence of another mutualistic relationship between an invading solitary, leaf-cutter bee, *Megachile apicalis* Spinola and yellow star-thistle wherein the bee is using the extensive populations of this weed species as corridors of invasion throughout the state (Barthell et al. unpublished manuscript-b). This species was first recorded on SCI by one of us (Robbin W. Thorp) and its pattern of invasion appears to be dictated by the distribution of yellow star-thistle (Thorp et al. 1999, this volume). Similar associations, even entire communities of invading species, remain to be examined from this perspective on Santa Cruz Island and elsewhere.

Island ecosystems may be especially susceptible to invasion by introduced species (Fritts and Rodda 1998). In addition, endemic species and subspecies are commonly found on islands. There are eight endemic plant taxa on SCI, for example, and 37 that are endemic to the Channel Islands (Junak et al. 1995). Conserving these species will require an understanding of these taxa as mutualistic assemblages of plants and pollinators (Kearns et al. 1998). Ironically, the nonnative mutualisms that introduced honey bees contribute to may threaten their native counterparts through range expansion of noxious weed species. This scenario has unfolded on SCI between honey bees and yellow star-thistle and the same relationship may exist between honey bees and other introduced weed species there. Such relationships may place conservationists in the position of having to identify nonnative mutualisms (such as honey bees and yellow star-thistle) for elimination in order to preserve native ones. As difficult as such decisions may be, involving expertise from multiple disciplines, conservationists will need to resolve this paradox to effectively preserve native ecosystems.

ACKNOWLEDGMENTS

Lyndal Laughrin (University of California) greatly assisted our efforts on Santa Cruz Island. Staff of The Nature Conservancy (TNC) cooperated with our efforts as well. Daniel Bromberger, Denise Fruitt, Michael Polakoff, Katherine Schick, Christopher Spohrer, and Alex Rapp provided field assistance. The work was primarily supported by a National Science Foundation grant to Adrian M. Wenner and Robbin W. Thorp along with earlier support from a TNC grant to John F. Barthell and John M. Randall. The Entomology Department of the University of California, Davis, provided residence and support to the senior author during the field portion of the project.

LITERATURE CITED

Barthell, J. F., G. W. Frankie and R. W. Thorp. 1998. Invader effects in a community of cavity nesting megachilid bees (Hymenoptera: Megachilidae). Environmental Entomology 27:240-247.

Barthell, J. F. and J. H. M. Knops. 1997. Visitation of evening primrose by carpenter bees: evidence of a "mixed" pollination syndrome. Southwestern Naturalist 42:86-93.

Bronstein, J. L. 1994. Our current understanding of mutualism. Quarterly Review of Biology 69:31-51.

Butz Huryn, V. M. 1997. Ecological impacts of introduced honey bees. Quarterly Review of Biology 72:275-297.

Crosby, A. W. 1986. Ecological imperialism: the biological expansion of Europe, 900-1900. Cambridge University Press, Cambridge, England.

Daly, H. V., K. Hoelmer and P. Gambino. 1991. Clinal variation in feral honey bees in California, USA. Apidologie 22:591-609.

Elton, C. S. 1958. The ecology of invasions by animals and plants. Methuen and Co., Ltd., London, England.

Frankie, G. W., R. W. Thorp, L. E. Newstrom-Lloyd, M. A. Rizzardi, J. F. Barthell, T. L. Griswold, J.- Y. Kim and S. Kappagoda. 1998. Monitoring solitary bees in modified wildland habitats: implications for bee ecology and conservation. Environmental Entomology 27:1-12.

Fritts, T. H. and G. H. Rodda. 1998. The role of introduced species in the degradation of island ecosystems: a case history of Guam. Annual Review of Ecology and Systematics 29:113-140.

Hendry, G. W. and M. K. Bellue. 1936. An approach to southwestern agricultural history through adobe brick analysis. Symposium on Prehistoric Agriculture, University of New Mexico Bulletin, New Mexico University Press, Albuquerque, NM.

Hurlbert, S. H. 1984. Pseudoreplication and the design of field experiments. Ecological Monographs 54:187-211.

Irving, W. 1956. A tour on the prairies. University of Oklahoma Press, Norman, OK.

Junak, S., T. Ayers, R. Scott, D. Wilken and D. Young. 1995. A flora of Santa Cruz Island. Santa Barbara Botanic Garden, Santa Barbara, CA.

Kearns, C. A., D. W. Inouye and N. M. Waser. 1998. Endangered mutualisms: the conservation of plant-pollinator interactions. Annual Review of Ecology and Systematics 29:83-112.

Kraus, B. and R. E. Page Jr. 1995. Effect of *Varroa jacobsoni* (Mesostigmata: Varroidae) on feral *Apis mellifera* (Hymenoptera: Apidae) in California. Environmental Entomology 24:1473-1480.

Maddox, D. M., D. B. Joley, D. M. Supkoff and A. Mayfield. 1996. Pollination biology of yellow starthistle (*Centaurea solstitialis*) in California. Canadian Journal of Botany 74:262-267.

Maddox, D. M. and A. Mayfield. 1985. Yellow starthistle infestations are on the increase. California Agriculture 39:10-12.

Nielsen, D., R. W. Page and M. W. J. Crosland. 1994. Clinal variation and selection of MDH allozymes in honey bee populations. Experentia 50:867-871.

Roubik, D. W. 1983. Experimental community studies: time-series tests of competition between African and neotropical bees. Ecology 64:971-978.

Thorp, R. W., A. M. Wenner and J. F. Barthell. 1994. Flowers visited by honey bees and native bees on Santa Cruz Island. Pages 259-286 *in* W. L. Halverson and G. J. Maender (eds.), Fourth California Islands Symposium: Update on the Status of Resources. Santa Barbara Museum of Natural History, Santa Barbara, CA.

Thorp, R. W., A. M. Wenner, and J. F. Barthell. Pollen and nectar resource overlap among bees on Santa Cruz Island. Pages 261 to 268 *in* Browne, D. R., K. L. Mitchell, and H. W. Chaney, (eds.), Proceedings of the Fifth California Islands Symposium, 29 March to 1 April 1999. Santa Barbara Museum of Natural History, Santa Barbara, CA. Sponsored by the U. S. Minerals Management Service, Pacific OCS Region, 770 Paseo Camarillo, Camarillo, CA 93010. OCS Study No. 99-0038.

Vitousek, P. M. and L. R. Walker. 1989. Biological invasion by *Myrica faga* in Hawaii: plant demography, nitrogen fixation, and ecosystem effects. Ecological Monographs 59:247-265.

Vivrette, N. J. and C. H. Muller. 1977. The mechanisms of invasion and dominance of coastal grassland by *Mesembryanthemum crystallinum*. Ecological Monographs 47:301-318.

Watkins, L. H. 1968. California's first honey bees. American Bee Journal 108:190-191.

Wenner, A. M. and R. W. Thorp. 1994. Removal of feral honey bee (*Apis mellifera*) colonies from Santa Cruz Island. Pages 513-522 *in* W. L. Halverson and G. J. Meander (eds.), Fourth California Islands Symposium: Update on the Status of Resources. Santa Barbara Museum of Natural History, Santa Barbara, CA.

Wenner, A. M., R. W. Thorpe, and J. F. Barthell. 1999. Removal of European honey bees from the Santa Cruz Island ecosystem. Pages 256 to 260 *in* Browne, D. R., K. L. Mitchell, and H. W. Chaney, (eds.), Proceedings of the Fifth California Islands Symposium, 29 March to 1 April 1999. Santa Barbara Museum of Natural History, Santa Barbara, CA. Sponsored by the U. S. Minerals Management Service, Pacific OCS Region, 770 Paseo Camarillo, Camarillo, CA 93010. OCS Study No. 99-0038

SOURCES OF UNPUBLISHED MATERIALS

Barthell, J. F., J. M. Randall, R. W. Thorp and A. M. Wenner. Exclusion studies of yellow star-thistle pollinators in the western USA: seed-set depression results from removing honey bees. Unpublished Manuscript-a.

Barthell, J. F., R. W. Thorp, G. W. Frankie and J.-Y. Kim. Impacts of introduced solitary bees on natural and agricultural systems: the case of the leaf-cutter bee, *Megachile apicalis*. *In*: K. Strickler, J. Cane and J. Brown (eds.), Proceedings of the 1998 Meeting of the National Entomological Society of America: For nonnative crops, whence pollinators of the future? Unpublished Manuscript-b.

ARGENTINE ANTS (HYMENOPTERA: FORMICIDAE) INVADE SANTA CRUZ ISLAND, CALIFORNIA

J. Andrew Calderwood[1], Adrian M. Wenner[2], and James K. Wetterer[3]

[1]Santa Barbara Museum of Natural History, 2559 Puesta del Sol Road, Santa Barbara, CA 93105
Current address: 428 Foxen Drive, Santa Barbara, CA 93105, (805) 682-7097
[2]967 Garcia Road, Santa Barbara, CA 93103, (805) 963-8508
[3]Center for Environmental Research and Conservation, Columbia University, New York, NY 10027
Current address: Honors College, Florida Atlantic University, 5353 North Parkside Drive, Jupiter, FL 33418
(561) 691-8648, FAX (561) 691-8535, E-mail: wetterer@fau.edu

ABSTRACT

The ecologically destructive Argentine ant, *Linepithema humile*, was discovered on Santa Cruz Island, California, in January 1996. By inspection of ground cover and potential foraging sites, we mapped its range in July 1997, finding it restricted to two sites on the southeast section of the island, covering areas of approximately 1.5 km^2 and 0.05 km^2, respectively. Follow-up surveys employing baited traps in 1998 confirmed the limit of infestation, and documented both the exclusion of most native ant species within colonized zones and a relatively stable boundary to infestation. We estimate the age of the infestation to be five to ten years.

Keywords: *Linepithema humile*, Argentine ant, tramp ant, Santa Cruz Island.

INTRODUCTION

Tramp ants are ant species that associate with humans and are spread by human commerce. They travel the world hidden in our plant products, packaging material, building supplies, and heavy machinery such as logging and military equipment (Williams 1994). The ecological importance of most tramp ant species remains undocumented. Several, however, are known to have dramatic impacts. When these ants invade, the entire biological community is transformed, as native invertebrate species are replaced by an impoverished set of ant-tolerant and usually non-native species (Williams 1994). Here we report the spread of a highly destructive tramp ant species, the Argentine ant, *Linepithema humile*, to Santa Cruz Island of the California Channel Islands.

Linepithema humile, a native of South America, is an important pest ant in many subtropical and temperate regions, such as the southern U.S. from Florida to California (Newell and Barber 1913; Barber 1916; Ward 1987). In areas where this ant invades, native invertebrates are heavily impacted (Erickson 1971; Ward 1987; Cole et al. 1992; Gillespie and Reimer 1993; Human and Gordon 1997). Newell and Barber (1913) described how *L. humile* attacks

birds: "the workers swarm over young chicks in such numbers as to cause their death...nests of many birds are frequented by the ants in the same way, and the number of young birds destroyed in this manner must be considerable."

Linepithema humile was first introduced to California earlier this century and has been steadily moving across the state, exterminating native invertebrates throughout lowland areas (Ward 1987; Human and Gordon 1997). In January 1996, Wenner first discovered *L. humile* on Santa Cruz Island of the California Channel Islands. *L. humile* was already known on two other Channel Islands, the populated islands of Santa Catalina and San Clemente (Miller, pers. comm.). Santa Cruz Island is of special concern because it is entirely a nature reserve. The western 90% of the island is owned by The Nature Conservancy and the remainder is owned by the National Park Service. At 245 km^2, Santa Cruz Island is the largest of the Northern Channel Islands and has the most diverse habitats (Miller 1985). *L. humile* is the only destructive tramp ant known to have invaded Santa Cruz Island, and it is likely that the previous absence of tramp ants has permitted many native invertebrates to persist there. Many terrestrial plants and animals are endemic to the Channel Islands, including more than 100 insect species (Miller 1985). Also found on Santa Cruz Island are more than 140 species of land birds (Power 1976; Diamond and Jones 1980), several terrestrial and marine mammals (Wenner and Johnson 1980), and 34 species of ants (Wetterer et al., In prep.).

MATERIALS AND METHODS

Three surveys were conducted. The first, conducted July 1997 by Calderwood with Emily Hebard of The Nature Conservancy, consisted of walking a number of transects through areas around known or suspected *Linepithema humile* infestations, looking for ants under ground cover such as rocks, logs, and boards, and inspecting potential foraging sites such as the branches of *Quercus agrifolia* and *Baccharis pilularis*, plants housing aphids and other homopterans attractive to some ants, including *L. humile*. Transects were chosen based on topography and ground cover, utilizing roads, stream beds, and pig trails where dense foliage prevented overland travel. In the Sacramento Valley in northern California, this method of inspection was as effective as baiting or leaf litter sifting in detecting the presence of *L. humile* (Ward 1987). Early in the survey, we discovered that only two ant species, a species of *Solenopsis* and a species of *Monomorium*, later identified as *S. molesta* and *M. ergatogyna* (Wetterer et al., In prep.), were taken with *L. humile* at sampling points. Therefore, the absence of *L. humile* could be reasonably assumed whenever an ant other than the above three was taken at a site, at least away from the margins of the range of *L. humile*. The only inconclusive sampling points were those in which no ants, or only *S. molesta* or *M. ergatogyna*, were taken.

In the second survey, led by Wetterer in March 1998, we laid baited traps, each consisting of a small piece of tuna and some cookie crumbs (Pecan Sandies™) on an index card which was collected approximately 1 hr later. In addition to reinforcing the data gathered on the known infestations, the second survey examined other parts of the island, particularly sites most likely to harbor recent infestations such as landings, roads, and buildings which were not explored in the first survey.

The third survey, led by Wetterer in May 1998, focused on the small upper infestation, mapping its margins with a tape measure to the nearest meter at six of eight compass points in preparation for a test of an eradication technique using hydramethylnon.

RESULTS

The July 1997 survey found that *Linepithema humile* occurred on two separate areas surrounding two dismantled Navy facilities (Figure 1). The areas of the two infestations were approximated at 1.5 km² and 0.04 km² in area, respectively.

After the follow-up survey in March 1998, we found the area occupied by *L. humile* had not changed measurably. Flags placed in 1997 to mark the ant's distribution still accurately marked the boundary (Figure 1). The broadened search of the island turned up no new infestations (Figure 1, inset). The Stanton Ranch Houses (now occupied by The Nature Conservancy), the University of California Field Station, Prisoners Harbor, the road running the length of the central valley, and the perimeter of an active Navy base just east of the smaller infestation site were all examined and found free of *L. humile*.

The third survey, of May 1998, a resurvey of the smaller upper site, mapped the margins of the range of *L. humile* at six of eight compass points as radial distances from a dead peach tree near the cliff on the former site of the Navy facility: N, 130 m; NE, 93 m; E, 121 m; SE, inaccessible; S, 233 m; SW, inaccessible; W, 130 m; NW, 134 m. The treacherous scree slope to the south was explored by Wetterer and was found to harbor *L. humile*. The least polygon connecting these six points covers approximately 0.05

km² and serves as a conservative minimum. Rounding the corners of the curve yields an area of approximately 0.06 km².

In summary, the larger of the two infestations presumably radiated from the lower dismantled Navy site (Figure 1) and now occupies the entire Three-Fork Canyon watershed from sea level to approximately 230 m elevation, the deep canyon adjacent to the west to the same elevation, Cañada Pomona and the surrounding valley west to nearly Rancho del Sur (where an orchard exists today), and to the southwest, up the tributaries of Cañada Pomona to less than 100 m elevation, covering approximately 1.5 km². The ridge west of Ceanothus Canyon lies just east of the eastern boundary of the range of *L. humile* at this lower site. The smaller infestation occupies the area within approximately 100 to 200 m radius of the center of the upper dismantled Navy site (Figure 1) reaching the road which passes north of the site at only one point, near the access driveway, a total of 0.05 to 0.06 km².

DISCUSSION

Both sites of infestation of *Linepithema humile* appear to radiate from sites of Navy installations which were dismantled in 1995. The heavy equipment used in such an operation suggests a possible source for the infestation. However, the rate of spread of these infestations appears to be, at least recently, much less than the 100 m/yr reported by Erickson (1971). Extrapolating this rate of growth back to the center of the range of *L. humile* requires nearly ten years of expansion, with a low estimate of five years. Either the populations of *L. humile* underwent rapid initial expansion which has since stabilized or they are much older than the dismantling operation of 1995. If the populations have stabilized, altitude may be playing a role. The larger site is restricted to elevations under 250 m. Ward (1987) found no populations above 300 m in his northern California study area. The much smaller size of the upper site suggests that at 380 m elevation, *L. humile* may be near its altitudinal limits there, though the vigor of that infestation may be further reduced by the lack of any permanent source of water except ridgetop dew. Since no clear factor is limiting the spread of *L. humile*, the more parsimonious hypothesis is that the lower infestation is old and its spread has been slow. The hypothesis of an infestation originating in 1995 would require an initial speed of spread of >500 m/yr, greater than ever recorded.

If the small upper infestation began at the now-dismantled Navy site, it has radiated much farther southward (down a steep slope) than in any other direction. If this reflects the fact that lower elevations are more favorable to *L. humile*, there is a threat that the population may release southward and accelerate its advance. Any eradication effort must pay greatest attention to this boundary. Of course, it may also be that gravity is responsible for the rapid spread of *L. humile* southward. This possibility demands that any monitoring of an eradication attempt must include an

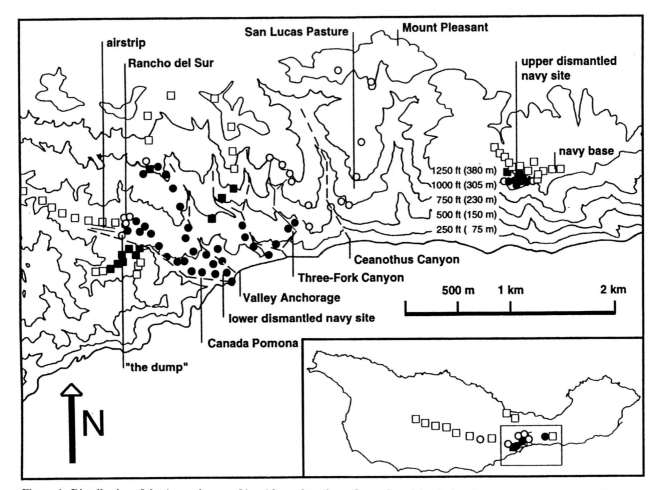

Figure 1. Distribution of the Argentine ant, *Linepithema humile*, on Santa Cruz Island, showing results of both July 1997 survey (circles) and March 1998 survey (squares). Inset: map of Santa Cruz Island indicating area of main map. Key: solid lines-topography at 250 ft (approximately 80 m) intervals, dashed lines- stream courses, grey circles or squares- sites with *L. humile*, white circles or squares- sites without *L. humile*.

examination of the slope all the way down to sea level in order to rule out a jump dispersal by way of tumbling rocks or logs infested with ants.

Linepithema humile on Santa Cruz Island has displaced most native ants within its range (Wetterer, Wetterer, and Hebard, In prep.), as was found in the Sacramento Valley (Ward 1987). Clearly, these surveys confirm the grave threat posed by *L. humile* to Santa Cruz Island biodiversity, especially to the 34 species of ants now known from the island (Wetterer et al., In prep.), and justify attempts to eradicate it.

We hope to test the use of chemical toxins for controlling *L. humile* on the island. Chemicals are commonly used for controlling tramp ants. Chemical control of ants may be particularly useful on small islands or with very localized populations as on Santa Cruz Island. Chemical methods are currently being employed to control the much larger infestation in Haleakala National Park on Maui, Hawaii (Krushelnycky and Reimer 1996). Hydramethylnon has been found to be effective against *L. humile* in citrus groves (Gaston and Baker 1984) and has full EPA approval (Krushelnycky and Reimer 1996). Hydramethylnon has been

used in many situations to control other tramp ants as well. For example, application of hydramethylnon has controlled the tramp ant *Wasmannia auropunctata* on Santa Fe Island in the Galapagos (Abedrabbo 1994).

In future research, we plan to resurvey the island to monitor the effectiveness of control measures and the expected recovery of invertebrate biodiversity if *L. humile* is removed from the island. In addition, we plan to survey ants on the other California Channel Islands to determine whether any tramp ants have invaded. We plan to start with surveys of abandoned military facilities, such as the dismantled military base on Santa Rosa Island. It is important that any invasions by *L. humile* or other tramp ants are detected and stopped as soon as possible, before they spread any further.

ACKNOWLEDGMENTS

We wish to thank A. Anderson, A. Aronwitz, K. Bartniczak, M. Bemon, J. Burger, C. Dunning, J. Gallagher, A. Ghaneker, L. Geschwind, D. Han, J. Howarth, E. Hebard, M. Hill, R. Lee, C. Mealey, A. Mingo, L. Patterson, M.

Patton, S. Riseman, J. Rowe, A. Southern, and A. Wetterer for field assistance.

We thank L. Laughrin of the University of California Field Station, D. Devine and R. Klinger of The Nature Conservancy, and T. Coonan of the National Park Service for logistical support and accommodations on Santa Cruz Island. The Santa Barbara Museum of Natural History and Columbia University provided financial support.

LITERATURE CITED

Abedrabbo, S. 1994. Control of the little fire ant, *Wasmannia auropunctata*, on Santa Fe Island in the Galapagos Islands. Pages 219-227 *in* Williams, D. F. (ed.), Exotic Ants: Biology, Impact, and Control of Introduced Species. Westview Press, Boulder, CO.

Barber, E. R. 1916. The Argentine ant: distribution and control in the United States. United States Department of Agriculture Bulletin 377:1-23.

Cole, F. R., A. C. Medeiros, L. L. Loope, and W. W. Zuehlke. 1992. Effects of the Argentine ant on arthropod fauna of Hawaiian high-elevation shrubland. Ecology 73:1313-1322.

Diamond, J. M. and H. L. Jones 1980. Breeding land birds of the Channel Islands. Pages 597-612 *in* Power, D. M. (ed.), The California Islands: Proceedings of a Multidisciplinary Symposium. Santa Barbara Museum of Natural History, Santa Barbara, CA.

Erickson, J. M. 1971. The displacement of native ant species by the introduced Argentine ant *Iridomyrmex humilis* Mayr. Psyche 78:257-266.

Gaston, L. K. and T. C. Baker 1984. Toxic bait to control Argentine ant field tested. Citograph: 188.

Gillespie, R. G. and N. J. Reimer 1993. The effect of alien predatory ants (Hymenoptera: Formicidae) on Hawaiian endemic spiders (Araneae: Tetragnathidae). Pacific Science 47:21-33.

Human, K. G. and D. M. Gordon 1997. Effects of Argentine ants on invertebrate biodiversity in northern California. Conservation Biology 11:1242-1248.

Krushelnycky, P. D. and N. J. Reimer 1996. Efforts at control of the Argentine ant in Haleakala National Park, Maui, Hawai'i. Cooperative National Park Resources Study Unit, University of Hawai'i Technical Report 109:1-33.

Miller, S. E. 1985. The California Channel Islands—past, present, and future: an entomological perspective. Pages 3-27 *in* Menke, A. S. and D. R. Miller (eds.), Entomology of the California Channel Islands. Santa Barbara Museum of Natural History, Santa Barbara, CA.

Newell, W. and T. C. Barber 1913. The Argentine ant. U. S. Department of Agriculture Bulletin 221:1-98.

Power, D. M. 1976. Avifauna richness on the California Channel Islands. Condor 78:394-398.

Ward, P. S. 1987. Distribution of the introduced Argentine ant (*Iridomyrmex humilis*) in natural habitats of the lower Sacramento Valley and its effects on the indigenous ant fauna. Hilgardia 55:1-16.

Wenner, A. M. and D. L. Johnson 1980. Land vertebrates on the California Channel Islands: sweepstakes or bridges? Pages 497-530 *in* Power, D. M. (ed.), The California Islands: Proceedings of a Multidisciplinary Symposium. Santa Barbara Museum of Natural History, Santa Barbara, CA.

Williams, D. F. (ed.) 1994. Exotic Ants: Biology, Impact, and Control of Introduced Species. Westview Press, Boulder, CO.

SOURCES OF UNPUBLISHED MATERIALS

Miller, S. E. International Centre of Insect Physiology and Ecology, Box 30772, Nairobi, Kenya and National Museum of Natural History, Smithsonian Institution, Washington, DC 20560. Personal communication.

Wetterer, J. K., A. L. Wetterer, and E. Hebard. In preparation. Impact of the Argentine ant, *Linepithema humile*, on the native ants of Santa Cruz Island, California.

Wetterer, J. K., A. L. Wetterer, P. S. Ward, J. T. Longino, J. C. Trager, and S. E. Miller. In preparation. Ants (Hymenoptera: Formicidae) of Santa Cruz Island, California.

CALIFORNIA ISLAND DEER MICE:
GENETICS, MORPHOMETRICS, AND EVOLUTION

Oliver R. W. Pergams[1] and Mary V. Ashley[2]

[1]Department of Biological Sciences, University of Illinois at Chicago,
845 W. Taylor Street, Chicago, Illinois 60607-7060
(312) 996-5446, FAX (312) 413-2435, E-mail: operga1@uic.edu
[2]Department of Biological Sciences, University of Illinois at Chicago,
845 W. Taylor Street, Chicago, Illinois 60607-7060
(312) 413-9700, FAX (312) 413-2435, E-mail: ashley@uic.edu

ABSTRACT

Deer mice, *Peromyscus maniculatus*, are found on all eight California Channel Islands and are classified as separate subspecies on each island. Distinct mitochondrial DNA haplotypes, identified by restriction enzyme analysis, were found in island deer mice, and on five of the eight islands deer mice have unique haplotypes, suggesting genetic isolation and independent evolution of several island subspecies. Founder effects on mtDNA diversity in island populations relative to mainland populations are evident. The connectivity of the deer mouse populations on East, Middle, and West Anacapa Islands (*P. m. anacapae*) was assessed using sequence data from the mitochondrial cytochrome *c* oxidase subunit II gene (COII). A common haplotype was found on all three Anacapa Islets, although Middle and East Anacapa each had an additional unique haplotype. This suggests that deer mice on Anacapa are functioning as a metapopulation, with some gene flow or extinction/recolonization occurring among the islets. Discriminant function analysis of cranial and external morphological characters for three island subspecies, *P. m. anacapae*, *P. m. santacruzae*, and *P. m. elusus*, produced a high rate of correct classification, indicating strong morphological as well as genetic differentiation. The specimens used for the morphometric study were museum specimens collected at different times during the past century. A surprising result of the morphological analysis was that each subspecies had exhibited extremely rapid change in several characters over this time period.

Keywords: Morphological change, temporal variation, California Channel Islands, deer mice (*Peromyscus maniculatus*), morphometrics, discriminant function analysis, mitochondrial cytochrome *c* oxidase subunit II (COII) sequences, gene flow, evolutionarily significant units (ESU), restriction enzymes, founder effect, metapopulations.

INTRODUCTION

Deer mice, *Peromyscus maniculatus*, are an important component of the terrestrial fauna of the California Islands. Deer mice are the only nonvolant vertebrate that occurs on all eight islands and their high abundance on several of the islands necessarily dictates that they influence the ecology of those islands. Further, the modest radiation of *Peromyscus maniculatus* into multiple genetically and morphologically distinct subspecies contributes much to the biodiversity of the islands and makes them an important subject for investigations of evolutionary history and adaptive radiations on the California Islands. It is therefore not surprising that California Island deer mice have been investigated by scientists for a century (Mearns 1897), and that these investigations continue today (Pergams and Ashley 1999; Pergams et al. 2000).

The focus of this report will be recent genetic and morphological research on California Island deer mice, but we will begin with a brief review of earlier morphological and genetic investigations. Mearns (1897) identified California Island mice as *Peromyscus texanus medius*. Elliot (1903) gave the deer mice from Santa Catalina and Santa Cruz single, separate species status as *Peromyscus catalinae*. Mearns (1907) essentially renamed the remaining mice from San Clemente, San Nicolas, Santa Rosa, and San Miguel as *Peromyscus texanus clementis*. Osgood's extensive and general revision of the genus (1909) placed California Islands deer mice as the same species but two different subspecies: *Peromyscus maniculatus clementis* and *P. m. catalinae*. Later, mice from Santa Barbara, San Nicolas, and Santa Cruz were described as separate subspecies, *P. m. elusus*, *P. m. exterus*, and *P. m. santacruzae*, respectively, and mice from Santa Rosa and San Miguel together were described as *P. m. santarosae* (Nelson and Goldman 1931). von Bloeker (1940, 1941) described mice from Santa Rosa and Anacapa as separate subspecies, *P. m. santarosae* and *P. m. anacapae*, respectively.

Collins et al. (1979) commented that three of the present subspecies descriptions were made from samples which included specimens collected from other islands. Measurements for *P. m. catalinae* were taken from mice collected on Santa Catalina and Santa Cruz (Osgood 1909), measurements for *P. m. clementis* were taken from mice collected from San Clemente, San Miguel, San Nicolas, Santa

Barbara, and Santa Rosa, and measurements from *P. m. streatori* were taken from mice collected from San Miguel and Santa Rosa. Collins et al. (1979) recommended re-evaluation of these three subspecies. These authors also provide general phenotypic descriptives of California Islands deer mice, based on their own experience and other literature existing at the time. Deer mice from the California Islands have dark brownish-black tipped hairs dorsally which are subtended by a buffy band before grading into grey at the base. In general, island mice are darker than mainland mice. In terms of body size, the San Miguel and San Clemente subspecies are the smallest, and the Anacapa, San Nicolas, and Santa Barbara subspecies are the largest. All island subspecies, however, are larger than the adjacent mainland deer mice.

The first formal morphometric treatment of California Island deer mice was conducted by Gill (1980). She applied stepwise discriminant function analysis to 219 specimens from all eight islands, as well as the mainland subspecies *P. m. gambelli*. An 85% classification rate was achieved from 17 external and cranial measurements. The majority of misclassifications involved mice from San Miguel, Santa Rosa, and San Nicolas. In a second analysis, mice from these three islands were removed, and a 98% classification rate was then achieved using 12 external and cranial measurements. Gill (1980) concluded that California Island deer mice have undergone significant morphological divergence.

Gill (1980) also conducted the first genetic study of California Island deer mice, an examination of variation at 30 protein-coding loci among island and adjacent mainland deer mice. She reported that levels of genetic variation were relatively high on the islands (average mean heterozygosity, H=0.066), but reduced from that found among California mainland deer mice (H=0.083). Genetic distances (Nei's *D* 1972) were small among all comparisons, less than 0.10.

We have conducted additional genetic studies, employing rapidly evolving mitochondrial DNA (mtDNA), and have performed discriminant function analysis of morphological characters of California Island deer mice. The work we present here has three separate components that examine different aspects of the evolution of island deer mice. First, we summarize results of previous mtDNA restriction fragment analysis of all the subspecies of *P. maniculatus* that occur on the California Islands as well as the adjacent mainland. The mitochondrial genome is maternally inherited and evolves rapidly relative to nuclear genes, and thus provides greater resolution of patterns of differentiation, isolation, and colonization than do nuclear-coded markers such as allozymes. The mtDNA results are compared to previous genetic and morphometric studies. Second, sequences of a mitochondrial gene, cytochrome *c* oxidase subunit II (COII), were used to look at an even finer evolutionary scale, that of *P. m. anacapae* populations on the three small islets that comprise Anacapa Island. We were interested in determining whether East, Middle, and West Anacapa Island deer mouse populations were genetically isolated from each, or alternatively, whether they functioned as a metapopulation

connected by gene flow. Finally, we draw on the extensive collection of California Island deer mice specimens in museums taken over nearly a century to document rapid morphological evolution in three of the island subspecies, *P. m. elusus*, *P. m. anacapae*, and *P. m. santarosae*. Taken together, these results provide a relatively detailed picture of California Island deer mice evolution at different spatial and temporal scales and for both morphological and genetic characters.

MATERIALS AND METHODS

Mitochondrial DNA RFLP Analysis

Table 1 provides information regarding specimens used for various aspects of this study. Purified mtDNA samples from 131 island and mainland mice collected from 1983 to 1985 (Table 1) were analyzed for restriction fragment length polymorphisms (RFLPs). Fresh tissue samples (liver, heart, kidney and spleen) were used for mtDNA purification following differential centrifugation (Lansman et al. 1981; Ashley and Wills 1987). All samples were digested with nine restriction enzymes, *Eco*RI, *Hin*d III, *Bst*EII, *Pst* I, *Bgl* II, *Ava* I, *Ava* II, *Mbo* I and *Hin*f I. Approximately 15 nanograms of purified mtDNA were used for each digestion and fragments were end-labeled with ^{32}P using the large fragment of *E. coli* polymerase I. Fragments were electrophoresed on 1% horizontal agarose slab gels or in 3.5% vertical polyacrylamide gels along with a molecular weight size standard. After electrophoresis, gels were dried and autoradiographed using Kodak XAR-5 film (Ashley and Wills 1987).

Sequence divergence (*p*) was estimated from the proportion of shared restriction fragments using the formula of Upholt (1977) and weighting the estimation relative to the total number of base pairs recognized by each type of restriction enzyme. Restriction pattern diversity, *h*, was estimated using Nei and Tajima (1981).

The relationships between geographic distance, genetic differentiation and morphological divergence of the California island subspecies were examined (Ashley and Wills 1989). Four distances matrices were compared using Kendall's tau statistic, K_c. Significance levels of observed K_c values were estimated by 2,000 random permutations of the elements of matrices (Dietz 1983). The elements of the four matrices were: 1) genetic distances (Nei's *D*, 1972) based on allozymes (Gill 1980); 2) morphological distance measured as distance in canonical-variable units between subspecies (Gill 1980); 3) sequence divergence (*p*) based on mtDNA RFLP comparisons of the predominant mtDNA genotype in each subspecies; and 4) geographic distance between islands.

Mitochondrial COII Sequence Analysis

Sequences of the mitochondrial COII gene were obtained for a total of 35 samples (Table 1), representing *P. m. anacapae* from each of the Anacapa islets (East, Middle

Table 1. Samples used in this study.

Species/ Subspecies	Collection Location	Collection Year	N	mt RFLP	mt COII	Morpho- metrics
P. m. anacapae	West Anacapa Island	1940-1996	40		11	29
	Middle Anacapa Island	1940-1996	49	8	9	35
	East Anacapa Island	1917-1997	26		7	24
P. m. catalinae	Santa Catalina Island	1983	7	7		
P. m. clementis	San Clemente Island	1985	10	10		
P. m. elusus	Santa Barbara Island	1897-1983	56	14	1	42
P. m. santacruzae	Santa Cruz Island	1983	48	10	1	38
P. m. santarosae	Santa Rosa Island	1985	10	10	1	
P. m streatori	San Miguel Island	1983	13	13		
P. m. exterus	San Nicolas Island	1983-1984	14	14		
P. m. gambelii	Los Angeles Co.	1903	13			13
	Los Padres National Forest, Santa Barbara Co.	1983	1	1		
	La Jolla, San Diego Co.	1983-1985	28	28	1	
	Cleveland National Forest, Riverside Co.	1985	5	5		
	Idyllwild, Riverside Co.	1985	3	3		
	Jalama, Santa Barbara Co.	1985	1	1		
	Las Flores ranch	1985	3	3	1	
	Los Alamos	1985	4	4	1	

and West) as well as two additional island subspecies (*P. m. elusus* and *P. m. santacruzae*) and one mainland subspecies (*P. m. gambelii*). Samples consisted of either purified mtDNA isolated by differential centrifugation (those collected from 1983 to 1985), or total genomic DNA (those collected from 1996 to 1997) isolated from frozen heart or liver tissue by standard phenol-chloroform extractions. The COII gene (684 bp) was amplified via the polymerase chain reaction (PCR) with primers designed from tRNA^{Asp} and tRNA^{Lys} genes that flank COII in the mammalian mitochondrial genome (Adkins and Honeycutt 1994). Two external and two internal primers were also used for amplification and/or sequencing (Pergams et al. 2000). PCR amplifications were performed in $50\mu l$ reaction volumes which included $0.2\mu M$ of each primer, $0.2\mu M$ dNTPs, 1U Taq polymerase, 1X reaction buffer, and approximately 2ng of DNA. Amplification proceeded for 32 to 40 cycles of $94°C$ for 1 min, 50-$51°C$ for 1 min, and $72°C$ for 2 min. Excess primers and dNTPs were removed from successful PCR reactions and these were sequenced either manually or on an automated sequencer (ABI 373A; Pergams et al. 2000).

Levels of mitochondrial variation were examined using indices of nucleotide diversity, π (Nei 1987). Gene flow, Nm, an estimate of migration averaged over evolutionary time, was estimated for the Anacapa islet populations from COII sequence data using equation 2 of Nei (1982). Calculations were performed using the computer program DNAsp 2.9 (Rozas and Rozas 1998).

Morphometric Analysis

Skulls and skins of total of 151 adult mice were measured for a study of temporal variation in three subspecies of island deer mice, *P. m. elusus*, *P. m. anacapae*, and *P. m. santacruzae* (Table 1). The collection years of the specimens are as follows. *P. m. elusus*: 1897 (N = 2), 1919 (3), 1939 (13), 1940 (3), 1955 (1), 1972 (2), 1974 (1), 1978

(14), and 1979 (3). *P. m. anacapae*: 1940 (38), 1978 (35). *P. m. santacruzae*: 1917 (5), 1938 (3), 1939 (9), 1941 (2), 1967 (13), 1983 (2), 1986 (1), and 1988 (1).

Twelve cranial measurements were taken (Pergams and Ashley 1999): intermeatus width (IW), length of nasals (LN), length of palate plus incisor (LPI, measured as the greatest distance from the anterior edge of the alveoli of the incisors to the mesopterygoid fossa), breadth of rostrum (BR), alimentary toothrow (AL), length of incisive foramen (LIF), rostral width (RW, the narrowest width of the rostrum and premaxilla dorsally and directly anterior to the infraorbital foramen), zygomatic breadth (ZB), interorbital breadth (IB), depth of braincase (DBC), breadth of braincase (BB), and breadth of zygomatic plate (BZP). All cranial measurements were taken to the nearest 0.01 mm. The four standard external measurements were originally made by 18 different museum preparers and recorded from museum tags: total length (TOT), tail length (TAIL), hind foot length (HIND), and ear length (EAR). EAR was not available for six *P. m. elusus* and five *P. m. santacruzae*.

SYSTAT v. 7.0 (SPSS, Inc. 1997) was used for statistical analysis. Normality of data was determined by visual inspection of normal probability plots, following the method of Afifi and Clark (1996). We plotted 85% ellipses of concentration as group scatterplot matrices. To determine if temporal change had occurred, three data sets were created: data from all years 1897 to 1988 (N = 140), data from only 1897 to 1941 (68), and data from only 1955 to 1988 (72). Since no mice had been collected between 1941 and 1955, these years served as an obvious, albeit arbitrary, cut-off between "early" and "late" collections. One-way ANOVAs and complete discriminant analyses were performed on each data set. The year the specimen was collected was used as the time variable. Results from all ANOVAs were considered significant at the 95% confidence level.

To compare differentiation between subspecies to relative morphological change over time, we performed a two-way ANOVA with subspecies and time as factors. Time was included by comparing time classes 1897 to 1941 and 1955 to 1988. Mean squared errors (MSE, or the sum of squares over degrees of freedom) of the two factors were compared (Sokal and Rohlf 1997). The variable with the larger MSE was considered to have the greater variance.

We used discriminant function analysis to characterize the direction, degree, and nature of the morphological changes over time. Our discriminant analysis used the "Weight" function in SYSTAT's data handling component to assign a weighting of "0" or "1" to individuals and thereby apportion them to time class. Individuals collected from 1897 to 1941 were fully weighted, and individuals collected from 1955 to 1988 were given zero weight. A complete discriminant function was derived only from individuals from 1897 to 1941, but applied to individuals from 1955 to 1988 as well. Centroid coordinates of the late groups were calculated by hand as the means of individual canonical scores. Mahalanobis distances between the centroids of early and late groups were calculated by hand using the distance formula.

RESULTS

RFLP analysis of the mtDNA genome revealed a total of 26 different haplotypes (Table 2). Of these, 10 haplotypes were identified among the 87 island mice surveyed, and the remaining 16 were found among southern California mainland *P. maniculatus gambelii*. No haplotypes occurred in both mainland and island deer mice, and six of the island subspecies (*P. m. anacapae*, *P. m. exterus*, *P. m. santacruzae*, *P. m. clementis*, *P. m. catalinae*, and *P. m. elusus*) had one or two unique haplotypes. In the cases of *P. m. anacapae*, *P. m. clementis*, *P.m. catalinae*, and *P. m. elusus*, only haplotypes unique to each subspecies were found. A common haplotype (#3) was found on four of the islands, Santa Rosa, San Nicolas, San Miguel and Santa Cruz. At most, two haplotypes were found on any island, and a single haplotype was found on San Miguel, Santa Rosa, and Santa Barbara Islands. Heterogeneity, h, ranged from 0 to 0.44 (mean 0.20) within island samples and from 0.67 to 1.00 (mean 0.79) within mainland samples from a single location. Estimated percent sequence divergence, p, ranged from 0.32% to 0.95% for haplotype comparisons (Ashley and Wills 1987).

Tests of association among the various distance matrices indicated that only two pairs of matrices are significantly correlated: mtDNA divergence versus allozyme divergence (P=0.002) and geographic distance versus allozyme divergence (P=0.0005; Ashley and Wills 1989).

For COII sequence analysis, at least 606 bp of sequence were obtained for three island subspecies (*P.m. elusus*, *P.m. santarosae*, and *P. m. anacapae)* and one mainland subspecies (*P. m. gambelii).* A total of 18 sites were polymorphic within *P. maniculatus*, 14 of which represented silent substitutions. Among the *P. maniculatus* subspecies, nucleotide diversity π was less than 1%, reflecting levels of differentiation similar to those found using RFLP analysis. The distribution of haplotypes identified by sequences also confirmed the RFLP results, with each haplotype identified by restriction enzyme analysis of the entire mtDNA genome also exhibiting nucleotide differences within the COII gene. The RFLP analysis for Anacapa only included specimens from Middle Anacapa Island and had identified two unique haplotypes. All specimens from West Anacapa Island had the most common of these two haplotypes. Specimens from East Anacapa also shared this haplotype, but a third haplotype was also identified (Figure 1).

Gene flow, *Nm*, or the number of individuals per generation migrating, was estimated for the three Anacapa islets using the COII sequence data. Approximately seven individuals are estimated to migrate between West and Middle Anacapa per generation, approximately the same number are estimated to migrate between Middle and East Anacapa, and approximately two individuals are estimated to migrate between West and East Anacapa per generation.

Table 2. mtDNA RFLP haplotypes observed among the samples of *P. maniculatus*. Letters describing mtDNAs, from left to right, refer to restriction fragment patterns for the restriction enzymes *Eco*R l, *Hin*d lll, *Bst*E ll, *Pst* l, *Bgl* ll, *Ava* l, *Ava* ll, *Mbo* l, and *Hin*f l, respectively. Each composite haplotype is numbered. The last column shows the number of mice sampled that show a particular mtDNA composite haplotype.

	mtDNA Genotype	Collection Site	Number of Mice
	California Channel Islands:		
1)	AACAAAAAG	Anacapa	7
2)	BBAAAAAAM	Anacapa	1
3)	AAAAAAAAF	Santa Rosa	10
		San Nicolas	12
		San Miguel	13
		Santa Cruz	8
4)	AAAAAAACF	San Nicolas	2
5)	AAAAAAAGK	Santa Cruz	2
6)	AABAAAAAE	Santa Barbara	14
7)	BBAAAAACH	Santa Catalina	6
8)	AAAAAAAHA	Santa Catalina	1
9)	ABAAAAAJD	San Clemente	3
10)	ABAAAAAAD	San Clemente	8
	Southern California Mainland:		
11)	ABABAAAAA	La Jolla	1
12)	ABAAAABAB	La Jolla	1
		Los Padres National Forest	1
13)	ABCAAAAAA	La Jolla	1
14)	AAAAAAJAA	La Jolla	1
15)	BBAAAAACA	La Jolla	1
16)	ABAAAACAA	La Jolla	15
		Cleveland National Forest	1
		Idyllwild	1
		Los Alamos	2
17)	ABAAAAAAA	La Jolla	3
		Idyllwild	2
		Cleveland National Forest	2
		Las Flores ranch	1
18)	ABAAAADAC	La Jolla	1
19)	ABABAAAAB	La Jolla	2
20)	FBAAAAAAD	La Jolla	1
21)	ABAAAAAAE	Cleveland National Forest	1
22)	ABAAAAIEA	Cleveland National Forest	1
23)	ABAAADAAA	Los Alamos	2
24)	ABAAAAABA	Las Flores ranch	1
25)	ABAAAAADA	Las Flores ranch	1
26)	ABAAAAALA	Jalama	1

Morphometric Analysis

Measurements of all characters were determined to be approximately normal in distributions so no transformations were made to the raw data, thereby avoiding distancing ourselves from the data (Reyment 1972).

Results of analyses for identifying morphological change over time are given in Table 3. For *P. m. elusus*, six measurements (LN, AL, TOT, TAIL, HIND, & EAR) were significantly correlated with time. For *P. m. anacapae*, ten measurements (IW, BR, LIF, RW, DBC, BZP, TOT, TAIL,

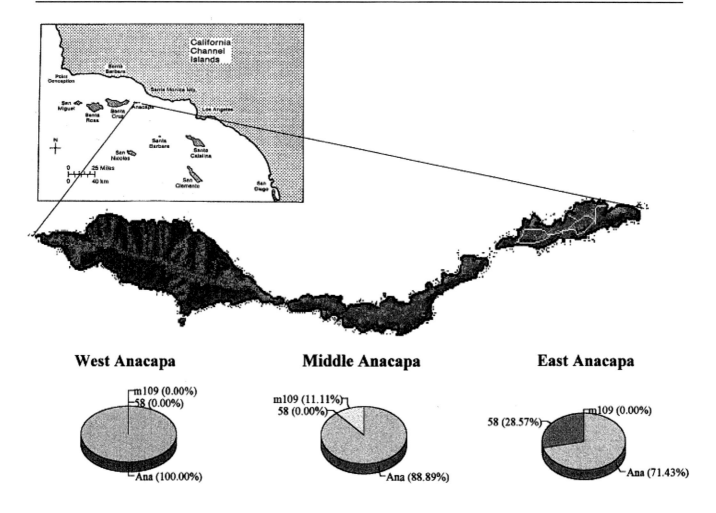

Figure 1. Map of Anacapa islets with distribution of haplotypes. *Ana* **is the common haplotype and corresponds to RFLP haplotype 1, Table 2.** *m109* **corresponds to RFLP haplotype 2, Table 2.** *58* **is a new haplotype.**

HIND, & EAR) were significantly correlated with time. For *P. m. santacruzae*, six measurements (IW, BR, TOT, TAIL, HIND, & EAR) were significantly correlated with time. On all three islands TOT, TAIL, HIND, & EAR showed significant change over time. Direction of change was the same for TOT, TAIL, and HIND (becoming smaller) but differed for EAR. Using our method of nested two-way ANOVA and comparing MSEs, we found that the temporal change in five characters (ZB, TOT, TAIL, HIND, & EAR) exceeded differentiation between subspecies. Complete discriminant analysis of data from all years (Figure 2a) correctly classified 85% (119/140) of individuals, whereas 1897 to 1941 data alone (Figure 2b) correctly classified 99% (67/68) and 1955 to 1988 data alone (Figure 2c) correctly classified 96% (69/72). Altogether, 97% (136/140) of individuals were correctly classified by correcting for temporal change. Had we not tested for temporal variation in this data, we would have lost the power to classify 12% (17/140) of our sample.

Given the extent of temporal change, we expected the discriminant function giving full weight to individuals from 1897 to 1941 and zero weight to individuals from 1955 to 1988 to be poor at classifying individuals from the later period (see Table 3). This is indeed the case. Only 40%

(29/72) of the individuals from 1955 to 1988 are correctly classified.

We compared the relative amounts of movement in morphology over time by calculating the Mahalanobis distances between old and new centroids for each island (Table 4). *P. m. elusus* and *P. m. anacapae* changed approximately the same amount, whereas *P. m. santacruzae* changed approximately 40% less. In Figure 3, arrows are drawn from the centroids of the 1897 to 1941 confidence ellipses to the centroids of the groupings of 1955 to 1988 individuals, illustrating the direction and magnitude of morphological change on the three islands. Although each subspecies exhibited rapid morphological change, they remain well differentiated, as shown by the high (96%) correct classification rate of the 1955 to 1988 group using the discriminant function from this period only.

DISCUSSION

The mtDNA haplotype analysis of California island deer mice was the first mtDNA study of an island vertebrate (Ashley and Wills 1987). Results demonstrated that mtDNA could be an extremely useful tool for recreating the

Table 3. Separate one-way ANOVA results for each subspecies, with time (year collected) as a factor. Significant values are in bold.

	P. m. elusus		*P. m. anacapae* (all)		*P. m. anacapae* (West)		*P. m. anacapae* (Middle)		*P. m. santacruzae*	
	F	p	F	p	F	p	F	p	F	p
IW	0.9769	0.47083	**14.8872**	**0.00025**	2.9725	0.09405	0.8020	0.38301	**2.78766**	**0.02477**
LN	**2.4767**	**0.03180**	0.2181	0.64191	2.5757	0.11805	0.2235	0.64236	0.38121	0.90551
LPI	0.7172	0.67483	1.2265	0.27183	1.6303	0.21057	1.9023	0.18569	0.81073	0.58590
BR	1.6126	0.15901	**4.5765**	**0.03585**	2.4699	0.12559	0.0000	0.99696	**2.49615**	**0.03988**
AL	**4.6440**	**0.00072**	1.5690	0.21446	1.1880	0.28362	1.1557	0.29739	0.88875	0.52826
LIF	0.5461	0.81306	**5.7802**	**0.01882**	0.1762	0.67742	2.0468	0.17066	0.63852	0.72031
RW	0.7136	0.67785	**4.7508**	**0.03260**	**5.5002**	**0.02518**	1.7817	0.19955	1.16060	0.35599
ZB	0.4880	0.85583	0.5749	0.45082	3.3917	0.07453	1.4432	0.24609	0.30255	0.94678
IB	1.7040	0.13448	1.9757	0.16421	0.0279	0.86829	**6.1161**	**0.02425**	0.18545	0.98620
DBC	1.8004	0.11252	**14.1596**	**0.00034**	3.8160	0.05929	1.8585	0.19058	2.27068	0.05791
BB	1.6882	0.13843	0.2077	0.64994	0.0247	0.87612	0.7202	0.40786	1.26373	0.30349
BZP	1.1043	0.38536	**6.5223**	**0.01280**	0.5222	0.47498	**9.6398**	**0.00644**	1.07835	0.40296
TOT	**7.6623**	**0.00001**	**5.1537**	**0.02623**	0.0279	0.86841	**5.3093**	**0.03410**	**7.49666**	**0.00004**
TAIL	**6.3124**	**0.00006**	**7.4039**	**0.00818**	0.2631	0.61145	**14.8551**	**0.00127**	**4.98064**	**0.00094**
HIND	**13.7525**	**0.00000**	**72.8647**	**0.00000**	**37.9775**	**0.00000**	**6.3659**	**0.02189**	**6.89603**	**0.00008**
EAR	**9.0280**	**0.00001**	**18.2799**	**0.00006**	**14.0332**	**0.00069**	**7.3880**	**0.01461**	**4.29155**	**0.00447**

Key: IW = intermeatus width, LN = length of nasals, LPI = length of palate plus incisor (see text). BR = breadth of rostrum, AL = alimentary toothrow, LIF = length of incisive foramen, RW = rostral width (see text), ZB = zygomatic breadth, IB = interorbital breadth, DBC = depth of braincase, BB = breadth of braincase, BZP = breadth of zygomatic plate, TOT = total length, TAIL = tail length, HIND = hind foot length, and EAR = ear length.

284

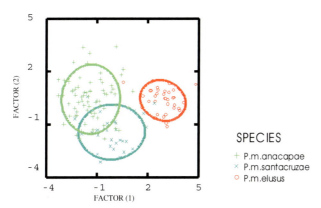

Figure 2a. Canonical scores plot for discriminant analysis of all years, 1897 to 1988.

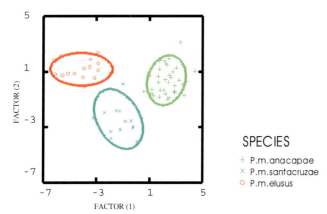

Figure 2b. Canonical scores plot for discriminant analysis of early period, 1897 to 1941.

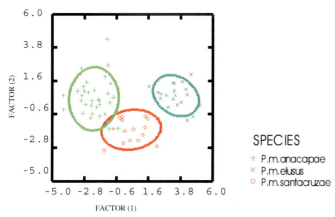

Figure 2c. Canonical scores plot for discriminant analysis of later period, 1955 to 1988.

evolutionary history of colonization and diversification of populations endemic to oceanic islands. Specifically for California Island deer mice, the islands are comprised of deer mice having haplotypes not found in mainland samples, and indicates they are genetically isolated from the mainland.

Table 4. Centroid coordinates and Mahalanobis distances between subspecies, from 1897 to 1941 and 1955 to 1988.

	early (1897 to 1941)	late (1955 to 1988)	Mahalanobis distance
P. m. elusus	-4.148, 1.184	0.460, 2.708	4.853
P. m. anacapae	2.242, 0.390	-2.350, -1.845	5.107
P. m. santacruzae	-1.344, -2.411	-4.354, -1.847	3.062

The presence of unique haplotypes on Anacapa, Santa Barbara, Santa Catalina, and San Clemente suggests that the subspecies of deer mice on these islands have been isolated from the mainland and other islands for a period of time sufficient for genetic differentiation to occur. The distribution of a common haplotype on Santa Rosa, San Nicolas, San Miguel and Santa Cruz suggests that recent gene flow or colonization events may have connected deer mice subspecies on these islands. In part this pattern may be explained by the geological history of the islands. The four northern islands (San Miguel, Santa Rosa, Santa Cruz, and Anacapa) were joined into the superisland of Santarosae a number of times during periods of lower sea level in the Pleistocene, and thus deer mice populations would have been in contact. This history does not, however, explain the unique haplotypes found on Anacapa nor the presence of this common haplotype on San Nicolas Island, which lies 80 km south of the northern islands.

Island subspecies of deer mice exhibited much lower levels of mtDNA variability than did mainland subspecies, although allozyme variability remains relatively high in island subspecies (Gill 1980). The explanation likely lies in differing transmission genetics of mitochondrial versus nuclear genomes. Because mtDNA is effectively haploid and maternally transmitted, founder effects and population bottlenecks will have a much greater effect on mtDNA variability than on diploid nuclear genes. Although this had been predicted from theoretical considerations (Birky et al. 1983), the California Island deer mouse investigation provided the first empirical demonstration of this phenomenon (Ashley and Wills 1987).

Allozyme and mtDNA differentiation among California Island deer mice subspecies are significantly correlated. The island subspecies have apparently been isolated long enough for differentiation to have occurred in both nuclear and mitochondrial genes through processes of genetic drift or natural selection. Neither of the genetic distance measures (allozyme distance or mtDNA divergence) was significantly correlated with morphological differentiation, suggesting that the evolution of morphological traits is not closely coupled with these types of genetic markers. A significant correlation between allozyme and geographic distance likely reflects the geological history of the islands and distance-dependent dispersal ability of deer mice. The lack of such an association for mtDNA and distance may reflect the role of rare founder events and other stochastic processes that shape distributions of mitochondrial haplotypes.

The advent of the polymerase chain reaction (PCR) and more efficient methods of DNA sequencing during the late 1980s and 1990s allowed mtDNA gene sequencing studies to largely replace RFLP studies. The COII sequence results obtained here for a subset of the RFLP-analyzed subspecies were in close agreement with the RFLP results. However, additional samples from West and East Anacapa allowed resolution of the metapopulation structure of *P. m. anacapae*. As shown in Figure 1, the connectivity of *P. m. anacapae* is demonstrated by the presence of one haplotype on all three islets, although unique haplotypes on Middle and West Anacapa suggest that the subspecies is not panmictic. Estimates of 2 to 7 migrants per generation were obtained, suggesting a metapopulation structure for this subspecies. Interestingly, deer mice from East Anacapa were thought to be extinct since 1981 to 1982 (Austin, pers. comm.), and very rare since 1966 (Collins et al. 1979). Deer mice were again collected on East Anacapa in 1997, but it was not known whether these mice represented recovery from a bottleneck on East Anacapa or whether deer mice had recolonized East Anacapa from elsewhere. Finding the common Anacapa mtDNA haplotype in East Anacapa deer mice suggest that they were not recolonized from outside Anacapa, but the presence of an additional unique haplotype not found on Middle or West Anacapa may indicate recovery from a bottleneck.

Collections of specimens of island deer mice over many years provided an opportunity to determine if morphological characters had changed over time (Pergams and Ashley 1999). We found that *P. m. elusus*, *P. m. santacruzae* and *P.m. anacapae* exhibited significant temporal change in several characters. Six characters in both *P. m. elusus* and *P. m. santacruzae* had changed over time, whereas ten characters in *P. m. anacapae* had changed. External body measurements (TOT, TAIL, HIND and EAR) exhibited temporal variation in all three subspecies, and two or more cranial characters also show significant temporal variation. Figure 3 illustrates that the subspecies are not converging on a

common phenotype but are remaining well differentiated. The finding that the change in several characters (ZB, TOT, TAIL, HIND and EAR) exceeded the level of differentiation between subspecies suggests that these characters are only useful for comparing specimens within a given time period. Discriminant analysis of data from the early years allowed correct classification of only 40% of the samples from the later years. Therefore the common practice of classification of modern specimens based on comparisons with much older museum type specimens is inappropriate in this case.

Clearly these island subspecies have undergone rapid phenotypic change during this century. The rate of change dramatically exceed those estimated from paleontological records (Gingerich 1983; Pergams and Ashley 1999) and are even higher than those reported in experimental selection studies (e.g. Losos et al. 1997). Although the changes were not associated with known selective forces, natural selection may be the most likely explanation for the observed morphological changes. Many changes have occurred on these islands, especially in the biotic components. For example, Santa Barbara had feral goats (Remington 1971), and sheep were introduced to all three islands in the 1800s (Brumbaugh 1980; Doran 1980; Federal Register 1997). European rabbits were introduced to Santa Barbara, and there were reports of feral pigs on Santa Cruz (Remington 1971, Federal Register 1997). Black rats (*Rattus rattus*) were accidentally introduced to Anacapa. Rats may have large effects on Anacapa mice because of their abundance and because they are both competitors and predators of deer mice (Collins et al. 1979). The introduction of exotic grasses for fodder, along with overgrazing, caused the extirpation of some native plants (Banks 1966). Examination of stomach contents of Anacapa and Santa Barbara deer mice showed that they were eating a mixture of native and exotic plants (Collins et al. 1979; Philbrick 1980; Federal Register 1997; CalFlora 8/2/98), thus dietary changes have occurred. However, none of these factors clearly stands out as a likely causal explanation for rapid morphological change. The island deer mouse populations are likely responding to differing combinations of stochastic and environmental factors that have resulted in rapid phenotypic change.

To summarize our findings on the evolution of California Island deer mice, it is clear that they represent a rich history of colonization, isolation, and evolutionary divergence in both genetic and morphological characters. Several of the islands have populations of deer mice that are morphologically and genetically distinct and have been following evolutionary trajectories independent of the mainland populations and other island populations. Nevertheless, they retain enough similarities for comparisons to be made and informative differences to be found. Our data also indicates recent contact among some of the island populations, including those of San Nicolas, San Miguel, and Santa Rosa and among East, Middle, and West Anacapa Islands. Finally, the California Island deer mice have served as an excellent "natural laboratory" for new and substantive evolutionary

Canonical Scores Plot

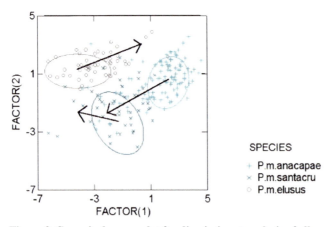

SPECIES
+ P.m.anacapae
× P.m.santacru
○ P.m.elusus

Figure 3. Canonical scores plot for discriminant analysis of all years, 1897 to 1988, but with discriminant function defined only by years 1897 to 1941.

findings, including different founder effects on nuclear and mitochondrial genomes and three of the most rapid cases of morphological evolution ever reported in natural populations. Now that we are entering the second century of research on California Island deer mice, we are certain that additional discoveries will emerge.

ACKNOWLEDGMENTS

We thank Greg Austin, Kate Faulkner, and the Channel Islands National Park. We thank the Santa Barbara Natural History Museum and the Natural History Museum of Los Angeles County for the generous access they gave us to their collections. We thank Dibyen Mujumdar and the Statistics Laboratory at UIC for their help with statistical analyses. We thank Paul Collins, Larry Heaney, and Bill Stanley for their help with morphometrics. We thank Dennis Nyberg, Jean Dubach, and Bruce Patterson for their comments. We thank many people for granting access to the islands and/or collecting mice, especially J. Engel, L. Laughrin, , R. McCluskey, K. Rindlaub, F. Ugolini, and A. Wenner. O. R. W. P. thanks his wife, Valerie Morrow, for her enduring support. This work was funded by a contract with Channel Islands National Park, National Park Service, U. S. Dept. of the Interior; and a subcontract with the Island Conservation and Ecology Group. This work was completed in partial fulfillment of the requirements for the masters degree (to O. R. W. P.) at the Graduate College of University of Illinois at Chicago.

LITERATURE CITED

Adkins, R. M. and R. L. Honeycutt. 1994. Evolution of the primate cytochrome *c* oxidase subunit II gene. Journal of Molecular Evolution 38:215-231.

Affifi, A. A. and V. Clark. 1996. Computer-aided Multivariate Analysis, 3rd edition, Chapman and Hall, London.

Ashley, M. V. and C. Wills. 1987. Analysis of mitochondrial DNA polymorphisms among Channel Island deer mice. Evolution 41:854-863.

Ashley, M. V. and C. Wills. 1989. Mitochondrial-DNA and allozyme divergence patterns are correlated among island deer mice. Evolution 43:646-650.

Banks, R. C. 1966. Terrestrial vertebrates of Anacapa Island, California. Transactions of the San Diego Society of Natural History 14:173-188.

Birky, C. W., T. Maruyama, and D. Fuerst. 1983. An approach to population and evolutionary genetic theory for genes in mitochondria and chloroplasts, and some results. Genetics 103:513-527.

Brumbaugh , R. W. 1980. Recent geomorphic and vegetal dynamics on Santa Cruz Island, California. Pages 139-158 *in* Power, D. M. (ed.), The California Islands: Proceedings of a Multidisciplinary Symposium. Santa Barbara Museum of Natural History, Santa Barbara, CA.

Calflora Database, "Dudleya caespitosa, Dudleya greenei, Dudleya traskiae, Marah macrocarpus, Opuntia littoralis, Opuntia oricola, Chenopodium californicum, Spergularia macrotheca, Coreopsis gigantea, Cakile maritima", http://elib.cs.berkeley.edu/cgi-bin/illus_query?table=calflora&like-char-textsoup=Dudleya+caespitosa, Dudleya+greenei,Dudleya+traskiae, Marah+macrocarpus,Opuntia+littoralis, Opuntia+oricola, Chenopodium+californicum, Spergularia+macrotheca, Coreopsis+gigantea, Cakile+maritima, [Accessed 2 August1998].

Collins, P. W., J. Storrer, and K. Rindlaub. 1979. Vertebrate zoology: biology of the deer mouse. Chapter XI *in* Power, D. M. (ed.), A Natural Resources Study of the Channel Islands National Park, California. Final Technical Report to the Denver Service Center, National Park Service, Washington, DC.

Dietz, E. J. 1983. Permutation test for association between two distance matrices. Systematic Zoology 32:21-26.

Doran, A. L. 1980. Pieces of Eight Channel Islands: A Bibliographic Guide and Source Book. Arthur H. Clark Co., Glendale, CA.

Elliot, D. G. 1903. A list of mammals collected by Edmund Heller in the San Pedro Martir and Hanson Laguna Mountains with the accompanying coast regions of lower California with descriptions of apparently new species. Field Columbia Museum Publications 79, Zoology Series, 3:199-232.

Federal Register, 1997. Endangered and threatened wildlife and plants; final rule for 13 plant taxa from the northern Channel Islands, California. 50 CFR Part 17. United States Fish and Wildlife Service, Washington, DC.

Gill, A. E. 1980. Evolutionary genetics of California Islands *Peromyscus*. Pages 719-744 *in* Power, D. M. (ed.), The California Islands: Proceedings of a Multidisciplinary Symposium. Santa Barbara Museum of Natural History, Santa Barbara, CA.

Gingerich, P.D. 1983. Rates of evolution: effects of time and temporal scaling: Science 222:159-161.

Lansmann, R. A., R. O. Shade, J. F. Shapira, and J. C. Avise. 1981. The use of restriction endonucleases to measure mitochondrial DNA sequence relatedness in natural populations. III. Techniques and potential applications. Journal of Molecular Evolution 17:214-226.

Losas, J. B., K. I. Warhelt, and T. W. Schoener. 1997. Adaptive differentiation following experimental island colonization in Anolis lizards. Nature 387:70-73.

Mearns, E. A. 1897. Descriptions of six new mammals from North America. Proceedings of the United States National Museum 19:719-724.

Mearns, E. A. 1907. Mammals of the Mexican boundary of the United States. United States National Museum Bulletin 56:1-530.

Nei, M. 1972. Genetic distance between populations. American Naturalist 106:283-292.

Nei, M. 1982. Evolution of human races at the gene level. Pages 167-181 *in* Bonne-Tamir, B., T. Cohen, and R. M. Goodman (eds.) Human genetics, part A: The unfolding genome. Alan R. Liss, NY.

Nei, M. 1987. Molecular Evolutionary Genetics. Columbia University Press, NY.

Nei, M. and F. Tajima. 1981. DNA polymorphism detectable by restriction endonucleases. Genetics 97:145-163.

Nelson, L., Jr. and E. A. Goldman. 1931. Six new white-footed mice (*Peromyscus maniculatus* group) from the islands off the Pacific coast. Journal of the Washington Academy of Science 21:532-535.

Osgood, W. H. 1909. Revision of the mice of the American genus *Peromyscus*. North American Fauna 28:1-285.

Pergams, O. R. W. and M. V. Ashley. 1999. Rapid morphological change in Channel Island deer mice. Evolution in press.

Pergams, O. R. W., R. C. Lacy, and M. V. Ashley. 2000 Conservation and management of Anacapa Island deer mice. Conservation Biology, in press.

Philbrick, R. 1980. Distribution and evolution of endemic plants of the California Islands. Pages 173-188 *in* Power, D. M. (ed.), The California Islands: Proceedings of a Multidisciplinary Symposium. Santa Barbara Museum of Natural History, Santa Barbara, CA.

Remington, C. l. 1971. Natural history and evolutionary genetics of the California Channel Islands. Discovery: Magazine of the Peabody Museum of Natural History at Yale University 7:3-18.

Reyment, R. A. 1972. The discriminant function in systematic biology. Pages 311-338 *in* Cacoullos, T. (ed.), Discriminant Analysis and Applications. Academic Press, NY.

Rozas, J. and R. Rozas. 1997. DnaSP v. 2.0: a novel software package for extensive molecular population genetics analysis. Computer Applications in Bioscience 13:307-311.

Sokal, R. R. and F. J. Rohlf. 1997. Biometry, 3rd edition. W. H. Freeman and Co., New York.

SPSS Inc. 1997. SYSTAT® 7.0 for Windows (computer program). SPSS, Inc., Chicago.

Upholt, W. B. 1977. Estimation of DNA sequence divergence from comparison of restriction endonuclease digests. Nucleic Acids Research 4:1257-1265.

von Bloeker, J. C. 1940. A new race of white-footed mouse from Santa Rosa island. Bulletin of the Southern California Academy of Science 39:172-174.

von Bloeker, J. C. 1941. A new subspecies of white-footed mouse from the Anacapa Islands, California. Bulletin of the Southern California Academy of Science 40:161-162.

POPULATION DECLINE OF ISLAND FOXES (*UROCYON LITTORALIS LITTORALIS*) ON SAN MIGUEL ISLAND

Timothy J. Coonan[1], Catherin A. Schwemm[1], Gary W. Roemer[2], and Greg Austin[3]

[1]National Park Service, Channel Islands National Park, 1901 Spinnaker Drive, Ventura, CA 93001
(805) 658-5776, FAX (805) 658-5798, E-mail: tim_coonan@nps.gov
[2]Institute for Wildlife Studies, P. O. Box 1104, Arcata, CA 95521
(707) 822-4258, FAX (707) 822-6300
and
Department of Biology, University of California, Los Angeles, CA 90024-1606
(310) 825-5014, FAX (310) 206-3987, E-mail: garyr@lifesci.ucla.edu
[3]U. S. Fish and Wildlife Service, Hopper Mountain National Wildlife Refuge, P. O. Box 5839, Ventura, CA 93005
(805) 644-5185, FAX (805) 644-1732, E-mail: greg_austin@mail.fws.gov

ABSTRACT

Annual population monitoring via capture-mark-recapture techniques revealed an abrupt decline in the island fox (*Urocyon littoralis littoralis*) population on San Miguel Island from 1994 to 1998. Adult fox density declined on all three grids monitored during the study period, and the range of decline was between 8.0 and 15.9 foxes/km². The estimated population on San Miguel declined from around 450 adults in 1994 to about 40 in 1998. The causes for the decline are unknown. However, the decline was not associated with changes in deer mice (*Peromyscus maniculatus*) density, with winter precipitation, or with seroprevalence to five canine diseases. Predation or other canine diseases or parasites may be factors in the decline. The population may be so low as to make recovery difficult.

Keywords: San Miguel Island, island fox, *Urocyon littoralis littoralis*, population decline.

INTRODUCTION

Since 1993, the National Park Service has conducted annual population monitoring of island foxes (*Urocyon littoralis littoralis*) on San Miguel Island, as part of the long-term ecological monitoring program at Channel Islands National Park. The island fox was a logical choice for monitoring. A diminutive relative of the mainland gray fox (*Urocyon cineroargenteus*), the island fox is found on the six largest of California's eight Channel Islands. Though individuals weigh less than 2.5 kg, the fox is the largest native mammal on the islands. The species has been listed as threatened by the state of California due to its small population size on several islands (California Department of Fish and Game 1987). The island fox was chosen as a key species to monitor at the Park because of its state-listed status, its apparently low population size, the general lack of demographic information about this species, and because of the relatively high amount of public interest in this unique canid. On San Miguel Island, island fox are annually monitored on three grids, using standard mark-recapture techniques.

In this paper we report on a catastrophic decline of island foxes on San Miguel Island, as indicated by the data from the annual population monitoring. We summarize six years of island fox monitoring data and investigate relationships between population parameters and other ecological factors, such as prey availability, weather, and seroprevalence for common canine diseases.

MATERIALS AND METHODS

Study Area

The National Park Service monitors island fox populations on San Miguel Island, the westernmost island of the Northern Channel Islands. At 38.7 km², San Miguel is the smallest of the islands on which island foxes occur. The island is a gently sloping plateau with long sandy beaches along the coastline. The island is fully exposed to the prevailing northwesterly wind, and is recovering from a period of severe overgrazing and erosion due to historic sheep ranching (Hochberg et al. 1979).

San Miguel's vegetation is currently dominated by grassland, which covers most of the deeper, stabilized soils on the island terrace (Hochberg et al. 1979). Introduced annuals (*Avena* spp. and *Bromus* spp.) dominate the grasslands. Native bunchgrasses such as *Nasella pulchra* occur more toward the eastern end of the island, but not in large stands. Shrub species, particularly coyote brush (*Baccharis pilularis*), are invading some grassland areas. The second most abundant vegetation type is *Isocoma* scrub, characterized by coast goldenbush (*Isocoma menziesii*), San Miguel Island locoweed (*Astragalus miguelensis*), California saltbush (*Atriplex californica*), and coyote brush. Coastal dune scrub vegetation occurs on the coast and extends well inland in some areas. Some inland sand dune areas are dominated by dense stands of silver lupine (*Lupinus albifrons*). Large bare areas on the island can be characterized as either unstabilized dunes ("sand stripes"), which are generally being colonized by coastal dune scrub species, or as erosion pavement where the soil cover has been removed, leaving a hardpan layer. Sea cliffs are dominated by coastal bluff scrub, including, in some areas, giant coreopsis (*Coreopsis gigantea*) and in others, introduced iceplant (*Mesembryanthemum crystallinum* and *M. nodiflorum*).

Three island fox trapping grids have been established on San Miguel Island (Schwemm 1995). The Dry Lakebed grid comprises primarily grassland cut by gentle ravines on the western end of the island. The western end of the Dry Lakebed grid extends onto a low area that is inundated in years of moderately high precipitation. The eastern end of the grid extends up the west flanks of Green Mountain. The San Miguel Hill grid extends eastward from San Miguel Hill and is the most varied of the three grids, both in topography and vegetation. More than a third of the grid is grassland, a third *Isocoma* scrub, and the remainder is canyon or unstabilized dune. The Willow Canyon grid comprises primarily grassland which is being invaded by *Baccharis*, although portions of the grid comprise *Isocoma* scrub, canyon, coastal bluff scrub, and unstabilized dune.

Island Fox Monitoring Methods

On San Miguel, island foxes are annually monitored with a standardized capture-recapture protocol developed for island foxes and also used on San Clemente, Santa Catalina, and Santa Cruz islands (Roemer et al. 1994). Fieldwork was conducted in mid- to late-summer (July to September) from 1993 to 1998. The Willow Canyon and San Miguel Hill grids each have 49 traps arrayed in a 7 x 7 grid. The Dry Lakebed grid has 48 traps arrayed in a 6 x 8 grid. In 1993, trapping on the Willow Canyon grid was conducted with 42 traps in a 6 x 7 array. Distance between traps is 250 m. Live traps (23 x 23 x 66 cm, Tomahawk Live Trap Co., Tomahawk, WI) were baited with dry cat food and a fruit scent (Knob Mountain Raw Fur Co., Berwick, PA). Traps were covered with burlap and placed to provide protection from sun, wind, and precipitation. A "chew tube" made of refrigerator (polyethylene) tubing was wired to the inside of each trap to provide captured foxes with a soft surface to chew upon. Each grid was trapped annually for six days, except for the Dry Lakebed grid, which was not trapped in 1993. During trapping, traps were checked once during every 24-hr period.

Upon first capture, foxes were weighed (±25 g), and sex, age, reproductive condition, presence of ectoparasites, and injuries were recorded. Foxes were aged according to tooth eruption and wear patterns on the first upper molar (Wood 1958) and were assigned to discrete age classes. Foxes were classified as pups (Age Class 0), young adults (Age Class 1: ca. 7 months to 2 years), adults (Age Class 2: ca. 2 to 3 years), mature adults (Age Class 3: ca. 3 to 4 years old) and old adults (Age Class 4: >4 years old). Foxes were marked with colored ear tags (Nasco-West, Modesto, CA) inserted in the pinna, and/or passive integrated transponder (PIT) tags (Biomark, Boise, ID) inserted subcutaneously between and just anterior to the scapulae. During the course of the study we shifted from use of ear tags to use of PIT tags because the latter have a lower loss rate (Schwemm 1996), result in fewer injuries to foxes, and are inconspicuous. During the study we caught foxes which had been marked during the design phase of the monitoring program (Fellers et al. 1988). These foxes were originally caught from 1985 to 1989 and were marked with collars made from 12 mm wide plastic cable ties. Collars were securely attached around the neck, and an identification number was permanently etched on the collar.

Estimation of Density and other Population Parameters

Island fox adult population sizes were estimated annually for each grid using closed population models from the program CAPTURE (version 2, White et al. 1982) as described by Roemer et al. (1994). Because CAPTURE's models for population size do not work well with very small population sizes, Chapman's modification of the Lincoln-Peterson (LP) estimator was used to estimate population size for the Dry Lakebed grid in 1996. Lack of adult captures prevented us from estimating population size, and thus densities, for the Dry Lakebed grid in 1997 and 1998, and the San Miguel Hill grid in 1998. To avoid counting animals twice, foxes that were captured on more than one grid in a given year were counted only on the grid where they were captured more frequently. This occurred only between the Willow Canyon and San Miguel Hill grids, which are contiguous. The number of adult foxes captured on both grids and subsequently assigned to one grid for 1993-1998 was 5, 2, 3, 4, 1, and 1, respectively.

Density of adult foxes (classes 1, 2, 3 and 4) was estimated for all grids and years, because adult density is a more conservative indicator of population change than total density. Pups were thus excluded from density estimates to reduce the variability introduced by interannual variation in pup survival. Adult density was estimated using the mean maximum distance moved (MMDM) method (Wilson and Anderson 1985). Naïve (or crude) density is calculated according to D = N/A, where N is the estimate of population size and A is the area of the trapping grid. Although closed population models assume that populations are closed both demographically and geographically, the naïve density estimator does not account for "edge effect" resulting from incomplete geographic closure. The size of the area trapped is actually larger than the size of the grid, due to the movements of animals residing on or just outside the grid. To account for this, the effective trap area A(W), where W is the boundary strip around the grid, was determined using estimates of MMDM provided by CAPTURE. MMDM is a measure of the maximum distance an animal moves between successive captures. A(W) was estimated by adding ½

MMDM to all sides of a grid. Density was estimated for each grid by dividing N by A(W). Standard errors of density estimates and 95% confidence intervals were estimated using the methods of Wilson and Anderson (1985).

To estimate annual island-wide population of adult foxes, average annual density from the three grids was multiplied by the island area (38.7 km²) except for 1998, when low number of adult captures prevented us from estimating density for two of the three grids. Some adults may have avoided traps in 1998, perhaps because the abundance of deer mice (*Peromyscus maniculatus*) was high enough to deter adults from investigating the traps as food sources. Pups, on the other hand, were readily caught in 1998. For example, we caught five pups on the Dry Lakebed grid in 1998, but no adults. Therefore, to estimate the island-wide population of adults in 1998, we reconstructed the adult population according to the number of pups that were caught (15). Assuming that adult fox pairs had two to three pups per litter, which is the approximate range of litter sizes from the previous five years on San Miguel Island (Coonan et al. 1998), then the adult population on the three grids was 10 to 14 foxes in 1998. Multiplying by the area of the island produces a range of 28 to 39 adult foxes, with an average of 33. This does not account for non-breeding adults.

Pup productivity was calculated as the number of pups recorded annually on each grid. Adult and pup survival rates were estimated with program MARK (White and Burnham 1997), which uses individual encounter histories to provide estimates of apparent survival for populations of marked animals. Apparent survival is the probability of recapturing an animal between encounter sessions. Apparent survival does not account for emigration, and thus may underestimate true survival, which is the probability of surviving between encounter sessions. For survival analysis, we pooled data for the Willow Canyon and San Miguel Hill grids, since there was considerable movement of individual foxes between those grids. During the study period, 23 foxes moved between the San Miguel Hill and Willow Canyon grids, as indicated by recaptures. In contrast, only one fox moved between the Dry Lakebed grid and any other grid during the study period.

Prey Availability

Data from the Park's long-term ecological monitoring program (Coonan 1995, 1996; Schwemm 1995, 1996; Austin 1996, 1998) were used as indices of population trend for vertebrate prey and vegetation food items. Collins and Laughrin (1979) report that island foxes on San Miguel Island are opportunistic omnivores, consuming a wide variety of plants and animals. Summer and fall diets comprised insects and the fruits and leaves of sea-fig, or iceplant (*Carpobrotus chilensis*), whereas winter diets were characterized by deer mice (*Peromyscus maniculatus*), birds, insects, and iceplant.

Spring and fall densities of deer mice were estimated with capture-recapture data from four permanent grids. Each grid comprised 100 Sherman traps in a 10 x 10

configuration, with 7 m spacing between traps. Mouse grids were monitored in both the spring and fall seasons, except when funding or personnel constraints prevented it. Deer mouse density was estimated using the program CAPTURE. To estimate relative abundance of ground-nesting birds, landbirds were monitored in spring and fall along permanent line transects that utilize the island's trail system (van Riper et al.1988). All birds within 100 m of the transect midline were recorded. For an index of annual abundance we used spring counts for horned larks (*Eremophila alpestris*) and western meadowlarks (*Sturnella neglecta*) from each line transect.

Relative cover of sea-fig was used as an index of availability for sea-fig fruits and leaves, though we do not know if sea-fig fruit and leaf availability is correlated with sea-fig relative cover. Data from the Park's vegetation monitoring program (Halvorson et al. 1988) were used to calculate relative cover of sea-fig. Vegetation was monitored annually on 16 permanent transects on San Miguel Island. Each 30 m transect comprises 100 points at which vegetation cover of all species is recorded. Relative cover of sea-fig was calculated as the number of sea-fig hits on each transect. Relative cover was averaged for habitat types with multiple transects. We did not collect data on abundance of insects and other arthropods.

Weather

Daily precipitation data were obtained from the daily weather log maintained at the Nidever Canyon Ranger Station, San Miguel Island.

Exposure to Canine Diseases

Fox blood samples were collected and tested for presence of antibodies to five lethal canine diseases. Three to 10 ml of blood were drawn from the femoral vein of unanesthetized captured foxes. Sera was obtained from 22 foxes in 1994, 15 foxes in 1995, and 18 foxes in 1997. Serum was separated from the cellular fraction by centrifugation, removed, and then frozen. Sera were tested for antibodies against canine adenovirus, canine distemper, canine parvovirus, *Leptospira canicola*, and *Leptospira ictero*. Serologic tests were conducted at the Washington Animal Disease Diagnostic Laboratory, Washington State University, Pullman, WA. Antibody titers of $\geq 1:5$ were considered evidence of previous exposure to canine adenovirus and canine distemper virus. Antibody titers of $\geq 1:25$ were considered evidence of previous exposure to canine parvovirus. Antibody titers of $\geq 1:100$ were considered evidence of previous exposure to *Leptospira canicola* and *Leptospira ictero*. Seroprevalence for each disease was calculated as the percentage of the total number of samples that tested positive.

Statistical Analysis

Differences among years were evaluated with analysis of variance (ANOVA) (SYSTAT 7.0, SPSS Inc., 1997). Repeated measures analysis of variance (rmANOVA) was used to evaluate trends in landbird and sea-fig abundance. Because island deer mouse density estimates for each grid and year were not replicated, analysis of variance could not be conducted to test for differences among years and grids. Instead, contrasts (Steel et al. 1997) were used to test for differences in deer mouse densities among years. Simple linear regression was used to test relationships between variables.

Percent or proportion data were transformed with the arcsine function prior to analysis. Significance levels were set at 0.05 for all tests except contrasts for comparison of abundance or density estimates, for which significance levels were set at 0.10, in order to minimize the chance of a type 2 error (failing to detect a decrease in abundance or density). In a long-term ecological monitoring program, failing to detect a problem (type 2 error) is at least as serious as a false report (type 1 error) (Steidl et al. 1997).

RESULTS

During the study period we captured 297 individual foxes a total of 904 times. Overall, density on each grid declined over time (Table 1, Figure 1). The rate of decline was similar on the three grids from 1995 to 1996 (approximately 5-6 foxes/km²). The islandwide population estimate for adults fell from near 450 in 1994 to approximately 40 in 1998 (Figure 2). Apparent annual survival of adults declined

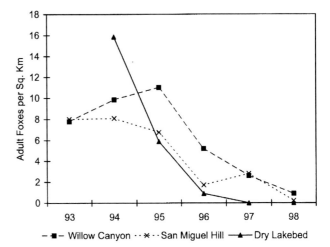

Figure 1. Adult island fox density estimates (number per km²) for three monitoring grids on San Miguel Island, 1993 to 1998.

Table 1. Total number of adults captured, population estimate (SE), model used, effective trap area [A(W)], density estimate, standard error, and 95% confidence interval for island fox trapping grids on San Miguel Island.

Grid/Year	Number of Adults	Population Estimate (SE)	Model[a]	A(W) km²	Density (foxes/km²)	SE	95% CI
Dry Lakebed							
1994	53	54 (1.6)	M(bh)	3.41	15.9	0.47	14.9-16.8
1995	14	21 (4.9)	M(h)	3.58	5.9	1.37	3.2-8.6
1996	2	2	n/a	n/a	0.9	n/a	n/a
1997	0	--					
1998	0	--					
San Miguel Hill							
1993	27	27 (0.1)	M(bh)	3.38	8	0.04	7.9-8.1
1994	27	27 (0.5)	M(bh)	3.34	8.1	0.15	7.8-8.4
1995	21	23 (3.2)	M(h)	3.4	6.8	0.93	4.9-8.6
1996	6	8 (1.8)	M(h)	4.67	1.7	0.39	1.0-2.5
1997	8	16 (5.3)	M(h)	5.7	2.8	0.92	1.0-4.6
1998	1	--					
Willow Canyon							
1993	26	28 (2.9)	M(bh)	3.59	7.8	0.8	6.2-9.4
1994	27	34 (7.3)	M(bh)	3.45	9.9	2.1	5.7-14.0
1995	28	34 (4.2)	M(h)	3.09	11	1.36	8.4-13.7
1996	13	17 (3.6)	M(h)	3.26	5.2	1.12	3.0-7.4
1997	10	12 (3.2)	M(h)	4.61	2.6	0.69	1.3-3.0
1998	4	5 (1.7)	M(o)	5.7	0.9	[b]	

[a]Refers to model used by program CAPTURE (White et al. 1982) to estimate population. M(h) = heterogeneous capture probability model; M(bh) = combination of behavior model and heterogeneous capture probability model.

[b]With only 1 recapture, SE and CI could not be estimated.

n/a = number of captures too low to use CAPTURE; Chapman's modifier of the Lincoln-Peterson estimator used instead.

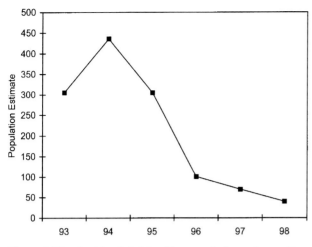

Figure 2. Island-wide adult island fox population estimate, San Miguel Island, 1993 to 1998.

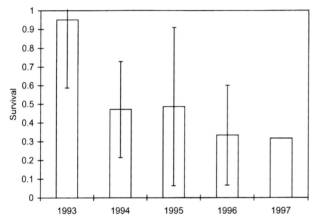

Figure 3. Annual estimates of apparent survival, with 95% confidence interval, for adult island foxes on the Willow Canyon and San Miguel Hills grids, San Miguel Island, 1993 to 1997. Survival estimates generated from program MARK (White and Burnham 1997).

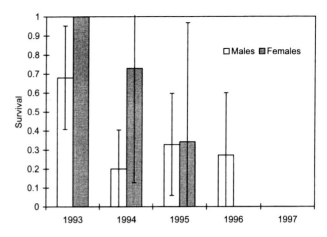

Figure 4. Annual estimates of apparent survival, with 95% confidence intervals, for island fox pups on the Willow Canyon and San Miguel Hill grids, San Miguel Island, 1993 to 1997. Survival estimates generated from program MARK (White and Burnham 1997).

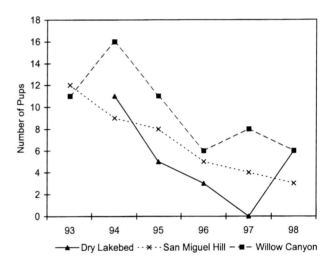

Figure 5. Total number of island fox pups captured on each of three trapping grids, San Miguel Island, 1993 to 1998.

over the study period (Figure 3). On the Dry Lakebed grid, no previously captured foxes were recaptured during monitoring in 1996, 1997, or 1998. Apparent survival of pups differed between sexes for the Willow Canyon/ San Miguel Hill grids (Figure 4). Female pup survival on those grids declined over time, and was apparently zero in 1997. Pup production generally decreased over the study period (Figure 5), except for an increase from 1997 to 1998 on the Dry Lakebed grid.

The fox population decline was not apparently associated with changes in prey availability. Linear contrasts showed that spring and fall mouse densities did not decrease or increase on the 4 mouse grids. Spring abundance of ground nesting birds did not decline over time (rmANOVA, F = 2.275, p = 0.121), although spring abundance of horned larks did decline (rmANOVA, F = 2.822, p = 0.099). Relative cover of sea-fig, or iceplant, generally increased on San Miguel Island between 1984 and 1996. On 6 permanent vegetation transects, sea-fig cover increased from 1984 to

1996 (rmANOVA, F = 5.572, p < 0.001). The increase after 1990 may reflect the higher precipitation during this period, in contrast to the drought years preceding this. During the study period, sea-fig cover did not change over time (rmANOVA, F = 1.187, p = 0.334).

Although annual precipitation varied over the six-year study period (Figure 6), adult density was not associated with previous winter's precipitation on either the Willow Canyon grid (f = 0.440, p = 0.544) or the San Miguel Hill grid (f = 0.023, p = 0.886), and adult survival was not correlated with winter precipitation (F = 0.066, p = 0.814).

The island fox population decline was not associated with changes in seroprevalence to canine diseases. Of the five diseases tested, antibodies were detected only for parvovirus and canine adenovirus (Table 2). Seroprevalence to canine adenovirus was high in all years tested, and was similar to seroprevalence in 1988 (Garcelon et al. 1992). Antibodies to canine parvovirus were detected in 2 of 22

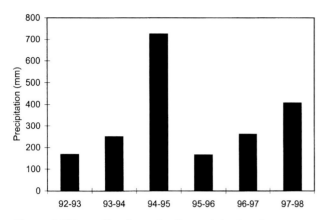

Figure 6. Winter (October - April) precipitation, San Miguel Island, 1992 to 1998.

Table 2. Prevalence of serum antibodies to canine diseases in island foxes, San Miguel Island.

		1988[a]	1994	1995	1997
	n	23	22	15	18
Canine adenovirus		96[b]	95	100	89
Canine distemper		0	0	0	0
Canine parvovirus		30	9	0	0
Leptospira canicola		0	0	0	0
Leptospira ictero		0	0	0	0

[a]Data from Garcelon et al. (1992).

[b]Prevalence = (Number of positive samples/total number of samples tested) x 100.

samples from 1994, but not in any samples from 1995 or 1997. Seroprevalence to canine parvovirus was 30% (7/23) in 1988.

DISCUSSION

Anecdotal information (Laughrin 1980) indicates that island fox populations have fluctuated widely in historic times, for unknown reasons. In this study we documented an abrupt decline in the island fox population on San Miguel Island from 1994 to 1998. Although other island fox populations have been shown to fluctuate, the range of the decline on San Miguel Island was greater than that reported for other island fox populations. Fox populations on San Clemente and Santa Catalina islands have fluctuated over time (Roemer et al. 1994). On those islands, within-grid density varied approximately 2 to 3 foxes/km² on four grids and approximately 6 foxes/km² on one grid. In contrast, the range of adult density on San Miguel Island during the recorded decline was 10.1 foxes/km² on the Willow Canyon grid, approximately 8.0 foxes/km² on the San Miguel Hill grid, and 15.9 foxes/km² on the Dry Lakebed grid.

On the eastern half of the island (Willow Canyon and San Miguel Hill grids), adult survival was initially high, but declined over the study period. The highest density was recorded on the Dry Lakebed grid in 1994, but survival was

low from 1994 to 1995, and apparently no foxes survived from 1995 to 1996 on the Dry Lakebed grid, or from 1996 to 1997. We did not document actual mortality of foxes in our study, and it is possible that foxes not seen in subsequent years may have dispersed from the grids. On the Willow Canyon and San Miguel Hill grids in 1997 we recaptured five individuals which had not been captured for two to four years previously. However, it is unlikely that a significant number of foxes not recaptured had dispersed away from the grids, because the proportion of the island sampled by the three grids was high, approximately 30% (see effective trap area estimates in Table 1).

We expected to observe declines in food availability, because such changes drive population dynamics of other fox populations, to varying degrees. Changes in food availability drive fox population dynamics primarily through effects on reproduction and nutritional status. Decline in prey availability can result in fewer females breeding, smaller litters, fewer pups, or lower pup survival to yearling stage. Such effects on reproduction have been observed for fox populations closely linked to single food sources (kit fox, *Vulpes macrotus*: Egoscue 1975, White and Ralls 1993; mainland arctic fox, *Alopex lagopus*: MacPherson 1969; insular red fox, *Vulpes vulpes*: Zabel and Taggart 1989; mainland red fox: Goszczynski 1989), as well as the generalist gray fox (Root and Payne 1985). Although we expected the decline in the fox population to be accompanied by declines in food, the prey items that we monitored did not decline over the study period. Like the mainland gray fox, the island fox is a generalist omnivore which does not rely on a single prey species (Moore and Collins 1995). Island fox diet changes seasonally according to availability of food items. The most important food items for island foxes on San Miguel Island are deer mice and the fruits of sea-fig. Deer mice, which were reported to be present in 11 to 76% of San Miguel Island fox scats (Collins and Laughrin 1979), did not decline over the study period.

Sea-fig has been reported to account for 30 to 90% volume of fox scats in all seasons (Collins and Laughrin 1979) and was most important in summer. Relative cover of sea-fig did not decline during the study period, although measurement of sea-fig cover may not accurately reflect fruit availability. Additionally, there is a scale-induced die-off of sea-fig occurring near Simonton Cove which the Park's vegetation monitoring program did not detect in its transects (K. McEachern, pers. comm. 1998).

We did not monitor invertebrate populations, and thus may have missed seasonal and annual fluctuation in invertebrates. Insects are seasonally important in San Miguel Island fox diets, occurring in 70 to 80 % of spring and fall scats, and accounting for 35% and 23% of the total volume of scats in those seasons, respectively (Collins and Laughrin 1979). It is possible that insect availability may have changed over the study period due to weather, and could have affected fox populations.

The only prey item that declined over the study period was horned larks. Birds are somewhat seasonally important in the diet of San Miguel Island foxes, occurring in 22% of spring scats, and accounting for an average of 13% of scat volume during spring (Collins and Laughrin 1979). Although horned larks declined over time, it is unlikely that this adversely affected nutrients available to foxes, since their diet is sufficiently diverse in the spring to allow them to switch to other food items, including seasonally abundant orthopterans.

We expected that annual precipitation could affect fox populations either positively, by increasing productivity and prey populations, or negatively, by affecting fox survival. San Miguel Island is subject to periodic drought caused by El Niño - Southern Oscillation events, but it is unknown whether this results in prey scarcity. We began monitoring foxes after a six-year drought had ceased, and thus cannot quantify the effects of drought on San Miguel Island foxes and their food base. However, record precipitation in 1995 did not result in higher mouse densities and higher fox densities. In fact, fox densities declined in the three years following the record precipitation. On the other hand, the high precipitation of winter 1994-1995 and winter 1997-1998 may have adversely affected fox survival on San Miguel Island. Precipitation was almost twice as high in winter 1994-1995 than in any other year, even the El Niño year of 1997-1998. Adult survival was lower in 1994-1995 than in 1993-1994, but, over the study period, adult survival was not correlated with winter precipitation. Unless changes in insect availability occurred, factors other than food availability and weather may have caused the observed island fox population decline.

The observed decline in the San Miguel fox population may be due to a disease agent. The pattern of population decline on the island (from west to east) suggests a disease spreading within the fox population in that same direction. Results from this and previous studies (Garcelon et al. 1992) indicate that island foxes on San Miguel Island have antibodies for canine parvovirus and canine adenovirus. Although exposure to canine adenovirus was high for all years, it is unknown whether this has impacted fox populations. Other free-ranging canids have also shown high seroprevalence to canine adenovirus, and the disease can cause high mortality rates in juveniles, according to Garcelon et al. (1992). Those authors documented high seroprevalence rates (72 to 97%) for four of the six island fox populations; Santa Cruz and Santa Catalina showed no antibodies to canine adenovirus. Garcelon et al. (1992) concluded that the high seroprevalence indicated that canine adenovirus may be enzootic in the island fox. In this study, female pup survival rates declined over time, and perhaps were influenced by canine adenovirus.

No antibodies to canine distemper have been found in any of the fox populations on the Channel Islands, suggesting either that distemper has never been introduced to island fox populations, or that island foxes are extremely susceptible to distemper and none survived exposure (Garcelon et al. 1992). Canine distemper has been identified as a factor in periodic local population declines of gray foxes on the California mainland (P. Swift, pers. comm. 1996) and has been identified as a significant mortality factor for some gray fox populations in the southeastern United States (Nicholson and Hill 1984, Davidson et al. 1992). On San Miguel Island, occasional visits by domestic dogs could expose island foxes to various diseases. Although domestic dogs are not allowed on the island, boaters have been observed bringing their pets ashore on San Miguel Island (I. Williams, pers. comm. 1996) and on nearby Santa Cruz Island (G. Roemer, pers. comm. 1994). During the decline, fox carcasses were not collected and necropsied, or examined for clinical evidence of disease. Without such evidence, it is difficult to rule out disease as a factor. Other diseases or parasites may have played a role in the observed population decline. We are currently investigating the occurrence in island foxes of a common canine parasite, heartworm (*Dirofilaria immitis*), and exposure to a calicivirus, San Miguel sea lion virus.

The extremely small adult population size estimated for San Miguel island foxes (40 adults) decreases the probability of this population persisting over time. Although a population viability analysis (PVA) has not been conducted for the San Miguel Island subspecies of island fox, the population's decrease to approximately 40 adults is alarming. Although such a small population size may compromise the maintenance of adequate genetic variation in the population (Franklin 1980; Lande and Barrowclough 1987), the demographic consequences for population persistence are more important in the short-term (Lande 1988). A population as low as 40 individuals may be subject to random demographic variation, as variation in individual birth and death rates causes the population to fluctuate, perhaps to extinction (Gilpin and Soule 1986).

Recent information indicates that island fox populations are declining on Santa Rosa and Santa Cruz Islands, as well as on San Miguel (G. Roemer and D. Garcelon, pers. comm. 1996). As on San Miguel, the reasons for the declines on Santa Rosa and Santa Cruz are not immediately apparent. The observed population decline of island fox on San Miguel Island comprises a "red flag" situation detected by a long-term ecological monitoring program. It also underscores the need for a monitoring program to marshal the fiscal and scientific support required to investigate cause and effect, after a red flag situation is discovered. Although the current island fox monitoring program provides a more complete dataset than any other terrestrial protocol at Channel Islands National Park, it is still insufficient to tease out the factors responsible for the observed population decline. Active and in-depth research is required to determine the roles that parasites and disease play in island fox population dynamics, and to directly determine mortality factors. Until factors for the decline can be established, and, if possible, mitigated, the data thus far raise the specter of a local extirpation of island fox on San Miguel Island, and perhaps on the other two islands where the fox occurs in the Park.

ACKNOWLEDGMENTS

This study was funded by the National Park Service, Channel Islands National Park. Heidi David, Mark Willett, and Keith Rutz served as lead field technicians during portions of this study. David Garcelon of the Institute for Wildlife Studies assisted in coordinating the serological survey for canine diseases, and Paul Geissler provided statistical advice. Fieldwork was conducted by Ethan Aumack, Terry Austin, Karen Beardsley, Winter Bonnin, Melissa Booker, Susan Coppelli, Julie Eliason, Kate Faulkner, Dave Garcelon, Jennifer Gibson, Julie Goldzman, Michael Hanson, Emily Hebard, Aaron Hebshi, Jeff Howarth, Joanna Iwanicha, Frans Juola, Marcia Kingsbury, Rob Klinger, David Kushner, Andrea Lehotsky, Marie Lindsey, Carmen Lombardo, Paige Martin, Ann Marx, LeeAnn Naue, Mark Philippart, Stella Quicoli, Bruce Rodriguez, Nancy Siepel, Grace Smith, Chris Starbird, Sandy Von Wedel, Ron Walder, and Ian Williams.

LITERATURE CITED

Austin, G. 1996. Terrestrial vertebrate monitoring, Channel Islands National Park, 1995 annual report. Channel Islands National Park Technical Report CHIS-96-04. National Park Service, Ventura, CA.

Austin, G. 1998. Terrestrial vertebrate monitoring, Channel Islands National Park, 1996 annual report. Channel Islands National Park Technical Report CHIS-98-02. National Park Service, Ventura, CA.

California Department of Fish and Game. 1987. Five-year status report on the island fox (*Urocyon littoralis*). Unpublished report, California Department of Fish and Game, Sacramento, CA.

Collins, P. W., and L. L. Laughrin. 1979. The island fox on San Miguel Island. Pages 12.1-12.47 *in* Power, D. M. (ed.), Natural resources study of the Channel Islands National Monument, California. Report submitted to the National Park Service. Santa Barbara Museum of Natural History, Santa Barbara, CA.

Coonan, T. J. 1995. Landbird monitoring, Channel Islands National Park, 1993 annual report. Channel Islands National Park Technical Report CHIS-94-03. National Park Service, Ventura, CA.

Coonan, T. J. 1996. Landbird monitoring, Channel Islands National Park, 1994 annual report. Channel Islands National Park Technical Report CHIS-96-02. National Park Service, Ventura, CA.

Coonan, T. J., G. Austin, and C. Schwemm. 1998. Status and trend of island fox, San Miguel Island, Channel Islands National Park. Channel Islands National Park Technical Report CHIS-98-01. National Park Service, Ventura, CA.

Davidson, W. R., V. F. Nettles, L. E, Hayes, E. W. Howerth, and C. E. Couvillion. 1992. Diseases diagnosed in gray foxes (*Urocyon cinereoargenteus*) from the southeastern United States. Journal of Wildlife Diseases 28:28-33.

Egoscue, H. J. 1975. Population dynamics of the kit fox in western Utah. Bulletin of the Southern California Academy of Sciences 74:122-127.

Fellers, G. M., C. A. Drost, and B. W. Arnold. 1988. Terrestrial vertebrates monitoring handbook. Channel Islands National Park, Ventura, CA.

Franklin, I. A. 1980. Evolutionary change in small populations. Pages 135-149 *in* Soule, M. E., and B. A. Wilcox (eds.), Conservation Biology: An Evolutionary-Ecological Perspective. Sinauer Associates, Sunderland, MA.

Garcelon, D. K., R. K. Wayne, and B. J. Gonzales. 1992. A serologic survey of the island fox (*Urocyon littoralis*) on the Channel Islands, California. Journal of Wildlife Diseases 28:223-229.

Gilpin, M. E., and M. E. Soule. 1986. Minimum viable populations: processes of species extinction. Pages 135-149 *in* Soule, M. E. (ed.), Conservation Biology: The Science of Scarcity and Diversity. Sinauer Associates, Sunderland, MA.

Goszczynski, J. 1989. Population dynamics of the red fox in central Poland. Acta Theriologica 34:141-154.

Halvorson, W. L., S. D. Veirs, Jr., R. A. Clark, and D. D. Borgais. 1988. Terrestrial vegetation monitoring handbook. Channel Islands National Park, Ventura, CA.

Hochberg, M., S. Junak, R. Philbrick, and S. Timbrook. 1979. Botany. Pages 5.1-5.91 *in* Power, D. M. (ed.), Natural resources study of the Channel Islands National Monument, California. Report submitted to the National Park Service. Santa Barbara Museum of Natural History, Santa Barbara, CA.

Lancia, R. A., J. D. Nichols, and K. H. Pollock. 1996. Estimating the number of animals in wildlife populations. Pages 215-253 *in* Bookhout, T. A. (ed.), Research and Management Techniques for Wildlife and Habitats. Fifth edition, revised. The Wildlife Society, Bethesda, MD.

Lande, R. 1988. Genetics and demography in biological conservation. Science 241:1455-1460.

Lande, R., and G. F. Barrowclough. 1987. Effective population size, genetic variation, and their use in population management. Pages 87-124 *in* Soule, M. E. (ed.), Viable Populations for Conservation. Cambridge University Press, Cambridge, Great Britain.

Laughrin, L. L. 1980. Populations and status of the island fox. Pages 745-749 *in* Power, D. M. (ed.), The California Islands: Proceedings of a Multidisciplinary Symposium. Santa Barbara Museum of Natural History, Santa Barbara, CA.

MacPherson, A. H. 1969. The dynamics of Canadian arctic fox populations. Canadian Wildlife Service Report Series No. 8. 52 pp.

Moore, C. M., and P. W. Collins. 1995. Urocyon littoralis. Mammalian Species 489:1-7.

Nicholson, W. S., and E. P. Hill. 1984. Mortality in gray foxes from east-central Alabama. Journal of Wildlife Management 48:1429-1432.

Roemer, G. W., D. K. Garcelon, T. J. Coonan, and C. Schwemm. 1994. The use of capture-recapture methods for estimating, monitoring and conserving island fox populations. Pages 387-400 *in* Halvorson, W. L. and G. J. Maender, (eds.), The Fourth California Islands Symposium: Update on the Status of Resources. Santa Barbara Museum of Natural History, Santa Barbara, CA.

Root, D. A., and N. F. Payne. 1985. Age-specific reproduction of gray foxes in Wisconsin. Journal of Wildlife Management 49:890-892.

Schwemm, C. A. 1995. Terrestrial vertebrate monitoring, Channel Islands National Park, 1993 annual report. Channel Islands National Park Technical Report CHIS-1994-02. National Park Service, Ventura, CA.

Schwemm, C. A. 1996. Terrestrial vertebrate monitoring, Channel Islands National Park, 1994 annual report. Channel Islands National Park Technical Report CHIS-96-03. National Park Service, Ventura, CA.

Steidl, R. J., J. P. Hayes, and E. Schauber. 1997. Statistical power in wildlife research. Journal of Wildlife Management 61: 270-279.

Steel, R.G. D., J. H. Torrie, and D. A. Dickey. 1997. Principles and procedures of statistics: a biometrical approach. Third edition, revised. McGraw-Hill, New York, NY.

Van Riper , C., III, M. K. Sogge, and C. Drost. 1988. Land bird monitoring handbook, Channel Islands National Park, California. National Park Service, Ventura, CA.

White, G. C., D. R. Anderson, K. P. Burnham, and D. L. Otis. 1982. Capture-recapture and removal methods for sampling closed populations. Los Alamos National Laboratory, LA-8787-NERP, Los Alamos, NM.

White, G. C., and K. P. Burnham. 1997. Program MARK – survival estimation from populations of marked animals. Online. Available at: http://www.cnr.colostate.edu/~gwhite/software.html.

White, P. J., and K. Ralls. 1993. Reproduction and spacing patterns of kit foxes relative to changing prey availability. Journal of Wildlife Management 57:861-867.

Wilson, K. R, and D. R. Anderson. 1985. Evaluation of two density estimators of small mammal population size. Journal of Mammalogy 66:13-21.

Wood, J. E. 1958. Age structure and productivity of a gray fox population. Journal of Mammalogy 39:74-86.

Zabel. C. J., and S. J. Taggart. 1989. Shift in red fox, *Vulpes vulpes*, mating system associated with El Niño in the Bering Sea. Animal Behavior 38: 830-838.

SOURCES OF UNPUBLISHED MATERIALS

Garcelon, D. K. Institute for Wildlife Studies, P. O. Box 1104, Arcata, CA 95518. Personal Communication 1996.

McEachern, K. U. S. Geological Survey, Biological Resources Division, Channel Islands Field Station, 1901 Spinnaker Drive, Ventura, CA 93001. Personal Communication 1998.

Roemer, G. W. Institute for Wildlife Studies, P.O. Box 1104, Arcata, CA 95518. Personal Communication 1996.

Swift, P. California Department of Fish and Game, Wildlife Investigations Laboratory, 1701 Nimbus Road, Suite D, Rancho Cordova, CA 95670. Personal Communication 1996.

Williams, I. Channel Islands National Park, 1901 Spinnaker Drive, Ventura CA 93001. Personal Communication 1996.

UPDATE ON THE STATUS OF THE ISLAND SPOTTED SKUNK

Kevin R. Crooks[1] and Dirk Van Vuren[2]

[1]Department of Biology, University of California, Santa Cruz, CA 95064
(619) 623-0086, E-mail: crooks@biology.ucsc.edu
[2]Department of Wildlife, Fish, and Conservation Biology, University of California, Davis, CA 95616
(530) 752-4181, E-mail: dhvanvuren@ucdavis.edu

ABSTRACT

The island spotted skunk, an insular endemic carnivore that occurs on only Santa Cruz and Santa Rosa islands, is listed as a subspecies of special concern by the State of California. Our prior research indicated that skunks were relatively rare, specialized in their resource use, and particularly sensitive to environmental perturbations. Consequently, we suggested that the continued existence of the island spotted skunk was precarious and recommended further monitoring of their population status. Surprisingly, trapping on Santa Cruz Island in 1998 revealed an overall trap success (3.8%) nearly seven times higher than our overall trap success in 1992 (0.57%). Although trapping design differed between years and sample sizes are small, the higher trap success of island spotted skunks, in conjunction with a recent increase in skunk sightings, suggests a population increase on Santa Cruz Island over the past six years. An increase in spotted skunks on Santa Cruz Island may be driven by a combination of factors, including normal variation in population size, a slow response to recovery of the island following removal of cattle and feral sheep, or the potential decline of island foxes, a direct competitor with skunks.

Keywords: Island spotted skunk, Santa Cruz Island, population increase.

INTRODUCTION

The island spotted skunk (*Spilogale gracilis amphiala*), a subspecies of the western spotted skunk, is an insular endemic carnivore that occurs on the two largest California Channel Islands, Santa Cruz and Santa Rosa. Due to small populations and limited distribution, the island spotted skunk is listed as a subspecies of special concern by the State of California. Prior to our published research on spotted skunks on Santa Cruz Island in 1992 (Crooks 1994a,b; Crooks and Van Vuren 1994, 1995), the status and ecology of the island spotted skunk was unknown. Our results indicated that skunks were relatively rare, specialized in their resource use, and were particularly sensitive to environmental perturbations. Consequently, we suggested that the continued existence of the island spotted skunk was precarious and recommended further monitoring of their population status. Herein we present recent data tentatively suggesting

a population increase in the island spotted skunk population on Santa Cruz Island.

STUDY AREA AND METHODS

Santa Cruz Island (250 km²) is located 40 km south of Santa Barbara, California. The island is 39 km long and 3 to 11 km wide. A system of interior valleys, including the large Central Valley, is oriented in an east-west direction and bounded by mountain ranges on the north (maximum elevation 750 m) and the south (465 m). Climate is a maritime Mediterranean-type, with hot, dry summers, and cool, wet winters.

In April and September 1998, we sampled island spotted skunks along road transects that totaled about 30 km in length throughout the central portion of the island. Skunks were live-trapped in single-door box-traps set every 250 to 500 m and baited with commercial cat food and fruit paste baits. Although population densities of skunks were not calculated, we obtained an index of their relative abundance through trap success, defined as number of captures divided by number of traps available (traps set minus traps sprung but empty). We calculated overall trap success for the entire study as well as separately for each trapping session (April and September).

RESULTS AND DISCUSSION

We captured one skunk during 130 trap nights in April (0.77% trap success) and nine skunks with no recaptures during 133 trap nights in September (6.7% trap success). Overall trap success was 3.8% (ten skunks in 263 trap nights). In comparison, we captured ten individual skunks 14 times during 2,457 trap nights (0.57%) in 1992 (Crooks 1994a). The trap success in 1998 therefore was nearly seven times higher than the trap success in 1992. Trap success in the winter (6 captures/939 trap nights = 0.64%) and spring (6/605 = 0.99%) of 1992 was similar to that in April 1998. However, in contrast to September 1998, trapping skunks was exceptionally difficult in summer (0/336 = 0.00%) and fall (2/577 = 0.35%) of 1992.

The higher overall trap success in 1998 suggests a population increase of island spotted skunks on Santa Cruz Island. We must caution, however, that trap success only provides an estimate of relative abundance and that we did not systematically survey the entire island for spotted skunks in either 1992 or 1998. Further, trapping design differed between years. Trap success was likely higher in 1998 because we placed traps at regular intervals along multiple transects throughout the island. In 1992, however, we heavily concentrated traps in smaller areas to capture skunks and foxes for a radio-telemetry study. In particular, in summer and fall 1992, trapping exclusively centered in two study areas to replace and remove radio-collars from study animals. Trap success therefore was lowered substantially because we had likely caught most skunks in each study area and recaptures proved difficult.

Nevertheless, the available data, although sparse, suggest a population increase in the past six years. Although trapping effort in 1998 was considerably less than in 1992, we caught the same number of individual skunks in both years. Further, although skunks were sighted only rarely on the island historically (Crooks 1994a), skunk sightings have recently increased markedly (L. Laughrin, pers. comm. 1998). An increase in the spotted skunk population on Santa Cruz Island may be driven by a combination of factors. For one, variable trap success may simply represent normal variation expected in any population. Skunk demography may also be influenced by environmental variables. Rainfall was exceptionally high on Santa Cruz Island in 1998, possibly stimulating an increase in reproduction and partially accounting for the higher trap success in September than in April 1998. Indeed, the western spotted skunk exhibits delayed implantation (Mead 1968), a reproductive mode that may allow skunks to increase fecundity in good years. The spotted skunk breeds in late September and early October, the blastocysts remain in a state of arrested development for approximately 200 days, the embryo is activated in March or April, and young are born from April to June.

Further, skunks may be slowly responding to recovery of the island. The removal of most sheep and cattle from the island in the 1980s, as well as the cessation of a prolonged drought, has stimulated a recovery of the island's plant communities. Unlike the island fox, which is relatively abundant and displays a wide range of resource use, the island spotted skunk is relatively rare and a resource specialist (Crooks 1994a,b; Crooks and Van Vuren 1994, 1995). Consequently, we predicted (Crooks and Van Vuren 1995) that although a generalist such as the island fox might initially respond more rapidly to island recovery, in the long-term skunks may benefit more as disturbed areas recover.

Lastly, resource overlap between skunks and foxes suggests some degree of interspecific competition between these two sympatric carnivores, and this competition likely affects skunks more than foxes (Crooks and Van Vuren 1995). For one, a generalist species such as the fox may have an advantage when its broad niche overlaps the narrow niche of a sympatric competitor such as the skunk. Also, the sheer numbers of foxes may magnify competitive effects on skunks. Interestingly, recent evidence suggests that island fox populations may be declining on the Channel

Islands (Coonan et al. 1998). If so, a reduction in competition with foxes may benefit the island spotted skunk.

Even though skunks may be increasing on Santa Cruz Island, they are still relatively uncommon on the island, are particularly sensitive to environmental disturbances due to their relatively specialized resource use, and are restricted to only two California Channel Islands. Thus, the status of the island spotted skunk remains precarious. The island spotted skunk has been classified only as a subspecies of special concern by the State of California, perhaps in part because its status and ecology were completely unknown. We again recommend further monitoring of the population status of the island spotted skunk on both Santa Cruz and Santa Rosa islands and suggest that the skunk should be considered for reclassification as a threatened subspecies.

ACKNOWLEDGMENTS

We thank L. Laughrin and the University of California Natural Reserve System, and R. Klinger and The Nature Conservancy for facilitating research on the island. C. Scott, L. Angeloni, L. Bowen, and E. Bowen provided valuable field assistance. This research was supported through an Environmental Protection Agency STAR Graduate Research Fellowship to KRC.

LITERATURE CITED

Coonan, T. J., G. Austin, and C. Schwemm. 1998. Status and trend of island fox, San Miguel Island, Channel Islands National Park. Technical Report 98-01. Channel Islands National Park, CA.

Crooks, K. R. 1994a. Demography and status of the island fox and the island spotted skunk on Santa Cruz Island, California. The Southwestern Naturalist 39:257-262.

Crooks, K. R. 1994b. Den site selection in the island spotted skunk of Santa Cruz Island, California. The Southwestern Naturalist 39:354-357.

Crooks, K. R., and D. Van Vuren. 1994. Conservation of the island spotted skunk and island fox in a recovering island ecosystem. Pages 379-386 in Halvorson, W. L. and G. J. Maender (eds.), The Fourth California Islands Symposium: Update on the Status of Resources. Santa Barbara Museum of Natural History, Santa Barbara, CA.

Crooks, K. R., and D. Van Vuren. 1995. Resource utilization by two insular endemic mammalian carnivores, the island fox and island spotted skunk. Oecologia 104:301-307.

Mead, R.A. 1968. Reproduction in the western forms of the spotted skunk (genus *Spilogale*). Journal of Mammalogy 49: 373-390.

SOURCE OF UNPUBLISHED MATERIALS

Laughrin, L. Natural Reserve System, University of California, Santa Barbara, CA 93106. Personal Communication 1998.

ERADICATION OF FERAL PIGS (*SUS SCROFA*) FROM SANTA ROSA ISLAND, CHANNEL ISLANDS NATIONAL PARK, CALIFORNIA

Carmen A. Lombardo[1] and Kate R. Faulkner[2]

[1]AC/S EMD (Fish and Wildlife Division), Marine Corps Base, PSC Box 20004, Camp Lejeune, NC 28542-0004
(910) 451-7226, FAX (910) 451-5836, E-mail: lombardoc1@clb.usmc.mil
[2] Channel Islands National Park, 1901 Spinnaker Drive, Ventura, CA, 93001
(805) 658-5709, FAX (805) 658-5799, Email: kate_faulkner@nps.gov

ABSTRACT

Feral pigs were eradicated from Santa Rosa Island, Channel Islands National Park between July 1990 and March 1993. The eradication occurred in three phases. Phase I included planning and design of a monitoring program. Phase II was testing and refinement of the monitoring program. Monitoring involved recording the frequency and distribution of pig sign on eighty-two belt transects stratified by habitat. Removal of pigs, through baiting and shooting, was compared to shifts in distribution and changes in relative abundance of pigs. Phase III involved pig eradication by contract hunters. Prior to implementation of Phase III, aerial surveys estimated the pig population at 1,400 (SE=±400). A total of 1,175 pigs were killed. Eradication strategies included systematic ground hunts (n=816), systematic hunts with dogs (n=88), road hunts (n=4), aerial hunts (n=261) (including forward-looking infrared cameras (n=2), and trapping (n=6). National Park Service personnel expended 700 hours in search of pigs during Phase II. Contractors expended 7,000 hours in search of pigs during Phase III. Since March 1993, no pigs or fresh pig signs have been found on the island. Observations and preliminary data from post-eradication monitoring indicate a favorable response by some fleshy-rooted plants and vegetation communities.

Keywords: Santa Rosa Island, feral pigs, monitoring, eradication strategies.

INTRODUCTION

The origin of feral pigs on the California Channel Islands is uncertain. Pigs are presently found on Santa Catalina, Santa Cruz, and formerly on San Clemente and Santa Rosa islands (SRI). Many authors have suggested that Spaniards introduced pigs to the Channel Islands during the late 1600s in order to have a supply of fresh meat during subsequent landings. Early writings pertaining to SRI fail, however, to mention the presence of pigs prior to the mid-1800s (Holland 1962; Collins 1981). The origin of SRI pigs is most likely from an 1853 introduction by a former landowner.

San Clemente and Santa Catalina island populations are from original SRI stock (Overholt and Sargent 1971). A syndactyl breed of pig was introduced to Santa Catalina during the 1960s, although very few pigs currently remain on the island with this morphological characteristic (D. Garcelon, pers. comm. 1990). A transfer of pigs during the 1930s from Santa Rosa Island to Santa Catalina Island and a subsequent introduction from Catalina Island to San Clemente Island in the mid-1950s represents the anthropogenic expansion of feral pigs within the northern Channel Islands during the twentieth century.

The ecological effects of feral pig populations vary greatly from area to area, depending upon the density of pigs and relative sensitivity of the ecosystems (Singer 1981). In general, impacts are more severe where pig densities are high and within sensitive plant communities, especially where invasive exotic plants prevail and where sensitive surface-dwelling terrestrial vertebrates occur (Bratton 1975). The impacts of feral pigs on island ecosystems are well documented (Hochberg 1980; Baber 1985; Baber and Coblentz 1986; Coblentz and Baber 1987; Sterner 1990). Feral pig impacts on SRI were qualitatively determined to be increases in siltation and soil erosion along stream courses, damage to the island's rangelands, and severe soil erosion which undermined the root systems of endemic island oaks (*Quercus tomentilla*). Pig foraging on acorns prevented natural regeneration of island oak. Areas of pig rooting create optimum growing conditions for invasive exotic plants such as spiny clotbur (*Xanthium spinosum* L.), milk thistle (*Silybum marianum* L.), and burr thistle. Additionally, a number of native plant species had been impacted by feral pigs (Table 1). Archaeological sites, especially those located in caves, had been heavily impacted by feral pig rooting and bedding behavior (D. Morris, pers. comm. 1990; C. Lombardo, pers. obs. 1990).

In 1949 and again in the early 1950s, hog cholera was introduced to SRI as a means of controlling pig numbers. The first introduction produced about 80% mortality in the pigs, the second introduction was less effective (N.R. Vail, pers. comm. 1990). A survey of sera and tissues from 61 pigs collected from Santa Rosa in 1987 indicated that the virus was no longer active on the island (Nettles et al. 1989). During the period from the early 1960s until government ownership of the island in 1986, the Vail and Vickers Company maintained a shoot-on-sight policy in an effort to

Table 1. Plant species impacted by feral pigs on Santa Rosa Island, Channel Islands National Park.

Species	Common Name	Status[a]
Arabis hofmannii	Hoffman's rock cress	E
Arctostaphylos confertiflora	SRI manzanita	E
Castilleja hololeuca	island paintbrush	
Castilleja mollis	soft-leaved paintbrush	E
Coreopsis gigantea	giant coreopsis	
Dudleya blochmaniae s. insularis	SRI Island live-forever	
Galium buxifolium		E
Gilia tenuiflora hoffmanii		E
Helianthemum greeni	island rushrose	T
Heuchera maxima	island allum-root	
Lyonothamus floribundus	Santa Cruz Island ironwood	
Berberis pinnata s. Brachyloba	island barberry	E
Orobanche parishii s. Insularis	shortlobed broomrape	
Phacelia insularis s. Insularis	island phacelia	E
Pinus torreyana s. Insularis	Torrey pine	
Quercue tomentella	island oak	
Salvia branegei	SRI sage	

[a] Federal status reported only. E=Federally Endangered T=Federally Threatened

control pig numbers. Even with this action, pig numbers were affected more by the seasonal availability of food and water than by direct reduction (N. R. Vail, pers. comm. 1990).

National Park Service (NPS) management policies direct the control or eradication of exotic animal species which have a detrimental impact upon native ecosystems and ecological processes. The policy states: "Manipulation of population numbers of exotic plant and animal species, up to and including total eradication, will be undertaken whenever such species threaten protection or interpretation or resources being preserved in the park."

Many national parks are implementing control and eradication programs for feral/wild pigs with varied success. The goal of feral pig management on SRI was eradication of the population and eventual restoration of native ecosystems to pre-European conditions. The compounding effects of other large herbivores on the island may partially mask the recovery of SRI communities post-eradication, however, feral pig removal was identified as the highest natural resource management priority by both private and Federal interests within the Channel Islands.

The complete eradication of an exotic species such as feral pigs from large areas (>1000 hectares) is a huge endeavor. Eradication programs of the magnitude of the SRI program have been conducted on private and public lands, but never documented to any great degree (Goatcher 1989; C. Winchell, pers. comm., 1992). Successful control programs have been instituted on larger areas (Korn 1986; Hone and Stone 1989).

STUDY AREA

Channel Islands National Park (CHIS) was established to protect the nationally significant natural, scenic, wildlife, marine, ecological, archeological, cultural, and scientific values of the Channel Islands off the coast of southern California (P.L. 96-199, Title II, March 5, 1980). CHIS includes the northernmost five of the eight California Channel

Islands (Anacapa, Santa Barbara, Santa Cruz, San Miguel, and SRI) and the surrounding one nautical mile of ocean. SRI was purchased from the Vail and Vickers Company in December 1986. Vail and Vickers continues a commercial hunt for nonnative deer and elk on SRI under a Special Use Permit. Between 2,500 and 5,000 cattle were on the island during the period of eradication.

SRI lies 72 km west of Ventura, and 48 km southwest of Santa Barbara, California. Approximately 21,450 hectares in size, the topography of SRI is dominated by an east-west trending highlands region with an impressive array of lateral canyons trending primarily north and south. The northern side of the island has an extensive marine terrace rising gently from steep sea bluffs to the central highlands. The south side possesses shorter, steeper and more narrow canyons extending from the highlands to the ocean. The coastline of SRI is dominated by rocky intertidal areas, with well developed sandy beaches and dunes on the southwestern and northeastern shores. A small tidal marsh is present on the eastern portion of the island.

Eighteen distinct plant communities have been documented on SRI (Clark et al. 1990). Grassland accounts for over 65% of the total area, mixed-oak woodland comprises 0.35% of the island. The remainder of the island is covered by either low growing shrubs (25.2%; coastal sage scrub, mixed chaparral, and baccharis scrub) or is devoid of vegetation due to erosion and blowing sand (6.9%).

A depauperate native mammal fauna includes island fox (*Urocyon littoralis santarosae*), deer mice (*Peromycus maniculatus santarosae*), and spotted skunk (*Spirogale gracilis amphalia*). Introduced alien herbivores include cattle (*Bos taurus*), horses (*Equus caballus*), elk (*Cervus elaphus* spp.), mule deer (*Odocoileus hemionus*), and feral pigs. All sheep (*Ovis aries*) had been removed from the island by the late 1950s. Land birds are abundant locally as residents or seasonal migrants, 31species are known or conjectured to breed on the island (Diamond and Jones 1980). There are only four recorded species of reptiles and amphibians.

METHODS

Phase I Planning (Early efforts)

Davis (1987), in cooperation with pig removal experts and park managers, developed an initial strategy for removal of feral pigs from SRI which included: 1) dividing the island into six management units by erecting new pig proof fencing or modifying existing cattle fencing, 2) removal of 60 to 70% of pigs within each unit by trapping, 3) remove remaining pigs with coordinated teams of shooters, and 4) assure complete removal by hunting with trained pig dogs and population monitoring. This eradication strategy was a fail safe operation. If complete removal of pigs within an individual unit was not achieved, fencing would serve to limit future population expansion. In contrast to Davis (1987), Goatcher (1989) proposed trapping and the use of highly trained pig dogs as the primary means of effecting complete eradication on SRI. Fencing was not considered a critical component of Goatcher's plan, rather it was viewed as providing a false sense of security for actual accomplishments.

In 1990, after redefining eradication objectives, a new strategy was developed which combined functional aspects of Davis (1987), Goatcher (1989), and other eradication programs. The resultant strategy was more or less an all or nothing approach and relied heavily on intensive eradication pressure applied evenly, although differential by method, throughout the program. The extensive use of helicopters as a shooting platform early in the eradication was viewed as an important first step in reducing pig numbers prior to more labor intensive eradication strategies.

Fencing to prevent or reduce pig movement was not used during the eradication program. Hone and Atkinson (1983) tested fence designs for their ability to stop feral pig crossings and reported that certain design and electrification configurations were effective in reducing or virtually eliminating pig movement, but only a complete wire mesh fencing was totally pig-proof. Davis (1987) estimated that approximately 40 miles of similar pig-proof fencing as either new construction or modification of existing cattle fencing would be needed to divide SRI into manageable units. The estimated cost for fencing would have exceeded $400,000.

Monitoring and Evaluation

For the pig eradication, the island was divided into seven management zones based upon geographical boundaries and existing cattle fencing (Figure 1). Two island-wide aerial surveys for pigs were conducted in early to mid-January 1991, at one week intervals. Surveys were begun in the early morning (0700 hrs) and concluded shortly after noon each day. Late afternoon/early evening (1500 to1700 hrs) searches were also conducted. Surveys were begun on the eastern portion of the island, covering each canyon/drainage at a low altitude (approx. 50 m) and slow forward air speed. Areas with broad flat terraces were surveyed at a higher altitude using the methods of Davis (1987). The approximate stopping point for the morning survey was the start point for the late afternoon search. Weather conditions at the time of survey (85° F) suggested that diurnal movements of pigs would be minimal or would not occur. This was substantiated during late morning when the majority of pigs were "flushed" from the cooler portions of lower canyons and from under dense brush. On each survey, the color of individual pigs, group size, and sex/age associations were carefully recorded. This survey methodology appeared to reduce double counting during afternoon surveys.

The distribution of pig sign (dung, tracks, rooting, wallows, and observations) was surveyed at three month intervals and in response to management actions by walking 82 belt transects (2 m wide and up to 5 km long) stratified by habitat important to pigs. Areas of particular concern for transect location were canyon bottoms, coastal sage scrub,

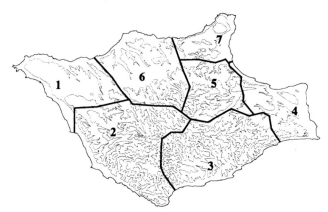

Figure 1. Management Zones for feral pig eradication, Santa Rosa Island, Channel Islands National Park.

baccharis scrub, and mixed woodland communities. Transect locations were established to be sensitive to shifts in habitat use, including daily, seasonal, and environmentally determined patterns such as prolonged drought. All dung was removed from transects to avoid double counting on subsequent runs.

It was apparent that the absence of impermeable boundaries, such as pig proof fencing, would enable pigs to immigrate to already searched areas. Therefore, partial transect surveys (n=7) within individual management units and in adjacent units were conducted to detect immigration and shifts in distribution by pigs in response to management activities. Partial surveys also were used as a measure of contractor effort and performance evaluation. Additionally, aerial searches within individual management units were conducted by NPS personnel to evaluate contractor performance.

Eradication Techniques

Two separate phases of pig removal were conducted, systematic ground hunts and trapping by NPS employees, and a three phase contract for eradication conducted by professional hunters. NPS employees utilized box traps (Williamson and Pelton 1971) and conducted systematic ground hunts in selected areas for pigs to test the efficacy of the monitoring design. Pigs were dispatched island-wide over a four month period. During this time period, the frequency of pig sign on transects was surveyed to monitor changes in relative abundance and pig distribution.

The techniques used to remove pigs during the contract phase of the program were dependent upon pig densities and local environmental conditions such as precipitation and fog. Aerial hunts, trapping, ground hunts, and ground hunts with trained pig dogs were employed systematically throughout the contract phase of the eradication. The dogs used in this program were primarily of the Catahoula breed and were trained to avoid non-target species.

During a one week period in February 1992, a Forward Looking Infrared (FLIR) system mounted to the underbelly of a Hughes 500E helicopter was used as an additional search method. FLIR technology, first developed for military and law enforcement applications, utilizes a thermal imaging system which registers heat reflectance from a viewing area. Dependent upon surrounding surface temperatures of the biotic (vegetation, trees, etc.) and abiotic (rocks, earth, etc.) community, warm-blooded organisms register as white-hot images and in many cases can be identified to the species level. FLIR technology has been employed in Hawaii on goats and pigs with varying success (L. Katahira, pers. comm. 1992).

The methods employed to eradicate pigs were the most humane available to accomplish the goal of a pig free island. Pig carcasses were left in the field to decompose as the California Department of Agriculture and the USDA-Animal Plant Health Inspection Service opposed the relocation or transportation of feral pigs from SRI because of the prevalence of pseudorabies (Glosser, unpublished 1988). Also, it is unlikely that live capture would have achieved the goal of eradication of pigs from SRI. Butchering of pigs was not a feasible option due to USDA's standards for human consumption of meat, the need for onsite inspectors, special handling procedures, disease free certification of individual animals, costly refrigeration units on the island and on transport vessels, and the logistical constraints of such an operation.

Necropsies were performed on a majority of the pigs dispatched during the initial phase of this program. Biological data collected from necropsied animals included pelage color, sex, age, reproductive condition, rump fat thickness, and presence or absence of internal and external parasites. Data concerning animal behavior, movements, and other ancillary biological information were collected through observation and post-mortem examinations.

RESULTS

Monitoring and Evaluation

Nine 8-hour days, utilizing a two person crew, were required to survey all monitoring transects. The time required to complete partial surveys (n=7; x=20.26±10.3 hr) was dependent upon local topography and transect length. Complete transect surveys were conducted at milestones throughout the program. Two complete surveys were conducted during Phase II of eradication and three were conducted during Phase III. Following Phase III, a final survey of all monitoring transects was conducted over a six-month period. Significant decreases (P < 0.10) in overall pig sign were noted between transect surveys (Table 2). The frequency of pig dung on transects appeared to provide the most reliable measure of reduction in pig numbers (Table 3). Data collected during partial surveys were used to assess shifts in pig distribution and to help direct contractor efforts. These data are not presented. Shifts in pig distribution were most apparent during Phase III of the program when intensive systematic ground hunts were concentrated within individual units.

The reliability of transects to detect reductions in pig numbers became questionable as the pig population was reduced to remnant (≤ 20) animals within individual management units. At this point in the eradication effort, transects were shifted to perceived "refuge" areas which feral pigs seemed to migrate to in response to management actions. Transects surveys within these areas were coordinated with active eradication efforts to increase the likelihood that encountered pigs were dispatched.

Table 2. Summary of feral pig sign along 82 belt transects on Santa Rosa Island, Channel Islands National Park.

Sign Type[b]	Transect Surveys[a]				
	T1	T2	T3	T4	T5
Observation	76 A[c]	81 A	10 B	0 C	0 C
Scats	1254 A	462 B	92 C	15 C	0 C
Wallows	126 A	86 B	15 C	1 C	0 C

a Information is reported for transect surveys during Phase II and Phase III.

b Total observations of individual sign types.

c Within row valyes with the same letter designation are not significantly different at P<0.10.

Table 3. Number of scats found along 82 belt transects, stratified by zone, Santa Rosa Island, Channel Islands National Park.

Zone	Transect Surveys				
	T1	T2	T3	T4	T5
1	83 A[a]	51 B	22 C	1 C	0 C
2	503 A	127 B	16 C	0 C	0 C
3	207 A	71 B	0 C	2 C	0 C
4	105 A	28 B	33 C	2 C	0 C
5	109 A	34 B	0 C	10 B	0 C
6	230 A	66 B	16 C	0 C	0 C
7	17 A	85 B	5 C	0 C	0 C
Totals	1254	462	92	15	0

a Within row values with same letter designation are not significantly different at P<0.10.

Eradication Techniques

A total of 1,175 pigs were killed during the course of this program; 455 by NPS staff, 450 by contractors, and 270 by non-government personnel linked with the private cattle ranch located on the island. NPS removal techniques included ground hunts (n=447) and trapping (n=8). A total of 700 hours (1.6 hrs per pig) were expended by NPS personnel conducting ground hunts. An additional 120 hours (15 hrs per pig) were devoted to trapping. Twenty pigs were dispatched enroute to hunt area destinations and are included in ground hunt totals.

Contractors expended a total of 7,000 hours in search of pigs over a 12-month period. Aerial hunts, used exclusively during Phase III, accounted for 263 pigs (Table 4). One hundred thirty-four hours were devoted to aerial hunts for a per unit effort of 0.51 hrs/pig. Systematic ground hunts accounted for 97 pigs with a per unit effort of 22 hrs/pig. Searches with trained pig dogs yielded 87 pigs with a corresponding effort of 54.1 hrs/pig. Eradication techniques were not employed simultaneously, therefore, comparisons between methods provide limited value.

Contractor search effort increased in relative proportion to total pigs killed expressed as per unit effort except during the last four months of the eradication when the pig population was reduced to remnant animals (Figure 2). A dramatic increase in search effort occurred for pigs 434 to 443 which was followed by a decrease in effort. An explanation for the prominent fluctuation in effort is explained in the Discussion section below.

NPS personnel expended forty hours of helicopter searches to monitor contractor effort within individual zones and to provide additional eradication pressure on the pig population. After the contractor had completed work in an individual management zone, on ground transect surveys were conducted to document reductions in pig numbers and to determined whether an aerial search was necessary. Pigs (n=6) encountered during these aerial searches were dispatched.

Pig activity during Phase II and the early stages of Phase III of the eradication was generally associated with the availability of water and the presence of artificial food supplements that were distributed throughout the island for

Table 4. Pigs killed, by method, during Phase III of feral pig eradication, Santa Rosa Island, Channel Islands National Park.

| Method | Number of Pigs Killed | | | | |
	Adult	Juvenile	Piglet	Totals	Hours
Helicopter	136	64	61	261	134
Ground Searches	55	22	20	97	2150
Ground Searches with Traind Dogs	52	16	20	88	4704
Driving	4	0	0	4	12
Totals	247	102	101	450	7000

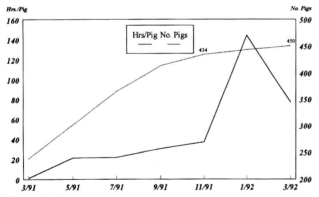

Figure 2. Search effort in relation to cumulative number of pigs killed during Phase III of feral pig eradication, Santa Rosa Island, Channel Islands National Park.

cattle and horses. The location of these artificial supplements was a convenient starting point for searches. The majority of pigs dispatched during Phase II and the beginning of Phase III of the program were found within 400±100 meters (P <0.05) of artificial supplements. Behavioral changes in response to eradication pressure later in the program resulted in opportunistic, rather than routine, use of artificial supplements by pigs.

Population Parameters and Sex/Age Structure

Most pigs appeared to be in good to fair body condition at the onset of the eradication (Riney 1960). Approximately one-third of pigs in the oldest age class of each sex were rated as excellent. Environmental parameters (excessive drought) contributed to the poor physical condition of pigs early in the eradication, but with increasing precipitation and milder temperatures, the physical condition of pigs improved as reflected by our data.

The sex ratio of pigs dispatched during Phase II was 1:0.9 (237M:218F) and differed slightly from 1:1 (Table 5). The extensive use of helicopters early in Phase III precluded sex identification on each downed pig due to excessive cost. Of the 450 pigs dispatched during Phase III, sex determinations were made on 291. The sex ratio of the these was 1:0.76 (165M:126F) and differed slightly from 1:1.

The age structure of the necropsied sample (n=415) was similar to that reported in the literature (Table 5) (Barrett 1978; Sterner 1990). Coat coloration suggested a feral/hybrid cross. Black and white spotted (37.5%) and all black (32.3%) was the most common coloration pattern. The wild/grizzled or agouti coat coloration, characteristic of wild boar, was present in 12.5% of the sample. Stippled coats on juveniles were present in 5 out of 120 piglets.

Table 5. Age and sex of feral pigs killed during Phase II of pig eradication, Santa Rosa Island, Channel Islands National Park.

Age (months)	n	%	Male	Female	Sex Ratio (M:F)
<12	252	55.4	132	120	1:0.9
12-24	102	22.4	47	55	1:1.1
25-36	57	12.5	32	25	1:0.8
37-48	31	6.8	16	15	1:1.06
49-60	10	2.2	7	3	1:2.3
>60	3	0.7	3	0	-
Totals	455	100	237	218	1:0.9

DISCUSSION

Feral Pig Population

Environmental conditions existing at the beginning of the eradication were near optimum for the task of removing all pigs from SRI. A natural reduction in pig numbers due to drought stress, reduced vegetation which improved visibility, and the extent of grassland on SRI maintained by other large herbivores presented a unique opportunity for success. Goatcher (1989) estimated the pig population on SRI to be 3,200 pigs and conjectured that persistent drought conditions would further reduce the population. At the start of the eradication, it was estimated that the pig population was at its lowest level in 12 years.

Monitoring and Search Effort

The monitoring strategy used during the eradication provided the level of detail necessary to document a relative decrease in pig numbers and provided a broad measure for detecting shifts in pig distribution. Barrett et al. (1988) utilized a comparable monitoring strategy as an index to pig reduction at Annandel State Park, California. A similar method was reported for national park areas in Australia and Hawaii (Hone and Stone 1989).

The relationship of shifts in distribution to search effort, and the ability to recognize and modify standard monitoring strategies, was highlighted during the last few months of the eradication. During Phase II of the eradication, distribution shifts were less apparent than during the mid- to later stages of Phase III. The shifts in distribution appeared to be in a roughly west to east direction, which followed the general pattern of hunting activity. A partial explanation could be that pigs had been previously exposed to limited intensity hunting (one to two shooters) during Phase II and were more likely to return to a particular drainage/canyon than when repeatedly pressured by a larger hunting party or a hunting party utilizing dogs as a method of search.

Search effort during Phase III of the eradication, as expected, increased as pig numbers decreased except for the last few pigs removed by contractors. The tendency of pigs to migrate toward areas with limited disturbance was identified through monitoring transects and field observations. Area specific searches within these "refuge" areas reduced per unit effort expenditures. The amount of effort to remove the last pig recorded during Phase III, although greater than the first 400 pigs, was less than anticipated. The documented last pig removed during Phase III, was located in an area which had been identified as a "refuge" area.

Surveillance on monitoring transects continued at infrequent intervals over a one year period following Phase III of the eradication. Nine months after Phase III was complete and the last pig was thought to have been killed, a barely discernable wallow was discovered in the same drainage as the documented last pig of Phase III. An intensive search in the surrounding drainages uncovered no addtional pig activity. Three months later, a two to three day old wallow and a single pig track was found at the same location. Two days later, a pack of dogs ran down the last feral pig on SRI. Since March 1993, no pigs or fresh pig sign have been found on the island.

Coat Coloration

Mayer (1983) and Mayer and Brisbin (1990) used various multivariate analyses to categorize pigs based upon phenotypic and morphologic characteristics. The percentage of pigs on SRI which exhibited the wild/grizzled agouti coloration (12.5%) is consistent with the lower end range of values reported for a feral/hybrid cross. Goatcher (1989) reported the wild/grizzled agouti coat coloration was present in 20% of SRI pigs. A reduced population size and the fact that coat coloration was not recorded during Phase III of the eradication may explain the small difference between our estimate and that of Goatcher (J. J. Mayer, pers. comm.

1996). Although no documentation exists to reflect an introduction of European wild boar to SRI (N. Vail, pers. comm. 1990), a previous introduction is realistic in terms of commercial hunting activities on the island prior to Federal ownership and the pattern of agouti coat coloration in adult pigs.

MANAGEMENT IMPLICATIONS

The methods used to eradicate feral pigs from SRI have broad usage for eradication programs elsewhere, although site specific conditions will play a large role in their timing, duration, and intensity. An intense, unrelenting eradication effort will, in the long run, be more cost and labor efficient than long-term or sporadic control.

ACKNOWLEDGMENTS

We would like to thank G. E. Davis, W. H. Halvorson, C. P. Stone, R. H. Barrett, and B. Goatcher for preliminary surveys and development of initial eradication strategies. Field assistance was provided by C. C. Kessler, J. A. Robbins, E. C. Smith, L. K. Fongemie, and many employees of Channel Islands National Park. The Vail and Vickers Company are thanked for their cooperation and assistance throughout the eradication. Funding for this eradication program was provided by the Natural Resource Preservation Program (NRPP), National Park Service, U.S. Department of the Interior.

LITERATURE CITED

Baber, D. W. 1985. Ecology of feral pigs on Santa Catalina Island. Ph.D. Dissertation, Oregon State University, Corvallis. 91 pp.

Baber, D. W., and B. E. Coblentz. 1986. Denisty, home range, habitat use, and reproduction in feral pigs on Santa Catalina Island. Journal of Mammalogy 67(3):512-525.

Barrett, R. H. 1978. The feral hog on Dye Creek Ranch, California. Hilgardia 46(9):283-355.

Barrett, R. H., B. L. Goatcher, and E. L. Fitzhugh. 1988. Removing feral pigs from Annadel State Park. Transactions Western Section the Wildlife Society.

Bratton, S. P. 1975. The effect of European wild boar, (*Sus scrofa*), on gray beech forest in the Great Smoky mountains. Ecology 56:1356-1366.

Coblentz, B. E., and D. W. Baber. 1987. Biology and control of feral pigs on Isla Santiago, Galapagos, Ecuador. Journal of Applied Ecology 24:403-418.

Collins, P. 1981. The origin and present status of feral pigs on the California Channel Islands. Santa Barabara Museum of Natural History. 5 pp.

Clark, R. A., W. L. Halvorson, A. Sado, and K. C. Danielson. 1990. Plant communities of Santa Rosa Island, Channel Islands National Park. Cooperative Park Studies Unit, Technical Report No. 42. University of California Davis, CA. 88 pp.

Davis, G. E. 1987. SRI feral pig removal plan. Channel Islands National Park, Ventura, CA. 22 pp.

Diamond, J. M., and H. L. Jones. 1980. Breeding landbirds of the Channel Islands. Pages 597-612 *in* Power, D. M. (ed.), California Channel Islands: Proceedings of a Symposium. Santa Barbara Museum of Natural History.

Goatcher, B. L. 1989. A report on the feasibility of feral pig eradication, SRI. Channel Islands National Park, Ventura, CA. 45 pp.

Hochberg, M. S., S. Juank, and R. Philbrick. 1980. Botanical study of Santa Cruz Island for the Nature Conservancy. Santa Barbara Botanic Garden, Santa Barbara, CA. 90 pp.

Holland, F. R. 1962. Santa Rosa Island: An archaeologic and historical study. Journal of the West 1:45-62.

Hone, J., and C. P. Stone. 1989. A comparison and evaluation of feral pig management in two national parks. Wildlife Society Bulletin 17:419-425.

Hone, J., and B. Atkinson. 1983. Evaluation of fencing to control feral pig movement. Australia Wildlife Research 10:350-357.

Korn, T. 1986. Control of feral pigs in the Macquarie Marshes. International Symposium on Wetlands.

Mayer, J. J. 1983. Wild Pigs, their history, morphology, and current status in the United States. Ph.D. Dissertation, University of Connecticut, Storrs. 368 pp.

Mayer, J. J., and I. L. Brisbin. 1990. Wild Pigs in the United States, their history, comparative morphology, and current status. University of Georgia Press, Athens, GA. 313 pp.

Nettles, V. F., J. L. Corn, G. A. Erickson, and D. A. Jessup. 1989. A survey of wild swine in the United States for evidence of hog cholera. Journal of Wildlife Diseases 25:61-65.

Overholt, A., and J. Sargent. 1971. The Catalina Story. Catalina Museum Society, Avalon, CA. 88 pp.

Singer, J. D. 1981. Wild pig populations in national parks. Environmental Management 5(3):263-270.

Sterner, J. D. 1990. Population characteristics, home range and habitat use of feral pigs on Santa Cruz Island, California. M. S. Thesis, University of California, Berkeley, CA. 111 pp.

Williamson, M. J., and M. R. Pelton. 1971. New design for a large portable mammal trap. Proceedings Annual Conference Southeast Association Fish and Wildlife Agencies 25:315-312.

SOURCES OF UNPUBLISHED MATERIAL

Garcelon, D., Institute for Wildlife Studies, Arcata, P.O. Box 127, CA 95521. Personal Communication 1990.

Glosser, J. W. 1988. Letter to Mr. William Penn Mott, Jr., Director, National Park Service. Unpublished.

Katahira, L. Hawaii Volcanos National Park. Personal Communication 1992.

Lombardo, C. A. Channel Islands National Park, 1901 Spinnaker Drive, Ventura, CA 93001. Personal Observation 1990.

Morris, D. Channel Islands National Park, 1901 Spinnaker Drive, Ventura, CA 93001. Personal Communication 1990.

Mayer, J. J. Westinghouse, Savannah River Ecology Lab, Aiken, GA. Personal Communication 1996.

Vail, N. R. Vail and Vickers Company. Santa Barbara, CA. Personal Comminication 1990.

Winchell, C. C. NAS North Island, San Diego, CA 92135. Personal Communication 1992.

STABILITY AND CHANGE IN THE BIRD COMMUNITIES OF THE CHANNEL ISLANDS

Hartmut S. Walter

Department of Geography, University of California, Los Angeles, CA 90095-1524
(310) 825-3116, FAX (310) 206-5976, E-mail: walter@geog.ucla.edu

ABSTRACT

Avifaunal datasets from the California Islands played a prominent role in the development of the equilibrium theory of island biogeography. I have re-analyzed these data using a functional spatial approach and separating short-term ecological from long-term evolutionary processes and dynamics. I distinguish between insular and continental taxa found on islands and define the concept of biotic space as a crucial functional element of persistence. Insular taxa are restricted to a particular island or archipelago. They have evolved and adapted within an island's environment. Continental island populations are connected to a larger mainland complex of populations; individual satellite or island populations may be quite unstable and non-viable over longer time scales. The continental taxa of the Channel Islands have experienced frequent turnover within and between taxa. By contrast, the insular taxa have been stable and have persisted with few exceptions. These findings contradict basic assumptions of the theory of island biogeography. The application of the concept of functional insularity to the problem of conserving mainland remnants and fragments shows that these isolate habitats and their biotic communities face survival problems that differ substantially from those of true oceanic islands and their insular biota.

Keywords: Island biogeography; extinction; turnover rates; functional areography; insular species; Channel Islands, California.

INTRODUCTION

The avifauna of the eight Channel Islands of southern California has played a significant role in contemporary ecology and conservation biology. Diamond's analysis of long-term changes in the bird communities of each of the Channel Islands (Diamond 1969) contributed crucial evidence supporting the concept of island biotas maintaining dynamic equilibrium numbers of species depending on island size and isolation. This was a fundamental requisite for the development of the *theory of island biogeography* (MacArthur and Wilson 1967; Simberloff 1974). Diamond's paper also sparked a controversy on the proximate and ultimate causes of the observed avian turnover rates (Lynch and Johnson 1974; Jones and Diamond 1976; Diamond and Jones 1980). Did the data accurately portray actual turnover and were such turnovers between species a consequence of natural or anthropogenic factors?

In hindsight and in the presence of new conceptual developments, this heated debate has lost relevance. Chaos theory and widespread evidence for the existence of non-equilibrium ecological communities (Lack 1976; Gilbert 1980; Williamson 1981; Case and Cody 1983; Wiens 1989; Pimm 1991; Simberloff 1994; Thornton 1996; Brown and Lomolino 1998) have shifted the focus of biogeographers and conservation biologists to a closer examination of the general processes underlying biotic change. The simplistic and mechanistic approach of the MacArthur-Wilson school has given way to a more differentiated and multi-factor approach to the different taxonomic, trophic, ecological, and functional elements of island life (Minelli 1990; Solem 1990; Rosenzweig 1995; Tilman and Kareiva 1997). Viewed from this context, a re-examination of the avifauna of the Channel Islands may offer valuable insights for a better understanding of spatio-temporal dynamics on islands and continents.

In this paper I attempt to accomplish three objectives:

1) A *functional areographic analysis* of the Channel Islands avifauna will divide the avifauna into different spatial sets and subsets. This will facilitate a discussion on the causes of turnover, colonization and extinction in this archipelago.

2) A *separation of scales and processes* in the temporal dynamics of avifaunas will lead to the distinction between seasonal or annual dynamics of the various bird taxa on an island and long-term adaptation and selection processes leading to evolutionary divergence, speciation, and persistence.

3) The *results* of this analysis will then be used to evaluate contemporary concepts of survival and extinction in isolated and connected communities.

AREOGRAPHIC CONCEPTS

Areography concerns itself with the structure of biotic distribution areas (Rapoport 1982). In the following, I have expanded this subfield by the addition of a functional component. Each taxon occupies a distinct *biotic space* composed of its geographic dispersion, the resources contained therein that are required for survival, and the functional interactions between different elements of the taxon (individuals, families, subpopulations, etc.) that their spacing behaviors permit. Of great importance for the conservation management of populations and species is a fundamental dichotomy between taxa occupying *insular* and *continental* spaces.

An *insular* taxon is confined to a geographic island; isolated from other lands it functions and thrives in its island environment. The latter meets all its needs and enables its long-term viable persistence. In many cases, an island's isolation and protection from continental factors (like mammal predators) has resulted in unique adaptations to the island environment (example: flightlessness in many island bird species). Insular taxa (Figure 1A) exist only because of the very existence and physical and biotic landscape of islands; often, they can only function and remain viable as long as the island maintains its isolation from the continental source region of other biota. Many but not all insular taxa are island endemics such as the dodo of Mauritius, the Darwin finches of the Galapagos Islands, or the landbirds of the Revillagigedo Islands (Walter 1998). The terrestrial animals of remote oceanic islands are generally completely insular.

A *continental* taxon occupies a geographic area on a mainland (Figure 1A). Its biotic space differs from that characteristic for insular biota because its distribution area is not defined by an island's perimeter and saltwater barrier. A large variety of continental factors (predators, competitors, diseases, parasites) will interact with such a taxon. Continental taxa may expand or contract, fragment or connect part of their distribution area over time. Their very persistence can be explained by the opportunities for survival in a complex continental setting and functional spatial response to the many adverse limiting factors of continental environments. Habitat fragments on continents do not qualify as islands sensu strictu because they cannot harbor insular species; they are *isolates* and contain isolate populations of continental origin.

A third set of species can be called *global* in terms of the functional relevance of space. These species breed on islands and/or continents; it does not matter to them whether they are isolated by saltwater barriers or not because their spacing behavior and area structure does not recognize such a barrier.

Many continental species occur also on islands but their persistence on the latter is often dependent on recruitment from and links to continental populations of the same species. Source-sink systems and metapopulation dynamics may support island components of these species. Most continental islands are occupied by such populations (Figure 1B). Some populations, however, thrive on continental or landbridge islands and become spatially and numerically independent from their conspecific mainland population

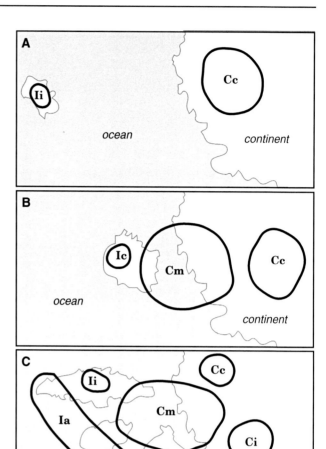

Figure 1. A simplified model of biotic space on islands and continents. A. Oceanic island and continent. B. Continental island and continent. C. Channel Islands and mainland coast of California. The spatial subsets are: Cc = continent-confined, Ci = functional continental, of island origin (rare), Cm = continental, mainland-dependent; Ii = functional insular endemic on single island, Ia = functional insular endemic within archipelago, Ic = functional insular, of continental origin.

areas. Very rarely do endemic island taxa colonize part of a continent and become functionally continental.

A simple functional classification of biotic space (with examples from the Channel Islands) has three sets and six subsets:

1. Insular(I)
   Ii - island endemic, on one island only (island scrub jay, *Aphelocoma insularis*)
   Ia - archipelago endemic, only on a particular archipelago or island group (horned lark, *Eremophila alpestris insularis*)
   Ic - continental origin but independent from continental area (chipping sparrow, *Spizella passerina*)
2. Continental(C)
   Cc - on mainland only, not on island(s) (wrentit, *Chamaea fasciata*)

Cm - Occupies island(s) but dependent on mainland area for island existence (American kestrel, *Falco sparverius*)

Ci - island origin but independent from island area (orange-crowned warbler, *Vermivora celata sordida*, Allen's hummingbird, *Selasphorus sasin sedentarius*; both breed in coastal mainland habitats of southern California)

3. Global(G)
No Channel Islands landbird taxon falls into this category.

DATA SOURCES AND METHODOLOGY

The paper concerns itself only with the landbirds of the eight Channel Islands lying off the coast of Santa Barbara and Los Angeles. Aquatic, seabirds, and other birds acquiring most or all of their energy sources at sea or below the high tide zone are not considered to be landbirds. Table 1 in Diamond and Jones (1980) is the principal data source for this paper. Bald eagle, osprey, peregrine falcon, American oystercatcher, and black oystercatcher were deleted from the list of landbirds due to their principal foraging of marine creatures. This leaves a total of 51 landbird species breeding at least once on one or more of the eight islands. In addition, Table 1 in Johnson's (1972) valuable paper provided the essential reference on endemic island taxa. These lists were complemented by further analysis and field observations found in Howell (1917), Miller (1951), Townsend (1968), Hunt and Hunt (1974), Jones and Diamond (1976), and Power (1980). Recent insights on the role of humans and their livestock in the modification of the vegetation of Santa Cruz Island were summarized by Junak et al. (1995).

The author has studied the landscapes and abundant bird populations on two of the islands: he spent several days on Santa Cruz Island approximately every two years since 1972. He has camped on Santa Catalina twice for a week-long stay in 1987 and 1997. He is currently engaged in bird surveys of all Channel Islands.

Bird species will be listed as *regular* breeders (symbol: X) if there is no record or a low probability of their disappearance in historic time. Birds colonizing an island for the first time during the past 50 years of observation and persisting there are listed separately as *new* regular breeders (N). *Occasional* breeders are classified as such (O), vanished island populations of taxa still existing elsewhere are listed as *disappeared* (D), and vanished populations of an endemic island taxon are classified as *extinct* (E).

Based on general guidelines from basic conservation biology and more recent evidence from persisting small and isolated bird populations (Walter 1990 and unpublished) a viable island population for short-term persistence should have at least 20 (large birds) to 50 (small birds) breeding pairs. Such a population is considered resistant to short-term extinction, relies solely on island resources in its realized

ecological niche, and therefore occupies an insular biotic space.

RESULTS

Endemic Taxa

Thirteen species have 57 island populations on the eight Channel Islands (Table 1) belonging to seventeen endemic subspecies and one endemic species (island scrub jay). Eight of these taxa are confined to a single island. All of these populations show morphological distinctions that set them apart from continental conspecific or congeneric relatives on the mainland. A few show clear behavioral differences in song, phenology, and foraging behavior; the others are likely to possess them as well but comparative studies have not been carried out for most taxa. These are the insular taxa (I) with the subsets Ii (8 taxa) and Ia (49 populations of 11 taxa).

Forty-six of 57 populations (81%) are considered regular breeders on their respective islands. Only two verified colonizations of formerly unoccupied islands have occurred resulting in viable populations of Allen's hummingbird on San Miguel and of the orange-crowned warbler on San Nicolas. The five disappeared and extinct taxa (8.8%) vanished from two islands for rather unnatural reasons: 1) on *Santa Barbara Island* the island vegetation was heavily overgrazed by rabbits and consumed by a human-caused wildfire (Hunt and Hunt 1974), and 2) on *San Clemente Island* overgrazing by goats and introduced predators (cats) severely degraded the integrity of the island's ecosystems. Only two taxa have gone extinct in the traditional sense of this term: they will not come back. This is the Santa Barbara Island subspecies of the song sparrow, *Melospiza melodia graminea*, and the San Clemente Island subspecies of the Bewick's wren, *Thryomanes bewickii leucophrys*. Only four islands have been listed as occasionally harboring breeding populations of the endemic loggerhead shrike and rufous-crowned sparrow (Table 1).

Rather unusual in island biogeography is the fact that two of the island subspecies have established viable 'beachheads' on the mainland coast near the islands. Allen's hummingbird is currently expanding its population size and overall density in the Los Angeles area (Walter, unpublished data). Less is known of the population size of the island taxon of the orange-crowned warbler in southern California's coastal habitats. Both taxa occupy continental biotic space Ci (see Figure 1C).

Non-Endemic Taxa

Among the 38 non-endemic breeding landbirds (Table 2) at least 136 breeding populations have been documented (Diamond and Jones 1980, Jones and Diamond 1976) for the Channel Islands. Only 81 (60%) are considered regular breeders; 18 new island colonizations (13%) have been documented. Some 34 populations are listed as occasional breeders. All of these populations are continental in origin. Only

Table 1. Endemic landbird taxa of the Channel Islands.

	Islands Occupied by Taxon								
Taxon	MIG	ROS	CRU	ANA	BAR	CAT	NIC	CLE	Total Islands
Horned Lark	X	X	X	X	X	X	X	X	8
Orange-crowned Warbler	X	X	X	X	X	X	N	X	8
Allen's Hummingbird	N	X	X	X	~	X	~	X	6
Loggerhead Shrike A	O	X	X	O	O	X	~	~	6
Western Flycatcher	~	X	X	X	~	X	~	X	5
House Finch	~	~	~	~	D	X	X	X	4
Bewick's Wren A	~	X	X	X	~	~	~	~	3
Spotted Towhee	~	X	~	~	~	X	~	D	3
Song Sparrow A	~	X	X	X	~	~	~	D	4
Rufous-crowned Sparrow	~	~	X	O	~	~	~	~	2
Loggerhead Shrike B	~	~	~	~	~	~	~	X	1
Bewick's Wren B	~	~	~	~	~	X	~	~	1
Bewick's Wren C	~	~	~	~	~	~	~	E	1
Song Sparrow B	X	~	~	~	~	~	~	~	1
Song Sparrow C	~	~	~	~	E	~	~	~	1
Sage Sparrow	~	~	~	~	~	~	~	X	1
California Quail	~	~	~	~	~	X	~	~	1
Island Scrub Jay	~	~	X	~	~	~	~	~	1
Subtotals									
Regular Breeders	3	8	9	6	2	9	2	7	46
Occasional Breeders	1	~	0	2	1	~	~	~	4
Disappeared	~	~	~	~	1	~	~	2	3
Extinct	~	~	~	~	1	~	~	1	2
New Colonization	1	~	~	~	~	~	1	~	2
Grand Total	5	8	9	8	5	9	3	10	57

X = regular, O = occasional, N = new regular, D = former, and E = extinct breeding population.

three of 136 breeding populations have apparently vanished: the house sparrow (*Passer domesticus*) from Santa Rosa (after an earlier successful colonization), the raven (*Corvus corax*) from San Miguel, and the bushtit (*Psaltriparus minimus*) from Santa Catalina.

Insular Space versus Continental Space

Many of the non-endemic island populations are quite large and meet the criteria for viable island populations (31 regular and 7 recent colonists, or 23%). They persist without any apparent support from the mainland source populations at present and occupy therefore the insular continental biotic space (Ic). When we add all populations occupying an insular biotic space (subsets Ii, Ia, and Ic) we have 53 endemic and 38 non-endemic populations. Among these, there have only been five disappearances and extinctions. Thus, 86 (95%) viable bird populations, each with more than 20 breeding pairs per island, have persisted over historic time.

A total of 61 old and new regular breeders as well as the 34 occasional breeders are classified as mainland-dependent taxa (Cm biotic space); these 95 populations (70% of all non-endemic populations) consist of one to fewer than

20 breeding pairs per island. These are by definition the less abundant, rare and irregular breeders of the Channel Islands.

DISCUSSION

Areography

The Channel Islands and the adjacent mainland coast contain all of the insular and continental subsets of functional biotic space (Figure 1C). This archipelago was not connected to the mainland during the last ice ages; although lying close to the Santa Barbara coastline, the islands remained isolated and preserved the insular spaces of many endemic taxa. The narrow distance to the islands enabled many birds, however, to cross the water barrier and to attempt colonization. Today, the islands contain an avifauna that is a composite of insular and continental areographic elements.

Persistence of Insular Endemics

The insular endemics (Table 1) have persisted everywhere except where massive human-caused interference has eliminated the resource base and or/ the island was overrun

Table 2. Non-endemic breeding landbird species.

Island	Breeding Status				
	Regular	New Regular	Occasional	Disappeared	Total No. Species
San Miguel	5 (2)	2 (0)	3	1	11
Santa Rosa	13 (6)	2 (0)	2	1	18
Santa Cruz	21 (11)	4 (3)	4	~	29
Anacapa	6 (0)	2 (0)	6	~	14
Santa Barbara	4 (0)	1 (0)	5	~	10
Santa Catalina	19 (8)	3 (2)	4	1	27
San Nicolas	4 (2)	2 (2)	6	~	12
San Clemente	9 (2)	2 (0)	4	~	15
Total No. of Populations	81 (31)	18 (7)	34	3	136 (38)

( ) = Estimated number of viable island populations [insular, of continental origin (Ic)]

Sources: Diamond and Jones (1980), Johnson (1972), Power (1980)

with introduced house cats. These insular populations (Ii and Ia) have therefore demonstrated a remarkable stability and resiliency over historic time as well as prehistoric time. They are as stable as the endemic landbirds of the Revillagigedo Islands in the Mexican Pacific (Walter 1998). It is highly probable that all the prehistoric endemic island populations would be more abundant today were it not for the potent transformation and degradation of the Channel Islands during the past 200 years (Junak et al. 1995). One element favoring the survival of these endemics is the often less specialized nature of island taxa compared to continental relatives. This adaptation to island life may help these taxa to cope with many anthropogenic modifications; nothing, of course, can be done in situ if scrub and woodland birds are faced with a bare island and hundreds of hungry cats as has been the case of S. Clemente Island and its extinct and vanished bird taxa (Table 1).

MacArthur-Wilson biogeography cannot account for the stability of this endemic avifauna but Lack's alternate theory of the 'ecological poverty' of island faunas (Lack 1976; Walter 1998) predicts a high level of stability for island landbirds in undisturbed landscapes.

The insular continental populations (Ic) are also unlikely candidates for disappearance from one or more islands because they are buffered by large numbers of breeding pairs (often hundreds of pairs); several of the recent immigrant taxa have become highly successful colonists and possess functional insularity. These are net additions to the avifauna of the islands that are the result of diffuse factors operating on the islands as well as on the continent. It may sound elementary but it has to be stated that common or abundant island birds normally do not vanish or suffer 'local extinction' unless there is anthropogenic destruction of habitats and predation or outright persecution.

Instability of Continental Taxa

The subset of mainland-dependent taxa (Cm) is responsible for most of the reported turnovers (Jones and Diamond 1976). This subset has also been the subject of many works dealing with island biogeography (see Pimm 1991). Four systems of spatial dynamics may be responsible for the persistence of these types of permanent or temporary mainland and island distributions:

1. Source-sink systems where an island population has low ecological fitness and regularly receives extra progeny from a continental source population (Ritchie 1997).

2. Primary-secondary habitat selection favors the continental habitat but many birds will choose the secondary habitat in some years due to overcrowding or unfavorable physical conditions in the primary area. This spatial dispersion system has been documented in German populations of the pied flycatcher (*Ficedula hypoleuca*) by Berndt and Winkel (1974).

3. Metapopulation dynamics with one or more islands as breeding patches in a largely continental system of loosely connected satellite areas. One or more of the patch populations may disappear at one time and be recolonized again from other patches in the future. Song sparrow populations in the San Juan Islands of British Columbia fit this spatial system (Smith et al. 1996).

4. Satellite populations on an island that are simply an isolate of a large continental distribution area.

The saltwater barrier separates the two populations but the island area is just as good or bad as the mainland area. The only difference is the much smaller population size on the island.

We do not know at present to which of the above spatial systems the non-viable and occasional breeders of the Channel Islands belong. But the possibilities for causing repeated presence-absence patterns are enormous: (a) Favorable breeding conditions on the mainland may flood the islands with year-old breeders during the next breeding season; (b) cold winter and spring seasons may thin the continental breeding population and drain the island population; (c) the same bird may breed on mainland and island in alternate years; (d) a single pair breeding on an island may just be a random event, a statistical outlier, or the beginning of a colonization trend. All these scenarios deal with ecological time scales and the spatio-temporal dynamics of bird populations. They tell us much about the aut- and demecology of birds, of their islands, and even more about their continental ranges but very little about island biogeography, because the driving forces regulating long-term island occupancy, evolution, and diversity overlap only slightly with these short-term population dynamics of mainland-dependent taxa.

Relevance for Conservation Management

The landbird data from the Channel Islands show that the usually scant breeding populations of the mainland-dependent subset (Cm) are responsible for most of the observed turnovers (species loss and species gain), not the more typical and more abundant island dwellers that have become functionally insular. The latter are buffered by their numbers and by island adaptation. We should perhaps disregard all non-viable populations and include only large insular taxa in our discussions of island ecology and biogeography. This might provide a more accurate representation of resource-adapted island diversity.

The landbirds of the Channel Islands cannot be used as an island model for the study and management of continental habitat isolates such as fragments of forest, prairie or chaparral.

First, fragments are not islands at all. They are connected in many ways to the surrounding terrestrial matrix or 'Umfeld' (a German term for spatial environment) that is rich in predators, competitors, parasites, etc. which can and will invade and impact the fragment sooner or later. Basically, a continental fragment lacks the protective isolation that is characteristic of all true islands (Laurance 1991:85-86).

Second, the biotic taxa found in continental fragments have evolved and persisted in continental biotic space containing extensive and contiguous habitats with the required resources over hundreds and thousands of square kilometers. Many large carnivores and herbivores need this kind of functional space over their evolutionary life span to avoid extinction due to global and regional climate and biotic change. Being trapped in a human-caused habitat fragment would mean the loss of their ability to use their large functional space for purposes of persisting in the optimal portions of the range. By contrast, the insular species of islands need isolation and thrive in restricted areas because they have been selected for this functional space over evolutionary time periods (Walter 1998).

Third, the insular taxa of the Channel Islands have proved to be remarkably resistant to disappearance and extinction. These islands have suffered from overgrazing, erosion, invasions by alien weeds and predators, human disturbance, and other common extinction factors. Yet, most insular taxa have tolerated this disturbance and destruction.

It is doubtful that similar impacts would be tolerated by continental biota in restricted continental fragments; more likely is that they would attempt to evade these extinction factors by leaving the fragment. A likely explanation for the high persistence of the endemic avifauna of the Channel Islands may be found in the natural rigor of the physical and biotic environment of this southern Californian archipelago. At the end of the extremely long and dry summer months even the undisturbed habitats appear ecologically stressed. This natural phenomenon may predispose the insular endemics of this archipelago to possess an ecological valency that tolerates some environmental disturbance. Similarly, the long-term presence of fox and skunk as well as of Amerindian encampments on the major islands may have resulted in less predator-naïve island birds than we expect to find on remote oceanic islands.

Finally, considerable attention should be given to all insular endemics; they have nowhere else to go and need the functional space of the Channel Islands. Hopefully, the environmental abuse of the past 200 years has abated forever. Of particular urgency is the plight of the endangered landbirds of San Clemente and San Nicolas Island. With regard to the likely fate of continental biota trapped in remnant habitats, this discussion of island birds has shown how precarious and dangerous life in a continental fragment must be compared to the relative security that functional insularity provides for many island dwellers.

ACKNOWLEDGMENTS

My heartfelt thanks go to the many students who shared my Channel Islands experiences over many seasons. Dan Kahane, Walter Wehtje, Caitlin Dempsey, Lisa Jerez, Tiki Baron, Kathy Hansen, Tom Gillespie, and Mike Starr were especially helpful and enthusiastic students. Santa Cruz Island Natural Reserve manager Lyndal Laughrin was always supportive of my island ventures. On Santa Catalina, Misty Gay of the Santa Catalina Island Conservancy was very helpful in arranging visits and vehicles. I am very appreciative of the enthusiasm for island studies shown by the directors and scientific staff of the Santa Barbara Museum of Natural History. At a conceptual level, I have gained much from the Channel Islands-related works of Jared M. Diamond, Ned K. Johnson, and Dennis M. Power.

LITERATURE CITED

Berndt, R. and W. Winkel. 1974. Oekoschema, Rivalitaet und Dismigration als oeko-ethologische Dispersionsfaktoren. Journal fuer Ornithologie 115:398-417.

Brown, J. H. and M. V. Lomolino. 1998. Biogeography, 2nd edition. Sinauer. Sunderland, Massachusetts.

Case, T. J. and M. L. Cody. 1983. Synthesis: pattern and processes in island biogeography. Pages 307-341 in Case, T. J. and M. L. Cody (eds.), Island Biogeography in the Sea of Cortéz. University of California Press. Berkeley, Los Angeles, and London.

Diamond, J. M. 1969. Avifaunal equilibria and species turnover rates on the Channel Islands of California. Proceedings of the National Academy of Sciences 64:57-73.

Diamond, J. M. and Jones, H. L.1980. Breeding land birds of the Channel Islands. Pages 597-612 in Power, D. M. (ed.), The California Islands: Proceedings of a Multidisciplinary Symposium. Santa Barbara Museum of Natural History, Santa Barbara, CA.

Gilbert, F. S. 1980. The equilibrium theory of island biogeography: fact or fiction? Journal of Biogeography 7:209-235.

Howell, A. B. 1917. Birds of the islands off the coast of southern California. Pacific Coast Avifauna, No. 12:1-127.

Hunt, G. L. and M. W. Hunt. 1974. Trophic levels and turnover rates: the avifauna of Santa Barbara Island, California. Condor 76:363-369.

Johnson, N. K. 1972. Origin and Differentiation of the avifauna of the Channel Islands, California. Condor 74:295-315.

Jones, H. L. and J. M. Diamond. 1976. Short-time-base studies of turnover in breeding bird populations on the California Channel Islands. Condor 78:526-549.

Junak, S., T. Ayres, R. Scott, D. Wilken and D. Young.1995. A flora of Santa Cruz Island. Santa Barbara Botanical Garden, Santa Barbara, CA.

Lack, D. 1976. Island biology: illustrated by the land birds of Jamaica. Studies in Ecology, Vol. 3. University of California Press, Berkeley and Los Angeles, CA.

Laurance, W. F. 1991. Ecological correlates of extinction proneness in Australian tropical rain forest mammals. Conservation Biology 5:79-89.

Lynch, J. F. and N. K. Johnson. 1974.Turnover and equilibria in insular avifaunas, with special reference to the California Channel Islands. Condor 76:370-384.

MacArthur, R. H. and E. O. Wilson, 1967. The Theory of Island Biogeography. Princeton University Press, Princeton, NJ.

Miller, A. H. 1951. A comparison of the avifaunas of Santa Cruz and Santa Rosa islands, California. Condor 53:117-123.

Minelli, A. 1990. Faunal turnover and equilibrium models in island biogeography: some problems in the study of species diversity in island biota. Atti dei Convegni Lincei 85:85-95.

Pimm, S. L. 1991. The balance of nature: ecological issues in the conservation of species and communities. University of Chicago Press, Chicago, IL.

Power, D. M. 1980. Evolution of land birds on the California Islands. Pages 613-649 in Power, D. M. (ed.), The California Islands: Proceedings of a Multidisciplinary Symposium. Santa Barbara Museum of Natural History, Santa Barbara, CA.

Rapoport, E. H. 1982. Areography: geographical strategies of species. Pergamon Press, NY.

Ritchie, M. E.1997. Populations in a landscape context: sources, sinks, and metapopulations. Pages 160-184 in Bissonette, J. A. (ed.), Wildlife and Landscape Ecology: Effects of Pattern and Scale. Springer, New York, NY.

Rosenzweig, M. L. 1995. Species diversity in space and time. Cambridge University Press, Cambridge, MA.

Simberloff, D. S. 1974. Equilibrium theory of island biogeography and ecology. Annual Review of Ecology and Systematics 5:161-182.

Simberloff, D. 1994. Habitat fragmentation and population extinction of birds. Ibis 137:S105-S111.

Solem, A. 1990. Limitations of equilibrium theory in relation to land snails. Atti dei Convegni Lincei 85:97-116.

Smith, J. N. M., M. J. Taitt, C. M. Rogers, P. Arcese, L. F. Keller, A. L. E. V. Cassidy and W. M. Hochachka. 1996. A metapopulation approach to the population biology of the song sparrow Melospiza melodia. Ibis 138:120-128.

Tilman, D. and P. Kareiva. 1997. Spatial ecology: the role of space in population dynamics and interspecific interactions. Princeton University Press, Princeton, NJ.

Thornton, I. 1996. Krakatau: The destruction and reassembly of an island ecosystem. Harvard University Press, Cambridge, MA.

Townsend, W. C. 1968. Birds observed on San Nicolas Island, California. Condor 70:266-268.

Walter, H. S. 1990. Small viable population: the red-tailed hawk of Socorro Island. Conservation Biology 4:441-443.

Walter, H. S. 1998. Driving forces of island biobiodiversity: an appraisal of two theories. Physical Geography 19: 351-377

Wiens, J. A. 1989. The Ecology of Bird Communities. Vol. 2: Processes and Variations. Cambridge University Press, Cambridge, MA.

Williamson, M. 1981. Island Populations. Oxford University Press, Oxford, United Kingdom.

APPENDIX

**List of scientific names of endemic landbird taxa of the
Channel Islands (see Table 1)**

California Quail (*Lophortyx californica catalinensis*)
Allen's Hummingbird (*Selasphorus sasin sedentarius*)
Western Flycatcher (*Empidonax difficilis insulicola*)
Horned Lark (*Eremophila alpestris insularis*)
Island Scrub Jay (*Aphelocoma insularis*)
Bewick's Wren (*Thryomanes* bewickii)
        Subspecies A (*T. b. nesophilus*)
        Subspecies B (*T. b. catalinae*)
        Subspecies C (*T. b. leucophrys*)
Loggerhead Shrike (*Lanius ludovicianus*)
        Subspecies A (*L. l. anthonyi*)
        Subspecies B (*L. l. mearnsi*)
Orange-crowned Warbler (*Vermivora celata sordida*)
House Finch (*Carpodacus mexicanus clementis*)
Spotted Towhee (*Pipilo maculatus clementae*)
Rufous-crowned Sparrow (*Aimophila ruficeps obscura*)
Sage Sparrow (*Amphispiza belli clementae*)
Song Sparrow (*Melospiza melodia*)
        Subspecies A (*M. m. clementae*)
        Subspecies B (*M. m. micronyx*)
        Subspecies C (*M. m. graminea*)

PRELIMINARY SURVEY OF PHYSICAL, GENETIC, PHYSIOLOGICAL AND BEHAVIORAL TRAITS OF FERAL HORSES (*EQUUS CABALLUS*) ON SANTA CRUZ ISLAND

Karen M. Blumenshine[1], Suzanne V. Benech[2], Ann T. Bowling[3], and Ned K. Waters[4]

[1]Santa Barbara Equine Practice, 15 St. Ann Drive, Santa Barbara, CA 93109
(805) 962-4414, FAX (805) 899-4160, E-Mail: kmblumenshine@vmth.ucdavis.edu
[2]Benech Biological, 487 Lincoln Drive, Ventura, CA 93001
(805) 643-2755, FAX (805) 643-1378, E-Mail: ajfield@msn.com
[3]Veterinary Genetics Lab, School of Veterinary Medicine, University California, Davis, CA 95616
(530) 752-2211, FAX (530) 752-3556, E-Mail: atbowling@ucdavis.edu
[4]Department of Radiology, School of Veterinary Medicine, Veterinary Medical Teaching Hospital,
University of California, Davis, CA 95616
(530) 752-3753, FAX (530) 752-9815, E-Mail:nkwaters@ucdavis.edu

ABSTRACT

Horses were first introduced to Santa Cruz Island (SCI) in the 1830s. A feral horse population developed by 1984, after cessation of ranching operations. This wild population provided a unique opportunity to study island adaptations on traits in feral horses. Preliminary field observations of physiological and physical traits, social structure, and behavior were studied from 1995 to 1998. Forty-one survey days were completed during all seasons. Physical collections, written records, video, and photographic documentation were analyzed. Migratory habits were mapped. Polymerase Chain Reaction (PCR) amplification of DNA was conducted on hair follicle and blood samples to determine familial relationships, consort behavior, and genetic variation. Urine and manure samples were analyzed to determine reproductive and parasite status. Long-bone (metacarpal) measurements were compared to data from mainland horses. Results indicate the SCI feral horse population resembles other wild horse herds in 1) matriarchal social structure, 2) elimination-marking sequence, 3) consort behavior, and 4) hoof wear patterns. However, SCI wild horses were unique from other wild horse populations in 1) a shift in reproductive season, 2) closer familial relationships, 3) high foal survival rate, 4) decreased long-bone length, and 5) genetic character. These differences appear to be a result of environmental adaptation and genetic isolation.

Keywords: Feral, wild, horse, behavior, physiology, genetics, bones, Santa Cruz, island, California.

INTRODUCTION

Horses (*Equus caballus*) were first introduced to Santa Cruz Island, off the southern California coast, in approximately 1830 when convicts from Mexico were dispatched there to live (de la Guerra Ord 1856). The court petition by Andres Castillero to secure confirmation of his title to Santa Cruz Island confirms his transport of horses to the island along with cattle and sheep in 1851 (Case #176, 1852). Horses were used in the construction of roads and buildings, and remained an integral part of every agricultural operation on the island ever since (M. Daily, pers. comm., 1996). The feral horse herd studied was released into the wild when the last commercial sheep ranching operation was discontinued in the early 1980s (F. Gherini, pers. comm. 1997). It was determined by the ages of the current herd that all 16 members were born in a wild state. The natural range of the horses consisted of approximately 2,549 hectares of primarily grassy coastal plateau of both volcanic and sedimentary origin, gradually inclining to the east to steep basaltic hills. There is no historical evidence that the population was manipulated by man in any way before this study except 20 to 40 members (approximate, from historic accounts, J. Owens, pers. obs. 1997) were apparently culled during a severe drought lasting from 1986 through 1991. Although genetic studies of the Channel Island fox (Wayne 1995) provide a cogent example "that small populations can persist for long time periods, even in the near absence of genetic variability," a benchmark genetic reference point for the Santa Cruz horses will allow appropriate paradigms to be applied in population discussions. This feral horse herd presented a unique opportunity to study the effects of this island ecosystem on feral horse behavior and physiology, and the effects of isolation and culling on genetic makeup. In October 1998, all of the horses were removed from the island. Thus these preliminary results represent the only behavioral, physical, and physiological studies conducted on this wild horse herd while it was intact on Santa Cruz Island.

METHODS

The social behaviors, familial relationships, grazing habits, seasonal migratory habits, reproductive patterns, genetic character and variation, long bone dimensions and hoof wear patterns in the wild horse population on Santa Cruz Island were studied. In order to efficiently cover their 2,549-hectare range, scouting on foot began in an area where the animals were last seen or near common water holes. Observations of the herd were made over a three-year period (1995 to 1998), in both wet and dry seasons. Severe weather conditions prohibited island access during portions of some years. Some herd information was collected by interviewing visitors and park rangers to more precisely pinpoint dates of birth or death. The herd was generally observed at a distance of 6 to 30 m. Behaviors such as social interactions, grazing habits, and migratory patterns were recorded by the investigator and knowledgeable volunteers, using field notes, video, and photographic documentation. Over the period of the study, the herd grew from about 11 to 17 horses.

Biological material used for initial genetic analysis of the feral horses included hair follicle cells from mane or chin hairs, which were used for determination of microsatellite variation by DNA fragment length analysis. These samples were taken from individuals without restraint. Follicle samples were collected from mature stallions (Buck Bay and El Dorado), mares (Tinker, Inez, Albina, Blanca, and Freckles), and young stock (Delphine, Primo and Miguel). During the period of capture and relocation from the island, blood samples were taken from all members of the herd, including the mature mare Panocha and from the youngest foals, and were used for both analysis of blood typing and DNA markers. DNA testing was conducted using the Polymerase Chain Reaction (PCR) method and 15 loci of dinucleotide repeat microsatellites (11 loci discussed in Bowling [1997]) augmented with LEX3, LEX33, ASB2, and UCDEQ425). After PCR amplification, an Applied Biosystems 373 DNA Sequencer with 672 Genescan Analysis software was used to analyze the fluorescently-tagged fragments for length polymorphisms. Due to difficulty in collecting hairs in the field from Panocha, the #1 herd alpha mare, and the foals born from 1996 to 1998, genetic information was not available until after the blood samples were received at the time of capture and relocation efforts. In this manuscript we describe only the results of the DNA analysis. However, familial relationships were determined from analysis of genetic variation (at least 30 loci) detected by a combination of DNA and blood typing methods (Bowling and Clark 1985).

Physical condition was monitored in several ways. The skin and coat on all individuals of the herd were visually examined to determine external parasite status. Fecal samples from six out of the 11 individuals comprising the heard at the start of the study were collected from the ground and examined. Fecal parasite egg counts were performed by flotation method using sodium nitrate (sp. gr. 1.20)

(Fecalsol - Evsco Reno, NV) to check for internal parasites. Hoof wear was observed and photographed during both wet and dry seasons. For comparison of cross sectional area of long bone to that of domestic horses, a specimen was taken from the carcass of a 12 year-old mare which had died of natural causes. The specimen was stripped with a NaOH solution and allowed to dry before sections. The midshaft of the cannon bone (metacarpal) was cut through and the cross-sectional area traced and measured by plani-meter. The cross-sectional area at the level of 50% of the distance from the proximal end of the metacarpal bone to the tip of the distal saggital ridge was measured so as to be comparable to existing data compiled from several breeds (Piotrowski et al. 1983). Further metacarpal measurements were acquired from Computerized Axial Tomography (CAT scan) images (General Electic 9800 Quick C.T. scanner). Eight third-metacarpal bones from domestic horses and one third-metacarpal bone from the SCI mare (Inez) were imaged and compared. The longitudinal (mid-saggital) measurement was made from the radiographic center of the carpo-metacarpal joint proximally to the radiographic center of the distal margin of the condyles of the third metacarpus. Cross-sectional areas from three transverse images were measured: midshaft (equidistant from either end of the longitudinal measurement), and 20 mm proximal and distal to midshaft. All cross-sectional measurements were acquired at 120 kvp and 100 ma. Measurements included cross-sectional area, shortest medulary diameter, longest dorsopalmar and mediolateral diameters, and thickest dorsal, medial, and lateral cortices.

Reproductive patterns were traced by collecting fresh urine and manure samples from mares to determine pregnancy status. These data were utilized in the pilot program for immunocontraception, developed to manage herd size. Immunocontraception was administered to one alpha mare for one season. Two doses of porcine zonae pellucidae vaccine were administered intramuscularly by a remote darting system, three weeks apart, during the last month before the time that foaling was predicted. This followed the protocol developed for the Assateague National Seashore feral horses. (Kirkpatrick et al.1992). Pregnancy status was evaluated by urinary oestrone level in EIA assay (Kirkpatrick et al. 1991). Urine samples were aspirated fresh from the ground by syringe. Foaling dates and survival rates were recorded (Tables 1 and 3).

RESULTS

Genetic Characteristics and Variation

For the 15 tested loci, the SCI feral horse population had two to four genetic variants (alleles), all previously identified in recognized domestic breeds. Nine loci had four variants, including an X-chromosome locus (LEX3). This observation suggested that at its smallest (genetic) size, regardless of the number of founder animals, the "bottleneck" population was at least three and likely four or more animals. The average number of variants per locus was 3.0.

Observed heterozygosity for the four adults El Dorado, Buck Bay, Tinker, and Inez ranged from 0.50 to 0.71 with an average of 0.61. The offspring sired by Buck Bay (Table 1) were genetically excluded to be sired by El Dorado, and could not be excluded to be sired by Buck Bay.

Social Organization

The general social unit of the feral horse herd consisted of a stallion, an alpha mare and her offspring, and other mares and their offspring. The stallions acted as sentinels guarding their harems, but did not take the lead in most herd decisions. Alpha mares tended to lead the herd to drink or to pastures. If a threat was perceived, the alpha mares lead the entire band away while a lead stallion was observed to stay behind to face and ward off danger. During the first two years of study, the alpha mares were the only mares producing foals (Table 1).

During most of the study (1995 to 1997) there were only two herds (Table 1). There was a predominance of females in each herd (Table 1). This may have been in part due to human intervention (culling) prior to the study. Neither stallion expended substantial energy in the defense of their mares from conspecific male attention. For instance, when one stallion was observed to be grazing closely to the mare from the other stallion's herd, the second stallion often responded by directing his path of grazing so as to position himself between the first stallion and the mares of the second stallion. This would often occur without any threat posturing. If the first stallion displayed increased interest and drew closer to a mare in the second herd, the second stallion

would respond with threatening gestures such as ear pinning, vocalizations, and flexation of the muscles of the neck and chest. If the first stallion responded to these threatening gestures, the interaction tended to intensify with "striking" motions with the front limbs followed by rearing onto the hind limbs and "striking." These more energetic confrontations were observed primarily during spring months.

Harem Stability and Territoriality

Social organization of the SCI wild horses during the study consisted of two comparably stable harems, displaying harem changes of two mares, 6.2% instability (Table 2). The first to move was Albina. Albina was a subordinate mare, closely bonded to another subordinate mare (Blanca). Blanca delivered a healthy foal in January 1997 and was elevated in social status. She and her foal (Rubio) were fiercely defended from Albina by the harem #2 (H#2) stallion (Buck Bay). Evidence of aggression (hair loss from bites) was observed on Albina when she was ostracized from H#2. She was then observed nuzzling with H#1 stallion (El Dorado) and was subsequently accepted into his harem and bore his foal the subsequent year. The second move observed over three years was a filly from H#2 to a new harem (H#3) which was established in 1998 (Table 1). This harem consisted of two animals, a 1.5-year-old colt (Pedro) and 2.5-year-old filly (Vera), both previously from H#1. Prior to the formation of H#3, the H#1 stallion began showing interest (genital sniffing) in Vera. During the formation of H#3, there were no physical signs of nonspecific fighting such as hair loss over the rump and sides. Harem #3 moved into previously

Table 1. Santa Cruz Island wild horse population structure, 1994 to 1998.

Name	Sex/Social Position	Est. Age in 1998	Birth**	Sire	Dam	Herd	Consort
El Dorado	alpha male	14 years	unkn	unkn	unkn	#1	
Panocha	alpha mare	unkn	unkn	unkn	unkn	#1	Buck Bay
Delphine	mare	6-7 years	unkn	Buck Bay	Inez	#1	
Freckles	mare	6 years	unkn	Buck Bay	Panocha	#1	
Albina	mare	4.5 years	Early 94	Buck Bay	unkn	#1	
Miguel*	male	3.5 years	1/2/95	Buck Bay	Panocha	#1*	
Cricket	male	1 year	10/7/97	El Dorado	Panocha	#1	
El Nino	male	foal	2/19/98	El Dorado	Albina	#1	
Last stand on S.C.	filly	foal	9/9/98	El Dorado	Panocha	#1	
Buck Bay	alpha male	12 years	unkn	El Dorado	unkn	#2	
Inez-deceased 2/97	alpha mare	12 years	unkn	El Dorado	unkn	#2	
Tinker	mare	5.5 years	Early 93	El Dorado	unkn	#2	
Blanca	mare	4.5 years	Early 94	Buck Bay	Inez	#2	
Primo	male (gelded 6/96)	3 years	11/24/95	Buck Bay	Inez	#2	
Rubio	male	1.5 years	1/29/97	El Dorado	Blanca	#2	
Nickels	filly	foal	1/29/98	Buck Bay	Blanca	#2	
Vera	mare	3 years	12/2/95	El Dorado	Panocha	#3	
Pedro	male	2 years	10/25/96	El Dorado	Panocha	#3	

* Adopted out of the herd as a yearling.

** Dates prior to 1995 were determined from oral histories from caretakers.

Table 2. Harem instability for the Santa Cruz Island wild horses.

Year	#Changed Harems/Total # Mares	% Instability	% Stability
1994	0/7	0%	100%
1995	0/7	0%	100%
1996	0/7	0%	100%
1997	1/6	17%	83%
1998	1/7	14%	86%
Ave. 5yr	**2/34**	**6.20%**	**93.8%**

unoccupied territory known as "No Man's Land," a rocky basaltic ridge approximately 500 m high, that forms a natural barrier to the west. Manure and tracks were first seen on the crest of this range in April 1998. Seasonal water was plentiful there in the spring. In June, with diminished water sources in the highlands, H#3 was observed in a confrontation with H#1 and H#2 on the plain, and after July, frequented a region near a vernal pool on Cavern Point (Figure 1). During mid-summer 1998, H#1 and H#2 were also observed in the vicinity of the vernal pool water source at Cavern Point. Subsequent to these observations, both members of H#3 and the stallions and some mares of H#1 and H#2 displayed hair loss on their rumps and sides, indicating conspecific fighting and evidence of territorial behavior. Harem #1 and H#2 were not observed on Cavern Point after this occurrence.

Although territoriality per se was not observed between H#1 and H#2, if a subordinate horse would pass manure or urine, a more dominant animal (usually a stallion) was observed smelling the excrement and showing a flehmen response. This investigative behavior would be followed by a period of increased activity or excitement, culminating in the passage of manure onto the top of the subordinate's pile. This "male-typical-elimination-marking-response" (S. McDonnell, pers. comm. 1998) has been associated with sexual behavior and territoriality (Rubenstein 1981; Turner and Kirkpatrick 1986).

Consort Behavior

Consort behavior was evaluated by determining genetic microsatellite loci using genetic material from hair follicles and blood collected from the individuals in the herd and comparing these to herd relationships observed in the field. Throughout the study from 1995 until April 1998 when a colt and young mare left to form a third harem, there were two distinct stallion-dominated harems. The stallion in H#2 (Buck Bay) was sired by the stallion in H#1 (El Dorado). Before 1996, the Harem #2 stallion sired all offspring tested during this study for both H#1 and H#2, after which the H#1 stallion sired all foals in H#1 and one foal in H#2 (Blanca's 1997 colt). Each stallion guarded the mares in his harem and their offspring. During our observations, we did not witness sexual posturing (such as thigh nuzzling, licking, genital sniffing, flehmen, or mounting) by a stallion from

one herd to a mare of another herd without a protective response (walking between individuals, ear pinning, flexation of chest muscles, striking or rearing behavior). The genetic data show, however, that the alpha mare of H#1 consorted with the alpha stallion of H#2, since the two of her progeny tested were both sired by him. Blanca of H#2 has born foals by the alpha stallions from both H#1 and H#2. Previous to the beginning of the study, the three eldest individuals in H#2 (Buck Bay, Inez, and Tinker) were all sired by the alpha stallion in H#1 (Table 1).

Grazing Patterns

Grazing observations indicated that the herd foraged primarily on grasses. Species of *Avena, Bromus, Hordeum* and *Nassella* appeared to predominate their rangelands although numerous other grasses such as *Phalaris, Koeleria, Gastridium, Lolium, Polypogon, Lamarckia, Piptatherum,* and *Poa* were also present and utilized. Forbes such as *Erodium* and *Medicago polymorpha* were also eaten. During the spring (wet season observations), the horses appeared highly selective and targeted the inflorescence of the abundant *Avena*. During the fall (dry season observations), grazing patterns were more diverse. Not only did they feed on stems of dry *Avena*, they also targeted the still green (more nutrious) blades of the perennial grass *Nassella*. Occasionally, during the dry season, they were observed eating and sometimes specifically targeting forbes such as *Brassica, Sonchus* and *Cirsium*. Most foraging behavior took place on the relatively level eastern plateaus. There were no apparent differences in foraging habits between sexes or among ages.

The study area was grazed by both feral sheep (est. 3,500 head) (Channel Islands National Park, pers. comm. 1997) and horses (12 to16 head). Horses grazed primarily the lower, flatter regions along the eastern plateaus. During this survey, these grasslands appeared to be in good condition in both the wet and dry seasons. Bare ground from overgrazing was not apparent in the plateau region. Bare ground occurred as access roads, rock outcrops, areas of feral pig rooting, and animal trails along canyon walls to water sources. During the wet season, grasses formed dense turf. In late fall, residual dry matter was still abundant. The native perennial bunch grasses (*Nassella*) were selectively grazed during the late summer and fall, but did not display any deformities typical of overgrazing.

Migration Patterns

There was an obvious trend for the herd to be found on the plateau (greater San Pedro Point) when local stream or pond water was available. After plateau water sources disappeared during the dry season, the tendency was to graze nearer either Scorpion or Smugglers Canyons where water was provided by a National Park Service watering trough (Figure 1). They were never observed utilizing perennial springs to the south, which were frequented by feral sheep.

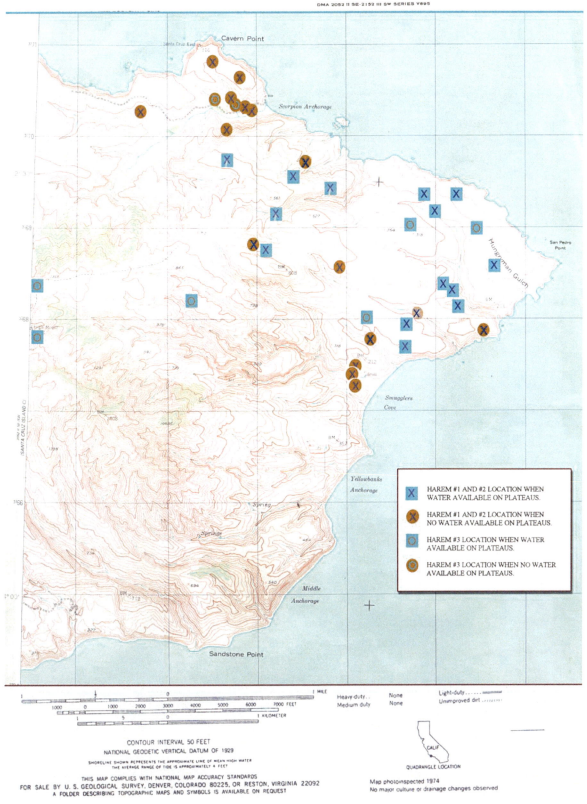

Figure 1. Migratory patterns of the Santa Cruz Island wild horses.

Physical and Physiological Traits

Condition/health of the herd was excellent by all standards. Haircoats were shiny and body scores, a standardized indicator of body weight (Mowrey 1993), were rated at 7 to 8, which is well above average weight. Survival rates (98% for adults and 100% for foals) were remarkable (Table 3). There was a pattern of foaling and breeding between the short photoperiod months of October and February (Table 1). No parasite eggs were seen in any of the fecal examinations and no external parasites were found. (D. Jensen, pers. comm. 1996). The weight bearing surface of the hoof remained remarkably smooth and symmetrical during all seasons, whether the ground was moist or dry. Both hoof length and hoof angle were considered to be within normal limits for domestic horses.

The long bone (metacarpal) length of the deceased SCI mare was greater than four standard deviations below the mean length of the Thoroughbred (TB) population and greater than two standard deviations below the mean of the Quarter Horse (QH) population measured (Table 4). Although the SCI mare metacarpal cross-sectional area was not substantially larger than the areas in the population measured at the University of California Davis (UC Davis) (Table 4), it was greater than three standard deviations above the mean values reported in a mixed-breed population studied at the School of Veterinary Medicine in Gainsville, Florida (Piotrowski et al. 1983).

A remarkable difference was found between the shape of the transverse sections of the metacarpal bone of the SCI wild mare, which had traveled mainly at a walk on basalt and Monterey shale surfaces, and that of domestic breeds which have traveled on various surfaces. While the long-bone cross sections of the SCI mare showed remarkable symmetry, those of the patient population at the Veterinary Medical Teaching Hospital at UC Davis exhibited a marked thickening of the anterior medial cortex.

DISCUSSION

Grazing conditions during our preliminary observations appeared ideal in both quantity and quality and were reflected in the overall healthy condition of both the feral herd and the rangeland (Duncan 1992). Although steeper sheep-dominated regions displayed evidence of overgrazing (i.e., bare ground and erosion), horse-dominated grasslands appeared to be in good condition with dense grass cover in both wet and dry seasons.

The migratory patterns were predominantly influenced by the available water supply. If water was available, the herd was most likely to be found on the coastal plateau.

The pattern of foaling between October and February is distinctly different from that of any United States wild herd reported except for the wild burro herd living in the U.S. Virgin Islands, which breeds and foals all year around. While the difference in photoperiod at that latitude can explain the apparent anomaly in the Virgin Islands (J. Turner, pers. comm. 1997), it cannot explain why the SCI feral herd bred and foaled during the months with the shortest photoperiod, in sharp contrast with nearby mainland domestic horses. Foaling on SCI appeared to coincide with the availability of green grass. Grazing on green grasses increases reproductive success since nutritional levels are then high enough to support a developing fetus and production of milk for the foal (Coates-Markle, in press). This suggests that there may have been some adaptation to island environment. Any conclusions need to be made with caution, however, because of the limited number of animals studied.

Other studies suggest that availability of forage vegetation contributes to harem stability in island herds of feral horses. When forage availability decreased, as much as 30% of adult females left their harems (Stevens 1990). Considering these findings, the high stability (93.8%) of the SCI wild horse harems may have reflected the availability of ample range and suitable vegetation (Table 3).

In previous studies, 25% to 30% of mares in stable consort relations with particular harem stallions have been reported to produce foals sired by stallions from outside their harem (Kasada et al. 1996; Bowling and Touchberry 1990). Analysis of microsatellite variation provided the tool to confirm or rule out suggested relationships in the SCI herd based on coat color and anecdotal information. Preliminary findings in the study indicated that all foals born in H#1 between 1994 and 1996, were sired by Buck Bay (H#2), son of El Dorado (H#2), while those born in 1997 or after were sired by El Dorado (H#1). The 1997 offspring of a mare from H#2 (Blanca) was sired by stallion H#1, but her 1998 offspring was sired by stallion H#2 (Table 1). This resulted in 6.2% harem instability for this herd. In light of the fact that consort behavior was occurring, it is interesting that these harems remained closely affiliated with very little confrontation and competition between stallions, and that only alpha mares produced offspring during most years. This suggests that forage availability may have been a stronger factor than potential mates in conspecific competition in these herds. It also suggests that there may have been some prohibition of mating of subordinate mares by the alpha mares.

Table 3. Survival rates for the Santa Cruz Island wild horses.

Description	1995	1996	1997	1998	Ave. Survival Rate
Adults over 1 year (Survival/Total#)	09/09	11/11	11/12	13/13	98%
First year of age	03/03*	01/01	02/02	03/03	100%
*Adopted colt not included in this data.					

Table 4. Comparison of long-bone measurements between SCI horses and domestic breeds.

Breed	Age	Sex	Leg	Length	Ave. CX area	CX/length
TB	15 years	mare	right	27.3 cm	10.72 cm^2	0.39
TB	9 years	gelding	left	25.8 cm	9.28 cm^2	0.36
TB	20 years	stallion	left	25.8 cm	9.96 cm^2	0.39
TB	3 years	gelding	left	27.1 cm	10.10 cm^2	0.37
Mean TB				26.5 cm	10.02 cm	0.38
St. Deviation TB				0.812	0.590	0.591
QH	7 years	mare	right	23.4 cm	8.72 cm^2	0.37
QH	2 years	mare	right	24.6 cm	7.60 cm^2	0.31
QH	6 years	gelding	right	25.5 cm^2	9.34 cm^2	0.37
QH	8 years	gelding	left	24.3 cm	9.29 cm^2	0.38
QH	10 years	gelding	left	24.7 cm	8.58 cm^2	0.34
Mean QH				25.4 cm	8.71 cm^2	0.35
St. Deviation QH				0.758	0.704	0.704
Mean Total #				25.4 cm	9.29 cm^2	0.36
St. Deviation Total				1.283	0.924	0.026
SCI wild mare	15 years	mare	right	22.9 cm	8.94 cm^2	0.36

TB = Thoroughbred; QH = Quarter Horse.

Comparison of the metacarpal length of the deceased SCI mare to that of Quarter Horses is most significant since Quarter Horse stock was reportedly introduced onto the island in the 1980s (M. Daily, pers. comm. 1996). Thoroughbred metacarpi used in the comparison were substantially longer (Table 4), which underscored the diminution of stature of the island sub-species. The marked decrease in long-bone length may have resulted either from island environmental factors affecting selection or from the genetic influences of the horses brought to the island by early European settlers. Although Inez was the only SCI horse to perish during the study, providing only one sample for comparison, it would appear that her long bones were representative since she appeared to be above average in stature for adults in the island herd (Figure 2). These findings substantiate the obvious phenotypic differences between this island sub-species which is shorter in stature in relation to body size than mainland breeds.

The level of heterozygosity in the Santa Cruz Island horses can be regarded as moderately high, particularly considering the small number of animals, their island isolation and likelihood of inbreeding. Average heterozygosity was 0.61 compared to 0.75 average from 16 domestic breeds and 0.72 from seven feral populations (Bowling 1994). No attempt was made to determine genetic similarity to extant breeds since effects such as small population size; non-random mating or natural selection is likely to have produced significant changes in gene frequency from the founder group. The Santa Cruz Island horses should be considered to provide a collection of genes that has been selected for survival under conditions present in this particular habitat.

Figure 2. Phenotypical Santa Cruz Island wild horses (Inez is mare in the foreground guarding foal in grass).

That collection may be a valuable resource in the future for traits presently undefined that may have been lost in the modern studbook of recorded breeds.

The survival rates of the SCI wild horses during this study (adults 98% and first-year foals 100%) were remarkably higher than reported average survival rates in 18 other wild herds in six states (California, Colorado, Idaho, Nevada, Utah, and Wyoming) (Journal of Range Management 1980). Estimates of first-year survival rate ranged from 50 to 70%; adult survival rates ranged from 80 to 85%. The seasonally sparse availability of grasses, harsher climactic conditions, and potential presence of predators in the other herds studied may be responsible for the markedly lower survival rates. In spite of competition of approximately 3,000 feral sheep, the abundant grasslands, relatively mild climactic conditions, and absence of predators on Santa Cruz Island provided an optimal habitat for the horse herd.

CONCLUSIONS

Abundant suitable habitat within an isolated island environment resulted in a wild horse herd remarkable in seven ways: 1) timing of reproductive cycling in winter months in spite of photoperiod, 2) high harem stability of 93.8%, 3) low conspecific competition, 4) high adult (98%) and foal (100%) survival rate, 5) shorter long bone (metacarpal) length, 6) increased cross-sectional area (thickness) of metacarpi and 7) high level of general health.

LITERATURE CITED

de LaGuerra Ord, A. 1956. Occurrences in Hispanic California. MCMLVI Academy of American Franciscan History 5401 West Cedar Ln., Washington, DC.

Anonymous. 1980. Journal of Range Management 33(5):354-360.

Augustine, D. J. and S. J. McNaughton. 1998. Ungulate effects on the functional species composition of plant communities: herbivore selectivity and plant tolerance. Journal of Wildlife Management 62(4):1165-1183.

Bowling, A. T. 1994. Population genetics of Great Basin feral horses. Animal Genetics 25(1):67-74.

Bowling, A. T., M. L. Eggleston-Stott, G. Byrnes, R. S. Clark, S. Dileanis and E. Wictum. 1997. Validation of microsatellite markers for routine horse parentage testing. Animal Genetics 28:247-252.

Bowling, A. T. and R. S. Clark. 1985. Blood group and protein polymorphism gene frequencies for seven breeds of horses in the United States. Animal Blood Groups and Biochemical Genetics 16:93-108.

Bowling, A. T. and R. W. Touchberry. 1990. Parentage of Great Basin feral horses. Journal of Wildlife Management 54(3):424-429.

Coates-Markle, L. In press. Interactions Between Social Ranch and Forage use in Mainland Feral Horses, Oregon State University, Corvallis, OR 97331.

Duncan, P. 1992. Horses and Grasses: nutritional ecology of equids and their impact on the Camague. Springer-Verlag, New York, NY.

Kaseda, Y., K. Nozawa, 1996 Paternity tests with blood types in Misaki feral horses. Animal Science and Technology 67(2):198-203.

Kirkpatrick, J. F., I. M. K. Liu, J. W. Turner, and M. Bernoco. 1991. Antigen recognition in feral mares previously immunized with porcine zonae pellucida. Journal of Reproduction and Fertility. Supplement 44.

Kirkpatrick, J. F., I. M. K. Liu, J. W. Turner Jr., R. Naugle, and R. Keiper. 1992. Long-term effects of porcine zonae pellucidae immunocontraception on ovarian function in feral horses (Equus caballus). Journal of Reproduction and Fertility 94.

McDonnell, S. M., M. M. Lutz, E. H. Ewaskieweiz, and A. Ruducha. 1998. Ontogeny of Sexual Behavior of foals in a Semi-feral Pony Herd (all authors at University of Pennsylvania School of Veterinary Medicine, New Bolton Center, Kennett Square, PA 19348). In press.

Mowrey, R. A. 1993. Mare and Foal Nutrition. North Carolina Cooperative Extension Service. North Carolina State University College of Agriculture & Life Sciences 1-6.

Nunamaker, D. M., D. M. Butterweck, and M. T. Provost. 1989. Some geometric properties of the third metacarpal bone: a comparison between the throughbred and standardbred racehorse. Journal of Biomechanics 22:129-134.

Ovnicek, G., J. B. Erfle, and D. F. Peters. 1995. Wild horse hoof patterns offer a formula for preventing and treating lameness. Pages 258-260 in 41st Annual Proceedings of the American Association of Equine Practitioners Convention.

Piotrowski, G., M. Sullivan, and P. T. Colahan. 1983. Geometric properties of equine metacarpi. Journal of Biomechanics 16(2):129-139.

Rubenstein, D. I. 1981. Behavioural ecology of island feral horses. Equine Veterinary Journal 13(1):27-34.

Stevens, W. F. 1990. Instability of harems of feral horses in relation to season and presence of subordinate stallions. Behavior 112:3-4,149-161.

Transcript of the Proceedings in Case #176, Andres Castillero vs The United States for the Island of Santa Cruz (1852).

Turner, J. W. and J. F. Kirkpatrick. 1986. Hormones and reporduction in feral horses. Equine Veterinary Science 6(5):250-258.

Wayne, Robert K. 1995. Conservation genetics in the Canidae. Pages 75 to 118 in Avise, J. C. and J. L. Hamrick (eds.), Conservation Genetics; Case Histories from Nature. Chapman & Hall, New York, NY.

SOURCES OF UNPUBLISHED MATERIALS

Daily, M., Santa Cruz Island Foundation, 1010 Anacapa Street, Santa Barbara, CA 93101. Personal communication 1996.

Gherini, F., 162 South "A" Street, Oxnard, CA 93030. Personal observation 1997.

Jensen, D. H., DVM, P.O. Box 798, Los Alamos, CA 93440. Personal communication 1996.

McDonnell, S.M., University of Pennsylvania School of Veterinary Medicine, New Bolton Center, Kennett Square, PA 19348. Personal Communication 1998.

Channel Islands National Park 1901 Spinnaker Dr., Ventura, CA 93001-4354, Personal Communication 1997.

Owens, J., 308 Lion Street, Ojai, CA 93023. Personal Communication 1997.

Turner, J.W., Medical College of Ohio, Department of Physiology and Molecular Medicine, 3000 Arlington Avenue, Toledo, OH 43699-0008. Personal Communication 1997.

THIRTY YEARS OF RESEARCH ON CALIFORNIA'S CHANNEL ISLANDS: AN OVERVIEW AND SUGGESTIONS FOR THE NEXT 30 YEARS

Robert C. Klinger[1,3] and Dirk Van Vuren[2]

[1]The Nature Conservancy, 213 Stearns Wharf, Santa Barbara, California 93101
(805) 962-9111, E-mail: rckscip@aol.com
[2]Department of Wildlife, Fish, and Conservation Biology, University of California, Davis, 95616
(530) 752-4181, E-mail: dhvanvuren@ucdavis.edu
[3] Current Address: Section of Evolution and Ecology, University of California, Davis, CA 95616
(530) 752-1092, E-mail: rcklinger@ucdavis.edu

ABSTRACT

In the 32 years since the publication of the first symposium on the biology of the California Islands, there have been distinct stages that have emphasized different aspects of the biology and management of the islands. Using papers published in the proceedings, we describe these different stages in relation to broader contemporary themes in ecology, evolution, and conservation, and comment on how these themes may have shaped island research agendas. We compare and contrast earlier research on the islands to what is currently underway, then make suggestions on how greater coordination and integration of academic and management studies can lead to a broader understanding of California Island ecosystems, and unify conceptual themes for research and management across the eight islands.

Keywords: Anthropology, archaeology, biogeography, botany, California Islands, Channel Islands, conservation, ecology, evolution, geology, islands, research, zoology.

INTRODUCTION

The four symposia on the California Islands (Philbrick 1967; Power 1980b; Hochberg 1993; Halvorson and Maender 1994) represent an impressive collection of scientific information that spans a period of rapid and significant evolution of thought in the physical and biological sciences. In the more than 30 years since the first symposium on the California Islands was held, major conceptual and technological advances in the physical and biological sciences have occurred at a startling rate. In his introduction to the second symposium, Power (1980a) noted that in the 13 years since the first symposium there had been major changes in scientific concepts and techniques. These included the way scientists perceived the dynamic nature of biological and geological systems, the ways which taxonomic relationships could be tested and represented, and how computers were starting to be used to help analyze large and unwieldy data sets. Since Power's observations, not only have we seen these concepts and techniques increase in sophistication but also new ones have continued to be developed. For example,

relatively simple concepts of ecological succession have been largely superseded by more complex patch dynamic/disturbance driven mechanisms of community change (Pickett and White 1985), concepts of the dynamic equilibrium of island biogeography are now nested within the framework of metapopulations (Hanski and Gilpin 1997), the taxonomy and systematics of many groups of organisms are being revised based on analyses done at the genetic level (e.g., Burns 1998; Steppan 1998), and the cyclical nature of some populations is seen as a special case of more complex spatial and temporal patterns of population change (Korprimaki and Krebs 1996; Rohner and Krebs 1998).

Just as scientific techniques and concepts have evolved, so have ownership status, land use activities and management priorities on the islands. The National Park Service designated the Northern Channel Islands as a National Park, assumed management of San Miguel Island from the U.S. Navy, and bought Santa Rosa Island and part of Santa Cruz Island. The Nature Conservancy acquired ownership of the western 90% of Santa Cruz Island, and land use on Santa Catalina Island shifted away from ranching and hunting to ecological preservation and restoration. The U.S. Navy started an active natural resource management program on San Nicolas and San Clemente islands. And, as the human population of southern California has expanded, so have direct and indirect impacts to the islands associated with this growth. One result of these changes is that the physical and biological systems on the islands are also changing, and this has resulted in an increasing amount of research on a wider variety of topics.

In this paper we take an overview of the last 30 years of research on the California Islands. Our primary goal is to identify patterns in how research on the islands has evolved and characterize the dynamic nature of this intellectual evolution. By relating these changes to contemporary developments in scientific concepts, we can begin to identify significant gaps in our knowledge of particular processes or groups of organisms, and hopefully create a foundation for guiding research into the next 30 years.

METHODS

We based our analysis on a summary of the contents of the four previously published symposia (Philbrick 1967; Power 1980b; Hochberg 1993; Halvorson and Maender 1994). We limited the scope of our analysis to papers published in the four symposia because they are the only body of work that collectively represents the dynamic nature of research on the islands. Papers published in refereed journals or in special proceedings on specific topics (e.g. entomology, Menke and Miller 1985) are most likely not representative of the scope of research being conducted on the islands.

We tallied the number of papers and authors from the proceedings of each symposium. The affiliations of all co-authors on a paper were classified as Academic, Museum (including botanic gardens), Government, and Private (non-public trust organizations such as The Nature Conservancy or Catalina Island Conservancy, consulting businesses, etc.). Multiple publications by authors were treated independently.

We used all papers published in the first four symposia to define two sets of categories. The first was a set of seven general subject groupings, each defining a particular area of natural or cultural science that we felt best described the content of the paper. These categories included Anthropology (research focused on cultural systems predating European settlement of the islands), Botany (research focused on terrestrial and marine plants), Conservation (research focused on the preservation of natural resources), Ecosystem Processes (research focused on the relationship between physical and biological systems, and involving organisms spanning different phylogenetic kingdoms), Geology (research focused on earth structure/history), History (research focused on recent cultural systems), and Zoology (research focused on terrestrial and marine animals).

Next, we categorized papers into 11 groups based on the concept that we felt best described the content of the paper. These included Anthropology (same definition as above), Community Ecology (studies on patterns in the interrelationships of multiple species and the processes driving these patterns), Comparative/Descriptive Ecology (natural history observations or patterns for multiple species, but not analyzing the interrelationships among the species or the processes driving the patterns), Conservation Biology (studies focused on the preservation of natural systems, communities, and species), Ecosystem Processes (same definition as above), History (same definition as above), Island Biogeography (studies focused on factors determining species distribution, abundance, and persistence on the islands, and usually relative to the mainland), Paleontology (studies focused on the geologic record of organisms on the islands), Physical Geology (studies focused on geological processes, structure, and history of the islands), Population Biology/Ecology (studies focused on the ecology of individual species), and Systematics/Evolution (classification and evolution of organisms).

The classification scheme we used for the papers is admittedly subjective, but we feel it captures the most significant areas of research in the islands over the last four decades. Some of the categories we used to classify the papers overlap to a degree (for example, Comparative/Descriptive Ecology and Population Biology/Ecology), and we recognize that legitimate justification could be made for inclusion of some papers into more than one category. However, we did not encounter this situation very frequently.

RESULTS

The number of papers increased 153% from the first to the second symposia, but increased only 9% from the second to the third and 6% from the third to the fourth (Table 1). The number of authors increased 175% from the first to the second symposia, 18% from the second to the third, and 17% from the third to the fourth. Authorship was dominated by academics in the first two symposia (almost 90%) but decreased in the third and fourth (55% and 52% respectively). The percentage of authors affiliated with government organizations increased steadily with each symposium, while the percentage of authors affiliated with museums fluctuated from 7 to 17% (Figure 1). Authors from private organizations did not appear on any papers in the first two symposia, but comprised 14 to 17% in the last two symposia.

In terms of general subject categories, botany and zoology dominated the first and second symposia (76% and 71% respectively), but decreased 25 to 50% in the third and fourth symposia, although they still made up a higher proportion of papers than other categories (Table 1). Zoology papers dominated the second and third symposia. The percentage of papers on anthropology doubled in the last two symposia compared with the first two symposia, while the percentage of papers on geology remained relatively constant, except for a drop in the second symposium. The percentage of papers addressing conservation issues increased three to five fold in the fourth symposium compared with the first three symposia. History as a subject first appeared in the third symposium, and the percentage of papers in this

Table 1. The number of papers in seven subject categories published in the proceedings of the four California Islands symposia, 1967-1994.

Subject Category	Symposium				
	1st	2nd	3rd	4th	Total
Anthropology	1	2	5	5	13
Botany	7	7	6	7	27
Conservation	0	2	3	11	16
Ecosystems	0	5	2	4	11
Geology	3	3	7	7	20
History	0	0	3	5	8
Zoology	6	24	21	11	62
Total	17	43	47	50	157

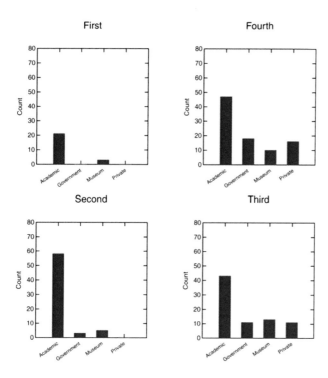

Figure 1. The organizational affiliation of authors of papers published in the proceedings of the four California Islands symposia, 1976-1994.

Table 2. The number of papers in eleven conceptual categories published in the proceedings of the four California Islands Symposia, 1967 - 1994.

Subject Category	Symposium				
	1st	2nd	3rd	4th	Total
Anthropology	1	2	5	5	13
Community Ecology	2	0	6	3	11
Conservation Biology	0	0	3	11	14
Descriptive Ecology	4	8	9	4	25
Ecosystems	0	6	1	6	13
Evolution	3	8	2	1	14
Geology	4	2	5	7	18
History	0	0	3	5	8
Island Biogeography	2	7	1	1	11
Paleontology	0	4	2	1	7
Population Biology	1	5	10	7	23
Total	17	43	47	50	157

category almost doubled from the third to the fourth symposia. A relatively low percentage of papers dealing with ecosystem processes appeared in the last three symposia.

Studies on marine organisms and invertebrates have shown an overall increase. Of the seven botany papers in the first symposium, two looked at components of the marine environment. Two of the six papers on zoology in the first symposium focused on marine animals, while 14 papers in the second symposium were related to marine organisms; proportionally this is about the same as in the first (about 25%). Only one botany paper dealing with marine organisms appeared in the third symposia, but in the fourth symposium three papers addressed marine plants directly and another three had aspects of marine plants incorporated in them. Sixteen papers in the third symposium were focused on marine animals, while only seven did in the fourth symposium.

There were very clear shifts between the four symposia in the 11 groups we used to describe the conceptual content of the paper (Table 2). In the first two symposia, island biogeography, evolution, and descriptive ecology made up about half of all of the papers presented. However, by the third and fourth symposia, island biogeography and evolution comprised less than 6% of the papers. About 20% of the papers in the third symposium were in the descriptive ecology category, but these fell to about 7% in the fourth symposium. The proportion of papers dealing with paleontology, ecosystem processes, and community ecology fluctuated widely among the four symposia, and in no discernible pattern. No papers on conservation biology appeared in

the first two symposia, but increased dramatically between the third and fourth ones. The proportion of papers on population biology increased two to four fold during the first three symposia, then declined about 50% from the third to the fourth symposia. With the exception of the second symposium, the proportion of papers on geology ranged from 10 to 23%. Although the proportion of papers on anthropology and history has never exceed 10% in any one symposium, the proportion has doubled in the third and fourth symposia when compared with the first two.

DISCUSSION

The symposia on the California Islands represent one of the more long-term and comprehensive collections of information on any area of the world. What makes this body of knowledge all the more impressive is that there has been no one single theme, process, or organism that has served to unify the tremendous variety of work being done on the islands. Also, there has been no formal group of people whose primary responsibility was seeing that the data were coordinated and presented professionally on a regular basis. Instead, it has been the nature of the islands themselves, and the multitude of issues associated with them, that has attracted so many scientists for so many years to devote themselves to bring about an understanding of the system, and consequently a better understanding of nature in general. Consequently, it has been the efforts of numerous dedicated people from many different organizations who have managed to find funding, and the time, to organize a forum and publish the results for most of the ongoing work in the islands.

The major patterns we observed among the four California Islands symposia reflect the evolution of scientific concepts, changes in ownership and management of the islands, and recognition of the influence of human use on the island's natural systems. The shifts that can be seen in the relative importance of different disciplines, concepts, and organizational affiliation of the authors all demonstrate these changes.

The clearest example of a dramatic shift in scientific thinking is away from the "islands as natural laboratories" philosophy which dominated the period from the 1960s through the early 1980s. Island biology has evolved beyond simply describing natural patterns and processes to increased interest in preserving island resources. Over the last 10 to 15 years conservation biology has emerged as an identifiable discipline, and as a result the "natural laboratory" philosophy has been modified and transformed into focusing on conserving the unique species and natural communities on the islands.

In the first two symposia, the dominant themes were evolution and island biogeography. This reflected the general interest in the type of adaptations characteristic of island populations (Carlquist 1974), and how these adaptations evolved. Similarly, the concept of island biogeography was one of the major ecological and evolutionary paradigms of the 1960s and 1970s (MacArthur and Wilson 1967). Of major importance in this shift in philosophy is that the theory of island biogeography has declined in importance as a freestanding paradigm (Hanski and Gilpin 1997). Although it served as the foundation for an increase in the theory and practice of conservation (Simberloff 1988; Shafer 1990), the underlying concepts of classical island biogeography have been absorbed and modified by other ideas and concepts in ecology and conservation biology. From a theoretical standpoint it is now generally considered as a variation of metapopulation dynamics within the context of fragmented habitats and populations (Harrison 1994; Hanski and Simberloff 1997). From a practical standpoint there has been an increased recognition that dispersal among many isolated populations at the landscape level is probably more important in the persistence of most species than classical immigration-extinction processes (Wiens 1997). Although there is still substantial interest in evolutionary adaptations of island populations, the functional context in which the species exist has taken on great importance, as has the importance of their conservation (Vitousek et al 1995).

Of note is the increase in the diversity of topics over the last 30 years. This has been especially true for studies on the marine environment, invertebrates, and the history of human cultures on the islands. Studies on marine organisms and systems increased in both scope and complexity, and by the fourth symposium an entire section was devoted to studies on the marine environment. Similarly, a very large component of the third symposium focused on invertebrates, a group of organisms that had not been well represented in the previous two symposia.

The first two symposia had a very small proportion of papers dealing directly with the patterns, trends, and impacts of human use on the islands. While the emphasis of the third and fourth symposia still remained natural science, the proportion of papers dealing with human culture has substantially increased. An excellent example of the importance of maintaining this interdisciplinary approach is Glassow's (1993) paper on archaeological evidence of long-term climate change on the northern islands.

The importance of ownership and land management on the types and emphasis of scientific research on the islands should not be underestimated. To varying degrees, the National Park Service, The Nature Conservancy, the Catalina Island Conservancy, the National Oceanic and Atmospheric Administration, and the U.S. Navy all have the protection and restoration of the biological diversity of the lands and waters of the islands they own as a management goal. In addition, various county, state and federal agencies have regulatory authority and responsibility on the islands. As ownership and land management on the islands changed over the last 30 years, so did the nature of some of the research. It is likely that the increase in the proportion of non-academic authors and increased emphasis on topics related to resource conservation are directly related to these ownership and land management changes.

A dominant theme of the early symposia was descriptive ecology. The collection of basic life history observations is a typical first step in the scientific process. This was probably facilitated by increased accessibility to the islands as a result of the changes in ownership and land use practices, as well as establishment of field stations for scientific research on Santa Cruz and Santa Catalina islands. However, in the fourth symposium papers dealing with descriptive ecology dropped by 65% from the previous three meetings. It would be unfortunate to see this trend continue because our knowledge of the basic life history of the majority of species on the islands needs further work, especially for many of the rare and/or endemic species.

Knowledge of the life history patterns of the plant and animal species on the islands is important from both scientific and management perspectives. For example, without these data scientists will not be able to compare the life history strategies of endemic and non-endemic species, or analyze how adaptations of island species evolved relative to conspecifics on the mainland. Two recent examples point out the importance for resource management of having basic life history information. Since the last symposium, over a dozen endemic plants on the northern Channel Islands have been listed as threatened or endangered by the U.S. Fish and Wildlife Service, and island foxes (*Urocyon littoralis*) on San Miguel and possibly Santa Cruz islands have undergone severe population declines (Coonan et al. 1998). The conservation of these species will depend directly on an understanding of their basic life history (e.g., reproductive biology, recruitment and mortality patterns, age structure, distribution, habitat requirements, diet).

We found it interesting that of the four symposia only the first had a stated focus (Philbrick 1967). Understanding how the subjects of research on the islands have changed over the last 30 years not only enables us to evaluate what has been done, but to also identify what hasn't been done. This in turn can lead to the development of a framework that could help to integrate and coordinate research among the islands over the course of the next 30 years. Not only would this be an effective step in the process of synthesizing a cohesive understanding of different ecological and evolutionary processes across the islands, but it would give resource managers an extensive database for developing, monitoring, and evaluating management programs. As an initial step in developing a research framework for the islands, we propose four general suggestions that we feel would be useful for optimizing the use of scientific expertise and resources.

Our first suggestion is, whenever possible, to set research and management projects in an appropriate theoretical framework. For example, despite an overall increase in the diversity of topics and the number of papers and authors, many important concepts in the fields of ecology, evolution, and conservation biology have been neglected in publications in the symposia. Some concepts that have direct importance to the islands include metapopulations, disturbance and patch dynamics, community assembly processes, the biology of small populations (Viable Population Theory), and landscape ecology. Studies focused around these concepts would give a theoretical foundation and empirical unity to a large array of potential research projects among the islands. For example, because of the many rare species on the islands, it would be worthwhile to identify which ones (if any) demonstrate metapopulation dynamics, or determine which ones are at risk from different deterministic or stochastic processes (e.g., habitat alteration, demographic stochasticity, etc.). Similarly, with the ongoing removal of feral animals and livestock, studies that focused on how species within the communities reassemble themselves against a backdrop of deterministic successional processes and stochastic disturbance events would have importance from both academic and practical perspectives.

Our second suggestion is that genetic, demographic, and evolutionary studies of rare populations be linked across all of the islands. The demographic trends should be collected over long time periods (>10 years) and associated closely with levels of genetic diversity and environmental variability (e.g., weather, habitat changes). Some aspects of this have been underway for several years (R. Klinger, unpubl. data; D. Wilken and K. McEachern, pers. comm.), but there is a need to initiate studies in a coordinated program across more islands. Ongoing and residual impacts from the degradation and loss of habitat from overgrazing by feral and domestic livestock will continue to occur on the islands for many years. Identifying which species are most at risk from particular impacts will be a tremendous tool for protecting or restoring these species, as well as contributing to a greater understanding of the biology of rare species.

Third, we recommend the continuation of basic life history studies of both plant and animal species. Basic data to collect would include distribution, habitat occurrence, relative abundance among habitat types, and reproductive patterns. Because it is unrealistic to expect to obtain detailed information on many species in a meaningful period of time,

we advocate a prioritization procedure based on species diversity within taxa, ecological importance, and management significance. For instance, there are relatively few species of herptiles and terrestrial mammals, so these species would be relatively high in priority. Among these species, the island spotted skunk (*Spilogale putorius littoralis*) is one of only two mammalian terrestrial predators on the islands, it only occurs on two islands, and it is thought to be low in abundance (Crooks and Van Vuren 1994). Based on the above criteria, spotted skunks would be a high priority species. Some alien plants such as fennel (*Foeniculum vulgare*), horehound (*Marrubium vulgare*), and milk thistle (*Silybum marianum*) would also be high priority because of their management significance.

Our final suggestion is that ecosystem studies based on resource monitoring programs be used as ways of integrating community and single species studies at multiple scales. Dramatic changes in the island's plant and animal communities can be expected to occur as different land management programs are phased out and others implemented. Relating these changes to biotic and abiotic variables at multiple scales will not only increase our understanding of how different ecological processes operate at different scales, but will provide resource managers with the basic data needed to prioritize, design and evaluate management programs in a specific ecological context (Klinger 1998). The most comprehensive monitoring program in the islands is that of Channel Islands National Park (Davis et al. 1994), and we recommend that many of the protocols they have developed be adopted on all of the islands.

Of importance in this discussion is a mechanism for implementing these suggestions. Of obvious importance are funding and personnel, but less obvious is how to structure and coordinate these programs among so many different organizations. Although proposing a detailed structure that deals with these issues is beyond the scope of this paper, we do offer some initial suggestions.

Probably the most important step is to expand the scope of activities of the Channel Islands Research Coordinating Committee (CIRCC). This group was originally set up as a steering committee for meetings, and as a way of disseminating information among the various agencies and organizations conducting research on the islands. Representatives from most of the organizations and agencies participate in CIRCC, and the more or less annual updates on respective research and management activities have been effective. However, CIRCC has never developed a process to truly coordinate research among the agencies. We propose that CIRCC hold a series of meetings to identify key ecological issues and questions common to all the islands, develop protocols for addressing the issues in an integrated program, and jointly present these recommendations to each organization and agency.

Funding is always a difficulty, but several groups exist that could possibly be useful in securing both private and public funding for research and management programs. The Friends of the Channel Islands (Park Service), Friends of

Santa Cruz Island (The Nature Conservancy), and the Santa Cruz Island Foundation have all been set up to support various research and management activities on the islands. Coordinating these groups with fund raising activities of various local organizations such as the University of California, Santa Barbara Museum of Natural History, and Santa Barbara Botanic Garden could provide valuable leverage in securing funds for coordinated, multi-island projects.

Over the last 30 years, a large amount of research has been done on the islands, which is a credit to the many scientists, students, and managers who have conducted the work. But research questions and resource management issues have become increasingly complex, expensive and varied. Just as the emphasis on different concepts and subjects has shifted over the years in the California Islands, so must the way we approach studying and managing the islands. We believe the time is right to introduce a programmatic approach to some of the ecological and conservation issues that are common to all of the islands. While not discouraging independent research, we think that focusing resources and effort in a coordinated, multi-island approach will deepen our understanding of certain ecological and evolutionary patterns and processes. In turn, we believe using this approach will build on the solid foundation of research done over the last four decades, and lead to more effective management of the natural and cultural resources of the islands.

LITERATURE CITED

Burns, K. J. 1998. Molecular phylogenetics of the genus *Piranga*: implications for biogeography and the evolution of morphology and behavior. Auk 115:621-634.

Carlquist, S. 1974. Island biology. Columbia University Press, New York, NY.

Coonan, T. J., G. Austin, and C. Schwemm. 1998. Status and trend of island fox, San Miguel Island, Channel Islands National Park. Channel Islands National Park Tech. Rep. 98-01. 27 pp.

Crooks, K. R. and D. Van Vuren. 1994. Conservation of the island spotted skunk and island fox in a recovering island ecosystem. Pages 379-386 *in* Halvorson, W. L. and G.J. Maender (eds.), The Fourth California Islands Symposium: Update on the Status of Resources. Santa Barbara Museum of Natural History, Santa Barbara, CA.

Davis, G. E., K. R. Faulkner, and W.L . Halvorson. 1994. Ecological monitoring in Channel Islands National Park, California. Pages 465-484 *in* Halvorson, W. L. and G. J. Maender (eds.), The Fourth California Islands Symposium: Update on the Status of Resources. Santa Barbara Museum of Natural History, Santa Barbara, CA.

Glassow, M. A. 1993. The occurrence of red abalone shells in Northern Channel Island archaeological middens: implications for climatic reconstruction. Pages 567-578 *in* Hochberg, F. G. (ed.) The Third California Islands Symposium: Recent Advances in Research on the California Islands. Santa Barbara Museum of Natural History, Santa Barbara, CA.

Halvorson, W. L., and G. J. Maender. (eds.), 1994. The Fourth California Islands Symposium: Update on the Status of Resources. Santa Barbara Museum of Natural History, Santa Barbara, CA.

Hanski, I. A. and M. E. Gilpin (eds.). 1997. Metapopulation Biology: Ecology, Genetics, and Evolution. Academic Press, San Diego, CA.

Hanski, I. A. , and D. Simberloff. 1997. Pages 5-26 *in* Hanski, I. A. and M. E. Gilpin (eds.), Metapopulation Biology: Ecology, Genetics, and Evolution. Academic Press, San Diego, CA.

Harrison, S. 1994. Metapopulations and conservation. Pages 111-128 *in* Edwards, P.J., N.R. Webb and R.M. May (eds.), Large-Scale Ecology and Biology. Blackwell, Oxford.

Hochberg, F. G. (ed.), 1993. The Third California Islands Symposium: Recent Advances in Research on the California Islands. Santa Barbara Museum of Natural History, Santa Barbara, CA.

Klinger, R. C. 1998. Santa Cruz Island monitoring program. Volume 1: Vegetation communities 1991-95 report. The Nature Conservancy, Santa Barbara, CA. 59 pp.

Koprimaki, E., and C. J. Krebs. 1996. Predation and population cycles in small mammals. Bioscience 46:754-764.

MacArthur, R. H. and E. O. Wilson. 1967. The Theory of Island Biogeography. Princeton University Press, Princeton, NJ.

Menke, A. and D. Miller. 1985. Entomology of the California Channel Islands. Santa Barbara Museum of Natural History, Santa Barbara, CA.

Philbrick, R. N. (ed.), 1967. Proceedings of the Symposium on the Biology of the California Islands. Santa Barbara Botanic Garden, Santa Barbara, CA.

Pickett, S. T. A. and P. S. White (eds.). 1985. The Ecology of Natural Disturbance and Patch Dynamics. Academic Press, NY.

Power, D. M. 1980a. Preface *to* The California Islands: Proceedings of a Multidisciplinary Symposium. Santa Barbara Museum of Natural History, Santa Barbara, CA.

Power, D. M. (ed.), 1980b. The California Islands: Proceedings of a Multidisciplinary Symposium. Santa Barbara Museum of Natural History, Santa Barbara, CA.

Rohner, C. and C. J. Krebs. 1998. Response of great horned owls to experimental "hot spots" of snowshoe hare density. Auk 115:694-705.

Shafer, C. L. 1990. Nature Reserves: Island Theory and Conservation Practice. Smithsonian Institution Press, Washington, DC.

Simberloff, D. 1988. The contribution of population and community ecology to conservation science. Annual Review of Ecology and Systematics 19:473-511.

Steppan, S. J. 1998. Phylogenetic relationships and species limits within *Phyllotis* (Rodentia: Sigmodontidae): concordance between mtDNA sequence and morphology. J. Mammal. 79:573-593.

Vitousek, P. M., L. L. Loope, and H. Adsersen (eds.), 1995. Islands: Biological Diversity and Ecosystem Function. Springer-Verlag, Berlin.

Wiens, J. A. 1997. Metapopulation dynamics and landscape ecology. Pages 43-68 *in* Hanski, I. A. and M. E. Gilpin (eds.), Metapopulation Biology: Ecology, Genetics, and Evolution. Academic Press, San Diego, CA.

SOURCES OF UNPUBLISHED MATERIALS

McEachern, Kathryn. Biological Resources Division, U.S. Geological Survey. Channel Islands National Park, 1901 Spinnaker Drive, Ventura, California, 93001. Personal Communication 1996.

Wilken, Dieter. Santa Barbara Botanic Garden. 1212 Mission Canyon Road, Santa Barbara, California, 93105. Personal Communication 1996.

ISLAND CONSERVATION ACTION IN NORTHWEST MÉXICO

C. Josh Donlan[1,2], Bernie R. Tershy[1,4], Brad S. Keitt[1,3], Bill Wood[1], José Ángel Sánchez[5], Anna Weinstein[1], Donald A. Croll[1,4], Miguel Ángel Hermosillo[5], and José Luis Aguilar[6]

[1] Island Conservation and Ecology Group, P. O. Box 141, Davenport, CA 95107
(831) 469-8651, FAX (831) 469-8651, E-mail: jdonlan@cats.ucsc.edu
[2] Dept. of Biology, A-316 E.M.S. Building, University of California, Santa Cruz, CA 95064
(831) 459-4581, FAX (831) 459-4882
[3] Dept. of Ocean Sciences, A-316 E.M.S. Building, University of California, Santa Cruz, CA 95064
(831) 459-4581, FAX (831) 459-4882
[4] Institute of Marine Sciences, A-316 E.M.S. Building, University of California, Santa Cruz, CA 95064
(831) 459-3610, FAX (831) 459-4882
[5] Grupo de Ecología y Conservación de Islas A. C., AP 71, Guerrero Negro, Baja California Sur 23940 México
011-52 (115) 7-11-20, FAX 011-52 (115) 7-11-20
[6] Departamento de Áreas Naturales Protegidas, Secretaría del Medio Ambiente
Recursos Naturales y Pesca, Delegación Baja California. Privada Riviera # 1-A,
Conjunto PRONAF, Zona Centro. Ensenada, Baja California 763510 México
011-52 (617) 6-35-10, FAX 011-52-(617) 6-09-77

ABSTRACT

Introduced mammals are present on many of the over 230 islands and islets in northwest México. Introduced mammals threaten many endemic species with extinction: of the 19 island vertebrate extinctions in northwest México, 18 can be attributed to introduced mammals. Over the past four years the Universidad Nacional Autónoma de México (UNAM) and the Island Conservation and Ecology Group (ICEG) have worked with Mexican government agencies (Mexican Office of National Protected Areas of Secretaría del Medio Ambiente Recursos Naturales y Pesca (SEMARNAP), Vizcaíno Biosphere Reserve, and the Gulf of California Islands Reserve) and local Mexican fishing cooperatives to protect island ecosystems. These collaborations have resulted in introduced mammal removal projects on nine islands in the region. Introduced mammals have been removed from nine islands: feral cats from Isabel, Asunción and Coronado Norte Islands; feral cats and rats from Isla San Roque; rats from Isla Rasa; goats and sheep from Isla Natividad; feral cats and rabbits from Isla Todos Santos Sur; and goats and burros from the Islas San Benito Oeste and Medio. Additional removal projects are currently in progress: feral cats from Isla Natividad and rats from Isla Isabel. To aid in the systematic prioritization of islands for conservation action and guide research activities, we have developed an island conservation relational database for the northwest México region that is available over the Internet via the World Wide Web at: http://islandconservation.org.

Keywords: Baja California, introduced mammals, endemic, extinction, seabirds, rats, cats, goats, rabbits, burros, relational database.

INTRODUCTION

Islands cover 2.7% of the earth's surface (AMNH 1998). Islands around the world are of critical importance to global biodiversity because they are rich in endemic species and important breeding areas for many wide-ranging marine animals (e.g., sea turtles, seabirds, and marine mammals). Furthermore, islands are natural habitat fragments to which species and communities have adapted. Unlike manmade habitat fragments in continental protected areas, natural ecological and evolutionary processes can persist on protected islands without intensive management. Thus by conserving island ecosystems, both significant biological diversity and important ecosystem processes are preserved with minimal land requirements (Tershy and Croll 1994).

The most serious threat to islands worldwide is the introduction of nonnative plants and animals. The majority of recorded animal extinctions (75%) have been on islands and most of these island extinctions can be attributed to introduced species (Diamond 1989; Groombridge 1992). Plants show a similar pattern: of the 250 plant species listed in the 1978 International Union for Conservation of Nature and Natural Resources Plant Red Data Book, 96 (38%) are from islands and many of these plants are threatened by introduced species (IUCN 1978). In addition to direct effects, introduced species can also lead to numerous indirect effects, which can have dramatic consequences on island communities and ecosystems (Elton 1958; Moors 1985; Mooney and Drake 1986; Cushman 1995).

There are over 230 islands and islets in northwest (NW) México. Overall, these islands harbor considerable biodiversity, including a wide taxonomic range of endemics (Huey 1964; Avise 1974; Soulé and Sloan 1966; Soulé and Yang 1973; Cody et al. 1983, Lawlor 1983; Murphy 1983;

Grismer 1993). These islands are considered by some bio-geographers to be one of the most ecologically intact non-polar archipelagos in the world (Case and Cody 1983). Despite this, introduced plants and animals threaten many of the region's island ecosystems. For example, the introduced iceplant *Mesembryanthemum crystallinum* and the introduced annual *Malva parviflora* have become common or dominant plants on some of the region's islands (Junak and Philbrick 1994a, 1994b, 1999; J. Donlan, pers. obs. 1998). Introduced mammals are responsible for 18 of the 19 animal extinctions that have taken place on islands in NW México (ICEG, unpublished 1998). Introduced mammals are present on at least 39 islands in NW México (ICEG, unpublished 1998). The most common nonnative mammals in this region include black rats (*Rattus rattus*), Norway rats (*Rattus norvegicus*), cats (*Felis catus*), dogs (*Canis familiaris*), european rabbits (*Oryctolagus cuniculus*), goats (*Capra hirca*), and burros (*Equus asinus*).

A number of groups have participated in introduced species removal projects on islands in NW México: the Mexican Office of National Protected Areas (ANP) of the Secretaría del Medio Ambiente Recursos Naturales y Pesca (SEMARNAP), Instituto Nacional de Ecología (INE), Universidad Nacional Autónoma de México (UNAM), Gulf of California Islands Reserve, Delegación SEMARNAP of Baja California, and the Island Conservation and Ecology Group/Grupo de Ecología y Conservación de Islas (ICEG/GECI). In this paper, we first review past and present introduced mammal removal projects in this region, with an emphasis on the projects of ICEG. We then discuss a recently developed island conservation database. This relational database, developed by ICEG, compiles relevant conservation data for islands in the region to help prioritize conservation action.

INTRODUCED SPECIES REMOVAL IN NORTHWEST MÉXICO

Gulf of California

Isla Rasa

The fall of 1994 marked the beginning of introduced species eradication on the islands of NW México. Jesús Ramírez (Centro de Ecología, UNAM) in conjunction with Enriqueta Velarde (INE) started the removal of Norway rats (*R. norvegicus*) and house mice (*Mus musculus*) from Isla Rasa (60 ha) in the central Gulf of California (Figure 1). Following techniques developed in New Zealand, Ramírez worked with a large team of undergraduate and community volunteers to set bait stations filled with Talon Weatherblock (0.05% brodifacoum). The bait stations were maintained for one year on this uninhabited island.

The eradication effort was successful; the island has been free of introduced mammals for over three years. Isla Rasa is one of the most important seabird colonies in North America with more than 90% of the global populations of

Figure 1. Islands in northwest México where introduced species have been removed or are currently being removed.

elegant terns (*Sterna elegans*) and Heermann's gulls (*Larus heermanni*). An estimated 360,000 gulls and terns breed on this small island between March and June (Velarde and Anderson 1994). Guano miners introduced rats and mice at the turn of the century. While rats and mice had minor impacts on the gulls and terns, they are possibly responsible for the absence of nocturnal hole and crevice nesting birds such as the Craveri's murrelet (*Synthliboramphus craveri*), black storm-petrels (*Oceanodroma melania*), least storm-petrels (*O. microsoma*), and black-vented shearwaters (*Puffinus opisthomelas*). Isla Rasa was the first island in NW México to receive protected status (in 1964) and since then has been a conservation success story.

Isla Isabel

Cristina Rodríguez Juarez and Hugh Drummond (Centro de Ecología, UNAM) led a program to remove cats and black rats (*R. rattus*) from Isla Isabel (98 ha) located at the mouth of the Gulf of California (Figure 1). This island, off the Pacific coast of the state of Nayarit, was once the largest sooty tern (*Sterna fuscata*) colony in México; however, over the last 60 years cat predation has decreased the size of the colony considerably. Feral cats prey on these terns as well as the native lizards *Sceloporus clarcki* and *Cnemidophorus costatus* (Rodríguez Juarez 1998).

Some 600 cats were removed from Isla Isabel between 1995 and 1998. Both poisoning, trapping, and hunting were used to remove cats from the island. As of winter 1999, the island appeared to be free of cats. Rats were poisoned using Talon Weatherblock. However, rat removal has not been successful due to native land crabs consuming much of the rat bait (invertebrates are not affected by Talon; Rodríguez Juarez 1998). Alternative methods for rat removal are being investigated.

Pacific Islands

Isla Coronado Norte

The Los Coronados Islands are located close to the México/U.S. border, approximately 13 km^2 offshore of Tijuana (Figure 1). This island group consist of four rocky islands: Isla Norte, Isla Sur, Isla Medio and a small unnamed islet (combined: 250 ha). While cats were recorded on Isla Coronado Sur as early as 1908 (Wright 1909), they were not introduced onto Isla Coronado Norte until the late 1970s or early 1980s (Everett 1991). However, earlier introductions and natural extirpations are a possibility (McChesney and Tershy, In press). Between 1995 and 1996, the Baja California State Office of ANP and ICEG removed feral cats from Isla Coronado Norte. A total of 22 cats were removed from the island and several subsequent follow-up trips have shown no sign of cat presence.

The impacts of the Isla Coronado Norte cat population on seabirds was substantial (Table 1). Leach's storm-petrel (*Oceanodroma leucorrhoa*) and Cassin's auklet (*Ptychoramphus aleuticus*) colonies have been extirpated from Isla Coronado Norte, most likely from cat predation. Cats are also responsible for the mortality of hundreds of Xantus' murrelets (*Synthliboramphus hypoleucus*) and black storm petrels (*O. melania*) annually (McChesney and Tershy, in press and references therein). In addition to important seabird colonies, Isla Coronado Norte is home to one endemic mammal, two endemic reptiles, and two endemic landbirds (Table 2). Given the diverse diet of feral cats (Jones and Coman 1981; Warner 1985; Churcher and Lawton 1987), it is likely that the feral cat population once prsent on Coronado Norte preyed upon all of these endemics.

Isla Todos Santos Sur

The Todos Santos Islands are located in the Bay of Ensenada 6 km north of Punta Banda, a promontory just south of Ensenada (Figure 1). These two islands are approximately 90 km south of the México/U.S. border. Todos Santos Sur (100 ha) is the larger of the two islands and is inhabited year-round by the abalone aquaculture business, Abulones Cultivados. A building is located on the northeast side of the island and is home to approximately 20 workers. There is also a small structure on the south end of the island used by several lobster fishermen from September to February.

The Todos Santos islands have a long history of introduced species. European rabbits (*O. cuniculus*) were introduced to the South island sometime between 1969 and 1979 (Moran, unpublished, 1979 ref. not seen by authors). Cats were introduced sometime between 1910 and 1923 (Howell 1912; Van Denburgh 1924). Both cats and rabbits were present in large enough numbers to be observed in 1978 and 1987 (Junak and Philbrick 1994a). On Todos Santos Sur, cat predation has been reported on Xantus' murrelets (Van Denburgh 1924; B. Tershy, pers. obs. 1997) and Cassin's auklets (J. Jehl, pers. comm., cited in Tershy and McChesney,

In press). This predation is likely the main cause for the extirpation of these two species from this island (Table 1).

In conjunction with the Baja California State Office of ANP, personnel from the Gulf of California Islands Reserve, and Abulones Cultivados, ICEG began a removal effort for both rabbits and cats on the South Island in November 1997. A combination of trapping and hunting was used to remove both rabbit and cat populations. Over 30 cats and 40 rabbits were removed on Isla Todos Santos Sur between November 1997 and July 1998. There has been no sign of rabbits or cats during several follow-up trips during the fall 1998 and winter 1999. On Todos Santos Norte, where a removal program is planned, rabbits and cats are present along with four burros.

While Todos Santos Sur is depauperate in botanical endemism (one multi-island endemic species, *Eschscholzia ramosa*), five endemic vertebrates until recently inhabited the island (Table 2; Van Denburgh 1924; Huey 1964; Mellink 1992; Grismer 1993; Junak and Philbrick 1994a). Unfortunately, it is very likely that introduced cats drove an endemic species and subspecies to global extinction prior to the removal program. While Van Denburgh (1924) reported the endemic Todos Santos packrat (*Neotoma anthonyi*) as being abundant, it has not been observed recently despite trapping efforts by Donlan (unpublished 1999) over the last two years and by Mellink in 1991 (Mellink 1992). The endemic subspecies of the rufous-crowned sparrow (*Aimophila ruficeps sanctorum*) appears also to be extinct, with predation by cats a likely cause. Mellink (1992) searched for the bird with the aid of bird-call recordings with no success. We have not seen the sparrow during two years of frequent visits. Todos Santos Sur is also home to two endemic snakes: the Todos Santos ringneck snake (*Diadophis punctatus anthonyi*) and the Todos Santos mountain kingsnake (*Lampropeltis zonata herrarae*). These endemic subspecies are unique to the island and introduced cats were likely a threat to their existence. Cats may also have competed for food resources with the kingsnake, by preying on island lizards and skinks. This kingsnake feeds primarily on lizards belonging to the genus *Sceloporus* and to a lesser degree skinks belonging to the genus *Eumeces* (Grismer 1993). Interestingly, the Todos Santos Islands are the only Pacific Baja California islands where these three taxa co-occur: *L. zonata herrarae*, *Sceloporus occidentalis longipes*, *Eumeces skiltonianus interparietalis*, the latter two occurring on both the north and south islands (Grismer 1993).

Islas San Benito

The San Benito Islands (combined: 640 ha) are approximately 65 km west of Punta Eugenia, the tip of the Vizcaíno peninsula (Figure 1). These three oceanic islands are 30 km northwest of Cedros Island. West San Benito is the largest of the group, possessing the most topographic and biological diversity. There is a lighthouse on West San Benito, which is maintained by one person year-round. In addition, there is a permanent fishing camp run by a fishing

Table 1. Nesting seabirds on nine northwest Mexican islands where introduced species were removed or are currently being removed[a]. An X indicates breeding presence, an E indicates the colony has been extirpated and an E? indicates the species may have nested historically and has been extirpated. Table is modified from McChesney and Tershy, in press.

	Isabela	Rasa	Coronado Norte	Todos Santos Sur	Natividad	San Benitos[b]	Asuncion	San Roque
Black-vented shearwater (*Puffinus opisthomelas*)		E?			X	X	E?	E?
Ashy storm-petrel (*Oceanodroma homocroa*)			X					
Black storm-petrel (*Oceanodroma melania*)		E?	X		E?	X	E?	E?
Leachs storm-petrel (*Oceanodroma leucorrhoa*)			E		E?	X	E?	E?
Least storm-petrel (*Oceanodroma microsoma*)		E?				X		
Magnificent frigatebird (*Fregata magnificens*)	X							
Red-billed tropicbird (*Phaethon aethereus*)	X							
Brown pelican (*Pelecanus occidentalis*)	X		X		X		E	X
Brown booby (*Sula leucogaster*)	X							
Blue-footed booby (*Sula nebouxii*)	X							
Red-footed booby (*Sula sula*)	X							
Brandts cormorant (*Phalacrocorax pencillatus*)			X	X	X		X	X
Double-crested cormorant (*Phalacrocorax auritus*)			X	X	X		X?	X
Heermanns gull (*Larus heermanni*)		X						X
Western gull (*Larus occidentalis*)			X	X	X	X	X	X
Elegant terns (*Sterna elegans*)		X						X
Sooty terns (*Sterna fuscata*)	X							
Royal terns (*Sterna maxima*)		X						
Brown noddy (*Anous stolidus*)	X							
Xantus murrelet (*Synthliboramphus hypoleucus*)			X	X		X	E	E?
Craveris murrelet (*Synthliboramphus craveri*)		E?				X		
Cassin auklet (*Ptychoramphus aleuticus*)			E	E	E	X	E	E

[a]Sources: Boswall 1978; Rodriquez Juarez 1998; ICEG, unpublished, 1998; McChesney and Tershy in press.

[b] West San Benito and Middle San Benito Islands.

cooperative based on Cedros Island, Pescadores Nacionales de Abulón. During abalone season there are as many as 70 people based at the Benito Camp; however, the area directly impacted on the island is relatively minimal (J. Donlan, pers. obs. 1998). Pescadores Nacionales de Abulón is actively participating with ICEG in the conservation projects on the Benito islands, providing housing and transportation.

While diversity is lower in comparison to the Pacific islands to the north, endemism is high on the San Benito Islands. The San Benito group harbors at least three endemic plants (one of which is restricted only to West San Benito), four endemic landbirds, and one endemic lizard (Table 2; Van Rossem 1943; Boswall 1978; Grismer 1993, 1996; Junak and Philbrick 1999). No native mammals are present on these islands. One of the endemic bird subspecies, the McGregor house finch (*Carpodacus mexicanus mcgregori*) is thought to be extinct (Boswall 1978). While the cause of the extinction is uncertain, cats were historically present on the San Benito Islands (Anthony 1925; Hanna 1925).

Introduced herbivores (i.e., goats and burros) have been reported on the San Benito islands as early as 1948; however, their presence has not been continuous (Junak and Philbrick 1999). Rabbits were introduced to West San Benito sometime during the early 1990s (Junak and Philbrick 1999). In addition to rabbits, seven goats and five burros were observed on West San Benito in December 1997 (J. Donlan, pers. obs. 1997). Rabbits were not introduced onto the East and Middle island until 1995 or 1996 (Junak and Philbrick 1999; B. Tershy and D. Croll, pers. obs. 1996). Introduced rabbits, goats and burros threaten many of the of the plants on the San Benito Islands. Introduced herbivores on West San Benito nearly drove the endemic Live-forever, *Dudleya linearis*, to extinction. Before the start of the removal campaign, very few individuals of this species were present on the island. Botanist S. Junak observed few live and many dead plants during a visit in 1996 (Junak and Philbrick 1999). During December 1997, J. Donlan (pers. obs. 1997) observed only 16 seedlings concentrated on one rocky slope.

Table 2. Animal endemics on nine northwest Mexican islands where introduced species were removed or currently are being removed[a]. An X indicates presence, an E indicates the species or subspecies is extinct. The Endemism column indicates the level of endemism.

	Isabela	Rasa	Coronado Norte	Todos Santos Sur	Natividad	San Benitos [b]	Asuncion	San Roque	Endemism
Birds									
San Benito horned lark (*Otocoris alpestris baileyi*)						X			Subspecies
San Benito rock wren (*Salpinctes obsoletus tenuirostris*)						X			Subspecies
San Benito savannah sparrow (*Passerculus sandwichensis sanctorum*)						X			Subspecies
Los Coronados song sparrow (*Melospiza melodia coronatorum*)			X						Subspecies
Todos Santos rufous-crowned sparrow (*Aimophila ruficeps sanctorum*)				E					Subspecies
Los Coronados house finch (*Carpodacus mexicanus clementis*)			X						Subspecies
McGregor house finch (*Carpodacus mexicanus mcgregori*)						E			Subspecies
Reptiles									
San Benito side-blotched lizard (*Uta stellata*)						X			Species
Los Coronados whiptail lizard (*Cnemidophorus tigris vividus*)			X						Subspecies
Los Coronados alligator lizard (*Elgaria multicarinata nana*)			X						Subspecies
Todos Santos ringneck snake (*Diadophis punctatus anthonyi*)				X					Subspecies
Todos Santos mountain kingsnake (*Lampropeltis zonata herrarae*)				X					Subspecies
Mammals									
Los Coronados white-footed mouse (*Peromyscus maniculatus assimilis*)			X						Subspecies
San Roque white-footed mouse (*Peromyscus maniculatus cineritius*)								E	Subspecies
Natividad white-footed mouse (*Peromyscus maniculatus dorsalis*)					X				Subspecies
Todos Santos white-footed mouse (*Peromyscus maniculatus dubius*)				X					Subspecies
Todos Santos wood rat (*Neotoma anthonyi*)				E					Species

[a] Sources: Van Rossem 1943; Huey 1964; Boswell 1978; Grismer 1993, 1996; ICEG, unpublished, 1998; Rodriguez Juarez 1998.

[b] West San Benito and Middle San Benito Islands

Introduced herbivores grazed heavily on the multi-island endemic, *Lavatera venosa*, (found on six islands) threatening the populations of the San Benito Islands (Junak and Philbrick 1999; J. Donlan, pers. obs. 1997). A San Benito endemic fishhook cactus, *Mammilaria neopalmeri* has also been heavily impacted by the introduced herbivores along with many of the non-endemic plants. In addition to these impacts on the island plants, rabbits may have competed for burrows with the many hole-nesting seabirds of the San Benito islands (Table 1).

In collaboration with the Baja California State Office of ANP and Pescadores Nacionales de Abulón, ICEG began removing rabbits and goats from West San Benito in January 1998. A combination of hunting and trapping was used for the removal. Over 400 rabbits were removed from West San Benito over a seven month period. During that same time period approximately 15 rabbits were removed from Middle San Benito. Seven goats were removed from West San Benito and the burros were permanently corralled, with processed food provided. Multiple follow-up trips were made over the fall of 1998 and will continue to be made throughout 1999. Presently, the West and Middle San Benito islands appear to be free of rabbits and goats. Many of the

impacted plant species have already shown sign of recovery (J. Donlan, unpublished 1999). ICEG plans to remove rabbits from East San Benito during the fall of 1999.

Isla Natividad

Isla Natividad (~1000 ha) is 5 km north of Punta Eugenia (Figure 1). There is a town of 400 permanent residents on the south end of the island; most inhabitants are members of the fishing cooperative, Buzos y Pescadores. In 1996 ICEG initiated a cooperative research project with the Vizcaíno Biosphere Reserve and Buzos y Pescadores to study the natural history and conservation of the Baja California endemic black-vented shearwater (*P. opisthomelas*; Keitt 1998). The island has a diverse assemblage of breeding birds including: osprey (*Pandion haliaetus*), peregrine falcons (*Falco peregrinus*), brown pelicans (*Pelecanus occidentalis*), Brandt's and double-crested cormorants (*Phalacrocorax penicillatus, P. auritus*), western gulls (*Larus occidentalis*), and over 90% of the world population of black-vented shearwaters (*P. opisthomelas*) (Table 1). Feral cats, and to a lesser extent introduced herbivores and human disturbance, pose a serious threat to this important breeding area (Keitt 1998).

Natividad has a long history of human inhabitation and consequently the first scientific reports mention the presence of introduced mammals (Brandegee 1900; Anthony 1925). In 1967 Delong and Crossin (unpublished 1968) reported cats on the island and remarked about the numerous shearwater carcasses scattered around the colony. During 1997 and 1998 feral cats were responsible for the mortality of hundreds of black-vented shearwaters (Keitt 1998). During 1997, we encountered a band of 40 goats and 15 sheep on the island along with a new mammal introduction, an antelope squirrel tentatively identified as *Ammospermophilus harrisi*. Goats and sheep were causing damage to native vegetation and impacting the black-vented Shearwater colony. It is unclear what impacts, if any, the antelope squirrels may be having on Natividad.

In addition to investigating the basic breeding biology of the black-vented shearwater, we conducted informal environmental education programs with island residents. Over the past two years, we have made presentations to the school children about the native animals on the island, conducted class field trips to see the breeding birds, and organized games to help raise awareness about island conservation (Keitt 1998). In 1997, with the cooperation of Vizcaíno Biosphere Reserve, we succeeded in moving all of the goats and sheep to a farm near Ensenada, México. In 1998, in part due to our education efforts and the unusually high numbers of shearwater carcasses found near town, island residents requested assistance from ICEG in removing cats from the island. By August 1998 only a few cats remained on the island. At the request of the island residents, ICEG and the Vizcaíno Reserve will assist in removing the few remaining cats from the island during 1999.

Islas Asunción and San Roque

Asunción (92 ha) and San Roque (38 ha) islands are located in Baja California Sur off the Vizcaíno Peninsula, inside Asunción Bay (Figure 1). These islands once had large nesting colonies of seabirds including the Xantus' murrelet (*S. hypoleucus*) and one of the five largest colonies of Cassin's auklets (*P. aleuticus*) in the world (Table 1; Everett and Anderson 1991; B. Tershy and D. Croll, unpublished 1994). Cats were likely introduced to Asunción and San Roque sometime during the 1970s. Predation on burrow-nesting seabirds by cats extirpated the population of Cassin's auklets and perhaps other species by 1992 (McChesney and Tershy, In press). Cat predation may have also caused the extinction of the San Roque endemic white-footed mouse, *Peromyscus maniculatus cineritius* (B. Tershy and D. Croll, unpublished 1994).

The SEDUE, predecessor of INE, began cat eradication efforts (with the participation of local fisherman) in the late 1980s; however, the project was terminated before all cats were removed. In 1994 a collaboration between the Vizcaíno Biosphere Reserve, the Cooperativa California de San Ignacio (the local fishing cooperative), and ICEG formed a restoration team that removed the remaining cats from

Asunción and San Roque Islands. In addition, black rats (*R. rattus*) were removed from San Roque Island. Cats were removed on both islands by trapping. Rats were poisoned with Talon Weatherblock containing brodifacoum and Vengeance Aquablocks containing bromethalin. Bait was placed in corrugated plastic pipe bait stations set on a 50 x 50 m grid across the island. Additional bait was placed in holes and crevices along the shoreline of the island where rats were thought to be more abundant. The bait stations were maintained for one year.

Concurrent with the removal programs, ICEG conducted a community education campaign with the fishing community on the mainland adjacent to the islands. The community involvement and education campaign was designed and conducted by L. Flores and R. Skydancer. They worked with local teachers to design a curriculum on island conservation for local school children, arranged a series of community presentations and produced a video for the local people on the importance of the local islands and the restoration project.

The education campaign facilitated the removal of introduced cats and black rats. Due in part to the education campaign, there was significant involvement and support by individuals and institutions in the community. The removal campaigns were successful on both islands. Automatic seabird vocalization playback devices were placed on the islands during December 1996 (e.g., Podolsky and Kress 1992). These solar-powered CD players and speakers were implemented to encourage the return of nesting seabirds. The light-activated devices play continuous recordings of nesting Cassin's auklet (*P. aleuticus*) and Leach's storm-petrel (*O. leucorrhoa*) colonies during the night hours. Follow-up trips planned for 1999 will begin to determine the success of the playback devices.

ISLAND CONSERVATION DATABASE

Since 1993 ICEG has been compiling data on the biotic and abiotic resources of the islands in NW México. The goal of these efforts has been to establish a central location for information on the islands, which can be used to assess and prioritize conservation efforts. This data have been recently loaded into a relational database and is available over the Internet via the World Wide Web (WWW).

Relational databases can be powerful conservation tools (Farr and Rossman 1996; Umminger and Young 1996). The ICEG database facilitates a means to provide data necessary for the Mexican government and non-governmental organizations (NGOs) to prioritize conservation action. The database contains information pertaining to the conservation and study of the NW México islands including: 1) geography and geology of the islands, 2) introduced species accounts, 3) zoological and botanical species accounts, 4) human use data, 5) endemism data, 6) extinction data, and 7) reference literature.

The data for the island conservation database was collected from a massive literature search, including published journal articles along with U.S. and México gray literature. Some of the data comes from the authors and other biologists' field notes on the islands. We are in the process of contacting experts from various fields to confirm and update the data. The accuracy of the data continues to be improved through communication with biologists.

The relational database is powered by ORACLE software and currently resides on a Windows NT Server. Dynamic HTML reports and queries are publicly available via the WWW (http://islandconservation.org). Full access to the database will be granted to the Mexican government, NGOs and other key conservation planners. In addition, the data residing in the database will be updateable over the WWW by experts in their field.

CONCLUSION

México is a megadiversity hotspot (Mittermeier 1988; Mittermeier et al. 1998). In assessing conservation priorities in México, Ceballos et al. (1998) ranks the Baja California islands an area of high priority. Not only do these islands support high endemism across taxa (Case and Cody 1983), they support the ecological and evolutionary processes that promote the differentiation of endemic forms (MacArthur and Wilson 1967; Lawlor 1983). By combining 1) on-the-ground restoration work with U.S. and Mexican collaborators, 2) sound environmental education and community involvement, and 3) the ability to assess and prioritize conservation needs at a macro level (e.g., ICEG Database), a platform is provided for a sustainable and permanent conservation program for an entire region. The Office of National Protected Areas of SEMARNAP, Instituto Nacional de Ecología, Gulf of California Islands Reserve, Universidad Nacional Autónoma de México, and the Island Conservation and Ecology Group have begun to develop such a platform.

While many islands in NW México remain threatened by introduced species, seven islands have been freed of introduced mammals: Rasa, Asunción, San Roque, Coronado Norte, Todos Santos Sur, West and Middle San Benito. Introduced mammals are currently being removed from two islands: Isabela (cats have been removed, rats remain), Natividad (goats and sheep have been removed, cats being removed). These islands should be free of introduced mammals in the near future. Thirteen terrestrial animal endemics along with many endemic plants are present on these nine islands (Table 2). Introduced mammals directly or indirectly threatened the majority of these endemics. These islands are important nesting sites for 22 species of seabirds (Table 1). While four extinctions have likely occurred, we expect other endemics and seabird species to recover on the restored islands in the near future.

ACKNOWLEDGMENTS

Research and restoration was funded by the Packard Foundation, Weeden Foundation, Switzer Foundation, Conservation International-México, Special Expeditions, Grant-in-Aid of Research from the National Academy of Sciences through Sigma Xi, Myers Oceanographic and Marine Biology Trust, and the American Museum of Natural History. Work was conducted under permits 750-10289, 750-10290, 750-10291, 750-11275 from SEMARNAP and 307 from Secretaría de Gobernación. We thank the Abulones Cultivados, Pescadores Nacionales de Abulón, and Buzos y Pescadores for their assistance and participation in the projects, along with the many field assistants whom provided excellent assistance on many of the projects. We also thank the ORACLE Research and Alliance for their support of the database project along with M. Donlan and M. Adlam of ORACLE Government, Education, and Health for providing technical consulting. We would like to thank S. Junak for his information, time, and enthusiasm during these projects. We thank B. Bedolfe, L. Flores, Q. G. Lozano, V. Sánchez, R. Skydancer and A. Zavala for their support and contributions to these projects. We also thank the ICEG board of Directors for their support: G. Anaya, L. Bourillón, D. Brimm, G. Ceballos, B. Heneman, A. Robles, M. Soulé, R. Terhsy, and S. Webster. We would especially like to express our gratitude to our partners in conservation: INE, SEMARNAP, ANP, Vizcaíno Biosphere Reserve and the Mexican Navy.

LITERATURE CITED

American Museum of Natural History (AMNH). 1998. Halls of Biodiversity. An exhibit at AMNH Museum. New York, NY.

Anthony, A. W. 1925. Expedition to Guadalupe Island, México, in 1922. The birds and mammals. Proceedings of the California Academy of Sciences (Fourth Series) 14:277-320.

Avise, J. C., M. H. Smith, R. K. Selander, T. E. Lawlor, and P. R. Ramsey. 1974. Biochemical polymorphism and systematics in the genus *Peromyscus*. V. insular and mainland species of the subgenus *Haplomylomys*. Systematic Zoology 23:226-238.

Boswall, S. 1978. The birds of the San Benito Islands, Lower California, México. Bristol Ornithology 11:23-32.

Brandegee, T. S. 1900. Voyage of the Wahlberg. Zoe 5:20-29.

Case, T. J. and M. L. Cody (eds.). 1983. Island Biogeography of the Sea of Cortez. University of California Press. Los Angeles, CA.

Cody, M. L., R. Moran and H. Thompson. 1983. The plants. Pages 49-99 *in* Island Biogeography of the Sea of Cortez. University of California Press. Los Angeles, CA.

Ceballos, G., P. Rodríguez and R. A. Medellín. 1998. Assessing conservation priorities in megadiverse México: mammalian diversity, endemicity, and endangerment. Ecological Applications 8:8-17.

Churcher, P.B. and J. H. Lawton. 1987. Predation by domestic cats in an English village. Journal of Zoology. 212:439-455, London.

Cushman, J. H. 1995. Ecosystem-level consequences of species additions and deletions on islands. Pages 135-147 *in* Vitousek, P. M., L. L. Loope and H. Anderson (eds.), Islands: Biological Diversity and Ecosystem Function. Springer-Verlag. New York, NY.

Diamond, J. M. 1989. Overview of recent extinctions. Pages 37-41 *in* Western, D., and M. C. Pearl (eds.), Conservation for the Twenty-first Century. Oxford University Press. New York, NY.

Elton, C. S. 1958. The Ecology of Invasions by Animals and Plants. Methuen, London.

Everett, W. T. 1991. Breeding Biology of the Black Storm-petrel at Islas Coronados, Baja California, México. M.S. Thesis, University of San Diego.

Everett, W. T. and D. W. Anderson. 1991. Status and conservation of the breeding seabirds on offshore Pacific islands of Baja California and the Gulf of California. Pages 115-139 *in* Croxall, J. P. (ed.), Seabird Status and Conservation: a Supplement. ICBP Technical Publications No. 11. Cambridge, England.

Farr, D. F. and A. Y. Rossman. 1996. Integration of data for biodiversity initiatives. Pages 475-490 *in* Reaka-Kudla, M. L., D. E. Wilson, and E. O. Wilson, eds. Biodiversity II: Understanding and Protecting our Biological Resources. Joseph Henry Press, Washington DC.

Grismer, L. L. 1993. The insular herpetofauna of the pacific coast of Baja California, México. Herpetological Natural History 1(2):1-10.

Grismer, L. L. 1996. *Cnemidophorus tigris* does not occur on Isla San Benito, Baja California. Herpetological Review 27(2):69-70.

Groombridge, B. (ed.). 1992. Global Biodiversity: Status of the Earth's Living Resources. Chapman and Hall. London.

Hanna, G. D. 1925. Expedition to Guadalupe Island, México, in 1922: general report. Proceedings of the California Academy of Sciences (Fourth Series) 14:217-275.

Howell, A. B. 1912. Notes from Todos Santos Island. Condor 19:187-191.

Huey, L. M. 1964. The mammals of Baja California. Transactions of the San Diego Society of Natural History 13(7):85-168.

International Union for Conservation of Nature and Natural Resources (IUCN). 1978. The IUCN Plant Red Data Book. Morges, Switzerland.

Jones, E. and B. J. Coman. 1981. Ecology of the feral cat, *Felis catus* (L.) in South-Eastern Australia I. Diet. Australian Wildlife Research. 8:537-47.

Junak, S. A. and R. Philbrick. 1994a. The vascular plants of Todos Santos Island, Baja California, Mexico. Pages 407-428 *in* Halvorson, W. L. and G. J. Maender (eds.), The Fourth California Islands Symposium: Update on the Status of Resources. Santa Barbara Museum of Natural History. Santa Barbara, CA.

Junak, S. A., and R. Philbrick. 1994b. The flowering plants of San Martin Island, Baja California, Mexico. Pages 429-447 *in* Halvorson, W. L., and G. J. Maender, (eds.) The Fourth California Islands Symposium: Update on the Status of Resources. Santa Barbara Museum of Natural History. Santa Barbara, CA.

Junak, S. A. and R. Philbrick. 1999. Flowering plants of the San Benito Islands, Baja California, Mexico. Pages 235 to 246 *in* Browne, D. R., K. L. Mitchell, and H. W. Chaney (eds.), Proceedings of the Fifth California Islands Symposium. 29 March to 1 April 1999. Santa Barbara Museum of Natural History, Santa Barbara, CA. Sponsored by the U.S. Minerals Management Service, Pacific OCS Region, 770 Paseo Camarillo, Camarillo, CA 93010. OCS Study No. 99-0038.

Keitt, B. S. 1998. Ecology and conservation biology of the Black-vented Shearwater (*Puffinus opisthomelas*) on Natividad Island, Vizcaíno Biosphere Reserve, Baja California Sur, México. M.S. Thesis. University of California Santa Cruz, CA.

Lawlor, T. E. 1983. The mammals. Pages 265-289 in Case, T. J., and M. L. Cody (eds.), Island Biogeography in the Sea of Cortéz. University of California Press. Los Angeles, CA.

MacArthur, R. H. and E. O. Wilson. 1967. The Theory of Island Biogeography. Princeton University Press. Princeton, NJ.

McChesney, G. J. and B. R. Tershy. In press. History and status of introduced mammals and impacts to seabirds on the California Channel and Northwestern Baja California Islands. Colonial Waterbirds.

Mellink, E. 1992. The status of *Neotoma anthonyi* (Rodentia, Muridae, Cricetinae) of Todos Santos Islands, Baja California, México. Bulletin of the Southern California Academy of Sciences 91(3):137-140.

Mittermeier, R. A. 1988. Primate diversity and the tropical forest: case studies from Brazil and Madagascar and the importance of megadiversity countries. Pages 145-154 *in* Wilson, E. O. (ed.), Biodiversity. National Academy Press. Washington, DC.

Mittermeier, R. A., N. Myers, J. B. Thomsen, G. A. B. da Fonseca, and S. Olivieri. 1998. Biodiversity hotspots and major tropical wilderness areas: approaches to setting conservation priorities. Conservation Biology 12:516-520.

Mooney, H. A. and J. A. Drake (eds.). 1986. Ecology of Biological Invasions of North America and Hawaii. Springer-Verlag. New York, NY.

Moors, P. J. (ed.). 1985. Conservation of Island Birds. International Council for Bird Preservation. Cambridge, England.

Murphy, R. W. 1983. The reptiles: origins and evolution. Pages 130-158 *in* Case, T. J., and M. L. Cody (eds.), Island Biogeography in the Sea of Cortéz. University of California Press. Los Angeles, CA.

Podolsky, R. and S. W. Kress. 1992. Attraction of the endangered Dark-rumped petrel to recorded vocalizations in the Galápagos Islands. Condor 94:448-453.

Rodríguez Juarez, Cristina. 1998. Erradicación de gatos y ratas en una isla tropical del Pacifico de México. M.S. Thesis. Universidad Nacional Autónoma de México.

Soulé, M., and A. J. Sloan. 1966. Biogeography and distribution of the reptiles and amphibians on islands in the Gulf of California, México. Transactions of the San Diego Society of Natural History 14:137-156.

Soulé, M., and S. Y. Yang. 1972. Genetic variation in side-blotched lizards on island in the Gulf of California. Evolution 27:593-600.

Tershy, B. R. and D. Croll. 1994. Avoiding the problems of fragmentation by preserving fragments: the benefits of conserving small islands. Page 158 in Abstracts, 1994 International Meeting of the Society for Conservation Biology and the Association for Tropical Biology. Guadalajara, Jalisco, México.

Umminger, B. L., and S. Young. 1996. Information management for biodiversity: a proposed U.S. national biodiversity information center. Pages 491-504 in Reaka-Kudla, M. L., D. E. Wilson, and E. O. Wilson (eds.), Biodiversity II: understanding and protecting our biological resources. Joseph Henry Press, Washington D.C.

Van Denburgh, J. 1924. The birds of Todos Santos Islands. Condor. 26:67-71.

Van Rossem, A. J. 1943. The Horned Lark and the Rock Wren of the San Benito Islands, Lower California. Condor 45:235-236.

Velarde, E. and D. W. Anderson. 1994. Conservation and management of seabird islands in the Gulf of California: setbacks and successes. Pages 229-243 in Nettleship, C. N., J. Burger and M. Gochfeld (eds.), Seabirds on Islands Threats, Case Studies and Action Plans, Birdlife Conservation Series No. 1. Birdlife International. Cambridge, United Kingdom.

Warner, R. E. 1985. Demography and movements of free-ranging domestic cats in rural Illinois. Journal of Wildlife Management 49(2):340-346.

Wright, H. W. 1909. An ornithological trip to Los Coronados Islands, México. Condor 11:96-100.

UNPUBLISHED MATERIALS

Moran, R., San Diego Museum of Natural History, P.O. Box 121390, San Diego, CA 92112-1390 USA. Field notes for 11 May 1979. Unpublished manuscript on file in the library.

Donlan, C. J., Island Conservation and Ecology Group, P. O. Box 141, Davenport, CA 95107 USA. Personal observation 1997.

Donlan, C. J., Island Conservation and Ecology Group, P. O. Box 141, Davenport, CA 95107 USA. Personal observation 1998.

Donlan, C. J., Island Conservation and Ecology Group, P. O. Box 141, Davenport, CA 95107 USA. Unpublished data 1999.

Delong, R. L. and R. S. Crossin. National Marine Mammal Laboratory, National Marine Fisheries Service, 7600 Sand Point Way NE, Seattle, WA. 98115. Status of seabirds on Islas de Guadalupe, Natividad, Cedros, San Benito and Los Coronados. Unpublished manuscript, 1968.

Island Conservation and Ecology Group (ICEG), P. O. Box 141, Davenport, CA 95107 USA. Unpublished data 1998.

Tershy B. T., Island Conservation and Ecology Group, P. O. Box 141, Davenport, CA 95107 USA. Personal observation 1997.

Tershy B. T. and D. A. Croll, Island Conservation and Ecology Group, P. O. Box 141, Davenport, CA 95107 USA. Unpublished data 1994.

Tershy B. T. and D. A. Croll, Island Conservation and Ecology Group, P. O. Box 141, Davenport, CA 95107 USA. Personal observation 1996.